ANNUAL REVIEW OF PSYCHOLOGY

ANNUAL REVIEW OF PSYCHOLOGY

MARK R. ROSENZWEIG, *Editor*
University of California, Berkeley

LYMAN W. PORTER, *Editor*
University of California, Irvine

VOLUME 25

1974

ANNUAL REVIEWS INC. 4139 EL CAMINO WAY PALO ALTO, CALIFORNIA 94306

ANNUAL REVIEWS INC.
Palo Alto, California USA

International Standard Book Number: 0-8243-0225-7
Library of Congress Catalog Card Number: 50-13143

Assistant Editor	Jean Heavener
Indexers	Mary A. Glass
	Susan Tinker
Subject Indexer	Dorothy Read

PRINTED AND BOUND IN THE UNITED STATES OF AMERICA

PREFACE

With this volume, the sixth to appear under his editorship, Paul Mussen retires as editor to gain time for his many other activities. Mark R. Rosenzweig will continue as an editor, and Lyman W. Porter moves from the Editorial Committee to become the other editor. The *Annual Review of Psychology* has benefitted greatly and in many ways from Paul Mussen's broad knowledge of both psychology and psychologists and from his incisive editing. The next two volumes will continue to show his contributions since he helped to guide the most important task in preparing these volumes—the selection of significant topics and able authors.

This volume also marks the end of the regular 5-year term of Professor W. D. Neff on the Editorial Committee. He has brought to the Committee his deep and wide-ranging knowledge and his dedication to the concept of the *Annual Reviews*. Lyman Porter's assumption of an editorship opened another position on the Committee. Conrad G. Mueller and Marian Radke-Yarrow have accepted the invitation of the Board to fill these positions for the next 5- and 6-year periods, respectively.

Another important contributor to the continuity of the *Annual Review of Psychology* is Miss Jean Heavener, who became assistant editor in 1968. She participates fully in every stage of the editorial enterprise, from the meetings of the Committee to the final corrections of page proof, and she responds cheerfully to the exigencies of a rapid production schedule and occasional strained deadlines. Christina Smillie ably assisted her with some of the copy editing for this volume.

M.R.R.

TOPICS AND AUTHORS
VOLUME 26 (1975)

CONTENTS

DEVELOPMENTAL PSYCHOLOGY

❖210

Donald M. Baer and John C. Wright[1]
Department of Human Development, University of Kansas, Lawrence

INTRODUCTION

A selective review of current developmental psychology obviously will hinge on the meaning of *developmental:* what is selected should be that work most relevant to the essence of the field. Developmental psychology may have a unique problem in this regard, in that it may represent the one chapter in an *Annual Review of Psychology* which needs to question whether it exists as a reviewable field. The alternative, taken in its extreme form, would be to argue that developmental psychology is nothing more that all psychology in the small, that is, located in children and other young organisms; consequently, such studies might well be reviewed as special cases (the young cases) in other chapters. For the most part, developmental psychology has proceeded as if this alternative were untenable. Theories such as Freud's and Piaget's have postulated uniquely developmental processes occurring in young children, to some extent qualitatively different from the processes typical of adults, and centrally important in determining the shape of adult psychology. These theories and similar logics have generated a very large amount of research, and that reasearch has constituted a developmental psychology, even if it did not prove that it always deserved the name. Its failure as a widely convincing proof is evident in the existence of a number of learning theories of child development as exemplified by Sears, Dollard, and Miller, Staats, and Bijou and Baer. Such theories suggest that much of developmental phenomena represent behavior change accomplished by the same environmental mechanisms that can and do produce behavior change in the adult organism. But these approaches, too, obviously fall short of widescale conviction of their audience, for research derived from the Piagetian paradigm clearly is increasing in relative frequency. And even if learning theories ordinarily do not cite different mechanisms of learning in the young organism from those in the adult, nevertheless they do typically point to a uniquely childlike

[1]The authors acknowledge with gratitude the assistance of Marilyn Shea and Ann Baer in searching the journals and screening and classifying articles for inclusion in this chapter.

content of what is learned, and thus take on a tactical significance within psychology requiring more than isolated paragraphs in an *Annual Review* chapter on learning.

In summary, the most critical research for review may well be those studies which suggest that there are uniquely developmental phenomena and those which suggest that there are not; however, whether or not there is a developmental psychology, there certainly is a child psychology. Even if the child is only a small case of the adult organism, he is an extremely common case (indeed, inevitable); the phenomena occurring in the child may not be different in kind from what will occur later, but they may very well have major import for what will happen later. They may be clearer in the child than in the adult; if there are troubles to be avoided or diminished for adults, the child may represent the best possible case in which to take preventive action. And, finally, the child is another case in which the generality of any principle may be tested—those laws that hold for adults but not for children are less general than those that hold for both. Thus a good deal of the research produced in this field is not aimed at a developmental psychology, but simply at a child psychology, and it also merits review.

The best organizing variables of a child psychology are probably age and sequence. Childhood is a process of change, and the change is very well organized (if not explained) by the child's age. Observation suggests that a great deal of that change occurs in very common sequences, highly similar from child to child. Consequently, a considerable amount of research in this area consists of age comparisons or descriptions of sequences and the difficulty of finding or producing different sequences. A large amount of the basic description required for this organization is already in hand (students in the field are regularly assigned the works of Gesell and his colleagues as the basic example and substance of the approach). However, as society changes, the situations within which children develop also change, and new descriptive research is required.

If a large part of the justification for a child psychology is the inevitability of children, another large part must be their sentimental and strategic value to us. Our affection for the child hardly needs comment, but our strategic commitment to intervention in his life does. Adults live in a society which children cannot join and maintain without extensive behavioral preparation. Thus we socialize and school them, formally and informally, and consequently much of a child psychology must be an applied psychology, a conclusion exemplified by the most recent edition of the *Review of Child Development Research* (48). Yet application, often undertaken for no more theory-serving purpose than because children exist in large numbers and have troubles (or will have, without intervention), may eventually have a profound effect on the issue of a developmental psychology. Behavior modification approaches to applied child psychology, for example, have been pointedly nondevelopmental in their views and their procedures; nevertheless, they have reported some striking successes in changing certain behaviors. Conceivably such applications may continue to demonstrate that a sufficient diversity of child behavior can be modified at such a range of ages and in such a wealth of sequences as to make a developmental psychology unimportant. This possibility has been suggested by Baer (10).

The review that follows will be organized in part around the issue of the existence of a developmental psychology, but in larger part according to the habitual topics of our existing child psychology, which only sometimes is concerned with whether it is a developmental psychology. Consequently, it will be seen that studies are grouped in honor of the fact that children perceive, learn, imitate, speak, symbolize, think, become socialized, and display personalities; and studies are chosen because they suggest that while all humans do these things, children may do them distinctively.

DEVELOPMENTAL PSYCHOLOGY AS A DISCIPLINE

The first topic of review is a sample of work especially relevant to the concept of a developmental psychology. Sometimes the relevance is explicit: it is research or commentary directly about the character that a developmental psychology has or should take on. Sometimes the relevance is implicit: the research or argument allows tentative conclusion that there are developmental issues per se; or, by contrast, suggests that what is called development (in the particular case at hand) may simply be a standard, nondevelopmental process which happens to be under study in a young organism. (Only a few examples of the studies that might be reviewed under this heading will be considered; most of the possible candidates instead are reviewed under some other substantive topic heading.)

That developmental psychology was itself a developing "organism" seemed to be the view of Looft (249). His article considered three handbooks of child psychology published at various points in the last 40 years, together with a recent handbook on the psychology of aging. A variety of measures were derived from the comparison, both quantitative and qualitative, to demonstrate a developmental ("evolutionary") process in the discipline. Looft suggested a three-part value in doing so: historical perspective avoids egocentrism; it sometimes shows that new ideas are in fact old ones; and, by demonstrating that the current state of the discipline is to some extent a function of its early history, it encourages understanding of the present (out of which understanding may come a new, perhaps better direction for the future?).

Riegel (326), in elaboration on a similar theme, made a fraternal twin study of the development of the discipline. He described two parallel trends, defining in effect two subdisciplines, by distinguishing the "capitalistic" orientation typical of English and American psychology from the "mercantilistic-socialistic" orientation of European psychology. The significant formative figures of the former ranged from Hobbes to Hall, and of the latter from Rousseau to Piaget. The central theme of the capitalistic orientation seemed to consider development as a homogeneous and continuous process, thereby allowing comparison of all individuals to a single normative standard (e.g. the intelligence test, as derived from white, achievement-oriented Americans). By contrast, the mercantilistic-socialistic orientation allowed and encouraged concurrent multiple models of growth; evaluation could well be specific to a generation or to a culture or subculture. Riegel's description of the two trends is followed by a strong recommendation for modern developmental psychology, based upon an interaction model emphasizing both sociocultural contingencies and biological process, to incorporate both of the earlier trends into a new integration. These recommendations require that a developmental psychology relate behavior not only to personal, individual time (age), but to historical time as well. Consequently, further recommendations result concerning the nature of research design in developmental psychology.

A similar dissatisfaction with much current research design was voiced by Lewis (239, pp. 75–76) in the introduction to a (1971 SRCD) symposium on cross-cultural studies of mother-infant interaction. Lewis argued that the proper task of developmental research was to delineate psychological process. But variables such as culture, sex, and social class are not psychological processes; instead, they are *carrier* variables within which psychological processes are likely to be located. Unfortunately, he noted, there was a strong tendency in modern research merely to demonstrate carrier variable differences (between cultures, sexes, classes): "Any test or procedure that can accomplish this end is held in esteem, regardless of whether the results add any substantial datum to our understanding" (239, p. 75). His argument applies equally well to age differences as to culture, sex, and class differences. In the symposium which followed, there were several examples of research in the mode recommended. Goldberg (144), for instance, noted that Zambian infants differ from American infants in that Zambian infants spend a great deal of their time in a sling on their mother's back. Goldberg theorized about the psychological processes altered by this practice and their consequent effect on motor, social, and cognitive development. She may not have proved her final point, but she had at least moved in the recommended direction.

Finally, the notion that our concept of developmental psychology can be a self-fulfilling prophecy with grave social consequences was voiced twice in the past year. Tulkin (401) couched the point in terms of the concept of cultural deprivation. The concept itself, he argued, ignored cultural relativism, which Riegel also had pointed out was unappreciated in American psychology yet well represented in European orientations. To the extent that "deprivation" was taken literally, social scientists found themselves obliged to accomplish "enrichment" in reply, and this made them missionaries rather than scientists. In that the problems underlying the invocation of a cultural deprivation theme were (Tulkin argued) a result of certain features of the majority culture, this misdirected the scientist from the more pertinent task of analyzing, recommending, and designing the needed social changes within that majority culture. Furthermore, the concept of cultural deprivation was not (in Lewis' terms) a psychological process but instead was a carrier variable and hence should be left behind in favor of more analytic studies. Those studies, very likely, would reinforce the idea of cultural relativism rather than deprivation.

Eisenberg (104) made a similar point in terms of aggression. He argued that a developmental discipline which conceives of man as instinctively aggressive (especially in the sense of inevitably aggressive) may not only be in error, but may in fact cause the error to approximate truth. In effect, Eisenberg argued for a developmental psychology in which biological and environmental variables are in constant interaction; and the environmental variables certainly include sociocultural, political variables as very potent factors in determining human development. Thus a culture whose science believes that its members are inevitably aggressive is likely to design itself in such a manner as to model, condone, and even reinforce the aggression of its members, thereby "proving" to itself that it was correct. On the other hand, "men and women must believe that mankind can become fully human in order for our species to attain its humanity" (104, p. 124). Consequently, the striving for ethological parallels across species becomes a dangerous exercise, because the uniformity of aggressive behavior across species is not accompanied by a uniformity of controlling mechanism.

> For example, attack behavior can be observed in organisms as varied as insect, bird, carnivore, ape, and man. In the first, it may be triggered by trace chemicals; in the second, by territorial defence, but only during the breeding season; in the third, by prey, but only if the appropriate internal state of arousal is present; in the fourth, by the appearance of a predator, if escape routes are unavailable and if the troop is threatened; and in man, by a mere verbal slur, if the social context and prior individual experience indicate attack as the socially appropriate response (104, p. 125).

Pointing to a remarkable variety of human behavior patterns across different but viable cultures, Eisenberg called for a developmental psychology that assumed that human behavior was thoroughly malleable, and suggested that studies of child behavior change were the proper arena in which to see not *if* behavior was plastic, but rather how *much* behavior change a given organism could tolerate and remain an integrated psychic entity. The issue was perhaps survival. (A much more academic but nonetheless pertinent parallel can be drawn from Eisenberg's argument. If the science of a culture thinks of its members as inevitably aggressive, the culture may make it true. Then if the science of a culture believes that its members' development is age scheduled, will the culture not make that true, too? And if the science of a culture believes that its members' development occurs in fixed sequences, can the culture also make that true?)

Seven studies will be considered next which are less commentary or argument about the nature of developmental psychology than they are powerful examples of one view or another at work.

To set the stage, consider a study by Brainerd (33), comparing age and stage (readiness) as factors in the training of a number conservation skill. Nonconserving kindergarteners were pretested; then they were either trained or not; and after a week of training (or waiting), they were posttested. As a group, the trained children improved in the conservation skill (relative to untrained children), but with considerable individual differences. A partial correlational analysis of those differences showed that the only variable predicting profit from training was the child's stage, not his age, at the outset of training. The implication was that there are certain prerequisites to being taught a conservation skill; in other words, development does come in fixed sequences (but not at fixed ages).

Next consider a study reported by Lane & Coon (231), dealing with reward-giving behavior by preschoolers. Children 4 and 5 years old performed a task, supposedly in collaboration with a partner; the partner's work was seen to be either better than, the same as, or worse than theirs. The children then received a number of rewards for the task and were instructed to give their partner a share. Four-year-olds generally took more than half for themselves, regardless of the partner's performance; by contrast, five-year-olds divided the rewards equally between themselves and the partner, again regardless of the partner's performance. Adults, it was claimed, would have allocated the rewards on an equity basis: whoever did more would receive more. The implication again is that there is a sequence of change in how rewards are given away, and in this instance, the sequence was roughly predictable by age.

Campbell & Spear (49) also pointed to age and sequence in their review of the ontogeny of memory. Their summary of a large number of studies indicated clear evidence that long-term memory capacity increases markedly with development. In offering an accounting of that fact, the authors invoked both neurological and behavioral mechanisms either known or presumed to be scheduled along the path of normal development.

The preceding three papers had much in common in terms of affirming (or assuming) that there is indeed a discipline of developmental psychology to be studied as such. Consider now four other studies of the past year which in this sense proceeded differently.

Groen & Parkman (157) offered a simple model as an analysis of addition skills in children and adults. They assumed that any organism, young or old, possesses a counter. Presented with an addition problem of the form add *m* and *n,* the organism sets the counter to the larger of the two, increments it a number of times equal to the smaller of the two, and reads the result. Latency in producing the answer should then be a function of how many times the counter must be incremented, and both children and adults yielded latencies in addition which corresponded to this prediction. Adults, however, have very much shorter latencies than children, even though ordered according to the same pattern. It was postulated then that adults have an auxiliary memory-based "look-up" process which they usually use, but that they sometimes revert to the counter-incrementing technique characterizing the child. In this approach, there is clearly a developmental sequence from child to adult, based on a memory process. If the Campbell & Spear account of memory is taken, then to the extent that memory is a developmental, sequenced process, so is the transition from childlike addition to adult addition. But at the same time, the Groen & Parkman model postulated a fairly specific memory process. If that "look-up" behavior can be translated into a teachable set of skills, then it might be found that with appropriate techniques, the skills could be taught relatively early in childhood, allowing transition at any (teachable) age, but always in the same sequence! On the other hand, it might also be shown that the memory process *alone* might be invoked sufficiently to give a child apparent addition skills in the absence of the counting mechanism. If so, then the counting mechanism might be added later on top of the memory technique (as schools do when they explain the concept of number line to a child who has already memorized a set of "addition tables"). Conceivably then, sequence would have been reversed, and a fast adder might become (for a time) a slow one, as he gave up memory for counter incrementing. Such a discussion is only speculative, of course. The Groen & Parkman model, if useful, simply illustrates the possibility that usual sequences need not prove to be necessary sequences—although the belief that they are may well determine the structure of the schools' curriculum in teaching addition.

Bond (29) reviewed studies dealing with infant visual perception, looking for evidence about the infant's capacity for form perception. This led her to consider visual discrimination behavior as well as visual scanning patterns. Despite her pursuit of the possibility, she could find no evidence requiring any belief in different infant perception processes than characterized the adult. She suggested that the qualitative equivalence of infant and adult perception was still the sound—as well as the prevailing—view.

Similarly, Kramer, Koff & Luria (225) examined child and adult speech to assess competence in the use of a grammatical exception rule (the minimal distance principle), and failed to find uniform competence anywhere between the ages of 8 and 20. The linguistic stage structure originally described for children below 8 years of age also characterized children and adults above age 8. Two years after the original assessment, those subjects who had not been competent in using the rule were retested. Improvement was found equally for all age levels within that group: "no evidence for greater improvement of competency for the younger 'language-plastic'-aged Ss was found" (p. 121). Thus these authors, like Bond, found no distinctively developmental phenomena in the area of behavior they examined. And these areas seem no more delimited or trivial than those in which developmental phenomena are asserted.

Finally, consider the report by Koegel & Covert (218) concerning the interaction between self-stimulatory behavior in three autistic children and their ability to learn discriminations under ordinary training procedures. In general, these authors found that when the children were engaged in self-stimulation (bizarre mannerisms, atavisms, etc), straightforward reinforcement contingencies frequently failed to establish a simple discrimination skill. However, if the self-stimulatory behavior was brought under control (by experimental punishment), the children then responded to those same contingencies and learned the discrimination. Furthermore, there were cases observed in which the reinforcement contingencies alone were sufficient to produce discrimination; in those cases, as the discrimination was learned, self-stimulatory behavior always was low. In other words, in these children, learning or its failure seemed to be under the direct control of the rate of another behavior. To the extent that their current environment failed to control that behavior, these children presumably would continue to fail under ordinary contingencies. If the interfering self-stimulatory behavior showed some developmental course of decline, then presumably positive development (learning the lessons presented by ordinary environmental contingencies) would begin. But self-stimulatory behavior, whatever its developmental course may be in such children, was demonstrably sensitive to environmental contingencies itself, specifically, punishment contingencies. For such children virtually any pattern of learning, or failure to learn, could be displayed, depending on what the environment chose to do about the children's self-stimulatory behavior. But as Koegel & Covert clearly demonstrate, the environment was in the hands of the children's caretakers for these purposes. Those caretakers could program punishment, reinforcement, or nothing for self-stimulatory behavior, and thereby would control what might otherwise appear to be a developmental process or a developmental anomaly.

The work presented in this field sometimes touches directly on the issue of whether there is a field here to be called developmental psychology, rather than one better labeled child psychology. What is striking is the relative rarity with which either side of the issue is directly attacked. Perhaps the most salient conclusion to be drawn from a review of the past year's research in this area is that it still has not demonstrated that it requires its chapter title, and it is not working very hard on doing so.

Developmental Prediction

The tradition of longitudinal study continues, and the most noteworthy publication was a study by Wilson & Harpring (426) of 261 pairs of twins from birth to 2 years, using the Bayley Scales. A quote from the abstract:

> The results showed that (a) with a small allowance for prematurity, the twins displayed essentially the same rate of progression in development as singletons; (b) the correlations between developmental scores obtained at successive ages were moderate and declined in size as the ages spread further apart; (c) at each age, however, the twins showed high within-pair correlations for mental and motor development, and they also displayed high concordance for the rate of gain across ages; (d) the correlations for monozygotic twins approached the reliability of the test itself, and most were significantly higher than the correlations for dizygotic twins; and (e) infant mental and motor development was temporarily retarded by low birth weight, but was not affected by the socioeconomic status of the home. The conclusion from these results is that while prenatal anomalies or an impoverished home environment may retard development, in the majority of cases the environmental conditions fall within the limits of sufficiency that permit the genetic blueprint to determine the course of infant development.

Another optimistic attempt at prediction has been launched, and a pilot study together with a promissory note has been published by Smith et al (369). A novel feature of this correlational study relating prenatal, perinatal, and postnatal events to developmental outcome at 7 years is the use of "sequential prediction stages" to limit the use of any predictor to that time interval beyond which its contribution to predictive accuracy is negligible.

Miscellaneous Methodology

An extremely heterogeneous group of studies are mentioned below because of their contribution of methodological innovations, cautions, or reassuring discoveries that certain variables traditionally a source of concern to research design needn't be.

With regard to spatial placement of the correct stimulus in two-choice discrimination tasks, Moody & Gollin (287) have demonstrated the inadequacy of the hoary Gellerman and the newer Fellows series. Apparently children are ingenious enough to develop response patterns (hypotheses?) which will gain unintended confirmation in almost any left-right sequence. Therefore, instead of offering a better sequence, the authors wisely suggest four methods of identifying, anticipating, or individually eliminating the systematically irrelevant patterning in children's responses. These are not panaceas, but all are potentially helpful.

Two of the "booming" areas in the field have produced seminovel methodological contributions: infancy and imitation. Infant head turning (67, 68) has soluble problems as a conditioning task. A debate on errors in the corneal reflection method of determining infant visual fixation was launched in a paper by Slater & Findlay (364). The replies of the Yale group and the continuing debate will doubtless be discussed in next year's *Annual Review of Psychology*. The continuing problem of locating drug-free neonates for research has led to increased attention to the effects of maternal perinatal pharmacology on neonatal behavior, and this effort has encountered its own methodological difficulties (224).

In the imitation arena, it has been demonstrated that an important determinant of both imitation and vicarious reinforcement effects is whether *S* knows during observation of *M* that he will later be expected to perform (394). Not surprisingly, the 20-year-old Asch technique for assessment of conformity has been applied to the study of imitation and perspective taking in the presence of peers (85, 417).

Finally, a study of normal and retarded children's P-A learning indicated fewest trials to criterion when items were presented by tape recorder; slower learning when they were presented by slides; and poorest learning when the venerable memory drum was used (214).

PERCEPTUAL DEVELOPMENT

In addition to the increasing number of studies of perceptual development bordering on the areas of learning and cognition discussed by subheads below, in 1972 there were studies of simple age changes in visual masking (160, 282); eidetic imagery (161); shape recognition under free vs sequentially self-programmed conditions (141); and hue, saturation, and brightness discrimination of colors (132). Two studies assessed auditory discrimination of speech sounds in early infancy (288, 399); and two extended the literature on olfaction in newborns (338, 351). Anchor effects in weight discrimination were studied developmentally by Wilkening, Sarris & Heller (425) in Germany.

Illusions

The temporal range within which apparent movement is perceived by preschool children declines with age when measured by a response-decrement model, but not when assessed by verbal report (246). The decline in strength of the Poggendorff illusion with age in relation to the fact that adults experience a successive-trials attenuation while children do not was discussed by Bayer (15). Pollack's theory of the ontogenetic development of illusions was tested by Matheny (262), using the Ponzo illusion (a secondary one that should increase with age) with MZ twins who differed in susceptibility. In support of Pollack's view, females, but not males, showed a within-twin correlation between susceptibility and nonverbal WISC subtests. Pollack fared less well in two other studies claiming to test his model. Hartmann and associates (175) failed to find correlations between the magnitude of the Müller-Lyer, allegedly a primary illusion, and age or IQ in children 6 to 9 years old. Brightness contrast and cognitive factors were examined in a study of the Delboef illusion by Weintraub & Cooper (418). who concluded that although the magnitude declined with increasing age, cognitive factors were implicated. Sjostrom & Pollack (363) criticized the adequacy and the assumption of equivalence of Weintraub & Cooper's methods in rejoinder.

Spatial Orientation

A lively continuing interest in children's perception with regard to orientation of objects, orientation of the body, localization with respect to the body, and spatial perspective is evidenced in the literature this year. McGurk (267) found that infants as young as 6 months of age (but not 3 months) can discriminate different orientations of the same form and can also recognize their identity. Adults were compared to 3- and 5-year-olds in a study by Gajzago & Day (133) when, following discrimination of a figure from its 180° rotation, the subject's head was inverted and he was required to identify the previously reinforced alternative. Only 50–75 percent of adults showed uprightness constancy under these conditions and fewer children did so, especially when the figure represented a different object in its inverted form.

Left-right discriminations were studied in the Piagetian context of development of logical relations by Harris (171), and horizontal vs vertical discrimination was analyzed by Mackay, Brazendale & Wilson (254). The latter found that the age of acquisition depended heavily upon task parameters and could develop in either order, depending upon the tests selected. Linear age effects and no sex differences in the development of directional concepts between ages 6 and 12 were found by Long & Looft (248), who ordered the various forms of directional competence in a sequence of development and confirmed previously obtained orders. Egocentric and nonegocentric comprehension of the spatial terms "front," "back," and "beside" were studied by Harris & Strommen (172).

Children's changing comprehension of spatial relations is mediated by both social and cognitive factors, according to a theoretical model proposed by Fishbein, Lewis & Keiffer (119). Older children make fewer errors than younger children, but a higher percentage of those they make are egocentric errors. Correct responses and egocentric errors have equal latencies, both shorter than those for nonegocentric errors. The analysis is reminiscent of White's temporal zones of automation and decision, respectively. Brodzinsky, Jackson & Overton (36) used Piaget's classic mountain scene perspective task to demonstrate that nonegocentric performance increases with age from 6 to 8 to 10 years. Reasoning that salient perceptual features of the scene as viewed may interfere with the transformations required for the construction of anticipatory images, they visually shielded *S* from temporarily uninformative features of the array in order to reduce their perceptual impact, and found that shielding facilitated performance for 8- and some 10-year-olds, but not for 6-year-olds.

Perception and Representation of Human Faces and Figures

The studies grouped under this heading use heterogeneous tasks, but have in common an interest in the social significance of human figure perception and drawing. Harris & Fleer (170) used full faces and half faces in a recognition memory task, and showed that retardates require full-face stimuli for accurate responding, unlike their matched M.A. controls. Odom & Lemond (297) predicted a developmental lag between the perception and the production of facial expressions from kindergarten to fifth grade children, but found instead that both age groups discriminated more of the eight expressions used than they could produce, and the difference *increased* with age, though older children excelled at both tasks.

Reasoning from a model based on language development, Goodnow & Friedman (149) designed a task in which children 3 to 6 years old were to complete a facial drawing presented to them as a circle containing two dots (eyes) placed either vertically on one side of the circle or horizontally but low in the circle. Resultant drawings could either follow figural cues (90° and 180° rotation, respectively) or could add details that made the face upright on the page in spite of the original display. The former solution was predominant, especially among the younger children. Analysis of this response as a qualitatively unique and developmentally intermediate pattern stressed the view that development in graphic representation, as in language, cannot be adequately described as successive approximation to adult behavior.

The failure of psychodynamic factors to influence the size of human figure drawings by children was emphasized in a study by Black (26) in which age, actual height, and numerically self-estimated height accounted for most of the variability. Viewed developmentally, the construction of human figures in a three-dimensional medium follows an orderly developmental sequence, according to the findings of Golomb (148) with children aged 2 to 6 years.

Cross-modal Perception

Cross-modal perceptual generalization is an increasingly utilized task setting from which to evaluate what is perceived and at what level of informational generality. Using the auditory and visual modalities, Vlietstra & Wright (404) demonstrated that certain stimulus properties such as intensity and interruptedness, trained in preschoolers as a discrimination within a visual or auditory dimension (with the other modality irrelevant), provided a basis for transfer to the previously irrelevant modality, but only if the previously reinforced value of the transmodal property remained correct in the new modality. Visual feedback training in auditory localization brought younger preschool children up to the level of both trained and untrained older children in auditory localization accuracy in a study by Warren & Judy (409). In a study of rhythm reproduction by 10- and 15-year-olds, Rileigh & Odom (327) showed that normal vs deficient hearing accounted for less variance than did salience of visually presented rhythm patterns in interaction with age. Beats were most salient for the 10-year-olds, followed by duration, and rhythm, which was most salient in the reproductions of 15-year-olds. Auditory-visual matches of pattern were more difficult than intramodal matches, and sequential spatial matches were still more difficult in a study of pattern-matching in relation to reading ability by Bryden (41). Poor readers were inferior to good ones on all kinds of match, and they showed a high within-group correlation between intermodal matching accuracy and reading ability, unlike the good readers. When between-modality matching tasks and within-modality matching tasks begin with the same modality, there are no differences between them in matching accuracy, but those that begin with visual and transfer to either auditory or visual are easier than those that begin with auditory and transfer to either modality, according to a study by Kuhlman & Wolking (228).

A number of studies considered transfer between the visual and tactual kinesthetic modalities. Fry & Craven (130) compared visual to active and passive tactual discrimination of horizontal and vertical discriminations. Jones (194) compared blind and sighted children on visual, cutaneous, and kinesthetic localization tasks. Rose, Blank & Bridger (331) found no differences in visual-visual, visual-tactual, tactual-tactual, and tactual-visual matching performances by 3-year-olds. Delays between presentation and matching, however, produced deficits for all conditions involving a tactual component, suggesting perhaps the greater potency of visual imagery in short-term memory. Even 6-month-old infants performing a Piaget-type, permanent-object assessment task, demonstrate the relative potency of visual over tactual cues, as demonstrated in an ingenious experiment by Gratch (151).

Attention: Stimulus Factors

This section is concerned with absolute stimulus features as determinants of selective attending, features leading to general statements about salience and preference, more or less regardless of the long- and short-term preceding experiences of the child. Color vs form preferences (with size as a third option) were investigated in first graders during three sessions spaced over 6 months in a study by Offenbach, Baecher & White (298). Form was consistently preferred to color, which was preferred to size, and of those *S*s who changed dominance patterns between sessions, about as many shifted from form to color as from color to form. Smiley (367) produced a convincing demonstration that intradimensional variance influences preference for color or form. Although no main effect of age (kindergarten vs first grade) appeared in initial preferences, making the cues on either dimension more similar induced preference shifts to the other dimension in a second test.

Normal and distorted faces and figures as three-dimensional stimuli were presented to 1-, 2-, and 3-year-olds in Boston and Yucatan by Finley, Kagan & Layne (118). One-year-olds looked longest at normal stimuli and 3-year-olds attended longest to the most distorted figures. Neither sex nor culture differences were observed. Bartol & Pielstick (12) found an age-by-sex interaction in a study of looking time at ambiguous and unambiguous figures. The former elicited more attention in general, especially among sixth graders, as compared with second graders and adults, with males reaching their peak attention to ambiguity earlier than females. Dots, stripes, and checkerboards at three levels of complexity were shown to infants aged 6 and 11 weeks by Greenberg & O'Donnell (152). In all cases the 11-week-olds spent more time fixating the complex patterns and less time on the simple patterns than did the 6-week-olds.

McGurk (268) showed that preschoolers readily discriminated between stimuli differing only in orientation, but when color and size were covaried with orientation, the latter came out a poor third. Kessen, Salapatek & Haith (210) explain on the basis of scanning patterns their finding that vertical contours attract the newborn's visual attention, while horizontal ones appear to have no effect whatever. A procedure for independently assessing attention-getting vs attention-holding properties of checkerboard designs was devised for infants by Cohen (71). He demonstrated that latency of turning toward the pattern (getting) was more determined by overall size of the stimulus, while duration of fixation (holding) was more determined by the number of squares it contained. Jones-Molfese (199) compared full-term and premature neonates in their looking times at planometric vs stereometric checkerboard patterns presented in pairs. The two samples did not differ on planometric patterns varying in amount of contour, but they did differ on stereometric patterns varying in contour, texture, and shading.

Attention: Habituation and Novelty

The general discrepancy hypothesis as cited by Super et al (390) states that attention to a stimulus bears an inverted U-shaped relationship to the discrepancy between the actual stimulus and the person's schema for it. Their data support the hypothesis by demonstrating such a function describing infants' attention to a standard laboratory mobile as a function of its discrepancy from different mobiles to which the infants had been exposed daily for the preceding 3 weeks at home. A similar function approximately describes the relationship between the temporal and spatial unpredictability of sequential light flash patterns and the suppression of limb movements and sucking (components of the orienting response) in 4-month-old infants, but not in 2-month-olds, whose orienting responses were generally weaker (74). Response decrement to repeated exposure and recovery to stimulus change were demonstrated with checkerboards in neonates by Friedman (128). The same dishabituation to novel stimuli was demonstrated with upright faces in 5- and 6-month-old infants, especially females, by Fagan (109). The same faces presented less realistically or inverted were less well discriminated.

In a test of Jeffrey's serial habituation hypothesis for the formation of schemas, Miller (281) first determined (by looking times) the initial saliency of three components of a standard stimulus separately. She then presented her 4-month-old male *S*s with the standard repeatedly to produce habituation, following which the components were again presented separately. The dishabituation data suggested that habituation of the components had been occurring in the order of their initial saliency. Other theories, of course, might make the same prediction, but the design is ingenious and very worthy of replication and extension. Similar support for Jeffrey's hypothesis might be drawn from a study of infant cardiac responses to two-tone auditory sequences (184). Dishabituation (response recovery to novel stimuli) was obtained only when the first tone in the sequence was changed, and only then if sufficient habituation had occurred prior to presentation of the stimulus change. Berg (22) also demonstrated habituation and dishabituation of cardiac responses to auditory stimuli. Unusually rapid habituation was obtained, along with smaller orienting responses to offset of continuous stimuli.

Three studies explored novelty-familiarity preferences in more naturalistic settings. Twenty infants were studied repeatedly from 6 to 12 months of age by Schaffer, Greenwood & Parry (344). Familiarization with an intially strange object was followed by presentation of an incongruous object in each session, and visual responsiveness indicated within-session habituation and dishabituation. No effect of familiarity and congruousness on touching latency was observed until 8 months, after which prolonged hesitation in touching unfamiliar stimuli appeared. Parry (307) also studied visual fixation and manipulative latency to the same stimuli in familiar (home) and unfamiliar (lab) settings, finding more visual attention and higher latency of approach to novel stimuli in the familiar setting. Ross, Rheingold & Eckerman (336) demonstrated that 12-month-old infants entered the more novel of two rooms upon leaving their mothers, and played with the more novel of two equally available toys.

Finally, Siebold (356) demonstrated that fifth- and sixth-grade children prefer novel to familiar but meaningless stimuli (Welsh figures) as a function of degree of familiarization, regardless of the complexity of the stimuli or the length of delay between familiarization and rating (up to 7 days).

Attention: Patterns of Exploration

This rather heterogenous group of attention studies includes patterns and sequences of attending, scanning, or exploratory behavior that appear strongly to influence perception. Pick, Christy & Frankel (310) compared second and sixth graders' reaction times as they compared selected aspects of pairs of objects, either being informed of the relevant aspect before or after presentation. While the older children had faster reaction times, the difference between the times for the informed and the uninformed conditions was greater for the older than for the younger children. Deliberate selective attention thus becomes more discriminating and efficient with age. The spatial separation of manipulandum and locus of reinforcement was studied by Millar & Schaffer (279) in 6-, 9-, and 12-month-old infants using operant conditioning and a noncontingent pseudoconditioning control. All *S*s learned under zero and 5° displacements, but only the older two groups learned when the displacement was 60°.

Twins between 5 and 11 years of age were given a wide set of arrays to explore by Matheny (263). Although exploration became more systematic and less error-prone with age, no left-right patterns were observed for arrays with strong Gestalt properties, contrary to the previous finding of Elkind and Weiss. Left-to-right scanning has been implicated in the bowed serial position curve for recall of strings of letters presented tachistoscopically (left best; right next; middle worst). This finding is reversed for readers of Hebrew. In a study by Keenan (205), children from grades two, four, and six who read both Hebrew and English showed left primacy for recall of strings of English letters and right primacy when the letters were Hebrew.

Two experiments by Jones (195) illustrate the value of active, isomorphic movements in psychophysical judgements by school children. When *S*s moved their arms through a length, it was more accurately reproduced than when either their arm was moved passively or when no movement accompanied initial exposure. The effects were replicated in a second experiment with six-sided random forms. The results increase the credibility of feedback effects frequently reported informally by Zaporozhets.

One last study, an investigation of direction of serial processing of geometric stimuli, though hardly conclusive, may lead to interesting replications and extensions. Braine (32) studied recognition of figures as a function of vertical orientation (right-side-up vs upside-down). Stimuli were designed with a strong vertical axis so that a feature defined as focal for young children was always at one end and a distinguishing cue for recognition at the other end. Error analysis indicated that younger children start with the focal feature and proceed downward, regardless of its location, while older children and adults start at the top and process downward regardless of the location of focal features.

What is needed for this and many other types of studies of perceptual development is a practical, high-speed eye-movement recorder that uses a spare field of a Gerbrands-type tachistoscope without interfering with its other function. Designers note: the camera need only be activated during the few seconds before, during, and after each tachistoscopic exposure, and the child's head could be free to move at all other times.

LEARNING

A very considerable amount of research effort is still devoted to the demonstration that what is known about learning in general (usually derived from the animal laboratory) is also characteristic of children's learning. To some extent, this is open-minded research, asking a simple generality question: whether children fit the same principles as the usual laboratory subjects. However, such research can have profound implications for developmental theory, in that a learning analysis can be a nondevelopmental candidate to replace the more traditional developmental analysis (e.g. 10). Thus it is significant to note that new and increasingly complex behaviors of children have been brought under the control of environmental contingencies exemplifying both positive and negative reinforcement; that basic mechanisms of learning such as conditioned reinforcement have their existence in children's behavior; that familiar effects such as behavioral contrast can be seen even in infants; that different types of reinforcers have differential effectiveness, sometimes predictable by other characteristics of the child; and, inevitably, that many of the issues still debated within learning theory can also be contested in the arena of child behavior.

A New Method

This section of the review might well start with a bit of methodological ingenuity. In the operant analysis of learning (indeed, of behavior in general) the concept of steady state performance is of central importance (cf. 355, chap. 8). Steady state refers to an experimental situation within which the behavior being analyzed exists in a stable yet so delicate an interaction with the experimental setting that it is maximally sensitive to the widest variety of experimental variables applied to it; yet when these variables are discontinued, the behavior returns to its characteristic baseline, ready for further analysis. Several methods have been developed for maintaining samples of children's behavior in approximations to this experimental ideal (cf. 25); however, the collection could hardly be considered complete or even efficient. Thus a technique developed by DeCasper & Zeiler (87) is more than welcome. These experimenters secured agreement to develop special "locks" for the school lockers of young children. Access to the locker (to store clothing, obtain necessary school materials, etc) was accomplished only by responding on a manipulandum which turned on lights (displayed on the locker) according to one or another reinforcement schedule. When ten lights had been turned on, the locker opened. DeCasper & Zeiler were able to maintain steady, repeated performances in their subjects, using light onset as a reinforcer eventually signaling an open locker, presumably because access to the locker was an important, frequently repeated event in their school routines. In particular, the method showed that children would display the high-rate performance characteristic of fixed ratio schedules, as well as the low-rate performance characteristic of differential-reinforcement-of-low-rate schedules, but they did not at first show the temporal discrimination which fixed interval schedules ordinarily produce in laboratory animals. (This lack of temporal discrimination under the fixed interval schedule has been frequently noted by puzzled researchers pursuing operant analyses of child behavior). However, subsequent to sufficient experience with the differential-reinforcement-of-low-rate schedule, the children did display the low rate appropriate to fixed interval performance, thus demonstrating at least one experimental addition to fixed interval scheduling important to its generality of effect across species.

New Responses

Sucking by the neonate has been subjected to learning analyses often in recent years and with fruitful and meaningful results. In general, it appears to have the characteristics of an operant response. Brown (39) has shown that it also conforms to the Premack principle, in that she has demonstrated that contingent access to a typically high-rate sucking response can reinforce a usually low-rate sucking response, whereas contingent access to the low-rate sucking response will punish the high-rate response. Brown noted that non-nutritive sucking on a regular nipple is higher than (and preferred to) sucking on a blunt nipple. She then programmed 30-sec access to one nipple as a consequence of finishing a fixed ration of sucking on the other, and obtained the reinforcement and punishment effects just noted in the form of increased or decreased rates of sucking, depending on the consequence.

By contrast, Hillman & Bruner (180) analyzed the effects of reinforcement schedules on nutritive sucking in infants between 1 and 4 months of age. Their technique controlled milk delivery through the nipple according to a range of fixed interval schedules (maximum interval, 2 sec) and fixed ratio schedules (maximum ratio, four sucks). Sparse schedules (ratio and interval alike) produced shorter sucking bursts and longer pauses between bursts than richer schedules, an effect seen more clearly in the older infants than the younger ones. Arthythmic sucking in response to sparse reinforcement schedules was more characteristic of the younger infants. Since pausing in sucking is often correlated with increased scanning activity, the authors postulated increased alertness and information processing resulting from the sparse schedules.

Replication of a now familiar condition effect, reinforcement of vocal response in infants, was reported by Ramey, Hieger & Klisz (319). Their study involved two normal and two "failure-to-thrive" infants, the latter characterized by retarded growth (third percentile or lower for height and weight) without known organic basis, coupled with apathy or other developmental lags and some evidence of inadequate mothering. Successful conditioning, as seen in longer durations and higher rates of vocalizations, was shown across the subjects, suggesting generality of the operant conditioning process despite such presumably important individual differences.

Aggression in boys in the form of hitting a Bobo doll was related to punishment schedules by Parke & Deur (304). Punishment was offered in the form of a loud buzz contingent on hitting, on either a continuous (consistent) or intermittent (inconsistent) schedule, preceded by instructions that either equated the buzz to "playing badly" or simply to being a "bad noise" (the latter presumably avoiding the implications of failure confounded with the former). Previous findings with similar techniques were confirmed: consistent punishment was more effective than inconsistent; either form of stimulation was more effective than no stimulation (an extinction schedule for hitting the doll); and—not previously established—these effects were similar under either type of preceding instruction, thus extending the generality of the effect from the restricted sphere of failure effects.

Negative reinforcement of self-criticism by children in a game-playing situation was demonstrated by Grusec & Ezrin (159). After noting baseline levels of self-criticism by the children, the experimenters at first punished the children by either withdrawal of love or of material rewards. Self-criticism levels did not change simply as a result of punishment (which was not contingent on self-criticism), but they increased in those children for whom termination of the punishment was programmed contingent on self-criticism (in contrast to others for whom punishment was terminated noncontingently). Children reinforced for self-criticism appeared less disturbed by "errors" than children not so reinforced, suggesting the behavior had more than a trivial function for the children. In those children whose self-criticism was strengthened through negative reinforcement (escape from punishment), increased use of self-criticism was seen in subsequent session when the children played alone (i.e. in the absence of a punishing agent).

Discriminative control of attention span during task performance was shown in a study by Redd (322). He offered two retardates three tasks each, one task always associated with reinforcement for correct responding, another with noncontingent reinforcement, and the third with no reinforcement at all. In the course of training, the task associated with reinforcement for correct responding came to maintain steady task behavior; the other two did not. This control was shown in novel settings and with novel experimenters. Given a choice among the three tasks, the children chose either the contingently reinforced or the noncontingently reinforced tasks over the nonreinforced task, showing no preference between the first two. Thus it was seen that through an appropriate history of reinforcement, attention span could be maintained by the task itself, to some degree independently of the preference value of the task. (That is, contingently reinforced and noncontingently reinforced tasks were *preferred* equally, but only the contingently reinforced tasks came to control attentive, ongoing performance).

Finally, it may be noted that children's creativity, in one definitional form or another, became the subject of reinforcement. Goetz & Baer (143) studied the blockbuilding activities of three preschoolers, defined a list of block forms, and applied descriptive social reinforcement to the production of every new form displayed in each session's construction. (In other words, only the first appearance of any form was reinforced in each session; subsequent productions of the same form in that session were ignored.) The number of different forms made in each construction proved responsive to the reinforcement contingencies; furthermore, the emergence of new forms, never seen before in any prior constructions by the child, also increased during these reinforcement conditions. The combination of increased diversity of forms plus the emergence of new forms was postulated as a useful definition of "creative" blockbuilding and as a socially desirable outcome.

Rather different measures were involved in another study in which Stratton & Brown (387) reported that grade school children could be trained for both quality and quantity of the solutions they produced in a series of problem-solving tasks (a combination labeled "creative thinking" by the authors). Prior studies had developed one or the other of these dimensions, neither of which represents a desirable outcome if it is at the expense of the other. The present study showed the relative ease of programming for both aspects of problem solving in a factorial design combining production training, judgment training, both in combination, and neither. A behavioral mode of problem solving was suggested from the results.

Still another approach to creativity training was exemplified in a study which reported that children's ideational creativity was modifiable by reinforcement conditions (particularly by giving a penny for every successive idea generated in response to a task). Ward, Kogan & Pankove (408) noted that the penny was the most effective of several incentive techniques used, and that their current sample of low SES children yielded results highly similar to the middle class samples involved in earlier research. They also pointed out that under the uniform treatment conditions of their study, those children whose ideational creativity was increased maintained the same rank-ordering they had shown prior to the increase; from this finding, the authors argued for the "greater importance of capacity than of motivational variables" (408, p. 699). Their results would have allowed them to argue differently, however, if ideational creativity can be increased by reinforcement, for then application of much reinforcement to certain children and little to others should change their rank ordering. The next experimenter meeting the same children and applying uniform reinforcement to them would probably note that all increased but in the same rank order. However, *that* rank order would represent not capacity but the prior experimenter's differential reinforcement programs.

Basic Mechanisms

Classical conditioning of children has not been as frequently pursued as instrumental conditioning in recent years, perhaps because the mechanism is considered reasonably well known and because those responses susceptible to it are not considered as important to child development as are instrumental behaviors. Nevertheless, Werden & Ross (421) used eyelid conditioning in preschoolers to produce data of developmental significance. Their study utilized procedures of trace and delay conditioning of eyelid responses to pure tones; both paradigms were successful, but the delay procedure more so. Comparison of these data to those produced in earlier studies with retardates and college students showed similarities and differences in each direction, allowing the conclusion that developmental level (presumably the variable at issue among the three populations) was important in determining the effectiveness of a basic learning mechanism. What remains to be seen, of course, is whether these differences are relatively invariant or whether they can be erased (or even reversed) by theoretically minor adjustments of the conditioning procedures for each population (e.g. a change in UCS, or schedule, or interstimulus interval). Depending on how minor the adjustments could be, such demonstrations would tend to diminish the significance of developmental level differences.

Delay in reinforcement is usually considered to cause a decrement in learning, perhaps a failure of learning, relative to the effects of immediate reinforcement. There is a literature confirming this generalization for children and also a small body of studies indicating special cases in which delay has no (or even beneficial) effects on children's learning. To these Goldstein & Siegel (146) add another case: with a two-choice successive visual discrimination problem, they showed that forced preexposure of the discriminative stimuli during the delay and interstimulus intervals of the paradigm obviated the usual decrement produced by delayed reinforcement.

Millar (278) also offered a study of delayed reinforcement in young infants (4-8 months), using zero-, 1-, 2-, and 3-sec delays between a hand pull and "perceptual reinforcement." In general, a sequence of experiments appeared to show that the longer the delay, the less likely was successful conditioning; however, with extended experience and improved procedural controls, this gradient was nearly erased. Unfortunately, considering the response used by Millar, it is not clear whether to classify the study as one of delayed reinforcement or as one conditioning extended *duration* of the hand pull; and considering certain of his procedures, it might be considered a pause-shaping study. In the former case, the differences would probably be considered less informative of the basic nature of infant cognition than of the need to program successively longer response durations, a needed operative in any shaping study in any organism.

Conditioned reinforcement has been a mainstay concept in all learning approaches to child development, and it is common in such approaches for their treatment of socialization, language, and personality to hinge strongly, if not exclusively, on the process. Nevertheless, in the animal laboratory (where presumably the effect should be conditionable with powerful variables, such as food reinforcement in deprived animals), the effect is known as fragile and difficult to replicate. Perhaps the most robust displays of the phenomenon are in chain schedules, in which the conditioned reinforcer is never entirely divorced from the unconditioned reinforcement on which it depends in its initial shaping. (In such arrangements, the conditioned reinforcer is not literally *paired* with the unconditioned reinforcement, but instead serves as a discriminative stimulus for often extensive response performances which eventually gain the unconditioned reinforcer.) Thus a demonstration of conditioned reinforcement in children outside of the chain schedule arrangement is always significant. Just such a demonstration was offered by Favell & Favell (111), who placed children in a match-to-sample situation involving compound stimuli, which could be matched on the basis of either form or color. Form and color matches were reinforced by a token system equally often. One initially neutral stimulus was paired with each reinforcement delivery, and a second initially neutral stimulus was given at nonreinforcement times. The test of conditioned reinforcement consisted of programming the paired stimulus contingent on every match to a given dimension (e.g. form) and the nonpaired stimulus contingent on every match to the other dimension (e.g. color). Three of five children showed clear conditioned reinforcement control, preferring to match the paired-stimulus dimension, accomodating promptly to reversals of the dimension receiving the conditioned reinforcement and reversals of the roles of the initially paired and nonpaired stimuli. The remaining two children, however, showed only dimension and stimulus preferences, unaffected by the conditioning contingencies. Thus the Favells' study again demonstrated the existence of the conditioned reinforcement phenomenon, but also displayed its failure to produce uniform results outside of the chain schedule.

Nevertheless, the phenomenon has also been demonstrated in infants (an extremely high priority research need for learning approaches to infant socialization). Silverstein (361), working in Lipsitt's laboratory, taught 10-month-old infants a spatial discrimination on the basis of a conditioned reinforcer established within a single experimental session. First, tone was paired with cereal presentations as reinforcement for touching a target; after each successful touch, there was an intertrial interval during which a different tone was heard. Subsequently, the infants were presented with two targets simultaneously, and heard the first tone as a consequence of touching one and the second tone as a consequence of touching the other. The previously cereal-paired tone produced more responses to its target than did the tone previously paired with the intertrial interval, thus displaying an apparent conditioned reinforcement effect, and in a very straightforward, reality relevant situation. There remains to be seen, of course, the reliability of this effect across infants, and the development of techniques which could give it durability and generality.

Conditioned reinforcement within the chain schedule paradigm is generally a reliable phenomenon, and its apparent analogue in behavior modification, the token reinforcement system, is very widely used with typical success. (The token system may be considered an analogue of the chain schedule in that in the token system one set of responses is reinforced by tokens, which then serve as discriminative stimuli for another set of responses—trading them in—which produces already effective reinforcers.) Nevertheless, remarkably little *analytic* research has been reported on token systems, i.e. research establishing how/why the systems work. Thus a study by Smith (370) requires note, even though it is a study of a previously operating system rather than a currently operating one. Smith exposed two groups of children to a two-button discrimination task, reinforcing one group with tokens previously paired with trinkets and the other group with tokens not previously paired with anything, for pressing one of the two buttons. Subsequently, both groups underwent extinction, receiving nothing for pressing either button. During the final extinction condition, the group that had received unpaired tokens pressed the two buttons equally, but the group which had received previously paired tokens for pressing one button continued to press that button in preference to the other. The study, although not directly representative of most practically useful token systems, nevertheless does control for a number of variables typically confounded in token system applications.

Watson & Ramey (414) offered a speculative and novel suggestion about conditioned reinforcement in the young human infant on the basis of some unusual results in an infant conditioning study. In effect they suggested that a nonsocial reinforcer which successfully takes control of some instrumental behavior of the infant will subsequently be responded to as if it were a "social" stimulus. In that so much of the infant's behavior is coming under the control of social reinforcers, the generalized classing of all reinforcers as social reinforcers may well be a reasonable, if temporary, response. The idea clearly deserves further definition and research attention.

In general, the year produced a fair number of successful demonstrations of the conditioned reinforcement effect, most of which were treated by their authors as straightforward conditioning phenomena. Libb (243), however, reported success in showing acceleration of a candy-reinforced response by stimuli paired directly with candy presentation, but failed to find any increase in rate in the presence of a cue signaling that such conditioned reinforcers were available as response consequences. He interpreted that pattern of success of the conditioned reinforcer and failure of its cue as evidence for a frustration interpretation rather than a conditioned reinforcement interpretation (a not uncommon alternative view). Nevertheless, it must be remembered that his paradigm was attempting to develop discriminative function for a stimulus on the basis of a newly, perhaps weakly conditioned reinforcer; higher order conditioning with weak stimuli is always a difficult feat.

Behavioral contrast plays no particular theoretical role in current approaches to child development, but it is a familiar observation in learning; hence, it is reasonable to ask for demonstrations of it in children's learning in the interests of evaluating its generality as a phenomenon. In general, contrast is seen when behavior is weakened in one situation and consequently increases in another, despite the fact that the increased rate shown in the second setting will not gain any more reinforcement than was secured by the earlier rate. Previously no demonstrations of this effect had been noted for children (apart from one report of a brief, transient effect). In the past year, however, sustained contrast has been reported twice, once for children and once for infants. Waite & Osborne (405) presented children with alternating schedules of variable interval reinforcement, and observed the usual differential rates of response (the schedule with the shorter average interval yielding the higher rate of response). They then replaced one of the variable interval schedules with an extinction schedule, and noted a sustained rise in rate in the remaining variable interval schedule during subsequent alternations. This rise in rate could not earn more reinforcers for the children, yet it persisted, allowing a conclusion of behavioral contrast (a conclusion which is a label, not an explanation).

Working with neonates, Kobre & Lipsitt (217) used similarly alternating schedules of reinforcement with an experimental group, in this case, 5-min periods of sucking for a water solution alternating with 5-min periods of sucking for sucrose. Rather than alter the schedule for these infants, the experimenters estimated what their water-sucking rate would have been in the absence of the preferred sucrose schedule by observing a second group sucking on water exclusively. The water-sucking rate of the second group was higher than the water-sucking rate of the group alternating between water and sucrose, allowing a conclusion of negative behavioral contrast. The authors took this as evidence that "memorial processes are not absent in the neonatal child" (p. 81), a conclusion pertinent to recent hypotheses about very short memory contingencies in newborns (412).

Motivational Variables and Setting Effects

A number of studies continue to show that the operation of basic learning mechanisms can be affected by variables other than those directly involved in the conditioning contingencies. Babad (9) reported a further detail in the nature of the social deprivation/satiation procedures shown by Gewirtz & Baer (138, 139) to affect social reinforcement. In this study, children were exposed to a 10-min treatment period during which they received either 2 or 16 presentations of approval from the experimenter. Subsequently, the reinforcing effectiveness of approval was tested in a discrimination task, either by the same experimenter present during the treatment period or by a novel one. The 2-approvals children showed greater responsiveness to approval than the 16-approvals children only if the experimenter dispensing approval in the test was the same person who had given it during the treatment period. This was interpreted to mean that the children developed expectations about the experimenter present during treatment which did not generalize to the novel experimenter. Alternatively, it might be said (descriptively) that one human's approval is a different stimulus than another's, and thus each is subject to its own deprivation/satiation procedures (analogous to the way in which we may satiate for, say, chocolate ice cream but not for vanilla).

Working on the same problem, but from a somewhat different theoretical perspective, Warren & Cairns (411) showed that young children displayed a satiation effect (reduced response for a contingent social reinforcer subsequent to a high rate of presentation of that reinforcer) only if the satiation treatment was conducted in a manner which did not give the social reinforcer discriminative status for a specific task aimed at reinforcement. When, by contrast, satiation was attempted with contingent, discriminative use of approval ("right") as a guide to correct performance of a specific task, its effectiveness as a reinforcer was enhanced, not decreased. The study is open to a variety of interesting interpretations, one of which may be made within the same reference as the original hypothesis of social deprivation/satiation effects: satiation is a process which may be overlaid with opposite-function conditioning processes, such that as a stimulus is subjected to satiation procedures, it is simultaneously subjected to additional conditioning procedures (e.g. pairings) which will enhance its effectiveness.

A study by Kubose (227), relevant to "boredom" as a motivational setting effect, is also reminiscent of the satiation concept. Kubose required children to look at either colored squares or pictures for either 8 or 18 sec prior to a simple response task. Whether the following response was to be instrumental in securing reinforcement or merely obedient to instructions, it was faster following 18-sec exposures than following 8-sec exposures (of either colored squares or pictures), suggesting that lengthy periods of invariant stimulation have motivating ("boring") function.

Experiences of success or failure have received repetitive attention recently as setting events affecting subsequent performance, especially self-reinforcement practices. Masters & Peskay (261) compared black and white children from lower and upper SES backgrounds in their self-reinforcement rates, after success, failure, and neutral feedback in a game. Self-reinforcement was allowed in two forms, contingent (according to the child's opinion of how well he did) and noncontingent (as much as he wanted, independently of how well he did). In general, it was found that children from low SES levels, children experiencing success, and children allowed noncontingent self-reinforcement showed higher rates of self-reinforcement. In addition, black children were found to use self-reinforcement slightly more than white children did; but whereas white children used noncontingent self-reinforcement after both success and failure experiences, black children showed it primarily after success. Such findings hardly clarify the nature of socioeconomic status or race as variables in the learning processes, but they do invite analysis, serving presumably as the "carrier" variables cited by Lewis in a discussion of cross-cultural variables (239). In another, closely related study, Masters (260) showed that children experiencing success or failure on an initial task, as well as greater or less rewards than other children had been seen to receive, typically showed high rates of self-reinforcement on a later task after success, whether it was allowed in contingent or noncontingent form; and they showed high rates of self-reinforcement after failure only in its noncontingent form, or only on tasks quite different than the first one.

Deutsch & Stein (95) also found that failure on a task was effective setting event, this time in the realm of "private speech" (i.e. speech not addressed to anyone in particular or requiring a response from anyone). Preschoolers who failed a task showed higher rates and more articulate forms of private speech than children who were interrupted in the task (not through failure but because of inadequate materials) or children who performed the task successfully. It remains to be demonstrated what function private speech may have for any other behaviors of children; the authors did note a positive relationship to MA.

One of the most basic qualifiers of the effect of any learning contingency is the effectiveness of the reinforcer involved in that contingency. In the past year, several studies have aimed at the clarification of such reinforcer differences. Blair (27) used a size discrimination task with middle-class grade-school boys, offering either tangible, social, or performance (correctness) feedback as reinforcement. With boys who could be classified as normal achievers, social and performance reinforcers were most effective; with low achievers, tangible reinforcers were most effective. In a similar vein, Pawlicki (308) compared the effectiveness of contingent and noncontingent supportive comments, neutral comments, or silence in maintaining a simple marble-sorting task. Increases over prereinforcement baseline rates were obtained only in the case of contingent supportive comments, although subsequent comparisons of the reinforcers yielded no continuing differences. In this case, the differential effectiveness of the stimuli offered was presumably struggling to surface through a heavy overcast of obedience to instructions, which is probably not the optimal situation in which to compare reinforcers. Moffat, by contrast, may have obviated such instructional complications by using an avoidance situation to compare the value of two types of recorded music (285). His subjects listened to records and could respond to avoid a regularly scheduled interruption of that music. The music was rated as having high "interest value" for one group, low "interest value" for another. The group listening to high interest value music acquired steady avoidance responding better than the other group; but no differences were seen between the groups in the subsequent extinction of the avoidance response—an interesting disparity. Haugan & McIntire (176) offered a rare comparison of three reinforcers suitable for shaping infant vocalizations by evaluating food, tactile stimulation, and imitation of the infant's vocalizations by the experimenter. All proved effective, but imitation of the infant was clearly the most effective stimulus of the trio in increasing rate of vocalization. Such a finding immediately invokes the possibility that the function of the stimulus may have included evoking repeated subsequent vocalizations as well as (or even instead of) reinforcing prior vocalizations. The authors point out that vocal imitation may have been more effective because of its relative immediacy of delivery and greater variability of content, as well as the possibility that their subjects—institutionalized 3- to 6-month-olds—were somewhat deprived of such stimulation.

Discrimination Learning and Transfer

The bulk of publications in this area of relevance to developmentalists is still concerned with whether and how younger children perceive, organize the task, mediate, are attentionally biased, and therefore transfer discrimination training in ways that are qualitatively different from those utilized by older children. Flavell's production deficiency and Reese's mediational deficiency hypotheses have been appropriately regrouped and discussed developmentally by Kendler (208). She considers both as demonstrable forms of mediational deficiency, and accordingly redefines the latter as *control* deficiency, arguing that both are involved in the transition from sensorimotor to symbolic-representational levels of functioning.

Along with increased attention to discrimination skills in younger children has occurred a corresponding increase in the number of studies focussing on perceptual and attentional determinants of children's learning, including stimulus salience, dimensional dominance, and attentional training (37, 147, 235, 296, 366, 367, 388). In contrast to the generally positive findings of these studies, three studies that compared verbal and visual techniques directly found some advantages for the former (206, 207, 436). Fein (112) found kindergartners less sensitive to distinctiveness and verbal instructions than third graders in a transposition task, and Reese (324) found that ADC helped and AEC hurt discrimination in ways not attributable to rehearsal or perceptual differentiation. Distinctiveness of cues may thus be better viewed as a consequence than as an antecedent of dimensional and attentional processes in discrimination.

Reversal, ID and ED shifting continue to be studied in their own right, and optional reversal shifting appears to be a linear function of log age (209). It is not particularly stable over one week, but for that half of the kindergarten and second-grade children studied by Brier & Jacobs (35) who were stable, it was positively related to IQ. The use of half reversals or partial dimensional reversals was studied by Miller (283) and by Trinder et al (400). The trend toward finding surprising competence in younger and younger children is exemplified in an excellent study combining elements of oddity learning, transposition, and optional shifting by Brown & Scott (38). The authors conclude that their results are "inconsistent with theories of learning which posit a developmental progression from single-unit processes to complex mediational processes, unless that progression can be said to occur before 3 years of age" (Abstract).

Color or form dominance has again been shown to be modifiable by either differential reinforcement (FR 5 vs FR 2) or by instructions to verbalize in 4- to 7-year-olds (162). Better recall of previously discriminated positive than negative or neutral cues has been demonstrated in a design controlling differential frequency and recency of exposure (323), and the result is stable over three consecutive discrimination problems. Incidental recall of a redundant, relevant cue is superior to recall of an irrelevant cue following discrimination, and a recency explanation is offered by Anderson (4).

Various kinds of stimulus summation and compounding received attention in 1972 in multiple-cue and training-generalization studies. Simultaneous use of multiple cues with different assigned weights was demonstrated in a psychophysical judgment task for school-age children by Montanelli (286). Spiker's stimulus interaction hypothesis was further supported in a study by Berch (21). The range of stimuli used in stimulus generalization studies appears to directly affect discriminability of stimuli within that range, which in turn determines generalization gradients, according to Croll (80). Formal predictions for multidimensional generalization as a function of verbal pretraining on one dimension were derived and sustained in a study by Spiker, Croll & Miller (378). Bogartz (28) provided an alternative analysis of the same data using three cue-selection models which he claimed explained the data of Spiker et al equally well. Their reply (379) illustrates what may be the problems symptomatic of a field in which the number of theoretical formulations exceed the number of significant and reliably demonstrable phenomena.

Task, format, and other boundary conditions may be more potent than theoretically subtle differences among processes and mechanisms in determining the amount of transfer of discrimination training according to the results of four experiments reported by Campione & Beaton (50).

Concept Formation: A Strained Concept

Classical concept formation studies have almost disappeared from the literature, but the learning of conceptual classes, rules, and sequential-probabilistic patterns by children have all received research attention in 1972. Caruso & Resnick (53) exemplified a trend toward logical and sequential task analysis in place of abstract theorizing. Having logically defined an "optimal" sequence for three matrix classification tasks (simple to complex) they demonstrated most rapid learning and best transfer to new matrices with similar structure following "optimally" sequenced training. The Bower-Trabasso procedure was used to test for continuity vs. noncontinuity in concept acquisition in an excellent study by Tighe & Tighe (397). The procedure involves presolution reversals of reinforcement contingencies and should increase errors to criterion (as compared with no-reversal controls) if the child is continuously developing partial knowledge about the solution, but not if he is engaged in relevant cue selection, as are college-age subjects. Fifth graders showed no such interference attributable to presolution reversals, but kindergarteners and first graders did. Cue-selection, rather than logical hypothesis generation seemed to account for the effect.

Verbal processes continue to be implicated as determinants of the more elaborated concepts of older children (342). It is noteworthy, however, that the involvement and contribution of verbal behaviors to the formation of class concepts defined as perceptual sets in preschoolers (422) and toddlers (292) is beginning to merit consideration. Verbalization by a model facilitates vicarious rule learning, generalization, and retention (439). Modeling and instructions to imitate were more effective than rehearsal and initial probability in a rule-governed verbal association game (333). Modeling and rule provision were effective in the absence of extrinsic reinforcers of any kind in a dial-reading, numerical concept task (441).

Bogartz's attentional-mnemonic model of binary prediction received confirmation by Jones (198), and cue-utilization and achievement in one-and two-cue probabilistic tasks were studied developmentally by Deffenbacher & Hamm (88). The latter found that sensitivity to environmental regularity was high at all ages, that Weir's U-shaped function relating age and achievement obtains only when the task provides one partially informative cue, and that when two cues of different probabilistic validity were present, performance increased linearly with age.

Memory

The study of mnemonic capacities and processes in children has shown a remarkable surge in popularity, perhaps reflecting recent increases in concern with attention, information processing, and memory in adults; advances in studies of children's verbal mediation and imagery; concern with developmental psycholinguistics; and Piaget's recent concern with mnemonic processes. A discussion of memory as an epiphenomenon of various cognitive developments and social interactions was published by Meacham (273). In general it appears that most studies are concerned either with a variety of contextual effects or with various measurable, trainable, or otherwise inducible strategies for processing information in ways that make it more retrievable, and these two foci are used to summarize the literature below.

A few memory studies are noteworthy but do not fit in the two categories mentioned. Retention by preschoolers was studied by Rosner (335) in a task similar to the game of "concentration," where over successive tests, items are drawn from the same pool, placed face down in a row, one at a time, and then *S* is given a copy of one of them and must locate its copy by position in the face-down array. Experienced *S*s show primacy effects (like adults) when a new list is used. Repeated testing from a small pool reduces retention regardless of serial position, and, after the first test, shows no primacy effect with children. Analogously, in paired-associates (P-A) learning Cole & Kanak (73) demonstrated that while first and third graders learn slower than fifth and seventh graders, there are no age differences in recall, and R-S recall was as good as S-R recall at all ages. Short-term recognition time for words was corrected by subtracting simple naming time from decision time, the difference being termed "memory scanning time" by Kirsner (215), who found no age differences in memory scanning time by this procedure when presentation list and test word were given auditorily. There were developmental differences, however, when the recognition list and the test word were presented in different modalities. Thus apparent age changes in mnemonic latency may be more a result of perceptual and response factors than of developmental changes in memory scanning rate. Reinstatement of previously learned behavior was demonstrated in 7-year-olds by Hoving & Choi (186) when they presented the previously learned response, but not when they presented the previous stimulus. Hoving et al (187) also demonstrated reinstatement by repeating pairs in a story context, but found no differences between 5- to 8-year-olds and 8- to 11-years-old.

Initial and middle positions of the serial recall curve are more strongly dependent upon age and IQ than are terminal positions (110) suggesting that short-term memory is less influenced by development than long-term memory. Similarly Belmont (19) showed that acquisition and retrieval are strongly influenced by age and IQ, but that short-term forgetting rate is not.

Nonverbal context can clearly serve to organize and facilitate recall, especially in young children. Reese (325) demonstrated that acquisition of paired-associate pictures was facilitated by showing the stimulus and response figures in mutual interaction as compared to showing them merely side by side. Repetition of responses facilitated primacy position recall as well. A facial context within which various curved lines could be interpreted as smiles and frowns did *not* facilitate discrimination and recognition in a study by Pick et al (311). For children "too young to mediate verbally" (3- and 4-year-olds) Conrad (75) found that color and form differences were equally well recognized from short-term memory, and that recognition was improved when items were redundantly differentiated in both color and form.

Five studies this year were concerned in one way or another with words vs pictures as stimuli in children's memory tasks. Davies (86) showed 9-year-olds either names or pictures of objects. Pictures were more effective when *S*s had to identify the object immediately in an array, but words were more effective in subsequent written recall. Holyoak, Hogeterp & Yuille (182) found that the P-A learning and recall of interacting figures was superior to the same pair presented side by side (cf Reese 325), and that simultaneous *E*-verbalization of the names of the paired items connected by a *verb* was better than their connection by a *conjunction* for both acquisition and recall. Again there were no age differences. Rowe (339) showed that in a discrimination learning task pictures were more easily discriminated than words by both adults and fourth graders, regardless of whether the required response was verbal or nonverbal. Using 5-, 8-, and 12-year-olds, Randhawa (320) compared visual vs verbal input and verbal vs nonverbal output. Visual input and nonverbal (reconstruction) recall was the best combination; verbal input and verbal output was the worst. Only output mode interacted with age, with older children doing better on verbal. Perhaps the most comprehensive study on this topic is that by Lynch & Rohwer (252). Pictures as stimuli were better recognized and matched than words, and the difference was greater for sixth than for third graders. Sixth graders were also better at verbal recognition of pictorial stimuli. When *E* provided at exposure the names of stimuli, the grade-by-mode interaction vanished. In summary, it appears that pictorial beats verbal at all ages, and that relevant, meaningful verbalization at exposure, when added to pictorial presentation, may facilitate recall, especially when the recall task involves verbal stimuli or responses.

Within the domain of verbal memory, two studies demonstrated that both rapid and long-term recognition of words is facilitated when encoding makes use of the evaluative (good-bad) connotations of the words (57, 117). Meaningfulness of both stimuli and responses is positively associated with P-A retention (142). Free recall is superior and more clustering occurs with semantically related than with unrelated words, which in turn are recalled better than acoustically related words by third graders (443). Horvitz & Levin (185) found that maintaining semantic constancy of the sentence or phrase context in which verbal paired associates were presented to that in which they were tested facilitated recall. Imagery instructions facilitated performance of sixth but not third graders. In free recall first graders may cluster *more* than adults instead of *less* (94). If the relationship between words is one of functional complementarity, children cluster more, but if it is one of categorical similarity, then adults cluster more. The finding appears to be analogous to the syntagmatic-paradigmatic shift in word associations associated with increasing age. The same phenomenon may underlie a finding by Suzuki (391) that children (but not adults) learn noun pairs better in the syntactic context, noun-verb-noun-conjunction-pronoun than in the context, noun-conjunction-noun-verb-pronoun. That is, "*dog* bites *man* and me" creates a functional, syntagmatic relationship between the to-be-remembered items "dog" and "man," which is mnemonically helpful to children. However, "dog and *man* bite me" gives a similarity or paradigmatic link between the to-be-remembered items that is less useful to children. Similarly Ehri (103) found that deep grammatical structure relationships, but not surface structure ones, facilitated retrieval of noun pairs, and Thurlow & Turnure (396) found that elaborative contexts, especially semantic paragraphs, facilitated P-A acquisition and reversal.

A multibowed serial recall curve for lists of nine digits was produced by experimenter-imposed spatial and temporal groupings during presentation in a study by Harris & Burke (169) of elementary school children. Corsini (76) found that spatial-positional cues were not used for memory purposes by kindergarteners, but verbal and other perceptual cues were helpful. Heider & Olivier (177) studied color naming and color matching from memory in two cultures whose color names and categories differed markedly. Contrary to Wharfian expectations, memory matching was unaffected by color-name semantics, but, of course, language and culture differences showed up in the naming task. Deaf and hearing children were compared when using and not using vocal labels as an aid to recalling object arrangements by Chovan (61). Differences in MA rather than deafness or use of labels accounted for most of the variance in recall. Similarly, Kimball & Dale (212) found that although recognition for colors was related to ability to name them, again CA, MA, and IQ strongly interacted with both naming and recall.

A final group of memory studies has as a common feature the elicitation or observation of specific mnemonic strategies, as distinct from those which merely provided mnemonic aids. Marx (258) found that younger elementary children showed better *recall,* but older children showed better *recognition* for words whose spelling had been practiced 3 months earlier. He interpreted the interaction as a consequence of greater verbal elaboration by the older children. Mallory (256) compared kindergarten and second graders classed as verbalizers with those classed as visualizers in a P-A task where verbal, visual, or no elaboration was provided. Isomodal advantages of selective elaboration strategies were demonstrated, which generalized to no-elaboration items. Instructions to remember, to group phonetically vs semantically, to categorize, or to organize all have been demonstrated to facilitate recall (24, 78, 216, 265, 350). However, kindergarten and first-grade *S*s, unlike fifth graders, study no differently and recall no better when instructed to memorize than when instructed merely to look at the stimuli (5). Using labial vs nonlabial phonemes and labial EMG recordings with second and third graders, Goldstein, Locke & Fehr (145) found no evidence that subvocalizers excelled non-subvocalizers in free oral recall of pictures and words. Instructed "visual rehearsal" helps preschoolers remember (277), and spontaneous manual manipulation of objects to form "dynamic images" facilitates recall even in "preimagery" children (429, 430). Kindergarteners benefit from instructions to form images only when the objects are tactually available for manipulation, whether or not they are visually available (431).

The most convincing studies in general appear to be those which define a stimulus feature, task poverty, or ancillary behavior, manipulate and measure it directly, and then assess its effects on memory—all as a function of a carrier variable like age or intelligence. These development-by-treatment designs are particularly revealing when a contributory behavior has been identified correlationally as facilitating learning or memory in naturalistic settings at developmental level *n,* and can then be experimentally synthesized and separately observed as a potential facilitator at level $n - k$.

IMITATION

Imitation by children is a longstanding target of research, in part because of its importance in socialization and language development, in part because it is a wholesale method of behavior change, and no doubt because it is a complex behavior and thus appropriate to competing theoretical analyses. The past year's research on imitation can be organized into three main categories: studies of variables contributing to the development or modification of imitation as a behavior; comparison of imitation and direct reinforcement or punishment; and the use of imitation to develop other behaviors.

The Development and Control of Imitation

Schroeder & Baer (348) used operant techniques to teach two retarded children increasingly skillful vocal imitation by two different methods of direct shaping; they then compared the generalization of imitative skill resulting from each method. One method labeled "serial" consisted of teaching the child to imitate three words or phrases, each taught separately, until a criterion of mastery was achieved, then the next, etc. The other method called "concurrent" involved teaching three words or phrases intermixed, bringing all three to a criterion of mastery at roughly the same time. Each subject experienced both methods in repeated alternations. Interspersed tests of generalized imitative skill (with untrained words and phrases) showed consistent superiority of generalization resulting from each application of the concurrent method. Although the concurrent method is not the usual method of teaching language to deficient children, the authors suggested that it might prove to be advantageous for such skills. Replication is clearly in order, especially with both smaller and larger units of speech, and with generalizable skills other than vocal imitation.

Geshuri (137) added another detail to the literature concerning the facilitative effects on imitation of observed reinforcement of the model. He showed young children video strips of a model displaying certain behaviors; over repeated trials the model displayed either a steady rate of these responses or an increasing rate, and was seen to receive either approving comments, neutral comments, or no special stimuli. (An unusual feature of the study was a preliminary phase, during which the reinforcing function of the approving comments to be used in the video strips was evaluated for the subjects.) Only those children watching the model receive approving comments showed imitation of the model, matching the rate (constant or increasing) displayed by the model over trials. Thus it was concluded that observed reward of a model is a cue for matching the model.

Two other studies uncovered techniques for inhibiting imitative behavior. Jeffrey, Hartmann & Gelfand (190) had children watch a model make choices in a simple preference task. Some children were reinforced directly for matching the model's responses; some instead experienced a nurturant interaction with the model; and some had neither experience. Those children reinforced for doing so imitated the model; those who had just had a nurturant interaction with the model matched no more often than a chance level; and those who had experienced neither (i.e. who had encountered an unresponsive model immediately prior) showed negative imitation—they systematically mismatched the model's preferences. In a subsequent phase with the model absent, only the previously reinforced children continued to match; the others showed chance performances. Negative imitation, or systematic mismatching, is a little researched phenomenon, but its logical importance would seem equal to that of positive imitation. The method of this study might well prove fruitful for future investigations in greater detail.

Examining a different class of variables, Masters (259) also found a negative imitation effect. In his study, preschoolers interacted with an adult partner; different groups discovered that the partner received more, the same, or fewer rewards than they did. Subsequently, the adult modeled certain behaviors of an innocuous sort, and also gave away rewards to supposed "poor children." Then the children had their chance to imitate his behaviors, including the giving away of rewards to other children. The unusual finding was that children who had seen the adult receive fewer reinforcers than they had received imitated the model less than children in other conditions. Why this should be awaits analysis. Meanwhile, Masters recommended that a proper definition of altruism should require a demonstration that the child called altruistic give away *more* rewards than a model has been observed to do, to distinguish it from mere "imitated altruism."

Comparison with Direct Reinforcement and Punishment

Cheyne (59) compared direct experience of reward and punishment with imitation (vicarious reinforcement). In that study, young children either chose a word from a pair of words and were told directly whether the choice was right or wrong, or else they watched a model undergo the same experience. In a subsequent test of recall (of which word in each pair was correct), directly rewarded and imitating (observing) children did equally well in recalling correct items; but children who were directly punished recalled better those negative items than children who only observed those items punished. However, if a child were given explicit instructions about future matching during the observation phase, this difference was eliminated. Such studies help to emphasize that there are probably few, if any, *invariant* differences between learning by imitation and by direct contingencies: either can be done well or badly; thus comparisons can be made to show any outcome.

Use of Imitation to Affect Other Behaviors

In a simple and straightforward application of imitation and reinforcement techniques, Zimmerman & Pike (440) increased the question-asking behavior of disadvantaged Mexican-American second grade children. A comparison to the effects of praise alone, contingent on question-asking, showed that it was effective, but not so efficient as the combination of an adult model with the praise. An untreated control group showed no essential change in their rate of the same behavior over that span of time. Some generalization of the effect was seen with a new teacher who neither modeled nor praised question-asking. In addition to the experimental group-control group design, a multiple baseline design was used as well, marking one of the first appearances of this "behavior modification" design in the more abstractly oriented journals of the field. It may be presumed that question-asking eventually should be maintained by the intermittent reinforcement implicit in the answers the behavior produces; an interesting question for generalization theory is how to use techniques such as in the present study to bring the behavior into sufficient contact with those natural consequences for indefinite maintenance of the response class. The Zimmerman & Pike study at least suggests a strong start toward that goal.

The intersection of imitation phenomena and television phenomena are apparent in a study by Wolf & Cheyne (428), in which school boys were exposed to models who either conformed to or broke a rule not to perform a certain act. One modeling condition consisted of live peers behaviorally breaking or conforming to the rule; another was the televised versions of the same acts; and a third model consisted of a peer verbally describing breaking or conforming to the rule. Relative to a no-model control condition, the children generally did what their models did; the live and televised models proved most effective, and the verbal model least. Ominously, the effects of rule-breaking models were more apparent in a one-month later followup than were the effects of rule-conforming models. The study adds one more set of facts to the accumulating literature on the effect of television models currently under debate.

LANGUAGE

The obvious importance of language to child development need not be labored here. However, its role as the arena within which competing theoretical approaches to the study of development come into their clearest opposition might well be noted once again. In particular, as learning approaches have demonstrated increasing ability to theoretically and factually analyze more and more areas of child behavior, language has increasingly become the crucial test case. Language may be seen as the expressive, mediating handmaiden of the essentially cognitive, symbolic, internalizing child; alternatively, it may be seen as a remarkably complex repertoire of discriminated operants with special utility for mediating generalization and class organization of behaviors in general. At the very least, it will be recognized as uniquely human in its full blown form, and as a very large problem for any approach. In terms of this context, the past year was surprisingly quiet (although some of the work which might be summarized here will be considered instead under Applications). Three classes of research will be considered: a few examples of the conditions which may be arranged to produce one or another language skill; some consideration of the mediating function of language for the development of other behaviors; and some contributions toward the theory of language acquisition.

Control of Language Skills

The undifferentiated vocalization rate of 3- to 4-month-old infants again proved susceptible to social reinforcement in a study by Banikiotes, Montgomery & Banikiotes (11). The social reinforcement was vocal feedback by adults. Conditioning was very quick, occurring in two 3-min stages of reinforcement within a single session. A notable component of the study was the use of both male and female experimenters to supply vocal reinforcement: no differences were seen in their effectiveness as reinforcing agents, nor was any shift in the fundamental frequencies of the infants' voices noted as function of male vs female reinforcement. (There is some evidence to suggest that with older infants, the use of male or female voices as reinforcers could produce a shift in fundamental frequency toward matching that of the experimenter. Whether this study represents a fundamental age difference, or simply too brief a conditioning period to allow the shift, is not clear.)

By contrast, Whitehurst, Novak & Zorn (424) reported an experimental case study in which speech was improved by evocative rather than reinforcing contingencies. Their study began as an observational analysis within the home of a 3 year-old speech-retarded child, noting minimal levels of imitative prompts and conversation by the parents to the child. Experimental intervention consisted of prescribing relatively small increases in the parents' rates of using either conversation or imitative prompts with the child. Either tactic proved equally successful in accelerating the child's acquisition and steady use of new words, as evident in dinner table speech (when all recordings were made). The study is noteworthy for its results, its careful observation and quantification techniques, and its use of a natural setting and the natural events within that setting. In addition, its interpretation is clearer than that of many other natural setting researches, in that it could specify that the immediate controlling variable was evocative conversation or prompts rather than an increased use of social reinforcement (which was observed and noted as constant throughout the experimental phases of the study). The authors point out that laboratory analyses of language skills need not prove relevant to natural environment mechanisms of language development, and express a concern for questions ". . . that can only be answered by studying the development of language in situations where parents and children can interact in a normal manner, where variables are defined from the situation rather than imposed upon it" (424, p. 169). There remains, of course, the need for explication of why these natural parent behaviors had such potent evocative function for their child's speech. Conceivably these events rely upon the reinforcing consequences parents have programmed intermittently throughout the child's earlier history. If so, a final analysis may yet prove to resemble laboratory models quite closely. Nevertheless, there is no denying the validity or value of the authors' approach. It represents a rare intersection of psycholinguistic and behavior modification techniques (cf. 10).

Bennett & Ling (20) reported a simple study of language improvement with a noteworthy outcome. Their subject was a 3-year-old hearing-impaired girl whose speech was primarily telegraphic, lacking articles, auxiliary verbs, etc. Through experimentally controlled imitation techniques, she was taught to use "the" and "is" in her descriptions of pictures presented to her. In consequence of this short, simple training, she was then able to describe new, untrained pictures in well-formed sentences in the present progressive tense. In that telegraphic speech impresses its hearers as primitive and retarded, whereas well-formed sentences are taken as evidence of good symbolic development, the study represents a useful analysis of how simple the response analysis of an apparently complex step in development may be for a given child.

Language acquisition continues to be studied as an imitative process, with emphasis on the naturalistic language environment (127, 398) and the verbal behavior of the mother (183, 371). In laboratory settings, imitation and modeling have influenced grammatical rule learning and sentence complexity more strongly than has exposure, expansion, sex, and bilingualism (173, 257). Appropriate, novel, two-word responses by 2-year-olds can result from training involving imitation, differential reinforcement, and holding the first word constant. Whitehurst (423) describes this procedure as a "partially conditioned frame." Adults as interpreters of children's speech are more accurate if they are parents. (419). According to Silverman (360), the complexity of children's speech as judged by adults is not influenced by the context (egocentric vs social), but Moerk (284) has made a strong plea for the incorporation of more contextual nonverbal variables in the study of adult-child interaction and demonstrated the use of this strategy. One study of receptive language has important methodological implications. Kamil & Rudegeair (202) found much higher sound discrimination scores for 5- and 6-year-olds when either (*a*) stimuli were made more redundant, e.g. /bob/vs/dod/ instead of /b/vs/d/, or (*b*) multiple testing sessions were used to establish a familiar procedure and a strong discrimination set. In general, in this area there appears to be a healthy level of interaction and cumulativity of research between theoretical camps, between laboratory and naturalistic studies, and between correlational surveys and experimental interventions.

Mediation of Other Behaviors

Language, used as a tool of conceptual analysis, was modeled for young children in a study by Rosenthal, Alford & Rasp (332). The subjects (second graders) were unable to solve a novel clustering task presented to them. They then watched a model solve examples of the problem, with different groups experiencing a silent model or models providing varying degrees of clarity of explanation, to the point of supplying a rule to handle future instances. In general, the degree to which the children acquired the clustering concept at issue was a function of the clarity or strength of the model's verbal coding during the modeled performance, as was their generalization to new stimuli embodying the same concept. Thus, whereas imitation can be a potent developmental mechanism, such studies as these demonstrate clearly that there exist performances too complex for quick acquisition simply through observation; yet observation plus a fairly minimal amount of language "coding" relevant to it yields prompt mastery and generalization. This is a familiar function of language, of course, yet not a frequently researched one, especially from the point of view of developmental process.

However, a failure of language to improve mediation reported in the past year may hold some surprises. Quay (317) reported that administration of the Stanford-Binet to 50 4-year-old black children "selected from an extremely deprived, physically and socially isolated community" (p. 245), in either standard English or in Negro dialect, yielded no systematic differences. An analysis of item difficulty also displayed no differences. Thus an abstract cognitive task, highly dependent on language skills, was not facilitated by administration of it in the language forms presumably most familiar and most useful to these children, who were presumed to be severely disadvantaged and perhaps most susceptible to confusion by standard English dialect.

Perhaps the most thorough view of language as a mediator in the past year's literature (and many other years as well) was offered by Palermo & Molfese (302). Deliberately turning their attention away from the first 4 years, during which acquisition seems most rapid and dramatic, these authors pointed out that after age 5, language continues to develop in increasingly complex and sophisticated ways, typically involving phonological, syntactic, and semantic components. Furthermore, at each notable developmental stage subsequent to age 5, corresponding advances in language behavior have already been noted in the literature. Taken as a whole, these studies suggest that ongoing language elaboration remains integral to, perhaps essential to, the breadth of development yet to take place throughout the developmental span of the organism. The argument seems undeniable, and the comprehensive review and integration offered by Palermo & Molfese hopefully will serve to better distribute research attention across the age span and developmental levels available for the analysis of language.

Theoretical Argument

Early in the year, McNamara (272) presented a *Psychological Review* paper which may be considered a major essay in the theory of language development. His central thesis was that language serves meaning for the developing child only to the extent that meaning already exists. Thus if an infant can understand the meaning of another person, it is then possible to decode the language used by that other person and thereafter to use the language himself. It is not the case that meaning is derived from or built upon developing language skills, but rather that language is derived from and built upon developing meanings. McNamara's prime assumption is that a distinction can be drawn between intention and language. It seems to follow that the study of language development is essentially a study of an increasingly bright code-breaker at work. For McNamara the theory is an outgrowth of earlier statements by Brown (40); however, it is meant to add to that statement an integration of vocabulary, syntax, and phonology, and to add very recent findings in linguistics and psycholinguistics. In doing so, McNamara was less than satisfied with the result. He argued that to some extent the development of vocabulary, syntax, and phonology were interdependent, but not completely enough to assign simple sequences to their acquisition: ". . . the interdependencies are only partial, though it is important to appreciate that at present they are quite obscure" (272, p. 11). In summary, it was argued that a fair analogy can be drawn between the language-developing child and the linguist describing a new language, with the exception that the linguist is constrained to state rules and the child is not. At any rate, it is a language development theory which thrusts primary importance and priority on nonlinguistic cognitive development [in which context Piaget is cited approvingly (p. 11)]

Developmental Psycholinguistics

An article by Dan Slobin (365) in *Psychology Today* makes a strong plea for the universality of the processes of language acquisition, one that is rich in multicultural, multilingual comparisons, and one which would not be strongly contested by a verbal behavior theorist. In the presence of function words only, 4- and 6-year olds imitate grammatical sentences more accurately than ungrammatical ones (250). De Villiers & de Villiers (96) found that 2- and 3-year-olds could grammatically correct and appropriately carry out imperative instructions that were made semantically anomalous, but that only the most linguistically advanced *Ss* could do so when the commands contained syntactic errors (reversed word orders). The penetration of psycholinguistics into Genevan psychology is evidenced in a study by Sinclair & Bronckart (362) in which all orders of two nouns and a verb were presented to Genevan, French-speaking children from 3 to 7 years of age. A developmental trend was established toward interpreting the first noun as subject and the second as object, regardless of verb location.

A promising new direction in linguistic research is indicated by a series of articles on the development of the language of emotions (241, 242, 432, 433). The authors attempt to study how children come to name their feelings, using a theoretical framework that contains elements of Freud, Piaget, Luria, and Lenneberg.

Two studies attempted to elicit generalized syntagmatic or paradigmatic word associations in order to cast light on the developmental shift between these two modes of response. Routh & Tweney (337) used instructions, prompting, and examples together with candy rewards to train kindergarteners and fifth-graders to make paradigmatic free associations. The general shift was obtained in that the older children made more paradigmatic responses in all conditions. Training produced a small increase in paradigmatic responding to verbs and adjectives at both ages, but a slight decrease among younger *Ss* in paradigmatic responses to nouns. Francis (125) used a word-matching task and directed associations with 7-year-olds, but found that neither form-class knowledge nor semantic class knowledge was sufficient to account for the range of responses and reasons therefore given by the children. Apparently we still have a phenomenon in search of a verifiable explanation.

COGNITIVE DEVELOPMENT

The research boom in cognitive development appears to have not yet reached its peak, and work stimulated by and addressing itself to Piagetian questions still dominates the field. Replication (and failure to replicate), extension to new tasks or materials and training studies account for nearly equal portions of the literature in 1972. Various applications of Piagetian notions to testing, educational practice, etc are gaining in frequency.

In the journal literature, two integrative theoretical essays are of interest. Kagan (200) addressed himself to the cognitive development of infants, summarizing a germinal series of studies that have led him to conclude that infant cognitive development is both more extensive and more maturationally based than most recent theorists have held it to be. Like several other infant laboratories, Kagan's is finding the orienting response to be as widely useful in assessing infant information processing as its earliest proponents predicted it would become. The use of response decrement and recovery techniques together with the incorporation of state variables and expectation phenomena within the general discrepancy (or adaptation-level) format have enabled Kagan to investigate such processes as hypothesis forming as early as 9 months of age. In fairness to other investigators, and in support of Kagan's summary, it should be noted that numerous other investigators of infant attending have used essentially the same logic and methods and reached essentially the same conclusions.

The second theoretical contribution is a very thoughtful and tightly reasoned monograph by Flavell (120) on the logic of sequential acquisition of competencies. Both requirements for developmental theorizing and criteria of methodological adequacy are discussed in terms of the establishment of sequential invariance of development, both between and within stages. The article should be required reading for researchers attempting experimentally to disentangle the skeins of developmental process.

Smillie (368) takes Piaget to task regarding the notion of *perceptual tableaux* used to describe the experience of the young infant. Citing research by Bower, the author reinterprets Piaget's evidence and proposes an initial period of visual realism, followed by a period in which the infant explores the range and consequences of his own actions. Only later are the two systems coordinated, according to this analysis of sensorimotor development.

It should be noted that Piaget's perceptual theory regarding the error of the standard has been strongly challenged by Begelman & Steinfeld (17) on conceptual, methodological, and empirical grounds. The authors offer new data in support of their conclusion that the operation of an error of the standard is not a required assumption for interpretation of any data thus far obtained.

Replication and Nonreplication of Piaget

Object permanence continues to receive the major share of attention in studies of sensorimotor development. Evans & Gratch (108) demonstrated that the stage IV error (looking for a hidden object where it was last found instead of where it has just been hidden) is made as often when the previously found toy is hidden in a new place as when a different toy is hidden in the new place. They reinterpret the stage IV error as simply a position preference. Webb, Massar & Nadolny (415) noted the information from early hiding trials produced pro-active interference on the first-choice responses on subsequent trials, indicating memory effects, but adequate self-correction on second choices by 16-month-olds. Fourteen-month-olds also showed pro-active interference but lacked a self-correction strategy. Both are apparently important contributors to object constancy performance.

Classification and conservation remain the favorite skills of investigators of concrete-operational thinking. The types and sequences of free-classification responses found by Piaget & Inhelder, and also those found by Vygotsky, were not fully replicated in two studies by Denney (92, 93). Task requirements, instructions, and procedures appear to play a more important role than the early studies assumed, but even when the early procedures were replicated closely, discrepant results were obtained.

Equivalence and identity conservation as different processes were studied in 4- and 6-year-olds by Elkind & Schoenfeld (106), who found identity easier, especially for younger children. On the other hand, Moynahan & Glick (289) found that identity and equivalence co-occurred in number, quantity, and weight conservation tasks, and identity occurred first only in one length-conservation task.

Compensation, at least as assessed by verbal explanation, appears not to contribute to the acquisition of conservation of liquid, since conservation appears first, according to Gelman & Weinberg (136). However, compensation is found differentially depending upon whether it is assessed by verbal explanation or by instructions to pour liquids in a compensatory fashion.

Three- to 6-year-olds have a clear understanding of number invariance, at least for small numbers, though they may not show conservation of number on standard tasks, according to Gelman (135). The conclusion is supported by their surprise reactions to surreptitious number change as well as by verbal explanations of changes in number, length, and density. Again the subtlety and ingenuity of Gelman's experiments are models of conservation research that ought to be more widely imitated. Pufall & Shaw (316) further clarified the distinction between "true" conservation on equivalence problems and pseudoconservation on inequivalence number problems. Either U-shaped or flat developmental curves were obtained, but the information processing of 3- and 4-year-olds appeared to be based directly on salient stimulus differences, while that of 5- and 6-year-olds depended more on the relationship of spatial properties to number. Discrimination rather than conservation procedures were used by Siegel (357) to study number concepts in 3- and 4-year-olds. Oneness and linear magnitude (constant density) discriminations co-occur and appear earlier than discrimination of nonlinear magnitude. Brainerd & Brainerd (34) point out that differential difficulty data indicating that number conservation is easier than liquid quantity conservation do not necessarily establish that the former always develops prior to the latter. But they established that it does by within-subject ordinal analyses.

The study of formal-operational thought is gaining interest, especially in relation to the roles of logic and language. Jones (196) demonstrated that sixth-grade boys of equal IQ but differing verbal ability and the use of tentative statements were equally skilled at hypothetical reasoning. Piaget will doubtless be pleased by these results. He is probably not as pleased with the results of a study by Bynum, Thomas & Weitz (47), who used the Inhelder-Piaget protocol on invisable magnetism and the original authors' method of analysis, and found in that protocol evidence for only 8 of the 16 binary operations of truth-functional logic. Eight of the Inhelder-Piaget analyses were deemed faulty, and six of the operations were alleged never to occur or be needed in any complex reasoning tasks. Indeed those six operations can be performed more simply by various combinations of the other ten. Additional credence is lent to this analysis by the fact that the first two authors are logicians and logic teachers. Finally, a contribution to the understanding of negation as both a concrete and a formal operation was made in an excellent monograph by Feldman (114).

Piagetian Innovations

Grouped in this section are studies in which new concepts, tasks, materials, methods, variables, or types of subject were studied more or less within the framework of Piagetian theory. Among new methods of developmental assessment are the use of a trick violation of object permanence to elicit varying amounts of puzzlement and searching in infants (233), and the use of movie presentation of conservation demonstrations to assess attainment of conservation (295).

The ingenuity of Bruner and his colleagues was again demonstrated in the devising of novel tasks, such as a lever to be used by 1- year-olds to rotate a turntable which thereby brought a toy within reach (223), or the use of seriated nesting cups to study the development of rulebound strategies in 1- and 2-year-olds (154). In both studies the now familiar outcomes of greater-than-expected orderliness and competency and earlier-than-expected development of skills were obtained.

The role of language in Piaget-type cognitive attainments continues to be studied, and not just at the symbolic and operational levels. For example, Sullivan (389) showed that children from 4 to 10 years old increasingly used constrained causal connectives and attended to the order of events presented in pairs of pictures. Ability to explain the temporal order as a clue to causal relatedness also increased with age. However, an experimental study will be needed to establish the contribution (as distinct from covariance) of language over the ages studied. Another language correlation was reported by Roberts & Black (330), who found that if children 1½ years old can follow an object through a sequence of invisible displacements (SM stage 6), then they tend to prefer and manipulate toys that are named by *E* to toys not named.

Integration of Piaget-type and learning-theory-based conceptions is continuing to appear in the literature. Transposition learning was related to seriation competency in studies of size (358) and of happy-to-sad faces (211). Figurative vs operative knowing and the relationship between logical and perceptual knowing were studied in 4- to 9-year-olds in two contrasting studies. Overton & Brodzinsky (301) showed that while there are no direct influences of figural or perceptual features that enhance two-way classification (conjunctive concepts) prior to the attainment of logical multiplication, there is a transitional period prior to the attainment of logical multiplication during which minimization of perceptual features enhances logical solution. However, in a simple drawing task with familiar objects, Freeman & Janikoun (126) demonstrated a developmental change between 7 and 8 years from intellectual realism (drawing what is known) to visual realism (drawing what is seen). Apparently the child can either be distracted by or corrected by visual cues more easily in a transition period than when he is intuitively certain (before) or logically certain (after).

Finally, two innovative studies deserve mention simply because they extend Piagetian research into new domains. Rubin (340) confirmed Piaget's prediction that children whose speech is less egocentric will be more popular with their peers, and thereby disconfirmed Vygotsky's implication of an opposite relationship: that active and cooperative participants in peer interaction use more egocentric speech. As always in comparing Piaget with Vygotsky, the contention that their definitions of "egocentric" are equivalent and their theories are in simple, direct opposition is somewhat strained. In a life-span developmental study, Papalia (303) demonstrated a progressive loss of conservation of substance, weight, and volume, but not of number in subjects over 65 years of age.

Training Studies

Recent training studies have generally gone beyond the simple contention that if training facilitates performance on Piagetian tasks, then Piaget is wrong, and if it doesn't, he is right. This year's crop provides some outstanding examples of ingenuity and subtlety in experimental acquisition studies. First consider the contribution of rules and feedback provided to the nonconserving child. Siegler & Liebert (359) demonstrated facilitation of conservation of liquid quantity, both in terms of correct answers and in terms of explanations, by either presenting relevant rules or complete feedback or both. The two treatments operated additively; a nonconservation series demonstrated that the facilitation was not merely a consequence of rote response acquisition; and the results were maintained a week later. Rosenthal & Zimmerman, (334) on the other hand, found that instruction did not facilitate conservation, and that providing a rule facilitated performance when both judged equivalence and verbal explanation were required, but not when judgment alone was required. Moreover, the same study demonstrated that observation of a conserving model alone and without further training facilitated conservation and generalization of conservation to new (unmodeled) stimuli. Praise of the model's responses had no effects, but a nonconserving model reduced the scores of initially conserving children. Peer-modeling effects were demonstrated by Murray (291) in an Asch-type experiment where one nonconserver and two conservers had to reach a consensus on standardized conservation problems. Gains in conservation judgment by the nonconservers were demonstrated in subsequent individual testing on the original problems and on new ones. Kuhn (229), on the other hand, failed to find strong effects of modeling of classification performances even when the model demonstrated performances at various levels relative to the child's own previously assessed level.

Next we consider three studies, one on the role of compensation as an ingredient of readiness for conservation training, one on the effects of cognitive conflict in inducing conservation, and one on the role of true reversibility in acquisition of number conservation. Not only are they all training studies, but they all direct their modification efforts toward an alleged developmental prerequisite of conservation, rather than directly toward conservation performance itself. Curcio et al (82) found that 27 of 67 children tested for conservation of discontinuous quantity and compensation of height-width dimensions showed compensation but not conservation, whereas only one showed conservation without compensation. Training in conservation produced gains for previously nonconserving compensators, as compared with untrained compensators and trained noncompensators. Post hoc, the degree to which compensators profited from training was predictable from the explicitness of their verbal justifications for compensation answers in the pretest.

LeFebvre & Pinard (234) demonstrated acquisition of conservation of liquid conservation by the use of cognitive conflict based on compensation, addition-subtraction, or both, compared to a control group. On two successive posttests (2 and 4 months later) all three experimental groups maintained gains over the control group but did not differ among themselves.

A very ingenious procedure was used by Schnall et al (346) to distinguish, as Piaget does, between operational reversibility and mere empirical return to previous state as contributors to number conservation. Induction of conservation was not accomplished by three displacement procedures providing empirical return: (*a*) *E* spread elements and returned them by hand; (*b*) *S* did the same; and (*c*) *S* spread and returned them by a cardboard device. Induction was obtained, however, when *S* spread and returned the elements by stretching an elastic strip to which the elements were attached. The authors claim that the elasticity condition, because of the bidirectional tension involved, modeled the characteristic of operational reversibility, rather than merely empirical return, and therefore was successful.

A deliberate application of individually programmed instruction to the acquisition of multiple-classification skills was compared by Parker, Sperr & Rieff (305) with a terminal behavior training program. The individually sequenced instruction was based on a task analysis of prerequisite behaviors, while the terminal program trained criterion performances only, and a third group served as a contact control. Both training programs produced better improvements than the contact control but did not differ from each other. Six- and 7-year-olds benefited more from training than 5-year-olds.

Formalization, Application, and Assessment Based on Piaget

In this section are grouped a variety of studies which either formalize certain Piagetian notions, apply them in an educational context, or use them to assess individual differences in cognitive development. Case (54) has extended Pascual-Leone's *M,* or "mental operator," as the set measure of Piaget's field of centration, referring to the maximum number of activated schemes that can be coordinated at any one time. Case demonstrates that by doing some empirical curve fitting, he can confirm for a different task than Pascual-Leone had used that estimates of M show an increase in value of one unit for every Piagetian substage. Furby (131) presented a Piaget-based pretheoretical model for cognitive development, drawing heavily on Gagné's model of cumulative learning sequences, and stressing not maturational readiness, but acquisition of an ordered set of capabilities. Case (55) further linked Gagné's model with Piaget's by predicting (based on Pascual-Leone's framework) that his experimental kindergartners would perform at the same level as regular fourth graders on a verbal classification task and at the same level as regular second graders on a gestural classification task. The predictions were confirmed. This trend toward maintaining what has come out of Piagetian investigations as sequential invariance of acquisitions, while viewing with skepticism allegations of maturational necessity for that sequence, may indicate that cognitive developmental research is moving toward Gagné-like descriptions of cumulative learning sequences and away from the concept of development per se as a fundamental conception. On a more pragmatic level, Denis-Prinzhorn, Kamii & Mounoud (89) have discussed various pedagogical implications of Piaget's theory.

In the domain of assessment, Pinard & Sharp (312) have provided a long-needed statement in English of the rationale behind (and some examples of) the Piaget-based intelligence test under development at the University of Montreal's Institute of Psychology. The standardization of its 25 subtests or items on 500 children from 4 to 12 is described. In a factor-analytic study Stephens et al (384) studied 27 Piagetian reasoning variables together with achievement, and intelligence scores, MA, and CA. In general the Piaget items were loaded on different factors than were the standard intelligence and achievement scores. Kaufman & Kaufman (204) found that Lorge-Thorndike MA, a Gesell battery, and a Piaget battery, administered in kindergarten, all predicted Stanford Achievement Test scores at the end of first grade with positive correlations approximating .60.

The relation of Piagetian developmental status to MA and IQ is one of the most frequent questions raised by students and practitioners in both fields. One of the clearest examples to date is a well-designed study by Gruen & Vore (158) comparing familial retardates at MA 5, 7, and 9 years with normal children matched for MA and for CA. This highly quotable study used number, liquid, and weight conservation problems and found that most of the variance in resulting performances could be attributed to MA and not IQ. Weight was more difficult than liquid, which was in turn more difficult than number, but exceptions were noted. Inequality (pseudoconservation) problems were used as well as equality ones, which is another feature of the experiment that makes it a model for students. Like most investigators since the Mehler-Bever vs Flavell controversy, these investigators found that inequality was less difficult than equality at the ages studied.

One final study comparing IQ (especially verbal) to Piagetian stage-wise development deserves separate mention because of its longitudinal design. Little (247) compared average and superior IQ children on three tasks each of conservation, seriation, and class inclusion at age 4½ to 5, and repeated the assessment 2 years later. IQ was associated with qualitative differences at both ages, but with stage differences only at the follow-up ages. The superior IQ children verbalized better at both ages: first in defense of their intuitive (and mostly wrong) responses, and later in explanation of their correct choices. Average IQ children were notably more dependent upon perceptual configurations at both ages. Unfortunately, the subjects were matched on CA rather than MA.

Individual Differences: Styles and Strategies

Studies of cognitive style and tempo, many stemming from Kagan's work on reflection-impulsivity, have become a popular subject variable in the study of cognitive development. In particular, attention to the information processing strategies differentially characterizing reflectives (or analytic responders) vs impulsives and the modifiability of styles have received increased attention. Following discussion of these studies, investigations of creativity, field independence, and a number of other cognitively evaluated individual difference measures are discussed in this section.

Katz (203) used Kagan's MFF test to identify reflective and impulsive preschool children, who then were given color- and form-matching tasks. Reflectives spontaneously discriminated forms more than impulsives, though both could do so when prodded. In general the tendency to discriminate was related to form preference and proposed as an explanation of the greater form preference of reflective children. Denney (90) used second graders and the Kagan CST to identify analytic vs relational responders. Exposure to reflective vs impulsive models or analytic vs relational models change the styles and tempos of the children, and effects generalized to unmodeled tasks. Relational models produced more immediate change, while analytic models produced more durable change.

A number of additional pieces of evidence support the general superiority of reflective children in information processing efficiency. Nuessle (294) found that reflective fifth and ninth graders were more proficient focusers in a concept identification task, that is, they were better able to eliminate irrelevant hypotheses. They also had longer latencies between feedback and next response, especially following negative feedback. Once again the inhibition of irrelevant response to make time for hypothesis revision appears to be their major advantage over impulsives. The visual scanning and search strategies employed by reflective and impulsive 9-year-olds on the MFF were studied by Zelniker et al (438) and by Ault, Crawford & Jeffrey (8). In addition to demonstrating that impulsives are poorer at sustaining attention than reflectives, they showed that the visual fixation patterns of impulsives and reflectives differ on the MFF. Moreover, when the logic of the task was reversed (find the different instead of the matching alternative) in a "DFF" task, subsequent MFF performance was altered. The main effect of DFF was an increase in comparison of alternatives and a decrease in looks at the standard during the DFF. This is a trend toward a pattern naturally characteristic of reflectives at this age. On the subsequent MFF, however, only the impulsives showed generalization of this shift in search strategy, and a reduction in errors among impulsives resulted. The second study included the subjects in the off-cells (fast-accurate and slow-inaccurate) who are customarily not included in studies of reflection-impulsivity. No difference was found between comparision of standard and a variant and comparison of two variants, unlike previous studies, but both of these relatively systematic patterns of search were more common in reflective and fast-accurate 9-year-olds than in their impulsive and slow-inaccurate age mates.

Adams (2) used the MFF to compare reflective and impulsive 6- and 8-year-olds on a probability learning task. Several patterns of guessing strategies were identified and defined empirically as more or less mature. As expected, for 6-year-olds, impulsives showed less mature strategies than reflectives. Eight-year-olds, however, did not show such differences.

One hypothesis about conceptual tempo states that the failure of impulsives to inhibit rapid and automated responding generalizes beyond the cognitive domain and characterizes their behavior in a variety of other settings as well. The motoric inhibition of reflective and impulsive black middle-class preschoolers was studied by Harrison & Nadelman (174), who used the MFF and Maccoby's Draw-a-Line-Slowly and Walk-Slowly tests, scored for both slowness (instructed) and irregularities. Reflectives were better able than impulsives to inhibit motor movement, and the latter ability was positively correlated with MFF latency and negatively with MFF errors. Bucky, Banta & Gross (43), however, found no such relationship among 5-, 10-, 15-, and 20-year-olds, using the Maccoby motor tasks, the MFF, and an Embedded Figures Test. Motivational variables were considered important determinants of motor inhibition among the older *S*s. On the hypothesis that nonanalytic children on the CST are more anxious than their analytic peers, Chiu (60) gave the CST to American and Taiwanese fourth and fifth graders together with the CMAS. No anxiety differences were found as a function of cognitive style for the American sample, but among the Taiwanese, nonanalytic children were more anxious than analytic ones.

Conceptual strategies continue to interest developmental psychologists, and methods for their detection seem to become more subtle each year. Bruner's distinction between hypothesis-seeking and constraint-seeking strategies in a 20 questions game was used by Denney (91) in a strategy-modeling study. Six-, 8-, and 10-year-old boys were shown videotaped models who demonstrated hypothesis seeking and two kinds of constraint seeking, one based on perceptible attributes, the other on functional attributes. Age was a determinant of susceptibility to modeling of strategies, but mere observation of the model was not in general adequate for acquisition of a previously unused strategy.

Gholson, Levine & Phillips (140) used a blank-trials probe procedure after each trial of several discrimination problems to detect hypothesis testing strategies in kindergarten, second, fourth, sixth grade, and college students. Hypothesis testing appeared at grade two. Hypotheses used were classified as strategic (focusing, dimension checking, and hypothesis checking) or stereotypic (stimulus preference, position preference, and position alternation). The kindergarten children showed mostly stereotypes; second to sixth graders used mostly strategic hypotheses, but never the focusing strategy, which is the most efficient. College students used almost exclusively focusing and dimension-checking strategies.

Analogous results were obtained by McKinney (270) using educable retardates at the MA 5–6 and 7–8 levels. Two strategies, conservative focusing and successive scanning were presented to two training groups, while a control group got no training. At the MA 5–7 level training in focusing did not facilitate conjunctive concept attainment, while scanning training increased efficiency but did not facilitate concept attainment. At the MA 7–8 level both kinds of training facilitated concept attainment, with the focusing strategy being more effective than the scanning strategy.

Coincidentally, two independent, five-year, longitudinal studies of creativity were published in 1972. Kogan & Pankove (219) retested in the tenth grade children who had been tested with the Wallach-Kogan tasks at grade five. Individual and group testing were used. Ideational productivity and uniqueness scores showed substantial stability over the interval for males retested by group administration and for females tested individually. IQ unrelated to creativity at grade five, remained so for females at grade ten, but became positively correlated for males. Cropley (81) had given six creativity tests to a sample of seventh graders, and followed them up 5 years later. Combining the tests into a single composit creativity predictor, he found correlations of .52 for boys and .46 for girls between that predictor and a composit achievement score based on extracurricular accomplishments in art, drama, literature, and music.

Witkin's field independence, as measured by the Embedded Figures Test, was correlated with performance on the Stroop color-word interference test (fixity vs mobility) at five different age levels ranging from 10 to 86 years in a study by Eisner (105). Field independence is an inverted U-shaped function of age and is associated with mobility, while field dependence is associated with fixity. Fleck (121) used the Children's Embedded Figures Test and a reversal-nonreversal task to identify field dependence vs independence and verbal mediation-nonmediation among kindergarten, first, and second grade boys. They were then given a variety of commercially produced Piagetian conservation tasks. Age and field independence were positively associated with conservational competence; verbal mediation was not.

The last three studies to be cited in this section are concerned with personality and social behavior characteristics as determinants of individual cognitive competencies. Crandall & Lacey (79) found that internal (vs external) control, defined as perception of academic success that is due to their own behavior (vs other causes), is related to speed and accuracy of Embedded Figures Test performance for girls, but not for boys, when age and IQ are partialled out. Ruble & Nakamura (341) compared field-dependent and field-independent children's performance in a game during which relevant cues were sometimes provided by the experimenter. According to the authors, the field-dependent children, because of their more social and less task-oriented approach, were better able to profit from the social cues given by *E*. The usual sex differences in field independence failed to have differential effects on attention to relevant social cues. In a study of the relationship between preschool social and emotional functioning and early school intellectual achievement, Kohn & Rosman (220) used rating scales to assess interest-participation vs apathy-withdrawal and cooperation-compliance vs anger-defiance in 323 preschoolers. Interest-participation was correlated positively with school readiness and first and second grade achievement. For boys anger-defiance vs cooperation-compliance was not related to achievement, but anger-defiance was negatively related to intellectual achievement in girls, beginning at the second grade. Perhaps such findings should be discussed under the heading of teacher bias rather than cognitive styles.

An efficient concept formation task originally developed by Huttenlocher was extended to younger children by Daehler (83). In this two-trial procedure, a conjunctive concept can be logically identified when there are two dimensions or properties with two values each if two of the four instances are presented on trial 1 and *S* is told whether the positive instance is present, followed by a second trial in which one of the instances is reversed and the other is presented unchanged and *S* is again told whether the target instance is present or not. For example, if the stimuli are black or white and large or small, then a concept (e.g. large, black) can be identified in any of four different ways: it can be present in the pair of instances of both trials (+ +), present on only one trial (+ – or – +), or present on neither trial (– –). Typically – + problems have been shown to be easiest, since the novel element on the most recent (second) trial *is* the concept. The – – problem has generally been the hardest, since the concept is never embodied in an instance actually presented, unless a matrix of all possibilities is also available to *S,* or the missing instance is by some other means logically indicated as the untried possibility. By using faces differing in sex and miscellaneous features, Daehler was able to obtain better than chance solutions to all types of problems by 5- to 7-year-olds, and by 4-year-olds on the – + and + + problems only. A response bias favoring the cue added on the second trial and the cue present on both trials was implicated for preschoolers. When the concept was simply one of four different cues (not a dimensionally organized, 2 X 2 conjunctive concept), or when older children were used on the conjunctive concept, the – – problem requiring solution by negative instances was the easiest.

SOCIAL AND PERSONALITY DEVELOPMENT

A number of topics, potentially includable under this heading, have been excluded from review, including studies of adolescence, clinical summaries, case studies, and evaluation of various instruments and tests. Studies of the effects of birth order have also been eliminated because of the publication of a comprehensive review of such studies by Adams (1). The literature reviewed in this section is organized both in terms of subjects studied (ethnic, cultural, SES, and sex comparisons) and in terms of popular clusters of behaviors, traits, and influences (attachment, achievement, moral development, and social communication). It is inevitable that certain studies included here deal as much with cognitive development as they do with personality and social development, and with increased concern for applied research in settings where whole children develop, we may expect more of the traditional topical boundaries to crumble in the next few years.

Racial and Cultural Comparisons

Strictly racial comparisons of children's performances in a variety of tasks are sometimes unfortunately confounded with SES differences, and the conclusions reached have correspondingly limited certainty. Slightly better are a number of studies in which SES is matched and held constant in order to make racial comparisons, though the generality of results is often limited by the restriction in range of SES levels studied. The most conclusive studies, of course, systematically co-vary race and SES.

The first group of studies to be considered have to do with racial attitudes per se. Cantor (51) developed a conflict paradigm for studying children's associations between the terms "good" or "bad" and pairs of faces of white and black children. Choices and latencies of response consistently supported the hypothesis of stereotyping among white second graders and demonstrated the general utility of the method for nonverbal attitude assessment. McMurtry & Williams (271) demonstrated that training designed to weaken white children's positive associations with light-skinned human figures and to strengthen their positive associations with dark-skinned figures generalized to reduce negative associations with dark skin. These and other similar results are discussed in the context of Osgood's evaluation factor in the domain of affective meaning among preschoolers. Cantor (52) also demonstrated that the ratings of liking or willingness to associate with children is determined jointly by familiarity and race. Familiarity enhanced the 9- to 11-year-old white children's ratings of black but not white children's pictures.

Behaviors associated with cognitive competence were evaluated in a number of ethnic comparison studies. Zimmerman & Rosenthal (442) found that modeling and rule repetition facilitated concept attainment and generalization in both Mexican-American and Anglo-American fifth graders, the latter outperforming the former. Bucky & Banta (42) found that although black and white preschoolers differed on a test battery assessing motor impulse-control, reflectivity, innovative behavior, and curiosity (the whites doing "better"), the race of the tester was critical. For both groups of *S*s white testers elicited better performances than black testers, and were rated from videotapes as providing a more positive social atmosphere, regardless of race of child. In a comparison of Canadian Indian children from a remote community with Canadian whites from several social and geographic groups, Schubert & Cropley (349) found that the lower WISC scores of the Indian group could be accounted for by reduced use of verbal regulation of behavior, which, in turn, varied as a function of contact with the white, urban culture. Taylor & Thweatt (393) found greater distortion in the Bender-Gestalt productions of Navajo 6- and 7-year-olds than in those of Anglos, but by age 12 there were no differences.

Two studies made ethnic comparisons of performance on the Illinois Test of Psycholinguistic Abilities. Kirk (213) compared blacks, American Indians, and Mexican-Americans and found that blacks were superior in short-term auditory sequential memory, while the Indian and Mexican-American groups were superior in short-term visual sequential memory. Differing child-rearing practices are cited to account for the obtained differences. Stephenson & Gay (385) compared black and white children matched at four SES levels and found that SES accounted for little variance in ITPA performance among the blacks, but that SES is related to scores of white children. No visual-motor vs auditory-vocal differences were found in this study.

Two studies made ethnic comparisons on the age of achievement of Piagetian conservation. Gaudia (134) found that black children achieved conservation about a year later than Indian and white children (all lower SES), and that all lower SES groups are delayed in comparison to norms based on a racially and socially heterogeneous population. Conservation was positively related to CA and IQ in all groups studied. Dasen (84) compared Australian Aboriginal children with Genevan whites and found that the order of acquisition was the same, except for a reversal of continuous quantity and weight, but that the Aborigines' concepts developed more slowly.

Black and white lower SES preschoolers and white middle SES preschoolers were compared by Guttentag (164) in a study of spontaneous movement under a variety of controlled conditions. The black children emitted a greater number and variety of movement responses than did either of the white groups.

A number of experimental studies treated ethnic group as a subject variable and examined its interaction with various treatment conditions, and these experiments appear to promise a more effective means of disentangling and explaining ethnic differences than do the strictly comparative or normative studies. The effects of setting and procedural variables, experimenters and observers, and stimulus materials used in comparing young, low-income, and minority children with others were reviewed by Dickie & Bagur (97) in relation to language development. Digit span and short-term memory were used by McCarver & Ellis (266) to compare middle-SES whites and lower-SES blacks, both of which showed the expected effects of verbal rehearsal on short-term recall to the same degree, in spite of the markedly superior performance of middle-SES whites in IQ. Sharp & Cole (354) compared West African children to previously reported European and U.S. children on the developmental shift from syntagmatic to paradigmatic response patterns in word association. The shift occurs in a language structurally different from English, as predicted; paradigmatic responding is greater if the child has attended school; and the shift appears in general to occur later among West African children. Ciborowski & Cole (63) compared Liberian and American *S*s varying in age and educational background in a disjunctive concept formation task. Ethnic differences found in the first experiment were eradicated in the second by the addition of a verbalization memory aid. Recall of printed language passages was studied by Nolen (293) as a function of the use of standard English, standard Negro dialect, and nonstandard Negro dialect. Second grade low-SES whites and blacks did not differ from each other, but the whites recalled more at fourth grade. There were no effects of translation of the materials into the dialects studied.

The effects of adults, teachers, models, etc have also been studied in relation to socioethnic variables. Race of *E* was implicated in the Bucky & Banta (42) article cited above. In contradiction to their findings, Solkoff (372) found that black examiners elicited higher performances than white ones on certain WISC tests administered to black and white 8- to 11-year-olds. The other tests showed no differences attributable to race of *E*. Black children scored lower than whites on those scales where differences associated with race of *S* were found, and race of child interacted with race of examiner on only one test. Liebert, Sobol & Copemann (245) found that black first- and second-grade boys imitated and recalled the choices of white models more than of black ones, and showed the same pattern of effects of vicarious reward and punishment to the model as had been previously demonstrated with white boys of the same age. White advantaged and black disadvantaged third and fourth graders were exposed by Portuges & Feshbach (314) to white female teachers displaying distinctive mannerisms and the use of positive vs negative reinforcement techniques. After observing the films, the children assumed the teacher role. The advantaged whites, the girls, and those who watched a positively reinforcing teacher showed the greatest imitation of her incidental behaviors.

Contrary to the predictions of some students of the "disadvantaged" child, the enrichment of the preschool classroom with a variety of additional materials and equipment designed to stimulate perceptual and cognitive growth had no consistent effects on the 123 black children studied by Busse et al (46). The dependent variables included the Stanford-Binet, WPPSI (performance), and four scales from the ITPA.

Black and white fifth-graders, half each of middle and lower SES, were given noncontingent feedback (success, failure, or no information) following a reading test by Friend & Neale (129). Then they were asked to attribute performance to some combination of ability, effort, task difficulty, and luck. White children judged that ability and effort were more important than difficulty or luck, while the reverse was true for blacks. Kagan & Madsen (201) used four experimental conflict situations to compare cooperation and competition among urban Anglos and rural Mexican children. No differences in motivation and ability to cooperate were found. The Anglos were more inclined to lower another child's outcomes when no gain to self would result, but both groups would take a toy from another if they could keep it for themselves. Anglos were more conflicted when a peer displayed rivalrous intent, but Mexican children were avoidant of conflict. Similar results were obtained by Miller & Thomas (280) in a comparison of rural Blackfoot Indian with urban Canadian children. Under group reward conditions, both groups cooperated effectively. When reward was delivered on an individual basis, the Indian children were even more cooperative, while the urban children showed disruptive competition.

Finally, a study by Baumrind (14) compared the patterns of parental authority and behavior of preschool children in black vs white families. The black parents appeared more authoritarian, but unlike their white counterparts, the most authoritarian of these families produced the most independent and self-assertive girls.

Socioeconomic Status Comparisons

Although obviously of importance in the preceding section, SES has been studied as the primary subject variable in the studies to be considered next. The first group contains correlational and survey comparisons; the second is composed of experimental studies. Tulkin & Kagan (402) found minimal differences between middle and working class mothers in nonverbal interaction at home with their 10-month-old firstborn daughters, whereas every verbal behavior observed was more frequent among the middle-class mothers. Radin (318) observed fathers at home with their 4-year-old sons, and compared middle- with lower-SES fathers on restrictiveness and nurturance and their sons on intelligence and masculinity-femininity. Over all, boys' IQ was positively related to nurturance and negatively related to restrictiveness. Middle-SES boys scored higher on IQ than lower-SES boys, and the latter showed a negative relationship between IQ and male sex role preference. Paternal behavior correlated with SES is concluded to be a more central determinant than other SES-related variables. Jones (197) compared high- and low-verbal ability fifth-grade boys matched on general intelligence. The high-verbal boys came from homes with greater opportunities for the use and development of language, as well as from homes scoring higher on parental interaction rate, parents' academic and vocational aspirations, and occupational status.

Deprived (D) and privileged (P) Israeli preschoolers were grouped together in three preschools (mixed), while D-only children comprised a fourth. Free-play social interactions were observed at the beginning and end of the 2-year project. Deprived children in the mixed classes showed higher rates of social interaction than those in the D-only school, but in the mixed schools both Ds and Ps interacted mainly within their own social group. The D-only children and the Ps in the mixed groups showed gains in cooperation with peers, while the Ds in the mixed groups remained very dependent upon adults (113).

In a study of visual information processing speed, Bosco (31) used the tachistoscopic masking threshold to compare middle- with lower-SES first, third, and sixth graders. The disadvantaged children required more time to process the same visual information, but the difference declined with increasing grade level. Spence (377) compared middle- and lower-SES preschoolers in four experimental and one control condition during a two-choice discrimination series. Control *S*s were shown the correct stimulus after each choice response. Experimentals received verbal or nonverbal reward for correct responses or verbal or nonverbal punishment following errors. There was a large effect of social class favoring the middle SES group, but no main effects or interactions involving treatments. On the other hand, Figurelli & Keller (116) compared middle- and lower-SES black children ages 6 to 8 on conservation tasks before and after training (vs no training). Middle-SES children scored higher on both the pre- and post-tests than lower-SES children. Training facilitated improvement as a main effect in both SES groups, but lower-SES children required more training task repetitions to criterion than did middle-SES children.

Fourteen months after completion of a 20-hour systematic conceptual learning program with preschool children from poverty backgrounds, Jacobson & Greeson (189) retested with the Stanford-Binet for retention of IQ gains. Not only were most of the gains retained in the follow-up study, but the original differential treatment effects (e.g. reinforcement only vs reinforcement plus additional information) were still discernable in the follow-up data.

Communication and Social Verbalization

Two studies reported this year were concerned with infant vocalization as a function of social and acoustic stimulation. Dodd (98) presented 9- to 12-month-old infants with 15 min of prerecorded vocal, social-vocal, or social-only auditory stimulation, followed by 15 min during which their vocalizations were recorded. Vocal and social-only had no effects, but vocal-social stimulation increased the number and length of utterances containing consonants, though there was no evidence of imitation of the particular consonant phonemes presented. Webster, Steinhardt & Senter (416) presented 7-month-old infants with vowel sounds spoken at either high or low pitch. Fewer vocalizations were produced during high-pitch stimulation than either before or after than stimulation, and an increase in fundamental frequency occurred from baseline to high-pitch stimulation periods, but no decrease was observed from baseline to low-pitch stimulation.

Three studies were concerned with the development of communication skills in children. Peterson, Danner & Flavell (309) found that both 4- and 7-year-olds reformulated an initial message when explicitly requested to do so, and both failed to do so when confronted only with nonverbal facial expressions of listener noncomprehension. Only the 7-year-olds, however, reformulated messages in response to an implicit verbal request, such as "I don't understand." Shantz & Wilson (352) trained 7-year-olds in trios (speaker, listener, and observer roles rotated) on tasks requiring verbal communication of critical cues to guide listener response. Peer discussion followed each of the six sessions. Trained *S*s subsequently exceeded controls in communication of useful information and overall message quality and showed moderate transfer of communications skills. Hoemann (181) compared the quality and accuracy of peer communications in 8- and 11-year-old deaf and hearing children, the former using manual methods and the latter using spoken English. Poorer performances by the deaf children were attributed to experiential deficits which adversely affect communications skills.

The likelihood of receiving a reply in response to a spontaneous verbal remark by one preschooler to another was studied in a free-play setting by Mueller (290). The most powerful predictors of whether a given communication would receive a reply were its technical quality and whether the speaker had the visual attention of the listener at its beginning. Nearly all communications aroused social interest in the listener and most of them received replies. A developmental trend was found by Solomon & Ali (373) characterizing which features of verbal evaluation statements are most important in the listener's perception of objective meaning, recipient's consequent feelings, and speaker's liking for the recipient. Positive, neutral, and negative levels of content and intonation were presented to subjects ranging from kindergarten to college age. Content was most influential for all three perceptions for young children, followed by differential usage of content and intonation depending upon which kind of perception was asked for. The adults relied most of all on intonation for affective meaning, though content, of course, still determined objective meaning.

Sex Differences

Corinne Hutt (188) makes a strong case for the biological determination of a number of sex differences in humans and other mammals. Physical growth and maturation, motor activity, and sensory capacities in infancy, mother-infant interaction, the onset of fear, social behavior of preschoolers, exploration, play, creativity, and other intellectual functions are reviewed in terms of neuroendocrinological processes of sexual differentiation prior to birth. For example, it is argued that the female relies principally on linguistic skills in intellectual functioning and that the higher parent-daughter than parent-son IQ correlation typically found reflects this fact (together with the earlier maturation of the female) rather than greater genetic control of IQ in girls. Her review can be expected to produce extensive replies and some argument.

Females at ages ranging from 2 years to adulthood consistently outperformed males in the task of filling form boards with red, green, and blue disks in a study by Guttman & Kahneman (165). At each age the females scored higher (more like adults) in number of colors used, order of color placement, and integration of final pattern, although there were no instructions as to correct or desirable responses. In a study of concept indentification in which availability of past correct vs past incorrect instances was the experimental variable, Pishkin (313) found that females outperformed males; availability of past-correct instances facilitated performance; and older females (9 years) profited from availability of past instances, especially correct ones, more than their male peers and more than 6-year-olds.

Broverman et al have previously stated the thesis that sex differences in cognitive abilities reflect sex-related differences in physiology. Their thesis has been once criticized and the criticism replied to in previous years. This year Parlee (306) renews the attack on the Broverman position in a more comprehensive and factually based manner. She criticizes their review of the literature on sex differences in cognitive abilities as being selective and arbitrary in characterizing those facts which it does include. She further points out that the pharmacological studies they cite are based on "dubious cross-species analogies" and that they have made a factual error in citing evidence in support of their proposed mechanism by which sex hormones might affect autonomic activity. Clearly the debate is just beginning.

Several studies this year have been concerned with sexual stereotypes, most notably those associated with body build. Lerner & Korn (238) asked chubby and average build males at three age levels (5–6, 14–15, and 19–20 years) to attribute items from a verbal checklist to pictures of an endomorph, a mesomorph, or an ectomorph, and then to judge the items as to good and bad connotations and applicability to themselves. Later *S*s identified their own body build and indicated their preference for one physique. In general at all age levels *S*s of both body types had a favorable view of the mesomorph, a very unfavorable view of the endomorph, and a somewhat less negative, but still unfavorable, view of the ectomorph. Staffieri (382) found analogous results for females aged 7 to 11 years who were asked to attribute adjectives to figures representing endomorphic, ectomorphic, and meso-dysplastic female body builds. A common set of behavioral and personality descriptions associated with the body types was found at all ages: all adjectives assigned significantly more often to the mesodysplastic body type were positive and all assigned differentially to the endomorphic type were negative. Clearly desirable and undesirable body-type stereotypes for one's own sex are well established by age 5 to 7 and reflect the rater's own preferences. Both same-sex and cross-sex stereotyping of both body build and facial expression were supported in a study of elementary school children by Felker (115).

In a study employing Brown's IT Scale, Fling & Manosevitz (122) found low correlations between parents' scores and those of their 4-year-old children. In general parents discouraged cross-sexed play interests in boys more than in girls, and parents of the same sex as their child reported more encouragement of sex typing than did opposite sex parents. A masculine bias in children's responses to the standard "IT" card was also reported.

Meyer & Sobieszek (276) used videotapes of 17-month-old children sometimes described as boys and sometimes as girls to secure ratings and judgments from adults, including sex-role items. While there was little evidence that attributed sex of child influences the judgments of tapes directly, the judges described a child said to be of their own sex as having more qualities, both male and female.

Social Behavior of Infants

Following closely upon the rediscovery of infants' perceptual and cognitive capacities has been the study of their preverbal vocal behavior and receptive speech abilities. Accompanying this second wave is increased attention to the nonverbal social behaviors of infants, especially crying, smiling, and laughing. The following section will then review studies of mother-infant attachment. One apparent trend in infant work is the tendency to treat the state of arousal of the infant as a datum, rather than as an annoyance to the investigator. Korner (221) discussed state as a mediator of infant stimulation, and Lewis (240) considered it as an index of infant-environment interaction. Both made strong pleas that state, like other individual differences, not merely be considered as error variance. Another trend is the use of well-developed visual fixation methodology to study infants' social attending and social object permanence when animate stimuli are compared with inanimate ones (153).

Dyadic interaction between adopted infants and their mothers was observed by Beckwith (16), who also obtained PARI protocols from the mothers. Responsiveness of babies to the mother in social play was a negative function of how suppressive and critical the mother was, and was also negatively correlated with responsiveness to a stranger. Quantity of contact between mother and infant was negatively related to infant self-stimulation rate and to frequency of ignoring maternal social overtures.

Crying of infants, a behavior usually studied under hospital or laboratory conditions, was studied normatively in the home setting over full days of tape recordings by Rebelsky & Black (321). Although the sample was small (10), the thoroughness, naturalistic setting, and duration of the study (1 week to 3 months) make these normative data useful. Contrary to a simple reinforcement model, Bell & Ainsworth (18) found that consistency and promptness of maternal response is associated with a decline in frequency of crying over the first year of life. Close physical contact was found to be the most effective means of terminating crying. Development of noncrying modes of communication to the mother also is associated with maternal responsiveness (both consistency and promptness) to infant signals. Korner & Thoman (222) compared vestibular-proprioceptive and close contact methods of soothing newborn infants. Unlike Bell & Ainsworth's older infants, they found that newborns' crying rates during and after soothing were sharply reduced by vestibular stimulation, while contact was less effective during and ineffective after the soothing period. The procedure used, unlike that of other studies, carefully controlled contact and vestibular stimulation both separately and in combination, and the authors suggest that the vestibular component in uncontrolled studies of soothing by contact may be the controlling factor. Bell & Ainsworth, however, indicate that significant learning to be soothed takes place over the first year, so Korner & Thoman's conclusion must for now be restricted to newborns.

The Meaning of Smiling and Vocalizing in Infancy was the title of an APA symposium in 1970, belatedly published in 1972 (166). In it Watson (413) discusses smiling and cooing as social indicators that the child has discovered a contingency relationship between two or more recurring events in his environment. The significance of this process for the development of cognitive and social schemas is discussed. Zelazo (437) emphasized the nonsocial determinants of smiling and vocalizing, such as moderate novelty in both social and nonsocial stimuli. McCall (264) sums up the cognitive position on these behaviors, reminding us that our definitions distinguishing smiling as an operant from smiling as social communication, from smiling as an index of cognitive processes involving recognition and novelty are not so clearly distinguished by infants, but are components of an emergent perceptual-cognitive process.

Finally, Sroufe & Wunsch (381) have traced developmental changes in classes of stimuli that elicit laughter during the first year of life. Tactile and auditory stimuli are effective with younger infants and become less potent in the second half-year. Most visual and some social stimuli become increasingly effective in the latter part of the first year.

Attachment and Mother-Infant Relationships

The following studies are ordered by age of child and range from neonatal breast feeding interactions to stranger-reactions in the third year of life. The experimentally studied determinants of attachment usually pit the mother against a cognitively interesting but nonsocial stimulus, while the dependent variables are distress upon separation or following and approaching the mother. Thoman, Leiderman & Olson (395) compared breast feeding of 2-day-old infants by primiparous vs multiparous mothers and found that the former spent more time in nonfeeding activities; spent more time feeding male infants; changed activities more often; provided more stimulation, including verbal, and especially with females; and smiled more at female infants. In turn the primiparous infants spent less time attached to the nipple and less of that actively sucking. For primiparous mothers, the number of weeks the mother continued breast feeding was correlated positively with the amount of time the mothers spent talking to their infants at the 2-day-old feeding observation.

Premature infants who remain in the hospital for the first 3 to 12 weeks of life are subsequently smiled at and held close to their mothers' bodies less than full-term babies in a study by Leifer et al (236). But within the premature group those who had full sensory contact with the mother during hospitalization did not differ from those who had visual contact only during that interval in the degree to which they were subsequently smiled at and held closely. Corter, Rheingold & Eckerman (77) found that the number and novelty of toys available in a strange room governed the promptness with which 10-month-old infants followed their mother upon her departure from the room.

Two studies by Coates, Anderson & Hartup (69, 70) investigated attachment behaviors at 10, 14, and 18 months of age. While touching and proximity to the mother were stable attachment indicators over both long and short terms, almost no stability over either duration was found for visual regard, vocalizing, crying, or orientation to the locus of the mother's disappearance. Visual regard, touching, and proximity were mutually associated behaviors that increased after separation, whereas crying and orientation to locus of disappearance increased during separation.

Messer & Lewis (275) studied 13-month-old infants in a standard playroom with available toys in the presence of the mother and found SES and sex differences. Lower SES infants vocalized much less in these sessions than did middle SES infants, and lower SES infants showed smaller sex differences. Girls showed more attachment behaviors in general, vocalized more, and showed more mobility than boys. Wenar (420) confirmed that exploration of the physical environment takes precedence over initiating social interaction with the mother in a free choice situation with 2-year-olds, but found no relationships among extensity, duration, and level of the alternate activities.

An excellent monograph by Maccoby & Feldman (253) studied attachment behaviors during the third year of life in American and Kibbutz-reared Israeli children. The two populations did not differ in general; disturbance over separation declined from age 2 to age 3; distal attachment behaviors toward both mother and stranger increased with age; but looking at them did not. At age 2 friendly interaction with a stranger was contigent on mother presence; by 3 it was not.

Family Structure, Child Rearing, and Personality

What used to be the hard core of correlational developmental psychology is represented this year by a diverse group of articles. The child-rearing and familial antecedents of specific behavioral characteristics is simply no longer regarded as the chief business of developmental psychology. At least the articles discussed below will illustrate the heterogeneity of methods and concerns that characterize the field. Antecedents of social desirability response tendencies in 6 to 12-year-olds were studied by Allaman, Joyce & Crandall (3), using the children in the Fels longitudinal study. Using the same population, Battle & Lacey (13) studied parental antecedents and behavioral correlates of hyperactivity throughout childhood, adolescence, and young adulthood.

Using fourth- to eighth-grade lower SES children's reports of parental childrearing behavior, Armentrout & Burger (6) found the same factor structure (for both sexes) as had been found earlier: acceptance vs rejection, psychological autonomy vs control, and firm vs lax control. Sex and age differences in factor scores were also reported.

Little or no support for a sex-by-birth-order interaction was found in a study of sex-role preferences and intelligence by Laosa & Brophy (232), in some instances because the expected birth-order differences were not found. Other variables which did show sex differences did so more with first- than with later-born children, confirming that sometimes first-borns are more thoroughly socialized. Burton (44) studied sex-typing in Barbados children as a function of degree of father absence. Controlling a host of demographic variables did not modify the fact that availability of male-role models did not systematically determine sex-role behaviors, while the status-envy hypothesis fared better. Both conflict of cross-sex identity and consistent feminine identification do occur in father-absent males in that culture. The critical period for absence appears to be the first 2 years of life.

In a reversal of the usual design, Osofsky & O'Connell (300) studied the effects of the behavior of 5-year-old girls on that of their parents in a laboratory task varying in dependency producing features. The parents interacted more and were more controlling when their daughter was dependent. Mothers were more encouraging and fathers more directly helping under dependency conditions.

Sex and sibling status influence the effectiveness of child-teachers of concepts, according to Cicirelli (64). Males got higher concept attainment scores than females as learners, but female sibs were more effective teachers than male sibs or female nonsibs, regardless of the sex of the learner.

A study of still more applied significance was reported by Woods (434) on the unsupervised activities of fifth-grade ghetto children whose mothers were employed. A battery of psychological tests, teacher ratings, and school and community records indicated positive influences associated with full-time employment of the mother, quality of mothering, mother-child relationships, and mother's attitude toward employment. More girls than boys were unsupervised, and unsupervised girls showed impoverished cognitive development.

Finally, it should be noted that a friendly debate is in progress between Burton (45) and Cohler (72) regarding the validity, utility, and interpretability of retrospective accounts by parents and grandparents of child-rearing attitudes and behaviors in the study of intergenerational attitudes and changes in prevailing cultural values. The debate is constructive and a useful caution to both students of culture change and life-span developmentalists as well as to the investigators of child-rearing to whom it is directed.

Achievement Motivation

Concern with achievement and level of aspiration has focused heavily this year on the effects of evaluations by, and expectations of, significant adults. Achievement motivation was contrasted with fear of failure in 9- and ten-year-olds by Hermans, ter Laak & Maes (179) in a study of parent child interactions during task performance in the home. Parents of high achievement-motivation children gave less specific help, but more nonspecific help and reinforcement than those of low achievement-motivation children. The high achievement-motivation children more often refused help than the lows. The parents of the high-anxious children responded less to the child's insecurity, provided more negative tension release, and witheld more reinforcement than those of low-anxious children. The combination of high motivation and low anxiety was characteristic of children whose parents had high expectations of their child's performance. Other correlations confirmed with Dutch children the behavior patterns established previously with American children associated with achievement motivation and fear of failure.

Children who perceive themselves as responsible for their own degree of success (high accountability or internality) do better than others on spelling, vocabulary, and math tests on which they set their own level of difficulty, according to Clifford & Cleary (66). These relationships held at each grade level studied (fourth through sixth), and internality predicted performance better than IQ did for boys, while the reverse was true for girls. Experimentally varying internal vs external evaluation, Maehr & Stallings (255) found that under internal conditions children showed a continuing interest in working on difficult tasks, especially if they were high achievement-motivation boys. Performance was not as systematically influenced as was interest in continuing.

Two studies have shown still more effects of adult expectancy on children's performances. Entwisle, Cornell & Epstein (107) found that positive expectations by a male principal following a first test facilitated performance on a second test for boys, but not for girls. In a marble-dropping task, Dusek (101) found that adult social reinforcing agents led to believe that the 9- to 10-year-old boys would outperform the girls they tested did not produce *E*-bias effects favoring boys. The experimenters told that girls would do better produced an *E*-bias effect, but only among low-anxious *Ss*. High-anxious *Ss* of both sexes were more responsive to reinforcement, regardless of *E*-bias.

Finally, a correlational study by Cattell, Barton & Dielman (56) showed that using objective measures of motivation and factored personality tests, personality, motivation, and ability variables each contribute independently and significantly to school achievement tests administered 3 months later. The potency of the three types of predictors varied with the academic area assessed on the achievement tests given to sixth and seventh grade children.

Moral Judgment and Behavior

An offshoot of the Piagetian tradition is the study of the development of moral judgment, which has been generally studied independently of moral behavior. The latter, however, stems from an older theoretical concern with identification and behavioral inhibition found in both psychoanalytic and social learning theory. The topics are reviewed in that order, followed by a discussion of the intersect of the two, which is beginning to receive some overdue attention in this most popular and relevant area of investigation. For this purpose considerable latitude has been used in the definition of what behaviors and judgments are considered to be "moral."

Shantz & Pentz (353) asked 6-, 10-, and 13-year-old boys to indicate the amount of punishment that aggressive boys in stories should receive, manipulating type of provocation, amount of retaliation in the story, and target retaliated against. Ten- and 13-year-olds found retaliation against sibs and peers less punishable than retaliation against fathers regardless of provocation, while 6-year-olds made such target distinctions only following physical provocation. All *S*s indicated that retaliation matched to provocation (physical vs verbal) was more acceptable than mismatched retaliation if the provocation came from a father. But when physical provocation came from peers, they judged that verbal was preferable to physical retaliation.

A similar method was used by Gutkin (163) to study moral judgments of fourth graders concerning the moral justifiability of stories in which the intentions of the protagonist were either good or bad and the damage done was either high or low. The judgments were scalable and yielded an apparent developmental sequence of four stages: (*a*) intentions irrelevant, damage determining; (*b*) intentions relevant, but damage more important; (*c*) intentions more important than damage, but damage still relevant; and (*d*) intentions alone relevant, damage irrelevant.

Jensen & Rytting (191) used systematic story variation in a study of immanent justice attribution by second-graders. In each story a misdeed was followed by an accident to the perpetrator that could be seen as impersonal punishment (immanent justice). The stories varied in whether naturalistic information was provided that could explain the real causes of the misfortune and whether the misdeed and the subsequent misfortune were presented as related. The more directly related were misdeed and subsequent misfortune, the less immanent justice was seen. The inclusion of naturalistic information only reduced immanent justice responding in stories that also provided a direct relation between the two events.

Merchant & Rebelsky (274) selected two groups of kindergarten and first-grade children on age and sex, all of whom had reached Piaget's stage of moral realism (morality of constraint) and none of whom had yet developed a consistent response characteristic of moral relativism (morality of cooperation) with regard to game rules. In the participation group each child made up rules for a new game, while his counterpart in the nonparticipation group was taught the rules made up by the child in the first group. As a check on this manipulation each child was then asked who made up the rules, and as intended the participation *S*s reported that they did, while nonparticipation *S* reported that *E* had made them up. Then all children were given a flexibility-of-rules test on which the participation group scored higher. Surprisingly, the first graders were not more flexible than the kindergarteners, and a pre-posttest comparison of flexibility on another game showed declines for all subgroups except the kindergarten participation group.

Next are considered studies of moral behavior defined as both production of prosocial behaviors and/or inhibition of antisocial behaviors. Although often somewhat artificial and of limited ecological validity in laboratory studies, sharing and generosity with limited resources is the most popular prosocial behavior studied. Poulos & Liebert (315) found that modeling and verbalization by *E* each increased the number of shared tokens and the number of children who shared. Surveillance by an adult did not enhance the children's sharing behavior, but it enhanced the positive effects of adult verbalization on that behavior. The particular standard of sharing modeled or preached was not differentially adhered to as a function of treatment, though *S*s exposed to it could recall it later.

Solomon & Druckman (375) conducted an ingenious study in which pairs of peers age 7 to 9, 10 to 12, and 13 to 15 played a game in which the total earnings of one member A from a previous game were distributed between the previous player A and his partner B. The A members were designated as winners or losers depending upon whether they had won more or less than their opponent in the previous game, and the B members knew how the A members had fared previously. A members who had been losers the first game wound up with less money than B members in younger dyads, more than B members in older dyads, and about the same as B members in intermediate age dyads.

Using essentially the same games, the first-game performances of A subjects who knew they would later share their winnings with a B partner (whom they represented, in a sense, in the first game) played that first game more cautiously, persistently, and competitively than did *S*s who did not represent a partner. This difference in responsiveness to role obligations held only for males, however (100).

In a highly artificial situation Fouts (124) gave 10- and 11-year-olds the opportunity to pull a lever that delivered money into a box labeled charity or one that delivered the money into a neutral box. The children responded more to the charity box in general, and the presence of an observing adult had no significant effect on responding in either situation, contrary to literature-based expectations.

On the antisocial side, Liebert and Baron (244) exposed 5- and 6-year-old and 8 and 9-year-old boys and girls to excerpts from actual TV programs depicting either aggressive or nonagressive scenes, and they were then given an opportunity to allegedly hurt a peer. Frequency of aggressive behaviors in subsequent free play was also recorded. Children exposed to aggressive TV engaged in longer attacks against an ostensible child victim than those exposed to nonaggressive TV. The aggressive program also produced higher frequencies of aggression in free play, especially among the younger boys.

Stein & Bryan (383) used a televised model who verbally encouraged either conformity or violation of rules concerning rate of self reward. In each model verbalization condition the model himself then either conformed with or violated the rules. The child's verbal explanations were mainly affected by the model's verbal stance, but the child's behavioral conformity or violation depended upon an interaction between the model's words and deeds. The greatest rule violation occurred when *M* was inconsistent, preaching violation but practicing conformity. The next greatest violation occurred when *M* was also inconsistent, but in the reverse direction. Models whose words and deeds matched elicited still less violation by *S*s, but more when *M* practiced and preached violation than when *M* practiced and preached conformity.

Academic cheating in fifth graders was studied by Johnson & Gormly (192) as a function of the obviousness vs subtlety of the measure used to assess cheating. Obviousness of the measure used in previous studies accounts for the reported relationship between academic ability and cheating. While a main effect of sex was not obtained in this study, the interaction of sex with other variables suggested that females were more likely to cheat when they were characterized as having unfavorable self perceptions, while males were more influenced by immediate situational factors.

Stouwie (386) had two adults give children conflicting instructions in a resistence-to-temptation task, one permissive and the other prohibitive. One adult was always dominant and the other nurturant. Most resistence followed dominant prohibitions and most deviation followed dominant permissive instructions. All *S*s increased in deviant responding over time. The role of maternal verbal communication style and content as an antecedent of resistance to temptation in Canadian and Italian families was analyzed in a monograph by Greenglass (155). Cheating was higher in Canadian than Italian boys, but no difference was obtained for girls, and no overall sex difference was found. Cheating was not related to motivation to succeed or to actual earned scores. Italian mothers were more authoritarian and restrictive than Canadian mothers with their sons. Canadian mothers used more reasoning with their sons. In both cultures mothers were more authoritarian and restrictive with their daughters than with their sons, and girls in both cultures who perceived parents as exerting control over them cheated less.

In a study of Mexican-American children in grades 2 through 8, Solomon et al (374) assessed five democratic values by interview and again behaviorally in a group-problem-solving and dart-throwing session. Four of the values showed age increases when assessed verbally but not when assessed behaviorally. These were equality of representation, equality of participation, assertion, and compromise. The fifth value, equality of resource distribution, was relatively high and invariant over ages when assessed verbally, while its behavioral index was the only one to show an increase as a function of age.

Greenglass (156) found that altruistic lying (to protect another who has given the child unauthorized help in a prior task) increased as a function of age.

Turiel & Rothman (403) pretested seventh and eighth grade boys with Kohlberg's moral judgment interview, then offered them a choice between two actions. Prior to choosing, each *S* heard one choice supported by reasoning at the stage just above his own on the Kohlberg scale, and the other choice supported by reasoning at the stage just below his own. The *S* then made his choice and gave a rationale for it. A posttest showed no significant overall stage changes, but reasoning at a stage above *S*'s own led to a shift upwards for stage 4 children.

A direct comparison of judgment and behavior was made by Saltzstein, Diamond & Belenky (343). Seventh-grade children were assessed by the Kohlberg interview and then tested for conformity in an Asch-type group-influence situation. Stage 3 children conformed more than either higher or lower stage children, and high stage children made very few conforming responses. Stage 3 is an intermediate one characterized as mostly "good-boy, good-girl, approval-seeking morality." Fodor (123) conducted a similar study relating Kohlber's stages to susceptibility to influence by others and to delinquency. A great many more such studies bridging the gap between the development of judgment and the adoption of behaviors will be needed (and are beginning to appear) before the relationship between these two domains is adequately clarified. A further bridge needs to be built between moral behavior and judgment on the one hand and modeling and TV influences on the other, so that the practice vs preach variable in the latter studies can be coordinated with the behavior vs judgment relationship in the former.

REJOINDERS, REBUTTALS, CORRECTIONS, AND CAUTIONS

This section of the review will cite a number of the past year's publications whose special characteristic is their attempt to correct an error in fact, logic, or method, or to alert the field to potential future errors of that sort. Certainly such reports could be summarized under the substantive topic headings to which they refer. On the other hand, they often represent a very special, quite valuable type of professional behavior—a sort of self-control mechanism for the field as a whole. Primarily for that reason, they will be treated as an area of their own. Since grouping by topic would accomplish virtually no grouping at all, the reports will be presented roughly in rank order along a dimension of specificity-generality, the most specific first.

Sostek, Sameroff & Sostek (376) have summarized very carefully conducted, throughly controlled research on the conditionability of the Babkin reflex and concluded that it is not a conditionable reflex. The Babkin reflex is a gaping response of the infant's mouth, accompanied by a turning of the head to midline while raising it (sometimes accompanied by eye closing and arm flexion). The response is elicited by a simultaneous pressing of the infant's palms. Earlier studies had suggested that it could be conditioned to a CS of passive motion of the infant's arm. Such studies lacked appropriate evaluation of the unconditioned effects of their CS over repeated trials and of the relationship of the infant's state (alert vs drowsy) to the response. The present study included such measures. It found no evidence for conditioning; instead, there appeared a positive correlation between drowsiness and the probability of the response, and state measures indicated that infants typically grew drowsier as the "conditioning" session progressed. Furthermore it was found that some infants displayed the Babkin reflex as an unconditioned response to arm movement, rendering it thoroughly unsuitable as a CS.

Warren (410) has noted that there is a general belief that African infants (defined as black peoples of sub-Saharan Africa) show precocious development in their first year of life; the belief is based on a number of studies measuring African infant characteristics and comparing them to test norms. However, studies which compare samples of African infants to similar samples of non-African infants, measured directly for purposes of comparison, do not show systematic differences. Warren suggests that better assessment techniques, more directly applied, are required for a final conclusion. Meanwhile, Lusk & Lewis (251) once again reported precocity for African infants; as Warren's argument predicted, their comparison was to norms.

Chandler & Greenspoon (58) on the one hand and Borke (30) on the other have presented some mutual suggestions for corrections of conclusions and terms concerning their research on egocentrism. Borke had previously presented data suggesting that children display empathy with others' viewpoints as early as 4 years of age. Chandler & Greenspoon, in the cited paper, argued that if this were correct, it would "force a major revision in the theories of Piaget and his co-workers" (58, p. 104). Chandler & Greenspoon then presented data based on a distinction between role-taking or perspective-taking skill and the more primitive ability to predict the feelings of others; their data suggested that while the latter ability (presumably Borke's "empathy") might be seen in quite young children, the former skill (the critical one in denying egocentrism, in their opinion) was still not solidly developed by middle childhood. In reply, Borke (30) acknowledged Chandler & Greenspoon's data and the definitional logic of their approach, but argued against the utility of making the distinction they had. Instead, she suggested that empathy be viewed as a steadily developing concept, one in which early manifestations were predominantly predictions of others' affect, but which increasingly became more complex until it encompassed the perspective-taking skills cited by Chandler & Greenspoon as the critical characteristic. In effect, the argument was largely resolved in terms of what the course of such development was; what remained for Borke were the social implications of the semantic attribution of "egocentrism" to children until adolescence. Her argument was reminiscent of Eisenberg's on aggression: "What we believe of man affects the behavior of men" (104, p. 124). Perhaps Borke was arguing that if the (agreed on) characteristics of young children are labeled "egocentric" by developmental science, the children will be made more so than they are.

A recent book by Easton & Dennis (102), entitled *Children in the Political System; Origins of Political Legitimacy,* has obvious relevance for developmental psychology. Krause (226), however, has taken the authors to task. He pointed out that they have sought a psychological cause of any general affection or respect that people may have for governmental and other authoritative social offices, but in doing so have strained both their data and their logic. Krause offered instead a psychologist's reconsideration and caution.

Infantile autism has been a busy focus in the past year for rebuttals. Two such were inspired by Ward's (407) postulation of an essentially environmental or psychogenic etiology of infantile autism. L'Abate (230) argued that Ward's conclusions were derived from too selective a review of the relevant literature, and consequently neglected the possibility of more than environmental factors interacting in the causation of autism. Furthermore, L'Abate hoped that newer treatment techniques would eventually produce a clearer definition of the entire syndrome, which inevitably would make arguments about etiology more precise. Rimland (328) also objected, arguing that Ward's use of the term "autism" was too broad and allowed consideration of irrelevant literature, that he had misinterpreted some classical behavioral specifications of autism and that there were several recent references suggesting biological factors in the etiology of autism. In that both rebuttals gave strong emphasis to the widespread lack of agreement on how to use the term "autism," it appears that many such arguments will continue to be arguments about definitional issues.

Measurement problems were cited for several locus-of-control studies in a caution by Gorsuch, Henighan & Barnard (150). They pointed out that many locus-of-control scales are often used with children of low verbal ability, and that while the reliability of such scales may amount to .60 with verbal fourth and fifth graders, their reliability is not even susceptible of estimation in the case of younger or nonverbal children. Such scales, characterized by different reliabilities in different subgroups of an experimental design, will yield misleading data under either of two conditions: when the mean of reliably measured children differs from a random response level, or when the variable identifying the subgroups interacts with the target of the scale. Both conditions are usually met in locus-of-control studies with children of systematically varying verbal abilities. Although issue was joined specifically with the procedures of certain locus-of-control studies, it is clear that the caution offered is a general one with many applications.

Longitudinal vs cross-sectional approaches to the study of development were the subject of two cautions. Bergman (23) argued on technical grounds that longitudinal samples with repeated measurements yielded better results than independent samples; his report also offered a regression approach to deal with the problem of large groups "dropping out" of longitudinal samples. Schaie (345) presented a more complicated caution in the same vein, specifically citing data from the Harvard growth study which, upon reanalysis, indicated serious limitations on their generalizability, even though estimated over such short spans of time as 4 months.

The entire literature of birth order effects came under question twice in the past year, once with a possible reinterpretation, and once with a severe challenge to its existence as other than a statistical artifact. McGurk & Lewis (269), reporting some birth order effects with young children, found that second-borns sought more adult help and approval, spent more time in individual activity, were more talkative, and displayed negative affect more often than comparison children. However, these authors also found that their second-borns on the average were only 18 months younger than their older sibs, but 30 months older than their nearest younger sibs. Thus, they argued, mothers should have more time to attend to first-and third-borns; relatively, they deprive second-borns of attention and so contribute to their dependency. By contrast, Schooler (347) questioned the existence of the phenomenon, pointing out that if recently hypothesized biases in long-term population trends are taken into account, it may be the case that first-borns and second-borns are drawn from distinctively different populations and differ less because of their birth order than because of the different characteristics prevalent in populations choosing to have one child rather than more than one. It would seem that Schooler's argument, while highly dependent upon some complex assumptions about population trends and attitudes about family size within different social classes, nevertheless is a familiar example of a general problem in biased sampling. No doubt the issue will recur in the future reports.

Finally, Wozniak (435) cautions us not to misinterpret an entire source of research—Soviet studies of the development of verbal inhibition of motor behavior. The frequent failures to replicate such findings, noted in the literature, may be a result of misinterpretation of the usual Soviet methodology and of its underlying assumptions. In short, the caution suggests that in these cases, nationality correlates strongly with systematic psychophilosophical assumptions and a consequent methodology.

APPLICATIONS

A total review of all child applications would be too lengthy to serve as a section of this chapter, nor would it be entirely appropriate; large sections of it would prove redundant with the chapters reviewing clinical and educational psychology. Nevertheless, children are an extraordinarily important target of application; certain applications are virtually unique to children; and some of those applications have direct or indirect implications for the concept of development (as argued earlier). Consequently, a highly selective and very brief survey will be presented, beginning with the scholarly discussion offered by Atkinson & Paulson (7) on the general problem of translating learning theory into a theory of instruction. Proceeding through a series of examples, these authors illustrated some generalizable procedures for deriving instructional strategies from learning principles. Significantly, their examples displayed the derivation of instructional sequences which take account of the individual differences of their students, relative to the difficulty of their various curricular units. In general, they suggested an intersection between learning theory, computer technology, and programmed instruction, and some tactics specific to that intersection which could lead to a radically different educational technology in the future. The implications of such a development for children are immense. In that a developmental psychology is conditioned by the culture within which the children it studies are socialized, and in that the culture's schools may presently become a much more potent behavior-changing medium than at present, then future developmental textbooks may have to cite articles such as this as key historical points.

At the same time that we cite careful data-based predictions about future child behavior problems, we must note the ongoing nonsolution of many current ones. Spinetta & Rigler (380), for example, have gathered together the literature dealing with child abuse, especially that descriptive of the abusing parent. They point out several behavioral (or potentially behavioral) characteristics of the abusing parent, and thereby help to define a problem for modification. In general, their survey suggests that abusing parents generally come from deprived environments, possess incorrect beliefs about the nature of child rearing expressed in various malpractices, and have generally high rates of improperly discriminated aggression of dangerous topography. Socioeconomic stresses were considered contributing but not essential factors in the parent's final descent into abuse.

Nevertheless, experimental application has proceeded into a number of fairly new settings. For example, Doke & Risley (99) and LeLaurin & Risley (237) reported two more details in an ongoing chain of experimental analyses of day care techniques. The first study demonstrated the conditions necessary for maintenance of optimal child involvement when their activities are to be prescribed and scheduled rather than allowed as free choices, and specified tactics allowing two teachers to maintain optimal child involvement even with a precisely specified sequence of activities. The second study compared two staffing patterns useful in accomplishing the transition from lunch through bathroom routines and into nap time, using the degree of child participation in the activities as the criterion. A pattern in which teachers staffed areas (the "zone" procedure) was found clearly superior to one in which teachers conducted specific groups of children through the sequence (the "man-to-man" procedure).

A number of studies have pressed experimental applications directly into homes, placing the techniques of child management in the hands of parents. Christophersen et al (62) taught two sets of parents to set up token systems within their homes and use them to ameliorate a lengthy series of child behavior problems (household chores, personal grooming, backtalk, etc). In a very similar application, Hall et al (167) taught four parents to use various behavior modification techniques (several forms of reinforcement, mild punishment, and extinction) to improve such behaviors as wearing correct orthodontic retainers, helping with household tasks, stopping crying, whining, and complaining, and getting dressed on time. Each parent was instructed to conduct an experimental reversal of the techniques used and then to recover the desirable behavior by reinstating the experimental practices. Herbert & Baer (178) taught parents to manage their social contingencies in a generalized correct manner, attending almost exclusively to all classes of desirable behavior by their child while ignoring almost completely all classes of undesirable behavior. The technique used involved the use of a counter on which the parent recorded all instances of attention to desirable behavior. (Recording errors—i.e. instances of attention to undesirable child behaviors—proved not to be an effective technique.) Those parents who profited by the technique seemed to be stable in their new practices after its discontinuation.

Clark, Burgess & Hendee (65) moved child behavior modification into the national parks and forests. They set up a reinforcement system for children in a campground, such that the children could eventually choose from a variety of readily available reinforcers. The responses required were the collection and proper disposal of litter in the campgrounds of the park. The experimenters went so far as to plant litter as part of the experiment to aid in the evaluation of the children's efficiency. The technique appeared to be thoroughly effective in recollecting such litter. On a simple cost basis, it may represent an attractive solution to littering in such settings.

Ritschl, Mongrella & Presbie (329) took a simple contingency in the school bus to maintain in-seat behavior (pointing out that out-of-seat behavior is dangerous in a moving bus). Their subjects were an unruly group of retarded (educable) children ranging in age from 6 to 15. Rock-and-roll music was played as long as the bus was moving and as long as no child was out of his seat. Each observed instance of out-of-seat resulted in 5 sec interruptions of the music. A marked effect was noted and experimentally analyzed as due to the new technique by experimental discontinuations of the procedure. (It is not yet clear, of course, whether the stimulus would work equally well with children in general, or if it is specific to retardates.)

School applications are probably the majority case, but only two will be cited, chosen for their relevance to the perceptual development of children. Halliwell & Solan (168) have reported a perceptual training program for reading skills, suitable for first grade. They evaluated its effectiveness by comparing a group of children exposed to it with other groups given traditional (nonperceptual) reading instruction as a supplement to their regular first grade curriculum, or else given no supplemental instruction at all. The perceptually based supplemental program led to better reading (primarily among the boys exposed to it) than was seen in the other groups. The authors pointed out that perceptual training for reading is largely a result of the influence of developmental psychology. In the same vein, Tawney (392) presented a much more molecular analysis of some perceptual responses involved in reading, specifically, letter discrimination. His training program was based on an analysis of presumably critical features of letter shapes which facilitate their discrimination from one another. Using a match-to-sample paradigm, Tawney reinforced some children for discriminating and matching the critical features (presented divorced from letters) and others for responding to presumably noncritical features; in addition, he utilized a control group who experienced neither program. A posttest of letter discrimination ability was then administered. All groups improved over their pretests; but children who had received discrimination training in the presumably critical features of letters did better than the others (including those who had undergone discrimination training in supposedly noncritical features). A detailed analysis of the children's errors gave some indications of the nature of letter confusions. Although letters are highly arbitrary visual stimuli, a successful program promoting their discrimination may well have implications for visual-perceptual development in general, at least in terms of a model of analytic procedure.

Generalization of desirable behavior changes, from the remediating environment to all other settings in which the child operates, is an enduring and difficult problem for application. It has been recognized as such only in recent years; more important, it has begun to appear as another item on lists of behavior to change, as if "to generalize" were a response in itself. Consequently, techniques for developing "to generalize" have begun to appear; eventually, it seems, a technology of generalization will result. The past year's research produced two notable examples. Johnston & Johnston (193) found that they had developed an effective token-mediated reinforcement system for improving severe articulation problems in the speech of young children in a classroom setting. However, generalization of the improved articulation outside of the training setting was poor. A technique was developed which succeeded in producing generalized correct articulation. Children were trained in pairs, such that one child was a discriminative stimulus for the correct articulation of the other, and vice-versa. To the extent that the children shared many environments other than the training setting, good articulation became generalized. Clearly, there remain several inviting problems, such as how to generalize control from a particular child to children in general and people in general. Walker & Buckley (406), coping with the same basic problem, evaluated several different techniques for obtaining generalization after a remedial experience ended. Their basic situation revolved around a remedial classroom, operating on a token reinforcement system, which produced desirable classroom behavior in difficult subjects. When the subjects returned from the remedial classroom to their regular classrooms, generalization was not always sufficient. Four groups of subjects were compared: a control group of remedial classroom graduates was simply returned to the regular classroom; another group was subjected to peer-reprogramming (in which children were taught to apply appropriate contingencies to the subjects in the regular classroom); others returned to a classroom in which many stimuli had been equated to those encountered in the remedial classroom; and the final group returned to a teacher who had meanwhile been subjected to training in behavior management techniques. At least some generalization was apparent in even the control group; but the two groups encountering equation of stimuli between the two settings and peer reprogramming did much better than that. Teacher training, however, was associated with no better results than were apparent in the control group. The peer reprogramming procedure was somewhat reminiscent of the Johnston & Johnston technique (just discussed), although more elaborate. In general, the two studies suggest practical and effective use can be made of peers, both as discriminative stimuli and as sources of reinforcement for behaviors to be generalized.

Finally, it is pertinent to note a critical comment on one aspect of child behavior modification and a reply to it. Late in the year, Winett & Winkler (427) presented a review of school behavior modification applications, and concluded with an indictment succinctly stated in their title: "Current behavior modification in the classroom: Be still, be quiet, be docile." The conclusion was derived from a survey of the research reported since 1968 in the *Journal of Applied Behavior Analysis* (a prime outlet for such studies). That survey indicated that inappropriate classroom behaviors invariably seemed to be those that were disorderly, loud, or disobedient of the teacher. It was suggested that behavior modification applications might well turn themselves toward different goals, e.g. the maintenance of "open" classrooms. A reply by O'Leary (299) accompanied the Winett & Winkler review. O'Leary suggested that their indictment was based on selective reviewing; he then presented a series of examples in which behavior modification techniques had been used for innovation and change rather than maintenance or strengthening of the status quo. Furthermore, O'Leary questioned whether the "open" classroom (in which children presumably sing, laugh, whistle, etc) was in fact known to be a desirable or effective learning environment for certain children, especially those with large social and academic deficits. However, O'Leary joined Winett & Winkler in warning against indulgent alliance with any request to change children's behavior by any representative of the educational establishment. In general, it would seem that the issue hinges very largely on knowing at the level of facts what behaviors lead to what consequences in classrooms. Unfortunately, the field of child applications is remarkably free so far of any empirical evaluations of whether education, socialization, or any other aspects of development proceeds better in quiet, orderly, obedient classrooms than in unruly, noisy, permissive ones. This situation, it appears, is about to change; factual investigations seem on the verge of appearance. Meanwhile, there is an abundance of opinion on both sides of the issue, so strong as to take on the appearance if not the substance of fact.

Literature Cited

1. Adams, B. N. 1972. Birth order: A critical review. *Sociometry* 35:411–39
2. Adams, W. V. 1972. Strategy differences between reflective and impulsive children. *Child Develop.* 43:1076–80
3. Allaman, J. D., Joyce, C. S., Crandal, V. C. 1972. The antecedents of social desirability response tendencies of children and young adults. *Child Develop.* 43:1135–60
4. Anderson, D. R. 1972. The effects of prior training on the incidental discriminative learning of children. *J. Exp. Child Psychol.* 14:416–26
5. Appel, L. F. et al 1972. The development of the distinction between perceiving and memorizing. *Child Develop.* 43:1365–81
6. Armentrout, J. A., Burger, G. K. 1972. Children's reports of parental child-rearing behavior at five grade levels. *Develop. Psychol.* 7:44–48
7. Atkinson, R. C., Paulson, J. A. 1972. An approach to the psychology of instruction. *Psychol. Bull.* 78:49–61
8. Ault, R. L., Crawford, D. E., Jeffrey, W. E. 1972. Visual scanning strategies of reflective, impulsive, fast-accurate, and slow-inaccurate children on the matching familiar figures test. *Child Develop.* 43:1412–17
9. Babad, E. Y. 1972. Person specificity of the "social deprivation effect." *Develop. Psychol.* 6:210–13
10. Baer, D. M. 1973. The control of developmental process: Why wait? In *Life-Span Developmental Psychology,* ed. J. Nesselroade, H. W. Resse, 185–93. New York: Academic. 364 pp.
11. Banikiotes, F. G., Montgomery, A. A., Banikiotes, P. G. 1972. Male and female auditory reinforcement of infant vocalizations. *Develop. Psychol.* 6:476–81
12. Bartol, C. R., Pielstick, N. L. 1972. The effects of ambiguity, familiarization, age and sex on stimulus preference. *J. Exp. Child Psychol.* 14:21–29
13. Battle, E. S., Lacey, B. 1972. A context for hyperactivity in children, over time. *Child Develop.* 43:757–73
14. Baumrind, D. 1972. An exploratory study of socialization effects on black children: Some black-white comparisons. *Child Develop.* 43:261–67
15. Bayer, C. A. 1972. An explanation of developmental differences in the successive trials effect of the Poggendorff illusion. *Psychon. Sci.* 26:85–86
16. Beckwith, L. 1972. Relationships between infants' social behavior and their mothers' behavior. *Child Develop.* 43:397–411
17. Begelman, D. A., Steinfeld, G. J. 1972. Is there an error of the standard? A critique of Piaget's perceptual theory. *Genet. Psychol. Monogr.* 86:81–117
18. Bell, S. M., Ainsworth, M. D. S. 1972. Infant crying and maternal responsiveness. *Child Develop.* 43:1171–90
19. Belmont, J. M. 1972. Relations of age and intelligence to short-term color memory. *Child Develop.* 43:19–29
20. Bennett, C. W., Ling, D. 1972. Teaching a complex verbal response to a hearing-impaired girl. *J. Appl. Behav. Anal.* 5:321–27
21. Berch, D. B. 1972. Stimulus interaction and problem difficulty in children's discrimination learning. *J. Exp. Child Psychol.* 13:115–27
22. Berg, W. K. 1972. Habituation and dishabituation of cardiac responses in 4-month-old, alert infants. *J. Exp. Child Psychol.* 14:92–107
23. Bergman, L. R. 1972. Inferential aspects of longitudinal data in studying developmental problems. *Hum. Develop.* 15:287–93
24. Bernstein, A., Luria, Z. 1972. Variables affecting associative recall in children. *Child Develop.* 43:288–92
25. Bijou, S. W., Baer, D. M. 1966. Operant methods in child behavior and development. In *Operant Behavior: Areas of Research and Application,* ed. W. Honig, 718–89. New York: Appleton-Century-Crofts. 865 pp.
26. Black, F. W. 1972. Factors related to human figure-drawing size in children. *Percept. Mot. Skills* 35:902
27. Blair, J. R. 1972. The effects of differential reinforcement on the discrimination learning of normal and low-achieving middle-class boys. *Child Develop.* 43:251–55
28. Bogartz, R. S. 1972. Three cue-selection models applied to multidimensional stimulus classification: Alternatives to the Spiker, Croll & Miller analysis. *J. Exp. Child Psychol.* 13:573–84
29. Bond, E. K. 1972. Perception of form by the human infant. *Psychol. Bull.* 77:225–36
30. Borke, H. 1972. Chandler & Greenspoon's "Ersatz egocentrism": A rejoinder. *Develop. Psychol.* 7:107–9
31. Bosco, J. 1972. The visual information processing speed of lower- and middle-class children. *Child Develop.* 43:1418–22

32. Braine, L. G. 1972. A developmental analysis of the effect of stimulus orientation on recognition. *Am. J. Psychol.* 85:157–86
33. Brainerd, C. J. 1972. The age-stage issue in conservation acquisition. *Psychon. Sci.* 29:115–16
34. Brainerd, C. J., Brainerd, S. H. 1972. Order of acquisition of number and quantity conservation. *Child Develop.* 43:1401–6
35. Brier, N., Jacobs, P. I. 1972. Reversal shifting: Its stability and relation to intelligence at two developmental levels. *Child Develop.* 43:1230–41
36. Brodzinsky, D. M., Jackson, J. P., Overton, W. F. 1972. Effects of perceptual shielding in the development of spatial perspectives. *Child Develop.* 43:1041–46
37. Brown, A. L., Scott, K. G., Urbano, R. C. 1972. Psychophysically scaled cue differences, learning rate, and attentional strategies in a tactile discrimination task. *J. Exp. Child Psychol.* 13:283–302
38. Brown, A. L., Scott, M. S. 1972. Transfer between the oddity and relative size concepts: Reversal and extradimensional shifts. *J. Exp. Child Psychol.* 13: 350–67
39. Brown, J. 1972. Instrumental control of the sucking response in human newborns. *J. Exp. Child Psychol.* 14:66–80
40. Brown, R., Ed. 1958. *Words and Things.* New York: Free Press
41. Bryden, M. P. 1972. Auditory-visual and sequential-spatial matching in relation to reading ability. *Child Develop.* 43:824–32
42. Bucky, S. F., Banta, T. J. 1972. Racial factors in test performance. *Develop. Psychol.* 6:7–13
43. Bucky, S. F., Banta, T. J., Gross, R. B. 1972. Development of motor impulse control and reflectivity. *Percept. Mot. Skills* 34:813–14
44. Burton, R. V. 1972. Cross-sex identity in Barbados. *Develop. Psychol.* 6: 365–74
45. Burton, R. V. 1972. The interpretation of intergenerational attitudes. *Merrill-Palmer Quart.* 18:61–62
46. Busse, T. V. et al 1972. Environmentally enriched classrooms and the cognitive and perceptual development of negro preschool children. *J. Educ. Psychol.* 63:15–21
47. Bynum, T. W., Thomas, J. A., Weitz, L. J. 1972. Truth-functional logic in formal operational thinking. *Develop. Psychol.* 7:129–32
48. Caldwell, B., Ricciutti, H., Eds. 1973. *Review of Child Development Research.* Univ. Chicago Press. In press
49. Campbell, B. A., Spear, N. E. 1972. Ontogeny of memory. *Psychol. Rev.* 79: 215–36
50. Campione, J. C., Beaton, V. L. 1972. Transfer of training: Some boundary conditions and initial theory. *J. Exp. Child Psychol.* 13:94–114
51. Cantor, G. N. 1972. Use of a conflict paradigm to study race awareness in children. *Child Develop.* 43:1437–42
52. Ibid. Effects of familiarization on children's ratings of pictures of whites and blacks, 1219–29
53. Caruso, J. L., Resnick, L. B. 1972. Task structure and transfer in children's learning of double classification skills. *Child Develop.* 43:1297–1308
54. Case, R. 1972. Validation of a neo-Piagetian mental capacity construct. *J. Exp. Child Psychol.* 14:287–302
55. Case, R. 1972. Learning and development: A neo-Piagetian interpretation. *Hum. Develop.* 15:339–58
56. Cattell, R. B., Barton, K., Dielman, T. E. 1972. Prediction of school achievement from motivation, personality, and ability measures. *Psychol. Rep.* 30: 35–43
57. Cermak, L. S., Sagotsky, G., Moshier, C. 1972. Development of the ability to encode within evaluative dimensions. *J. Exp. Child Psychol.* 13:210–19
58. Chandler, M. J., Greenspoon, S. 1972. Ersatz egocentrism: A reply to H. Borke. *Develop. Psychol.* 7:104–6
59. Cheyne, J. A. 1972. Direct and vicarious reinforcement: A note on punishment and negative instances. *J. Educ. Psychol.* 63:63–68
60. Chiu, L. H. 1972. Manifest anxiety in children with analytic and nonanalytic cognitive style. *Percept. Mot. Skills* 35: 406
61. Chovan, W. L. 1972. Role of vocal labeling in memory for object arrangements by deaf and hearing children. *Percept. Mot. Skills* 34:59–62
62. Christophersen, E. R., Arnold, C. M., Hill, D. W., Quilitch, H. R. 1972. The home point system: Token reinforcement procedures for application by parents of children with behavior problems. *J. Appl. Behav. Anal.* 5: 485–97
63. Ciborowski, T., Cole, M. 1972. A cross-cultural study of conjunctive and disjunctive concept learning. *Child Develop.* 43:774–89
64. Cicirelli, V. G. 1972. The effect of sibling relationship on concept learning of

young children taught by child-teachers. *Child Develop.* 43:282–87
65. Clark, R. N., Burgess, R. L., Hendee, J. C. 1972. The development of antilitter behavior in a forest campground. *J. Appl. Behav. Anal.* 5:1–5
66. Clifford, M. M., Cleary, T. A. 1972. The relationship between children's academic performance and achievement accountability. *Child Develop.* 43: 647–55
67. Clifton, R. K., Meyers, W. J., Solomons, G. 1972. Methodological problems in conditioning the headturning response of newborn infants. *J. Exp. Child Psychol.* 13:29–42
68. Clifton, R. K., Siqueland, E. R., Lipsitt, L. P. 1972. Conditioned headturning in human newborns as a function of conditioned response requirements and states of wakefulness. *J. Exp. Child Psychol.* 13:43–57
69. Coates, B., Anderson, E. P., Hartup, W. W. 1972. Interrelations in the attachment behavior of human infants. *Develop. Psychol.* 6:218–30
70. Ibid. The stability of attachment behaviors in the human infant, 231–37
71. Cohen, L. B. 1972. Attention-getting and attention-holding processes of infant visual preferences. *Child Develop.* 43:869–79
72. Cohler, B. J. 1972. The role of retrospective accounts on the study of intergenerational attitudes. *Merrill-Palmer Quart.* 18:59–60
73. Cole, L. E., Kanak, N. J. 1972. Paired-associate learning and bidirectional associative recall in first, third, fifth, and seventh graders. *J. Exp. Child Psychol.* 13:128–37
74. Collins, D., Kessen, W., Haith, M. 1972. Note on an attempt to replicate a relation between stimulus unpredictability and infant attention. *J. Exp. Child Psychol.* 13:1–8
75. Conrad, R. 1972. Form and color as short-term memory codes in preschool children. *Psychon. Sci.* 27:225–26
76. Corsini, D. A. 1972. Kindergarten children's use of spatial-positional, verbal, and nonverbal cues for memory. *J. Educ. Psychol.* 63:353–57
77. Corter, C. M., Rheingold, H. L., Eckerman, C. O. 1972. Toys delay the infant's following of his mother. *Develop. Psychol.* 6:138–45
78. Cramer, P. 1972. A developmental study of errors in memory. *Develop. Psychol.* 7:204–9
79. Crandall, V. C., Lacey, B. W. 1972. Children's perceptions of internal-external control in intellectual-academic situations and their embedded figures test performance. *Child Develop.* 43: 1123–34
80. Croll, W. L. 1972. Generalization as a function of the range of test stimuli: The roles of discriminability and response bias. *J. Exp. Child Psychol.* 13:404–12
81. Cropley, A. J. 1972. A five-year longitudinal study of the validity of creativity tests. *Develop. Psychol.* 6:119–24
82. Curcio, F., Kattef, E., Levine, D., Robbins, O. 1972. Compensation and susceptibility to conservation training. *Develop. Psychol.* 7:259–65
83. Daehler, M. W. 1972. Developmental and experimental factors associated with inferential behavior. *J. Exp. Child Psychol.* 13:324–38
84. Dasen, P. R. 1972. The development of conservation in aboriginal children: A replication study. *Int. J. Psychol.* 7: 75–85
85. Davidson, E. S., Liebert, R. M. 1972. Effects of prior commitment on children's evaluation and imitation of a peer model's perceptual judgments. *Percept. Mot. Skills* 35:825–26
86. Davies, G. M. 1972. Quantitative and qualitative aspects of memory for picture stimuli. *J. Exp. Child Psychol.* 13: 382–93
87. DeCasper, A. J., Zeiler, M. D. 1972. Steady-state behavior in children: A method and some data. *J. Exp. Child Psychol.* 13:231–39
88. Deffenbacher, K. A., Hamm, N. H. 1972. An application of Brunswik's lens model to developmental changes in probability learning. *Develop. Psychol.* 6:508–19
89. Denis-Prinzhorn, M., Kamii, C., Mounoud, P. 1972. Pedagogical applications of Piaget's theory. *People Watching* 1: 68–71
90. Denney, D. R. 1972. Modeling effects upon conceptual style and cognitive tempo. *Child Develop.* 43:105–19
91. Ibid. Modeling and eliciting effects upon conceptual strategies, 810–23
92. Denney, N. W. 1972. A developmental study of free classification in children. *Child Develop.* 43:221–32
93. Ibid. Free classification in preschool children, 1161–70
94. Denney, N. W., Ziobrowski, M. 1972. Developmental changes in clustering criteria. *J. Exp. Child Psychol.* 13: 275–82
95. Deutsch, F., Stein, A. H. 1972. The effects of personal responsibility and task interruption on the private speech

of preschoolers. *Hum. Develop.* 15: 310–24
96. de Villiers, P. A., de Villiers, J. G. 1972. Early judgments of semantic and syntactic acceptability by children. *J. Psycholing. Res.* 1:299–310
97. Dickie, J., Bagur, J. S. 1972. Considerations for the study of language in young low-income minority group children. *Merrill-Palmer Quart.* 18:25–38
98. Dodd, B. J. 1972. Effects of social and vocal stimulation on infant babbling. *Develop. Psychol.* 7:80–83
99. Doke, L. A., Risley, T. R. 1972. The organization of day-care environments: Required vs. optional activities. *J. Appl. Behav. Anal.* 5:405–20
100. Druckman, D., Solomon, D., Zechmeister, K. 1972. Effects of representational role obligations on the process of children's distribution of resources. *Sociometry* 35:387–410
101. Dusek, J. B. 1972. Experimenter-bias effects on the simple motor task performance of low- and high-test anxious boys and girls. *Psychol. Rep.* 30:107–14
102. Easton, D., Dennis, J. 1969. *Children in the Political System: Origins of Political Legitimacy.* New York: McGraw-Hill
103. Ehri, L. C. 1972. Sentence contexts as facilitators of noun pair learning in children. *J. Exp. Child Psychol.* 14:242–56
104. Eisenberg, L. 1972. The *human* nature of human nature. *Science* 176:123–28
105. Eisner, D. A. 1972. Developmental relationships between field independence and fixity-mobility. *Percept. Mot. Skills* 34:767–70
106. Elkind, D., Schoenfeld, E. 1972. Identity and equivalence conservation at two age levels. *Develop. Psychol.* 6:529–33
107. Entwisle, D. R., Cornell, E., Epstein, J. 1972. Effect of a principal's expectations on test performance of elementary-school children. *Psychol. Rep.* 31:551–56
108. Evans, W. F., Gratch, G. 1972. The stage IV error of Piaget's theory of object concept development: Difficulties in object conceptualization or spatial localization? *Child Develop.* 43:682–88
109. Fagan, J. F. 1972. Infants' recognition memory for faces. *J. Exp. Child Psychol.* 14:453–76
110. Fagan, J. F. 1972. Rehearsal and free recall in children of superior and average intelligence. *Psychon. Sci.* 28: 352–53
111. Favell, J. E., Favell, J. E. 1972. Control of preference in children by conditioned positive reinforcement. *J. Exp. Anal. Behav.* 18:107–12
112. Fein, G. G. 1972. The effect of within-pair variation and instructions on the transposition behavior of kindergarten and third grade children. *J. Exp. Child Psychol.* 14:379–97
113. Feitelson, D., Weintraub, S., Michaeli, O. 1972. Social interactions in heterogeneous preschools in Israel. *Child Develop.* 43:1249–59
114. Feldman, S. S. 1972. Children's understanding of negation as a logical operation. *Genet. Psychol. Monogr.* 85:3–49
115. Felker, D. W. 1972. Social stereotyping of male and female body types with differing facial expressions by elementary school boys and girls. *J. Psychol.* 82:151–54
116. Figurelli, J. C., Keller, H. R. 1972. The effects of training and socioeconomic class upon the acquisition of conservation concepts. *Child Develop.* 43: 293–98
117. Finley, G. E., Frenkel, O. J. 1972. Children's tachistoscopic recognition thresholds for and recall of words which differ in connotative meaning. *Child Develop.* 43:1093–1103
118. Finley, G. E., Kagan, J., Layne, O. 1972. Development of young children's attention to normal and distorted stimuli: A cross-cultural study. *Develop. Psychol.* 6:288–92
119. Fishbein, H. D., Lewis, S., Keiffer, K. 1972. Children's understanding of spatial relations: Coordination of perspectives. *Develop. Psychol.* 7:21–33
120. Flavell, J. H. 1972. An analysis of cognitive-developmental sequences. *Genet. Psychol. Monogr.* 86:279–350
121. Fleck, J. R. 1972. Cognitive styles in children and performance on Piagetian conservation tasks. *Percept. Mot. Skills* 35:747–56
122. Fling, S., Manosevitz, M. 1972. Sex typing in nursery school children's play interests. *Develop. Psychol.* 7:146–52
123. Fodor, E. M. 1972. Delinquency and susceptibility to social influence among adolescents as a function of level of moral development. *J. Soc. Psychol.* 86:257–60
124. Fouts, G. T. 1972. Charity in children: The influence of "charity" stimuli and an audience. *J. Exp. Child Psychol.* 13: 303–9
125. Francis, H. 1972. Toward an explanation of the syntagmatic-paradigmatic shift. *Child Develop.* 43:949–58
126. Freeman, N. H., Janikoun, R. 1972. Intellectual realism in children's drawings of a familiar object with distinctive features. *Child Develop.* 43:1116–21

127. Friedlander, B. Z., Jacobs, A. C., Davis, B. B., Wetstone, H. S. 1972. Time-sampling analysis of infants' natural language environments in the home. *Child Develop.* 43:730–40
128. Friedman, S. 1972. Habituation and recovery of visual response in the alert human newborn. *J. Exp. Child Psychol.* 13:339–49
129. Friend, R. M., Neale, J. M. 1972. Children's perceptions of success and failure: An attributional analysis of the effects of race and social class. *Develop. Psychol.* 7:124:28
130. Fry, C. L., Craven, R. B.1972. A developmental examination of visual and of active and passive tactual horizontal-vertical illusions. *J. Genet. Psychol.* 121:127–32
131. Furby, L. 1972. Cumulative learning and cognitive development, elaboration and implications of a pretheoretical model. *Hum. Develop.* 15:265–86
132. Gaines, R. 1972. Variables in color perception of young children. *J. Exp. Child Psychol.* 14:196–218
133. Gajzago, C., Day, R. H. 1972. Uprightness constancy with head inversion in young children and adults. *J. Exp. Child Psychol.* 14:43–52
134. Gaudia, G. 1972. Race, social class, and age of achievement of conservation on Piaget's tasks. *Develop. Psychol.* 6: 158–65
135. Gelman, R. 1972. Logical capacity of very young children: Number invariance rules. *Child Develop.* 43:75–90
136. Gelman, R., Weinberg, D. H. 1972. The relationship between liquid conservation and compensation. *Child Develop.* 43:371–83
137. Geshuri, Y. 1972. Observational learning: Effects of observed reward and response patterns. *J. Educ. Psychol.* 63:374–80
138. Gewirtz, J. L., Baer, D. M. 1958. The effect of brief social deprivation on behavior for a social reinforcer. *J. Abnorm. Soc. Psychol.* 56:49–56
139. Ibid. Deprivation and satiation of social reinforcers as drive conditions, 165–72
140. Gholson, B., Levine, M., Phillips, S. 1972. Hypotheses, strategies, and stereotypes in discrimination learning. *J. Exp. Child Psychol.* 13:423–46
141. Girgus, J. S., Hochberg, J. 1972. Age differences in shape recognition through an aperture in a free-viewing situation. *Psychon. Sci.* 28:237–38
142. Glidden, L. M. 1972. Meaningfulness, serial position and retention interval in recognition short-term memory. *J. Exp. Child Psychol.* 13:154–64
143. Goetz, E. M., Baer, D. M. 1971. Descriptive social reinforcement of "creative" block building by young children. In *A New Direction for Education: Behavior Analysis 1971,* ed. E. A. Ramp, B. I. Hopkins, 1:72–79. Lawrence: Univ. Kansas Support and Development Center for Follow Through
144. Goldberg, S. 1972. Infant care and growth in infant Zambia. *Hum. Develop.* 15:77–89
145. Goldstein, J., Locke, J. L., Fehr, F. S. 1972. Children's prerecall phonetic processing of pictures and printed words. *Psychon. Sci.* 26:314–15
146. Goldstein, S. B., Siegel, A. W. 1972. Facilitation of discrimination learning with delayed reinforcement. *Child Develop.* 43:1004–11
147. Gollin, E. S., Schadler, M. 1972. Relational learning and transfer by young children. *J. Exp. Child Psychol.* 14: 219–32
148. Golomb, C. 1972. Evolution of the human figure in a three-dimensional medium. *Develop. Psychol.* 6:385–91
149. Goodnow, J. J., Friedman, S. 1972. Orientation in children's human figure drawings: An aspect of graphic language. *Develop. Psychol.* 7:10–16
150. Gorsuch, R. L., Henighan, R. P., Barnard, C. 1972. Locus of control: An example of dangers in using children's scales with children. *Child Develop.* 43:579–90
151. Gratch, G. 1972. A study of the relative dominance of vision and touch in six-month-old infants. *Child Develop.* 43: 615–23
152. Greenberg, D. J., O'Donnell, W. J. 1972. Infancy and the optimal level of stimulation. *Child Develop.* 43:639–45
153. Greenfield, P. M. Playing peekaboo with a four-month-old: A study of the role of speech and nonspeech sounds in the formation of a visual schema. *J. Psychol.* 82:287–98
154. Greenfield, P. M., Nelson, K., Saltzman, E. 1972. The development of rule-bound strategies for manipulating seriated cups: A parallel between action and grammar. *Cogn. Psychol.* 3:291–310
155. Greenglass, E. R. 1972. A cross-cultural study of the relationship between resistance to temptation and maternal communication. *Genet. Psychol. Monogr.* 86:119–39

156. Greenglass, E. R. 1972. Effects of age and prior help on "altruistic lying." *J. Genet. Psychol.* 121:303–13
157. Groen, G. J., Parkman, J. M. 1972. A chronometric analysis of simple addition. *Psychol. Rev.* 79:329–43
158. Gruen, G. E., Vore, D. A. 1972. Development of conservation in normal and retarded children. *Develop. Psychol.* 6:146–57
159. Grusec, J. E., Ezrin, S. A. 1972. Techniques of punishment and the development of self-criticism. *Child Develop.* 43:1273–88
160. Gummerman, K., Gray, C. R. 1972. Age, iconic storage, and visual information processing. *J. Exp. Child Psychol.* 13:165–70
161. Gummerman, K., Gray, C. R., Wilson, M. 1972. An attempt to assess eidetic imagery objectively. *Psychon. Sci.* 28: 115–16
162. Gusinow, J. F., Price, L. E. 1972. Modification of form and color responding in young children as a function of differential reinforcement and verbalization. *J. Exp. Child Psychol.* 13:145–53
163. Gutkin, D. C. 1972. The effect of systematic story changes on intentionality in children's moral judgments. *Child Develop.* 43:187–95
164. Guttentag, M. 1972. Negro-white differences in children's movement. *Percept. Mot. Skills* 35:435–36
165. Guttman, R., Kahneman, I. 1972. Age- and sex-related variation in performance on a figural-conceptual task. *Develop. Psychol.* 7:4–9
166. Haith, M. M. 1972. The forgotten message of the infant smile. *Merrill-Palmer Quart.* 18:321–22
167. Hall, R. V. et al 1972. Modification of behavior problems in the home with a parent as observer and experimenter. *J. Appl. Behav. Anal.* 5:53–64
168. Halliwell, J. W., Solan, H. A. 1972. The effects of a supplemental perceptual training program on reading achievement. *Except. Child.* 613–17
169. Harris, G. J., Burke, D. 1972. The effects of grouping on short-term serial recall of digits by children: Developmental trends. *Child Develop.* 43: 710–16
170. Harris, G. J., Fleer, R. E. 1972. Recognition memory for faces by retardates and normals. *Percept. Mot. Skills* 34: 755–58
171. Harris, L. J. 1972. Discrimination of left and right, and development of the logic of relations. *Merrill-Palmer Quart.* 18:307–20
172. Harris, L. J., Stommen, E. A. 1972. The role of front-back features in children's "front," "back" and "beside" placements of objects. *Merrill-Palmer Quart.* 18:259–72
173. Harris, M. B., Hassemer, W. G. 1972. Some factors affecting the complexity of children's sentences: The effects of modeling, age, sex, and bilingualism. *J. Exp. Child Psychol.* 13:447–55
174. Harrison, A., Nadelman, L. 1972. Conceptual tempo and inhibition of movement in black preschool children. *Child Develop.* 43:657–68
175. Hartmann, D. P., Gelfand, D. M., Courtney, R. J., Malouf, R. E. 1972. Successive presentations of elements of the Mueller-Lyer figure and CA, MA, IQ: An age extension and unsuccessful replication. *Child Develop.* 43:1060–66
176. Haugan, G. M., McIntire, R. W. 1972. Comparisons of vocal imitation, tactile stimulation, and food as reinforcers for infant vocalizations. *Develop. Psychol.* 6:201–9
177. Heider, E. R., Olivier, D. C. 1972. The structure of the color space in naming and memory for two languages. *Cogn. Psychol.* 3:337–54
178. Herbert, E. W., Baer, D. M. 1972. Training parents as behavior modifiers: self-recording on contingent attention. *J. Appl. Behav. Anal.* 5:139–49
179. Hermans, H. J. M., ter Laak, J. J. F., Maes, P. C. J. M. 1972. Achievement motivation and fear of failure in family and school. *Develop. Psychol.* 6:520–28
180. Hillman, D., Bruner, J. S. 1972. Infant sucking in response to variations in schedules of feeding reinforcement. *J. Exp. Child Psychol.* 13:240–47
181. Hoemann, H. W. 1972. The development of communication skills in deaf and hearing children. *Child Develop.* 43:990–1003
182. Holyoak, K., Hogeterp, H., Yuille, J. C. 1972. A developmental comparison of verbal and pictorial mnemonics in paired-associate learning. *J. Exp. Child Psychol.* 14:53–65
183. Holzman, M. 1972. The use of interrogative forms in the verbal interaction of three mothers and their children. *J. Psycholing. Res.* 1:311–17
184. Horowitz, A. B. 1972. Habituation and memory: Infant cardiac responses to familiar and discrepant auditory stimuli. *Child Develop.* 43:43–54

185. Horvitz, J. M., Levin, J. R. 1972. Semantic and imaginal factors in learning as related to age. *J. Exp. Child Psychol.* 14:11–20
186. Hoving, K. L., Choi, K. 1972. Some necessary conditions for producing reinstatement effects in children. *Develop. Psychol.* 7:214–17
187. Hoving, K. L., Coates, L., Bertucci, M., Riccio, D. C. 1972. Reinstatement effects in children. *Develop. Psychol.* 6:426–29
188. Hutt, C. 1972. Sex differences in human development. *Hum. Develop.* 15: 153–70
189. Jacobson, L. I., Greeson, L. E. 1972. Effects of systematic conceptual learning on the intellectual development of preschool children from poverty background: A follow-up study. *Child Develop.* 43:1111–15
190. Jeffrey, D. B., Hartmann, D. P., Gelfand, D. M. 1972. A comparison of the effects of contingent reinforcement, nurturance, and nonreinforcement on imitative learning. *Child Develop.* 43: 1053–59
191. Jensen, L., Rytting, M. 1972. Effects of information and relatedness on children's belief in immanent justice. *Develop. Psychol.* 7:93–97
192. Johnson, C. D., Gormly, J. 1972. Academic cheating: The contribution of sex, personality, and situational variables. *Develop. Psychol.* 6:320–25
193. Johnston, J. M., Johnston, G. T. 1972. Modification of consonant speech-sound articulation in young children. *J. Appl. Behav. Anal.* 5:233–46
194. Jones, B. 1972. Development of cutaneous and kinesthetic localization by blind and sighted children. *Develop. Psychol.* 6:349–52
195. Jones, B. 1972. Facilitation of visual perception through voluntary movement in elementary school children. *J. Exp. Child Psychol.* 14:408–15
196. Jones, P. A. 1972. Formal operational reasoning and the use of tentative statements. *Cogn. Psychol.* 3:467–71
197. Jones, P. A. 1972. Home environment and the development of verbal ability. *Child Develop.* 43:1081–86
198. Jones, S. J. 1972. Test of Bogartz's model on binary prediction by children. *Psychon. Sci.* 27:77–78
199. Jones-Molfese, V. J. 1972. Individual differences in neonatal preferences for planometric and stereometric visual patterns. *Child Develop.* 43:1289–96
200. Kagan, J. 1972. Do infants think? *Sci. Am.* 226:74–82
201. Kagan, S., Madsen, M. C. 1972. Experimental analyses of cooperation and competition of Anglo-American and Mexican children. *Develop. Psychol.* 6:49–59
202. Kamil, M. L., Rudegeair, R. E. 1972. Methodological improvements in the assessment of phonological discrimination in children. *Child Develop.* 43: 1087–91
203. Katz, J. M. 1972. Cognitive tempo and discrimination skill on color-form sorting tasks. *Percept. Mot. Skills* 35: 359–62
204. Kaufman, A. S., Kaufman, N. I. 1972. Tests built from Piaget's and Gessell's tasks as predictors of first-grade achievement. *Child Develop.* 43: 521–35
205. Keenan, V. 1972. Effects of Hebrew and English letters on children's perceptual set. *J. Exp. Child Psychol.* 13:71–84
206. Kendler, H. H., Glasman, L. D., Ward, J. W. 1972. Verbal-labeling and cue-training in reversal-shift behavior. *J. Exp. Child Psychol.* 13:195–209
207. Kendler, H. H., Ward, J. W. 1972. Reversal learning: The effects of conceptual and perceptual training in the absence of differential observing responses. *Psychon. Sci.* 28:346–47
208. Kendler, T. S. 1972. An ontogeny of mediational deficiency. *Child Develop.* 43:1–17
209. Kendler, T. S., Ward, J. W. 1972. Optional reversal probability is a linear function of the log of age. *Develop. Psychol.* 7:337–48
210. Kessen, W., Salapatek, P., Haith, M. 1972. The visual response of the human newborn to linear contour. *J. Exp. Child Psychol.* 13:9–20
211. Kier, R. J., Harter, S. 1972. Children's ability to order facial and nonfacial continua as a function of MA, CA, and IQ. *J. Genet. Psychol.* 120:241–51
212. Kimball, M. M., Dale, P. S. 1972. The relationship between color naming and color recognition abilities of preschoolers. *Child Develop.* 43:972–80
213. Kirk, S. A. 1972. Ethnic differences in psycholinguistic abilities. *Except. Child.* 112
214. Kirk, W. J., Johnson, J. T. 1972. Negative transfer as a function of IQ and mode of presentation in paired-associate learning. *J. Exp. Child Psychol.* 14: 233–41
215. Kirsner, K. 1972. Developmental changes in short-term recognition memory. *Brit. J. Psychol.* 63:109–17

216. Kobasigawa, A., Middleton, D. B. 1972. Free recall of categorized items by children at three grade levels. *Child Develop.* 43:1067–72
217. Kobre, K. R., Lipsitt, L. P. 1972. A negative contrast effect in newborns. *J. Exp. Child Psychol.* 14:81–91
218. Koegel, R. L., Covert, A. 1972. The relationship of self-stimulation to learning in autistic children. *J. Appl. Behav. Anal.* 5:381–87
219. Kogan, N., Pankove, E. 1972. Creative ability over a five-year span. *Child Develop.* 43:427–42
220. Kohn, M., Rosman, B. L. 1972. Relationship of preschool social-emotional functioning to later intellectual achievement. *Develop. Psychol.* 6:445–52
221. Korner, A. F. 1972. State as variable, as obstacle, and as mediator of stimulation in infant research. *Merrill-Palmer Quart.* 18:77–94
222. Korner, A. F., Thoman, E. B. 1972. The relative efficacy of contact and vestibular-proprioceptive stimulation in soothing neonates. *Child Develop.* 43:443–53
223. Koslowski, B., Bruner, J. S. 1972. Learning to use a lever. *Child Develop.* 43:790–99
224. Kraemer, H. C., Korner, A. F., Thoman, E. B. 1972. Methodological considerations in evaluating the influence of drugs used during labor and delivery on the behavior of the newborn. *Develop. Psychol.* 6:128–34
225. Kramer, P. E., Koff, E., Luria, Z. 1972. The development of competence in an exceptional language structure in older children and young adults. *Child Develop.* 43:121–30
226. Krause, M. S. 1972. A critical analysis of children in the political system. *Hum. Develop.* 15:253–60
227. Kubose, S. K. 1972. Motivational effects of boredom on children's response speeds. *Develop. Psychol.* 6: 302–5
228. Kuhlman, E. S., Wolking, W. D. 1972. Development of within- and cross-modal matching ability in the auditory and visual sense modalities. *Develop. Psychol.* 7:365
229. Kuhn, D. 1972. Mechanisms of change in the development of cognitive structures. *Child Develop.* 43:833–44
230. L'Abate, L. 1972. Early infantile autism: A reply to Ward. *Psychol. Bull.* 77:49–51
231. Lane, I. M., Coon, R. C. 1972. Reward allocation in preschool children. *Child Develop.* 43:1382–89
232. Laosa, L. M., Brophy, J. E. 1972. Effects of sex and birth order on sex-role development and intelligence among kindergarten children. *Develop. Psychol.* 6:409–15
233. LeCompte, G. K., Gratch, G. 1972. Violation of a rule as a method of diagnosing infants' levels of object concept. *Child Develop.* 43:385–96
234. LeFebvre, M., Pinard, A. 1972. Apprentissage de la conservation des quantities par une methode de conflit cognitif. *Can. J. Behav. Sci.* 4:1–12
235. Lehman, E. B. 1972. Selective strategies in children's attention to task-relevant information. *Child Develop.* 43:197–209
236. Leifer, A. D., Leiderman, P. H., Barnett, C. R., Williams, J. A. 1972. Effects of mother-infant separation on maternal attachment behavior. *Child Develop.* 43:1203–18
237. LeLaurin, K., Risley, T. R. 1972. The organization of day-care environments: "Zone" vs. "man-to-man" staff assignments. *J. Appl. Behav. Anal.* 5:225–32
238. Lerner, R. M., Korn, S. J. 1972. The development of body-build stereotypes in males. *Child Develop.* 43:908–20
239. Lewis, M. 1972. Introduction. (Cross-cultural studies of mother-infant interaction: Description and consequence.) *Hum. Develop.* 15:75–76
240. Lewis, M. 1972. State as an infant-environment interaction: An analysis of mother-infant interaction as a function of sex. *Merrill-Palmer Quart.* 18:95–122
241. Lewis, W. C., Wolman, R. N., King, M. 1972. The development of the language of emotions: II. Intentionality in the experience of affect. *J. Genet. Psychol.* 120:303–16
242. Ibid. The development of the language of emotions: III. Type of anxiety in the experience of affect, 325–42
243. Libb, J. W. 1972. Stimuli previously associated with reinforcement: Reinforcing or frustrating to the mentally retarded? *J. Exp. Child Psychol.* 14: 1–10
244. Liebert, R. M., Baron, R. A. 1972. Some immediate effects of televised violence on children's behavior. *Develop. Psychol.* 6:469–75
245. Liebert, R. M., Sobol, M. P., Copemann, C. D. 1972. Effects of vicarious consequences and race of model upon imitative performance by black children. *Develop. Psychol.* 6:453–56
246. Linder, F. I. 1972. Developmental study of apparent movement in preschool children. *Percept. Mot. Skills* 34:107–18

247. Little, A. 1972. A longitudinal study of cognitive development in young children. *Child Develop.* 43:1024–34
248. Long, A. B., Looft, W. R. 1972. Development of directionality in children: Ages six through twelve. *Develop. Psychol.* 6:375–80
249. Looft, W. R. 1972. The evolution of developmental psychology. *Hum. Develop.* 15:187–201
250. Love, J. M., Parker-Robinson, C. 1972. Children's imitation of grammatical and ungrammatical sentences. *Child Develop.* 43:309–19
251. Lusk, D., Lewis, M. 1972. Mother-infant interaction and infant development among the Wolof of Senegal. *Hum. Develop.* 15:58–69
252. Lynch, S., Rohwer, W. D. 1972. Grade interactions with words and pictures in a paired-associate task: A proposed explanation. *J. Exp. Child Psychol.* 13: 413–21
253. Maccoby, E. E., Feldman, S. S. 1972. Mother-attachment and stranger-reactions in the third year of life. *Monogr. Soc. Res. Child Develop.* 37:No. 1, Serial No. 146
254. Mackay, C. K., Brazendale, A. H., Wilson, L. F. 1972. Concepts of horizontal and vertical: A methodological note. *Develop. Psychol.* 7:232–37
255. Maehr, M. L., Stallings, W. M. 1972. Freedom from external evaluation. *Child Develop.* 43:177–85
256. Mallory, W. A. 1972. Abilities and developmental changes in elaborative strategies in paired-associate learning of young children. *J. Educ. Psychol.* 63: 202–17
257. Malouf, R. E., Dodd, D. H. 1972. Role of exposure, imitation, and expansion in the acquisition of an artificial grammatical rule. *Develop. Psychol.* 7:195–203
258. Marx, M. H. 1972. Recall/recognition differences as a function of elementary school grade. *Psychon. Sci.* 27:230–31
259. Masters, J. C. 1972. Effects of social comparison upon the imitation of neutral and altruistic behaviors by young children. *Child Develop.* 43:131–42
260. Masters, J. C. 1972. Effects of success, failure, and reward outcome upon contingent and noncontingent self-reinforcement. *Develop. Psychol.* 7:110–18
261. Masters, J. C., Peskay, J. 1972. Effects of race, socioeconomic status, and success or failure upon contingent and noncontingent self-reinforcement in children. *Develop. Psychol.* 7:139–45
262. Matheny, A. P. 1972. Cognitive factors associated with the Ponzo illusion: a study using the co-twin method. *Psychon. Sci.* 29:91–92
263. Matheny, A. P. 1972. Perceptual exploration in twins. *J. Exp. Child Psychol.* 14:108–16
264. McCall, R. B. 1972. Smiling and vocalization in infants as indices of perceptual-cognitive processes. *Merrill-Palmer Quart.* 18:341–48
265. McCarver, R. B. 1972. A developmental study of the effect of organizational cues on short-term memory. *Child Develop.* 43:1317–25
266. McCarver, R. B., Ellis, N. R. 1972. Effect of overt verbal labeling on short-term memory in culturally deprived and nondeprived children. *Develop. Psychol.* 6:38–41
267. McGurk, H. 1972. Infant discrimination of orientation. *J. Exp. Child Psychol.* 14:151–64
268. McGurk, H. 1972. The salience of orientation in young children's perception of form. *Child Develop.* 43:1047–52
269. McGurk, H., Lewis, M. 1972. Birth order: A phenomenon in search of an explanation. *Develop. Psychol.* 7:366
270. McKinney, J. D. 1972. Developmental study of the acquisition and utilization of conceptual strategies. *J. Educ. Psychol.* 63:22–31
271. McMurtry, C. A., Williams, J. E. 1972. Evaluation dimension of the affective meaning system of the preschool child. *Develop. Psychol.* 6:238–46
272. McNamara, J. 1972. Cognitive basis of language learning in infants. *Psychol. Rev.* 79:1–13
273. Meacham, J. A. 1972. The development of memory abilities in the individual and society. *Hum. Develop.* 15:205–28
274. Merchant, R. L., Rebelsky, F. 1972. Effects of participation in rule formation on the moral judgment of children. *Genet. Psychol. Monogr.* 85:287–304
275. Messer, S. B., Lewis, M. 1972. Social class and sex differences in the attachment and play behavior of the year-old infant. *Merrill-Palmer Quart.* 18:295–306
276. Meyer, J. W., Sobieszek, B. I. 1972. Effect of a child's sex on adult interpretations of its behavior. *Develop. Psychol.* 6:42–48
277. Millar, S. 1972. Effects of instructions to visualize stimuli during delay on visual recognition by preschool children. *Child Develop.* 43:1073–75
278. Millar, W. S. 1972. A study of operant conditioning under delayed reinforcement in early infancy. *Monogr. Soc. Res. Child Develop.* 37:Serial No. 147

279. Millar, W. S., Schaffer, H. R. 1972. The influence of spatially displaced feedback on infant operant conditioning. *J. Exp. Child Psychol.* 14:442–53
280. Miller, A. G., Thomas, R. 1972. Cooperation and competition among Blackfoot Indian and Urban Canadian children. *Child Develop.* 43:1104–10
281. Miller, D. J. 1972. Visual habituation in the human infant. *Child Develop.* 43:481–93
282. Miller, L. K. 1972. Visual masking and developmental differences in information processing. *Child Develop.* 43:704–9
283. Miller, S. A. 1972. Bidimensional solution shifts in children and adults. *Psychon. Sci.* 26:195–96
284. Moerk, E. 1972. Principles of interaction in language learning. *Merrill-Palmer Quart.* 18:229–58
285. Moffat, G. H. 1972. Avoidance conditioning in young children with interruption of a positive stimulus as the aversive event. *J. Exp. Child Psychol.* 13:21–28
286. Montanelli, D. S. 1972. Multiple-cue learning in children. *Develop. Psychol.* 7:302–12
287. Moody, M., Gollin, E. S. 1972. Problems of control in simultaneous discrimination tasks. *Develop. Psychol.* 6:416–25
288. Morse, P. A. 1972. The discrimination of speech and nonspeech stimuli in early infancy. *J. Exp. Child Psychol.* 14:477–92
289. Moynahan, E., Glick, J. 1972. Relation between identity conservation and equivalence conservation within four conceptual domains. *Develop. Psychol.* 6:247–51
290. Mueller, E. 1972. The maintenance of verbal exchanges between young children. *Child Develop.* 43:930–38
291. Murray, F. B. 1972. Acquisition of conservation through social interaction. *Develop. Psychol.* 6:1–6
292. Nelson, K. 1972. The relation of form recognition to concept development. *Child Develop.* 43:67–74
293. Nolen, P. S. 1972. Reading nonstandard dialect materials: A study at grades two and four. *Child Develop.* 43:1092–97
294. Nuessle, W. 1972. Reflectivity as an influence on focusing behavior of children. *J. Exp. Child Psychol.* 14:265–76
295. O'Bryan, K. G., Boersma, F. J. 1972. Movie presentation of Piagetian tasks: A procedure for the assessment of conservation attainment. *J. Genet. Psychol.* 121:295–302
296. Odom, R. D., Guzman, R. D. 1972. Development of hierarchies of dimensional salience. Develop. Psychol. 6:271–87
297. Odom, R. D., Lemond, C. M. 1972. Developmental differences in the perception and production of facial expressions. *Child Develop.* 43:359–69
298. Offenbach, S. I., Baecher, R., White, M. 1972. Stability of first-grade children's dimensional preferences. *Child Develop.* 43:689–92
299. O'Leary, K. D. 1972. Behavior modification in the classroom: A rejoinder to Winett and Winkler. *J. Appl. Behav. Anal.* 5:505–11
300. Osofsky, J. D., O'Connell, E. J. 1972. Parent-child interaction: Daughters' effects upon mothers' and fathers' behaviors. *Develop. Psychol.* 7:157–68
301. Overton, W. F., Brodzinsky, D. 1972. Perceptual and logical factors in the development of multiplicative classification. *Develop. Psychol.* 6:104–9
302. Palermo, D. S., Molfese, D. L. 1972. Language acquisition from age five onward. *Psychol. Bull.* 78:409–21
303. Papalia, D. E. 1972. The status of several conservation abilities across the life-span. *Hum. Develop.* 15:229–43
304. Parke, R. D., Deur, J. L. 1972. Schedule of punishment and inhibition of aggression in children. *Develop. Psychol.* 7:266–69
305. Parker, R. K., Sperr, S. J., Rieff, M. L. 1972. Multiple classification: A training approach. *Develop. Psychol.* 7:188–94
306. Parlee, M. B. 1972. Comments on "roles of activation and inhibition in sex differences in cognitive abilities" by D. M. Broverman, E. L. Klaiber, Y. Kobayshi, and W. Vogel. *Psychol. Rev.* 79:180–84
307. Parry, M. H. 1972. Infants' responses to novelty in familiar and unfamiliar settings. *Child Develop.* 43:233–37
308. Pawlicki, R. E. 1972. The influence of contingent and noncontingent social reinforcement upon children in a simple operant task. *Child Develop.* 43:1423–28
309. Peterson, C. L., Danner, F. W., Flavell, J. H. 1972. Developmental changes in children's response to three indications of communicative failure. *Child Develop.* 43:1463–68
310. Pick, A. D., Christy, M. D., Frankel, G. W. 1972. A developmental study of visual selective attention. *J. Exp. Child Psychol.* 14:165–75
311. Pick, A. D., Hales, J. J., Christy, M. D., Frankel, G. W., Glick, J. A. 1972. The effect of a human facial contest on the

discrimination and recognition of curved lines. *Psychon. Sci.* 27:239–40
312. Pinard, A., Sharp, E. 1972. I.Q. & point of view. *Psychol. Today* 6:65–90
313. Pishkin, V. 1972. Concept identification with mnemonic cues as a function of children's sex and age. *J. Educ. Psychol.* 63:93–98
314. Portuges, S. H., Feshbach, N. D. 1972. The influence of sex and socioethnic factors upon imitation of teachers by elementary school children. *Child Develop.* 43:981–89
315. Poulos, R. W., Liebert, R. M. 1972. Influence of modeling, exhortative verbalization, and surveillance on children's sharing. *Develop. Psychol.* 6:402–8
316. Pufall, P. B., Shaw, R. E. 1972. Precocious thoughts on number: The long and the short of it. *Develop. Psychol.* 7:62–69
317. Quay, L. C. 1972. Negro dialect and Binet performance in severely disadvantaged black four-year-olds. *Child Develop.* 43:245–50
318. Radin, N. 1972. Father-child interaction and the intellectual functioning of four-year-old boys. *Develop. Psychol.* 6:353–61
319. Ramey, C. T., Hieger, L., Klisz, D. 1972. Synchronous reinforcement of vocal responses in failure-to-thrive infants. *Child Develop.* 43:1449–55
320. Randhawa, B. S. 1972. Nonverbal information storage in children and developmental information processing channel capacity. *J. Exp. Child Psychol.* 13: 58–70
321. Rebelsky, F., Black, R. 1972. Crying in infancy. *J. Genet. Psychol.* 121:49–57
322. Redd, W. H. 1972. Attention span and generalization of task-related stimulus control: Effects of reinforcement contingencies. *J. Exp. Child Psychol.* 13: 527–39
323. Rees, R., Babbitt, B. 1972. Children's recall of S+, S–, S^0 as a function of feedback frequency. *Psychon. Sci.* 29: 253–54
324. Reese, H. W. 1972. Acquired distinctiveness and equivalence of cues in young children. *J. Exp. Child Psychol.* 13:171–82
325. Ibid. Imagery and multiple-list paired-associate learning in young children, 310–23
326. Riegel, K. F. 1972. Influence of economic and political ideologies on the development of developmental psychology. *Psychol. Bull.* 78:129–41
327. Rileigh, K. K., Odom, P. B. 1972. Perception of rhythm by subjects with normal and deficient hearing. *Develop. Psychol.* 7:54–61
328. Rimland, B. 1972. Comment on Ward's "early infantile autism." *Psychol. Bull.* 77:52–53
329. Ritschl, C., Mongrella, J., Presbie, R. J. 1972. Group time-out from rock and roll music and out-of-seat behavior of handicapped children while riding a school bus. *Psychol. Rep.* 31:967–73
330. Roberts, G. C., Black, K. N. 1972. The effect of naming and object permanence on toy preferences. *Child Develop.* 43: 858–68
331. Rose, S. A., Blank, M. S., Bridger, W. H. 1972. Intermodal and intramodal retention of visual and tactual information in young children. *Develop. Psychol.* 6:428–86
332. Rosenthal, T. L., Alford, G. S., Rasp, L. M. 1972. Concept attainment, generalization, and retention through observation and verbal coding. *J. Exp. Child Psychol.* 13:183–94
333. Rosenthal, T. L., White, G. M. 1972. Initial probability, rehearsal, and constraint in associative class selection. *J. Exp. Child Psychol.* 13:261–74
334. Rosenthal, T. L., Zimmerman, B. J. 1972. Modeling by exemplification and instruction in training conservation. *Develop. Psychol.* 6:392–401
335. Rosner, S. R. 1972. Primacy in preschoolers' short-term memory: The effects of repeated tests and shift-trials. *J. Exp. Child Psychol.* 13:220–30
336. Ross, H. S., Rheingold, H. L., Eckerman, C. O. 1972. Approach and exploration of a novel alternative by 12-month-old infants. *J. Exp. Child Psychol.* 13:85–93
337. Routh, D. K., Tweney, R. D. 1972. Effects of paradigmatic response training on children's word associations. *J. Exp. Child Psychol.* 14:398–407
338. Rovee, C. K. 1972. Olfactory cross-adaptation and facilitation in human neonates. *J. Exp. Child Psychol.* 13: 368–81
339. Rowe, E. J. 1972. Discrimination learning of pictures and words: A replication of picture superiority *J. Exp. Child Psychol.* 14:323–28
340. Rubin, K. H. 1972. Relationship between egocentric communication and popularity among peers. *Develop. Psychol.* 7:364
341. Ruble, D. N., Nakamura, C. Y. 1972. Task orientation versus social orientation in young children and their attention to relevant social cues. *Child Develop.* 43:471–80

342. Saltz, E., Soller, E., Sigel, I. E. 1972. The development of natural language concepts. *Child Develop.* 43:1191–1202
343. Saltzstein, H. D., Diamond, R. M., Belenky, M. 1972. Moral judgment level and conformity behavior. *Develop. Psychol.* 7:327–36
344. Schaffer, H. R., Greenwood, A., Parry, M. H. 1972. The onset of wariness. *Child Develop.* 43:165–75
345. Schaie, K. W. 1972. Limitations on the generalizability of growth curves of intelligence. *Hum. Develop.* 15:141–52
346. Schnall, M., Alter, D., Swanlund, T., Schweitzer, T. 1972. A sensory-motor context affecting performance in a conservation task: A closer analogue of reversibility than empirical return. *Child Develop.* 43:1012–23
347. Schooler, C. 1972. Birth order effects: Not here, not now! *Psychol. Bull.* 78: 161–72
348. Schroeder, G. M., Baer, D. M. 1972. Effects of concurrent and serial training on generalized vocal imitation in retarded children. *Develop. Psychol.* 6: 293–301
349. Schubert, J., Cropley, A. J. 1972. Verbal regulation of behavior and IQ in Canadian Indian and white children. *Develop. Psychol.* 7:295–301
350. Scribner, S., Cole, M. 1972. Effects of constrained recall training on children's performance in a verbal memory task. *Child Develop.* 43:845–57
351. Self, P. A., Horowitz, F. D., Paden, L. Y. 1972. Olfaction in newborn infants. *Develop. Psychol.* 7:349–63
352. Shantz, C. U., Wilson, K. E. 1972. Training communication skills in young children. *Child Develop.* 43:693–98
353. Shantz, D. W., Pentz, T. 1972. Situational effects on justifiableness of aggression at three age levels. *Child Develop.* 43:274–81
354. Sharp, D., Cole, M. 1972. Patterns of responding in the word associations of West African children. *Child Develop.* 43:55–65
355. Sidman, M., Ed. 1960. *Tactics of Scientific Research.* New York: Basic Books
356. Siebold, J. R. 1972. Children's rating responses as related to amount and recency of stimulus familiarization and stimulus complexity. *J. Exp. Child Psychol.* 14:257–64
357. Siegel, L. S. 1972. The development of concepts of numerical magnitude. *Psychon. Sci.* 28:245–46
358. Siegel, L. S. 1972. Development of the concept of seriation. *Develop. Psychol.* 6:135–37
359. Siegler, R. S., Liebert, R. M. 1972. Effects of presenting relevant rules and complete feedback on the conservation of liquid quantity task. *Develop. Psychol.* 7:133–38
360. Silverman, E. M. 1972. Syntactic complexity of preschoolers' egocentric and socialized speech. *Percept. Mot. Skills* 35:247–49
361. Silverstein, A. 1972. Secondary reinforcement in infants. *J. Exp. Child Psychol.* 13:138–44
362. Sinclair, H., Bronckart, J. P. 1972. S.V.O. a linguistic universal? A study in developmental psycholinguistics. *J. Exp. Child Psychol.* 14:329–48
363. Sjostrom, K., Pollack, R. H. 1972. The role of lightness contrast in determining the magnitude of the Delboeuf Illusion: A rejoinder to Weintraub and Cooper. *Develop. Psychol.* 6:198–200
364. Slater, A. M., Findlay, J. M. 1972. The measurement of fixation position in the newborn baby. *J. Exp. Child Psychol.* 14:349–64
365. Slobin, D. I. 1972. They learn the same way all around the world. *Psychol. Today* 5:71–82
366. Smiley, S. S. 1972. Instability of dimensional preference following changes in relative cue similarity. *J. Exp. Child Psychol.* 13:394–403
367. Ibid. Optional shift behavior as a function of dimensional preference and relative cue similarity. 14:313–22
368. Smillie, D. 1972. Piaget's constructionist theory. *Hum. Develop.* 15:171–86
369. Smith, A. C., Flick, G. L., Ferriss, G. S., Sellmann, A. H. 1972. Prediction of developmental outcome at seven years from prenatal, perinatal, and postnatal events. *Child Develop.* 43:495–507
370. Smith, T. D. 1972. Development of tokens as secondary reinforcers. *J. Exp. Child Psychol.* 14:133–38
371. Snow, C. E. 1972. Mother's speech to children learning language. *Child Develop.* 43:549–65
372. Solkoff, N. 1972. Race of experimenter as a variable in research with children. *Develop. Psychol.* 7:70–75
373. Solomon, D., Ali, F. A. 1972. Age trends in the perception of verbal reinforcers. *Develop. Psychol.* 7:238–43
374. Solomon, D., Ali, F. A., Kfir, D., Houlihan, K. A., Yaeger, J. 1972. The development of democratic values and behavior among Mexican-American children. *Child Develop.* 43:625–38
375. Solomon, D., Druckman, D. 1972. Age, representatives' prior performance, and

the distribution of winnings with teammates. *Hum. Develop.* 15:244–52
376. Sostek, A. M., Sameroff, A. J., Sostek, A. J. 1972. Evidence for the unconditionability of the Babkin reflex in newborns. *Child Develop.* 43:509–19
377. Spence, J. T. 1972. Verbal and nonverbal rewards and punishments in the discrimination learning of children of varying socioeconomic status. *Develop. Psychol.* 6:381–84
378. Spiker, C. C., Croll, W. L., Miller, A. A. 1972. The effects of verbal pretraining on the multidimensional generalization behavior of children. *J. Exp. Child. Psychol.* 13:558–72
379. Ibid. On the comparison of psychological theories: A reply to Professor Bogartz, 585–92
380. Spinetta, J. J., Rigler, D. 1972. The child-abusing parent: A psychological review. *Psychol. Bull.* 77:296–304
381. Sroufe, L. A., Wunsch, J. P. 1972. The development of laughter in the first year of life. *Child Develop.* 43:1326–44
382. Staffieri, J. R. 1972. Body build and behavioral expectancies in young females. *Develop. Psychol.* 6:125–27
383. Stein, G. M., Bryan, J. H. 1972. The effect of a television model upon rule adoption behavior of children. *Child Develop.* 43:268–73
384. Stephens, B., McLaughlin, J. A., Miller, C. K., Glass, G. V. 1972. Factorial structure of selected psycho-educational measures and Piagetian reasoning assessments. *Develop. Psychol.* 6:243–348
385. Stephenson, B. L., Gay, W. O. 1972. Psycholinguistic abilities of black and white children from four SES levels. *Except. Child.* 38:705–9
386. Stouwie, R. J. 1972. An experimental study of adult dominance and warmth, conflicting verbal instructions, and children's moral behavior. *Child Develop.* 43:959–71
387. Stratton, P. R., Brown, R. 1972. Improving creative thinking by training in the production and/or judgement of solutions. *J. Educ. Psychol.* 63:390–97
388. Strayer, J., Ames, E. W. 1972. Stimulus orientation and the apparent developmental lag between perception and performance. *Child Develop.* 43:1345–54
389. Sullivan, L. 1972. Development of causal connectives by children. *Percept. Mot. Skills* 35:1003–10
390. Super, C. M., Kagan, J., Morrison, F. J., Haith, M. M., Weiffenbach, J. 1972. Discrepancy and attention in the five-month infant. *Genet. Psychol. Monogr.* 85:305–31
391. Suzuki, N. S. 1972. Noun-pair learning in children and adults: Underlying strings and retrieval time. *Child Develop.* 43:299–307
392. Tawney, J. W. 1972. Training letter discrimination in four-year-old children. *J. Appl. Behav. Anal.* 5:455–65
393. Taylor, H. D., Thweatt, R. C. 1972. Cross-cultural developmental performance of Navajo children on the Bender-Gestalt test. *Percept. Mot. Skills.* 35:307–9
394. Thelen, M. H., Rennie, D. L., Fryrear, J. L., McGuire, D. 1972. Expectancy to perform and vicarious reward: Their effects upon imitation. *Child Develop.* 43:699–703
395. Thoman, E. B., Leiderman, P. H., Olson, J. P. 1972. Neonate-mother interaction during breast-feeding. *Develop. Psychol.* 6:110–18
396. Thurlow, M. L., Turnure, J. E. 1972. Elaboration structure and list length effects on verbal elaboration phenomena. *J. Exp. Child Psychol.* 14:184–95
397. Tighe, T. J., Tighe, L. S. 1972. Reversals prior to solution of concept identification in children. *J. Exp. Child Psychol.* 13:488–501
398. Tizard, B., Cooperman, O., Joseph, A., Tizard, J. 1972. Environmental effects on language development: A study of young children in long-stay residential nurseries. *Child Develop.* 43:337–58
399. Trehub, S. E., Rabinovitch, M. S. 1972. Auditory-linguistic sensitivity in early infancy. *Develop. Psychol.* 6:74–77
400. Trinder, J., Metzger, K. R., Sherman, A. E., Richman, C. L. 1972. Development of stimulus organization. *Develop. Psychol.* 6:26–31
401. Tulkin, S. R. 1972. An analysis of the concept of cultural deprivation. *Develop. Psychol.* 6:326–39
402. Tulkin, S. R., Kagan, J. 1972. Mother-child interaction in the first year of life. *Child Develop.* 43:31–41
403. Turiel, E., Rothman, G. R. 1972. The influence of reasoning on behavioral choices at different stages of moral development. *Child Develop.* 43:741–56
404. Vlietstra, A. G., Wright, J. C. 1971. Sensory modality and transmodal stimulus properties in children's discrimination learning and transfer. *Ann. Rep. Kansas Center Res. Early Childhood Educ.* Univ. Kansas
405. Waite, W. W., Osborne, J. G. 1972. Sustained behavioral contrast in children. *J. Exp. Anal. Behav.* 18:113–17
406. Walker, H. M., Buckley, N. K. 1972. Programming generalization and maintenance of treatment effects across time

and across settings. *J. Appl. Behav. Anal.* 5:209–24

407. Ward, A. J. 1970. Early infantile autism. *Psychol. Bull.* 73:350–62
408. Ward, W. C., Kogan, N., Pankove, E. 1972. Incentive effects in children's creativity. *Child Develop.* 43:669–76
409. Warren, D. H., Judy, S. J. 1972. Visual feedback training in auditory localization by nursery school children. *Percept. Mot. Skills* 35:311–18
410. Warren, N. 1972. African infant precocity. *Psychol. Bull.* 78:353–67
411. Warren, V. L., Cairns, R. B. 1972. Social reinforcement satiation: An outcome of frequency or ambiguity? *J. Exp. Child Psychol.* 13:249–60
412. Watson, J. S. 1967. Memory and contingency analysis in infant learning. *Merrill-Palmer Quart.* 13:55–76
413. Ibid. 1972. Smiling, cooing, and "the game." 18:323–40
414. Watson, J. S., Ramey, C. T. 1972. Reactions to response-contingent stimulation in early infancy. *Merrill-Palmer Quart.* 18:219–28
415. Webb, R. A., Massar, B., Nadolny, T. 1972. Information and strategy in the young child's search for hidden objects. *Child Develop.* 43:91–104
416. Webster, R. L., Steinhardt, M. H., Senter, M. G. 1972. Changes in infants' vocalizations as a function of differential acoustic stimulation. *Develop. Psychol.* 7:39–43
417. Weinheimer, S. 1972. Egocentrism and social influence in children. *Child Develop.* 43:567–78
418. Weintraub, D. J., Cooper, L. A. 1972. Coming of age with the Delboeuf Illusion: Brightness contrast, cognition, and perceptual development. *Develop. Psychol.* 6:187–97
419. Weist, R. M., Stebbins, P. 1972. Adult perception of children's speech. *Psychon. Sci.* 27:359–60
420. Wenar, C. 1972. Executive competence and spontaneous social behavior in one-year-olds. *Child Develop.* 43:256–60
421. Werden, D., Ross, L. E. 1972. A comparison of the trace and delay classical conditioning performance of normal children. *J. Exp. Child Psychol.* 14:126–32
422. West, H., Abravenal, E. 1972. Evidence for class-concept mediation of perceptual sets on preschool children. *Child Develop.* 43:1242–48
423. Whitehurst, G. J. 1972. Production of novel and grammatical utterances by young children. *J. Exp. Child Psychol.* 13:502–15
424. Whitehurst, G. J., Novak, G., Zorn, G. A. 1972. Delayed speech studied in the home. *Develop. Psychol.* 7:169–77
425. Wilkening, F., Sarris, V., Heller, O. 1972. Contrast effects in the child's judgment of lifted weight. *Psychon. Sci.* 28:207–8
426. Wilson, R. S., Harpring, E. B. 1972. Mental and motor development in infant twins. *Develop. Psychol.* 7:277–87
427. Winett, R. A., Winkler, R. C. 1972. Current behavior modification in the classroom: Be still, be quiet, be docile. *J. Appl. Behav. Anal.* 5:499–504
428. Wolf, T. M., Cheyne, J. A. 1972. Persistence of effects of live behavioral, televised behavioral, and live verbal models on resistance to deviation. *Child Develop.* 43:1429–36
429. Wolff, P. 1972. The role of stimulus-correlated activity in children's recognition of nonsense forms. *J. Exp. Child Psychol.* 14:427–41
430. Wolff, P., Levin, J. 1972. The role of overt activity in children's imagery production. *Child Develop.* 43:537–47
431. Wolff, P., Levin, J. R., Longobardi, E. T. 1972. Motoric mediation in children's paired-associate learning: Effects of visual and tactual contact. *J. Exp. Child Psychol.* 14:176–83
432. Wolman, R. N., Lewis, W. C., King, M. 1972. The development of the language of emotions: 1. Theoretical and methodological introduction. *J. Genet. Psychol.* 120:167–76
433. Ibid. The development of the language of emotions: IV. Bodily referents and the experience of affect. 121:65–81
434. Woods, M. B. 1972. The unsupervised child of the working mother. *Develop. Psychol.* 6:14–25
435. Wozniak, R. H. 1972. Verbal regulation of motor behavior—Soviet research and non-Soviet replications. *Hum. Develop.* 15:13–57
436. Yussen, S. R. 1972. The effects of verbal and visual highlighting of dimensions on discrimination learning by preschoolers and second graders. *Child Develop.* 43:921–29
437. Zelazo, P. R. 1972. Smiling and vocalizing: A cognitive emphasis. *Merrill-Palmer Quart.* 18:349–66
438. Zelniker, T., Jeffrey, W. E., Ault, R., Parsons, J. 1972. Analysis and modification of search strategies of impulsive and reflective children on the matching familiar figures test. *Child Develop.* 43:321–35
439. Zimmerman, B. J., Bell, J. A. 1972. Observer verbalization and abstraction in

vicarious rule learning, generalization, and retention. *Develop. Psychol.* 7: 227–31

440. Zimmerman, B. J., Pike, E. O. 1972. Effects of modeling and reinforcement on the acquisition and generalization of question-asking behavior. *Child Develop.* 43:892–907

441. Zimmerman, B. J., Rosenthal, T. L. 1972. Concept attainment, transfer, and retention through observation and rule-provision. *J. Exp. Child. Psychol.* 14: 139–50

442. Zimmerman, B. J., Rosenthal, T. L. 1972. Observation, repetition, and ethnic background in concept attainment and generalization. *Child Develop.* 43: 605–13

443. Zupnick, J. J., Forrester, W. E. 1972. Effects of semantic and acoustic relatedness on free recall in normal children and retardates. *Psychon. Sci.* 26:188–89

DERIVED MOTIVES[1,2]

M. R. D'Amato
Rutgers University, New Brunswick, New Jersey

There is no surer prescription for a prolonged bout of humility than to accept an assignment to review a well-defined, neatly circumscribed area of psychological research. When the area has no clear demarcations, no discernible beginning or end, and can include virtually everything or almost nothing, humility becomes leadened with despair. The project was partially rescued by the editorial wisdom of a mercifully small page allotment, but its final survival required a number of more or less arbitrary decisions regarding topics to be covered in the review. Conditioned appetitive drives were included because the topic had not been reviewed in this series recently and because of the opportunity presented by such a review to relate traditional work in this area to highly related research efforts that in the past have dangled far apart. Conditioned reinforcement seemed a natural enough followup to conditioned appetitive drives, and in addition some interesting recent developments could be recounted. For some reason the "contrafreeloading" phenomenon—the fact that animals often work for food when free food is available—has escaped attention in past reviews though it seems quite relevant to the topic at hand. Solomon & Corbit's (129) opponent-process model of motivation is treated in some detail because it is a very recent development and because of the continuing dearth of fresh, sensible, and suggestive models of acquired motivation. The last section is a brief digression which acknowledges certain current upheavals in the field of learning and, in general terms, assesses their significance for developments in acquired motivation.

CONDITIONED APPETITIVE DRIVES

As pointed out by Brown & Farber (24), the possibility of conditioning such basic need states as hunger and thirst has long entertained psychologists interested in

[1]Preparation of this chapter was supported in part by National Science Foundation Grant GB-24386X.

[2]The following abbreviations are used without prior definitions: CS (conditioned stimulus); CR (conditioned response); US (unconditioned stimulus); UR (unconditioned response); S+, S– (positive and negative stimulus, respectively, in a discriminative task).

acquired motivation. No purer realization of the latter concept seems possible than to show that, through appropriate conditioning techniques, hunger and thirst can be produced in an organism at will. However, joining Cofer & Appley (33) and Bolles (17), Brown & Farber concluded from their review that "the reality of the phenomenon (conditioned hunger) remains to be established" (p. 107). Perhaps because of this consensus of skepticism—reinforced by a subsequent review and methodological analysis by Cravens & Renner (35)—as well as a general disenchantment with the concept of drive itself (3), the topic of conditioned appetitive drive vanished from the subsequent two reviews of derived motives (3, 19). Largely owing to the work of Seligman and his associates (95, 115, 117, 119), the subject now appears to deserve at least a temporary reprieve.

Conditioned Thirst

Where previous investigators managed to produce at best fragile evidence for conditioned hunger or thirst (35), Seligman and associates have reported conditioned drinking in massive amounts: 50 to 1000% increases in drinking observed in virtually all of the 150 or more rats tested by them (119). Moreover, in sharp contrast to the evanescent character of earlier evidence of appetitive conditioning, they were able to produce conditioned drinking that was often virtually "inextinguishable." The conditioning technique employed by Seligman and associates is simplicity itself.

During a series of baseline sessions rats, deprived of water for 1 hour, were placed into a distinctive test box in which water was readily available. There followed a number of conditioning sessions in which a solution of hypertonic saline (15%) plus procaine (2%) was injected subcutaneously, and after some 15 minutes, the animal was placed into the test box for 45 minutes. Subcutaneous injections of 15% saline solutions are known to induce avid drinking in a matter of minutes (80, 141). Procaine, an anesthetic, was added in an attempt to alleviate the irritation caused by hypertonic saline injections (140, 141). It is important to note that during these conditioning sessions water was not available in the test chamber. At the termination of conditioning, the animals entered an "extinction" series during which, again 1 hour water-deprived, they were placed into the test chamber with water available but with no prior injections. If thirst had been conditioned to the cues of the test chamber as a result of the conditioning experience, the animals should consume more water during extinction than they had during the baseline sessions, which indeed they did.

It was not very long, however, before this pleasantly straightforward situation was disturbed by unforeseen complications. First, substantial conditioned drinking was produced by *isotonic* procaine injections (117; cf. 34). And though there was some indication that the combination of hypertonicity and procaine yielded more conditioning than procaine alone (117; cf. 34), it must have come as a surprise that unadulterated hypertonic saline injections yielded little, if any, evidence of conditioned drinking (119). Moreover, hypothalamic injections of angiotensin, which produce rapid and marked unconditioned drinking (47), acted like hypertonic saline injections in producing at best only evanescent conditioned drinking (119).

The interpretation of this complex pattern of results offered most recently by Seligman and his associates is that there are two different mechanisms responsible for the conditioned drinking observed in their experiments. On the one hand, there is the classical conditioning of "real" thirst. "Stimuli paired with the very rapid induction of thirst caused by angiotensin injected into the hypothalamus can themselves later produce increased drinking" (119, p. 119). The conditioned drinking based on this mechanism, however, is small in extent and quick to extinguish. The really striking conditioned drinking obtained in their experiments (cf. 139) is attributed not to classically conditioned thirst, but to operant conditioning of the drinking response motivated by the procaine component of the injections, which presumably acts as a "poison." The assumption is that the procaine causes physical distress which is somehow relieved by ingestion of water. Because in their early experiments (115, 117, 119) water was not available in the test cages during conditioning sessions, it must be assumed that the animals learned the connection between water ingestion and alleviation of the procaine-induced distress by drinking water available in the home cages. In any event, the proposal is that "If the rat learns to anticipate illness and also learns that drinking relieves or prevents illness, it should continue to drink during extinction in order to prevent that illness" (95, p. 384). Going one step further, such conditioned drinking is extremely resistant to extinction because drinking in this situation is essentially an avoidance response, and the parallel is drawn to the (alleged) high resistance to extinction of more conventional avoidance behavior (cf. 36, pp. 358–9).

It appears that the evidence for "true" thirst conditioning is no less equivocal in the present series of studies than in earlier attempts. Although a small amount of conditioned drinking was reported when hypertonic saline solutions alone were employed (119), this result was marred by the fact that drinking was allowed during the conditioning trials. Moreover, in the very same report the authors state that "We have replicated this experiment without water available in the test cage during injections and have not found conditioning in the hypertonic groups" (119, p. 113). Similarly, the conditioned drinking produced by angiotensin injected into the lateral hypothalamus (presumably mediated by conditioned thirst) enjoyed the benefit of conditioning sessions in which water was freely available. And even then, as noted earlier, only a relatively small amount of conditioned drinking was observed, which dissipated quickly. Whether any conditioned drinking would occur if water were denied during the conditioning sessions remains to be determined.

In a recent study, unfortunately lacking the controls necessary to be totally convincing, the suggestion was advanced that hypertonic saline-procaine injections result in a conditioned "nonspecific increase in motor excitability" (34, p. 219), which, if circumstances allow, can trigger eating and running as well as drinking. This is a significant methodological point. Our confidence that drinking was selectively aroused by their earlier conditioning experience would doubtlessly increase if, during extinction, Seligman's animals had been provided with the opportunity to engage in dominant alternative activities.

Conditioned Hunger

Typically, the conditioning of hunger has been attempted by subjecting a rat to some sort of food deprivation procedure and then placing the animal in a distinctive test chamber, on the assumption that by this procedure (backward conditioning?) hunger would somehow become classically conditioned to the cues of the test chamber. In a very recent attempt, the evidence obtained for conditioned hunger again shows that, the use of modality-relevant CSs notwithstanding, "it is at best a rather ephemeral effect" (94).

A somewhat more direct approach makes use of the observation that in man and animals exogenous insulin induces both hypoglycemia and hunger (21, 23, 64, 66). Since hypoglycemia can apparently be classically conditioned (2, 72, 148–150; but see 57, 122), the possibility of classically conditioning hunger by means of insulin injections immediately suggests itself. The indicated experiment, similar in conception and design to the conditioned drinking studies, was performed by Balagura (9), who found that rats subjected to daily insulin injections during a conditioning series showed augmented lever pressing for food in a later extinction series in which normal saline was substituted for insulin. Like the conditioned drinking reported for hypertonic saline and angiotensin, the conditioned eating observed in this study was short-lived.

Noting that Balagura allowed his subjects to work for food during the conditioning sessions, Siegel & Nettleton (123) later showed that augmented bar pressing did not occur in extinction if the animals had been denied the opportunity to lever press for food during the conditioning trials. They concluded that classical conditioning of hunger had not been demonstrated by Balagura, that the observed conditioned lever pressing and eating was an operantly conditioned "escape or avoidance response to the aversive stimulus of hyperinsulinism" (123, p. 391; cf. 86).

Conclusions

Despite continued and sometimes ingenious experimentation the case for classically conditioned appetitive drive states is still unimpressive. In part the problem lies in the vexing ambiguity of the concepts of hunger and thirst (50). Even a limited perusal of the relevant literature is sufficient to drive home the point that a large number of factors determine the eating and drinking behavior of animals and humans (26, 47, 49, 52, 74, 81, 98, 109, 131, 133, 151, 152). What subsets of these factors are to enter into the definition of hunger and thirst have never been adequately specified. As a consequence, it is not at all clear what, if anything, would constitute ironclad evidence for the conditioning of hunger or thirst, especially in animals.

"We agree with . . . prior reviewers and believe that the term drive has been bandied about to the point where it is not only useless but is actually meaningless and confusing . . . [It] serves no scientific purpose and should be abandoned" (138, p. 54). Inasmuch as a scuttled ship takes down hull and superstructure alike, perhaps the terms conditioned hunger and conditioned thirst ought to share the fate of basic drives. Rather than searching for conditioned appetitive drives, it might be more profitable to turn our attention to how eating and drinking can come under the control of learning mechanisms, particularly classical and operant conditioning. Pursuit of this enterprise brings us in contact with areas of research that have for too long remained apart from the traditional conditioned drive literature.

Classical Conditioning of Regulatory Eating and Drinking

Substantial evidence exists that certain aspects of regulatory eating and drinking (i.e. eating and drinking related to metabolic needs) can be conditioned within a format suggestive of the classical conditioning paradigm. For example, Fitzsimons & Le Magnen (53) found that in a stable feeding situation the drinking patterns of rats were closely keyed to the future metabolic water needs generated by the size or the constitution of the meal. Because of the time course of the adjustments in water intake, they maintained that this "food-associated" drinking was not triggered by appropriate systemic regulatory stimuli ("primary thirst") but rather was the result largely of the conditioning of drinking to some features of the ingested food (e.g. oropharyngeal stimuli). However Deaux, Sato & Kakolewski (39) sacrificed rats a few minutes after completing an accustomed 1.5 g meal of dry food (at the very instant that the animals commenced drinking) and found that their plasma osmolality was significantly higher than that of unfed controls. They suggested that this systemic cue, rather than conditioning, could account for the initiation of food-associated drinking. Another possibility is that the increased plasma osmolality was itself a conditioned rather than an unconditioned response to the ingested food, developed in accordance with the classical conditioning model sketched below. If so, the drinking in question may be regarded as conditioned despite the presence of a relevant systemic cue.

The conditioning of satiety [the regulation of meal size in accordance with its caloric content before this information can be systemically registered (20)] has also been reported in rats (20, 81). As pointed out by Booth (20), many of the earlier studies offered as evidence for conditioned satiety (e.g. 81) are susceptible to an interpretation in terms of conditioned taste aversions (105). His own studies, which avoided this difficulty, showed that the size of a feeding bout could come under the control of oral cues paired with different caloric densities. Moreover, the differentiation remained when two diets were offered alternately, equal in caloric value but tagged with olfactory or taste cues which formerly were associated with diets of high and low caloric density.

A more general effect of oropharyngeal factors on satiety has been reported by Jordan (76), who in intragastric feeding experiments with humans found that subjects given intragastic food loads did not compensate fully for them by the amount that they consumed orally, nor were they as satisfied by the intragastric intake as by normal ingestion (cf. 137). "Apparently there is a separate oral aspect of satiety that remains unsatisfied in intragastric feeding" (76, p. 505).

The precise nature of the processes involved in the conditioning of regulatory eating and drinking remains to be specified. Most accounts do little more than state that appropriate consummatory and satiety behaviors become anticipatory, or that they come under the control of oropharyngeal stimuli (20, 53, 91). If learned regulatory eating and drinking are based on classical conditioning, two explicit models suggest themselves. In the first, taking food-associated drinking as an example, the role of US is served by the systemic cues that regulate drinking (cf. 81), drinking itself being the UR. Then, in accordance with the classical conditioning paradigm, drinking moves forward as an anticipatory (conditioned) response to the CS of food and its ingestion. The second model views the systemic regulatory "cues" as URs to the metabolic conditions which produce them, just as hypoglycemia is a response to insulin. Through classical conditioning these systemic regulatory processes (or some fraction of them) become anticipatory (much in the way that hypoglycemia can be classically conditioned), and in the present case presumably elicit drinking. This, apparently, was the model employed by Balagura (9) in his attempt to demonstrate conditioned hunger.

The notion that the conditioning of regulatory eating and drinking resides in the classical conditioning of appropriate systemic regulatory processes [either directly or indirectly (cf. 38)], rather than in the classical conditioning of consummatory behavior, enjoys certain advantages. For one thing, conditioned satiety is perhaps more easily handled by this formulation. Rather than conceiving the CR as being the cessation of eating, as one must, given the first model, the second view requires only that the appropriate post-ingestive systemic processes, perhaps including in part hyperglycemia (cf. 98), become conditioned in greater force to diets of higher caloric intensity. For another, the model makes contact with the conditioned taste-aversion literature, which, as pointed out below, is not totally unrelated to the problem at hand. That certain neurohumoral and even "non-neural" physiological processes are capable of modification via classical conditioning seems likely (2, 72, 148–150; cf. 29), although, as Gantt (56) points out, there are distinct limits to the conditionability of physiological processes.

There are two other points that should be mentioned before leaving this topic. In the natural course of eating and drinking the cues that serve as conditioned stimuli for the control of regulatory eating and drinking are modality relevant, as they have been in related laboratory experiments (20, 81). It is interesting in this connection that the lastest attempt at hunger conditioning using the traditional conditioning paradigm (94) produced some evidence for conditioning only when gustatory cues formed part of the CS complex. In view of the critical role played by modality relevance in the establishment of conditioned aversions (43, 58, 63, 121, 143), it perhaps is little wonder that the traditional conditioned hunger and thirst studies, most of which employed arbitrary CSs, produced such meager results. The second observation is that classical conditioning of regulatory eating and drinking extinguishes fairly rapidly (20, 81), which is what one would expect from the functional requirements of these acquired behaviors. If conditioned satiety, conditioned drinking, and other such processes are to serve usefully in food and water regulation they must adapt adroitly to changes in diet and in other relevant conditions.

Operant Conditioning of Nonregulatory Eating and Drinking

That eating and drinking can come under the control of operant conditioning procedures hardly needs documentation. And, although subject to special contraints (14), consummatory behavior established by appropriate contingencies can be extremely resistant to extinction, as was perhaps illustrated by the conditioned drinking studies (e.g. 117, 139). The excessive eating by obese people doubtlessly is sometimes the result of operant conditioning (but see 99), which in turn has been used successfully to reduce eating to more acceptable levels (e.g. 100). Although interpretations differ (27), there can be little doubt that the profound depression of eating behavior often observed in anorexia nervosa, which has a mortality rate as high as 15% (15), is frequently shaped and maintained by operant contingencies. As in the case of obesity, behavior modification based on operant conditioning principles has been successfully used in restoring more acceptable eating behavior, often with striking weight gains (11, 15, 112).

A tempting, though clearly premature, generalization is that classically conditioned eating and drinking behaviors are likely to be regulatory whereas operantly conditioned consummatory behavior tends to be nonregulatory. By anticipating the post-absorptive effects of ingested food and water, classical conditioning enables the organism more quickly and more accurately to adjust its consummatory behavior to its metabolic needs (20, 22, 53, 81, 91).

The potential for operantly conditioned consummatory behavior to serve nonregulatory ends resides in the fact that such acquired behavior can rather easily come under the control of stimulus conditions far removed from metabolic needs and can be reinforced by consequences which bear little relationship to the satisfaction of metabolic requirements, such as parental approval, anxiety reduction, and the like (15, 100). The despair expressed from time to time by concerned nutritionists with regard to the American diet, both with respect to quality and quantity, is testimony of how far consummatory behavior can drift from regulatory ends.

Extending the classical conditioning model a bit further, perhaps conditioned taste aversions based on vitamin-deficient, or poisoned, diets may also be viewed as classically conditioned regulatory eating and drinking. According to this view, the illness that results from ingestion of vitamin-deficient or contaminated food is characterized by certain physiological processes which serve as the URs. Some portion of the latter become conditioned to the oropharyngeal cues produced by the defective diet, becoming anticipatory and thereby inhibiting consummatory behavior (cf. 106). In a recent study bearing directly on this point, Zahorik (155) worked with taste aversions induced by thiamine deficiency, one of the most prominent symptoms of which is bradycardia. She found that rats, either in a thiamine-deficient or a recovered state, drank more of a "control" solution than of one that had been paired with thiamine deprivation, and drank still more of a third solution that had been paired with thiamine injections [known to produce rapid temporary recovery from some deficiency symptoms (155, 156)]. However, the important point is that the animals' heart rates reflected their drinking behavior, being slowest in the second condition and most rapid in the third, as if the bradycardia characteristic of thiamine deficiency became classically conditioned to the solution with which it had been associated and the increased heart rate which attended recovery from thiamine deficiency became conditioned to the solution with which it had been paired. Although these results offer some support for the classical conditioning model outlined above, they are in clear need of verification and extension.

Perhaps a sharper distinction between classical and operant conditioning has been drawn than can be justified by recent empirical and theoretical developments (12, 16, 18, 93, 132; but see 40). Nevertheless, the distinction may still be of heuristic value in sorting out the learning mechanisms which contribute to the control of regulatory and nonregulatory consummatory behaviors.

Conditioned Aversive States

Although the relevant literature continues to mount, because of space limitations this topic will not be covered. Apart from the usual journal sources, detailed treatment of various aspects of the topic can be found in a number of recent edited volumes (13, 28, 62, 92).

CONDITIONED REINFORCEMENT AND THE INFORMATION HYPOTHESIS

The quest for the essential nature of positive conditioned, or secondary, reinforcement is still very much alive. According to the classical view of conditioned reinforcement, appropriately pairing a previously neutral stimulus with primary reinforcement is a sufficient condition for establishing a secondary reinforcer, which thereafter functions, at least for a time, in much the same way as a primary reinforcer. The pros and cons of this interpretation have already been dealt with in considerable detail and need not be recounted here (69, 85, 142). A strong challenge is offered to the traditional view by what may be referred to as the information hypothesis; this holds that neutral stimuli acquire reinforcing properties not simply because they have been paired with primary reinforcement but rather because they provide relevant information about such events. Thus, for example, a stimulus may consistently precede the presentation of food but if its information is redundant, in the sense that the same information is conveyed by an immediately antecedent stimulus, it may develop little in the way of conditioned reinforcement properties (44, 45). The information hypothesis of conditioned reinforcement has gained increasing support in recent years, though by no means to the extent of eradicating competing interpretations (41, 103). A nakedly cognitive theory of conditioned reinforcement has been advanced by Longstreth (85), who went beyond the information hypothesis in arguing that secondary reinforcers are really only means for securing desired rewards in the future. "People do not work for money because it has been paired with rewards in the past. They work for it only if they believe it will bring rewards in the future" (p. 76).

Despite the crossfire of conflicting opinions regarding the conceptual status of conditioned reinforcement, cultivation of its empirical basis continues. Thus, for example, token reinforcement in kindergarten children has been demonstrated within a setting that eliminates an interpretation in terms of response facilitation exerted by the presence of the tokens themselves. Children took longer to extinguish pressing a button that had delivered a token previously paired with trinkets than a button that earlier produced a token with no such prior history (128). Although this study was apparently motivated by the traditional view of conditioned reinforcement, it seems vulnerable to the cognitive interpretation suggested by Longstreth

(85). Perhaps the children pressed the first button longer simply because they believed they might subsequently be allowed to exchange any tokens they earned for trinkets.

Be that as it may, the cognitive hypothesis, which emphasizes the subject's ability to reason, would have to be pushed a bit to account for the establishment in 10-month-old infants of a spatial discrimination solely on the basis of conditioned reinforcement (124). Infants were first exposed to a short training period in which each time they touched an illuminated target on a feeding table a tone was sounded, followed shortly by the delivery of a Froot Loop reinforcement; a second, distinctively different, tone was also presented but not in association with reinforcement. Two target stimuli were then presented, one of which when touched produced the "positive" tone (but not Froot Loops), the other, the "negative" tone. The infants showed a clear preference for touching the target that produced the positive tone. As in other studies using the same general paradigm, there may be a question as to whether the control exhibited by the positive tone should be attributed to a reinforcing or to an eliciting function of that stimulus. This is one of a number of troublesome methodological points that must be kept in mind when designing studies aimed at demonstrating conditioned reinforcement effects (85, 142).

Turning to developments in methodology, Albert & Mah (1) recently reported a novel method of illustrating one-trial learning based on conditioned reinforcement. Water-deprived rats were first habituated to a bare black box which contained a pyramid-shaped nook. An empty drinking spout (of the same kind used in the home cages) was then inserted into the nook and the animals allowed to explore the spout for a maximum of 15 seconds. During a 5-minute test session given 48 hours later with the water spout removed, these animals showed much more exploration within the area of the nook than control subjects. This very simple experimental task was also shown to be sensitive to motivational variables, in that the water deprivation condition at the time of testing proved to be quite important in determining exploration of the nook area, while deprivation conditions during training, and the amount of time spent by the animals exploring the empty spout during training, were less effective variables. Because it produces clear evidence of learning with an exposure "trial" of only a few seconds, this paradigm might prove useful in areas other than conditioned reinforcement, e.g. memory consolidation. Somewhere at the opposite end of the complexity continuum, schedule interactions within the token-reinforcement paradigm have been investigated in rats, with ordinary glass marbles serving as tokens (136). [See (69) for a useful review of the methods currently in use for studying conditioned reinforcement.]

Conditioned Reinforcement and Observing Behavior

As already indicated, the conflict between the traditional analysis of conditioned reinforcement and the information hypothesis can be reduced to the question of whether stimuli achieve reinforcing properties because in the past they occurred contiguously with positive reward or because they provide information regarding subsequent reinforcing events. [Some writers, it should be pointed out, apparently allow for both pairing and information in determining the strength of a conditioned reinforcer (e.g. 145).] To its credit, the traditional interpretation is reasonably objective in specifying the conditions under which a previously neutral stimulus achieves the status of a conditioned reinforcer. On the other hand, in spite of demonstrated applications of formal information theory to psychological research (e.g. 4, 60), the information hypothesis of conditioned reinforcement has developed largely out of an intuitive grasp of informational concepts, although there are signs that this situation is changing (16, 147). There is also a definite movement afoot to extend the scope of the information hypothesis from conditioned reinforcement to a much wider range of phenomena, including partial reinforcement effects (145), classical and operant conditioning, and their interactions (16).

A major impetus for the application of information concepts to conditioned reinforcement has come from investigations of observing behavior. These are studies in which the presentation of discriminative stimuli (S+, S–, or both) are made contingent upon the performance of an "observing" response. In a pioneer study verified many times, Wyckoff (153) found that pigeons would emit substantial numbers of observing responses which served to produce the discriminative stimuli of a multiple schedule (which otherwise became a mixed schedule). He attempted to accommodate this result within the traditional interpretation of secondary reinforcement by assuming that the strength of a positive conditioned reinforcer is related to percentage of reinforcement by an increasing exponential function (154). Since that time, however, there have been numerous attacks on Wyckoff's analysis, all suggesting that the information provided by the stimuli produced by observing responses (or the attending uncertainty reduction) constitute the source of reinforcement for observing behavior (e.g. 37, 83, 146; cf. 68).

One issue that has recently been brought into focus by the rival viewpoints is the degree to which S– can maintain observing behavior. An unmodified information hypothesis would have to acknowledge that if S– produces as much information (i.e. as much uncertainty reduction) as S+, it should sustain observing behavior to the same degree as the latter stimulus. Quite the contrary deduction flows from the traditional interpretation of conditioned reinforcement, in which S– qualifies as a secondary aversive stimulus, one which very likely would tend to punish immediately preceding responses. The empirical data regarding this issue still are not clear. On the one hand, there have been reports that observing behavior can be maintained when its only consequence is to produce S– (83, 110). These results have been criticized, however (41), even by critics friendly to the information hypothesis (145). Moreover, Dinsmoor, Browne & Lawrence (41) reported just the opposite result, that when only S– was produced by observing responses, the latter declined to near-zero levels.

A less direct attack on the same problem takes advantage of the fact that under appropriate circumstances the average amount of information available in the discriminative stimuli (S+ or S–) is related to the probability of S+ (and reward) by an inverted U function, symmetrical around 0.50. Thus if observing responses are reinforced by the quantity of information they produce, rather than by the nature of the information ("good news" vs "bad news"), observing response rate ought to produce a symmetrical, inverted U function when probability of S+ is appropriately manipulated. This seems not to be the case. Wilton & Clements (147) manipulated probability of S+ (and primary reward) from 20 to 80% and found a higher rate of observing responses in the latter condition. They suggest that the asymmetry arises because the same amount of information has different reinforcing effects on the observing response depending upon whether it signals reward or nonreward. As the authors point out, an asymmetrical function relating observing response rate to probability of S+ (and reward) is presumptive evidence that more than the informational content of the discriminative stimulus determines its ability to reinforce observing behavior. But by the same token, such a function does not necessarily mean that S– has zero positive reinforcing ability. More than likely, we are dealing with a common situation in behavioral research, namely, any one of a variety of results can be obtained depending upon the particular parameter values chosen. In the present case it is likely that the reinforcement schedules associated with S+ and S–, scheduling of the observing response, the duration of discriminative stimuli produced by each reinforced observing response, the level of deprivation, and possibly other variables, determine the degree to which S– contributes to the maintenance of observing behavior. Trying to establish that S– never reinforces observing responses will probably prove fruitless. Good news *is* probably more reinforcing than bad news, but if the information provided by bad news were entirely without positive reinforcing effect, weather forecasters, at least in the part of the country in which I reside, would long since have gone out of business.

Preference for Signaled Reinforcement

There are a large number of studies, closely related to the observing response research in all but terminology, which clearly show that animals and humans very generally prefer signaled to unsignaled reinforcement. To cite several of the most recent of these experiments, rats prefer signaled (positive) electrical brain stimulation to unsignaled stimulation (30, 31), and humans, bathed in hot, humid, air from the chin up, prefer signaled to unsignaled 15-second cooling air puffs delivered to the face (54). Turning to aversive stimuli, rats prefer signaled to unsignaled shock whether or not the shock is escapable (5, 6), and show the same kind of preference in a shock avoidance task (8). The greater aversiveness of unsignaled over signaled shock has also been verified using a response rate measure (87). The magnitude of the difference in the aversiveness of the two types of shock is indicated by the fact that in one study rats chose signaled shock 4 to 9 times longer in duration than unsignaled shock of the same intensity, and with duration held constant they chose signaled shock 2 to 3 times more intense than unsignaled shock (7). Although the consensus is strong, preference for signaled reinforcement is not a unanimous finding. Hershiser & Trapold (70) reported that their rats consistently preferred unsignaled to signaled reinforcement, which took the form of sucrose solution injected directly into the mouth by means of a permanent oral fistula. Apparently, however, such exceptions are rare.

Taken as a whole, these experiments, particularly those dealing with aversive stimulation, seem to offer striking support for the information hypothesis. In many of these studies the subject had two classes of responses available, one of which led to signaled reinforcement and the other to a physically equivalent reinforcement but minus the signal. The indicated conclusion, from the point of view of the information hypothesis, is that the first response class was chosen over the second because of the extra reinforcement provided by the information residing in the signal. The information hypothesis can also point to a number of situations in which a stimulus signaling an aversive event was eagerly sought out, perhaps producing at last the needed evidence that bad news can be strongly reinforcing.

Unfortunately, the situation is not that simple. In the first place, the signal, apart from any reinforcing value it might possess, appears to influence the subjective value of the primary reinforcement itself. This is suggested by the rat's preference for signaled shock even at the cost of far longer or much more intense shocks (7); it seems unlikely that the marked disparity in the physical values of the signaled and unsignaled shocks could be completely compensated for by the reinforcement supplied by the information in the signal, i.e. by uncertainty reduction. The same point is illustrated in the case of positive reinforcement by the finding that an otherwise nonreinforcing electrical brain stimulation can be rendered reinforcing by having it preceded by a brief signal (31). One could perhaps complement the information hypothesis with a mechanism such as Perkins' (101) "preparatory responses," thereby accounting for both the reinforcement residing in informative stimuli and the effects that such stimuli sometimes have on the subjective intensity of subsequent primary reinforcing events. It is questionable, though, whether given a satisfactory explanation of the second class of phenomena, any need would exist for a separate accounting of the first. Further eroding the apparent support for the information hypothesis, some investigators have argued that the important informative stimulus in signaled aversive paradigms is not the signal heralding the advent of shock, but rather its absence which, serving as a cue for nonshock periods, constitutes a "safety" signal (7; cf. 70). So there is a question about how firmly these studies support a positive reinforcing role for bad news.

Rescorla (103) has recently taken aim at the information hypothesis as that conceptual system has been applied to Pavlovian conditioning. He pointed to a number of developments, all seeming "to suggest that by itself contiguity between a CS and US is insufficient for Pavlovian conditioning. Rather, for a CS to become conditioned, it must in some sense provide 'information' about the coming of the US" (p. 2). Rescorla went on to analyze the implications of these suggestions, ultimately coming to the conclusion "that although it may sometimes be useful to describe conditioning in informational terms, in the end that intuition is incomplete and incorrect" (p. 43). As a substitute for informational concepts, he presented a quantitative theory that was developed jointly with Wagner (e.g. 104). Although some may feel that the theory bears a distressing resemblance to Hull's classical learning theory and to first-generation mathematical models, it does a suprisingly good job of accounting for at least some of the results (e.g. blocking) that appear to call for an informational analysis of Pavlovian conditioning.

If the informational analysis of conditioned reinforcement, Pavlovian conditioning, and related behavioral processes (16) is to resist assimilation by more traditional behavior theory, it will have to show that its scope of application is at least as wide as that of the latter. To accomplish this expansion it probably will have to assign reinforcement value to stimuli, not only on the basis of the amount of information transmitted, but also in terms of the nature of the event addressed by the information. Surely not all information (defined in technical terms) is equally valuable. The cost of achieving the information must also be considered. Not many people would trouble to learn the time of day if they had to purchase a Tiffany wristwatch each time to do so. It is also important to learn whether the reinforcement function assigned to uncertainty reduction can, in the interests of parsimony and objectivity, be transferred to more peripheral processes, such as preparatory responses, tension reduction, and the like.

Several years ago this reviewer (37) reported that when monkeys were either extinguished or reversed on a simple discrimination problem they increased enormously their rate of observing responses which, because both S+ and S– followed each observing response, produced only redundant information. In informational terms it looked as though the nonreinforcement that suddenly accompanied the onset of extinction or reversal induced a state of uncertainty in the animals which they attempted to reduce by a search for relevant information. (Frustration seemed unable to account for the increase in observing behavior.) This is the kind of result that still poses problems for traditional reinforcement views, and the kind that must be handled in considerable detail by the informational analysis if it is to prove a viable alternative.

THE WORK ETHIC IN ANIMALS AND CHILDREN

A number of studies have reported that rats (both normal and with septal or ventromedial hypothalamic lesions), pigeons, and children (Caucasian and American Indian) will perform an instrumental response to obtain precisely the same reward that is available to them with no work requirement. Rats will run down an alley tripping over hundreds of food pellets to obtain a single, identical, pellet in the goal box (134), press a lever on various schedules to obtain pellets of food which can be had without work in the nearby vicinity (32, 75, 96, 125, 126), and pigeons will peck a key, even on intermittent schedules of reinforcement to secure exactly the same food that is freely available in a nearby food cup (96, 97). Given the option of receiving marbles merely by waiting an equivalent amount of time for their delivery, children tend to prefer to press a lever (on a fixed-ratio 10 schedule) to obtain the same marbles (125, 127).

As noted by Taylor (135), there are two related but separable issues involved in these work vs "freeloading" studies. With reference to animal subjects, the first is whether, and to what extent, animals will work for food when identical food is freely available; the second, which is really a special case of the first, is whether animals *prefer* to work for food rather than to freeload. If verified, this stronger version places animals, and by implication humans, in a far more sanguine light with regard to their motivational systems than heretofore suspected by many.

That animals and children will indeed spend part of their time working for the same rewards that are available with no work requirement is unquestioned, even by

Taylor (135). And something is known about the conditions that modulate this phenomenon: (*a*) The instrumental behavior is not maintained simply by "intrinsic" reinforcement, for if the instrumental response fails to produce the reward object, its rate drops off precipitously in pigeons and rats (96) and children bar press less (127). (*b*) Increasing the work requirement (32; but see 97, 126) or increasing the rate of delivery of free food (125) increases freeloading. (*c*) On the other hand, higher levels of training on the instrumental response tend to reduce the amount of subsequent freeloading (75, 134). (*d*) Prior operant training is not required, however, for pigeons living in an experimental chamber with food continuously available will acquire and maintain (for at least 20 days) a key-pecking or lever-pressing response which produces identical food (96). (*e*) Finally, in the single study that employed water as reward, rats showed very little disposition to work for water when free water was available (135).

The evidence that animals prefer work over freeloading, in the sense that during a given experimental period they consume more earned than free food, is less firm (135). Yet, striking instances have been reported (32, 75, 125). An analogous preference in children (for marbles) has been observed by Singh (125, 127). Apart from their potential significance for certain touchy social issues, these results are interesting because they seem to be counter-intuitive and counter-theoretical, at least for many behavioristic theories (96, 125).

Following Kavanau (77), Singh (125, 127) has proposed that controlling the environment, that is, "manipulating, and altering relationships with any susceptible environmental features" (77, p. 1623) is an important factor in behavior determination. Animals enjoy a substantial degree of control over their natural environment, reflected in such activities as obtaining food, building and maintaining nesting sites, avoiding and escaping predators, and so on. Exerting control over the environment is so essential to the survival of animals that it is not implausible that exercising such control is itself reinforcing. Consequently, if in a laboratory situation an opportunity for environmental control presents itself, an animal will ordinarily take advantage of it, as in the work vs freeloading studies. One implication of this hypothesis is that if means of controlling the environment were provided in addition to working for food [such as manipulating the illumination level (77)], animals will enage in these activities at the expense of working for food and hence show a greater propensity for freeloading. Apparently, no such study has been reported.

Another possibility is that the two sources of reward available in freeloading studies, although physically identical, are not perceived as identical by the animals. The very same wine often tastes better when drunk from a stem glass than from a paper cup. Perhaps there is something about the temporal sequencing (or other properties) of earned food that differentiates it from free food. Assuming that animals prefer some degree of variability in their diets, one would expect that they would occasionally work for food even though free food was available. However, a preference for earned food cannot be explained on this basis alone. It might be interesting, nevertheless, to tag the earned and free food with different odors or flavors, which if the present hypothesis has substance, ought to decrease freeloading.

Obviously, a great deal remains to be learned about "contrafreeloading" (135), its persistence (most demonstrations have involved only a small number off sessions), its relationship to exploratory and manipulatory behavior (46), to autoshaping, or more generally behavior maintained by noncontingent reinforcement (25, 55, 111, 132, 144), and to the phenomenon of "self-reinforcement" which, recently demonstrated in pigeons (90), is a self-management technique currently employed in behavior modification (89).

AN OPPONENT-PROCESS THEORY OF ACQUIRED MOTIVATION

Anyone consulting the reviews of derived motives in this series for enlightenment regarding the possible basis of human acquired motivation must have come away sorely disappointed. The vast majority of studies cited in these papers relate to animal, and in particular rat, research. The reasons for this emphasis are not hard to find. Most of the reasonably rigorous conceptualizations of acquired motivation have, after all, derived from traditional learning theory, which was itself heavily rooted in rat research. Moreover, such motivationally relevant concepts as conditioned appetitive and aversive drives, incentive motivation, and conditioned reinforcement did not develop because of a basic concern with motivation itself but rather as a response to the needs of an expanding theory of learning. It is little wonder, then, that these concepts have never been forged into a convincing theory of acquired motivation.

Quite recently, however, Solomon & Corbit (129) have proposed an opponent-process theory of motivation which, being stimulated by problems of motivation rather than of learning, makes contact with virtually the full range of acquired motivational phenomena, from the "joy" experienced by dogs when an accustomed strong aversive event is terminated, to the abstinence agony that torments addicts upon drug withdrawal. Because of its potential theoretical significance and its relevance, the model and its applications will be described here in a little detail.

An important feature of the model is the assumption of hedonic or motivational homeostasis, hardly a novel innovation. (In the current version of the model hedonic value, emotion, affect, motivation, and related concepts are not distinguished.) What is novel is the nature of the mechanism that is postulated to accomplish hedonic homeostasis. In effect, much of what is considered acquired motivation is created from the failure, or at least the over-zealousness, of the homeostatic mechanism. Their notion, in brief, is that whenever a significant departure from hedonic equilibrium occurs due to the presentation of an affect-producing stimulus, a negative feedback system is activated which generates "an affective process which is, in some abstract sense, the opposite of that precipitated by the stimulus input." Thus we have a primary affective or motivational process, also referred to as affective state *A,* which is elicited by an appropriate stimulus situation; elicitation of state *A* leads immediately to a secondary affective process which, because it is opposite in affective value, is termed an opponent process. The affective state identified with the opponent process may be referred to as state *B.* Although the opponent process is assumed to be "sluggish in its latency, recruitment, and decay," with repeated elicitation of state *A* it is assumed to grow in intensity, occur with shorter latency, and decay to affective zero less rapidly. Given these assumptions, it is not difficult to see that with proper parameter values the opponent process could overshoot its target of establishing hedonic equilibrium and overwhelm the primary affective process, whether it be positive or negative.

To cite an illustration given by Solomon & Corbit, dogs initially subjected to strong noncontingent shocks behave in such a way as to suggest a state of terror (extreme negative affect) while shock is present, reverting to a state of stealth, submission, and caution upon termination of shock. After the dogs have had considerable experience with shock, a dramatic change takes place in their behavior. Upon application of shock, terror is replaced by a far less aversive state (unhappiness, anxiety), and when shock is terminated, a distinctly positive affect state seems to result, the animals appearing euphoric, active, social and happy. The opponent-process model manages to accommodate these striking changes in behavior, and in inferred affective states, by its assumption that repeated application of shock (resulting in repeated elicitations of state *A*) serve to strengthen greatly the opponent process (state *B*). As a result, the negative affect generated by the shock stimulus is greatly attenuated and upon termination of shock, because state *A* is thereby eliminated and only a greatly exaggerated state *B* remains, the animals are left in a state of euphoria.

This same type of interaction between a primary affective process and an immediately reacting secondary opponent process can be applied to a wide variety of phenomena in the general area of acquired motivation. Parachutists frequently experience considerable fear on initial jumps and at the termination of a jump may appear "stunned" and "stony-faced" (129). After much experience, however, during which the opponent process gains in strength, the terror associated with the jump gives way to tense expectancy, and at the termination of the jump, which leaves only a heightened state *B* to express itself, feelings of exhilaration and jubilation result, often lasting for considerable lengths of time. [By way of comparison, Epstein and Fenz's anxiety inhibition principle (cf. 48, 51) can account for the reduction of fear in experienced parachutists but not for the development of positive affect.]

Cigarette and drug addiction are handled in much the same way, only in these cases state *A* has positive affect and state *B* is an unusually long-lasting negative affect state. Since another assumption of the model is that state *B* can be eliminated or reduced by reinstitution of state *A*, addiction may be viewed as behavior in the service of escaping an aversive state *B* by inducing (via cigarettes, drugs, etc.) its antidote, state *A*. Unfortunately, however, grossly unlike antidotes, the reinstitution of state *A* only means that state *B* will become that much stronger. Thus the addict is slowly crushed under an opponent process which becomes more massive each time it is temporarily dislodged.

There are other features of the model that are worthy of note. Although changes in the strength of the opponent process forms the core of acquired motivation within the model, there is a second way in which learning enters. Both state *A* and state *B* are assumed to be conditionable by Pavlovian conditioning techniques, though quite different consequences are associated with the conditioning of the two states.

The major difference is that a stimulus which, through conditioning, is capable of eliciting state *A* will have a "biphasic" effect. It will first elicit state *A* and, because of the unconditioned coupling of the primary and opponent affective processes, state *B* will also make an appearance. This implies that when state *A* is negative, conditioned elicitation of state *A* will result in a negative hedonic state followed by a state of positive affect, e.g. "anxiety" followed by "relief." Conditioning of *B* states leads to no such reversal of affect.

Because the model applies equally to positive and negative affect states, the possibility exists for developing an exaggerated opponent process to a negative *A* state. In such a case, an individual might deliberately inflict an aversive *A* state upon himself in order to achieve the associated positive *B* state. The potential of this implication for interpreting behaviors ranging from acquired tastes for initially aversive substances to outright masochism should be apparent.

Although it is far too early to judge the theoretical and pragmatic fruitfulness of the opponent-process model, it seems to incorporate the kinds of mechanisms that can be articulated into a viable structure of acquired motivation, if not for the entire class of such phenomena, at least for an important subset. Whether addictive behavior can be meaningfully handled by the theory is perhaps open to question. Solomon & Corbit (129) have some interesting things to say about cigarette addiction and its treatment, an area greatly in need of fresh insights (10, 71). On the other hand it may be stretching things a bit to apply the opponent-process model to drug addiction. A major assumption of the theory is that the opponent process (state *B*) is weakened by disuse. Consequently, if a heroin addict could by some means be prevented from taking heroin for an extended period of time, his craving for the drug (state *B*) should ultimately dissipate, i.e. he should no longer be an addict. This seems not to be the case.

Dole (42), a pioneer of methadone maintenance treatment, points out that addicts who have been on methadone maintanance for as long as three or four years, during which time their craving for heroin is apparently extinguished, almost always experienced "heroin hunger" upon withdrawal of methadone. "They felt that they were so far away from drug addiction and so far beyond wanting heroin anymore that they would have no need for methadone. For them the return of a heroin hunger was terrifying" (p. 24). Dole (42) also observes, "Addicts who have been locked up for 5 years in jail, totally abstinent, are likely to get re-addicted within the first month after they are out. I believe one has to reckon with the fact that heroin hunger is probably a symptom of a pharmacological imprint that may last for a man's life" (p. 24).

Possibly the opponent-process model can accommodate permanent addiction, when it occurs, by postulating that extra-potent *B* states may not be completely reversible. However, this assumption [like the closely related "principle of partial irreversibility of anxiety" used by Solomon & Wynne (130) in a completely different context] is vulnerable to ad hoc applications. Despite this and other potential problems, the opponent-process model is likely to figure importantly in future theoretical and research developments in acquired motivation.

LEARNING, REVOLUTION, AND DERIVED MOTIVATION

Since derived motivation, by definition, rests on acquired mechanisms, it cannot avoid being affected by significant conceptual and empirical developments in learning. It will not come as a surprise to anyone who still reads the relevant literature that the area of learning is in the midst, or perhaps at the tail end, of a pair of revolutions, which, although starting from quite different bases, sometimes share a common front. Like all other revolutions, these two have well-developed roots in the past and both have caused more heads to roll than was perhaps necessary.

The major impact of the first of these revolutions has been to reinsert biology and evolution into the learning equation. The divergent lines of inquiry that successfully mounted this effort are nicely represented in the recent volume *Biological Boundaries of Learning* (116), to which may be added Razran's monograph (102) and a spate of recent articles which converge on the topic from a variety of angles (18, 49, 56, 59, 61, 79, 106, 113, 114, 120, 132). This development finally came to a head because we could no longer afford merely to nod to certain facts, among them, (*a*) that when it comes to serving as discriminative stimuli in learning situations not all stimuli are equivalent, or even approximately so—the principle of nonequivalence of stimuli; (*b*) that depending upon the response system chosen, the effectiveness with which instrumental behavior is acquired can vary enormously—the principle of nonequivalence of responses; and (*c*) that there is a profound difference in the readiness with which associations can be formed, particularly over long temporal intervals, which seems to depend upon the "modality" of the association [see (120) for a detailed review of the evidence relating to these issues]. Another contributing factor was a decreasing confidence in reinforcement as an agent which impartially and mindlessly strengthens selectively the most recent behaviors and in the assumption that it holds an exclusive franchise on this function (e.g. 18, 132).

All of the nonequivalences made sense when looked at from the point of view of the biological and behavioral endowments of the organism as handed down by evolution and natural selection; and, of course, all had been recognized for some time inside and outside the area of learning. Why they, and certain closely related issues, suddenly erupted to alter theoretical conceptions in learning to an extent that makes the term "revolution" quite proper is a matter for future reflection to decide. But in any event, these changed attitudes are here to stay and are likely to have a deep impact on our conceptualizations of acquired motivation.

The second revolution is the extraordinary proliferation and development of cognitive concepts in psychology. If Tolman were alive today he could only revel in the fury of the cognitive assault that threatens to capture almost the full range of nonreflexive behavior in both humans and animals (12, 18, 65, 67, 73, 78, 84, 85, 88, 107, 118); not even among the pages of the *Journal of the Experimental Analysis of Behavior* can one any longer find complete refuge (108). While the variety of cognitive concepts employed today is richer than in the past, the rigor with which these concepts are defined and applied varies enormously (e.g. 18 vs 73), and at times one cannot help wondering whether much more is being accomplished than relabeling. Nevertheless, this development too promises to alter permanently long-held conceptions regarding learning and motivational processes (79).

One common ground on which the biological-evolutionary and cognitive developments join forces is the belief that many cognitive abilities are themselves the products of evolution responding to the pressures of natural selection. They are, to use a term endangered by overuse, species-specific behaviors. As Lenneberg (82) has put it, "every animal species must be assumed to have cognitive specificities," a general thesis developed more recently in considerable detail by Razran (102).

Against this background of conceptual reorientation—if not revolution—it requires little foresight to predict striking changes in our formulations of acquired motivation. We probably will see less of conditioned drives and conditioned reinforcers established automatically by conventional conditioning techniques and thereafter controlling behavior in much the same way as the real things. We will see less effort devoted to reducing all motivational states to some common core drive, and still less of the tacit assumption that acquired motivation, whatever it might be, develops in essentially the same way across species and situations. On the other hand, we are likely to witness much more emphasis on the adaptive significance of acquired motivation, particularly within the ecological niche of the organism, more attention paid to the special conditions that foster the acquisition of derived motives in different species, and greater sensitivity toward the structural and cognitive requirements of different systems of learned motives. Out of this web of increasing complexity there may one day emerge a theoretically satisfying, yet useful, general formulation of acquired motivation.

Literature Cited

1. Albert, D. J., Mah, C. J. 1972. An examination of conditioned reinforcement using a one-trial learning procedure. *Learn. Motiv.* 3:369–88
2. Alvarez-Buyalla, R., Carrasco-Zanini, J. 1960. A conditioned reflex which reproduces the hypoglycemic effect of insulin. *Acta Physiol. Lat. Am.* 10:153–58
3. Appley, M. H. 1970. Derived motives. *Ann. Rev. Psychol.* 21:485–518
4. Attneave, F. 1959. *Applications of Information Theory to Psychology.* New York: Holt. 120 pp.
5. Badia, P., Culbertson, S. 1970. Behavioral effects of signaled versus unsignaled shock during escape training in the rat. *J. Comp. Physiol. Psychol.* 72: 216–22
6. Badia, P., Culbertson, S. 1972. The relative aversiveness of signalled vs unsignalled escapable and inescapable shock. *J. Exp. Anal. Behav.* 17:463–71
7. Badia, P., Culbertson, S., Harsh, J. 1973. Choice of longer or stronger signalled shock over shorter or weaker unsignalled shock. *J. Exp. Anal. Behav.* 19:25–32
8. Badia, P., Culbertson, S., Lewis, P. 1971. The relative aversiveness of signalled vs unsignalled avoidance. *J. Exp. Anal. Behav.* 16:113–21
9. Balagura, S. 1968. Conditioned glycemic responses in the control of food intake. *J. Comp. Physiol. Psychol.* 65: 30–32
10. Bernstein, D. A. 1969. Modification of smoking behavior: an evaluative review. *Psychol. Bull.* 71:418–40
11. Bianco, F. J. 1972. Rapid treatment of two cases of anorexia nervosa. *J. Behav. Ther. Exp. Psychiat.* 3:223–24
12. Bindra, D. 1972. A unified account of classical conditioning and operant training. See Ref. 13, 453–81
13. Black, A. H., Prokasy, W. F., Eds. 1972. *Classical Conditioning II: Current Theory and Research.* New York: Appleton-Century-Crofts. 497 pp.

14. Black, A. H., Young, G. A. 1972. Constraints on the operant conditioning of drinking. See Ref. 62, 35–50
15. Blinder, B. J., Freeman, D. M. A., Stunkard, A. J. 1970. Behavior therapy of anorexia nervosa: effectiveness of activity as a reinforcer of weight gain. *Am. J. Psychiat.* 126:1093–98
16. Bloomfield, T. M. 1972. Reinforcement schedules: contingency or contiguity? See Ref. 62, 165–208
17. Bolles, R. C. 1967. *The Theory of Motivation.* New York: Harper & Row. 546 pp.
18. Bolles, R. C. 1972. Reinforcement, expectancy, and learning. *Psychol. Rev.* 79:394–409
19. Bolles, R. C., Moot, S. A. 1972. Derived motives. *Ann. Rev. Psychol.* 23:51–72
20. Booth, D. A. 1972. Conditioned satiety in the rat. *J. Comp. Physiol. Psychol.* 81:457–71
21. Booth, D. A., Brookover, T. 1968. Hunger elicited in the rat by a single injection of bovine crystalline insulin. *Physiol. Behav.* 3:439–46
22. Booth, D. A., Lovett, D., McSherry, G. M. 1972. Postingestive modulation of the sweetness preference gradient in the rat. *J. Comp. Physiol. Psychol. Monogr.* 78:485–512
23. Booth, D. A., Pitt, M. E. 1968. The role of glucose in insulin-induced feeding and drinking. *Physiol. Behav.* 3:447–53
24. Brown, J. S., Farber, I. E. 1968. Secondary motivational systems. *Ann. Rev. Psychol.* 19:99–134
25. Brown, P. L., Jenkins, H. M. 1968. Auto-shaping of the pigeon's key peck. *J. Exp. Anal. Behav.* 11:1–8
26. Bruch, H. 1969. Hunger and instincts. *J. Nerv. Ment. Dis.* 149:91–114
27. Bruch, H. 1971. Anorexia nervosa in the male. *Psychosom. Med.* 33:31–47
28. Brush, F. R., Ed. 1971. *Aversive Conditioning and Learning.* New York: Academic. 626 pp.
29. Bykov, K. M. 1957. *The Cerebral Cortex and the Internal Organs,* transl. W. H. Gantt. New York: Chemical Publ. 448 pp.
30. Cantor, M. B., LoLordo, V. M. 1970. Rats prefer signaled reinforcing brain stimulation to unsignaled ESB. *J. Comp. Physiol. Psychol.* 71:183–91
31. Ibid 1972. Reward value of brain stimulation is inversely related to uncertainty about its onset. 79:259–70
32. Carder, B., Berkowitz, K. 1970. Rats' preference for earned in comparison with free food. *Science* 167:1273–74
33. Cofer, C. N., Appley, M. H. 1964. *Motivation: Theory and Research.* New York: Wiley. 958 pp.
34. Cott, A., Wayner, M. J., Millner, J. 1972. Conditioned drinking: a specific or nonspecific response? *Physiol. Behav.* 9:219–27
35. Cravens, R. W., Renner, K. E. 1970. Conditioned appetitive drive states: empirical evidence and theoretical status. *Psychol. Bull.* 73:212–20
36. D'Amato, M. R. 1970. *Experimental Psychology: Methodology, Psychophysics and Learning.* New York: McGraw-Hill. 727 pp.
37. D'Amato, M. R., Etkin, M., Fazzaro, J. 1968. Cue-producing behavior in the capuchin monkey during reversal, extinction, acquisition, and overtraining. *J. Exp. Anal. Behav.* 11:425–33
38. Deaux, E., Kakolewski, J. W. 1970. Emotionally induced increases in effective osmotic pressure and subsequent thirst. *Science* 169:1226–28
39. Deaux, E., Sato, E., Kakolewski, J. W. 1970. Emergence of systemic cues evoking food-associated drinking. *Physiol. Behav.* 5:1177–79
40. DiCara, L. V., Braun, J. J., Pappas, B. A. 1970. Classical conditioning and instrumental learning of cardiac and gastrointestinal responses following removal of neocortex in the rat. *J. Comp. Physiol. Psychol.* 73:208–16
41. Dinsmoor, J. A., Browne, M. P., Lawrence, C. E. 1972. A test of the negative discriminative stimulus as a reinforcer of observing. *J. Exp. Anal. Behav.* 18:79–85
42. Dole, V. P. 1971. Research on methadone maintenance treatment. In *Methadone Maintenance,* ed. S. Einstein, 13–27. New York: Marcel Dekker. 249 pp.
43. Domjan, M., Wilson, N. E. 1972. Specificity of cue to consequence in aversion learning in the rat. *Psychon. Sci.* 26:143–45
44. Egger, M. D., Miller, N. E. 1962. Secondary reinforcement in rats as a function of information value and reliability of the stimulus. *J. Exp. Psychol.* 64:97–104
45. Egger, M. D., Miller, N. E. 1963. When is a reward reinforcing?: an experimental study of the information hypothesis. *J. Comp. Physiol. Psychol.* 56:132–37
46. Eisenberger, R. 1972. Explanation of rewards that do not reduce tissue needs. *Psychol. Bull.* 77:319–39

47. Epstein, A. N., Fitzsimons, J. T., Rolls, B. J. 1970. Drinking induced by injection of angiotensin into the brain of the rat. *J. Physiol. London* 210:457–74
48. Epstein, S. 1967. Toward a unified theory of anxiety. In *Progress in Experimental Personality Research,* ed. B. A. Maher, 4:1–89. New York: Academic. 323 pp.
49. Falk, J. L. 1971. The nature and determinants of adjunctive behavior. *Physiol. Behav.* 6:577–88
50. Falk, J. L. 1971. Determining changes in vital functions: ingestion. In *Methods in Psychobiology,* ed. R. D. Myers, 1: 301–29. New York: Academic. 356 pp.
51. Fenz, W. D., Jones, G. B. 1972. Individual differences in physiologic arousal and performance in sport parachutists. *Psychosom. Med.* 34:1–8
52. Fitzsimons, J. T. 1972. Thirst. *Physiol. Rev.* 52:468–561
53. Fitzsimons, J. T., Le Magnen, J. 1969. Eating as a regulatory control of drinking in the rat. *J. Comp. Physiol. Psychol.* 67:273–83
54. Furedy, J. J., Klajner, F. 1972. Preference for information about an unmodifiable but rewarding outcome. *J. Exp. Psychol.* 95:469–71
55. Gamzu, E., Schwartz, B. 1973. The maintenance of key pecking by stimulus-contingent and response-independent food presentation. *J. Exp. Anal. Behav.* 19:65–72
56. Gantt, W. H. 1972. Organ-system responsibility, homeostasis and the conditional reflex. *Cond. Reflex* 7:1–10
57. Gantt, W. H., Katzenelbogen, S., Loucks, R. B. 1937. An attempt to condition adrenalin hyperglycemia. *Bull. Johns Hopkins Hosp.* 60:400–11
58. Garcia, J., Koelling, R. A. 1966. Relation of cue to consequence in avoidance learning. *Psychon. Sci.* 4:123–24
59. Garcia, J., McGowan, B. K., Green, K. F. 1972. Biological constraints on conditioning. See Ref. 13, 3–27
60. Garner, W. R. 1962. *Uncertainty and Structure as Psychological Concepts.* New York: Wiley. 369 pp.
61. Gilbert, R. M. 1972. Variation and selection of behavior. See Ref. 62, 263–76
62. Gilbert, R. M., Millenson, J. R., Eds. 1972. *Reinforcement: Behavioral Analyses.* New York: Academic. 288 pp.
63. Green, L., Bouzas, A., Rachlin, H. 1972. Test of an electric-shock analog to illness-induced aversion. *Behav. Biol.* 7:513–18
64. Greenwood, F. C., Landon, J., Stamp, T. C. B. 1966. The plasma sugar, free fatty acid, cortisol, and growth hormone response to insulin. I. In control subjects. *J. Clin. Invest.* 45:429–36
65. Grings, W. W. 1973. Cognitive factors in electrodermal conditioning. *Psychol. Bull.* 79:200–10
66. Grossman, M. I., Stein, I. F. Jr. 1948. Vagotomy and the hunger-producing action of insulin in man. *J. Appl. Physiol.* 1:263–69
67. Hammond, K. R., Summers, D. A. 1972. Cognitive control. *Psychol. Rev.* 79:58–67
68. Hendry, D. P., Ed. 1969. *Conditioned Reinforcement.* Homewood, Ill.: Dorsey. 454 pp.
69. Ibid. Introduction, 1–33
70. Hershiser, D., Trapold, M. A. 1971. Preference for unsignaled over signaled direct reinforcement in the rat. *J. Comp. Physiol. Psychol.* 77:323–28
71. Hunt, W. A., Ed. 1970. *Learning Mechanisms in Smoking.* Chicago: Aldine. 237 pp.
72. Hutton, R. A., Woods, S. C., Makous, W. L. 1970. Conditioned hypoglycemia: pseudoconditioning controls. *J. Comp. Physiol. Psychol.* 71:198–201
73. Irwin, F. W. 1971. *Intentional Behavior and Motivation: A Cognitive Theory.* New York: Lippincott. 201 pp.
74. Jacobs, H. L., Sharma, K. N. 1969. Taste versus calories: sensory and metabolic signals in the control of food intake. *Ann NY Acad. Sci.* 157: 1084–1125
75. Jensen, G. D. 1963. Preference for bar pressing over "freeloading" as a function of number of rewarded presses. *J. Exp. Psychol.* 65:451–54
76. Jordan, H. A. 1969. Voluntary intragastric feeding: oral and gastric contributions to food intake and hunger in man. *J. Comp. Physiol. Psychol.* 68:498–506
77. Kavanau, J. L. 1967. Behavior of captive white-footed mice. *Science* 155: 1623–39
78. Kimble, G. A. 1971. Cognitive inhibition in classical conditioning. In *Essays in Neobehaviorism: A Memorial Volume to Kenneth W. Spence,* ed. H. H. Kendler, J. T. Spence, 69–87. New York: Appleton-Century-Crofts. 345 pp.
79. Kimble, G. A. 1973. Scientific psychology in transition. See Ref. 92, 1–19
80. Kutscher, C. 1966. Effect of hypertonic saline injections and water deprivation

on drinking, serum osmolality and gut water. *Physiol. Behav.* 1:259–68
81. LeMagnen, J. 1969. Peripheral and systemic actions of food in the caloric regulation of intake. *Ann. NY Acad. Sci.* 157:1126–57
82. Lenneberg, E. H. 1969. On explaining language. *Science* 164:635–43
83. Lieberman, D. A. 1972. Secondary reinforcement and information as determinants of observing behavior in monkeys (*Macaca mulatta*). *Learn. Motiv.* 3: 341–58
84. Lockhart, R. A. et al 1973. Classical conditioning and the cognitive processes: a symposium. *Psychophysiology* 10:74–122
85. Longstreth, L. E. 1972. A cognitive interpretation of secondary reinforcement. In *Nebraska Symposium on Motivation,* 1971, ed. J. K. Cole, 33–80. Lincoln: Univ. Nebraska Press. 304 pp.
86. Lovett, D., Goodchild, P., Booth, D. A. 1968. Depression of intake of nutrient by association of its odor with effects of insulin. *Psychon. Sci.* 11:27–28
87. MacDonald, L., Baron, A. 1973. A rate measure of the relative aversiveness of signalled vs unsignalled shock. *J. Exp. Anal. Behav.* 19:33–38
88. Macnamara, J. 1972. Cognitive basis of language learning in infants. *Psychol. Rev.* 79:1–13
89. Mahoney, M. J. 1972. Research issues in self-management. *Behav. Ther.* 3: 45–63
90. Mahoney, M. J., Bandura, A. 1972. Self-reinforcement in pigeons. *Learn. Motiv.* 3:293–303
91. McFarland, D. J. 1970. Recent developments in the study of feeding and drinking in animals. *J. Psychosom. Res.* 14:229–37
92. McGuigan, F. J., Lumsden, D. B., Eds. 1973. *Contemporary Approaches to Conditioning and Learning.* Washington: Winston. 321 pp.
93. Miller, N. E. 1969. Learning of visceral and glandular responses. *Science* 163: 434–45
94. Mineka, S. 1972. *Conditioned appetitive drives: some new evidence and a new theoretical status.* Presented at Eastern Psychol. Assoc. Meet., Boston
95. Mineka, S., Seligman, M. E. P., Hetrick, M., Zuelzer, K. 1972. Poisoning and conditioned drinking. *J. Comp. Physiol. Psychol.* 79:377–84
96. Neuringer, A. J. 1969. Animals respond for food in the presence of free food. *Science* 166:399–401
97. Ibid 1970. Many responses per food reward with free food present. 169:503–4
98. Nicolaïdis, S. 1969. Early systemic responses to orogastric stimulation in the regulation of food and water balance: functional and electrophysiological data. *Ann. NY Acad. Sci.* 157:1176–1203
99. Nisbett, R. E. 1972. Hunger, obesity, and the ventromedial hypothalamus. *Psychol. Rev.* 79:433–53
100. Penick, S. B., Filion, R., Fox, S., Stunkard, A. J. 1971. Behavior modification in the treatment of obesity. *Psychosom. Med.* 33:49–55
101. Perkins, C. C. Jr. 1968. An analysis of the concept of reinforcement. *Psychol. Rev.* 75:155–72
102. Razran, G. 1971. *Mind in Evolution: An East-West Synthesis of Learned Behavior and Cognition.* Boston: Houghton Mifflin. 430 pp.
103. Rescorla, R. A. 1972. Informational variables in Pavlovian conditioning. In *The Psychology of Learning and Motivation: Advances in Research and Theory,* ed. G. H. Bower, 6:1–46. New York: Academic. 312 pp.
104. Rescorla, R. A., Wagner, A. R. 1972. A theory of Pavlovian conditioning: variations in the effectiveness of reinforcement and nonreinforcement. See Ref. 13, 64–99
105. Revusky, S., Garcia, J. 1970. Learned associations over long delays. In *The Psychology of Learning and Motivation: Advances in Research and Theory,* ed. G. H. Bower, 4:1–84. New York: Academic. 339 pp.
106. Rozin, P., Kalat, J. W. 1971. Specific hungers and poison avoidance as adaptive specializations of learning. *Psychol. Rev.* 78:459–86
107. Saltz, E. 1971. *The Cognitive Bases of Human Learning.* Homewood, Ill.: Dorsey. 510 pp.
108. Salzinger, K. 1973. Inside the black box, with apologies to Pandora. A review of Ulric Neisser's *Cognitive Psychology. J. Exp. Anal. Behav.* 19:369–78
109. Schachter, S. 1971. *Emotion, Obesity, and Crime.* New York: Academic. 195 pp.
110. Schaub, R. E. 1969. Response-cue contingency and cue effectiveness. See Ref. 68, 342–56
111. Schwartz, B. 1972. The role of positive conditioned reinforcement in the maintenance of keypecking which prevents

delivery of primary reinforcement. *Psychon. Sci.* 28:277–78

112. Scrignar, C. B. 1971. Food as the reinforcer in the outpatient treatment of anorexia nervosa. *J. Behav. Ther. Exp. Psychiat.* 2:31–36
113. Segal, E. F. 1972. Induction and the provenance of operants. See Ref. 62, 1–34
114. Seligman, M. E. P. 1970. On the generality of the laws of learning. *Psychol. Rev.* 77:406–18
115. Seligman, M. E. P., Bravman, S., Radford, R. 1970. Drinking: discriminative conditioning in the rat. *Psychon. Sci.* 20:63–64
116. Seligman, M. E. P., Hager, J. L., Eds. 1972. *Biological Boundaries of Learning.* New York: Appleton-Century-Crofts. 480 pp.
117. Seligman, M. E. P., Ives, C. E., Ames, H., Mineka, S. 1970. Conditioned drinking and its failure to extinguish: avoidance, preparedness, or functional autonomy? *J. Comp. Physiol. Psychol.* 71:411–19
118. Seligman, M. E. P., Johnston, J. C. 1973. A cognitive theory of avoidance learning. See Ref. 92, 69–110
119. Seligman, M. E. P., Mineka, S., Fillit, H. 1971. Conditioned drinking produced by procaine, NaCl, and angiotensin. *J. Comp. Physiol. Psychol.* 77:110–21
120. Shettleworth, S. J. 1972. Constraints on learning. In *Advances in the Study of Behavior,* ed. D. S. Lehrman, R. A. Hinde, E. Shaw, 4:1–68. New York: Academic. 217 pp.
121. Shettleworth, S. J. 1972. Stimulus relevance in the control of drinking and conditioned fear responses in domestic chicks (*Gallus gallus*). *J. Comp. Physiol. Psychol.* 80:175–98
122. Siegel, S. 1972. Conditioning of insulin-induced glycemia. *J. Comp. Physiol. Psychol.* 78:233–41
123. Siegel, S., Nettleton, N. 1970. Conditioning of insulin-induced hyperphagia. *J. Comp. Physiol. Psychol.* 72:390–93
124. Silverstein, A. 1972. Secondary reinforcement in infants. *J. Exp. Child Psychol.* 13:138–44
125. Singh, D. 1970. Preference for bar pressing to obtain reward over freeloading in rats and children. *J. Comp. Physiol. Psychol.* 73:320–27
126. Ibid 1972. Preference for mode of obtaining reinforcement in rats with lesions in septal or ventromedial hypothalamic area. 80:259–68
127. Singh, D., Query, W. T. 1971. Preference for work over "freeloading" in children. *Psychon. Sci.* 24:77–79
128. Smith, T. D. 1972. Development of tokens as secondary reinforcers. *J. Exp. Child Psychol.* 14:133–38
129. Solomon, R. L., Corbit, J. D. 1973. An opponent-process theory of motivation: II. Cigarette addiction. *J. Abnorm. Psychol.* 81:158–71
130. Solomon, R. L., Wynne, L. C. 1954. Traumatic avoidance learning: the principles of anxiety conservation and partial irreversibilty. *Psychol. Rev.* 61:353–85
131. Spatz, C., Jones, S. D. 1971. Starvation anorexia as an explanation of "self-starvation" of rats living in activity wheels. *J. Comp. Physiol. Psychol.* 77:313–17
132. Staddon, J. E. R., Simmelhag, V. L. 1971. The "superstition" experiment: a reexamination of its implications for the principles of adaptive behavior. *Psychol. Rev.* 78:3–43
133. Stellar, E. 1967. Hunger in man: comparative and physiological studies. *Am. Psychol.* 22:105–17
134. Stolz, S. B., Lott, D. F. 1964. Establishment in rats of a persistent response producing a net loss of reinforcement. *J. Comp. Physiol. Psychol.* 57:147–49
135. Taylor, G. T. 1972. A limitation of the contrafreeloading phenomenon. *Psychon. Sci.* 29:173–74
136. Waddell, T. R., Leander, J. D., Webbe, F. M., Malagodi, E. F. 1972. Schedule interactions in second-order fixed-interval (fixed-ratio) schedules of token reinforcement. *Learn. Motiv.* 3:91–100
137. Walike, B. C., Jordan, H. A., Stellar, E. 1969. Preloading and the regulation of food intake in man. *J. Comp. Physiol. Psychol.* 68:327–33
138. Wayner, M. J., Carey, R. J. 1973. Basic drives. *Ann. Rev. Psychol.* 24:53–80
139. Wayner, M. J., Cott, A. 1971. Conditioned drinking and the effects of saccharin on its recovery after lateral hypothalamic lesions. *Physiol. Behav.* 7:201–6
140. Wayner, M. J. Jr., Emmers, R. 1959. A test of the thirst-deprivation hypothesis in the hooded rat. *J. Comp. Physiol. Psychol.* 52:112–15
141. Wayner, M. J., Gawronski, D., Mueller, R. 1967. Effects of procaine-HCl on the salt arousal of drinking. *Physiol. Behav.* 2:249–54
142. Wike, E. L. 1970. Secondary reinforcement: some research and theoretical issues. In *Nebraska Symposium on*

Motivation, 1969, ed. W. J. Arnold, D. Levine, 39–84. Lincoln: Univ. Nebraska Press. 334 pp.
143. Wilcoxon, H. C., Dragoin, W. B., Kral, P. A. 1971. Illness-induced aversions in rat and quail: relative salience of visual and gustatory cues. *Science* 171:826–28
144. Williams, D. R., Williams H. 1969. Auto-maintenance in the pigeon: sustained pecking despite contingent nonreinforcement. *J. Exp. Anal. Behav.* 12:511–20
145. Wilton, R. N. 1972. The role of information in the emission of observing responses and partial reinforcement acquisition phenomena. *Learn. Motiv.* 3:479–99
146. Wilton, R. N., Clements, R. O. 1971. Observing responses and informative stimuli. *J. Exp. Anal. Behav.* 15:199–204
147. Ibid. The role of information in the emission of observing responses: a test of two hypotheses. 16:161–66
148. Woods, S., Makous, W., Hutton, A. 1968. A new technique for conditioned hypoglycemia. *Psychon. Sci.* 10:389–90
149. Woods, S. C., Makous, W., Hutton, R. A. 1969. Temporal parameters of conditioned hypoglycemia. *J. Comp. Physiol. Psychol.* 69:301–7
150. Woods, S. C., Shogren, R. E. Jr. 1972. Glycemic responses following conditioning with different doses of insulin in rats. *J. Comp. Physiol. Psychol.* 81: 220–25
151. Wooley, O. W., Wooley, S. C., Dunham, R. B. 1972. Can calories be perceived and do they affect hunger in obese and nonobese humans? *J. Comp. Physiol. Psychol.* 80:250–58
152. Wooley, S. C. 1972. Physiologic versus cognitive factors in short term food regulation in the obese and nonobese. *Psychosom. Med.* 34:62–68
153. Wyckoff, L. B. Jr. 1952. The role of observing responses in discrimination learning. Part 1. *Psychol. Rev.* 59: 431–42
154. Ibid 1959. Toward a quantitative theory of secondary reinforcement. 66:68–78
155. Zahorik, D. M. 1972. Conditioned physiological changes associated with learned aversions to tastes paired with thiamine deficiency in the rat. *J. Comp. Physiol. Psychol.* 79:189–200
156. Zahorik, D. M., Maier, S. F. 1969. Appetitive conditioning with recovery from thiamine deficiency as the unconditioned stimulus. *Psychon. Sci.* 17: 309–10

ANIMAL LEARNING—VISCERAL AND AUTONOMIC CONDITIONING ❖212

Alan H. Harris and Joseph V. Brady[1]
The Johns Hopkins University School of Medicine, Baltimore, Maryland

This chapter will be concerned with the effects of behavioral conditioning procedures, both classical and instrumental, upon physiological response measures commonly referred to as "visceral" and autonomic (e.g. heart rate, blood pressure, gastric motility). Within this general framework, the laboratory animal research to be reviewed can be divided into three broad investigative categories based upon the relationship between the physiological measures and the conditioning procedures. In the first *Classical Autonomic Conditioning* category, the physiological event that is conditioned appears initially as an unconditioned response (e.g. salivation) to an unconditioned stimulus (e.g. food) and is subsequently observed to occur (though not necessarily in identical form) during presentation of a conditioned stimulus (e.g. bell) which has been paired repeatedly with the unconditioned stimulus. The second *Concurrent Autonomic Conditioning* category is defined by experimental approaches that depend primarily upon operant conditioning procedures to establish and maintain ongoing performances (e.g. lever pressing) while concurrently measuring physiological changes (e.g. hormone elevations) which show systematic relationships to the conditioned instrumental behavior. And in the third *Instrumental Autonomic Conditioning* category, an essential feature of the procedure emphasizes a contingency relationship between antecedent physiological changes (e.g. heart rate increase) and experimentally programmed environmental consequences (e. g. food delivery and/or shock avoidance).

Over the past decade, animal learning studies within the framework of these three autonomic conditioning paradigms clearly have focused more upon some physiological response systems (e. g. cardiovascular) than others (e.g. gastrointestinal), and this differential emphasis will of necessity be reflected in the ensuing categorical review. To a considerable extent, this uneven distribution of physiological measures

[1]We gratefully acknowledge the assistance of Mrs. Joan Harris in the preparation of this chapter. This work was supported in part by Grant No. HE-06945 from the National Heart and Lung Institute.

is a function of the technological and methodological developments which have paced the emergence of a scientifically operational laboratory psychophysiology. In this regard it is appropriate to acknowledge at least some of the major innovations and refinements upon which this burgeoning research domain depends. Particularly noteworthy have been the technical advances in the recording and measurement of heart rate (30, 48, 63, 87, 98, 147, 193, 202, 207), blood pressure (74, 107, 120, 146, 149, 201, 245, 264), hormone levels (166), and electromyographic activity (77, 118) in both restrained and free-moving animals. As these and other psychophysiological developments (50) have increased the ease and accessibility of visceral and autonomic measurement techniques, an ever-broadening range of biological events have been exposed to experimental scrutiny in relationship to behavioral conditioning procedures.

CLASSICAL AUTONOMIC CONDITIONING

The historical roots of an extensive research literature on classical autonomic conditioning can be traced at least as far back as the early studies of Pavlov and Sherrington before the turn of the century. Numerous volumes have been devoted to a broad range of psychophysiological experiments which document the central role of such conditioning processes in the adaptations and adjustments of the internal environment (1, 17, 81, 140, 195, 196, 204, 208). Despite this illustrious heritage, the past decade has produced a host of research reports which appear to justify few generalizations about the classical conditioning of autonomic responses and contribute more to the complexity of the process than to its clarification. This confusing state of affairs is nowhere more evident than in the veritable tidal wave of classical cardiac conditioning studies which have all but inundated the literature in this once-pristine area of experimental inquiry.

Shearn's 1961 answer to his own rhetorical question "Can the heart learn?" provided convincing evidence of the wide-ranging variability in the *form* (i.e. acceleration or deceleration) of the classically conditioned heart rate response (226). A most charitable characterization of the research on this problem over the past 10 years would represent the reported studies as an attempt to examine the conditions under which such form variations are seen to occur. In this regard, both aversive (e.g. electric shock UCS) and appetitive (e.g. food UCS) cardiac conditioning experiments have confirmed that all possible outcomes can be observed under some conditions. Conditioned cardiac responses to a stimulus paired with shock continue to be reported as an acceleration in heart rate by some authors (29, 51, 86, 136, 182, 254) and as a deceleration in heart rate by others (64, 96, 125, 194, 215, 248). Similar variability in the form of the conditioned cardiac response have been reported (222) with a procedure involving tone-milk pairings which produce both accelerative and decelerative changes in heart rate within experimental sessions, though the occurrence of the conditioned response (regardless of its form) was found to be a reliable predictor of subsequent consummatory behavior. There is, of course, some basis in these conflicting reports for considering the role of species differences (i.e. between rodents, carnivores, and primates), but both increases and decreases have been reported within the same species by investigators using essentially the same procedures (21, 31, 168, 176, 182, 254) and even with the same animal (29, 160, 222).

In this latter regard, several authors (82, 205, 206, 222, 234, 236, 266) using several different species (i.e. laboratory rats, dogs, and monkeys) and CS durations (i.e. 12–60 seconds) have all reported a characteristically biphasic cardiac response pattern which emerges after repeated CS-UCS pairings. The form in which this pattern has been observed is that of an early heart rate acceleration (during the initial seconds of the CS) followed by a deceleration in heart rate during the terminal seconds of the CS interval before UCS presentation. On a different time scale, the experiments reported by Black & Black (29) using a tone-shock pairing procedure with rats confirmed this biphasic variation in the form of the conditioned cardiac response over successive trials, the heart rate change appearing in decelerative form during early trials and developing into an accelerative CR during later trials. To some extent at least, these results suggest the possibility that separable response components (e.g. "orienting") may participate differentially in the temporal course of cardiac conditioning (135), or that extraneous procedural factors (e.g. "effect of person") involving ongoing subject-experimenter interactions (161, 162) may influence the emergent form of the conditioned cardiac response (13).

Although the results of some studies (169, 269) have indicated that the parametric dimensions of the UCS (e.g. shock intensity) may account, at least in part, for some of the conditioned cardiac response variability, others (56, 153) suggest that the direction of the conditioned cardiac rate change is independent of UCS (electric shock) intensity. The most constructive methodological suggestion to emerge from recent experimental reports may be the attempt by Lynch (160) to confront the variability in heart rate as a lawful datum in providing a functional description of the cardiac classical conditioning process. With dogs given tone-shock pairings, heart rate *variability* was found to be consistently decreased during tone presentations as compared to non-tone periods, the day-to-day variability measures proving to be a more reliable index of cardiac conditioning than the heart rate per se, which showed no systematic change over the succession of conditioning trials.

Several cardiac conditioning studies over the past decade have explored the application of the *Law of Initial Values* (LIV) as a factor in determining the effects of classical autonomic conditioning procedures. In at least three reports (26, 206, 236) some support was provided for a dependence of CR magnitude upon pre-CS heart rate level, an inverse relationship having been observed between the classically conditioned heart rate change and the cardiac rate during the time interval immediately preceding the CS presentation. Controlling the pre-CS heart rate with a cardiac pacemaker, however, did not reveal systematic relationships between the classically conditiond heart rate response and the paced pre-CS heart rate level (236), suggesting that the interactions which define LIV effects reflect more the participation of central than peripheral factors. A more recent study by Downer & Thompson (78), on the other hand, with four different primate species (i.e. baboons, rhesus monkeys, spider monkeys, and squirrel monkeys) failed to confirm the LIV effects which have been so well documented in cardiovascular experiments with humans (126, 150), and reiterated in yet another dimension the conflicts and confusions which characterize this classical autonomic conditioning field.

Trace and *Delay* procedures of long-standing interest have continued to receive experimental attention in classical cardiac conditioning studies concerned with the relative power of these alternative paradigms. Several reports based upon both appetitive (e.g. light-food pairings) conditioning procedures (222) and aversive (e.g. tone-shock pairings) conditioning procedures (95, 248) have confirmed the superiority of the delay procedure over the trace procedure with regard to the magnitude and reliability of the classically conditioned heart rate response. The differences between the two procedures do appear to be attenuated, however, in aversive classical conditioning experiments as the intensity of the UCS (i.e. shock) is increased (95, 248).

Procedural parameters related to *trial frequency* and *reinforcement schedule* (i.e. UCS intermittency) have also continued to receive experimental attention as determinants of classically conditioned cardiac response magnitude and durability. Single-trial conditioning has been reported (182) in dogs with one tone-shock pairing producing heart rate changes in response to tone presentations which persisted over extended time intervals and during repeated extinction trials. Partial reinforcement effects upon resistance to extinction (19, 183) have generally been confirmed in more recent studies (93, 94, 96, 97, 123, 253), although in at least one instance (252) no difference was found in this regard between partial and continuous reinforcement conditions. Similarly, classically conditioned cardiac accelerative responses in rhesus monkeys have been reported to show no difference between partial and continuous reinforcement procedures, though discrimination of a negative (non-shocked) stimulus (CS–) appears to be more readily established when the CS+ is continuously reinforced (176).

Such *generalization* and *discrimination* effects have been investigated in several other classical cardiac conditioning studies over the past decade with the usual range of form and magnitude divergencies in evidence. To some extent at least, procedural variables appear to account for recurrent inconsistencies in the findings from different studies, and the relationship between CS+ (i.e. CS presentations followed by the UCS) and CS– (i.e. CS presentations not followed by the UCS) trials emerges as an important determinant of the reported outcomes with the conditioned cardiac response to the CS+ significantly greater than to the CS– in all cases (21, 64, 83, 136, 176, 191, 194, 234, 246). An additional study (266), however, appeared to identify discrimination difficulty as a parameter influencing the magnitude of the conditioned heart rate response regardless of the training procedure used, while another (83) reported that blood pressure discriminations were less stable than heart rate discriminations to the same CS+ and CS–.

Several recent reports have also described both correlated and uncorrelated changes in *other circulatory measures* during classical conditioning based, for the most part, upon traditional tone-shock pairings. Blood pressure (83, 88, 156, 181, 198, 268), blood flow (198), catecholamine levels (88), and peripheral vasomotor changes (110, 111) have all been shown to be affected by such classical conditioning procedures, though agreement is somewhat less than unanimous with regard to differentiation of the "orienting" or "startle" components from the "true" conditioned autonomic response pattern (135). The results of one of these studies (181), however, involving determinations made with dogs under both curarized and non-curarized conditions, suggest at least some degree of independence between such classically conditioned cardiovascular responses on the one hand and respiratory and skeletal muscle changes on the other.

Classically conditioned cardiac *response mechanisms* have been recurrently analyzed with the aid of neurophysiological and neuropharmacological research techniques for selectively evaluating the role of central and peripheral factors in the establishment and maintenance of such heart rate changes. Several studies (228, 249, 254) have shown, for example, that direct stimulation of the brain can serve effectively as a UCS for cardiac conditioning, though direct peripheral stimulation of the ventricular myocardium has been reported (200) ineffective as a UCS for the classical conditioning of extrasystoles. "Centrally mediated" extrasystoles, however, apparently can be conditioned (197, 199). Additional evidence for the central role of selective brain mechanisms in the mediation of cardiovascular conditioning effects has also been provided by ablation studies (79, 80) implicating both the ventromedial and dorsolateral tegmentum in control of the classically conditioned heart rate response. Neuropharmacological analysis of classical cardiac conditioning has also confirmed the role of central neural influences in the control of such heart rate changes, Hein (119) having found that the conditioned cardiac response was blocked by atropine but not by succinylcholine-induced muscle paralysis. Blockade of the sympathetic innervation has also been found to produce only a small reduction in the conditioned heart rate response even though a striking reduction in cardiac contractility change follows such sympathetic blockade (128). In a related series of studies, Schneiderman et al (216, 217) have analyzed the effects of alpha-adrenergic and cholinergic blockade upon both conditioned and unconditioned cardiovascular responses (e.e. blood pressure and heart rate) in the albino rabbit. Although the results of these experiments showed clearly that blood pressure changes contributed importantly to both conditioned and unconditioned heart rate changes, it was also demonstrated that conditioned cardiac responses could occur in the absence of conditioned blood pressure changes.

The documented role of such regulatory homeostatic mechanisms in the control of classically conditioned cardiovascular responses would seem to require that a broader biological perspective be maintained with regard to the range of *interacting visceral and somatic systems* which in concert provide for the adjustments and adaptations of the internal environment. Within this context, the relationship between heart rate and other visceral and motor components of a "total" classically conditioned response has been the primary focus of several researchers (21, 28, 57, 61, 64, 83, 99, 119, 129, 159, 184–186, 190, 194, 209, 234, 238, 243, 250, 267, 268, 270). Not unexpectedly, something less than a completely consistent account of these complex interactions appears to emerge, with some experimental reports emphasizing the independent variations of multiple interacting systems (21, 28, 61, 64, 83, 129, 190, 194, 234, 238, 250, 267, 270), while others focus upon the interdependent correlations between response measures (57, 99, 119, 159, 184–186, 209, 268). Probably the most parsimonious view of this obviously complex process would recognize that all possible combinations and permutations can and do occur under some circumstances, and that it remains a continuing research challenge to delineate and define the range of independent conditions under which such classical autonomic learning is established.

CONCURRENT AUTONOMIC CONDITIONING

Though lacking the long-standing and prestigious laboratory background enjoyed by Classical Autonomic Conditioning, an active and productive research interest in the measurement of performance-related concurrent autonomic conditioning effects has emerged over the past several decades. Significantly, this investigative emphasis can be seen to bear a close relationship to the development of instrumental or operant learning analysis techniques which focus more directly upon behavioral interactions with the external environment. In an initial review of the area, Brady (34) surveyed several groups of laboratory studies which at the time appeared to define and delineate such research applications as they related to the experimental production of altered physiological states. For the most part, the emphasis upon endocrine, cardiovascular, and gastrointestinal changes that was apparent in those early studies has continued to characterize investigative progress over the past decade. In this regard, significant methodological advances related particularly to the analysis of hormone response patterns (166) and the measurement and recording of blood pressure (201, 245, 264) have contributed importantly to these developments. In addition, increasing emphasis upon enduringly chronic preparations (33, 90, 102, 121) has provided for more extended observation and experimental manipulation. Aversive behavioral control procedures of established effectiveness, including conditioned suppression (85) and free-operant avoidance (259), have continued to receive increasing psychophysiological attention, and a progressively more refined analysis of the observed interactions is reflected in major groups of concurrent conditioning studies concerned with endocrine and cardiovascular changes on the one hand, and gastrointestinal effects on the other.

Endocrine and Cardiovascular Changes

Systematic increases in plasma 17-hydroxycorticosteroid (17-OH-CS) levels have now been described, for example, in relationship to the acquisition of *conditioned suppression* (i.e. "conditioned emotional response" or CER) with monkeys (167), and the course of cardiovascular changes during the development and maintenance of such conditioned suppression has also been extensively studied in chronically catheterized primates with monitoring of heart rate and both systolic and diastolic blood pressure (45). Dramatic reversals in both the direction and magnitude of such blood pressure and heart rate changes were observed to occur in response to repeated clicker-shock pairings. Initially the development of conditioned behavioral suppression over the first 8 to 10 trials for all 5 rhesus monkeys in the study was accompanied by a consistent and systematic decrease in both heart rate and blood pressure in response to the 3-minute clicker presentations. Continued daily pairings of clicker and shock superimposed upon the lever-pressing performance, however, produced abrupt and sustained reversals in both the direction and magnitude of the cardiovascular response. Significantly, these changes were observed to persist as large magnitude increases in heart rate and both systolic and diastolic blood pressure in response to the behaviorally suppressing clicker presentations for from 50 to 100 daily conditioning trials. The results were interpreted as reflecting the differential temporal development of the early CER instrumental performance suppression (with the initial cardiovascular "suppression" related to decreases in motor activity during the clicker) followed by the later-appearing "conditioned cardiac respondent" component as sustained cardiovascular activation during clicker presentations. It is also of some interest to contrast the form of these concurrent biphasic cardiovascular changes with the biphasic form of the classically conditioned heart rate response described in the first section of this review. To some extent at least, these several findings provide a basis for explaining the recurrent conflicting reports (62, 64, 65, 180, 194, 233, 234, 237, 240, 243, 265) regarding CER effects upon the cardiovascular system and point conspicuously to the temporal course over which some experimental observations are made as a critical source of contributory variance. More importantly, the results of these studies seem to argue for "causal independence" of the separable but interacting physiological and behavioral responses defining such "emotional" conditioning.

The extended analysis of behaviorally induced endocrine and cardiovascular changes over the past decade has focused even more intensively upon *conditioned avoidance* models, predominantly of the free-operant or Sidman variety (229). In addition to multiple reconfirmations (33, 35) of the twofold to fourfold elevations in 17-OH-CS levels associated with even relatively brief, shock-free experimental exposures to this performance requirement, marked differences in the hormone response have been observed (167) when the free-operant avoidance procedure includes a discriminable exteroceptive warning signal or when "free" shocks are superimposed upon the performance baseline. Significantly, the corticosteroid response was consistently reduced during "discriminated" avoidance sessions including an exteroceptive auditory stimulus presented 5 seconds before shock whenever 15 seconds had elapsed since a previous response, though removal of the "warning signal" resulted in the immediate reappearance of the steroid elevations. Conversely, superimposing "free" or unavoidable shocks upon a well-established avoidance performance without a "warning signal" has been reported to produce more than a 100% increase over the elevated corticosteroid levels observed during the regular nondiscriminated Sidman avoidance procedure.

Significant advances have also been made during the past decade in determining the endocrine and cardiovascular consequences of free-operant avoidance performance requirements during long-term studies over months and even years. A report by Brady (33), for example, describes the effects of repeated exposure to continuous 72-hour avoidance over periods up to, and in some cases exceeding, one year upon patterns of thyroid, gonadal, and adrenal hormone secretion in a series of five chair-restrained rhesus monkeys. Two of the five monkeys participated in the 72-

hour avoidance experiment on six separate occasions over a 6-month period with an interval of approximately 4 weeks between each exposure. The remaining three animals performed on a schedule which repeatedly programmed 72-hour avoidance cycles followed by 96-hour nonavoidance or "rest" cycles (3 days "on" and 4 days "off") for periods up to and exceeding one year.

The two animals exposed to repeated 72-hour avoidance at monthly intervals for 6 months showed a progressively increasing lever-pressing response rate with each of the six successive 72-hour avoidance sessions. In contrast, shock frequencies over this same period showed a sharp decline within the first two 72-hour avoidance sessions and remained at a stable low level for the remaining four 72-hour avoidance cycles. Hormone changes related to the repeated 72-hour avoidance cycles showed consistent and replicable patterns over the 6-month experimental period for both animals. During the initial experimental sessions both monkeys showed approximately threefold elevations in 17-OH-CS levels during 72-hour avoidance and returned to near baseline levels about 6 days afterwards. The remaining four monthly experiments were characterized by substantial though diminished steroid responses (approximately twofold elevations in 17-OH-CS levels) during avoidance, with essentially the same 6-day period required for recovery of basal levels. Significant changes related to the extended avoidance performance were also observed in catecholamine, gonadal, and thyroid hormone levels, with recovery cycles extending in some instances (thyroid) for 3 weeks following the 72-hour avoidance period. A detailed experimental and interpretive analysis of such multiple hormone changes induced by exposure to the 72-hour Sidman procedure has been provided in an exhaustive multiauthored monograph (166) describing this most systematic laboratory study series yet to appear in the psychoendocrine literature.

The three remaining monkeys described in the Brady (33) report as performing on the 3 days "on," 4 days "off" avoidance schedule showed an initial increase in lever-pressing response rates for approximately the first 10 avoidance sessions similar to that seen with the two animals described above. By approximately the 20th weekly session with these animals, however, lever-pressing response rates during the 72-hour avoidance period had decreased to a value well below that observed during the initial avoidance sessions, and the performance tended to stabilize at this new low level for the ensuing weeks of the experiment. In contrast, shock frequencies for all animals quickly approximated a stable low level within the first two or three exposures to the avoidance schedule and seldom exceeded a rate of two shocks per hour for the remainder of the experiment. The initial 72-hour avoidance sessions were also characterized by significant elevations in 17-OH-CS levels. In the succeeding weeks, 17-OH-CS levels gradually declined but rose again by the 30th week. The general pattern obtained was replicated with all three animals with only minor variations, though the change in responsivity of the pituitary-adrenal system to the avoidance stress with continued exposure to this procedure over extended time periods was perhaps the most consistent and striking observation. These findings are somewhat at variance with the repeated observations made in many previous acute studies (33, 35, 167) of a close positive relationship between steroid elevations and avoidance performance, and indicate that continued exposure to this repeated performance requirement on the time schedule programmed in this experiment produces an apparent dissociation between the avoidance performance and the 17-OH-CS response. Although a definitive analysis of such interactions is not possible on the basis of these data alone, a critical role of the temporal parameters (work-rest cycles) is clearly indicated, and the relationship of these phasic hormone changes to the previously described classical and concurrent cardiovascular conditioning effects would seem to require detailed investigation.

A trend toward more extended periods of experimental observation and measurement has been apparent also in concurrent avoidance studies focusing upon cardiovascular changes, particularly in primates. Both rhesus (102) and squirrel monkeys (121) have been reported to develop hypertensive blood pressure levels with recurrent exposure to free-operant avoidance requirements for periods up to and exceeding 12 months. Chair-restrained baboons (91) performing on a discrete-trial fixed ratio instrumental escape-avoidance procedure, however, were not found to maintain elevated blood presure levels over the year or more during which they participated in the study (90). Indeed, the baboons in this extended study did show substantial pressure increases during the actual escape-avoidance performance intervals within the daily experimental sessions, and there were some periods during the first several months on the program which were characterized by general elevations in both blood pressure and heart rate. But the chronically high cardiac output levels (i.e. heart rate) maintained apparently by the extended exposure to work-activity requirements of the ratio escape-avoidance schedule in this study suggest procedural differences which may account, at least in part, for the long-term return to normotensive pressure levels not recovered in previous studies (102, 121) with exposures of comparable duration to less demanding free-operant avoidance requirements.

A recent series of studies on cardiovascular changes associated with operant avoidance procedures (7–12) provides further evidence which is at least consistent with the hypothesized relationship between muscle activity and the dynamic interplay between cardiac output and peripheral resistance in the behavioral pathogenesis of hypertensive conditions. The focus of these studies with dogs has been upon continuous monitoring of blood pressure and heart rate during free-operant (panel press) shock avoidance and, significantly, during a fixed-interval *pre-avoidance* period systematically programmed to precede the required avoidance performance. Under these conditions a unique divergence between heart rate and blood pressure changes was observed during pre-avoidance intervals up to 15 hours in length, with virtually all animals showing a characteristic systolic and diastolic increase and either a decrease or no change in heart rate. Comparisons involving similar performance requirements on a variable interval food reinforcement schedule revealed a markedly different pre-performance cardiovascular pattern characterized by systematic increases in both heart rate and blood pressure. And this differential "preparatory" pattern was confirmed both between individual animals maintained separately on each of the procedures and "within" the same animal alternately performing on the avoidance and food reinforcement schedule. Moreover, direct measurements of cardiac output in dogs prepared with aortic flow probes during exposure to the avoidance program confirmed that the pre-avoidance pressure changes were attributable to increased peripheral resistance while the pressure increases during the avoidance performance per se occurred as the peripheral resistance was actually observed to decrease and the cardiac output increased markedly. Additional studies involving beta-adrenergic blockade with the drug propranolol during the same experimental procedure, however, clearly showed that peripheral resistance levels do increase to maintain elevated pressure levels during avoidance when drug-induced heart rate reductions produce decreases in cardiac output (10).

The results of these experiments establish firm relationships between a broad range of endocrine and cardiovascular response processes and free-operant behavioral performances. Both general and specific support for these findings have now been provided by numerous published reports with rodents, carnivores, and primates (15, 20, 27, 35–39, 41–44, 46, 53, 54, 58, 101, 103–106, 109, 113, 114, 122, 124, 130, 132, 139, 145, 151, 154, 155, 163, 165, 175, 177, 179, 239, 241, 242, 244, 251, 261). In many respects, the changes in absolute levels of selected hormones and autonomic activity can be viewed as reflecting relatively undifferentiated consequences of arousal states associated with behavioral responses under aversive conditions. The definite temporal course of visceral and steroid changes under such conditions and the quantitative nature of the relationship between degree of behavioral involvement and level of physiological response have been well documented. In addition, the critical role of an organism's behavioral history in determining the nature and extent of autonomic-endocrine response to performance situations has been convincingly demonstrated. Clearly, however, the most meaningful dimension for hormone and visceral analysis in relationship to more chronic behavioral interactions would appear to be the broader patterning or balance of secretory and visceral changes in many interdependent autonomic and endocrine systems which in concert regulate metabolic events. The extensive and prolonged participation of these fundamental systems in behavioral interactions suggests a relationship between such physiological activity and the more durable consequences of performances under aversive control. Indeed, the differentiation of such autonomic-endocrine response patterns in relationship to the historical and situational aspects of behavioral events may well provide a first approximate step in the direction of identifying distinguishable intraorganismic consequences associated with both episodic and persistent behavioral interactions.

Gastrointestinal Effects

While the obvious constraints imposed upon laboratory studies of behaviorally induced somatic changes have continued to limit the range of experimental activity in this general area over the past decade, the recent research literature does reflect an abiding concern with concurrent conditioning effects involving the gastrointestinal system (2, 235). Of particular interest would seem to be the rather prominent controversy over the factors that influence the incidence of peptic ulcers in rodents and primates under *aversive behavioral control.* Some further support for the efficacy of *"conflict"* and related conditioning procedures in the production of gastric lesions in laboratory rats has been provided by studies focusing upon a variety of social-psychological and physiological parameters (158, 210–214), but replication and confirmation of the reported relationships continue to present problems (3, 4, 189). Similarly, recurrent descriptions of *avoidance conditioning* effects upon the gastrointestinal system have characteristically presented something less than a consistent picture with regard specifically to the conditions under which erosions of the gastric mucosa are most likely to occur. The reported incidence of peptic ulcers in rhesus monkeys intermittently exposed to a free-operant shock-avoidance procedure (47) has proved difficult to repeat under some laboratory conditions (100), including those under which the study originated (32). Additionally, several investigations with laboratory rats on escape-avoidance procedures have failed to find an incidence of gastric lesions in experimental animals which exceeded that of controls, and in some instances yoked control animals receiving unavoidable shocks alone showed a greater degree of ulceration than their avoiding partners (178, 192, 256).

To some extent a clarification and at least partial reconcilation of these apparently conflicting developments in the delineation of behavioral conditioning effects upon the gastrointestinal system has been suggested by Weiss in a systematic series of published experimental reports from the Rockefeller University (255–258). Starting with the observation that laboratory rats receiving intermittent tail shock following presentation of a 10-second beeping tone developed significantly less gastric ulceration than animals receiving the same shock without the "predictability" provided by the pre-aversive "warning" stimulus, Weiss examined the effects of adding an operant escape-avoidance ("coping") panel-press to the procedure. Under these conditions markedly fewer gastric lesions were found in the experimental animals when compared with "helpless" controls similarly exposed to warning signals and shocks (one per minute for 21 hours) but without escape-avoidance "coping." When the interactions between warning signals and the escape-avoindance responses were tested in a subsequent experiment involving groups differentiating between two types of pre-aversive stimuli ("beeping" tone and an "added clock"), presence or absence of escape-avoidance wheel-turning, and appropriate "yoked" controls, the results provided Weiss with a basis for proposing a "theory" to reconcile the apparent contradictions between the rat and monkey studies. While the outcome of this rather mammoth 180-rat experiment confirmed the prepotence of the operant escape-avoidance conditioning in reducing the incidence of ulcers, the addition of a warning signal to the procedure was found to attenuate the development of gastric pathology even further. It is of some interest to note that a similar warning stimulus procedure has been found to reduce the steroid response to operant avoidance performance requirements in the monkey (167).

In Weiss' view, these findings indicate that the incidence of peptic ulcers may be a function of the interaction between strength of the escape-avoidance performance (i.e. the frequency of "coping" responses) and the probability of discriminable response-contingent signals associated with the absence of aversive stimuli (i.e. "feedback" about shock-free conditions). Within the framework of this interpretive analysis, the incidence of peptic ulcers in free-operant avoidance monkeys would be accounted for in terms of a high response frequency in the absence of warning stimuli and the relatively low "feedback" discriminability of "safe" signals produced by those responses. The yoked-control monkeys, in contrast, characteristically emitted "avoidance" responses only infrequently, received only a few shocks well distributed in time (due to the high performance rates of the experimental animals), and were found to be free of gastrointestinal pathology. Some further confirmation of this formulation has been provided by Weiss in a subsequent series of experimental manipulations which increased the frequency of ulcers in avoidance rats punished with shock for responding, and decreased the incidence of ulcers in animals producing a brief tone with each shock-postponing panel-press (257, 258).

It is perhaps worth noting (though a bit out of place in the "systems" organization of this section) that Weiss and his colleagues at the Rockefeller University have also found hormonal and body weight changes which reflect the interactions suggested by the ulcer studies, and that levels of brain norepinephrine are increased in escape-avoidance animals and decreased in nonperforming ("helpless") shocked rats (259–261).

INSTRUMENTAL AUTONOMIC CONDITIONING

Animal studies concerned with the experimental analysis of instrumental autonomic conditioning represent a relatively recent development in the visceral learning field, with laboratory roots originating in the work of Neal Miller and his students at Yale in the mid-1960s. Indeed, several earlier reports with human subjects (60, 108, 131, 141, 143, 157, 208, 224, 227) had foretold of such "operant" learning effects involving visceral and autonomic processes, and an extensive literature on "voluntary" physiological control by Yoga meditation and breathing techniques (5, 6, 14, 262, 263) has long been available. But the experimental analysis of such instrumental autonomic conditioning effects in the animal laboratory has clearly activated a new research era in the investigation and application of such "visceral learning" phenomena.

The earliest reported animal learning experiments on instrumental autonomic conditioning involved an attempt by Miller & Carmona (172) to change the rate of *salivation* in a water-deprived dog by operantly reinforcing both increases and decreases in this antecedent autonomic response with a contingent environmental consequence (i.e. water reward). Although the results of this study showed clearly that such autonomic responses could be operantly controlled, attention was focused upon the possible role of skeletal muscle activity as a "mediator" of the observed visceral changes. Since the curarization technique used to control such skeletal muscle mediation produced direct effects upon salivation, an experiment by Trowill (247) explored the operant control of *heart rate* in curarized laboratory rats using rewarding electrical brain stimulation (medial forebrain bundle at the level of the posterior hypothalamus) as a contingent reinforcing consequence. Although the actual changes were small, both increases and decreases in heart rate were successfully conditioned. A subsequent study by Miller & DiCara (173) showed that the magnitude of the instrumentally conditioned heart rate response could be influenced dramatically (producing changes approximating 20% of basal values) by a "shaping" procedure which required the animals to meet a progressively more difficult criterion in order to obtain the rewarding brain stimulation. In addition, this experiment also demonstrated that such operantly conditioned autonomic changes could be brought under discriminative control of the specific stimulus complex which provided the occasion for reinforcement of either the heart rate raising or lowering response. In a further confirmation of this instrumental heart rate conditioning effect, Hothersall & Brener (127), using curarized rats and electrical brain stimulation reward, incorporated a feedback light whenever the prescribed criterion was met, and extended their investigation to include a demonstration of operant extinction when the instrumentally conditioned heart rate response was no longer reinforced with brain stimulation.

Persistent concern with the degree of skeletal involvement in such instrumental autonomic conditioning was reflected in a series of experiments by Black (22) with dogs initially trained on a lever-pressing shock-avoidance task and subsequently curarized for operant conditioning of either *electromyographic* or heart rate responses. The level of curarization insured little or no overt movement but did not completely eliminate the EMG response. The results showed that the instrumentally conditioned heart rate changes were closely associated with the conditioned EMG changes which readily transferred to affect the performance in the noncurarized state. In a later report, however, Black (24) concluded that the heart rate response could be conditioned independently of overt movement, without conceding that the operantly controlled autonomic changes occurred in the absence of some central events related to the initiation and performance of skeletal motor responses. DiCara & Miller (68) had in fact hypothesized that such central activity (e.g. motor cortex impulses) classically conditioned to elicit heart rate changes might account for the demonstrated autonomic effects, but on the basis of an experiment with curarized rats using a tail-shock control, they argued that such indirect skeletal motor influences could not provide a sufficient account of the instrumentally conditioned heart rate change. They further showed (68) that the completely curarized rat (i.e. no EMG responses from the gastrocnemius muscle) could learn to both increase and decrease heart rate as an operant shock-avoidance response, thus establishing that the instrumental autonomic conditioning effect was not an artifact of the electrical brain stimulation reinforcer. The results of this study also showed that discriminative control over the conditioned heart rate change could be developed and maintained by a stimulus that always preceded shock presentation. Such instrumentally learned heart rate changes have also been shown to persist in the absence of reinforced practice trials over extended periods (e.g. 3-month retention tests) and to be relearned after extinction (71).

Transfer of learning effects have also been demonstrated in a series of studies by DiCara & Miller (72, 73) in which heart rate changes instrumentally conditioned under curare were subsequently (one week later) observed in free-moving rats, and additional training in the noncurarized state was shown to produce changes of even greater magnitude. Similar transfer was also demonstrated from the noncurarized to the curarized state, and the differences in respiration and gross movement were found to decrease as the differences in heart rate increased. This emergent response specificity has also been documented in an experiment by Miller & Banuazizi (171) in which independent operant control of both heart rate changes and *intestinal contractions* was demonstrated, and Fields (89) has subsequently demonstrated the remarkable specificity of such conditioning effects by producing instrumentally learned increases or decreases in the *P-R interval of the EKG* independently of changes in the P-P interval. That the issues related to a linkage between somatomotor and cardiovascular activities in the instrumental autonomic conditioning process have not been definitively settled, however, is clearly evident in a recent report by Goesling & Brener (112) which showed that two different training procedures (i.e. immobility training vs activity training) can have a greater effect upon heart rate changes in curarized rats than the reinforcement contingencies per se. Prior discrimination training, however, appears to have no effect upon the magnitude of the changes produced by subsequent instrumental heart rate conditioning in curarized animals (230).

Interaction effects involving operant heart rate conditioning and other related psychophysiological processes have been investigated in a number of animal learning studies. Curarized rats operantly pretrained to decrease heart rate, for example, have been shown to subsequently acquire (in the noncurarized state) shuttle-box escape-avoidance behavior more readily than rats similarly pretrained to increase their heart rate (76). It has also been reported (84) that blood pressure changes were significantly positively correlated with heart rate decreases instrumentally conditioned as an avoidance response in rhesus monkeys, but such blood pressure effects were uncorrelated with instrumentally conditioned heart rate increases in the same animals. Differences in the opposite direction have been reported with respect to epinephrine and norepinephrine by DiCara & Stone (75), who found higher endogenous cardiac and brainstem catecholamine levels in rats operantly trained to increase heart rate as compared to rats instrumentally conditioned to decrease heart rate. Cardiac H^3-norepinephrine retention studies by these same authors, however, suggested that rats trained to decrease heart rate under curare were subjected to greater stress than rats trained to increase heart rate. Of additional interest in this regard is the finding by DiCara et al (67) that an intact neocortex is essential for instrumental autonomic conditioning, though this appears not to be the case with respect to the classical conditioning of the same heart rate and gastrointestinal responses.

The instrumental conditioning of *blood pressure* in the curarized rat was convincingly demonstrated by DiCara & Miller (69) using a shock avoidance procedure to reinforce both increases and decreases in systolic pressure levels independently of changes in heart rate and rectal temperature. And in a subsequent study, these same investigators (70), using electrical brain stimulation as a reinforcer with the curarized rat, dramatically confirmed the specificity of such instrumental autonomic learning by selectively conditioning vasomotor tone increases in one ear and vasomotor tone decreases in the other ear of the same animal. Significantly, these conditioned *blood flow* changes were not correlated with heart rate, rectal temperature, or vasomotor tone in the tail, suggesting a remarkable and previously unrecognized localization of sympathetic action. Following a replication of these findings, (69), Pappas et al (188) further demonstrated that instrumentally conditioned systolic blood pressure increases and decreases in noncurarized rats did not transfer to the curarized state, but that retraining the same animals after curarization produced even larger magnitude pressure changes than in the noncurarized state. Similar observations with respect to the specificity of instrumentally conditioned cardiovascular changes previously reported by DiCara & Miller (69, 72) received additional support from the finding by Pappas et al (188) that the operantly conditioned blood pressure effects were independent of heart rate and gross skeletal activity.

Large magnitude diastolic blood pressure elevations (50-60 mm Hg) conditioned instrumentally as a shock avoidance response in the rhesus monkey were first reported by Plumlee (203), though the relatively short duration of the changes and the observed postural effects suggested mediation by a Valsalva maneuver (i.e. alteration of intrathoracic pressure by abdominal muscle contraction). Somewhat more modest elevations in mean arterial pressure (e.g. 25 mm Hg) were maintained in squirrel monkeys by Benson et al (18) for periods of 20 minutes or longer as a result of an operant reinforcement contingency arrangement which required the indicated pressure change as a shock avoidance response. And Harris et al (115) have also shown that substantial elevations in both systolic and diastolic blood pressure (e.g. 50-60 mm Hg) could be established and maintained in dog-faced baboons by an operant conditioning procedure which provided for food delivery and shock avoidance programmed as environmental consequences contingent upon prescribed increases in diastolic pressure levels. The instrumentally conditioned blood pressure changes were sustained for intervals up to and exceeding 5 minutes and appeared to bear somewhat systematic but complex temporal relationships to variations in heart rate. More recently, these same authors (116) have extended this basic instrumental autonomic conditioning procedure with the baboon to produce more sustained and clinically relevant increases (30-40 mm Hg) in both systolic and diastolic blood pressure throughout daily 12-hour experimental sessions. Significantly, the maintained instrumentally conditioned blood pressure increases were accompanied by elevated but progressively decreasing heart rate levels.

Instrumentally conditioned *glandular response* changes have also been demonstrated in an experiment with curarized rats rewarded by electrical brain stimulation for both increases and decreases in the rate of *urine formation* by the kidney (174). Using inulin-^{14}C and tritiated *p*-aminohippuric acid, it was also determined that both *glomerular filtration* rate and *renal blood flow* were systematically altered by the operant conditioning procedure, though heart rate, blood pressure, and peripheral blood flow were not, confirming the high degree of specificity and localization of action emphasized in previous reports (69, 70, 89, 171). More recently, Banuazizi (16) has extended the experimental analysis of selectively conditioned intestinal contractions in the curarized rat by demonstrating discriminative stimulus control of both short- and long-duration intestinal responses operantly reinforced by shock avoidance. Significantly, the study also included a control for the unconditioned effects of the electric shock as a possible "state dependent" influence upon the contractile response, and confirmed the instrumental intestinal conditioning under even these more stringent requirements.

The role of *feedback* stimulation in the establishment and maintenance of instrumentally conditioned visceral and autonomic response changes has been emphasized in several recent studies (115, 116, 127, 144, 152) despite the somewhat equivocal status of the "interoceptive discrimination" issue as reflected in the literature of the past decade (133, 134, 164, 231, 232). The early and more recent studies of Miller and his students as reviewed above involved reinforcing stimulus changes (e.g. electric brain stimulation) which provided immediate feedback following visceral or autonomic response variations. As instrumental autonomic conditioning effects of more extended duration have been investigated, however, exteroceptive stimuli (e.g. lights, tones) linked with the internal environment by advanced electrophysiological recording and amplification techniques (52, 55, 117, 148) have provided both digital and analogue representations of critical interoceptive events and processes. In addition, such feedback stimuli serve as conditioned reinforcers bridging the temporal gap between the visceral response and its maintaining environmental consequences. The effectiveness of such stimulus feedback applications has been convincingly demonstrated in the instrumental heart rate conditioning studies of Hothersall & Brener (127) with curarized rats, and the operant blood pressure conditioning experiments of Harris et al (115, 116) with laboratory baboons.

Despite this emergent operational orientation, *interpretive* and *theoretical accounts* of instrumental autonomic conditioning procedures and results continue to focus upon "mediational" issues as these have been reviewed and discussed at length in several recent reports (59, 137, 138, 142, 219, 220). As fruitless as the resulting regress to "pure" operant status may now appear, the controversies surrounding experimental attempts to control such "voluntary mediators" in instrumental autonomic conditioning studies have at least emphasized the need to reexamine some basic formulations regarding conventional distinctions between "the two types" of learning (218, 221). With respect to more focused concern involving the interrelationship between autonomic-visceral and somatomotor activity, two more or less distinguishable points of view can be identified. On the one hand, Miller, DiCara, and associates (66, 68-70, 170, 171, 188, 247) have appeared to take the position that evidence from their own experiments and those of others (223, 225) supports the independence of somatomotor and autonomic-visceral control. Black (22–24), Brenner & Goesling (49), and Obrist et al (187), on the other hand, prefer to represent autonomic-visceral and somatomotor activities as two components of a more general, centrally controlled response process. That the dividing line between the two formulations may not be too firmly drawn, however, would seem to be indicated by the fact that virtually all the adherents to the latter school of thought (25, 112, 187) appear willing to concede that the postulated "normal" linkage between the two systems may be modified in a variety of ways. Indeed, a more moderate "separable but interacting" formulation (40) of the observed psychophysiological relationships may better serve the purposes of both clinical and experimental investigators concerned with the conditions under which dissociation or decoupling of the two systems can and do occur in the course of ongoing behavioral transactions between organism and environment.

A cautionary note must be inserted before concluding the review of instrumental autonomic conditioning. As Neal Miller pointed out in his 1972 presidential address to the Society for Neuroscience, and has reported in print (170a), there has been a progressive decline in the magnitude of learned changes in heart rate from the first experiment conducted in 1966 (173) through those of 1972. A number of factors are being investigated in order to try to account for this "extraordinarily perplexing and vexing phenomenon," as Miller terms it, but no proposed explanation for the decline has yet been confirmed.

Be all this as it may, the fact remains that the field of animal learning appears now to be extending the horizons of conditioning to probe the depths of "inner space" (92) with the same incisive methodological approach that has proved so productive in analyzing more conventional behavioral interactions with the external environment. The potential of this investigative endeavor to provide new insights into the behavioral control of physiological processes holds the promise of an active participant role for man in learning to deal effectively with his proverbial "worst enemy."

Literature Cited

1. Ádám, G. 1967. *Interoception and Behavior.* Budapest:Akademiai Kiado, Publ. House Hung. Acad. Sci. 152 pp.
2. Ader, R. 1971. Experimentally induced gastric lesions. *Advan. Psychosom. Med.* 6:1–39
3. Ader, R., Beels, C. C., Tatum, R. 1960. Social factors affecting emotionality and resistance to disease in animals. II. Susceptibility to gastric ulceration as a function of interruptions in social interactions and the time at which they occur. *J. Comp. Physiol. Psychol.* 53:455–58
4. Ader, R., Tatum, R., Beels, C. C. 1960. Social factors affecting emotionality and resistance to disease in animals. I. Age of separation from the mother and susceptibility to gastric ulcers in the rat. *J. Comp. Physiol. Psychol.* 53:446–54
5. Anand, B., Chhina, G. 1961. Investigations on yogis claiming to stop their heart beats. *Indian J. Med. Res.* 49: 90–94
6. Anand, B. K., Chhina, G. S., Singh, B. 1961. Some aspects of electroencephalographic studies of Yogi. *Electroencephalogr. Clin. Neurophysiol.* 13: 452–56
7. Anderson, D. E., Brady, J. V. 1971. Pre-avoidance blood pressure elevations accompanied by heart rate decreases in the dog. *Science* 172:595–97
8. Anderson, D. E., Brady, J. V. 1972. Differential preparatory cardiovascular responses to aversive and appetitive behavioral conditioning. *Cond. Reflex* 7(2):82–96
9. Anderson, D. E., Brady, J. V. 1973. Prolonged preavoidance upon blood pressure and heart rate in the dog. *Psychosom. Med.* 35:4–12
10. Ibid. Effects of beta blockade on cardiovascular responses to avoidance performances in dogs, 84
11. Anderson, D. E., Daley, L. A., Findley, J. D., Brady, J. V. 1970. A restraint system for the psychophysiological study of dogs. *Behav. Res. Methods Instrum.* 2:191–94
12. Anderson, D. E., Tosheff, J. 1973. Cardiac output and total peripheral resistance changes during pre-avoidance periods in the dog. *J. Appl. Physiol.* 34:650–54
13. Anderson, S., Gantt, W. H. 1966. The effect of person on cardiac and motor responsivity to shock in dogs. *Cond. Reflex* 1:181–89
14. Bagchi, B. K., Wenger, M. A. 1957. Electrophysiological correlates of some Yoga exercises. *Electroencephalogr. Clin. Neurophysiol. Suppl.* 7: 132–49

15. Banks, J. H., Miller, R. E., Ogawa, N. 1966. The development of discriminated autonomic and instrumental responses during avoidance conditioning in the rhesus monkey. *J. Genet. Psychol.* 108:199–211
16. Banuazizi, A. 1972. Discriminative shock avoidance learning of an autonomic response under curare. *J. Comp. Physiol. Psychol.* 80:236–46
17. Beecroft, R. S. 1966. *Classical Conditioning.* Goleta, Calif.: Psychonomic Press. 198 pp.
18. Benson, H., Herd, J. A., Morse, W. H., Kelleher, R. T. 1969. Behavioral inductions of arterial hypertension and its reversal. *Am. J. Physiol.* 217:30–34
19. Bersh, P. J., Notterman, J. N., Schoenfeld, W. N. 1953. The effect of randomly varying the interval between conditioned and unconditioned stimuli upon the production of experimental anxiety. *Proc. Nat. Acad. Sci. USA, 1953.* 39:553–70
20. Black, A. H. 1959. Heart rate changes during avoidance learning in dogs. *Can. J. Psychol.* 13:229–42
21. Black, A. H. 1965. Cardiac conditioning in curarized dogs: The relationship between heart rate and skeletal behavior. In *Classical Conditioning: A Symposium,* ed. W. F. Prokasy, 20–47. New York: Appleton-Century-Crofts. 421 pp.
22. Black, A. H. 1967. Operant conditioning in curarized dogs. *Cond. Reflex* 2:158
23. Black, A. H. 1967. Transfer following operant conditioning in the curarized dog. *Science* 155:201–3
24. Black, A. H. 1968. Operant conditioning of autonomic responses. *Cond. Reflex* 3(2):130
25. Black, A. H. 1971. Autonomic aversive conditioning in infrahuman subjects. In *Aversive Conditioning and Learning,* ed. F. R. Brush, 3–104. New York: Academic
26. Black, A. H., Carlson, N. J., Solomon, R. L. 1962. Exploratory studies of the conditioning of autonomic responses in curarized dogs. *Psychol. Monogr.* 76:1–31
27. Black, A. H., Dalton, A. J. 1965. The relationship between the avoidance response and subsequent changes in heart rate. *Acta Biol. Exp. Warsaw* 25:107–19
28. Black, A. H., Lang, W. M. 1964. Cardiac conditioning and skeletal responding in curarized dogs. *Psychol. Rev.* 71:80–85
29. Black, R. W., Black, P. E. 1967. Heart rate conditioning as a function of interstimulus interval in rats. *Psychon. Sci.* 8(5):219–20
30. Blizard, D., Welty, R. 1970. A technique for monitoring the heart rate of mice. *Psychophysiology* 7:143–44
31. Bloch-Rojas, S., Toro, A., Pinto-Hamuy, T. 1964. Cardiac versus somatomotor conditioned responses in neodecorticate rats. *J. Comp. Physiol. Psychol.* 58:233–36
32. Brady, J. V. 1964. Behavioral stress and physiological change. A comparative approach to the experimental analysis of some psychosomatic problems. *Trans. NY Acad. Sci.* 26:483–96
33. Brady, J. V. 1965. Experimental studies of psychophysiological responses to stressful situations. *Symposium on Medical Aspects of Stress in the Military Climate,* 271–89. Walter Reed Army Inst. Res. Washington, D.C.: GPO. 622 pp.
34. Brady, J. V. 1966. Operant methodology and the production of altered physiological states. In *Operant Behavior: Areas of Research and Application,* ed. W. Honig, 609–33. New York: Appleton-Century-Crofts. 865 pp.
35. Brady, J. V. 1967. Emotion and the sensitivity of the psychoendocrine systems. In *Neurophysiology and Emotion,* ed. D. Glass, 70–95. New York: Rockefeller Univ. 234 pp.
36. Brady, J. V. 1969. Recent developments in the measurement of stress. In *Explorations in the Psychology of Stress and Anxiety,* ed. B. P. Rourke, 131–64. New York: Longmans. 178 pp.
37. Brady, J. V. 1970. Emotion: Some conceptual problems and psychophysiological experiments. In *Feelings and Emotions,* ed. M. Arnold, 69–100. New York: Academic. 339 pp.
38. Brady, J. V. 1970. Endocrine and autonomic correlates of emotional behavior. In *Physiological Correlates of Emotion,* ed. P. Black, 95–125. New York: Academic. 309 pp.
39. Brady, J. V. 1971. Emotion revisited. *J. Psychiat. Res.* 8:343–84
40. Brady, J. V. 1972. Emotion: Some conceptual problems and psychophysiological experiments. In *Current Status of Physiologic Psychology: A Book of Readings,* ed. D. Singh, C. T. Morgan,

63–78. Monterey, Calif.: Brooks/Cole. 398 pp.
41. Brady, J. V. Psychophysiological syndromes resulting from overly-rigid environmental control: Concurrent and contingent animal models. In *Symp. Exp. Behav. Basis Ment. Disturb.*, Ireland. In press
42. Brady, J. V., Anderson, D. E., Harris, A. H., Stephens J. H. 1973. The effects of classical and instrumental conditioning upon blood pressure and heart rate in mongrel, monkey, and man. *Cond. Reflex* 8(3):174–75
43. Brady, J. V., Findley, J. D., Harris, A. H. 1971. Experimental psychopathology of emotion. *In Experimental Psychopathology,* ed. H. D. Kimmel, 119–46. New York: Academic. 264 pp.
44. Brady, J. V., Harris, A. H., Anderson, D. E. 1972. Behavior and the cardiovascular system in experimental animals. In *Neural and Psychological Mechanisms in Cardiovascular Disease,* ed. A. Zanchetti, 47–74. Milano: Il Ponte. 387 pp.
45. Brady, J. V., Kelly, D., Plumlee, L. 1969. Autonomic and behavioral responses of the rhesus monkey to emotional conditioning. *Ann. NY Acad. Sci.* 159:959–75
46. Brady, J. V., Nauta, W. J. H. 1972. *Principles, Practices, and Position in Neuropsychiatric Research.* New York: Pergamon. 548 pp.
47. Brady, J. V., Porter, R., Conrad, D., Mason, J. 1958. Avoidance behavior and the development of gastroduodenal ulcers. *J. Exp. Anal. Behav.* 1: 69–72
48. Brener, J. M. 1965. The measurement of heart rate. In *Manual of Psychophysiological Methods,* ed. P. H. Venables, I. Martin. New York: Elsevier. 557 pp.
49. Brener, J. M., Goesling, W. J. 1968. *Heart rate and conditioned activity.* Presented at Soc. Psychophysiol. Res. Meet., Washington, D.C.
50. Brown, C. C., Ed. 1967. *Methods in Psychophysiology.* Baltimore: Williams & Wilkins. 502 pp.
51. Brown, C. C., Peters, J. E. 1967. The effects of different durations of conditional stimulus on the magnitude of conditional cardiac acceleration. *Cond. Reflex* 2(2):159
52. Brown, C. C., Thorne, P. 1964. An instrument for signaling heart rate to unrestrained human subjects. *Psychophysiology* 1(2):192–94
53. Brown, G. M., Schalch, D. S., Reichlin, S. 1971. Patterns of growth hormone and cortisol responses to psychological stress in the squirrel monkey. *Endocrinology* 88:956–63
54. Brush, F. R., Levine, S. 1966. Adrenocortical activity and avoidance learning as a function of time after fear conditioning. *Physiol. Behav.* 1: 309–11
55. Budzynski, T. H., Stoyva, J. M. 1969. An instrument for producing deep muscle relaxation by means of analog information feedback. *J. Appl. Behav. Anal.* 2:231–37
56. Church, R., LoLordo, V., Overmier, J. B., Solomon, R. L., Turner, L. H. 1966. Cardiac responses to shock in curarized dogs: Effects of shock intensity and duration, warning signal, and prior experience with shock. *J. Comp. Physiol. Psychol.* 62:1–7
57. Cohen, D. H., Durkovic, R. G. 1966. Cardiac and respiratory conditioning, differentiation, and extinction in the pigeon. *J. Exp. Anal. Behav.* 9(6): 681–88
58. Coover, G. D., Goldman, L., Levine, S. 1971. Plasma corticosterone increases produced by extinction of operant behavior in rats. *Physiol. Behav.* 6(3):261–63
59. Crider, A., Schwartz, G. E., Shnidman, S. 1969. On the criteria for instrumental autonomic conditioning: A reply to Katkin and Murray. *Psychol. Bull.* 71(6):455–61
60. Crider, A., Shapiro, D., Tursky, B. 1966. Reinforcement of spontaneous electrodermal activity. *J. Comp. Physiol. Psychol.* 61:20–27
61. DeToledo, L. 1968. *Changes in heart rate and skeletal activity during conditioned suppression in rats.* PhD dissertation. McMaster Univ., Ontario
62. DeToledo, L. 1971. Changes in heart rate during conditioned suppression in rats as a function of US intensity and type of CS. *J. Comp. Physiol. Psychol.* 77:528–38
63. DeToledo, L., Black, A. H. 1965. A technique for recording heart rate in moving rats. *J. Exp. Anal. Behav.* 8(3):181–82
64. DeToledo, L., Black, A. H. 1966. Heart rate: Changes during conditioned suppression in rats. *Science* 152:1404–6
65. DeVietti, T. L., Porter, P. B. 1970. Heart rate responses during aversive

conditioning. *Psychol. Rep.* 27(2): 651–58
66. DiCara, L. V. 1970. Learning in the autonomic nervous system. *Sci. Am.* 222(1):30–39
67. DiCara, L. V., Braun, J. J., Pappas, B. A. 1970. Classical conditioning and instrumental learning of cardiac and gastrointestinal responses following removal of neocortex in the rat. *J. Comp. Physiol. Psychol.* 73(2):208–16
68. DiCara, L., Miller, N. E. 1968. Changes in heart rate instrumentally learned by curarized rats as avoidance responses. *J. Comp. Physiol. Psychol.* 65:1–7
69. DiCara, L., Miller, N. E. 1968. Instrumental learning of systolic blood pressure responses by curarized rats: Dissociation of cardiac and vascular changes. *Psychosom. Med.* 30(5, Pt.1):489–94
70. DiCara, L., Miller, N. E. 1968. Instrumental learning of vasomotor responses by rats: learning to respond differentially in the two ears. *Science* 159:1485–86
71. DiCara, L. V., Miller, N. E. 1968. Long term retention of instrumentally learned heart-rate changes in the curarized rat. *Commun. Behav. Biol.* 2(Pt.A):19–23
72. DiCara, L. V., Miller, N. E. 1969. Heart-rate learning in the noncurarized state, transfer to the curarized state, and subsequent retraining in the noncurarized state. *Physiol. Behav.* 4: 621–24
73. DiCara, L. V., Miller, N. E. 1969. Transfer of instrumentally learned heart-rate changes from curarized to noncurarized state: Implications for a mediational hypothesis. *J. Comp. Physiol. Psychol.* 68(2, Pt.1):159–62
74. DiCara, L., Pappas, B. A., Pointer, F. 1969. A technique for chronic recording of systemic arterial blood pressure in the unrestrained rat. *Behav. Res. Methods Instrum.* 1(6):221–23
75. DiCara, L. V., Stone, E. A. 1970. Effect of instrumental heart-rate training on rat cardiac and brain catecholamines. *Psychosom. Med.* 32(4): 359–68
76. DiCara, L. V., Weiss, J. M. 1969. Effect of heart-rate learning under curare on subsequent noncurarized avoidance learning. *J. Comp. Physiol. Psychol.* 69:368–74
77. Dixon, C., De Toledo, L., Black, A. H. 1969. A technique for recording electromyographic activity in freely-moving rats using an all-purpose slip ring commutator. *J. Exp. Anal. Behav.* 12(3):507–9
78. Downer, T. B., Thompson, W. D. 1972. Test of the law of initial values in four species of primates. *Psychol. Rep.* 30:191–95
79. Durkovic, R. G., Cohen, D. H. 1969. Effect of caudal midbrain lesions on conditioning of heart- and respiratory-rate responses in the pigeon. *J. Comp. Physiol. Psychol.* 69(2):329–38
80. Ibid. Effects of rostral midbrain lesions on conditioning of heart- and respiratory-rate responses in pigeons. 68(2, Pt.1):184–92
81. Dykman, R. A. 1967. On the nature of classical conditioning. In *Methods in Psychophysiology,* ed. C. C. Brown, 234–90. Baltimore: Williams & Wilkins. 502 pp.
82. Dykman, R. A., Gantt, W. H. 1958. Cardiovascular conditioning in dogs and in humans. In *Physiological Bases of Psychiatry,* ed. W. H. Gantt, 171–95. Springfield, Ill.: Thomas. 344 pp.
83. Dykman, R. A., Mack, R. L., Ackerman, P. T. 1965. The evaluation of autonomic and motor components of the nonavoidance conditioned response of the dog. *Psychophysiology* 1(3):209–30
84. Engel, B. T., Gottlieb, S. H. 1970. Differential operant conditioning of heart rate in the restrained monkey. *J. Comp. Physiol. Psychol.* 73(2):217–25
85. Estes, W. K., Skinner, B. F. 1941. Some quantitative properties of anxiety. *J. Exp. Psychol.* 29:390–400
86. Fehr, F. S., Stern, J. A. 1965. Heart rate conditioning in the rat. *J. Psychosom. Res.* 8:441–45
87. Ferraro, D. R., Silver, M. P., Snapper, A. G. 1965. A method for cardiac recording from surface electrodes in the rat during free-operant procedures. *J. Exp. Anal. Behav.* 8(1):17–18
88. Ferreira, S. H., Gollub, L. R., Vane, J. R. 1969. The release of catecholamines by shocks and stimuli paired with shocks. *J. Exp. Anal. Behav.* 12(4): 623–31
89. Fields, C. 1970. Instrumental conditioning of the rat cardiac control systems. *Proc. Nat. Acad. Sci. USA* 65(2):293–99
90. Findley, J. D., Brady, J. V., Robinson, W. W., Gilliam, W. J. 1971. Continuous cardiovascular monitoring in the baboon during long-term behavioral

performances. *Commun. Behav. Biol.* 6:49–58

91. Findley, J. D., Robinson, W. W., Gilliam, W. J. 1971. A restraint system for chronic study of the baboon. *J. Exp. Anal. Behav.* 15:69–71
92. Fischer, R. 1971. A cartography of the ecstatic and meditative states. *Science* 174:897–904
93. Fitzgerald, R. D. 1963. Effects of partial reinforcement with acid on the classically conditioned salivary response in dogs. *J. Comp. Physiol. Psychol.* 56:1056–60
94. Fitzgerald, R. D. 1966. Some effects of partial reinforcement with shock on classically conditioned heart-rate in dogs. *Am. J. Psychol.* 79:242–49
95. Fitzgerald, R. D., Teyler, T. J. 1970. Trace and delayed heart-rate conditioning in rats as a function of US intensity. *J. Comp. Physiol. Psychol.* 70(2, Pt.1):242–53
96. Fitzgerald, R. D., Vardaris, R. M., Brown, J. S. 1966. Classical conditioning of heart-rate deceleration in the rat with continuous and partial reinforcement. *Psychon. Sci.* 6(9):437–38
97. Fitzgerald, R. D., Vardaris, R. M., Teyler, T. J. 1966. Effects of partial reinforcement followed by continuous reinforcement on classically conditioned heart rate in the dog. *J. Comp. Physiol. Psychol.* 62(3):483–86
98. Fitzgerald, R. D., Vardaris, R. M., Teyler, T. J. 1968. An on-line method for measuring heart rate in conditioning experiments. *Psychophysiology* 4(3):352–53
99. Fitzgerald, R. D., Walloch, R. A. 1966. Changes in respiration and the form of heart-rate CR in dogs. *Psychon. Sci.* 5:425–26
100. Folz, E. L., Miller, F. E. Jr. 1964. Experimental psychosomatic disease states in monkeys. I. Peptic ulcer "executive monkeys." *J. Surg. Res.* 4: 445–53
101. Forsyth, R. P. 1968. Blood pressure and avoidance conditioning. *Psychosom. Med.* 30(1):125–35
102. Ibid 1969. Blood pressure responses to long-term avoidance schedules in the restrained rhesus monkey. 31:300–9
103. Forsyth, R. P. 1971. Regional blood-flow changes during 72-hr. avoidance schedules in the monkey. *Science* 173: 546–48
104. Forsyth, R. P. 1972. Sympathetic nervous system control of distribution of cardiac output in unanesthetized monkeys. *Fed. Proc.* 31(4):1240–44
105. Forsyth, R. P., Harris, R. E. 1970. Circulatory changes during stressful stimuli in rhesus monkeys. *Circ. Res.* 27(Suppl. 1):1–13
106. Forsyth, R. P., Hoffbrand, B. I., Melmon, K. L. 1971. Hemodynamic effects of angiotensin in normal and environmentally stressed monkeys. *Circulation* 44:119–29
107. Forsyth, R. P., Rosenblum, M. A. 1964. A restraining device and procedure for continuous blood pressure recordings in monkeys. *J. Exp. Anal. Behav.* 7(5):367–68
108. Fowler, R. L., Kimmel, H. D. 1962. Operant conditioning of the GSR. *J. Exp. Psychol.* 63:563–67
109. Frazier, T. W., Weil-Malherbe, H., Lipscomb, H. S. 1969. Psychophysiology of conditioned emotional disturbances in humans. *Psychophysiology* 5(5):478–503
110. Fromer, R. 1963. Conditioned vasomotor responses in the rabbit. *J. Comp. Physiol. Psychol.* 56:1050–55
111. Gale, E. N., Stern, J. A. 1968. Classical conditioning of the peripheral vasomotor orienting response. *Psychophysiology* 4(3):342–48
112. Goesling, W. J., Brener, J. 1972. Effects of activity and immobility conditioning upon subsequent heart-rate conditioning in curarized rats. *J. Comp. Physiol. Psychol.* 81:311–17
113. Graham, L. A., Cohen, S. I., Shmavonian, B. M. 1967. Urinary catecholamine excretion during instrumental conditioning. *Psychosom. Med.* 29(2):134–43
114. Granger, L. 1970. Variation of heart rate in different types of visual attention stiuations. *Can. J. Psychol.* 24(5):370–79
115. Harris, A. H., Findley, J. D., Brady, J. V. 1971. Instrumental conditioning of blood pressure elevations in the baboon. *Cond. Reflex* 6:215–26
116. Harris, A. H., Gilliam, W. J., Findley, J. D., Brady, J. V. Instrumental conditioning of large magnitude daily 12-hour blood pressure elevations in the baboon. *Science.* In press
117. Hefferline, R. F., Keenan, B. 1963. Amplitude-induction gradient of a small-scale (covert) operant. *J. Exp. Anal. Behav.* 6:307–15
118. Hefferline, R. F., Keenan, B., Harford, R. A., Birch, J. 1960. Electronics in

psychology. *Columbia Eng. Quart.* 13:10–15

119. Hein, P. L. 1969. Heart rate conditioning in the cat and its relationship to other physiological responses. *Psychophysiology* 5(5):455–64
120. Herd, J. A., Barger, A. C. 1964. Simplified technique for chronic catheterization of blood vessels. *J. Appl. Physiol.* 19:791
121. Herd, J. A., Morse, W. H., Kelleher, R. T., Jones, L. G. 1969. Arterial hypertension in the squirrel monkey during behavioral experiments. *Am. J. Physiol.* 217:24–29
122. Higgins, D. J. 1971. Set and uncertainty as factors influencing anticipatory cardiovascular responding in humans. *J. Comp. Physiol. Psychol.* 74(2):272–83
123. Hilton, A. 1967. *Partial reinforcement of a conditioned emotional response.* PhD dissertation. McMaster Univ., Ontario
124. Hokanson, J. E., DeGood, D. E., Forrest, M. S., Brittain, T. M. 1971. Availability of avoidance behaviors in modulating vascular-stress responses. *J. Pers. Soc. Psychol.* 19(1):60–68
125. Holdstock, T. L., Schwartzbaum, J. S. 1965. Classical conditioning of heart rate and galvanic skin response in the rat. *Psychophysiology* 2(1):25–38
126. Hord, D. J., Johnson, L. C., Lubin, A. 1964. Differential effect of the law of initial value (LIV) on autonomic variables. *Psychophysiology* 1:79–87
127. Hothersall, D., Brener, J. 1969. Operant conditioning of changes in heart rate in curarized rats. *J. Comp. Physiol. Psychol.* 68(3):338–42
128. Howard, J. L., Obrist, P. A., Martin, P. L., Smithson, K. W., Sutterer, J. R. 1969. Differential influence of the cardiac innervations during classical aversive conditioning in dogs. Presented at: 9th Ann. Meet. Soc. Psychophysiol. Res., Monterey, Calif. Abstr. 1970. *Psychophysiology* 6:645
129. Jaworska, K., Kowalska, M., Soltysik, S. 1962. Studies on the aversive classical conditioning, I. Acquisition and differentiation of motor and cardiac conditioned classical defensive reflexes in dog. *Acta Biol. Exp. Warsaw* 22:23–24
130. Jennings, J. R., Averill, J. R., Opton, E. M., Lazarus, R. S. 1970. Some parameters of heart rate change: Perceptual versus motor task requirements, noxiousness, and uncertainty. *Psychophysiology* 7(2):194–212
131. Johnson, R. J. 1963. Operant reinforcement of an automatic response. *Diss. Abstr.* 24:1255–56
132. Jolley, A. 1970. Effects of food deprivation and consummatory activity on the heart rate of the rat. *Anim. Behav.* 18(1):92–95
133. Kadden, R. M., Schoenfeld, W. N., Snapper, A. G. 1970. Cardiac pacing in the rhesus monkey: A technique and some behavioral data. *Proc. 78th Ann. Conv. APA* 5(2):259–60
134. Kadden, R. M., Snapper, A. G., Schoenfeld, W. N., Kop, P. 1970. Transvenous intracardiac pacing in the rhesus monkey. *Commun. Behav. Biol.* 5:255–58
135. Kakigi, S. 1971. Cardiovascular generalization and differentiation—The relationship between heart rate and blood pressure. *Cond. Reflex* 6:191–204
136. Kakigi, S., Newton, J. E., Gantt, W. H. 1968. Stimulus generalization in cardiovascular conditioning. *Cond. Reflex* 3(2):133–34
137. Katkin, E. S., Murray, E. N. 1968. Instrumental conditioning of autonomically mediated behavior: theoretical and methodological issues. *Psychol. Bull.* 70(1):52–68
138. Katkin, E. S., Murray, E. N., Lachman, R. 1969. Concerning instrumental autonomic conditioning: A rejoiner. *Psychol. Bull.* 71(6):462–66
139. Kelleher, R., Morse, W., Herd, J. A. 1972. Effects of propranolol, phentolamine, and methylatropine on cardiovascular function in the squirrel monkey during behavioral experiments. *J. Pharmacol. Exp. Ther.* 182:204
140. Kimble, G. A., Ed. 1967. *Foundations of Conditioning and Learning.* New York: Appleton-Century-Crofts. 696 pp.
141. Kimmel, E., Kimmel, H. D. 1963. Replication of operant conditioning of the GSR. *J. Exp. Psychol.* 65:212–13
142. Kimmel, H. D. 1967. Instrumental conditioning of autonomically mediated behavior. *Psychol. Bull.* 67(5):337–45
143. Kimmel, H. D., Hill, F. A. 1960. Operant conditioning of the GSR. *Psychol. Rep.* 7:555–62
144. Kimmel, H. D., Kimmel, E. 1970. An instrumental conditioning method for

the treatment of enuresis. *J. Behav. Ther. Exp. Psychiat.* 1(2):121–23
145. Krahenbuhl, G. S. 1971. Stress reactivity in tennis players. *Res. Quart. Am. Assoc. Health Phys. Educ.* 42(1):42–46
146. Krausman, D. 1969. Automatic online print out of peak systolic and diastolic blood pressures. *Psychophysiology* 5(3):337–41
147. Ibid. 1970. Heart rate derived from blood pressure and other physiological signals. 7:503–7
148. Krausman, D. T. 1972. A system for providing an on-line analogue display of beat-by-beat cardiac output. *Med. Biol. Eng.* 10:81–88
149. Krausman, D., Ehrlich, W., Brady, J. V. 1972. Preprocessor adapts cardiovascular signals to a minicomputer. *Psychophysiology* 9(5):554–63
150. Lacey, J. I., Lacey, B. C. 1962. The law of initial value in the longitudinal study of autonomic constitution: Reproducibility of autonomic responses and response patterns over a four-year interval. *Ann. NY Acad. Sci.* 98: 1257–89
151. Laforge, H. 1971. The influence of random reinforcement on heart rate during extinction. *J. Psychol.* 77(1):89–99
152. Lang, P. J. 1970. Autonomic control or learning to play the internal organs. *Psychol. Today* 4(5):37–41
153. Lang, W., Black, A. H. 1963. *Cardiac conditioning in dogs as a function of US intensity and difficulty of differentiation.* Presented at East. Psychol. Assoc. Meet., New York
154. Lawler, J. E., Meyers, K. A., Obrist, P. A. 1972. *Cardiovascular integration during performance on a Sidman avoidance schedule.* Presented at: Ann. Meet. Soc. Psychophysiol. Res., Boston
155. Levine, M. D., Gordon, T. P., Peterson, R. H., Rose, R. M. 1970. Urinary 17-OHCS response of high- and low-aggressive rhesus monkeys to shock avoidance. *Physiol. Behav.* 5(8): 919–24
156. Lico, M. C., Hoffman, A., Corian, M. R. 1968. Autonomic conditioning in the anesthetized rabbit. *Physiol. Behav.* 3(5):673–75
157. Lisina, M. I. 1958. The role of orientation in the transformation of involuntary reactions into voluntary ones. In *Orienting Reflex and Exploratory Behavior,* ed. L. G. Voronin, A. N. Leontiev, A. R. Luris, E. N. Sokolov, O. S. Vinogradova, 339–44. Wash: Am. Inst. Biol. Sci.
158. Lower, J. S. 1967. *Approach-avoidance conflict as a determinant of peptic ulceration in the rat.* PhD dissertation. Western Reserve Univ., Cleveland, Ohio
159. Lynch, J. J. 1966. Overtraining in classical conditioning: A comparison of motor and cardiac systems. *Cond. Reflex* 1(4):266–79
160. Lynch, J. J. 1968. Heart rate variability of dogs in classical conditioning. *Psychol. Rec.* 18(1):101–6
161. Lynch, J. J., Gantt, W. H. 1968. The heart rate component of the social reflex in dogs: The conditional effects of petting and person. *Cond. Reflex* 3(2):69–80
162. Lynch, J. J., McCarthy, J. F. 1969. Social responding in dogs: Heart rate changes to a person. *Psychophysiology* 5(4):389–93
163. Malcuit, G., Ducharme, R., Belanger, D. 1968. Cardiac activity in rats during bar-press avoidance and "freezing" responses. *Psychol. Rep.* 23(1):11–18
164. Mandler, G., Kahn, M. 1960. Discrimination of changes in heart rate: Two unsuccessful attempts. *J. Exp. Anal. Behav.* 3(1):21–26
165. Mason, J. W., Brady, J. V., Rose, R. M. 1969. Adrenal responses to maternal separation and chair adaptation in experimentally-raised Rhesus monkeys (*Macaca Mulatta*). *Proc. 2nd Int. Congr. Primatol.* 1:211–18
166. Mason, J. W. et al 1968. Organization of psychoendocrine mechanisms. *Psychosom. Med.* 30:565–808
167. Mason, J. W., Brady, J. V., Tolson, W. W. 1966. Behavioral adaptations and endocrine activity. In *Proceedings of the Association for Research in Nervous and Mental Diseases,* ed. R. Levine, 227–48. Baltimore: Williams & Wilkins. 475 pp.
168. McDonald, D. G., Stern, J. A., Hahn, W. W. 1963. Classical heart rate conditioning in the rat. *J. Psychosom. Res.* 7:97–106
169. Meredith, A. L., Schneiderman, N. 1967. Heart rate and nictitating membrane classical discrimination conditioning in rabbits under delay vs. trace procedures. *Psychon. Sci.* 9:139–40
170. Miller, N. E. 1969. Learning of visceral and glandular responses. *Science* 163:434–45
170a. Miller, N. E. 1972. Interactions between learned and physical factors in

mental illness. *Seminars Psychiat.* 4: 239–54

171. Miller, N. E., Banuazizi, A. 1968. Instrumental learning by curarized rats of a specific visceral response, intestinal or cardiac. *J. Comp. Physiol. Psychol.* 65:1–7
172. Miller, N. E., Carmona, A. 1967. Modification of a visceral response, salivation in thirsty dogs, by instrumental training with water reward. *J. Comp. Physiol. Psychol.* 63:1–6
173. Miller, N. E., DiCara, L. 1967. Instrumental learning of heart rate changes in curarized rats: Shaping and specificity to discriminative stimulus. *J. Comp. Physiol. Psychol.* 63:12–19
174. Miller, N. E., DiCara, L. 1968. Instrumental learning of urine formation by rats; changes in renal blood flow. *Am. J. Physiol.* 215:677–83
175. Miller, R. E., Banks, J. H., Caul, W. F. 1967. Cardiac conditioned responses in avoidance and yoked-control rats. *Psychosom. Sci.* 9:581–82
176. Miller, R. E., Caul, W. F. 1969. Influence of uncertainty on conditioned heart rates of monkeys. *Physiol. Behav.* 4(6):975–80
177. Miyata, Y., Soltysik, S. 1968. The relations between salivary, cardiac and motor responses during instrumental performance. *Acta Biol. Exp. Warsaw* 28(4):345–61
178. Moot, S. A., Cebulla, R. P., Crabtree, J. M. 1970. Instrumental control and ulceration in rats. *J. Comp. Physiol. Psychol.* 71(3):405–10
179. Morse, W. H., Herd, J. A., Kelleher, R. T., Gross, S. A. 1971. Schedule-controlled modulation of arterial blood pressure in the squirrel monkey. In *Experimental Psychopathology: Recent Research and Theory,* ed. H. D. Kimmel, 147–64. New York: Academic. 264 pp.
180. Nathan, M. S., Smith, O. A. Jr. 1968. Differential conditional emotional and cardiovascular responses—A training technique for monkeys. *J. Exp. Anal. Behav.* 11(1):77–82
181. Newton, J. E. 1967. Blood pressure and heart rate changes during conditioning in curarized dogs. *Cond. Reflex* 2(2):158
182. Newton, J. E., Gantt, W. H. 1966. One-trial cardiac conditioning in dogs. *Cond. Reflex* 1(4):251–65
183. Notterman, J. M., Schoenfeld, W. N., Bersh, P. J. 1952. Partial reinforcement and conditioned heart rate response in human subjects. *Science* 115:77–9
184. Obrist, P. A. et al 1972. Alterations in cardiac contractility during classical aversive conditioning in dogs—methodological and theoretical implications. *Psychophysiology* 9:242–61
185. Obrist, P. A., Webb, R. A. 1966. Heart rate and somatic-motor changes during classical conditioning in dogs: Effects of experimental conflict. *Proc. 74th Ann. Conv. APA* 1:143–44
186. Obrist, P. A., Webb, R. A. 1967. Heart rate during conditioning in dogs: relationship to somatic-motor activity. *Psychophysiology* 4(1):7–34
187. Obrist, P. A., Webb, R. A., Sutterer, J. R., Howard, J. L. 1970. The cardiac-somatic relationship: Some reformulations. *Psychophysiology* 6(5):569–87
188. Pappas, B. A., DiCara, L. V., Miller, N. E. 1970. Learning of blood pressure responses in the noncurarized rat: Transfer to the curarized state. *Physiol. Behav.* 5(9):1029–32
189. Paré, W. 1964. The effect of chronic environmental stress on stomach ulceration, adrenal function, and consummatory behavior in the rat. *J. Psychol.* 57:143–51
190. Paré, W. P. 1967. The role of gross locomotor restriction in the acquisition of motor and cardiac constitutional discrimination in the dog. *Cond. Reflex* 2(4):277–84
191. Paré, W. P. 1969. *The development of a three-stimulus cardiac discrimination problem in three mammalian species.* Presented at 9th Ann. Meet. Soc. Psychophysiol. Res., Monterey, Calif. Abstr. 1970. *Psychophysiology* 6: 629–30
192. Paré, W. P. 1971. Six-hour escape-avoidance work shift and production of stomach ulcers. *J. Comp. Physiol. Psychol.* 77(3):459–66
193. Paré, W. P., Isom, K. E., Reus, J. F. 1970. Recording the electrocardiogram from the squirrel monkey, Saimira Sciureus. *Physiol. Behav.* 5: 819–21
194. Parrish, J. 1967. Classical discrimination conditioning of heart rate and bar-press suppression in the rat. *Psychon. Sci.* 9:267–68
195. Pavlov, I. P. 1927. *Conditioned Reflexes,* transl. G. V. Anrep. London: Oxford Univ. 430 pp.
196. Pavlov, I. P. 1928. *Lectures on Conditioned Reflexes,* transl. W. H. Gantt. New York: International. 414 pp.

197. Perez-Cruet, J. 1962. Conditioning of extrasystoles in humans with respiratory maneuvers as unconditional stimulus. *Science* 137:1060
198. Perez-Cruet, J., Gaertner, R. 1967. Cardiodynamics of cardiac conditioning. *Cond. Reflex* 2(2):156
199. Perez-Cruet, J., Gantt, W. H. 1964. Conditional reflex electrocardiogram of bulbocapnine conditioning of the T wave. *Am. Heart J.* 67:61
200. Perez-Cruet, J., Jude, J. R., Gantt, W. H. 1966. An attempt to condition extrasystoles using direct myocardial electrical stimulation as an unconditional stimulus. *Cond. Reflex* 1(2): 104–16
201. Perez-Cruet, J., Plumlee, L., Newton, J. E. 1966. Chronic basal blood pressure in unanesthetized dogs using the ring-catheter technique. *Proc. Symp. Biomed. Eng.* 1:383–86
202. Perez-Cruet, J., Tolliver, G., Dunn, G., Marvin, S., Brady, J. V. 1963. Concurrent measurement of heart rate and instrumental avoidance behavior in the rhesus monkey. *J. Exp. Anal. Behav.* 6(1):61–4
203. Plumlee, L. A. 1969. Operant conditioning of increases in blood pressure. *Psychophysiology* 6:283–90
204. Prokasy, W. F., Ed. 1965. *Classical Conditioning: A Symposium.* New York: Appleton-Century-Crofts. 421 pp.
205. Ramsay, D. A. 1969. *Cardiac activity in the rhesus monkey under several classical conditioning procedures and operant avoidance.* PhD dissertation. Columbia Univ. New York
206. Ramsay, D. A. 1970. Form and characteristics of the cardiovascular conditional response in rhesus monkeys. *Cond. Reflex,* 5(1):36–51
207. Ramsay, D. A., Pomerleau, O. F., Snapper, A. G. 1968. Two methods of obtaining electrocardiograms of chair-restrained monkeys. *Cond. Reflex.* 3(3):200–4
208. Razran, G. 1961. The observable unconscious and the inferable conscious in current Soviet psychophysiology: Interoceptive conditioning, semantic conditioning, and the orienting reflex. *Psychol. Rev.* 68:81–147
209. Santibanez, H., Saavedra, M. A., Middleton, S. 1963. Cardiac and respiratory concomitants in classical defensive conditioning in cats. *Acta Biol. Exp. Warsaw* 23:165–70
210. Sawrey, W. L., Long, D. H. 1962. Strain and sex differences in ulceration in the rat. *J. Comp. Physiol. Psychol.* 55:603–5
211. Sawrey, W. L., Sawrey, J. M. 1963. Fear conditioning and resistance to ulceration. *J. Comp. Physiol. Psychol.* 56:821–23
212. Ibid 1964. Conditioned fear and restraint in ulceration. 57:150–51
213. Sawrey, J. M., Sawrey, W. L. 1964. Ulcer production with reserpine and conflict. *J. Comp. Physiol. Psychol.* 57:307–9
214. Ibid 1966. Age, weight, and social effects on ulceration rate in rats. 61: 464–66
215. Schneiderman, N., Smith, M. C., Smith, A. C. 1966. Heart rate classical conditioning in rats. *Psychon. Sci.* 6(5):241–42
216. Schneiderman, N., Vandercar, D., Yehle, A. 1967. Role of the compensatory vagal reflex in heart rate classical conditioning of rabbits. *Psychon. Bull.* 1(2):30
217. Schneiderman, N. et al 1969. Vagal compensatory adjustment: relationship to heart rate classical conditioning in rabbits. *J. Comp. Physiol. Psychol.* 68(2, Pt. 1):175–83
218. Schoenfeld, W. N. 1966. Some old work for modern conditioning theory. *Cond. Reflex* 1:219–23
219. Ibid 1970. *Oyepk* on mediating mechanisms of the conditioned reflex. 5: 165–70
220. Ibid 1971. Conditioning the whole organism. 6:125–28
221. Ibid 1972. Problems of modern behavior theory. 7:33–65
222. Schoenfeld, W. N., Matos, M. A., Snapper, A. G. 1967. Cardiac conditioning in the white rat with food presentations as unconditional stimulus. *Cond. Reflex* 2(1):56–67
223. Schwartz, G. E., Shapiro, D., Tursky, B. 1971. Learned control of cardiovascular integration in man through operant conditioning. *Psychosom. Med.* 33(4):57–62
224. Shapiro, D., Crider, A. B., Tursky, B. 1964. Differentiation of an autonomic response through operant conditioning. *Psychon. Sci.* 1:147–48
225. Shapiro, D., Tursky, B., Schwartz, G. E. 1970. Differentiation of heart rate and systolic blood pressure in man by operant conditioning. *Psychosom. Med.* 32(4):417–23

226. Shearn, D. W. 1961. Does the heart learn? *Psychol. Bull.* 58:452–58
227. Shearn, D. W. 1962. Operant conditioning of heart rate. *Science* 137: 530–31
228. Sideroff, S., Schneiderman, N., Powell, D. A. 1971. Motivational properties of septal stimulation as the US in classical conditioning of heart rate in rabbits. *J. Comp. Physiol. Psychol.* 74(1):1–10
229. Sidman, M. 1953. Avoidance conditioning with brief shock and no exteroceptive warning signal. *Science* 118:157–58
230. Slaughter, J., Hahn, W., Rinaldi, P. 1970. Instrumental conditioning of heart rate in the curarized rat with varied amounts of pretraining. *J. Comp. Physiol. Psychol.* 72(3):356–59
231. Slucki, H., Adam, G., Porter, R. W. 1965. Operant discrimination of an interoceptive stimulus in rhesus monkeys. *J. Exp. Anal. Behav.* 8(6):405–14
232. Slucki, H., McCoy, F. B., Porter, R. W. 1969. Interoceptive SD of the large intestine established by mechanical stimulation. *Psychol. Rep.* 24(1): 35–42
233. Smith, O. A., Nathan, M. S. 1967. The The development of cardiac and blood flow conditional responses during the acquisition of a differentiated "conditioned emotional response" in monkeys. *Cond. Reflex* 2(2):155–56
234. Smith, O. A., Stebbins, W. C. 1965. Conditioned blood flow and heart rate in monkeys. *J. Comp. Physiol. Psychol.* 59:432–36
235. Smith, R. M., Hain, J. D. 1970. Relationship between somatization and effects of stress on electrogastric waveforms in humans. *Psychol. Rep.* 27(3):755–65
236. Snapper, A. G., Kadden, R. M., Schoenfeld, W. N. 1971. Cardiac pacing and the law of initial value in rhesus monkeys. *Cond. Reflex* 6(4):227–35
237. Snapper, A. G., Pomerleau, O. F., Schoenfeld, W. N. 1969. Similarity of cardiac CR forms in the rhesus monkey during several experimental procedures. *Cond. Reflex* 4(3):212–20
238. Soltysik, S., Jaworska, K. 1962. Studies on the aversive classical conditioning. 2. On the reinforcing role of shock in the classical leg flexion conditioning. *Acta Biol. Exp. Warsaw* 22: 181–91
239. Soltysik, S., Kowalski, M. 1960. Studies on the avoidance conditioning: Relations between cardiac (Type I) and motor (Type II) effects in the avoidance reflex. *Acta. Biol. Exp. Warsaw* 22:157–70
240. Stebbins, W. C., Smith, O. A. 1964. Cardiovascular concomitants of the conditioned emotional response in the monkey. *Science* 144:881–83
241. Stern, J. A., Word, T. J. 1962. Heart rate changes during avoidance conditioning in the male albino rat. *J. Psychosom. Res.* 6:167–75
242. Stoyva, J., Forsyth, R. P., Kamiya, J. 1968. Blood pressure during sleep in the rhesus monkey before and after stress. *Am. J. Physiol.* 214(5):1122–25
243. Sutterer, J. R., Howard, J. L., Loth, E., Obrist, P. A. 1970. Alterations of heart rate and general activity during aversive conditioning procedures. *Psychophysiology* 6:635–36
244. Swadlow, H. A., Hosking, K. E., Schneiderman, N. 1971. Differential heart rate conditioning and lever lift suppression in restrained rabbits. *Physiol. Behav.* 7(2):257–60
245. Swinnen, M. E. T. 1968. Blood pressure digitizer. *Proc. Ann. Conf. Eng. Med. Biol.* 10:18
246. Tighe, T. J., Graves, D. M., Riley, C. A. 1968. Successive reversals of a classically conditioned heart rate discrimination. *J. Exp. Anal. Behav.* 11(2):199–206
247. Trowill, J. A. 1967. Instrumental conditioning of the heart rate in the curarized rat. *J. Comp. Physiol. Psychol.* 63(1):7–11
248. Tyler, T. J., Fitzgerald, R. D. 1967. Trace versus delay conditioning of heart rate in rats as a function of US intensity. *Psychon. Bull.* 1(2):30
249. Vandercar, D. H., Elster, A., Schneiderman, N. 1970. Heart-rate classical conditioning in rabbits to hypothalamic or septal US stimulation. *J. Comp. Physiol. Psychol.* 72(1):145–52
250. Vandercar, D. H., Schneiderman, N. 1967. Interstimulus interval functions in different response systems during classical discrimination conditioning of rabbits. *Psychon. Sci.* 9(1):9–10
251. Vanderwolf, C. H., Vanderwart, M. L. 1970. Relations of heart rate to motor activity and arousal in the rat. *Can. J. Psychol.* 24(6):434–41
252. Vardaris, R. M. 1970. Partial reinforcement of heart rate CR in rats with motivation and stimulus change controlled. *Proc. 78th Ann. Conv. APA* 5(1):31–2

253. Wagner, A. R., Seigel, L. S., Fein, G. G. 1967. Extinction of conditioned fear as a function of percentage of reinforcement. *J. Comp. Physiol. Psychol.* 63:160–64
254. Weinberg, H. 1968. Temporal discrimination of cortical stimulation. *Physiol. Behav.* 3(2):297–300
255. Weiss, J. M. 1970. Somatic effects of predictable and unpredictable shock. *Psychosom. Med.* 32(4):397–408
256. Weiss, J. M. 1971. Effects of coping behavior in different warning signal conditions on stress pathology in rats. *J. Comp. Physiol. Psychol.* 77:1–13
257. Ibid. Effects of coping behavior with and without a feedback signal on stress pathology in rats, 22–30
258. Ibid. Effects of punishing the coping response (conflict) on stress pathology in rats, 14–21
259. Weiss, J. M. 1972. Psychological factors in stress and disease. *Sci. Am.* 226(6):104–13
260. Weiss, J. M., McEwen, B. S., Silva, M. T., Kalkut, M. 1970. Pituitary-adrenal alterations and fear responding. *Am. J. Physiol.* 218(3):864–68
261. Weiss, J. M., Stone, E. A., Harrel, N. 1970. Coping behavior and brain norepinephrine level in rats. *J. Comp. Physiol. Psychol.* 72:153–60
262. Wenger, M. A., Bagchi, B. K. 1961. Studies of autonomic functions in practitioners of yoga in India. *Behav. Sci.* 6:312–23
263. Wenger, M. A., Bagchi, B. K., Anand, B. K. 1961. Experiments in India on "voluntary" control of the heart and pulse. *Circulation* 24:1319–25
264. Werdegard, D., Johnson, D. G., Mason, J. W. 1964. A technique for continuous measurement of arterial blood pressure in unanesthetized monkeys. *J. Appl. Physiol.* 19:519–21
265. Williams, J. L. 1969. Response contingency and effects of punishment: changes in autonomic and skeletal responses. *J. Comp. Physiol. Psychol.* 68:118–25
266. Wilson, R. S., Duerfeldt, P. H. 1967. Cardiac responsiveness and differential conditioning. *J. Comp. Physiol. Psychol.* 63(1):87–94
267. Yehle, A. L. 1968. Divergences among rabbit response systems during three-tone classical discrimination conditioning. *J. Exp. Psychol.* 77(3, Pt. 1):468–73
268. Yehle, A. L., Dauth, G., Schneiderman, N. 1967. Correlates of heart rate classical conditioning in curarized rabbits. *J. Comp. Physiol. Psychol.* 64(1):98–104
269. Yehle, A. L., Hsui-Ying, L., Hung-Mei, S. 1971. Maintenance of heart-rate responding during classical conditioning of the rabbit. *Psychol. Rep.* 29:1341–42
270. Yehle, A. L., Spaulding, L. E., Hsiu-Ying, L. 1970. Classical discrimination conditioning and reversal in the albino rabbit. *Psychon. Sci.* 20(3): 187–88

EXPERIMENTAL PSYCHOLINGUISTICS

❖213

P. N. Johnson-Laird
University of Sussex, Brighton, England

The fundamental problem in psycholinguistics is simple to formulate: what happens when we understand sentences? Most of the other problems would be half-way solved if only we had the answer to this question; and potential answers to it, of course, have accumulated rapidly ever since George Miller (125) introduced psychologists to the ideas of transformational grammar. The results of the initial phases of experimentation are well known (see, for example, 73, 83, 160); and since Fillenbaum (52) has recently contributed a wide-ranging survey of the area, including language acquisition and its biological bases, it is appropriate in the present review to concentrate on comprehension and its cognate problems.

Because meaning depends on words and syntax, there is a general consensus that comprehension involves processing both of them and combining the meanings of words according to the perceived syntactic relations between them. But comprehension is only a start: once an individual understands a sentence he may react to it. He may try to verify a statement, or to answer a question, or to carry out a command. He may simply remember the sentence or one of its implications. Many of his tangible responses are of immediate intrinsic interest to a psycholinguist. But the responses do have a further use. If an individual can decide that a sentence is true, then he is likely to have come to an understanding of it, and his performance may therefore be very revealing about this process. Such indirect approaches to the study of comprehension are extremely useful because there is no simple veridical index of when a sentence has been understood.

The literature continues to grow faster than knowledge, and in trying to epitomize its findings and foibles, we shall follow the progress of a sentence as its syntax is parsed, its word meanings retrieved from lexical memory, and its sense ultimately understood. We shall examine such matters as how sentences are verified, and how questions are answered. Finally, we shall turn to the ways in which sentences and larger units of discourse are remembered.

THE PERCEPTION OF SYNTAX

It was implicit in the initial phase of experimental psycholinguistics that the process of perception paralleled the levels of analysis in transformational grammar. Yet it was clear that there would have to be considerable interplay between these levels because purely semantic factors were known to affect the intelligibility of speech. Nevertheless, the pioneers believed that the linguistic distinction between surface and deep structure was likely to be reflected in the organization of the perceptual system, with one set of procedures designed to parse a sentence into its immediate constituents—nounphrases, verbphrases, etc.—and another set of procedures retrieving the underlying structure of a sentence, including such relations as its subject and object. The distinction was there from the start and it has proved vital to most of the work in the area, particularly the sustained investigations into perception carried out by Bever, Fodor, Garrett, and their colleagues at MIT.

The MIT group has made considerable use of a technique in which listeners are required to locate a click presented to one ear with respect to a sentence presented to the other ear. The subjects usually have to write down the sentence and then to indicate where the click occurred within it; however, comparable results appear to be obtained when they have merely to judge whether a click occurred in the same place in two sentences (cf. the unpublished MIT study cited in 84). The first studies with the technique, reviewed by Bever (14), indicated that the click was often perceptually relocated so as to minimize the number of surface constituents that it interrupted. It was as though extraneous noises were not permitted to violate the integrity of major constituents and were consequently preposed, or postposed, into the boundaries between them. The results of more recent studies, however, suggest that whatever it is that determines click location, it is *not* surface structure.

The Reality of Deep Structure

Reber & Anderson (148) certainly found a regression of clicks towards the major surface boundary within sentences. But they had purposely confounded this boundary with the midpoint of the sentences, and a similar regression occurred with both random strings of words and strings made up of bursts of white noise. Indeed, a distinct response bias towards this position was evident in the performance of a control group instructed to respond to "subliminal" but in fact nonexistent clicks. There is evidently a similar bias towards locating clicks within words rather than between them (109) which also tells against the hypothesis since words are surface constituents. Such findings naturally suggest that nonlinguistic attentional factors may be primarily responsible for the perceptual location of clicks. But although the MIT group subsequently failed to detect effects of surface structure, they have regularly reported another phenomenon that seems inexplicable without resort to linguistic principles. Clicks are consistently relocated so that they fall into or towards a boundary between the *underlying* clauses of sentences—even, Bever (14) claims, when such boundaries are unmarked in surface structure. A particularly striking finding involved a contrast between two superficially similar sorts of complement (18). With a nounphrase complement, an entire underlying clause is treated like a nounphrase, e.g. "The corrupt police can't bear *criminals to confess very quickly.*" A click actually located in the word "criminals" would often be reported to have occurred between "bear" and "criminals," i.e. at the point corresponding to the boundary between the two underlying clauses. With a verbphrase complement, on the other hand, there is no longer a distinct boundary between clauses, e.g. "The corrupt police can't force *criminals to confess very quickly.*" Here "criminals" serves as the object of "force" as well as the subject of "confess"; and a click located in the word "criminals" no longer showed any systematic tendency to be preposed. It is debatable whether or not there are concomitant differences in the surface structure of these two sorts of sentence. Chapin and his colleagues (30) were unhappy about this aspect of the materials and undertook a more direct test of Bever's conjecture. They found that clicks placed midway between a major surface boundary and a subsequent underlying clause boundary were attracted to the surface boundary; but when the clause boundary preceded the major surface boundary, locational errors were more or less equally divided between them. It seems likely that the technique will have to be refined in order to resolve these inconsistencies. One feasible modification would be to utilize the paradigms of signal detection, setting listeners to detect the presence of a faint click in a specified region of a sentence or forcing them to choose between a number of possible alternative locations. These procedures may show that there are genuine fluctuations in perceptual sensitivity during the syntactic analysis of sentences. Such a view is plausible because sensitivity to the location of a switch in speech from one ear to the other is greatest at boundaries between clauses (183), and similarly reaction times to clicks are faster when they occur in clause boundaries (84). Meanwhile, however, what are we to infer from the rather muddled history of clickology?

The story told by Bever (16) has considerable attraction. He argues that surface structure has a less direct perceptual reality than underlying structure. Surface structure is a derived construct, and it takes time to mature in the mind of the perceiver. Its effects on perceptual tasks such as the location of clicks occur only when there is sufficient delay for its mental derivation to take place. Ordinarily, when an individual listens to a sentence, he is gathering information about its underlying structure, and it is at the end of each clause that such structure is assigned—hence the relocation of clicks to clause boundaries. Bever goes on to argue that clauses are more directly perceived than individual words, since listeners recognize a target word in a list of sentences more quickly when they are told the sentence in which it will occur, even though it is the first word of the sentence (15). Moreover, Savin & Bever (154) argue that words are more directly perceived than phonemes. They found that listeners recognize a target phoneme in a list of syllables more quickly when they are told the syllable in which it will occur, even though it is the first phoneme of the syllable. This topsy-turvy conception, from which it seems to follow that deep structures are more directly apprehended than phonemes, makes it difficult to explain such everyday phenomena as the detection of mispronunciations, neologisms, and solecisms. Yet is is a useful supplement to the more conventional order of processing—from sound through syntax to sense. It embodies the important truth that the perceiver does not come empty-handed to his task. He is likely to have a number of conjectures about the meaning of a sentence, derived from his immediate or general semantic knowledge. He is likely to possess a variety of perceptual heuristics to aid him in the assignment of underlying structure, e.g. the occurrence of a noun-verb-noun sequence normally signifies the underlying roles of actor-action-object (14).

If a conventional order of processing is permitted to augment Bever's scheme, then it is feasible that a perceiver also exploits cues in the surface structure of a sentence in order to recover its underlying structure (55). Such cues appear to divide into two categories: the presence of grammatical formatives indicating explicit structure, and the presence of certain lexical items suggesting definite hypotheses about structure. Particular exemplars of both sorts of cue have been investigated using the phoneme-monitoring task devised by Foss (59). The technique rests on the assumption that all aspects of perceptual analysis are carried out to some extent by the same central processor; hence the time taken to recognize a target phoneme provides a useful index of the load placed on the processor by the syntax of a sentence. The general assumption appeared to be justified by the finding that responses were slower when a target followed a relatively infrequent word, although the effect only occurs with adjectives (24). One salient cue to underlying structure is the presence of relative pronouns in embedded sentences. For example, "The car that the man whom the dog bit drove crashed" seems easier to understand than "The car the man the dog bit drove crashed." Despite an early setback (62), Foss and Hakes and their co-workers have established that responses to a target phoneme in an embedded sentence are faster when it contains relative pronouns (77, 78). Hakes (76) has demonstrated in the same fashion that signaling the occurrence of a complement by the presence of "that" makes a sentence easier to parse.

The effects of lexical cues to underlying structure have been examined only with verbs, perhaps because they differ so markedly in the number and variety of structures they may take as objects. Verbs that can take complements should cause more difficulties than verbs that can take only simple direct objects, since whenever a complement verb occurs a greater number of structural hypotheses have to be tested (56). However, Hakes (75) failed to detect any effect of verb complexity upon a phoneme-monitoring task. A possible explanation for this failure is suggested by the results of an experiment carried out by Holmes & Forster (85). They used a technique invented by Forster (57) in which the words of a sentence are superimposed one after the other in a rapid serial visual presentation. Under this regime, the perception of sentences was influenced by the sort of verb they contained. Sentences with simple transitive verbs were easier to perceive accurately than sentences with nounphrase complement verbs, and when such a verb was followed by an actual complement, e.g. "Bill wanted his father to leave on the last bus," the sentence was still harder to perceive. A very different pattern of results emerged with verbphrase complement verbs. The presence of such a verb, e.g. "The judge warned the youth about the dangers of drugs," made a sentence more difficult to perceive, but this difficulty vanished completely when such a verb was followed by an actual complement, e.g. "His mother allowed the boy to swim in the pool." This surprising facilitation is probably due to the fact that verbphrase complements are much more constrained than nounphrase complements: they must contain an explicit subject, which is almost invariably animate. Since Hakes (75) had used an identical sentence frame for presenting both the simple and the complement verbs, his technique may have been insensitive to such subtle differences between them. This explanation may also account for a recent failure to find an effect of verb complexity on judgments of grammaticality (71).

The Unreality of Deep Structure

For obvious historical reasons most psycholinguists have maintained a continued intellectual loyalty to the basic tenets of transformational grammar. Yet if Chomsky and his colleagues had not postulated the existence of deep structure, psycholinguists might never have invented it. The studies of click location show that clicks migrate sometimes to the boundaries between underlying clauses and sometimes to boundaries between major surface constituents. A simple explanation for this apparent inconsistency is that the technique may be primarily sensitive, not to the assignment of syntax, but to the amalgamation of meaning. The bulk of semantic processing obviously takes place at the end of clauses and at the end of complicated nounphrases. Just such nounphrases attracted clicks in the study carried out by Chapin and his colleagues (30). Similarly, the effects of different sorts of verb on rapid serial visual perception may be attributable to semantic factors: verbphrase complements almost invariably have animate agents, but there is no comparable prediction for nounphrase complements.

This tentative conjecture is not a covert plea for a particular conception of linguistics, but is an argument for abandoning the idea that the deep structure of a sentence is separately perceived. It suggests instead that there is a single integrated analysis of syntax aimed at determining the meaning of a sentence. A listener attempts to assimilate the meaning of each incoming word to his current semantic representation of the sentence, or indeed to his representation of the discourse as a whole. He may well rely upon his knowledge of the likely meaning of a sentence and a variety of heuristic parsing strategies. Perhaps these two activities are conducted in parallel (cf. 14). But, if they are *both* geared to a semantic goal, it seems more likely that they will be conducted in serial fashion in order to avoid conflicts between them. Studies carried out by Rosenberg and his colleagues (e.g. 151) have indeed shown that general semantic expectations affect the intelligibility of sentences presented in noise. Forster & Ryder (58) have observed comparable effects upon rapid serial visual perception. Just as sentences with a complicated syntax were harder to perceive accurately than sentences with a simple syntax, so also sentences describing improbable situations were harder to perceive accurately than sentences describing mundane situations. However, when complex syntax was combined with improbable content, the resulting sentence was still harder to perceive, compatible with the view that hypotheses about sense and syntax are pursued serially.

To deny the perceptual reality of deep structure is tantamount to denying the reality of surface structure, since some admixture of both sorts of information must be involved in syntactic processing. In what situation might it be shown that individuals are sensitive to unadulterated surface structure? One answer is, of course, whenever there is enough time for its mental derivation. There are a number of studies that amply fulfil this requirement, yet which have failed to establish its psychological reality (cf. 111). Edwin Martin (118) found that when individuals were asked to sort the words of a sentence into "natural groups," their performance did not reflect the surface structure of the sentence. A comparable failure occurred in another study (120) in which subjects indicated the locations of intonation breaks in sentences. An interesting finding occurred in both of these studies: when the object of a sentence was a complicated nounphrase, it was often separated from the verb. Once again, it is possible that performance reflected semantic rather than syntactic processing.

THE COMPREHENSION OF WORDS

The comprehension of words is a prerequisite to the comprehension of sentences; and the meanings of words must be represented in memory in a way which is compatible with the meanings of sentences. Yet such is the profusion of hypotheses about meaning (e.g. 103, 157, 165), that thinkers of a positivistic persuasion might be tempted to argue that the notion is gratuitous. This position is advocated by certain contemporary philosophers (cf. 44), but it is unlikely to find much support among psycholinguists, though the drift of a recent work is at times in this direction (133). The more dominant tendency is to search for a parsimonious theory of the representation of meaning.

The Organization of Semantic Memory

The representation of a word in a mental dictionary must include a variety of information—its sound and orthography, its syntactic properties, its meanings and any relevant perceptual features, its emotional and factual connotations. The list is long, and granted the efficiency with which the information can be retrieved, the system must be highly organized (127). The heart of the problem for our purposes is the organization and retrieval of semantic information. But before the meaning of a word can be retrieved, it is first necessary to identify the word. It would take us too far afield to consider the vast literature on this process; and we note in passing only that the effect of even an apparently simple variable such as frequency of usage is a matter of considerable controversy (e.g. 29, 65, 108, 131).

Empirical studies of semantic memory are currently concerned with establishing the relative ascendancy of the psychological notion of an association, the linguistic notion of a semantic component, and the programming notion of a list structure. The traditional conception of an association has been reanimated by the work of Quillian (e.g. 147) in developing computer programs for the storage and retrieval of verbal information. Although this work was originally conceived as an exercise in artificial intelligence, Collins & Quillian (37, 40, 41) have used it as the basis for a model of human performance. They assume that the meaning of a word is its set of verbal associations, which may involve a variety of different sorts of associative link, including class-inclusion and part-whole relations. The organization of the complete associative network reflects the way in which information is initially acquired. An individual is unlikely to learn as a separate fact that, for example, poodles are animals; rather he learns that dogs are animals and, independently, that poodles are dogs. Hence, the representation of "poodle" is only indirectly linked to the representation of "animal"; and once the network has been entered, the retrieval of certain facts is direct (e.g. "dogs are animals"), whereas the retrieval of other facts requires additional associative links to be traversed (e.g. "poodles are animals"). The results of several experiments suggest that the network can be entered with equal ease at any point (66, 113, 114), and they support the notion of a hierarchical retrieval of facts (37, 39, 40, 161). One unexpected finding was that although the closeness of items in the semantic network facilitated positive judgments about them, it impeded negative judgments, e.g. it is harder to evaluate "a canary is an ostrich" than to evaluate "a canary is a fish." The difference has been consistently replicated (155, 156, 182) and perhaps constitutes the central regularity of semantic judgment: the greater the similarity in meaning between words, the easier it is to make a positive judgment, and the harder it is to make a negative judgment, about a semantic relation between them. The network model provides a natural account for the facilitation of positive judgment, but it is necessary to suppose that negative judgments are impeded by extraneous links between neighboring words (40).

The regularity is, however, open to alternative explanations. Schaeffer & Wallace (156) argue that it is a consequence of a comparison process rather than a retrieval process. The meaning of a word, according to this theory, is represented by a set of conceptual elements analogous to the semantic components of linguistic theory (101). In deciding whether an item is a member of a category, the sets of conceptual elements for both words are retrieved and compared. The comparison involves sampling a certain amount of information from both sets in order to satisfy a criterion of judgment. Since similar words will have some common elements, the sampling required to satisfy the criterion will be smaller for a positive judgment than for a negative judgment. A still simpler explanation of the facilitation of positive judgments is that an individual has to search through a list of items stored with the category label, and so the larger the size of the category, the longer it will take him. Such category size effects were discovered by Landauer & Freedman (106), and subsequently corroborated by others (e.g. 122). They may explain what appears to be an effect of an associative hierarchy simply because position in this supposed hierarchy tends to be confounded with category size. It may take longer to decide that a poodle is an animal than to decide that it is a dog because there are more animals than dogs to be examined.

Perhaps such a result simply reflects Marbe's classical law of associations. The law states that the more frequent the associative response to a given word, the faster it should be made; and presumably "poodle" is more likely to elicit "dog" than "animal." The existence of associative norms for categories (e.g. 9, 115) has led to direct tests of the law, and it has been emphatically sustained in studies of both the production of category members (66, 113, 116) and the categorization of given items (182). But what happens when associative frequency is controlled? A study by E. E. Smith and his colleagues (161) paired arbitrary digits with a hierarchy of categories and still detected hierarchical effects. Comparable results were obtained in other more naturalistic studies conducted by Carol Conrad. She found that when associative frequency was held constant, hierarchical effects were present for statements about class inclusion but absent for statements about the properties of items (42). There seems to be more than Marbe's law at work in categorization tasks; and of course it could never really explain the phenomena since it predicts that *any* item with a high associative frequency should be given as an instance of a category. The law is only a statement of a correlation between frequency and latency, and it cannot account for adherence to the logic of categorization. This failure brings us back to the three main competing approaches to semantic judgment. The attempts to tease them apart have been curiously unsatisfactory. No one theory has been conclusively vindicated, and they have all been confronted with some ugly facts.

Perhaps the major inconvenience for the hierarchical theory is a finding reported by Meyer & Ellis (cited in 107). They examined the times taken to categorize a variety of items including pronounceable strings of letters that were not actual words in the language. It took longer to decide that an item like "mafer" was not a "structure" than to decide that it was not a "building." Because "mafer" is not a word, it cannot be part of a semantic network, and the hierarchical theory cannot explain the result. The category size hypothesis, however, runs into comparable troubles. Collins & Quillian (38) investigated negative judgments involving items totally dissimilar in meaning and categories of different sizes. They found that it was just as easy to decide that an item such as "magnesium" was not an "animal" as to decide that it was not a "dog." There were equally disquieting results with some positive judgments, e.g. there was no difference between categorizing birds and categorizing animals. Finally, Landauer & Meyer (107) have cast doubt upon the main regularity of negative judgments, and consequently upon both the hierarchical theory and conceptual element theory. They obtained rankings of the closeness of meaning of items involved in a categorization task. Negative judgments were not appreciably affected by the degree of semantic similarity between item and category.

An empirically minded critic is likely to argue about the adequacy of these experiments and to try to draw up a balance sheet assessing their respective merits. Certainly there is a need for better data. No study appears to have utilized an entirely proper procedure for estimating category size, i.e. the number of items individual subjects actually recognize as members of a category. Yet a disinterested observer might draw a different moral. The seemingly contrary findings may reflect the flexibility of human semantic processing and the capability of subjects to adopt different strategies to meet the constraints of experimental situations. The experiments may even pass by the fundamental problem, since it is so rare in everyday life to have to ascertain the truth of a sentence such as "a dog is an animal." Of course, one can hardly understand such a sentence without verifying it. But there is a considerable distinction between these two transactions for ordinary contingent sentences like "a dog is expensive to keep" (cf. 152). In understanding this sentence, an individual presumably retrieves some information from the lexical entry for "dog," but what? It seems that for the most important semantic retrieval problem, we have no clear idea of what is retrieved, let alone how it is retrieved.

The Meaning of Words

It would be dangerous, even if it were possible, to decide between the competing theories of semantic memory solely upon the results obtained from studies of categorization. Other experimental tasks have, of course, been used to investigate lexical memory. They range from studies of judgments about whether or not strings of letters are words (e.g. 124, 153, 163) to procedures involving memory for words (e.g. 5, 74, 178). But these studies have been concerned mainly with matters other than a systematic assay of the alternative theories of semantic memory. From this point of view it is particularly unfortunate that the categorization studies have concentrated on the organization of nouns, since in them the distinction between linguistic and factual knowledge is especially blurred. On what basis, for instance, do we assign things to the category of "birds"? Are the criteria linguistic or factual? Indeed, perhaps there are no criteria, but merely a list of exemplars from whose shifting attributes a disjunctive set of family resemblances may be inferred. Yet some characteristics *are* more salient than others. Eleanor Heider (81) has shown that apparently there are different degrees of category membership. Her subjects considered that, for example, robins and eagles come closer to the ideal bird than do chickens and ducks. And, as the linguist George Lakoff has pointed out, we appear to recognize a variety of different sorts of criteria whenever we hedge our remarks in such characteristic ways as: "A robin is a typical bird"; "Strictly speaking, an ostrich is a bird"; "Superman is a regular bird."

Many of these complexities melt away when one turns to verbs or to relational terms in general. Apart from technical vocabulary, their meanings rarely embrace a fuzzy boundary between linguistic and encyclopedic knowledge, but the relations between them are correspondingly more complex. Simple hierarchies give way to intricate cross-classifications; for example, such verbs as "travel," "own," and "see" lack a causal component that is present in the meaning of "lift," "seize," and "look at," and these verbs in turn lack an intentional component that is present in "chase," "buy," and "look for." An alternative and more salient classification of these examples, which are taken from an unpublished analysis by George Miller and the present author, is simply into verbs of motion, verbs of possession, and verbs of perception. It is unlikely that mere lists of verbs in semantic memory could handle these subtleties. And since the network theory has no way of freeing meaning from the specific verbiage in which it is expressed, it seems committed to the dubious view that the meanings of verbs are acquired, in part, from explicit statements involving "cause" and "intention." Only a theory countenancing underlying conceptual elements seems to offer sufficient flexibility to account for the acquisition of meaning. Apart from such global considerations, however, it is difficult to distinguish between a semantic network and a set of conceptual elements. Studies of semantic judgment often yield evidence compatible with both theories. For instance, Steinberg (e.g. 164) found that sentences like "The husband is a wife" are considered to be contradictory, whereas sentences like "The chair is a husband" are considered to be nonsensical. The difference can be explained either by postulating an ordered set of semantic components representing the meaning of a word or by reference to the likely distance between words in the semantic network.

One factor that has undoubtedly shaped the direction of research into semantic memory, at least in a negative way, has been a lack of systematic knowledge about the meanings of words. It is difficult to study the organization and retrieval of information without a specification of what information is involved. Although a number of empirical techniques are helpful (e.g. 54, 136), there seems to be no substitute for painstaking linguistic analysis. Unfortunately, linguists have been reluctant to carry out such lexicographical projects in the detail required by psychologists. Perhaps the sort of approach that will have to be adopted is exemplified by George Miller's recent study of verbs of motion (128). Miller used a novel method of "incomplete definition" in which his intuitive choice of paraphrases revealed the major semantic elements of each verb. The resulting analysis was tested empirically at various points by using a technique in which a subject has to sort words according to his perception of their similarity in meaning. This technique has been developed over a number of years for use with both adults and children (e.g. 3, 126), since it provides a stringent test of semantic analyses. Once a beachhead into the English lexicon has been established in this way, it may be possible to devise suitable discovery procedures.

THE COMPREHENSION OF SENTENCES

A major obstacle to understanding the process of comprehension is its intangible nature—a fact borne out by the possible semantic contamination of studies of syntactic perception. It can, of course, be investigated by the use of such tasks as verification or paraphrase, since—to use a potent metaphor—a program must be compiled before it can be executed (45). But the way in which comprehension occurs may well depend upon which of these tasks is about to be performed. Perhaps the simplest and oldest technique is merely to time how long it takes an individual to decide that he has understood a sentence. It was with this procedure, for example, that Danks (43) showed that comprehension appears to be disrupted more by semantic anomaly than by grammatical deviance, and that the effort after meaning sometimes led subjects to misread lexical items. It is probably important whether the subjects read or listen to the material. A reader, unlike a listener, can adjust the depth of his processing to take into account fluctuations in the difficulty of a passage (46). Thus readers can make rapid and accurate assessments of the comprehensibility of a sentence, sometimes even before they have reached the end of it (158). A listener can, of course, elect not to pay too much attention to what someone is saying, but there is clearly no aural equivalent to rapid reading—it is speech that has to be speeded up to increase the efficiency of the system (63).

There is a direct parallel between judgments of comprehensibility and judgments of grammaticality; both sorts of judgment appear to be adversely influenced by semantic incongruities between noun and verb (e.g. 130, 170). The crucial syntactic factor appears to be simply the distance between subject and verb; hence sentences that are self-embedded, or that have a considerable Yngve depth, tend to be rated as hard to understand (79, 171). It is difficult to establish whether the nouns are more salient than the verb, or the verb is more salient than the nouns. But the verb does appear to be decisive for the control of the interpretative process; and when sentences are grouped together on the basis of their similarities in meaning, sameness of verb rather than sameness of subject is the potent factor (cf. 80).

Understanding Ambiguous Sentences

Most sentences considered in isolation are to some extent ambiguous; but it is only rarely that listeners are perplexed by ambiguity. In some mysterious way, the context of an utterance usually suffices to render its meaning plain. However, although only a single conscious interpretation of a sentence occurs, other interpretations may have been covertly considered and rejected. Certain results support such a conjecture; for example, Foss (60) found that responses in his phoneme-monitoring task were slower to ambiguous than to unambiguous sentences, and Garrett (67) found that the location of clicks within ambiguous words was less accurate than when they had been rendered unambiguous by the preceding context. But perhaps the most striking evidence for the partial processing of more than one meaning comes from a study by Lackner & Garrett (105). They presented an ambiguous sentence to one ear with a disambiguating sentence 5 dB softer to the other ear. Almost without exception the sentence was interpreted in accordance with its disambiguating context, yet the subjects were unable to report this unattended sentence. In order for the context to have such an effect, it seems that both meanings of the sentences must be to some extent available to the subjects. All of these findings lend support to McKay's theory (117) that the meanings of ambiguous sentences are processed in parallel and interact with one another in such a way that the perception of one meaning leads to the suppression of others.

Failures to detect effects of ambiguity have been reported in a number of studies. It seems to take no longer to paraphrase ambiguous sentences than unambiguous sentences (67); and it only takes longer to verify ambiguous descriptions on those occasions that the ambiguity is likely to have been noticed (27).

These superficially inconsistent findings have been resolved by Garrett (67) on the grounds that the experiments showing no effects of ambiguity tested subjects after they had understood the sentences, whereas experiments showing effects of ambiguity tested them during the process of comprehension. The one awkward phenomenon is the greater time required to complete an ambiguous rather than an unambiguous sentence fragment (117). However, a recent study (17) suggests that the effect appears only when the fragment ends in an incomplete clause. In other words, ambiguity is irrelevant once a clause boundary is passed, because a single meaning has generally been decided upon by then. There is, however, an alternative resolution of the experimental findings. An individual is likely to analyze more than one meaning of a sentence only if its context fails to provide a strong bias towards one reading. If there is such a bias, the sentence will be no harder to understand than an unambiguous one. If the bias turns out to be inappropriate, then the listener will have been led up the garden path and he will have to reconsider the sentence (cf. 47). It follows that where sentences are presented in contextual isolation, effects of ambiguity are likely to be detected; but where they are presented after a disambiguating context, no such effects are likely to be detected. The one awkward exception to this principle is the failure to find any difference in the time to paraphrase isolated ambiguous and unambiguous sentences. But although paraphrasing tasks are often revealing about the search for meaning (51, 68), they are relatively insensitive indices of perceptual processing (76). It seems, in general, that any procedure permitting sentences to be considered in tranquillity is unlikely to be affected by their ambiguity (129).

Students of ambiguity have been provided with a wide variety of materials by linguists, and they have investigated the effects of ambiguities in both words and syntax. It does not seem that there are any safe generalizations that can be made at present about the psychological relevance of the origin of an ambiguity in a sentence. However, the view that all the meanings of a sentence are analyzed to some extent seems more feasible when its ambiguity is structural rather than lexical in origin; certainly such a distinction would explain why it is harder to reinterpret sentences with lexical ambiguities (cf. the study by Cairns cited in 17).

The Verification of Sentences

The study of sentence verification has undergone a distinct shift of emphasis during the last few years. Originally the task was introduced in order to establish differences in the ease of understanding sentences, as in Wason's classic studies of negation (e.g. 172). But psycholinguists have become increasingly interested in *how* an individual determines whether a sentence is true or false. This development is due largely to the independent work of Clark (32, 36) and Trabasso (167, 168), although the differences between their approaches are largely terminological. Both theories agree that the process of verification can be separated into four main serial stages: the representation of a sentence, the representation of some state of affairs it purports to describe, the comparison of the two representations, and the mobilization of an appropriate response. The order of the first two stages depends upon the order of presentation of the materials or the order in which they are encoded. But this order has important consequences. If a visual display is presented first, it will usually be represented in a neutral affirmative way. It it is presented after its purported description, then the format of its representation will be contingent upon the nature of this sentence.

Verification tasks have shown that a variety of factors appear to influence the initial representation of a sentence. There is evidence that negative sentences take longer to understand than affirmative sentences (32, 168), that explicit negatives such as "none" or "not present" take longer to understand than implicit negatives such as "few" or "absent" (32, 99), and that passive sentences take longer to understand than active sentences (135). But the analysis of verification has also stimulated interest in other linguistic phenomena, including the distinction between *unmarked* items, such as "deep" or "long," which can be used in both a neutral and a contrastive sense, and *marked* items, such as "shallow" or "short," which can be used only in a contrastive sense. Marked items resemble negatives in that they tend to take longer to encode. However, there has been sharp controversy between

Huttenlocher (e.g. 87, 88) and Clark (e.g. 33) about lexical marking and the strategies individuals use to solve three-term series problems. The controversy has been fervent rather than enlightening, perhaps because the antagonistic positions may be reconcilable (96).

Although Clark (e.g. 35) originally argued that sentences are represented in the form of their underlying structures, the evidence for this view is sketchy and indirect and takes no account of the alternative hypothesis that they are represented in a more semantic form. No verification study has directly contrasted these two views; but evidently Clark (34) has partially abandoned this tenet of his theory.

There is also a latent controversy about possible differences in picture encoding. Chase & Clark (31) argue, for example, that whether a display is encoded as *X above Y* or as *Y below X* makes no difference to the duration of the operation. They found that instructing subjects to attend to the top or the bottom of the display had no effect on encoding time, though it obviously affected the form in which the display was represented. However, when Olson & Filby (135) ingeniously focused attention upon the depicted object of an action, encoding was in a form comparable to the passive voice and took longer to execute. It seems that verification like other choice reactions is influenced by information-theoretic aspects of the task, and the range of alternative stimuli may affect encoding time (134).

The core of the verification models is, of course, the stage when the two representations are compared. It is axiomatic in both models that a successful match depends upon complete congruency between representations; and this view naturally suggests an underlying abstract encoding common to both pictures and sentences. The challenge to the theorist is to devise a plausible set of operations that yields the appropriate responses and tallies with the data. Clark & Chase (36) argue that the comparison stage has a truth index which is initially set as "true," and that each mismatch reverses this index. A series of comparisons is required because the negative component of a sentence is not considered until after its basic unnegated proposition. The truth index obviously remains unchanged for a true affirmative. It is reversed once for a false affirmative because the representation of the sentence fails to match the representation of the picture. It is reversed once for a false negative because although its unnegated proposition matches the representation of the picture, its negative component does not. And it is reversed *twice* in the case of a true negative because first the unnegated proposition and then the negative component fail to match the representation of the picture. The resulting interaction between the form of the sentence and its truth value has been abundantly confirmed: true affirmatives are easier than false affirmatives, but true negatives are harder than false negatives (e.g. 32, 168). In some experiments, however, subjects rid themselves of negative sentences by converting them into equivalent affirmatives, e.g. the predicate "isn't odd" is changed to "is even." Naturally, such conversions are particularly prevalent with binary predicates (168). When subjects adopt such a strategy, their results are compatible with the models on the assumption that conversion modifies the representation of a sentence and takes an additional amount of time.

Contrary to the central assumption of the verification models, Tversky (169) has suggested that a name may be converted into a pictorial code or a picture into a verbal code; and Seymour (159) has similarly argued that the meaning of a word in a shape-naming task may be represented in some quasipictorial fashion. Such arguments may be correct for simple tasks where subjects are sensitive to the restricted nature of the linguistic materials. But if negative sentences were encoded pictorially, it would be extremely difficult to explain the standard interaction with truth value. Perhaps the real burden of these criticisms is that the boundary conditions of the verification models have yet to be clearly drawn. The majority of studies have been concerned with seeking confirmatory evidence, and critical tests of the serial nature of verification, using the additive factor method (166), have only recently been undertaken. Unfortunately, it does not seem too difficult to discover embarrassing interactions between factors, e.g. encoding a negative sentence appears to retard both picture encoding (104) and the retrieval of information from long-term memory (123).

Answering Questions

Answering a question is in many ways a comparable task to verifying a statement, especially when the interrogated information has only just been presented. Hence it is a simple matter in principle to modify the verification models so that they will account for this sort of question answering (35). But the actual details of such modifications are harder to establish since the experimental results are complicated. A surprising phenomenon was discovered by Patricia Wright (185) in a task where listeners heard a sentence followed 5 seconds later by a question about it. The main source of difficulty in giving a correct answer about the actor or object was a mismatch between the voice of the question and the voice of the original sentence. Consequently, passive sentences created difficulty only when the questions were active. When the action itself was queried—e.g. "what was done by X?"—the syntactic form of the question was much less relevant than which noun occurred in it. The task was easier when this noun was the first to be mentioned in the original sentence. It might seem that these effects are simply due to the verbatim retention of the sentences. In a subsequent replication, however, Wright (186) used an interpolated task to prevent rehearsal, but the pattern of results was identical. A further experiment suggested that even when the answer to a question is a single word, its production covertly involves a complete clause, and that the form of the question determines the form of this clause. This principle applies even where the action itself is queried: the noun that occurs in the question becomes the first noun of the answer.

There are still more complex results from studies of question answering. Some experiments conducted by Smith & McMahon (162) detected direct effects of voice: where the sentences and questions concerned the relative order of two participants, passive sentences took longer to encode than active sentences. There were also striking effects of both intricate semantic variables and the order of presentation of sentence and question. What makes such results particularly difficult to interpret is, as the authors acknowledge, the possibility that subjects adopted special strategies to deal with the task.

The Natural History of Negation

The main danger with the models of verification is that their very success in certain situations may lead to unjustified claims, such as that the comprehension of all forms of negation can be accounted for by a single model. The example of negation is instructive because Wason has argued for a number of years that its proper function is to deny misconceptions and misunderstandings. The reason that negative sentences are not ordinarily noted for their difficulty is perhaps because their interpretation requires the listener merely to consider changing the truth value of some proposition that he has already interpreted (174). Indeed, the ordinary negative seems analogous to the false negative of the laboratory, since it probably calls for only a single mental reversal of truth value (173). In evaluating a similar thesis, Greene (72) found that it was much easier to determine that an affirmative and a negative sentence differed in meaning than to determine that they were synonymous. It is also easier to appreciate that an assertion has been denied when the denial is an explicit negation rather than an implicit negation (98).

One tentative moral that might be drawn from this aspect of negation is that there are good psychological reasons for the existence of each sort of grammatical clause. If there are circumstances where negatives are easier than affirmatives, then there are likely to be favorable circumstances for any option within a clause. There may be no intrinsically difficult clause constructions, only difficult combinations of them.

LANGUAGE AND MEMORY

It is parsimonious to assume that sentences are remembered, at least initially, in the form in which they are interpreted; and such an assumption is often made, as Fillenbaum (53) has emphasized, when making inferences about comprehension from the results of memory experiments. But since these results so often depend upon the task the subjects have performed (26, 50, 187), there is uncertainty about whether the experimental procedure affects initial interpretation or subsequent memorial processes. Nevertheless, it is generally accepted that sentences are not normally retained as strings of unrelated words, and a variety of hypotheses have been put forward about their mode of organization in memory.

Memory and Syntax

A simple proposal is that sentences tend to be retained in "chunks" that correspond to their surface constituents (e.g. 94). Although effects of surface structure have been reported in the rote learning of connected discourse (4), their natural locus appears to be the short-term retention of sentences (82). When an individual is presented with a sentence spoken in normal intonation followed by a probe word to which he has to respond with the next word in the sentence, the latency of his response appears to reflect the surface structure of the sentence (1). Since pauses in linguistic and nonlinguistic materials have a comparable effect on the probe task (180, 181), the apparent effects of surface structure may be due to rhythmic aspects of the perceived or rehearsed intonation of the sentence (cf. 120, 121).

We saw previously that certain aspects of syntax affect comprehension, and several theorists have proposed that such features will also affect retention. A diversity of syntactic indices have been canvassed, including transformational complexity, Yngve depth, and lexical density (i.e. the proportion of content words in a sentence). Unfortunately, while Perfetti (142) found an effect of lexical density but no effect of depth in short-term retention, Bacharach & Kellas (7) holding lexical density and depth constant found an effect of transformational complexity, and, in more long-term tasks, Wearing (e.g. 176) found an effect of depth but little or no effect of transformational complexity. There is not likely to be any simple resolution of these results. It is difficult to see why any syntactic property should ordinarily be relevant to the retention of intelligible sentences, unless it is being deliberately used as an aid to memory. Paradoxically, unraveling the mechanisms of intentional memory could prove extremely difficult simply because of an enhanced sensitivity of subjects to the nature of the materials.

The obvious alternative to some sort of superficial segmentation is, of course, a deep structure representation of sentences. But since our earlier analysis of perception suggested that deep structure had no independent psychological validity, it should not be surprising to learn that recent work continues to cast doubt on this hypothesis. It was originally argued, for example, that the amount of storage space occupied by a sentence depended on the number of transformational "footnotes" such as Passive, Interrogative, and Emphatic specified in its underlying structure. This view has encountered a whole series of setbacks (e.g. 49, 61, 69). Deep structure theories about the efficacy of words as prompts to the recall of sentences have perhaps fared a little better, but they have not gone unchallenged. Certainly prompted recall can be affected by factors other than syntax. It is enhanced, for instance, by the presence of co-referential items in separate clauses (110), provided that the relation is conspicuously signposted by the use of a pronoun. The facilitation is not simply due to the greater ease of processing pronouns (119). On the contrary, children's memory is improved by explicit repetitions of nounphrases within the same sentence (100), presumably because they have yet to master the intricacies of pronominalization. The integrative function of pronouns is further corroborated by the observation that when a sentence is partially recalled, the presence of a pronoun rather than a noun is more likely to lead to its complete recall (10).

Perhaps the best illustration of the drift away from explanations in terms of deep structure is provided by the work of Rohrman and his colleagues on memory for nominalizations. Linguistic analysis shows that a subject nominalization such as "growling lions" has a simpler underlying structure than an object nominalization such as "digging holes," because the object nominalization requires an additional argument representing its deleted subject. Rohrman's original view (cf. 149) was that this difference explained why subject nominalizations were easier to remember than object nominalizations. However, it was evident in the experimental materials that the subject nominalizations generally involved animate nouns and intransitive verbs, whereas the object nominalizations generally involved inanimate nouns and transitive verbs. Subsequent tests showed that animate nouns were easier to remember than inanimate nouns, and that intransitive verbs were easier to remember than transitive verbs (144, 149). Rohrman concluded, with some justice (8, 150), that the critical factor was the lexical representation of nouns and verbs.

Just when it looked as though a plausible account of linguistic memory might be given in terms of undifferentiated syntactic factors on the one hand and semantic factors on the other hand, a quite separate conception of memory emerged.

Memory and Imagery

In a number of publications (e.g. 137, 138), Paivio has argued that imagery is a highly potent mode of representing sentences and other verbal materials. According to this hypothesis, certain so-called "concrete" sentences are represented in the form of sensory images, whereas other so-called "abstract" sentences are represented less efficiently in some form of verbal code. Particular situations are likely to inhibit the use of imagery (6), and particular individuals are likely to be incapable of forming sensory images (141). Nevertheless, imageability seems to be an important variable. Two independent studies, for example, have shown that Rohrman's subject nominalizations were rated as easier to image than his object nominalizations (139, 175); and when imageability was carefully manipulated, it was the only variable to have a consistent effect upon recall. Yet the interaction between imageability and type of nominalization, with its varying pattern from one experiment to the next, suggests that unknown factors are also at work.

There have been several other reappraisals of established findings in the light of the imagery theory. It was generally considered that the subjects of sentences are easier to recall than their objects, and that they differ in their efficacy as prompts in the same way (86). However, when imageability was controlled, these differences disappeared (89). Likewise, earlier studies had shown that the nouns in adjective-noun pairs tend to be better recalled than the adjectives (86), and that they differ in their efficacy as prompts in the same way (112). But when their imageability was equalized, the asymmetry in recall disappeared (12, 143).

It seems incontrovertible that sentences can be remembered in the form of images. But although such a view is often pitted against alternative linguistic explanations of experimental findings, it is not necessarily in fundamental conflict with them. When imagery is used, sentences have to be translated into images, and at recall the images have to be translated back again into sentences. The probability of error during these processes, as Paivio (139, 140) admits, may well be related to the complexity of the material to be remembered. Certainly linguistic factors seem to be necessary to account for the finding that the imagery value of the object noun is a better predictor of verb recall than the imagery value of the subject noun (89). And if the differences in rated imageability could be explained, they might depend upon linguistic complexity as well as more obvious perceptual attributes (102).

The task for the Imagist psychologists is to demonstrate conclusively that concrete sentences are encoded as sensory images, and that it is in virtue of this representation that they are better remembered than abstract sentences. Begg & Paivio (13) found that subjects were sensitive to changes in the meaning of concrete sentences, and merely sensitive to changes in the wording of abstract sentences. Such differences are consistent with the theory but inconclusive. A recent study has demonstrated that the abstract sentences were harder to understand and that changes in their meaning were correspondingly harder to detect (92). Hence, the most that can be safely concluded from the original experiment is that individuals retain the sense of sentences, as opposed to verbiage, in proportion to their grasp of it. More direct tests of encoding have also sometimes yielded results contrary to the imagery theory (e.g. 179). It seems incontrovertible that sentences can be remembered without recourse to imagery.

One of the consequences of the revival of interest in imagery, and in other forms of mnemonic, has been an enormous increase in the use of sensible linguistic materials in studies of associative learning; and there is wide-ranging evidence for an improvement in such tasks as paired-associate learning when subjects are encouraged to form a unifying image between stimulus and response (e.g. 19, 20). The study of sentences from an associative point of view—a topic too vast to be reviewed here—has revealed that in incidental learning tasks a sentence has a definite integrative function (2). Likewise, when subjects respond associatively to one word with another from the same sentence, the pattern of their responses is consistent with neither a surface nor a deep structure representation. It is best explained in terms of semantic processes (177).

Memory and Meaning

When subjects are unaware that their memory for a particular sentence is going to be tested, they rapidly lose the ability to recall its precise wording. In a series of studies, Jarvella (e.g. 90, 91) has investigated the ability of listeners to perform a running memory task in which from time to time they have to recall the immediately preceding part of a connected passage. Typically, memory is reasonably accurate only for the final sentence that was heard, and it is verbatim only for its final clause. Caplan (25) has shown that the latency to identify a probe word is faster if it, too, comes from the immediate clause rather than an earlier clause, regardless of the amount of interpolated material. Similarly, a study carried out by Goldman-Eisler (70) has established the importance of the clause in simultaneous translation. Such results bear out the thesis that verbatim information is normally lost to memory almost as soon as it has been used, and that the clause is the natural unit in such transactions.

One of the difficulties in evaluating the importance of the clause in perception is to determine whether its boundary is associated with the assignment of underlying structure or with a more general process of semantic interpretation. Its importance in memory is similarly ambiguous since the retention of meaning is often sufficient to enable a subject to reconstruct underlying structure. However, where sense and syntax are not confounded, it appears that underlying grammatical relations are rapidly forgotton. Fillenbaum (53) found that subjects in an incidental memory task readily confused sentences of the form "If you do that I'll hit you" with those of the form "Do that and I'll hit you." Another recent study obtained similar confusions between sentences of the form "John liked the painting and he bought it from the Duchess" and "The painting pleased John and the Duchess sold it to him" (97). The meaning of sentences in these studies and others (e.g. 11) was retained with remarkable accuracy. And, as Rosenberg and his colleagues have shown, purely semantic manipulations can affect the memorability of sentences. Semantically well integrated sentences such as "The doctor cured the patient" are better recalled than less well integrated sentences such as "The doctor shook the author" in both intentional and incidental tasks (e.g. 151).

Inference is likely to play an important part in comprehension, and it is from studies of memory that this fact first emerged in the psycholinguistic literature. It had been forced upon theorists by some of the problems of analyzing connected discourse. For example, Winograd (184) pointed out that there is no linguistic rule for relating anaphoric pronouns to their appropriate nounphrases. The listener relies upon a heuristic inference in order to appreciate the contrast between "Peter put the package on the table, but because it was round, it rolled off" and "Peter put the package on the table, but because it wasn't level, it slid off" (cf. 132). The role of inference in memory has been most notably demonstrated by Bransford & Franks and their colleagues (21). They observed that subjects presented with a sentence like "Three turtles rested on a floating log, and a fish swam beneath them" would readily assume in a recognition test that the sentence had read "Three turtles rested on a floating log, and a fish swam beneath *it.*" However, if the original sentence merely stated that the turtles were *beside* the log, such an inference is less plausible, and the subjects were much less likely to make the false recognition. Such inferences probably occur during the interpretation of a sentence; yet an unpublished study by Charles Jenkins (cited in 71) suggests, surprisingly, that they are made later.

Memory and Connected Discourse

It is debatable whether in the ordinary course of events individual sentences are remembered. It seems more likely that once their meaning has been grasped, they will be retained not as separate entities but by integration into the relevant stock of long-term memories. Bransford & Franks have shown that there appears to be a strong tendency for separately acquired information to become related in this fashion. Their subjects had considerable difficulty in distinguishing whether they had been originally presented with such sentences as "The ants ate the jelly" and "The jelly was on the table" or with more complex sentences such as "The ants ate the jelly on the table" (22, 64). A further study has established that such integrations occur in the spontaneous interpretation of connected discourse (93).

Psychologists have been interested for a long time in the ways in which coherent discourse is remembered, since it is a problem of both practical and theoretical significance (cf. 28 for a number of reviews from both orientations). The main topic that has been investigated experimentally is the effect of thematic knowledge upon retention. One of the first of these studies, carried out by Pompi & Lachman (145), showed that where the theme of a text was obvious, subjects would readily assume that words related to it had occurred in the passage. Dooling & Lachman (48) went on to demonstrate that the recall of a somewhat vague passage was considerably enhanced when it was given an appropriate and revealing title. A similar study by Bransford & Johnson (23) replicated such findings and also showed that the comprehension and retention of sentences could be improved by presenting a picture of the general situation they described. Few psychologists would be surprised by this result because without the picture to set the scene the sentences hardly appear to relate to one another—the reader is distinctly reminded of the White Rabbit's evidence in *Alice in Wonderland.* What is particularly interesting about such passages, and stands in need of further investigation, is the variety of linguistic devices that can be exploited to avoid having to make clear what is being discussed, e.g. the use of anaphoric pronouns in the absence of a prior specification of their reference, e.g. "It takes some skill but it's easy to learn," the use of abstract or generic descriptions for specific activities, e.g. "Too many people doing the same thing can also cause problems," and the deliberate omission of an underlying argument, e.g. "Rain, however, soaks in very fast." (All of these examples come from a passage about flying a kite.) It seems plausible that such variables would have a similar effect upon the memory of individual sentences; and, indeed, Dooling & Lachman (48) found such effects even when the passage was presented in a scrambled order.

The ultimate problem in the study of connected discourse is to discern what factors make for its maximum cohesion and how it is mapped into some form of memorial representation. We know that individuals tend to remember what is important (e.g. 95), and that they are sensitive to structural and cohesive factors in the text (e.g. 146), but we are almost totally ignorant about the processes involved in the long-term representation of discourse. We do not even know whether such linguistic memories entail different principles of organization from the episodic memories of daily life.

Literature Cited

1. Ammon, P. R., Ostrowski, B., Alward, K. 1971. Effects of task on the perceptual organization of sentences. *Percept. Psychophys.* 10:361–63
2. Anderson, J. R., Bower, G. H. 1972. Configural properties in sentence memory. *J. Verb. Learn. Verb. Behav.* 11: 594–605
3. Anglin, J. M. 1970. *The Growth of Word Meaning.* Cambridge, Mass.: MIT Press. 108 pp.
4. Anglin, J. M., Miller, G. A. 1968. The role of phrase structure in the recall of meaningful verbal material. *Psychon. Sci.* 10:343–44
5. Anisfeld, M. 1970. False recognition of adjective-noun phrases. *J. Exp. Psychol.* 86:120–22
6. Atwood, G. 1971. An experimental study of visual imagination and memory. *Cogn. Psychol.* 2:290–99
7. Bacharach, V. R., Kellas, G. 1971. Phrase versus base structure effects on short-term retention. *J. Verb. Learn. Verb. Behav.* 10:171–75
8. Bacharach, V. R., Kellas, G., McFarland, C. E. 1972. Structural properties of transitive and intransitive verbs. *J. Verb. Learn. Verb. Behav.* 11:486–90
9. Battig, W. F., Montague, W. E. 1969. Category norms for verbal items in 56 categories: a replication and extension of the Connecticut category norms. *J. Exp. Psychol. Monogr.* 80:1–46
10. Beatty, J., Borree, J. 1971. Effects of word class on the recall of sentences. *J. Verb. Learn. Verb. Behav.* 10:604–7
11. Begg, I. 1971. Recognition memory for sentence meaning and wording. *J. Verb. Learn. Verb. Behav.* 10:176–81
12. Ibid 1972. Recall of meaningful phrases. 11:431–39
13. Begg, I., Paivio, A. 1969. Concreteness and imagery in sentence meaning. *J. Verb. Learn. Verb. Behav.* 8:821–27
14. Bever, T. G. 1970. The cognitive basis for linguistic structures. In *Cognition and the Development of Language,* ed. J. R. Hayes, 279–362. New York: Wiley. 370 pp.
15. Bever, T. G. 1970. The influence of speech performance on linguistic structure. In *Advances in Psycholinguistics,* ed. G. B. Flores d'Arcais, W. J. M. Le-

velt, 4–30. Amsterdam: North-Holland. 454 pp.
16. Bever, T. G. 1971. The integrated study of language behaviour. In *Biological and Social Factors in Psycholinguistics,* ed. J. Morton, 158–209. London: Logos Press. 215 pp.
17. Bever, T. G., Garrett, M. F., Hurtig, R. The interaction of perceptual processes and ambiguous sentences. *Memory and Cognition.* In press
18. Bever, T. G., Lackner, J., Kirk, R. 1969. The underlying structures of sentences are the primary units of immediate speech processing. *Percept. Psychophys.* 5:225–34
19. Bower, G. H. 1970. Imagery as a relational organizer in associative learning. *J. Verb. Learn. Verb. Behav.* 9:529–33
20. Bower, G. H. 1972. Mental imagery and associative learning. In *Cognition in Learning and Memory,* ed. L. W. Gregg, 51–88. New York: Wiley. 263 pp.
21. Bransford, J. D., Barclay, J. R., Franks, J. J. 1972. Sentence memory: a constructive versus interpretive approach. *Cogn. Psychol.* 3:193–209
22. Bransford, J. D., Franks, J. J. 1971. The abstraction of linguistic ideas. *Cogn. Psychol.* 2:331–50
23. Bransford, J. D., Johnson, M. K. 1972. Contextual prerequisites for understanding: some investigations of comprehension and recall. *J. Verb. Learn. Verb. Behav.* 11:717–26
24. Cairns, H. S., Foss, D. J. 1971. Falsification of the hypothesis that word frequency is a unified variable in sentence processing. *J. Verb. Learn. Verb. Behav.* 10:41–43
25. Caplan, D. 1972. Clause boundaries and recognition latencies for words in sentences. *Percept. Psychophys.* 12: 73–76
26. Carey, P. 1971. Verbal retention after shadowing and after listening. *Percept. Psychophys.* 9:79–83
27. Carey, P., Mehler, J., Bever, T. G. 1970. Judging the veracity of ambiguous sentences. *J. Verb. Learn. Verb. Behav.* 9: 243–54
28. Carroll, J. B., Freedle, R. O., Eds. 1972. *Language Comprehension and the Acquisition of Knowledge.* Washington, D.C.: Winston. 385 pp.
29. Catlin, J. 1969. On the word-frequency effect. *Psychol. Rev.* 76:504–6
30. Chapin, P. G., Smith, T. S., Abrahamson, A. A. 1972. Two factors in perceptual segmentation of speech. *J. Verb. Learn. Verb. Behav.* 11:164–73
31. Chase, W. G., Clark, H. H. 1971. Semantics in the perception of verticality. *Brit. J. Psychol.* 62:311–26
32. Clark, H. H. 1970. *How we understand negation.* Presented at COBRE Workshop on Cognitive Organization and Psychological Processes, Huntington Beach, Calif.
33. Clark, H. H. 1971. More about "Adjectives, comparatives, and syllogisms": a reply to Huttenlocher and Higgins. *Psychol. Rev.* 78:505–14
34. Clark, H. H. 1971. *The chronometric study of meaning components.* Presented at CRNS Colloque International sur les Problèmes Actuels de Psycholinguistique, Paris
35. Clark, H. H. In press. Semantics and comprehension. In *Current Trends in Linguistics Vol. 12: Linguistics and Adjacent Arts and Sciences,* ed. T. A. Sebeok. The Hague: Mouton
36. Clark, H. H., Chase, W. G. 1972. On the process of comparing sentences against pictures. *Cogn. Psychol.* 3:472–517
37. Collins, A. M., Quillian, M. R. 1969. Retrieval time from semantic memory. *J. Verb. Learn. Verb. Behav.* 8:240–47
38. Ibid 1970. Does category size affect categorization time? 9:432–38
39. Collins, A. M., Quillian, M. R. 1970. Facilitating retrieval from semantic memory: the effect of repeating part of an inference. *Acta Psychol.* 33:304–14
40. Collins, A. M., Quillian, M. R. 1972. Experiments on semantic memory and language comprehension. See Ref. 20, 117–37
41. Collins, A. M., Quillian, M. R. 1972. How to make a language user. In *Organization of Memory,* ed. E. Tulving, W. Donaldson, 309–51. New York: Academic. 423 pp.
42. Conrad, C. 1972. Cognitive economy in semantic memory. *J. Exp. Psychol.* 92: 149–54
43. Danks, J. H. 1969. Grammaticalness and meaningfulness in the comprehension of sentences. *J. Verb. Learn. Verb. Behav.* 8:687–96
44. Davidson, D., Harman, G., Eds. 1972. *Semantics of Natural Language.* Dordrecht-Holland: Reidel. 769 pp.
45. Davies, D. J. M., Isard, S. 1972. Utterances as programs. In *Machine Intelligence,* ed. D. Michie, 7:325–39. Edinburgh Univ. Press

46. Deese, J. 1969. Behavior and fact. *Am. Psychol.* 24:515–22
47. Dooling, D. J. 1972. Some context effects in the speeded comprehension of sentences. *J. Exp. Psychol.* 93:56–62
48. Dooling, D. J., Lachman, R. 1971. Effect of comprehension on retention of prose. *J. Exp. Psychol.* 88:216–22
49. Epstein, W. 1969. Recall of word lists following learning of sentences and of anomalous and random strings. *J. Verb. Learn. Verb. Behav.* 8:20–25
50. Fillenbaum, S. 1970. On the use of memorial techniques to assess syntactic structures. *Psychol. Bull.* 73:231–37
51. Fillenbaum, S. 1971. On coping with ordered and unordered conjunctive sentences. *J. Exp. Psychol.* 87:93–98
52. Fillenbaum, S. 1971. Psycholinguistics. *Ann. Rev. Psychol.* 22:251–308
53. Fillenbaum, S. 1973. *Syntactic Factors in Memory.* The Hague: Mouton. 98 pp.
54. Fillenbaum, S., Rapoport, A. 1971. *Structures in the Subjective Lexicon.* New York: Academic. 278 pp.
55. Fodor, J. A., Garrett, M. F. 1967. Some syntactic determinants of sentential complexity. *Percept. Psychophys.* 2: 289–96
56. Fodor, J. A., Garrett, M. F., Bever, T. G. 1968. Some syntactic determinants of sentential complexity II. Verb structure. *Percept. Psychophys.* 3:453–61
57. Forster, K. I. 1970. Visual perception of rapidly presented word sequences of varying complexity. *Percept. Psychophys.* 8:215–21
58. Forster, K. I., Ryder, L. A. 1971. Perceiving the structure and meaning of sentences. *J. Verb. Learn. Verb. Behav.* 10:285–96
59. Foss, D. J. 1969. Decision processes during sentence comprehension: effects of lexical item difficulty and position upon decision times. *J. Verb. Learn. Verb. Behav.* 8:457–62
60. Ibid 1970. Some effects of ambiguity upon sentence comprehension. 9:699–706
61. Foss, D. J., Cairns, H. S. 1970. Some effects of memory limitation upon sentence comprehension and recall. *J. Verb. Learn. Verb. Behav.* 9:541–47
62. Foss, D. J., Lynch, R. H. 1969. Decision processes during sentence comprehension: effects of surface structure on decision times. *Percept. Psychophys.* 5:145–48
63. Foulke, E., Sticht, T. 1969. Review of research on the intelligibility and comprehension of accelerated speech. *Psychol. Bull.* 72:50–62
64. Franks, J. J., Bransford, J. D. 1972. The acquisition of abstract ideas. *J. Verb. Learn. Verb. Behav.* 11:311–15
65. Frederiksen, J. R. 1971. Statistical decision model for auditory word recognition. *Psychol. Rev.* 78:409–19
66. Freedman, J. L., Loftus, E. F. 1971. Retrieval of words from long-term memory. *J. Verb. Learn. Verb. Behav.* 10:107–15
67. Garrett, M. F. 1970. Does ambiguity complicate the perception of sentences? See Ref. 15, 48–60
68. Gear, S. E., Gleitman, H., Gleitman, L. 1972. Paraphrasing and remembering compound words. *J. Verb. Learn. Verb. Behav.* 11:348–55
69. Glucksberg, S., Danks, J. H. 1969. Grammatical structure and recall: a function of the space in immediate memory or of recall delay? *Percept. Psychophys.* 6:113–17
70. Goldman-Eisler, F. 1972. Segmentation of input in simultaneous translation. *J. Psycholing. Res.* 1:127–40
71. Gough, P. B. 1971. Experimental psycholinguistics. In *A Survey of Linguistic Science,* ed. W. O. Dingwall, 252–92. Univ. Maryland Linguistics Program. 810 pp.
72. Greene, J. M. 1970. Syntactic form and semantic function. *Quart. J. Exp. Psychol.* 22:14–27
73. Greene, J. M. 1972. *Psycholinguistics: Chomsky and Psychology.* Harmondsworth, Middlesex: Penguin. 208 pp.
74. Grossman, L., Eagle, M. 1970. Synonymity, antonymity, and association in false recognition responses. *J. Exp. Psychol.* 83:244–48
75. Hakes, D. T. 1971. Does verb structure affect sentence comprehension? *Percept. Psychophys.* 10:229–32
76. Hakes, D. T. 1972. Effects of reducing complement constructions on sentence comprehension. *J. Verb. Learn. Verb. Behav.* 11:278–86
77. Hakes, D. T., Cairns, H. S. 1970. Sentence comprehension and relative pronouns. *Percept. Psychophys.* 8:5–8
78. Hakes, D. T., Foss, D. J. 1970. Decision processes during sentence comprehension: effects of surface structure reconsidered. *Percept. Psychophys.* 8:413–16
79. Hamilton, H. W., Deese, J. 1971. Comprehensibility and subject-verb relations in complex sentences. *J. Verb. Learn. Verb. Behav.* 10:163–70

80. Healy, A. F., Miller, G. A. 1970. The verb as the main determinant of sentence meaning. *Psychon. Sci.* 6:372
81. Heider, E. R. On the internal structure of perceptual and semantic categories. In *Cognitive Development and the Acquisition of Language,* ed. T. M. Moore. New York: Academic. In press
82. Heisey, J. A., Duncan, C. P. 1971. Syntactical encoding in short term memory. *J. Verb. Learn. Verb. Behav.* 10:95–100
83. Herriot, P. 1970. *An Introduction to the Psychology of Language.* London: Methuen. 197 pp.
84. Holmes, V. M., Forster, K. I. 1970. Detection of extraneous signals during sentence recognition. *Percept. Psychophys.* 7:297–301
85. Holmes, V. M., Forster, K. I. 1972. Perceptual complexity and underlying sentence structure. *J. Verb. Learn. Verb. Behav.* 11: 148–56
86. Horowitz, C. M., Prytulak, L. S. 1969. Redintegrative memory. *Psychol. Rev.* 76:519–31
87. Huttenlocher, J., Higgins, E. T. 1971. Adjectives, comparatives, and syllogisms. *Psychol. Rev.* 78:487–504
88. Huttenlocher, J., Higgins, E. T., Milligan, C., Kauffman, B. 1970. The mystery of the "negative equative" construction. *J. Verb. Learn. Verb. Behav.* 9:334–41
89. James, C. T. 1972. Theme and imagery in the recall of active and passive sentences. *J. Verb. Learn. Verb. Behav.* 11:205–11
90. Jarvella, R. J. 1970. Effects of syntax on running memory span for connected discourse. *Psychon. Sci.* 19:235–36
91. Jarvella, R. J., Herman, S. J. 1972. Clause structure of sentences and speech processing. *Percept. Psychophys.* 11:381–84
92. Johnson, M. K., Bransford, J. D., Nyberg, S. E., Cleary, J. J. 1972. Comprehension factors in interpreting memory for abstract and concrete sentences. *J. Verb. Learn. Verb. Behav.* 11:451–54
93. Johnson, M. K., Bransford, J. D., Solomon, S. Memory for tacit implications of sentences. *J. Exp. Psychol.* In press
94. Johnson, N. F. 1969. Chunking: associative chaining versus coding. *J. Verb. Learn. Verb. Behav.* 8:725–31
95. Johnson, R. E. 1970. Recall of prose as a function of the structural importance of the linguistic units. *J. Verb. Learn. Verb. Behav.* 9:12–20
96. Johnson-Laird, P. N. 1972. The three-term series problem. *Cognition* 1:57–82
97. Johnson-Laird, P. N., Stevenson, R. 1970. Memory for syntax. *Nature* 227: 412–13
98. Johnson-Laird, P. N., Tridgell, J. M. 1972. When negation is easier than affirmation. *Quart. J. Exp. Psychol.* 24: 87–91
99. Just, M. A., Carpenter, P. A. 1971. Comprehension of negation with quantification. *J. Verb. Learn. Verb. Behav.* 10:244–53
100. Kamil, M. L. 1972. Memory for repeated words and parallel structure in compound sentences. *J. Verb. Learn. Verb. Behav.* 11:634–43
101. Katz, J. J. 1972. *Semantic Theory.* New York: Harper and Row. 464 pp.
102. Kintsch, W. 1972. Abstract nouns: imagery versus lexical complexity. *J. Verb. Learn. Verb. Behav.* 11:59–65
103. Kintsch, W. 1972. Notes on the structure of semantic memory. See Ref. 41, 247–308
104. Krueger, L. E. 1972. Sentence-picture comparison: a test of additivity of processing time for feature-matching and negation-coding stages. *J. Exp. Psychol.* In press
105. Lackner, J., Garrett, M. F. Resolving ambiguity: effects of biasing context in the unattended ear. *Cognition.* In press
106. Landauer, T. K., Freedman, J. L. 1968. Information retrieval from long-term memory: category size and recognition time. *J. Verb. Learn. Verb. Behav.* 7: 291–95
107. Landauer, T. K., Meyer, D. E. 1972. Category size and semantic-memory retrieval. *J. Verb. Learn. Verb. Behav.* 11:539–49
108. Landauer, T. K., Streeter, L. A. Some differences between common and rare words. *J. Verb. Learn. Verb. Behav.* In press
109. Larsen, S. F. 1971. The psychological reality of linguistic segments reconsidered. *Scand. J. Psychol.* 12:113–18
110. Lesgold, A. M. 1972. Pronominalization: a device for unifying sentences in memory. *J. Verb. Learn. Verb. Behav.* 11:316–23
111. Levelt, W. J. M. 1970. A scaling approach to the study of syntactic relations. See Ref. 15. 109–21
112. Lockhart, R. S. 1969. Retrieval asymmetry in the recall of adjectives and nouns. *J. Exp. Psychol.* 79:12–17
113. Loftus, E. F., Freedman, J. L. 1972. Effect of category-name frequency on the speed of naming an instance of the category. *J. Verb. Learn. Verb. Behav.* 11:343–47

114. Loftus, E. F., Freedman, J. L., Loftus, G. R. 1970. Retrieval of words from subordinate and supraordinate categories in semantic hierarchies. *Psychon. Sci.* 21:235–36
115. Loftus, E. F., Scheff, R. W. 1971. Categorization norms for 50 representative instances. *J. Exp. Psychol.* 91:355–64
116. Loftus, E. F., Suppes, P. 1972. Structural variables that determine the speed of retrieving words from long-term memory. *J. Verb. Learn. Verb. Behav.* 11:770–77
117. McKay, D. G. 1970. Mental diplopia: towards a model of speech perception at the semantic level. See Ref. 15, 76–98
118. Martin, E. 1970. Toward an analysis of subjective phrase structure. *Psychol. Bull.* 74:153–166
119. Martin, E., Walter, D. A. 1969. Subject uncertainty and word class effects in short-term memory for sentences. *J. Exp. Psychol.* 80:47–51
120. Martin, J. E., Kolodziej, B., Genay, J. 1971. Segmentation of sentences into phonological phrases as a function of constituent length. *J. Verb. Learn. Verb. Behav.* 10:226–33
121. Martin, J. G. 1970. Rhythm-induced judgments of word stress in sentences. *J. Verb. Learn. Verb. Behav.* 9:627–33
122. Meyer, D. E. 1970. On the representation and retrieval of stored semantic information. *Cogn. Psychol.* 1:242–300
123. Meyer, D. E. 1971. Verifying affirmative and negative propositions: effects of negation on memory retrieval. Presented at the 4th Int. Symp., Colorado, August 16–21. To appear in *Attention and Performance IV,* ed. S. Kornblum. New York: Academic. In press
124. Meyer, D. E., Schvaneveldt, R. W. 1971. Facilitation in recognizing pairs of words: evidence of a dependence between retrieval operations. *J. Exp. Psychol.* 90:227–34
125. Miller, G. A. 1962. Some psychological studies of grammar. *Am. Psychol.* 17: 748–62
126. Miller, G. A. 1969. A psychological method to investigate verbal concepts. *J. Math. Psychol.* 6:169–91
127. Miller, G. A. 1972. Lexical memory. *Proc. Am. Phil. Soc.* 116:140–44
128. Miller, G. A. 1972. English verbs of motion: a case study in semantic and lexical memory. In *Coding Processes in Human Memory,* ed. A. W. Melton, E. Martin, 335–72. Washington, D.C.: Winston. 448 pp.
129. Mistler-Lachman, J. L. 1972. Levels of comprehension in processing of normal and ambiguous sentences. *J. Verb. Learn. Verb. Behav.* 11:614–23
130. Moore, T. E. 1972. Speeded recognition of ungrammaticality. *J. Verb. Learn. Verb. Behav.* 11:550–60
131. Morton, J. 1969. Interaction of information in word recognition. *Psychol. Rev.* 76:165–78
132. Norman, D. A. 1972. *Memory, knowledge, and the answering of questions.* Presented at Loyola Symp. Cogn. Psychol., Chicago
133. Olson, D. R. 1970. Language and thought: aspects of a cognitive theory of semantics. *Psychol. Rev.* 77:257–73
134. Olson, D. R. 1972. Language use for communicating, instructing, and thinking. See Ref. 28, 139–67
135. Olson, D. R., Filby, N. 1972. On the comprehension of active and passive sentences. *Cogn. Psychol.* 3: 361–81
136. Osgood, C. E. 1970. Interpersonal verbs and interpersonal behavior. In *Studies in Thought and Language,* ed. J. L. Cowan, 133–228. Tucson: Univ. Arizona. 228 pp.
137. Paivio, A. 1969. Mental imagery in associative learning and memory. *Psychol. Rev.* 76:241–63
138. Paivio, A. 1971. *Imagery and Verbal Processes.* New York: Holt, Rinehart & Winston
139. Paivio, A. 1971. Imagery and deep structure in the recall of English nominalizations. *J. Verb. Learn. Verb. Behav.* 10:1–12
140. Paivio, A., Begg, I. 1971. Imagery and comprehension latencies as a function of sentence concreteness and structure. *Percept. Psychophys.* 10:408–12
141. Paivio, A., Okovita, H. W. 1971. Word imagery modalities and associative learning in blind and sighted subjects. *J. Verb. Learn. Verb. Behav.* 10:506–10
142. Perfetti, C. A. 1969. Lexical density and phrase structure depth as variables in sentence retention. *J. Verb. Learn. Verb. Behav.* 8:719–25
143. Peterson, M. J. 1971. Imagery and the grammatical classification of cues. *J. Exp. Psychol.* 88:307–13
144. Polzella, D. J., Rohrman, N. L. 1970. Psychological aspects of transitive verbs. *J. Verb. Learn. Verb. Behav.* 9: 537–40
145. Pompi, K. F., Lachman, R. 1967. Surrogate processes in the short-term re-

tention of connected discourse. *J. Exp. Psychol.* 75:143–50
146. Potts, G. R. 1972. Information processing strategies used in the encoding of linear orderings. *J. Verb. Learn. Verb. Behav.* 11:727–40
147. Quillian, M. R. 1969. The teachable language comprehender: a simulation program and theory of language. *Commun. A.C.M.* 12:459–76
148. Reber, A. S., Anderson, J. R. 1970. The perception of clicks in linguistic and nonlinguistic messages. *Percept. Psychophys.* 8:81–89
149. Rohrman, N. L. 1970. More on the recall of nominalizations. *J. Verb. Learn. Verb. Behav.* 9:534–36
150. Rohrman, N. L., Polzella, D. J., Ackart, L. A. 1970. The psychological status of some syntactic and semantic models. *Pap. Ling.* 2:267–78
151. Rosenberg, S., Jarvella, R. J. 1970. Semantic integration and sentence perception. *J. Verb. Learn. Verb. Behav.* 9:548–53
152. Rubenstein, H. An overview of psycholinguistics. See Ref. 35
153. Rubinstein, H., Garfield, L., Millikan, J. A. 1970. Homographic entries in the internal lexicon. *J. Verb. Learn. Verb. Behav.* 9:487–92
154. Savin, H., Bever, T. G. 1970. The nonperceptual reality of the phoneme. *J. Verb. Learn. Verb. Behav.* 3:295–302
155. Schaeffer, B., Wallace, R. 1969. Semantic similarity and the comparison of word meanings. *J. Exp. Psychol.* 82: 343–46
156. Ibid 1970. The comparison of word meanings. 86:144–52
157. Schank, R. C. 1972. Conceptual dependency: a theory of natural language understanding. *Cogn. Psychol.* 3:552–631
158. Schwartz, D., Sparkman, J. P., Deese, J. 1970. The process of understanding and judgments of comprehensibility. *J. Verb. Learn. Verb. Behav.* 9:87–93
159. Seymour, P.H.K. 1970. Order of fixation effects in classification of word-shape pairs. *Quart. J. Exp. Psychol.* 22:440–49
160. Slobin, D. I. 1971. *Psycholinguistics.* Glenview, Ill.: Scott, Foresman. 148 pp.
161. Smith, E. E., Haviland, S. E., Buckley, P. B., Sack, M. 1972. Retrieval of artificial facts from long-term memory. *J. Verb. Learn. Verb. Behav.* 11:583–93
162. Smith, K. H., McMahon, L. E. 1970. Understanding order information in sentences: some recent work at Bell Laboratories. See Ref. 15, 253–74
163. Snodgrass, J. G., Jarvella, R. J. 1972. Some linguistic determinants of word classification times. *Psychon. Sci.* 27: 220–22
164. Steinberg, D. D. 1970. Negation, analyticity, amphigory, and the semantic interpretation of sentences. *J. Exp. Psychol.* 84:417–23
165. Steinberg, D. D., Jakobovits, L. A., Eds. 1971. *Semantics: An Interdisciplinary Reader in Philosophy, Linguistics and Psychology.* Cambridge Univ. Press. 603 pp.
166. Sternberg, S. 1971. *Decomposing mental processes with reaction-time data.* Presented at Ann. Meet. Midwest. Psychol. Assoc., Detroit
167. Trabasso, T. 1972. Mental operations in language comprehension. See Ref. 28, 113–37
168. Trabasso, T., Rollins, H., Shaughnessy, E. 1971. Storage and verification in processing concepts. *Cogn. Psychol.* 2: 239–89
169. Tversky, B. 1969. Pictorial and verbal encoding in a short-term memory task. *Percept. Psychophys.* 6:225–33
170. Wang, M. D. 1970. Influence of linguistic structure on comprehensibility and recognition. *J. Exp. Psychol.* 85:83–98
171. Wang, M. D. 1970. The role of syntactic complexity as a determiner of comprehensibility. *J. Verb. Learn. Verb. Behav.* 9:398–404
172. Wason, P. C. 1961. Response to affirmative and negative binary statements. *Brit. J. Psychol.* 52:133–42
173. Wason, P. C. 1972. In real life negatives are false. *Logique et Analyse* 57–58: 17–38
174. Wason, P. C., Johnson-Laird, P. N. 1972. *Psychology of Reasoning: Structure and Content.* London: Batsford. Cambridge, Mass.: Harvard Univ. Press. 264 pp.
175. Wearing, A. J. 1971. Vividness and the recall of English nominalizations. *Psychon. Sci.* 22:121–22
176. Wearing, A. J. 1972. Remembering complex sentences. *Quart. J. Exp. Psychol.* 24:77–86
177. Weisberg, R. W. 1971. On sentence storage: the influence of syntactic versus semantic factors on intrasentence word associations. *J. Verb. Learn. Verb. Behav.* 10:631–44
178. Wickens, D. D. 1970. Encoding categories of words: an empirical approach

to meaning. *Psychol. Rev.* 77:1–15
179. Wickens, D. D., Engle, R. W. 1970. Imagery and abstractness in short-term memory. *J. Exp. Psychol.* 84:268–72
180. Wilkes, A. L., Kennedy, R. 1969. Relationship between parsing and retrieval latency in sentences of varying grammatical form. *J. Exp. Psychol.* 79: 241–45
181. Wilkes, A. L., Kennedy, R. A. 1970. The relative accessability of list items within different pause-defined groups. *J. Verb. Learn. Verb. Behav.* 9:197–201
182. Wilkins, A. J. 1971. Conjoint frequency, category size, and categorization time. *J. Verb. Learn. Verb. Behav.* 10:382–85
183. Wingfield, A., Klein, J. F. 1971. Syntactic structure and acoustic pattern in speech perception. *Percept. Psychophys.* 9:23–25
184. Winograd, T. 1972. *Understanding Natural Language.* New York: Academic. 191 pp. Also published in *Cogn. Psychol.* 3:1–191
185. Wright, P. 1969. Transformations and the understanding of sentences. *Lang. Speech* 12:156–66
186. Wright, P. 1972. Some observations on how people answer questions about sentences. *J. Verb. Learn. Verb. Behav.* 11:188–95
187. Wright, P., Kahneman, D. 1971. Evidence for alternative strategies of sentence retention. *Quart. J. Exp. Psychol.* 23:197–213

INSTRUCTIONAL PSYCHOLOGY

❖214

Wilbert J. McKeachie[1]
Department of Psychology, University of Michigan, Ann Arbor

The first problem in reviewing research on instructional psychology is determining what "instructional psychology" means. In this review we take it to mean those things relevant to teaching, educating, or instructing. The question we are trying to answer is "What factors influence the effectiveness of instruction?" Our structure is a relatively loose one in which we group together studies primarily dealing with: (*a*) the learner, including such variables as anxiety, aptitude, and social class (most of this section deals with attribute-treatment interactions); (*b*) the teacher and teacher style; (*c*) the teaching methods, technology, and characteristics of the class; (*d*) the objectives and content, including microfeatures of instruction such as feedback and reinforcement.

The two earlier reviews of instructional psychology in this series (Gagné & Rohwer 51, Glaser & Resnick 56) approached the subject in different ways, and this review obviously reflects my own interests and biases. As compared with the earlier chapters, this one probably gives greater weight to molar instructional variables and less to those variables traditionally associated with research in verbal learning and performance. This chapter supplements rather than supplants these excellent preceding reviews of instructional psychology. Most of my research and experience have been in the area of college teaching, and the reader should be warned that research dealing with college students and adults has received disproportionate emphasis in this review. And because I have a great interest in improving teaching, I trust I may be forgiven for occasional paragraphs directed more to the teacher than to researchers and theorists.

[1]I am indebted to Terry Miller, Nan Holmes, Margy Moffett, Yi-Guang Lin, Richard Mann, James Greeno, Stanford Erickson, Rob Seltzer, James Kulik, and Karl Zinn for helpful comments and to Bette DeKarske, who handled the onerous task of coordinating the bibliography with the text.

It is probably not pure chance that led me to start this chapter with a section on the student. The term "instructional psychology" is not one I like as well as "psychology of learning" or even "educational psychology," for "instruction" carries a connotation of teacher direction or building that is less pleasing to me than the emphasis on the student implied in "learning," or even the relationship of "leading from" implied in "educate." Even though the student as a person gets lost in this chapter's consideration of traits and attribute-treatment interactions, I still have some sense that the most important focus of instruction is a living, breathing, seeking, human being. Were I a sociologist I would no doubt begin with the broader social setting and the role of the school in society. Certainly much of the most important criticism of education in our society aims not at the specifics of instruction but at the bureaucratic nature of the school in inculcating values and knowledge and screening students for positions in our social and occupational heirarchies. Thus the author begs the reader to remind himself from time to time that "state and trait anxiety," "Keller plan," "inductive and deductive strategies," and our other topics have to do with the feelings and experiences of young people in an institution which may or may not fit well with the rest of their lives.

THE LEARNER

Anxiety

Learner anxiety has for some time been a major interest of educational researchers. In many situations anxiety seems to be detrimental to learning and/or to performance on tests, but the findings are inconsistent (see Martens 94), and the mechanisms by which anxiety may influence learning and performance have not been clarified despite conflicting theories. During the past 2 years some progress has been made in this area.

Researchers at two centers of activity, the City University of New York and Florida State, have used variations in programmed materials as the instructional method. In a typical but rather complicated study, Tobias & Abramson (158) compared the interactions between stress, anxiety, and response mode. The basic variable in response mode was whether the program required only reading or a constructed response. An additional variable was reinforcement or nonreinforcement (i.e. whether or not the correct answer was given on the next frame of the program). Anxiety and stress did interact, but the more anxious students learned familiar material *better* than less anxious students in the stressful condition. Note, however, that this was a learning situation with a relatively low error rate (3.7%). The expected interaction in the opposite direction should be more likely to occur with more difficult materials, as was demonstrated in the experiments by O'Neil et al (116) and Spielberger, O'Neil & Hansen (147).

Spielberger's approach differentiates the *state* of anxiety from the *trait* of anxiety. The *state* of anxiety consists of unpleasant consciously perceived feelings of nervousness, tension, and apprehension with concomitant physiological arousal. The *trait* of anxiety is the tendency to perceive a wide variety of situations as threatening and to respond with anxiety; i.e. trait anxiety is a relatively stable individual characteristic (Spielberger 146). Trait anxiety is the primary component of most tests of anxiety.

The distinction between state anxiety and trait anxiety is an important one, since one is thereby led to look at changing effects of anxiety in a given situation. One might expect, for example, that anxiety, when it is aroused, would first be disruptive for learning difficult materials, but that the course of the effect of anxiety might then depend upon what sort of defense mechanisms were used. Spielberger et al (147) and O'Neil (115) present evidence that students with high trait anxiety show diminishing state anxiety over time in stress conditions. Since this trend did not occur for low trait anxiety students, it suggests that high trait anxiety students may have learned to defend against anxiety relatively quickly in stressful situations or that they at least have defended against admitting they're anxious.

Do these defenses take hold as soon as the student begins a test, or only when he encounters difficult items? Do the defenses break down if the test is too difficult? Testing experts have usually advised a test sequence moving from easy to difficult items on the assumption that easy items increase confidence and reduce the amount of damage to performance likely to be caused by high anxiety. Munz & Jacobs (110) found that when sequencing achievement tests items, a hard-to-easy order is better than a random order, and perhaps even better than an easy-to-hard order for students high in trait anxiety. One explanation would be that the highly anxious students feel a great sense of relief when they come to easy items after trying to solve hard ones; with an easy-to-hard sequence, on the other hand, anxiety is increasing and thus likely to be more disturbing.

In programmed learning tasks it is difficult to separate the effects of anxiety upon learning and the effect on the responses required by the program. Moreover, there is the probability that being questioned arouses anxiety, particularly if one does not know the answer. The effects of anxiety on performance in a low error rate program may be quite different from effects on ordinary learning of text or upon performance on a difficult achievement test. Thus, for example, Ray, Katahn & Snyder (126) found no effect of trait anxiety on learning items of prose except when test items were interspersed. Anxiety not only affected original performance adversely but also affected retention with original learning controlled.

Tennyson & Wooley (155) compared the performance of high and low A-State subjects on a self-instructional poetry classification program in which an easy section followed a difficult section of poetry selections. Subjects initially low in A-State made fewer errors on the difficult section, but high A-State subjects made fewer errors on the easy section. These results are contradictory to those of O'Neil (115). However, O'Neil's subjects were all females, while those of Tennyson & Wooley included both males and females. Unfortunately, analysis of sex differences was not reported in the Tennyson & Wooley study, but it seems likely that this is an additional complicating factor.

These studies indicate that predictions about the effect of anxiety on performance are not really very simple. High anxiety is *not* necessarily detrimental to learning. Its effects depend not only upon task difficulty but upon sequence of tasks.

Helping the Anxious Student

In attempting to reduce the possibly deleterious effects of anxiety upon learning, two approaches have been used. One attempts to reduce the anxiety; the other accepts the anxiety and attempts to help the learner by providing aids for the specific damaging processes produced by anxiety.

An example of both the first and second approaches is that used by Sarason (141) in studies in which reassuring instructions preceded the learning task. In one such study "reassurance" (anxiety reducing), "task orientation," and "motivating task orientation" instructions all prevented the detriment to the performance of high test anxious subjects found under an achievement orientation condition, and there was no difference between the three positive conditions. In fact, under these conditions the performance of the high anxious subjects was superior to that of low test anxious subjects.

Wine (166) observed classroom behaviors of high and low test (trait) anxious children in an art class just before an important examination. In this situation high anxious children sought teacher approval, listened attentively to the teacher, and spent more time sitting idle. Wine summarizes her results by suggesting that the high test anxious children under stress become more alert to evaluative cues, less alert to task cues, and more concerned about self worth, while low test anxious students focus more fully on the task. Wine's theory, developed more fully in her review of previous research (165), helps account for the positive effects of Sarason's instructions, since his instructions deal with the areas in which anxious students should have difficulty. "Task orientation" and "motivating task orientation" instructions should help the test anxious student focus his attention on the task, thus diminishing the normal deficiency in this process.

Many of the Florida State studies also use the second approach of compensating for deficiences in information processing produced by high anxiety in programmed and computer-assisted-instruction (CAI). Since CAI offers a relatively well-controlled instructional situation, the Florida State group has been able to study quite carefully the particular functions which anxiety affects. For example, Leherissey et al (86) followed by Sieber's (144) argument that anxiety's disruptive effects may be through its effect on memory. To assist the anxious student, a list of previous errors on the material being studied was given as a memory support. The results of the experiment were complex. Unexpectedly memory support tended to increase state anxiety; presumably being reminded of errors was anxiety arousing. This complicates interpretation of results since memory support produced no overall improvement in performance. But students high in state anxiety did better in the memory support group than the high state anxious students without memory support. The study by Meyers & Dunham (104) also supports the theory that anxiety has a particular effect on memory. They found that while memory span and performance on a concept learning transfer task were positively correlated for low trait anxiety subjects, the relationship washed out for high anxiety subjects.

One of the basic questions relevant to practical application of knowledge of attribute-treatment interactions is who should determine which students get which treatments. Even if the interaction were clearer than it usually is, the task of fitting instruction to the varied students in a typical class may well be too difficult for teachers to perform. Thus it is attractive to hypothesize that students themselves can select the instruction optimal for themselves. O'Neil (114) provided support for this hypothesis by providing memory support at the option of anxious students. This condition was superior to one in which mandatory memory support was provided.

In the studies cited above the major concern has been to reduce the detrimental effects of high anxiety; thus the search for interactions between conditions and anxiety have focused on the high-anxious group. Tallmadge, Kasten & Shearer (154), however, in a complex study of interactions between inductive and deductive teaching styles, understanding and rote learning, two subject matters, and 39 learner characteristics, found only one interesting interaction. Low anxiety students achieved more with deductive rather than inductive instruction. This result is unexplained.

Aptitude

The attribute-treatment interaction of longest interest to psychologists has been the aptitude-treatment interaction—an area recently reviewed by Cronbach & Snow (31). One new study opens the possibility of progress in this area by differentiating differing kinds of aptitudes. Koran, Snow & McDonald (82) studied the interaction of student aptitude with three methods of training teacher trainees in "analytic questioning": (*a*) videotape portrayal of the skill; (*b*) written instructions; and (*c*) no special instruction. Both experimental treatments produced greater effects on behavior in microteaching situations than the control. Videotape presentation was the best of the three, particularly for students who had made high scores on the film memory test, but the written presentation was more effective for subjects who had scored well on the hidden figures test, a result surprising to the researchers. They suggest the possibility that a given treatment, in this case videotape, may either work well for those whose abilities fit that treatment, such as students high in "film memory," or it may serve a compensatory function, as for the low "hidden figures" students who may lack ability to visualize.

At the moment there seems to be a quiescence in the area of research on cognitive variables interacting with treatments. The Koran, Snow & McDonald study as well as the studies on anxiety suggest that more careful analysis of individual and treatment characteristics may pay off.

Achievement Orientation

Achievement motivation and various achievement orientations have been obvious candidates for investigation by those interested in instruction and education. Among the more widely used scales are Gough's Achievement via Conformance and Achievement via Independence Scales from the California Psychological Inventory. One of the few educational studies in which clear interaction effects were obtained was Domino's study (34) of interaction of these two characteristics with teaching style. Those students taught in a manner consistent with their achievement orientation, as indicated by the title of the scale, obtained significantly higher means (than students taught in a discordant manner) on multiple choice tests, essay questions involving factual knowledge, and on the students' ratings of the teacher effectiveness and value of the course. A somewhat similar result was obtained by Goldberg (57) using a criterion of amount of extra nonrequired reading completed. Thus a glimmer of hope for attribute-treatment interactions appears.

Socioeconomic Status and Early Education

The "best-seller" of the year in the area of instructional psychology was one by Jencks (70). His book has been so extensively reviewed and criticized that there is probably little point in an additional review here. However, it is worth pointing out that Jencks did *not* conclude from his review of the rather scanty research available that schools make no difference. Rather he concludes that not going to elementary school makes a marked difference for lower class children and that there *are* significant differences between elementary schools in effectiveness.

Despite the heat generated about the effects of early instruction, relatively little additional evidence seems to have emerged in the past 2 years. Jacobson et al (68) found that preschool children from poverty backgrounds could be systematically trained in concept learning in ways that increased scores on the Stanford-Binet as well as on tests of concept learning. Jacobson & Greenson (69) reported that half the IQ gains were maintained 14 months after the training ended. Unfortunately the control group was not retested.

What does a gain in IQ mean in studies such as this? One answer is that an intelligence test is a pretty good measure of generalized achievement and that gains in IQ thus indicate that the training has produced cognitive gains outside the specific tasks upon which the training was done. Another interpretation of IQ gains is that they largely represent changes in motivational and social factors affecting test taking, as suggested by the study of Zigler & Butterfield (171). But most readers of studies in which IQ gains are produced are probably reading more into the intelligence test scores. Intelligence tests are primarily used as predictive devices. The implication of a gain in IQ is that the individual who has made the gain has developed skills or aptitudes which will be predictive of later academic achievement. But when IQ scores are changing as a result of a training program, are the scores after the program better predictors than those obtained at the beginning of the program? The question is not whether IQ gains[2] persist but whether or not school and other intellectual performance is thereafter at a higher level.

To say that the gains in IQ should not be expected to persist without changes in the schools is a weak rejoinder. Intelligence tests were designed to predict achievement in conventional schools. If changes in intelligence (academic aptitude) have really been produced, it is in conventional schools that the effects should be most

[2]While many child psychologists have stressed the effects of early training on curiosity or achievement motivation, another effect may be the sheer pleasure of familiarity with words and schools. Zajonc has shown in several studies (170) that simple exposure leads to liking. A concept training task thus not only influences cognitive mechanisms involving concept formation but also increases liking for the concepts.

apparent. Rohwer (130) deals with this point when he shows that lower socioeconomic status black children are not as disadvantaged in certain kinds of learning not requiring conceptual elaboration as in IQ. Learning skills, such as conceptual elaboration, can be taught (Rohwer & Ammon 131) so that lower socioeconomic status children can learn more effectively in school. But in all of these efforts good longitudinal data are still needed.

Attribute-Treatment Interactions

The studies in this section have been based largely on the faith that instruction could be improved if it were adapted in terms of differences in student characteristics. The results of the research reported provide some empirical support of that faith. But the largest recent study of trait-treatment interactions produced relatively limited results. Goldberg (57) compared lecture and independent study methods and quizzes vs papers in two psychology courses. Rather than choosing personality variables on the basis of a theory about the personality characteristics of individuals likely to be differently affected by the two methods, he tested 350 different personality measures for interaction effects with the teaching methods. Not surprisingly only about one-third more significant interactions were found than would have been expected by chance.

Despite Goldberg's rather pessimistic view of attribute-treatment interactions, few citizens, few educators, and not even many researchers would reject the hope that educational environments can somehow be varied in ways that will permit adaptation to characteristics of the developing learner. A measure like an intelligence test designed to predict success with all sorts of schools and teachers is not likely to be effective in discriminating particular interactions, but other measures, dealing with changing and less general characteristics, may be more useful in interaction analyses. Glaser (55) has compared adaptive and selective (survival of the fittest) modes of education and concluded that our penchant for a fixed educational mode derives from the tendency to think of students as having fixed enduring traits. What we need, he suggests, are measures of new aptitudes—aptitudes that are trainable, aptitudes conceptualized in terms of processes.

THE TEACHER

Some aspects of the teacher's role in instruction are, of course, implied in the studies of Attribute-Treatment Interaction discussed above. In the studies reported in the previous section, however, our focus was upon learner characteristics, and the teacher was essentially the context. In this section the teacher moves to the foreground, and we look at ways in which teachers differ and how these differences affect learning.

Dimensions of Ratings of Teaching Effectiveness

The use of student ratings of teaching effectiveness is a topic which has generated a great deal of heat and research activity, particularly at the college level. Not all of the controversy is directly relevant to the topic of this chapter, but the question of dimensions of teacher characteristics related to student learning seems directly applicable to instruction. Costin, Greenough & Menges (29) have reviewed the research up to 1971. Recent studies have stirred up additional interest.

Feather (38) reported the results of factor analyses of a 22-item scale derived from the University of Washington scale. Three factor analyses were performed. The three samples were five first-year, five second-year, and seven third-year psychology courses at the Flinders University of South Australia.

1. The first factor, Instructional Competence, included items such as:
   "Is clear and understandable in his explanations";
   "Instructor's general teaching effectiveness in comparison to other psychology teachers";
   "Interprets abstract ideas and theories clearly."
2. The second factor, Interest, included:
   "Subject matter of the course is interesting";
   "Value of the course in comparison to other courses you have taken";
   "Has helped broaden my interests."
3. The third factor, Instructor Attitude to Students, included:
   "Has sympathetic attitude toward his students";
   "Treats his class as adults";
   "Is reasonable in his demands on student time."

These factors[3] seem comparable to those of previous factor analytic studies. Factor 1 appears to be comparable to one found by Field et al (39) and by Frey (46). Factor 2 also is comparable to one found by Frey. Factor 3 appears to be much the same as that found in Germany by Müller-Wolf & Fittkau (109) and in Australia by Field et al's multiple discriminant analysis. The third function found by Field et al is that labeled by Isaacson et al (67) as "Feedback."

Frey (46), whose study will be reviewed later, found six factors:

1. Student accomplishment
2. Organization planning
3. Work load
4. Grading
5. Teacher's presentations (comparable to Feather's "Instructional Competence")
6. Teacher accessibility (comparable to Feather's "Instructor Attitude to Students")

Frey's "Student Accomplishment" probably picks up much the same variance as Feather's "Interest" factor with its item "Value of the course . . ." and enters the area tapped more extensively by Hogan & Hartley's (63) items on student self-development. Hogan & Hartley's student self-development items yield three factors: General Cognitive Development, Field-Specific Development, and Relevance.

[3]Factor analytic results are limited by one methodological problem. Since within-class and between-teacher covariance are lumped together in these studies, factor analysis primarily tells us the dimensions used by students as they perceive a teacher, not necessarily the dimensions along which teachers differ. Multiple discriminant analysis seems less vulnerable in this respect (see Field et al 39).

An interesting feature of these results is that student ratings of *teaching* effectiveness are differentiated from those of the value of the *course,* with course value more closely tied to the important educational goal of developing broader interests. While "teaching effectiveness" ratings are not, as some critics have suggested, measures of cheap popularity, it is probably worthwhile to get a separate rating of course value, which seems to give greater weight to the total plan and organization of the course and less to classroom performance.

The point of these studies is presumably to determine how teachers and classes differ, and in terms of student perceptions the answer apparently is that they differ along eight or ten dimensions. Now we turn to the crux of the matter: "Do these differences among teachers perceived by students make a difference in instructional effectiveness?"

Probably the most publicized recent study in this area was that of Rodin & Rodin (129), which attracted attention both because its results were so surprising and because they supported the doubts many faculty members already had about student ratings. Rodin & Rodin reported a high *negative* correlation between mean student ratings of teaching assistants in a calculus course and the mean course grade of the students. Frey (46) repeated the study with a more carefully controlled research design and analysis and obtained results in the opposite direction; i.e. the teachers whose students achieved the most were rated as most effective.

All six of the factors on the Frey scale showed positive correlations with mean student performance. Even though the *N*'s of teachers were small (8 in introductory calculus, 5 in multidimensional calculus) three of the factors produced statistically significant correlations. These three factors were

1. Student accomplishment:
   "This course has enabled me to identify and analyze central issues in this field";
   "I can now understand relatively advanced presentations on this subject";
   "This course has developed my ability to examine the evidence in this field."
2. Teacher's presentation:
   "The teacher made good use of examples and illustrations";
   "The teacher discussed the course material in an insightful and penetrating fashion."
3. Organization-planning:
   "The teacher arranged the class schedule in an orderly way and followed it closely."

Frey's results indicate that students can report a teacher's effect on learning when they are asked to do so specifically. Note that the "Student Accomplishment" items do not ask the student to rate teacher effectiveness but rather to report effects of the course upon the student himself. This fits with the findings of McKeachie, Lin & Mann (99), who found less striking, but supportive, evidence for the validity of student ratings.

While student ratings can tell us something about how instructors differ and may also indicate which teachers are most effective for particular goals, to date they have not revealed any instructional characteristics which seem to be universally related to instructional effectiveness. Thus we find here, as in the preceding section on the student, a hint that simple, one-variable, linear relationships are not jumping out of the research data. Interactions between teacher characteristics, student characteristics, and outcomes are also not "bustin' out all over," but some tender buds are beginning to suggest possible fruitfulness.

Teacher Expectancy

Feather's third factor, Instructor attitude toward Students, represents a dimension found in many studies having to do with the teacher's relations with, and expectancies of, students. The most famous study of teacher expectancy was Rosenthal's *Pygmalion in the Classroom* (134), which continues to influence educators 5 years after publication. Recent studies agree with Claiborn (23) in failing to replicate the Pygmalion effect. Fleming & Anttonen (42) undertook a large scale replication with better controls and found that false information given the teacher about pupil IQs had no effect on later IQ measures. The study suggested that teachers tended to distrust information discrepant with their own assessment of student ability—a result according with that of José & Cody (74). Thus once again an exciting finding bites the dust. My Fair Lady in the classroom was really fairer than Rosenthal perceived.

Pellegrini & Hicks (123) also failed to find a significant effect of expectancy in a tutorial situation except when tutors were shown the test that would be used as a dependent variable. Rubovits & Maehr (139), however, were able to produce differences in teacher behavior in a situation in which college students were brought together with strange children for a one-hour teaching session. Students labeled as gifted were more likely to be asked questions and praised for their statements than were those labeled nongifted. This finding is not very convincing evidence of the ability of inaccurate information to influence behavior of teachers who are interacting with students over a semester.

Does this mean that teacher expectancies are unimportant? Probably not. The Fleming & Anttonen and José & Cody studies did not really disprove the effect of teacher expectancies on student learning, but rather indicated that false information did not produce a significant effect on teacher expectancy [as pointed out by Finn (40) in a thoughtful review of the expectancy literature]. Rothbart, Dalfin & Barrett (135) did find that teachers paid more attention to students designated as "better," and Finn demonstrated that in some settings teachers do hold expectations which bias their evaluations of pupil work. What the replications suggest is that the connection between teacher expectancies and changes in student academic ability is a good deal more complex and uncertain than the publicizers of *Pygmalion in the Classroom* led the public to believe. While it seems unlikely that Rosenthal's results can be fully replicated, it does seem that when the teacher's expectancies differ there may be ensuing differences in teacher behavior toward students. Strongly held stereotypes may indeed resist change from pupil-teacher interaction and make differences in teacher behavior which may in turn influence student achievement. Thus far, however, research has not been able to demonstrate these links.

TEACHING METHODS, TECHNOLOGY, AND CHARACTERISTICS OF THE CLASS

After our look at the student and the teacher, the two most important persons in instruction, we now turn to the classroom and the methods of instruction used in educational institutions. Lurking in the background of our reflection about classes and teaching methods should be the recognition of the context provided by the school. While we will cite relatively little research on characteristics of schools influencing instruction, there can be little doubt that the nature of schools in our society strongly conditions the effects of instructional methods, a point developed in theoretical detail by Getzels (53). Moreover, the very structure of the classroom suggests certain goals and patterns of interaction. The open classroom, the free school, the student-led class,—these are still deviant activities which carry a special burden of risk and a resulting aura of anxiety and excitement. And as Cohen (26) has pointed out, conventional classes differ in the degree to which the teacher's goal is obedience rather than learning.

In this section we deal with major instructional methods and characteristics of the class such as the Keller plan, programmed learning, computer-assisted instruction, simulation, class size, team teaching, homogeneous grouping, student options, and student-centered teaching. The next-to-last topic of the section is labeled *Student Activity* and should probably be with *Questioning* in the later section on Content, but it seems to flow from student-centered teaching, so here it is.

The Keller Plan

The brightest new star in the constellations of college teaching methods has been the Keller Plan (76), named after one of its major creators, but also variously called PSI (Personalized System of Instruction), "individualized instruction," "contingency-management instruction," or "modular instruction." (The system is not very personalized or individualized except in comparison with the large lecture, which is the favorite *bete noir* to which all new teaching methods wish to be compared.)

Although the first controlled studies of the Keller plan showed no superiority in achievement and less effective use of time as compared with conventional teaching, there are now empirical data indicating that the Keller plan can sometimes be superior to lectures in affecting student achievement and retention and is usually superior in student satisfaction (Born, Gledhill & Davis 17, Cooper & Greiner 27, McMichael & Corey 101, Rubinstein & Friedman 138, and Witters & Kent 167).

Attention is now shifting to research on modifications of the plan to further enhance learning. Sullivan & Hartley (152), for example, gave bonus points for reaching a given criterion on weekly tests, rather than requiring a certain criterion before a student could move to the next unit. The results indicated that bonus points had little effect on final examination scores. Knight (80) studied the effect of three motivational conditions. The control condition involved taking weekly 10-item tests. Students in the two experimental conditions were allowed to retake the test a second or third time, but if 100% correct answers were not attained on any one of the weekly tests by the third retake, students in one experimental group were punished by dropping one full grade in the course (e.g. from A to B), and students in the other group were given a grade of F (failure) for the course. The latter two groups performed better (on the first administrations of the tests), and there was no effect on performance in other courses. However, pacing students by giving quizzes made no difference in achievement in Lasco's study (85). Thus, of three attempts to increase motivation, the only successful one was a very strong threat.

What kind of students benefit from the Keller plan? Born, Gledhill & Davis (17) found that although the poorer students tended to drop out, those who stayed in the course tended to show the most gain from the Keller plan. Ability differences affecting gains were not found, however, by Hellström (62). Dogmatism did not interact with method in the study by Rubenstein & Friedman (138). Thus there is at present little indication of differential effectiveness of the Keller plan for differing types of students.

What kind of learning does the Keller plan help? One might expect the Keller plan to be most effective with simple memorization, but in fact Born et al (17), Morris & Kimbrell (108), and Rubinstein & Friedman (138) found it to be more effective than lecture for higher level cognitive objectives as well, and Stalling (148) found a favorable effect upon motivation for further learning as measured by intention to major in psychology. Kelley (77) found similarly wide-ranging favorable effects on achievement, test performance, and motivation to major in economics for his TIPS (Teaching Information Processing System), a similar method. As with most other methods of instruction, it thus appears that the Keller plan can be effective for a variety of goals if it is well planned and well administered. The Keller plan, well done, requires a great deal of planning and effort. To achieve higher level outcomes requires additional effort on the part of teachers and tutors. When the Keller plan fails, it is because of lack of such investment rather than inherent deficiencies in the method itself (which is propably true of discussions, lectures, and other methods as well).

Programmed Learning

The Keller plan is an attempt to gain some of the benefits of programmed learning while transcending its limitations. But traditional programmed learning continues to be a frequently used instructional tool. Costin (28), in an excellent review of lectures vs other methods of teaching, concludes that programmed study may have an advantage over lectures in promoting acquisition of information. Beard & Bligh's comprehensive review of research on college teaching (12) points to a similar conclusion.

Computer-Assisted Instruction (CAI)

Computer-assisted instruction in reading has been under development for over a decade. Fletcher & Atkinson (43) report the effects of adding 8 to 10 minutes a day of CAI to the normal instruction of 50 first graders for 5 1/2 months. The CAI produced substantially better performance both on tests tailored to the CAI objectives and on standardized achievement tests. Greater benefit for boys than for girls was found. Allen (2), however, found no significant differences between CAI and lecture in an introductory psychology course. Students who felt that lecture classes spend too much time on each topic and who liked to solve problems and take tests did better with CAI than with lecture.

Vinsonhaler & Bass (161) reviewed ten major reasonably well designed studies of the effectiveness of CAI drill and practice on learning in language and mathematics. In general the results indicate that 5 to 15 minutes of CAI added to regular instruction each day produce performance gains. Unfortunately only two studies used a control group with a comparable supplementation. In one (Suppes & Morningstar 153) classroom drill was as effective as CAI. In the other (Dick & Latta 33) programmed instruction was superior to CAI. Thus it appears that CAI has no special magic that will solve our instructional problems. It can relieve teachers of some time spent on drill (as can printed programmed instruction). Whether CAI is better in this respect than arranging for pupils to tutor one another is not known. Intuitively one feels that the computer should have great instructional potential, but apparently it is not going to be realized without a great deal of arduous work.

One promising direction for this research is the approach used by Pask and associates (Pask & Scott 121, 122), who carry R. C. Atkinson's (5) encouragement of response sensitive paradigms to the point of a colloquy between the computer and the learner to determine the learner's preferred learning strategy. Pask demonstrates that matching the structure of the learning program to the learning strategy (holist or serialist) of the student results in more effective instruction than learner control or an incompatible program. In general the research on learner control of CAI is inconclusive, leading Judd (75) to conclude his review with the suggestion that students may need specific training to exercise effective control of their own instruction.

An intriguing aspect of the effort of Pask and his colleagues is that their procedures are useful not only in teaching statistics but in helping the learner discover his own most effective learning strategy to be used both in CAI and non-CAI situations. As Zinn has suggested in oral presentations,[4] the most effective use of computers may not be in programming every detail of an instructional sequence but rather in using the computer in ways which will help learners make their own judgments and decisions more effectively. This does not necessarily imply matching instruction to a student's present cognitive style. It may mean finding where he is and helping him move to a more effective strategy or to more flexible uses of strategies appropriate for differing kinds of learning.

Simulation and Games

One of the more glamorous teaching methods is simulation. Used extensively during World War II in training pilots, naval command officers, and other personnel required to perform complex tasks, simulation is now used in a variety of instruc-

[4]Karl L. Zinn, University of Michigan: *A Technology for Instruction in the Age of Informatics,* presented at Lehr Systeme 72, Berlin, April 1972; and *Computer Learning Under Evaluation (Project CLUE) and an Attempt at Hyperspeech,* presented at RAND Corp. conference on Computers in Higher Education, October 1970.

tional situations. For example, teacher training programs often include experience in simulating instruction, frequently with videotape feedback. "Microteaching," a brief simulation involving a specific instructional skill, has been widely publicized as a potentially valuable tool for instructing prospective teachers. Jensen & Young (72) studied the effect on teaching behavior of a teacher training program. Both experimental and control groups had the same training experiences except for three 7-minute microteaching experiences given the experimental group. Teaching behavior during the following term of practice teaching was evaluated by raters unaware of the experimental variable. The microteaching group proved to be superior on five of the six factors of Sinha's Teacher Performance Evaluation Scale. Thus microteaching can be an effective training device. Unfortunately, research on microteaching has not produced evidence of its effectiveness in terms of ultimate impact on learning of the trainee's students. Despite the increasing popularity of simulation and educational games, little evidence on their instructional effectiveness has emerged.

Class Size

Class size is probably the hardiest perennial of instructional research. Following an initial spate of studies in the 1920s, interest shifted to teaching methods, and the popular generalization was that class size was not the important variable but rather what the teacher did in classes of different sizes. This reasonable conclusion dampened enthusiasm for studies of class size, but now after several decades of attention to teaching methods, class size again is beginning to emerge as an interesting variable which affects student learning, partly because it does have a potent effect on the teacher's choice and flexibility in use of teaching methods. McKeachie (98) reviewed research on class size at the college level and pointed out the consistency of direction of differences favoring small classes for higher level cognitive achievement and motivational and attitudinal outcomes. Moody, Bausell & Jenkins (107) carried out a parametric study of the effect of class size on the learning of mathematics at the fourth grade level. Using class sizes of 1, 2, 6, and 23, they found the smaller class sizes to produce greater learning than the larger classes, with the tutorial (1 to 1) class most effective. Similarly Bausell, Moody & Walzl (11) found individual tutoring to be more effective than classroom instruction. Thus the evidence supporting small classes continues to accumulate.

Team Teaching

Fifteen years of trial of team teaching in elementary schools has thus far produced no evidence of its instructional value. Rhodes (127) found in a well-controlled study that team teaching in grades K-6 was not only not superior to traditional, self-contained classes but was actually worse in affecting improvement in reading skill and pupil attitudes.

Homogeneous Grouping

The current social climate has placed the practice of homogeneous grouping, tracking, or streaming under severe pressure, largely in terms of its possible use to preserve segregation by race and social class. Homogeneous grouping may simply be based on the assumption that bright students can learn faster than students with less ability, but often there is an implicit assumption that the aptitude-treatment interactions (discussed in our section on the student) are so important that students of different ability levels need to be grouped so that they can be taught differently. This assumption finds less support in the ATI literature than in the studies of validity of student ratings of instruction, where there has been evidence that teachers rated as being more effective by bright students than by poorer students are more effective with bright students and vice versa. Research on the effects of homogeneous grouping on achievement was reviewed by Barker-Lunn (9), with the conclusion that most of the differences favored homogeneous grouping.[5] Clifford (24) studied the effect upon vocabulary list learning of competition in homogeneous fifth grade classes. The competitive treatments increased interest but not achievement or retention. Clifford presents a model emphasizing the importance of intrinsic motives rather than extrinsic reward.

SEX DIFFERENCES IN EFFECTS OF HOMOGENEOUS GROUPING BY ABILITY Levy & Tucker (89) present data suggesting that homogeneous grouping may be particularly effective for bright boys, while heterogeneous grouping was more effective for the less intelligent boys. For girls the results were reversed. House (65) has presented evidence that males are oriented toward testing out their abilities in social achievement situations, while females are more likely to avoid social competition. The tendency to seek competition was positively correlated with positive self-attributes for males but negatively correlated for females. If positive attributes correlate with intelligence as assessed in the Levy & Tucker study, and if homogeneous grouping increases competitive pressures, the Levy & Tucker study supports House's theory. Gjesme (54), working from the assumption that girls have subjective probabilities of success lower than objective reality, suggested that in a heterogeneous classroom high ability girls would have their achievement-related motives more strongly aroused since they would then subjectively perceive a moderate level of success, which according to J. W. Atkinson's theory (4) should be maximally motivating. Gjesme's results support this theory, as do those of Levy & Tucker.

Student Options and the Contract System

Somewhat more personalized than the "Personalized System of Instruction" is the increasing practice of offering students choices of various options for achieving course objectives and perhaps even some options with respect to objectives. As we saw in our review of learner control of computer-assisted instruction, neither psychologists nor learners are very good in choosing the most effective instruction. Pascal (120) studied the effects of three instructional options offered to students: lecture, lecture with discussion, and independent study. Although students given

[5]A comprehensive review by Findley & Bryan reaches negative conclusions about homogeneous grouping. Findley, W. G., Bryan, M. W. 1971. *Ability grouping: 1970.* Athens, Ga.: Center for Educational Improvement.

their preference developed more positive attitudes toward psychology, there was no effect on cognitive outcomes. The three methods did have different outcomes independent of the option aspect. The lecture group was superior on a test of knowledge, while the independent study group was superior in evaluation of a previously unread psychology article.

Another sort of option is the contract system of teaching in which the student negotiates a contract with the teacher. The contract normally specifies learning activities which the student will undertake and the method of evaluation and grading to be used. Poppen & Thompson (124) did not find significant differences in achievement on examinations or case study reports between students taking an educational psychology course under the contract method and a control group taught by undescribed traditional methods.

A different sort of option was provided in Fry's (49) study of student control of instruction. In this experiment students were given a deck of cards containing a list of questions about computers. For each question there was a videotape answer. The student could ask the questions in any order and could ask a tutor further questions after the videotape. Students in this condition were compared with students who received the questions and answers and videotapes of a yoked experimental subject's extra questions and answers in a sequence determined by experts. A third group received the materials in random order. Results showed that the subject-controlled group learned significantly *less* than the other two groups, although subject control worked well for high aptitude students who were also high in a measure of inquisitiveness. High aptitude subjects low in inquisitiveness did best with the sequence determined by experts. One suspects that one of the factors sometimes neglected in sequencing research is the motivational effect of surprisingness. Randomness may not make sense conceptually, but it may be more fun than a sequence so logical and with steps so small that one knows exactly what will be coming next. Such factors can be taken into account in planning a sequence of instruction, but as Atkinson (6) has suggested, the strategy likely to be most effective in ordering instructional materials is likely to be "response sensitive"; i.e. one using the subject's own responses from moment to moment to determine what should be done next. Such a program will be discussed later under the heading *Vocabulary List Learning.*

Student-Centered Teaching

Student-centered teaching was one of the most frequently studied teaching methods during the post-World War II period and showed some revival of interest as T-groups flourished during the 1960s. Lloyd (91) reviewed research on student-centered vs teacher-centered teaching at the college level and found consistency in results pointing to the superiority of student-centered teaching for higher level cognitive goals and for motivational and attitudinal changes. Three more recent diverse studies support this conclusion. Kohut (81) set up an experimental 6-week senior high school course in Colonial American History and found that a pupil-centric method was superior to teacher-centric on an essay examination (but not an objective test), and this superiority persisted in a test of retention. Dawson, Messe

& Phillips (32) manipulated two aspects of student-centered teaching—consideration and initiating structure—in a general psychology course. High consideration produced better performance than low consideration on all three criteria used—examination scores, bibliography, and research. Haddon & Lytton (59) followed up students who had been tested 4 years earlier just before completion of primary school in a study of the effects of "formal" and "informal" schools on divergent thinking. The original results had favored the "informal"[6] schools. On the follow-up 4 years later the differences persisted.

STUDENT ACTIVITY AND PEER INSTRUCTION One of the desired features of student-centered instruction is a high level of student activity. In addition to the studies cited above, there are other indications that increased student activity and interaction may improve instruction. Milbers (105), for example, found that participation in conversation groups involving active interaction produced better comprehension, fluency, and vocabulary in French than attending an audio laboratory. Oliver (112) found that demonstrations designed to stimulate discussion in psychology classes influenced student attitudes favorably, including motivation for majoring in psychology. Centra & Rock (22) found that colleges characterized by high degrees of faculty-student interaction were particularly effective as measured by student performance on Graduate Record Examination area tests. Cobb (25) found that children who talk about academic material to their peers are more likely to succeed academically than children who pay attention without interacting with peers. Talking with teachers may also help. Wood & Wilson (168) found that college students whose intellectual orientation increased during college reported more out-of-class interaction with faculty than did other students. Such students also reported more gains in specific academic skills. Thus interaction between students and peers and between students and faculty produces favorable educational outcomes at several levels.

Habits of interacting with teachers may be developed through modeling and reinforcement. Zimmerman & Pike (174) found that disadvantaged second-graders learned to ask more questions when they observed a model asking questions and were praised for the questions they themselves asked. Praise alone was not as effective. Some generalization to a new teacher occurred.

INSTRUCTION BY STUDENTS One method of stimulating student activity is through students teaching other students. In an earlier review of instructional psychology, Gagné & Rohwer (51) express some skepticism about the value of learning by teaching. Long (92), however, presents data indicating that serving as an experimenter in a paired-associate learning experiment has a beneficial effect on later learning of paired associates. Comparable time as experimenter with a nonresponding subject or as an observer did not produce the beneficial effect.

[6]The Free School movement has thus far produced more rhetoric than evidence. The August 1972 *Harvard Educational Review* is devoted entirely to "Alternative Schools" and has several interesting and provocative essays.

In a college English class, Romig (132) found that student-led discussions produced higher achievement by the students in the group on higher level cognitive outcomes (but not on knowledge), and Hamblin & Hamblin (60), working at the other end of the educational scale, found that peer tutoring was more effective than adult tutoring in teaching disadvantaged preschoolers to read. These results fit with earlier research summarized by McKeachie (98), indicating that student-led classes are effective—often more effective than teacher-led classes.

OBJECTIVES, CONTENT TESTING, AND FEEDBACK

The line between this and the preceding section is not always very clear in my own mind. Why questioning and testing are here rather than with the Keller plan and CAI is probably an arbitrary decision. To some extent the latter part of this section emphasizes what I call microaspects of instruction—variables, such as feedback, affecting learning in a single class period regardless of the general teaching method.

Objectives

Probably the single strongest pressure exerted by educational psychologists upon teachers is the importance of having specific behavioral objectives. While such an exercise may be good for the soul, it appears from the study of Jenkins & Deno (71) that it may not be particularly helpful for instruction. In a study in which (*a*) teachers, (*b*) students, or (*c*) both teachers and students were given either general or specific objectives of an instructional unit, no significant differences in student achievement were found. Similarly Olson (113) found that giving students specific behavioral objectives vs general understanding objectives did not make a difference in learning from an instructional program in interior design. Geis' sensible review (52) similarly finds no significant effects of behavioral objectives. Note that these results do not tell us that the process of working out objectives for oneself is useless; perhaps the experimenters were the ones who benefitted in the studies above.

Rothkopf & Kaplan (137), however, in a briefer instructional experiment found that more *intentional* learning resulted from specific than from broad objectives given learners. *Incidental* learning was not affected. Both incidental and intentional learning were favorably affected by explicit description of instructional goals as compared with directions simply to learn everything.

CURRICULUM A major national evaluation of a new physics course was reported by Welch & Walberg (164). In a well-designed controlled experiment, the Project Physics course proved not to be more effective than traditional courses in achieving the cognitive goals for which it was designed, but affective and attitudinal outcomes were favorable to the Project Physics course. An arithmetic program, Project SEED, was also evaluated in a large scale project and proved to be superior to conventional programs on standardized achievement tests (Dysinger & Rosenfeld 35).

STRUCTURE OF CONTENT AND INFORMATION PROCESSING STRATEGIES

Interest in cognitive structures and information processing strategies has generated research studies dealing with individual differences in the strategies used by learners and studies dealing with strategies of presenting content.

Audiovisual Elaboration

Mallory (93) showed that second-grade pupils were helped more than kindergarteners by presentation of noun pairs to be memorized in either auditory or visual elaborative contexts linking the two nouns. Children could be classified in terms of their use of the auditory or visual information processing strategy and this proved to be rather stable.

Increasing the elaborative context of material to be learned may not always be helpful. A realistic educational TV presentation, for example, proved to be less effective for college level students than a program with relatively plain, less realistic materials in the research of Barrington (10). This result may be surprising to those not familiar with earlier research on instructional films and television which showed that "bare bones" presentations were more effective than those in which color, realistic detail, or other features not essential to the learning desired were added (Adams, Carpenter & Smith 1, Carpenter & Greenhill 20). Increased meaningfulness aids learning up to a point, but complete realism may add too many irrelevant cues if the goal goes much beyond recognition. In summary, a structure of content which helps link critical features in some meaningful way aids retention and application; presentations which add complexity that is not relevant reduce effectiveness.

Classification Learning

When one is trying to teach a classification system such as biological types or types of music or literature, should one present several examples of one type first or should examples of the different types be intermixed? Sanders, DiVesta & Gray (140) confirmed the advantage of the former method but showed that this method was not particularly helpful for subjects who were not systematic in their formulation of hypotheses. Friedman & Greitzer (48) showed that presenting attributes before names was more effective than names before attributes, suggesting that this is conducive to a coding and retrieval strategy organized heirarchically. They point out that this advantage was not found in previous research in which there were more attributes than names. Similarly Stolurow (149) showed that children learned to identify parts of speech better when the sentence and part of speech were not varied simultaneously in the training program. Shifting both aspects complicated the task too much. All of these studies are reminiscent of the old controversy over part-whole learning and suggest a reformulation of part-whole problems in terms of a cognitive strategy in which a smaller, simpler set is learned before a larger or more complex related set of elements.

Vocabulary List Learning

When one is trying to teach a vocabulary list for a foreign language, such as Japanese, how should the lists of words be presented? English-Japanese? Japanese-English? Horowitz & Gordon (64), using the standard verbal learning premise that this task involves two components—associative learning and response learning—demonstrated the transfer value of pretraining on each component, i.e. training associations through presentation of Japanese-English pairs and training responses separately (such as by having subjects give the Japanese word when simply given some of its letters, no English). Such pretraining was not, however, as efficient as simple practice on the criterion English-Japanese pair learning. Intermingling the pretrained tasks improved pretraining effectiveness.

Atkinson & Paulson (8) describe the steps necessary for developing an optimal instruction strategy, using as an example the learning of Swahili vocabulary. A parameter-dependent strategy taking individual differences into account proved to be more efficient than an all-or-none model or a standard procedure not taking individual differences into account. Even more dramatic differences were found in an experiment by Atkinson (7) using the task of learning German vocabulary. In this case a random presentation of items produced correct responses a week later of 38%; when subjects had selected their own items for study the percent correct was 58%, a performance equivalent to that achieved when items were selected on the basis of values of parameters estimated on the basis of a pilot experiment; when a separate set of parameters was calculated for each item with the values determined by the subject's past performance on the item the percent correct rose to 79. Thus, despite our earlier discussion of the lack of effectiveness of simple programs, it appears that when one's theory of learning is good enough, takes account of individual differences, and is adjusted in terms of immediate past experience, planned instruction can be superior to a random order or student-selected presentation (at least for a single 2-hour lesson).

Learning by Discovery vs Learning by Rule and Inductive Method vs Deductive Method

Studies cited earlier have looked for interactions of student characteristics with inductive and deductive teaching methods affecting learning. It may well be that the paucity of clear results is due to the complication of another interaction—method by outcome, as exemplified in a complex study of learning the concept of trochaic meter in poetry (Tennyson, Wooley & Merrill 156).

Mayer & Greeno (95) found that in teaching the concept of binomial probability, students taught by being given the formula with rules performed better on transfer to familiar items, while those taught more conceptually were better able to identify unanswerable problems and to answer questions about the formula. Mayer & Greeno suggest that the instructional differences produce differences in the degree to which the concept is connected to internal mathematical structures (required in familiar problems) or to external cognitive structures resulting in general understanding. Shavelson (143) used diagraphs to analyze the content structure of a segment of high school physics and showed that the learner's cognitive structures came to correspond more closely to the content structure over the course of instruction—not an unexpected finding, but an interesting measure.

Egan & Greeno (36) found no differences in effectiveness of discovery and rule programs of teaching binomial probability, but found that individual differences in relevant abilities and knowledge were more predictive of success in learning by discovery than in learning by rule. Low ability subjects did better when instructed by rule. As in Mayer & Greeno's research, the discovery method was superior in transfer to problems requiring more interpretation or relating to previous knowledge ("external connectedness" in Greeno's terms). Learning by rule, however, was superior on familiar problems. Similarly, Goldman (58) found that psychology students using a logical strategy for learning statistics and experimental psychology did better on test scores and a research proposal than those using a mnemonic strategy.

However, in a larger field study comparing three English junior schools, Richards & Bolton (128) found that the schools stressing the discovery method produced poorer achievemement in mathematics both on traditional tests and on a test of understanding than schools using a traditional or a combination of traditional and discovery approaches. One of the problems of applying treatment-outcome interaction research in the schools is the probability that a further interaction term is added —the teacher.

Communication Style

Even though most classrooms are characterized by a high level of teacher talking, relatively little research has been done on what the teacher says or how it is said. Smothergill, Olson & Moore (145) manipulated the amount of elaboration of children's comments in a preschool. Positive effects of elaboration upon children's verbal performance were found. Types of examples used by teachers, such as those with a racial reference, made no difference in learning of black and white college students in a study by Trumpeter (159).

Despite the great current interest in the effects of models on children's behavior, a gap remains in research on the effect of a teacher's verbal and conceptual behavior on students. Moreover, the research on modeling has largely been focused at the younger ages. If models play an important part in development, college students should have well-learned skills in learning from models, yet, so far as I know, no one has studied the effects of different teacher models on cognitive outcomes of college courses or the variables which influence the extent to which students incorporate a cognitive model.

Questioning

The insertion of questions in prose materials has been shown by a number of studies to facilitate learning. In two nicely controlled studies McGaw & Grotelueschen (97) investigated the direction and generality of this effect, finding that the questions facilitated performance through stimulating review of material preceding the question and through increasing attention to the material following the question. Boyd's (18) results support this theory.

Other cues focusing attention or increasing meaningfulness can also aid learning. Johnson et al (73) found that adding diacritical marks to elementary school reading material improved performance both in reading (on nonmarked material) and spelling. These results on the effect of focusing attention fit with Rothkopf's concept of mathemagenic activities (136), those activities that give birth to learning. Rothkoff's concept grew out of his finding that knowledge of results does not affect learning directly but does affect inspection activities of students.

Rothkopf (136) replicated the earlier finding that questions asked by a teacher during individual study were more effective than written questions. The later study showed that the facilitative effect was dependent upon text relevant questions and not social interaction. If, as Zajonc (169) suggests, social facilitation involves increased arousal, the effect of the arousal is apparently focused by the questions.

Another theory relevant to the effect of questioning is Berlyne's theory of epistemic curiosity (13). In Berlyne's original demonstration (14) subjects given a questionnaire before reading statements with answers to the questions recalled more than subjects not given the questionnaire. Frick & Cofer (47) repeated the Berlyne study with a better control on the test items and obtained the same results. Watts & Anderson (163) found that questions requiring application of principles to new examples were more effective than those simply involving recall.

The use of questions in reading material thus helps focus the attention of the learner and stimulates review and application. In addition, questions can create motivation by arousing curiosity.

Testing and Grading

One of the classic studies of educational research is McCluskey's (96) finding that students studied more effectively for essay than for objective tests. This fits with the Watts & Anderson finding cited above if one assumes that students see objective tests as requiring recall more than application. Mellenbergh (103) failed to find McCluskey's difference. Students given weekly quizzes requiring eighth graders to draw inferences were compared by McKenzie (100) to students given quizzes on recall of facts. He found the inference quizzes to be more effective in terms of ability to draw new inferences, with no loss in recall of facts, a result very comparable to that found by McCluskey and to King & Russell's (78) finding that students instructed to study a passage for meaning remembered more verbatim details than a group instructed to memorize it. Thus here again we find that information processing strategies involving meaning and logic (as in Goldman's study reported above) are more efficient than those relying upon memorization.

Pack (118) compared the effects of norm-referenced vs criterion-referenced tests on student attitudes and found that criterion-referenced testing in which the student is not compared with others produced more favorable attitudes toward the subject matter. Veroff's theory of the development of achievement motivation (160) would suggest that one should expect age-level differences in responses to competitive vs criterion-referenced standards of achievement.

A neat, but probably not earthshaking, finding is that in grading essay tests, graders are affected by neatness in handwriting if they are themselves neat writers.

Graders whose own writing is messy are not biased by neatness (Huch & Bounds 66).

Pass-Fail Grading

At the college level, arguments about feedback and reinforcement have largely centered around grading systems. One commonly used system is to allow students to elect one course on a pass-fail rather than graded basis. In one of the few experimental studies of legal education, Lempert (87) found that students did not achieve as well in their pass-fail course as a control group who had also wished to take the course pass-fail, nor as well as would have been expected in terms of previous performance. Moreover, the pass-fail students' performance in graded courses did not improve. Similar results were obtained by Bronfenbrenner (19). Such results probably cannot be generalized to the situation where *all* courses are graded pass-fail or pass-no entry. When a pass-fail course is competing for student time with graded courses, pass-fail loses out when tests or due dates for term papers in the graded courses become imminent. Thus lower achievement on graded examinations for Pass-Fail students is not surprising. The question remaining is, "Are there gains in attitudinal or other types of outcomes?" To date few data are available.

Feedback, Reinforcement, Reward

Reinforcement has long been believed to affect learning, and in fact some experimenters define reinforcement as any condition that increases learning. Yet Bolles (16) and Lipe & Jung (90) review a variety of evidence indicating that contingent reinforcement is neither necessary nor sufficient for operant learning. I have followed Walker (162) and other theorists, e.g. Estes (37), in believing that some of the contradictory results in this area could be resolved by differentiating between the informational and motivational consequences of reinforcement. In this conception informational feedback is particularly crucial in cognitive learning. But, as the following section indicates, even informational feedback turns out to be more complicated than can be expressed in a simple principle that knowledge of results aids learning.

KNOWLEDGE OF RESULTS Programmed learning places much emphasis upon prompt feedback. Olson (113) found that giving college students knowledge of results on quiz items failed to produce generally better final performance than no knowledge of results, and Oner (117) also found no effect of feedback or praise in learning decimals in a programmed lesson. Moreover, feedback did not interact with anxiety in determining performance. Thus knowledge of results does not always aid learning. My guess is that the crucial factor is the amount of information given by knowledge of results and the learner's knowledge of what to do to achieve a better outcome. In typical programmed learning units with low probability of errors, knowledge of results conveys little information. We might expect more positive effects of feedback in situations in which the task is more difficult and the information provided thus greater.

CONTIGUITY Sassenrath (142) has manipulated feedback delay and found no advantage for immediate over delayed feedback. For those who know the classical nonsense and motor skill learning literature, such a finding may seem heretical, but studies of learning of meaningful verbal materials have not found that immediate feedback aided retention. Sturges (150) suggests that the advantage of delayed feedback found in these studies and in Sturges' own research may be due to the subject's exploration and organizaton of the material before feedback.

Programmed instruction proponents were understandably aghast to find that immediate knowledge of the correct response (expected to be a reinforcer) did not facilitate learning in programmed instruction. Like Sturges (151), Anderson, Kulhavy & Andre (3) suspected that the reason this result occurred was that when knowledge of the correct result is immediately available, students become inattentive and careless in trying to answer the question. Thus they used a computer to give knowledge of correct response only after the student gave an answer. Results in their experiments tended to be positive. Their hypothesis was further supported by finding that a group allowed to peek at the correct response scored lower than students who had no feedback of the correct response. Feedback of correct response after the student's response did not, however, produce superior performance on a delayed test of retention.

Delayed feedback was superior to immediate feedback in the experiment of Kulhavy & Anderson (83), and their design provided support for the theory that the delay permits potentially interfering errors to be forgotten as well as contributing to greater attention to the feedback.

These experiments casting doubt on the principle of contiguity suggest again that the importance of knowledge of results depends upon the information provided. Delayed knowledge of results may be more informative than immediate and may stimulate rehearsal. Delayed reinforcement should work as well as (or better than) immediate reinforcement if the relevant stimuli and responses are familiar and the subject can remember what he is being reinforced for.

The fact that delayed feedback can be effective does not necessarily suggest that a teacher should delay returning test papers. Most of the studies reported herein were carried out with delays much shorter than those common in school and often with programmed materials in which feedback gives little information because students already know most of the answers before getting the feedback. In school situations one is likely to have many students who are genuinely confused or misinformed before receiving feedback. Delay in returning papers may be damaging to their motivation and may be interpreted as evidence of the teacher's lack of commitment to the class.

INFORMATIONAL FEEDBACK VS PRAISE VS TANGIBLE REWARDS Tangible rewards can improve learning (Frase 45, O'Leary & Drabman 111, Rosenfeld 133), but consequences of responses differ in their effects upon learning for different children. Informing a child of the correctness of his response increases learning for middle-class, normally achieving children, but nonmiddle-class or nonachieving children may learn more effectively when given praise or tangible rewards (Terrell, Durkin & Wesley, 157, Zigler & deLabry 172, Zigler & Kanzer 173). Blair (15) similarly showed that normal achievers in the third grade learned more effectively for informational feedback or praise than for tangible rewards (toys or candy); low achieving children learned better with tangible rewards. Cradler & Goodwin (30) found that in groups of second and sixth graders, sixth grade middle-class subjects were more responsive to praise and symbolic feedback while second grade lower-class children were more responsive to candy. Portuges & Feshbach (125) found that advantaged children, especially girls, were more likely than disadvantaged children to imitate a teacher model, especially if the teacher had been positively reinforcing to children.

Since teachers are likely to emphasize symbolic and social rewards, differences in achievement between social classes may be due in some part to lack of effective rewards for learning and lack of teacher modeling by underachieving children.

OTHER VARIABLES INFLUENCING THE EFFECT OF FEEDBACK In addition to interaction with student characteristics, the effect of feedback depends on the type of course and the type of feedback given. Levin (88) found that praise for achievement-related skills helped spelling, but not achievement in arithmetic or language for underachieving elementary school children. Levin also found that praise for achievement was more effective than praise for effort.

The content of feedback was also an important variable for Means & Means (102), who found that for low grade-point-average students, being told that they had done well on an aptitude test produced better performance on the midterm in an adolescent psychology course. For high grade-point-average students, being told that they had done poorly produced better performance. Such results remind one of Atkinson's theory that achievement motivation is highest when probabilities of success are moderate.

Teachers can be learners too, and one presumed input to their learning to be more effective teachers is the use of student ratings of teaching. As in the case of feedback to students, feedback of student rating of teaching effectiveness to college instructors does not necessarily produce good effects. Miller (106) found positive results of such feedback in only one of three classes. Centra (21) also found no overall effect of feedback. He did, however, find that those teachers who rated themselves more favorably than their students did change (as perceived by students) in the direction suggested by the student ratings. Klein (79) found that teachers' positive or negatively toned verbal behavior was influenced by pupil feedback (smiling, attentiveness) in the classroom. Pambookian (119) found that feedback to instructors did not help those who were rated as highly effective or as ineffective but did help those rated as being moderately effective—again fitting Atkinson's theory.

Pambookian's results fit nicely with those of Flook & Robinson (44), who found that among students who were told their intelligence and anxiety test scores, those in the middle range of intelligence were the only group to show superior achievement during the freshman year as compared to a control group not told their scores. Hammer (61) showed that teacher comments on undergraduate physics papers had a positive effect on later performance and especially when the teacher slanted the comments depending upon the student's expected grade. These comments, from the examples given, seem to have been likely to move probability of success to an intermediate level, thus, in Atkinson's terms, increasing motivation. The effect of such comments was particularly great for students high in external control on Rotter's I-E Scale; presumably such students are more dependent upon external evaluation.

PRINCIPLES OF LEARNING AND INSTRUCTION

The past 2 years have been bad ones for those of us who attempt to apply traditional principles of learning to instruction. Thorndike's principles of learning seems to be crumbling. As we have seen:

1. Knowledge of results is not necessary for learning.
2. Delayed knowledge of results may be more effective than immediate knowledge of results.
3. Rewards seem not always to function to improve learning, and the effect depends upon the type of reward.
4. Errors do not seem to persist as expected (Kulhavy & Parsons 84).
5. Careful planning of a learning program may be no better than a random sequence.
6. Learning by a sequence of small steps may be less effective than learning by larger jumps.
7. Defining objectives may not help improve student learning.

In fact, each one of the principles confidently enunciated by Skinner in *The Science of Learning and the Art of Teaching* now turns out to be untrue—at least in as general a sense as he believed at that time. This does not mean that Skinner's attempts to influence education have been bad or that the principles are false; rather the attempt to make a really systematic effort of application has revealed that what we psychologists took to be verities are principles that hold only under limited conditions. This does not mean that the search for principles of learning is fruitless. One implication is that the traditional principles of learning apply to particular kinds of learning and that we now need to apply the same theoretical and experimental rigor to the study of principles of learning concepts and meanings. Moreover, attempts at application have forced us to confront the need for ways of classifying tasks and situations if we are to generalize from laboratory findings to other situations (Fleishman 41, Gagné 50).

Moreover, having demonstrated that the traditional principles of learning are not universally valid does not mean that they are valueless for instructional psychology.

Knowledge of results, I would aver, *is* important for learning when the knowledge provides information and the learner knows how to correct his behavior; it doesn't make much difference if the learner already has a pretty good idea of how well he has done or doesn't know what to do differently.

Contiguity probably makes a difference in learning if the learner soon forgets what he did, but it doesn't help when he can easily retrieve it from memory and continue to think about it.

Rewards probably do affect motivation for continuing learning, since from them the subject learns what activities lead to rewards, but extrinsic rewards which strengthen immediate motivation should not necessarily be expected to strengthen motivation for choosing learning activities in the absence of anticipation of the reward.

Planning and guidance of learning probably is useful within limits, but there may be too much as well as too little.

Moreover, some traditional principles do stand up fairly well in this more complex domain. For example: (*a*) active participation is better than passive learning if active means something more than writing out an answer one already knows; (*b*) meaningful learning is better than rote learning.

But the differences between the old and the new principles lies not only in better understanding of their limitations but also in a shift from an associationist, S-R, approach to an information processing approach. In such research as that on providing memory support to anxious students and on rote vs conceptual strategies for presenting content, we see how information processing models suggest analyses of instruction that have proved to be productive.

Without researchers' hardheaded studies of meaningful learning in the laboratory and in controlled natural settings, I could have continued making well-intentioned speeches to college teachers on the principles of learning. Now I believe that those principles apply most clearly to learning nonsense syllables or to the learning of animals in artificial situations. Meaningful learning is both more robust and more complex. But the complexity, so frustrating to those who wish to prescribe educational methods, is a reminder of the fascinating uniqueness of the learner. Fortunately, most educational situations are interactive situations in which a developing, learning human being engages with a situation in ways designed to meet his learning needs. Part of that situation is another human being who has some resources for instruction and some capacity to adapt to the learner. The educational outcome of their interaction over time depends upon many variables. I was reared in psychology with the dictum that most important relationships are linear. I am now an agnostic on linearity. I can contemplate the possibility that much of the educational world is characterized by complex nonlinear relationships. In each section of this review we have dealt with interactions—attribute-treatment interactions (ATI), teacher-test interactions (TTI), method-outcome interactions, and the three-way and four-way interactions resulting from combinations of these. The complexity is enormous, but education would be sterile, boring, and inhumane if the complexity were not there.

Do the limitations of our current work mean that instructional research has no useful role in education? Not so! On the one hand it provides a safeguard against easy oversimplifications; it can increase the instructor's ability to see new dimensions and to make finer differentiations. On the other hand it can help the instructor to avoid being overwhelmed by the enormity of the complexity, by providing some ways to structure perceptions of the learner, the group, the instructional task, the situation, and the teacher-student relationship. Models of the instructional process may limit one's awareness and ability to change, but properly conceived they can be tools to increase one's capacity for perceiving and understanding the complexity of this very special changing human interaction.

Literature Cited

1. Adams, J. C., Carpenter, C. R., Smith, D. R. 1958. *College Teaching by Television.* Washington, D.C.: Am. Counc. Educ.
2. Allen, M. W. 1971. The prediction of achievement in computer assisted instruction versus lecture instruction using linear multiple regression techniques. *Diss. Abstr. Int.* 32:6612
3. Anderson, R. C., Kulhavy, R. W., Andre, T. 1971. Feedback procedures in programmed instruction. *J. Educ. Psychol.* 62:148–56
4. Atkinson, J. W. 1964. *An Introduction to Motivation.* Princeton, N.J.: Van Nostrand
5. Atkinson, R. C. 1972. *Ingredients for a Theory of Instruction.* Tech. Rep. 187, Stanford Univ.
6. Atkinson, R. C. 1972. Ingredients for a theory of instruction. *Am. Psychol.* 27: 921–31
7. Atkinson, R. C. 1972. Optimizing learning a second vocabulary. *J. Exp. Psychol.* 96:124–29
8. Atkinson, R. C., Paulson, J. A. 1972. An approach to the psychology of instruction. *Psychol. Bull.* 78:49–61
9. Barker-Lunn, J. C. 1967. The effects of streaming and non-streaming in junior schools: second interim report. *New Res. Educ.* 1:46–75
10. Barrington, H. 1971. An evaluation of the effectiveness of instructional television presentation variables. *Brit. J. Educ. Psychol.* 41:219–20
11. Bausell, R. B., Moody, W. B., Walzl, F. N. 1972. A factorial study of tutoring versus classroom instruction. *Am. Educ. Res. J.* 9:591–97
12. Beard, R. M., Bligh, D. A. 1972. *Research into Teaching Methods in Higher Education.* Research into Higher Education Monographs. London: Soc. Res. Higher Educ. 3rd ed.
13. Berlyne, D. E. 1954. A theory of human curiosity. *Brit. J. Psychol.* 45: 180–91
14. Ibid. An experimental study of human curiosity, 256–65
15. Blair, J. R. 1972. The effects of differential reinforcement on the discrimination learning of normal and low-achieving middle-class boys. *Child Develop.* 43: 251–55
16. Bolles, R. C. 1972. Reinforcement, expectancy, and learning. *Psychol. Rev.* 79:394–409
17. Born, D. G., Gledhill, S. M., Davis, M. L. 1972. Examination performance in lecture-discussion and personalized instruction courses. *J. Appl. Behav. Anal.* 5:33–43
18. Boyd, W. M. 1973. Repeating questions in prose learning. *J. Educ. Psychol.* 64: 31–38
19. Bronfenbrenner, U. 1972. A Cornell study relating to grading conditions. *Center Improv. Undergrad. Educ. Notes* 4:2–4
20. Carpenter, C. R., Greenhill, L. P. 1958. An investigation of closed-circuit television for teaching university courses. *Inst. Telev. Res. Rep. Proj. 2,* Penn. State Univ.
21. Centra, J. A. 1972. The utility of student ratings for instructional improvement. *Educ. Test. Serv.* 74 pp.
22. Centra, J., Rock, D. 1971. College environments and student academic achievement. *Am. Educ. Res. J.* 8(4): 623–34
23. Claiborn, W. L. 1969. Expectancy effects in the classroom: A failure to replicate. *J. Educ. Psychol.* 60:377–83
24. Clifford, M. M. 1972. Effects of competition as a motivational technique in the classroom. *Am. Educ. Res. J.* 9:123–37
25. Cobb, J. A. 1972. Relationship of discrete classroom behaviors to fourth-grade academic achievement. *J. Educ. Psychol.* 63:74–80
26. Cohen, E. G. 1972. Sociology and the classroom: setting the conditions for teacher-student interaction. *Rev. Educ. Res.* 42:441–52
27. Cooper, J. L., Greiner, J. M. 1971. Contingency management in an introductory psychology course produces better retention. *Psychol. Rec.* 21(3): 391–400
28. Costin, F. 1972. Lecturing versus other methods of teaching: A review of research. *Brit. J. Educ. Tech.* 3:4–30
29. Costin, F., Greenough, W. T., Menges, R. J. 1971. Student ratings of college teaching: Realiability, validity, and usefulness. *Rev. Educ. Res.* 41:511–35
30. Cradler, J. D., Goodwin, D. L. 1971. Conditioning of verbal behavior as a function of age, social class, and type of reinforcement. *J. Educ. Psychol.* 62: 279–85
31. Cronbach, L. J., Snow, R. E. 1969. *Individual Differences in Learning Ability as a Function of Instructional Variables.* Off. Educ. Rep. OEC 4-6-061269-1217
32. Dawson, J. E., Messe, L. A., Phillips, J. L. 1972. Effect of instructor-leader be-

havior on student performance. *J. Appl. Psychol.* 56:369–76

33. Dick, W., Latta, R. 1969. *Comparative Effects of Ability and Presentation Mode in CAI and Programmed Instruction,* AD-694 021. Springfield, Va.: Clearinghouse Fed. Sci. Tech. Inform.
34. Domino, G. 1971. Interactive effects of achievement orientation and teaching style on academic achievement. *J. Educ. Psychol.* 62(5):427–31
35. Dysinger, D. W., Rosenfeld, M. 1972. *Evaluation of Project SEED: A Conceptually Oriented Mathematics Program for Elementary School Students.* Pittsburgh: AIR
36. Egan, D. E., Greeno, J. G. 1973. Acquiring cognitive structure by discovery and rule learning. *J. Educ. Psychol.* 64: 85–97
37. Estes, W. K. 1972. Reinforcement in human behavior. *Am. Sci.* 60:723–29
38. Feather, N. T. 1972. Teaching effectiveness and student evaluation. *Aust. Psychol.* 7:180–87
39. Field, T. W., Simpkins, W. S., Brown, R. K., Rich, P. 1971. Identifying patterns of teacher behavior from student evaluations. *J. Appl. Psychol.* 55: 466–69
40. Finn, J. D. 1972. Expectations and the educational environment. *Rev. Educ. Res.* 42:387–410
41. Fleishman, E. A. 1972. On the relation between abilities, learning, and human performance. *Am. Psychol.* 27:1017–32
42. Fleming, E. S., Anttonen, R. G. 1971. Teacher expectancy or my fair lady. *Am. Educ. Res. J.* 8:241–52
43. Fletcher, J. D., Atkinson, R. C. 1972. Evaluation of the Stanford CAI program in initial reading. *J. Educ. Psychol.* 63:597–602
44. Flook, A. J. M., Robinson, P. J. 1972. Academic performance with and without knowledge of scores on tests of intelligence, aptitude, and personality: A further study. *J. Educ. Psychol.* 63: 123–29
45. Frase, L. T. 1971. Effect of incentive variables and type of adjunct question upon test learning. *J. Educ. Psychol.* 62:371–75
46. Frey, P. W. 1973. Student instructional ratings and faculty performance. *Science.* In press
47. Frick, J. W., Cofer, C. N. 1972. Berlyne's demonstration of epistemic curiosity: An experimental re-evaluation. *Brit. J. Psychol.* 63:221–28
48. Friedman, M. P., Greitzer, F. L. 1972. Organization and study time in learning from reading. *J. Educ. Psychol.* 63: 609–16
49. Fry, J. P. 1972. Interactive relationship between inquisitiveness and student control of instruction. *J. Educ. Psychol.* 63:459–65
50. Gagné, R. M. 1965. *Conditions of Learning.* New York: Holt, Rinehart & Winston
51. Gagné, R. M., Rohwer, W. D. Jr. 1969. Instructional Psychology. *Ann. Rev. Psychol.* 20:381–418
52. Geis, G. L. 1972. Behavioral objectives: A selected bibliography and brief review. *ERIC Paper.* McGill Univ., Montreal, Quebec, Canada
53. Getzels, J. W. 1969. A social psychology of education. In *The Handbook of Social Psychology,* ed. G. Lindzey, E. Aronson. Reading, Mass: Addison-Wesley
54. Gjesme, T. 1973. Achievement-related motives and school performance for girls. *J. Pers. Soc. Psychol.* 26:131–36
55. Glaser, R. 1972. Individual and learning: The new aptitudes. *Educ. Res.* 13: 5–13
56. Glaser, R., Resnick, L. B. 1972. Instructional Psychology. *Ann. Rev. Psychol.* 23:207–76
57. Goldberg, L. R. 1972. Student personality characteristics and optimal college learning conditions: An extensive search for trait-by-treatment interaction effects. *Inst. Sci.* 1:153–210
58. Goldman, R. D. 1972. Effects of a logical versus a mnemonic learning strategy on performance in two undergraduate psychology classes. *J. Educ. Psychol.* 63:347–52
59. Haddon, F. A., Lytton, H. 1971. Primary education and divergent thinking abilities: Four years on. *Brit. J. Educ. Psychol.* 41:136–47
60. Hamblin, J. A., Hamblin, R. L. 1972. On teaching disadvantaged preschoolers to read: a successful experiment. *Am. Educ. Res. J.* 9:209–16
61. Hammer, B. 1972. Grade expectations, differential teacher comments, and student performance. *J. Educ. Psychol.* 63:454–58
62. Hellström, L. 1972. IMU-projektet: Forsök med individualiserad matematikundervisning pa grundskolans mellanstadium. [A study on individualized mathematics instruction in the comprehensive school, grades 4–6.] *Pedagogisk-Psykologiska Problem.* 76 pp.
63. Hogan, T. P., Hartley, E. L. 1972. Some additional factors in student evaluation of courses. *Am. Educ. Res. J.* 9:241–50

64. Horowitz, L. M., Gordon, A. M. 1972. Associative symmetry and second-language learning. *J. Educ. Psychol.* 63: 287–94
65. House, G. F. 1972. *Orientations to Achievement: Autonomous, Social Comparison and External.* PhD thesis. Univ. Michigan, Ann Arbor. 392 pp.
66. Huch, S. W., Bounds, W. G. 1972. Essay grades: An interaction between graders' handwriting clarity and the neatness of examination papers. *Am. Educ. Res. J.* 9:279–83
67. Isaacson, R. L. et al 1964. Dimensions of student evaluations of teaching. *J. Educ. Psychol.* 55:344–51
68. Jacobson, L. I. et al 1971. Effects of age, sex, systematic conceptual learning, acquisition of learning sets, and programmed social interaction on the intellectual and conceptual development of preschool children from poverty backgrounds. *Child Develop.* 42:1399–1417
69. Jacobson, L. I., Greeson, L. E. 1972. Effects of systematic conceptual learning on the intellectual development of preschool children from poverty backgrounds: a follow-up study. *Child Develop.* 43:1111–15
70. Jencks, C. 1972. *Inequality: A Reassessment of the Effect of Family and Schooling in America.* New York: Basic Books
71. Jenkins, J. R., Deno, S. L. 1971. Influence of knowledge and type of objectives on subject-matter learning. *J. Educ. Psychol.* 62:67–70
72. Jensen, L. C., Young, J. I. 1972. Effect of televised simulated instruction on subsequent teaching. *J. Educ. Psychol.* 63:368–73
73. Johnson, H., Jones, D. R., Cole, A. C., Walters, M. B. 1972. The use of diacritical marks in teaching beginners to read. *Brit. J. Educ. Psychol.* 42:120–26
74. José, J., Cody, J. J. 1971. Teacher-pupil interaction as it relates to attempted changes in teacher expectancy of academic ability and achievement. *Am. Educ. Res. J.* 8:39–50
75. Judd, W. A. 1973. Learner-controlled computer-assisted instruction. In *Computers in the Instructional Process: Report of an Instructional School,* ed. K. Zinn, M. Refice, A. Romano. Amsterdam: Elsevier
76. Keller, F. S. 1968. "Good-bye, Teacher." *J. Appl. Behav. Anal.* 1: 79–89
77. Kelley, A. C. 1971. *T.I.P.S. and Technical Change in Classroom Instruction Abstract.* Presented at Am. Econ. Assoc., New Orleans
78. King, D. J., Russell, G. N. 1966. A comparison of rote and meaningful learning of rote and meaningful learning of connected meaningful material. *J. Verb. Learn. Verb. Behav.* 5:478–83
79. Klein, S. S. 1971. Student influence on teacher behavior. *Am. Educ. Res. J.* 8: 403–22
80. Knight, J. M. 1972. *Two Varieties of Programmed Student Achievement.* Rep. Univ. Oklahoma, Norman
81. Kohut, S. 1972. A comparison of student achievement and retention on subjective versus objective examinations in the social studies as influenced by different instructional patterns. *Diss. Abstr. Int.* 32:6207
82. Koran, M. L., Snow, R. E., McDonald, F. J. 1971. Teacher aptitude and observational learning of a teaching skill. *J. Educ. Psychol.* 62:219–28
83. Kulhavy, R. W., Anderson, R. C. 1972. Delay-retention effect with multiple-choice tests. *J. Educ. Psychol.* 63: 505–12
84. Kulhavy, R. W., Parsons, J. A. 1972. Learning-criterion error perseveration in text materials. *J. Educ. Psychol.* 63: 81–86
85. Lasco, R. A. 1972. The effect of pacing of instruction on the effectiveness and efficiency of an individualized course serving college level geology. *Diss. Abstr. Int.* 32:6208
86. Leherissey, B. L., O'Neil, H. F., Hansen, D. N. 1971. Effects of memory support on state anxiety and performance in computer-assisted learning. *J. Educ. Psychol.* 62:413–20
87. Lempert, R. 1972. Law school grading: An experiment with pass-fail. *J. Legal Educ.* 24:251–308
88. Levin, W. J. 1972. The effectiveness and generalization of ability-oriented and effort-oriented reinforcement for improving the academic performance of underachievers. *Diss. Abstr. Int.* 32:(11-B)6652
89. Levy, P., Tucker, J. 1972. Differential effects of streaming on primary school attainment. *Brit. J. Educ. Psychol.* 42: 75–79
90. Lipe, D., Jung, S. M. 1971. Manipulating incentives to enhance school learning. *Rev. Educ. Res.* 41:249–80
91. Lloyd, K. E. et al 1972. A note on some reinforcing properties of university lectures. *J. Appl. Behav. Anal.* 5:151–55
92. Long, K. K. 1971. Transfer from teaching to learning. *J. Educ. Psychol.* 62: 167–78

93. Mallory, W. A. 1972. Abilities and developmental changes in elaborative strategies in paired-associate learning of young children. *J. Educ. Psychol.* 63: 202–17
94. Martens, R. 1971. Anxiety and motor behavior: a review. *J. Mot. Behav.* 3: 151–79
95. Mayer, R. E., Greeno, J. G. 1972. Structural differences between learning outcomes produced by different instructional methods. *J. Educ. Psychol.* 63: 165–73
96. McCluskey, H. Y. 1934. An experimental comparison of two methods of correcting the outcomes of examination. *Sch. & Soc.* 40:566–68
97. McGaw, B., Grotelueschen, A. 1972. Direction of the effect of questions in prose material. *J. Educ. Psychol.* 63: 580–88
98. McKeachie, W. J. 1972. Research on college teaching. *Educ. Perspect.* 11: 3–10
99. McKeachie, W. J., Lin, Y-G., Mann, W. 1971. Student ratings of teacher effectiveness: Validity studies. *Am. Educ. Res. J.* 8:435–45
100. McKenzie, G. R. 1972. Some effects of frequent quizzes on inferential thinking. *Am. Educ. Res. J.* 9:231–40
101. McMichael, J. S., Corey, J. R. 1969. Contingency management in an introductory psychology course produces better learning. *J. Appl. Behav. Anal.* 2:79–83
102. Means, R. S., Means, G. H. 1971. Achievement as a function of the presence of prior information concerning aptitude. *J. Educ. Psychol.* 62:185–87
103. Mellenbergh, G. J. 1972. A comparison between different kinds of achievement test items. *Nederl. T. Psychol.* 27: 157–58
104. Meyers, J., Dunham, J. L. 1972. Anxiety x aptitude interactions in concept learning. *Proc. 80th Ann. Conv. APA* 485–86
105. Milbers, A. 1971. "Functional French," a student-oriented course. *Learn. Develop.* 2(8):1–4. McGill Univ.
106. Miller, M. T. 1971. Instructor attitudes toward, and their use of, student ratings of teachers. *J. Educ. Psychol.* 62: 235–39
107. Moody, W. B., Bausell, R. B., Jenkins, J. R. 1972. *The Effect of Class Size on the Learning of Mathematics: A Parametric Study.* Presented at AERA Ann. Meet. New Orleans, 1973
108. Morris, C. J., Kimbrell, G. M. 1972. Performance and attitudinal effects of the Keller method in an introductory psychology course. *Psychol. Rec.* 22: 523–30
109. Müller-Wolf, H. M., Fittkau, B. 1971. Lehrverhalten von Hochschullehrern und seine Bedeutung fur Einstellungen and Verhalten von Studenten. (Teaching behavior of college professors and its meaning for attitudes and behavior of students.) *Z. Entwicklungspsychol. Pädagog. Psychol.* 3:165–80
110. Munz, D. C., Jacobs, P. D. 1971. An evaluation of perceived item-difficulty sequencing in academic testing. *Brit. J. Educ. Psychol.* 41:195–205
111. O'Leary, K. D., Drabman, R. 1971. Token reinforcement programs in the classroom: A review. *Psychol. Bull.* 75: 379–99
112. Oliver, L. W. 1972–73. The effect of discussion section demonstrations upon student achievement and attitudes in an introductory psychology course. *Mo. Psychol.* 21
113. Olson, G. H. 1972. A multivariate examination of the effects of behavioral objectives, knowledge of results, and the assignment of grades on the facilitation of classroom learning. PhD thesis. *Diss. Abstr. Int.* 32:6214–15
114. O'Neil, H. F. Jr. 1972. Anxiety reduction and computer-assisted learning. Presented at symp. "Anxiety in Educationally Relevant Situations," Ann. Meet. APA, Honolulu
115. O'Neil, H. F. Jr. 1972. Effects of stress on state anxiety and performance in computer-assisted learning. *J. Educ. Psychol.* 63:473–81
116. O'Neil, H. F. Jr., Spielberger, C. D., Hansen, D. N. 1969. Effects of state anxiety and task difficulty on computer-assisted learning. *J. Educ. Psychol.* 60: 343–50
117. Oner, N. P. 1972. Impact of teacher behavior and teaching technique on learning by anxious children. *Diss. Abstr. Int.* 32:6215
118. Pack, E. C. 1972. The effects of testing upon attitude towards the method and content of instruction. *J. Educ. Meas.* 33:195
119. Pambookian, H. S. 1972. The effect of feedback from students to college instructors on their teaching behavior. Unpublished disseration. Univ. Michigan
120. Pascal, C. E. 1971. Instructional options, option preference, and course outcomes. *Alberta J. Educ. Res.* 17: 1–11

121. Pask, G., Scott, B. C. E. 1972. Learning strategies and individual competence. *Int. J. Man-Mach. Stud.* 4:217–53
122. Ibid 1973. CASTE: A system for exhibiting learning strategies and regulating uncertainties. In press
123. Pellegrini, R. J., Hicks, R. A. 1972. Prophecy effects and tutorial instruction for the disadvantaged child. *Am. Educ. Res. J.* 9:413–19
124. Poppen, W. A., Thompson, C. L. 1971. The effect of grade contracts on student performance. *J. Educ. Res.* 64:420–24
125. Portuges, S. H., Feshbach, N. D. 1972. The influence of sex and socioethnic factors upon imitation of teachers by elementary school children. *Child Develop.* 43:981–89
126. Ray, W. J., Katahn, M., Snyder, C. R. 1971. Effects of test anxiety on acquisition, retention, and generalization of a complex verbal task in a classroom situation. *J. Pers. Soc. Psychol.* 20:147–54
127. Rhodes, F. 1971. Team teaching compared with traditional instruction in grades kindergarten through six. *J. Educ. Psychol.* 62:110–16
128. Richards, P. N., Bolton, N. 1971. Types of mathematics teaching, mathematical ability and divergent thinking in junior school children. *Brit. J. Educ. Psychol.* 41:32–37
129. Rodin, M., Rodin, B. 1972. Student evaluations of teachers. *Science* 177: 1164–66
130. Rohwer, W. D. Jr. 1971. Learning, race, and school success. *Rev. Educ. Res.* 41:191–210
131. Rohwer, W. D. Jr., Ammon, M. S. 1971. Elaboration training and paired-associate learning efficiency in children. *J. Educ. Psychol.* 62:376–83
132. Romig, J. L. 1972. An evaluation of instruction by student-led discussion in the college classroom. *Diss. Abstr. Int.* 32:6816
133. Rosenfeld, G. W. 1972. Some effects of reinforcement on achievement and behavior in a regular classroom. *J. Educ. Psychol.* 63:189–93
134. Rosenthal, R., Jacobson, L. 1968. *Pygmalion in the Classroom.* New York: Holt, Rinehart & Winston
135. Rothbart, M., Dalfen, S., Barrett, R. 1971. Effects of teacher's expectancy on student-teacher interaction. *J. Educ. Psychol.* 62:49–54
136. Rothkopf, E. Z. 1972. Variable adjunct question schedules, interpersonal interaction, and incidental learning from written material. *J. Educ. Psychol.* 63: 87–92
137. Rothkopf, E. Z., Kaplan, R. 1972. Exploration of the effect of density and specificity of instructional objectives on learning from text. *J. Educ. Psychol.* 63:295–302
138. Rubinstein, J., Friedman, M. J. 1972. The "Cafeteria of Learning"—an experience in informal learning and individualized instruction. *Div. Teach. Psychol. Newslett.*, Dec. 7–9
139. Rubovits, P. C., Maehr, M. L. 1971. Pygmalion analyzed: toward an explanation of the Rosenthal-Jacobson findings. *J. Pers. Soc. Psychol.* 19:197–203
140. Sanders, N. M., DiVesta, F. J., Gray, G. S. 1972. Effects of concept instance sequence as a function of stage of learning and learner strategy. *J. Educ. Psychol.* 63:235–41
141. Sarason, I. G. 1972. Experimental approaches to test anxiety: Attention and the uses of information. In *Anxiety: Current Trends in Theory and Research,* Vol. 2, ed. C. D. Spielberger. New York: Academic
142. Sassenrath, J. M. 1972. Effects of delay of feedback and length of postfeedback interval on retention of prose material. *Psychol. in Sch.* 9:194–97
143. Shavelson, R. J. 1972. Some aspects of the correspondence between content structure and cognitive structure in physics instruction. *J. Educ. Psychol.* 63: 225–34
144. Sieber, J. F. 1969. A paradigm for experimental modification of the effects of test anxiety on cognitive processes. *Am. Educ. Res. J.* 6:46–61
145. Smothergill, N. L., Olson, F., Moore, S. G. 1971. The effects of manipulation of teacher communication style in the preschool. *Child Develop.* 42:1229–39
146. Spielberger, C. D. 1972. Anxiety as an emotional state. In *Anxiety: Current Trends in Theory and Research,* ed. C. D. Spielberger. New York: Academic
147. Spielberger, C. D., O'Neil, H. F. Jr., Hansen, D. N. 1972. Anxiety, drive theory, and computer assisted learning. *Progr. Exp. Pers. Res.* 6:109–48
148. Stalling, R. B. 1971. A one-proctor programmed course procedure for introductory psychology. *Psychol. Rec.* 21:501–5
149. Stolurow, K. A. 1971. Experimental study of sequencing rules applied to instructional materials. Presented at Am. Educ. Res. Assoc. Ann. Conv., New York City
150. Sturges, P. T. 1972. Information delay and retention: effect of information in

feedback and tests. *J. Educ. Psychol.* 63:32–43
151. Ibid. Effect of instructions and form of informative feedback on retention of meaningful material, 99–102
152. Sullivan, A. M., Hartley, J. 1972. The effects of manipulating incentives on learning from a structured individualized psychology course. *Progr. Learn. Educ. Tech.* 8:235–44
153. Suppes, P., Morningstar, M. 1969. Computer-Assisted Instruction. *Science* 166:343–50
154. Tallmadge, G., Kasten, E. A., Shearer, J. W. 1971. Interactive relationships among learner characteristics, types of learning, instructional methods, and subject matter variables. *J. Educ. Psychol.* 62:31–38
155. Tennyson, R. D., Wooley, F. R. 1971. Interaction of anxiety with performance on two levels of task difficulty. *J. Educ. Psychol.* 62:463–68
156. Tennyson, R. D., Wooley, F. R., Merrill, M. D. 1972. Exemplar and nonexemplar variables which produce correct concept classification behavior and specified classification errors. *J. Educ. Psychol.* 63:144–52
157. Terrell, G., Durkin, K., Wesley, M. 1959. Social class and the nature of the incentive in discrimination learning. *J. Abnorm. Soc. Psychol.* 59:270–72
158. Tobias, S., Abramson, T. 1971. Interaction among anxiety, stress, response mode, and familiarity of subject matter on achievement from programmed instruction. *J. Educ. Psychol.* 62:357–64
159. Trumpeter, P. W. 1972. The effects of novelty and racial reference of illustrative examples in teaching psychological concepts to Black college students. *Diss. Abstr. Int.* 32:5625
160. Veroff, J. 1969. Social comparison and the development of achievement motivation. In *Achievement-Related Motives in Children,* ed. C. Smith. New York: Russell Sage
161. Vinsonhaler, J. F., Bass, R. K. 1971. *Ten Major Studies of the Evaluation of CAI Drill and Practice.* Inform. Syst. Lab. Rep. No. 21. Michigan State Univ., Lansing
162. Walker, E. 1969. Reinforcement—the one ring. In *Reinforcement and Behavior,* ed. J. L. Tapp. New York: Academic
163. Watts, G. H., Anderson, R. C. 1971. Effects of three types of inserted questions on learning from prose. *J. Educ. Psychol.* 62:387–94
164. Welch, W. W., Walberg, H. J. 1972. A national experiment in curriculum evaluation. *Am. Educ. Res. J.* 9:373–83
165. Wine, J. 1971. Test anxiety and direction of attention. *Psychol. Bull.* 76:92–105
166. Wine, J. 1972. Test Anxiety and Stress: Naturalistic Observation of Children in the Classroom. Presented at APA Meet., Honolulu
167. Witters, D. R., Kent, G. W. 1972. Teaching without lecturing: Evidence in the case for individualized instruction. *Psychol. Rec.* 22:169–75
168. Wood, L., Wilson, R. C. 1972. Teachers with impact. *Res. Rep.* 7:1–4. Univ. California, Berkeley
169. Zajonc, R. 1965. Social facilitation. *Science* 149:269–74
170. Zajonc, R. 1968. Attitudinal effects of mere exposure. *J. Pers. Soc. Psychol.* Monogr. Suppl. 9:1–27
171. Zigler, E., Butterfield, E. C. 1968. Motivational aspects of changes in IQ test performance of culturally deprived nursery school children. *Child Develop.* 39:1–14
172. Zigler, E., deLabry, J. 1962. Concept switching in middle-class, lower-class, and retarded children. *J. Abnorm. Soc. Psychol.* 65:267–73
173. Zigler, E., Kanzer, P. 1962. The effectiveness of two classes of verbal reinforcers on the performance of middle- and lower-class children. *J. Pers.* 30:157–63
174. Zimmerman, B. J., Pike, E. O. 1972. Effects of modeling and reinforcement on the acquisition and generalization of question asking behavior. *Child Develop.* 43:892–907

SPATIAL VISION

❖215

Robert Sekuler

Cresap Laboratory of Neuroscience and Behavior, Department of Psychology
Northwestern University, Evanston, Illinois

The period covered by this review held much ferment and progress for the field of spatial vision. This review emphasizes those major trends which I believe ought to be encouraged if progress is to be both solid and rapid. What are those trends? First, we have seen an increased awareness of the complexity of the anatomy and physiology that support spatial vision. This increased awareness has brought not only new insights but also recognition of the deficiencies of earlier explanations for complex phenomena. A second major development has been the growing cross-fertilization between clinicians and nonclinicians who share a common professional interest in spatial vision. This interaction has been fostered in part by program and publication policies of the Association for Research in Vision and Ophthalmology (*ARVO*). A third encouraging sign is the successful application of linear systems analysis to various problems in spatial vision. This includes the use of Fourier analysis both as a means of describing stimuli and as part of a model of what the visual system may be doing. Related to this last trend is the growing awareness that many of the problems of spatial vision can be profitably attacked with paradigms and insights derived from work on other sensory systems, particularly the auditory. As Gouras (88) suggested, this collaboration may indeed work for the benefit of all neuroscience: "... the over-all microscopic similarity of all parts of neocortex implies that some fundamentally similar plan is being followed for feature-detecting circuits in all sensory and motor modalities, and it would be exciting if vision research could provide the crucial insight into this master design" (88, p. 3). This growing interaction among specialists in various modalities would surely have delighted von Békésy, Nobel prize winning student of vision, audition, touch, and taste, who constantly urged such interaction (197) and who passed away recently.

Since this review's bibliography makes no claims to be all-inclusive, it may be well to indicate the usefulness of certain bibliographic compilations that may not be familiar to all readers. The various parts of the *Science Citation Index* are to be found in most large science libraries. The components permit searches to be made in a variety of modes while the catholicity of its multidisciplinary data base matches that of spatial vision itself. On this very score, a traditional bibliographic source for psychologists, *Psychological Abstracts,* is quite useless. Recently the Visual Science Information Center of the School of Optometry at Berkeley has begun to publish the *Vision Index,* drawing from a data base well suited to most interests in spatial vision. While users will find an occasional subject term a little odd, the *Index* is for the most part very valuable. Finally, the recent outstanding *Annual Review* chapters by Brown (41) and Leibowitz & Harvey (114) provide leads to some papers that readers might otherwise have missed.

MAJOR BOOKS AND MONOGRAPHS

During the period under review, there were three major publications of book or monograph size. The one that is likely to have the greatest impact, both on the literature and pocketbook, is the volume *Visual Psychophysics* (105) which Jameson & Hurvich edited for the *Handbook of Sensory Physiology.* While its price is an outrage, a good deal of the sting is reduced by its contents and copious illustrative material. Among the chapters that are of direct concern to the present review are those on dark and light adaptation (Barlow 9), signal detection theory (Nachmias 138), luminance difference thresholds by Blackwell (19), and Aulhorn & Harms' chapter on visual perimetry of all sorts (7), Heinemann's review of work on simultaneous brightness induction (96), and Westheimer's thoughtful and provocative treatment of visual acuity (212). This last chapter, a useful extension of Westheimer's *Annual Review* chapter on visual acuity of some years back (210), is nicely supplemented by Fiorentini's chapter on phenomena associated with Mach bands (77). While not directly concerned with spatial vision per se, three other chapters in the Jameson & Hurvich volume will be of particular interest to students of vision: Kelly's on flicker (109), Alpern's on eye movements (1), and the chapter by L. Matin (130) on the relationship between eye movements and perceived visual direction. Riggs & Wooten (156) have summarized much work on electrical and psychophysical data in humans, and their treatment of evoked responses can be nicely supplemented by Regan's encyclopedic book on this same topic (154). Finally, Enoch (70) provides an extraordinarily lucid presentation of the logic and assumptions that underlie Stiles' two-color, increment threshold technique. Since this procedure or others that resemble it in intent, if not in fact, is of use in studies of nonchromatic stimuli in spatial vision, Enoch's presentation is most welcome at this time. The whole volume, including the chapters on color vision which have not been cited here, provides a very useful addition to a vision researcher's reference library particularly since earlier volumes with which it might be compared seem to have aged rather badly (89, 113). The only quarrel I have with this volume is its uneven allocation of space. While some relatively minor topics are given unlimited chapter space, some major topics, like acuity, are held to about half the length they merit. In the near future we'll see the companion volumes of the *Handbook of Sensory Physiology* as well as the multivolume *Handbook of Perception,* edited by Carterette & Friedman.

A second major publishing event is the appearance of the proceedings of an interdisciplinary conference on visual prostheses (Sterling et al 183). A visual prosthesis is a device designed to substitute for (or supplement) impaired vision. The rapid development of integrated circuit technology makes possible serious discussion (196) of implanted electrocortical visual prostheses driven by the output of a miniature television camera mounted in the orbit. Such an unusual prosthesis would take advantage of the phenomenon known as visual phosphenes (visual sensations elicited by electrical stimulation of the brain) to produce a usable cortical representation of visual stimuli (163). Some of the book would read like intriguing, though not particularly well-written, science fiction were it not for the experiments of Brindley & Lewin (38), reprinted in that volume and amplified considerably by Brindley (37). Brindley & Lewin implanted a prototype visual phosphene prosthesis in the occipital cortex of a 52-year-old blind patient. When an electrode in the cortical matrix was energized the patient saw a small phosphene spatially localized in a position controlled by the electrode. Two important observations were made which seem to be critical if this phosphene procedure is to be used as the basis for a practical prosthesis: first, repeated stimulation of one electrode produced no habituation, and second, on each stimulation the phosphene was localized in the same place in the visual field. Brindley and Lewin were able to stimulate clusters of electrodes to produce recognizable phosphene "forms" (e.g. alphabetic characters). The patient was easily able to identify these forms. Several of the contributions to the conference show that present technology could produce a useful implanted cortical phosphene prosthesis (Sterling & Vaughan 184, Vaughan & Schimmel 196, Marg 126, Schimmel & Vaughan 163). Strongly influenced by research on image enhancement and pattern recognition, several contributions to this volume argue the importance of digital preprocessing, filtering, or normalizing of the visual imput to the prosthetic device (e.g. Sterling & Weinkam 185). Finally, a variety of nonphosphene prostheses are described, some using tactile inputs to substitute for vision (Bliss 27). Sprinkled throughout the reported interactions among speakers and discussants at the conference is considerable concern for the ethical implications and considerations of such research.

Another major volume which appeared during this review period is Julesz's *Foundations of Cyclopean Perception* (106). This beautifully produced and illustrated monograph covers not only the phenomena of stereo-depth that have become identified with the author's name, but also many other less well known aspects of Julesz's work. These include new motion phenomena discovered by Julesz and his collaborators, novel aspects of form perception, the analysis of symmetry and clusters, and a general extension of what Julesz calls "psychoanatomy." This term signifies the use of various experimental ploys to localize the site of various perceptual effects in the human visual system.

The book is an outstanding piece of work, provocative and impressive in its range. The monograph contains dozens of demonstrations, in the form of analglyphs, which permit the reader to see himself the phenomena Julesz describes. Most readers find that random-dot stereograms containing many depth planes require a considerable amount of time for the development of the stereo percept. For example, the "hyperbolic paraboloid with torus" or the multiturn spiral surface need to be viewed for many seconds before the figures fully emerge. What the visual system is doing during this prolonged period of incubation is one of the great puzzles that Julesz tries to model. Among the questions that are largely unexplored is why, after viewing one of these multidepth plane random-dot stereograms, there seems to be considerable "savings" in the latency required to see another, different stereogram. In general, I believe that many of the traditional paradigms of learning (massed vs distributed practice, savings, transfer, forgetting etc) could be studied profitably with the Julesz random-dot stereograms. The Julesz patterns lie on the interface between memory and vision, as may the McCollough effect (121) and its very long-lived relatives. Such patterns may provide novel and important insights into the research domains that lie on each side of that interface. Nonstereo random-dot patterns are beginning to receive increased attention in clinical and applied contexts (Gorian et al 87, Cunningham & Galbraith 62), a trend that is likely to accelerate.

The appearance in print of the Canberra Symposium on Vision within months of its occurrence presents a refreshing and fortunate precedent. The issues of *Investigative Ophthalmology* that contain the proceedings are veritable gold mines of significant and current developments in vision, with an emphasis on physiology and anatomy but with a sprinkling of psychophysics as well (Day 64, Julesz 107, Over 142, MacKay 123, Rushton 157).

THE "GREENING" OF VISUAL PHYSIOLOGY

Many of the Canberra papers on the anatomy and physiology of the mammalian visual system will be seen as a mixed blessing to those vision researchers who thought that Hubel & Wiesel (101, 102, 104) had provided at least the outline of a satisfactory understanding of the organization of the visual system. Just when the literature was on the threshold of assimilating the work of Hubel & Wiesel on receptive field organization, and just as nearly every psychophysical paper had at least one gratuitous reference to Hubel & Wiesel, we find that the gospel is in serious need of revision. The standard assumption made by those who use the Hubel & Wiesel hierarchy to "explain" spatial vision is that the visual system is primarily serial in its organization (Lindsay & Norman 116, Stent 181). This means that receptive field structure at the level of bipolar cells (Werblin 208) determines, via appropriate synaptic connections, receptive field structure at the level of the retinal ganglion cells (Cleland & Levick, 53), which are in turn the primary determinants of receptive field structure at the lateral geniculate nucleus (Levick, Cleland & Dubin 115). Somewhat closer to the focus of most students of spatial vision, the gospel proclaims that lateral geniculate cells begat simple cortical cells, which begat complex cortical cells, which begat hypercomplex cells (of Type I), which begat hypercomplex cells of Type II, etc.

At the risk of repeating well-known arguments, it may be worthwhile to outline the implications of some of these relationships as they bear on spatial vision. In repeating them here, the emphasis will be on the deficiencies of the standard interpretation given such physiological data. To anticipate somewhat, we can classify these deficiencies into three categories: first, earlier treatments largely ignored the role of midbrain structures in spatial vision; second, there is a growing recognition that the retinogeniculate pathway itself is not homogeneous—containing at least two major classes of subchannels, differing in latency, linearity, etc; third, there is a new emphasis on the potential of the visual system for parallel processing and information transfer.

Hubel & Wiesel and Their Misuse

Recordings from ganglion cells of the human retina (Weinstein, Hobson & Baker 204) as well as recordings from the intact human visual cortex (Marg, Adams & Rutkin 127, Marg & Adams 128) suggest that responses in our own visual systems are not dissimilar to the responses at comparable levels of the visual systems of lower animals. Given this presumptive evidence of the general similarity of the human visual system to those of cat and monkey, let's consider what Hubel & Wiesel say about the visual cortex.

In their beautiful pioneering work, Hubel & Wiesel described the basic nature of synaptic organization of the geniculostriate pathways of cat (101, 102) and monkey (104). Simple cortical cells, presumably as a result of the nature of their connections to lateral geniculate cells, respond most strongly to a visual stimulus of a certain orientation and luminance sign (i.e. whether it is lighter or darker than the background), and require that the stimulus be within a certain narrowly defined region in a frontoparallel projection. Simple cells have two other characteristics which are of interest. First, they respond to increasing length of stimulus with increasing response up to some critical length, beyond which response is invariant. Second, they respond to increasing width of a stimulus with increasing response up to a certain value, beyond which response may diminish. All of these characteristics may be developed in a straightforward manner from an understanding of the connections of the simple cell to the lateral geniculate cells from which it functionally rises. Such simple cortical cells have been termed "bar detectors," "line detectors," or "orientation detectors," and they have been treated by some psychologists as though "a single 'simple' cortical unit may signal for a rectangle of a certain orientation at or below a certain width and corresponding to a particular retinal locus" (Weisstein 205, p. 159). Somewhat less spectacular claims have often been made for single cells of the Hubel & Wiesel type. For example, in a standard text on physiological psychology the following statement is found: ". . . the characteristics of stimuli that are effective in activating cells are those what are often said to be mediated by 'higher' processes such as 'perception.' Perhaps the most fundamental importance of these experiments is that they remove much of the mystery from 'perception.' Abstract aspects of stimulus quality are coded by single nerve cells and do not require mysterious gestalt fields, a 'scanning sensor,' or a 'man-within-a-man' to do the perceiving" (Thompson 191, p. 351).

While such cells may very well play a role in the analysis of orientation or other stimulus aspects, it must be pointed out that any one of these cells cannot by itself signal uniquely either orientation or the length of the stimulation line or any other property to which it responds differentially. The reason for this is obvious. Since the response of a cell is in fact the joint outcome of several stimulus dimensions, variation in any of them cannot be signaled unequivocally or represented by the output of one simple cell. In other words, by judicious choice of stimulus values along all dimensions of the cell's sensitivity it would be theoretically possible to have a large number of stimuli all adjusted to produce exactly the same response from the simple cell. Perhaps an analogy with color vision might reinforce this idea. Imagine a retina with only one photopigment type. The response of that photopigment is jointly determined by the number of quanta and the photopigment's sensitivity to the wavelength of those quanta. We can produce exactly the same response in the photopigment by a combination of lots of quanta at a wavelength where the photopigment is not very sensitive (that is one at which the probability of a quantal absorption is low) or by stimulating with fewer quanta but at a wavelength to which the photopigment is more sensitive. Since its response is determined along two stimulus dimensions, we cannot derive wavelength related information from its output. We will return later to the implications of this point.

The next stage of analysis in the cortex results in receptive fields that seem to be the product of synaptic interaction among several simple cells. This stage of analysis is represented by the complex cell. Complex cortical cells show specificities for stimulus orientation and width approximately the same as those found in simple cells but differ from the latter in two major ways. First, complex cells show direction specificity—that, is a given cell may respond maximally to a stimulus moving in one direction and be totally unresponsive to movement in the opposite direction. Second, a complex cell seems less fussy about its *x–y* position requirements than is a simple cell. A complex cell will respond to an appropriately oriented line over a wide range of *x–y* positions. Such a lack of position specificity in the complex cell has frequently been used to explain the position invariance shown by various perceptual phenomena. Unlike simple cells, complex cell receptive fields did not appear to be composed of obvious on and off areas. Hubel & Wiesel went on to suggest that complex cells may be wired together to determine hypercomplex cell receptive field organization. Hypercomplex cells of Type I exhibit a novel property, namely an extreme sensitivity to length of line or stimulating bar. Such a cell will show increasing response as a function of the length of a properly positioned and oriented bar until a critical length is reached. Beyond this length, response drops, sometimes quite rapidly. This inhibition or "end stop" can be explained on the assumption of not too implausible presynaptic inputs from complex cells. An inhibitory input to the hypercomplex cell from a complex cell is adequate to explain the sharp drop in response as the stimulus is elongated beyond the excitatory region of the receptive field (Dreher 67). A second type of hypercomplex cell, perhaps deriving from Type I connections, shows sensitivity to stimulus angles. This rapid review of cortical organization ignores features that are of considerable importance to spatial vision. These features include the processing of retinal disparities (Pettigrew 148, Bishop & Henry 17) and the columnar organization so intensely characteristic of the visual and other sensory cortical volumes (24).

Parallel and Serial Organization

Because the hierarchical scheme described above may require some modification, a few remarks about it are in order here. First, it should be recognized that the existence of a hierarchy does not necessarily imply a strictly serial system. This rather obvious point is often forgotten (as is pointed out in the discussion by Hubel and Stone in 186). The fact that receptive field organizations of all kinds are found in the axons which cross the corpus callosum (Hubel & Wiesel 103) indicates that there may be a good deal of parallel organization along with the basic hierarchy which Hubel & Wiesel describe. While the precise connections of these fibers that carry visual information between hemispheres is quite complicated, the implications of their receptive field types is more clear: information from cells of all types—simple, complex, etc.—is available to whatever centers are interested in such information. This fact is quite slow to impress students of spatial vision who have found it more convenient to pretend the system was not only hierarchical, but also serial.

A related issue is raised by attempts to identify contrast analysis with the operation of retinal ganglion cells. It has often been assumed by psychophysicists and physiologists that by the time the retinal image is coded into impulses along the optic nerve, that code reflects substantial analysis of spatial contrast. For example, simultaneous contrast in man has been attributed to the spatially opponent organization of retinal ganglion cells. Observations by Maffei & Fiorentini (125) cast doubt on this thesis. They show that the inhibitory aspects of lateral geniculate cell receptive fields arise not from the inhibitory aspects of retinal ganglion cells (as had been thought) but rather from centers of retinal receptive fields, albeit different centers than give rise to the centers of the geniculate cell fields. They argue that the opponent organization at the retinal level is essentially a sensitivity control mechanism (see 208 for related arguments), and that the analogous opponent organization of the geniculate level does not arise from that of the preceding stage. Another important finding reported by Maffei & Fiorentini is that unlike their retinal ganglion cell counterparts, the strength of the opponent organization at the geniculate is unaffected by dark adaptation. The implications of these results for psychophysics will be considered later.

Bishop & Henry (18) expressed their dissatisfaction with two aspects of previous work on cortical receptive fields: first, as most readers will appreciate, there has been less than complete rigor and clarity in the manner of defining and classifying cell types; second, relatively little attempt has been made to describe the "intrinsic structure or regional organization within the receptive field" (18, p. 347), with most workers being satisfied merely to map the outlines of the field. This latter complaint has begun to be settled (Henry & Bishop 97), and there is yet hope that eventually we will know as much about the detailed regional organization of cortical cells as we know about that of retinal ganglion cells. Bishop & Henry (18) described their technique for plotting and classifying receptive fields with admirable clarity. While Bishop & Henry agree that the Hubel & Wiesel classificatory scheme is generally useful, they quarrel with certain details: first, they claim that fully three quarters of the simple cortical cells show directional selectivity in their response; second, they describe cells which are hypercomplex in that they show stopped-end inhibition but resemble simple cells in having distinct on and off subregions. These exchanges and disagreements among Hubel, Bishop & Henry in the Canberra Symposium (18, 97) give the reader a clear idea of the degree of agreement on the organization of the visual cortex.

Subchannels in the Primary Afferent Pathway

The distinction that Enroth-Cugell & Robson (71) made between two distinct types of retinal ganglion cells has been extended to the lateral geniculate nucleus. Enroth-Cugell & Robson characterized retinal ganglion cells as X-type (linear summation of center and surround, sustained responses, and slowly conducting axons) or as Y-type (nonlinear summation of center and surround, transient responses, and more rapidly conducting axons). Stone & Hoffman (187) and Cleland, Dubin & Levick (54) showed that X- and Y-type retinal ganglion cells tend to drive separate cells in the lateral geniculate of cat.

Moreover, such X- and Y-type lateral geniculate cells may constitute separate geniculostriate channels (differing in latency, for example) and perhaps even have different cortical cells subgroups as their target (Stone 186). Stone has argued, in addition, that complex cortical cells may derive primarily from the Y channel while simple and hypercomplex cells derive from the X channel. Certain properties of the receptive fields of the cortical cells in question are consistent with this speculation. This controversial argument is further complicated by Hoffman's (100) claims that X-type retinal ganglion cells do not project to the superior colliculus either directly or indirectly, but that Y-type cells do, after relaying through geniculate and cortex. While the value of this carefully preserved segregation of visual information into separate subchannels remains to be discovered, it is well to remember that neither all retinal ganglion cells nor all cells of the lateral geniculate nucleus are likely to prove equal.

Contributions of the Superior Colliculus

Several years ago it might nearly have been possible to draw a decent diagram of the main afferent pathways in the mammalian visual system (*a*) without lifting one's pencil from the paper and (*b*) without recrossing very many lines. The recognition that the colliculus is a structure to be reckoned with in the scheme of things (McIlwain 122, Gordon 86) makes this feat no longer possible. Introducing his survey of the anatomy of the superior colliculus, Lund described the colliculi as "concerned with aspects of visual attention and centering of the visual image on the retina" (119, p. 435). His paper reminds us that colliculi are anatomically (Sprague 179) and functionally heterogeneous structures. Virtually every investigator of the superior colliculus has found it useful to distinguish (at very minimum) between "superficial" and "deep" laminar divisions. Roughly speaking the superficial layers are concerned with strictly visual matters, receiving inputs from both contra- and ipsilateral retinas as well as from ipsilateral visual cortex. Its outputs go to several places in the visual system. Inputs to the less superficial regions of the colliculi carry information from several nonvisual modalities, from the superficial region of the ipsilateral colliculus, as well as from the contralateral colliculus. Gordon (86) summarized her work and that of her collaborator Sterling (Wickelgren, 214; Wickelgren & Sterling, 215) on both superficial and deep aspects of the colliculus. The duplication of retinotopic maps in midbrain and cortical structures presents a great puzzle to the casual observer, a puzzle which is not lessened by the probability of species differences in collicular function (Schiller 162). Cells in the superior colliculus are less fussy in their stimulus requirements than are cortical cells. For example, the sharp tuning to direction of movement or stimulus orientation, characteristic of so many cortical cells, seems to be absent in the colliculus. Studies of cortical ablation suggest that at least two visual receptive field characteristics of collicular cells, their binocular sensitivity and large receptive field diameters, derives from corticotectal rather than retinotectal influences. There is a general agreement on the point that the superior colliculus plays a role in target acquisition and tracking (162) but growing disagreement on the details of this formulation. Wurtz & Goldberg, for example, write "we think the colliculus is involved in a shift of attention and facilitation of movement to an area, but not the coding of the exact location of the eye movement target for two sets of reasons: one is that our monkeys with lesions can acquire the target perfectly, but only take longer to start. The other is that properties of the cells are more consistent with an attention-shifting role than with a fine-guidance role (218, p. 595)." Goldberg and Wurtz (85) have provided a superb model of how one might study as complex a phenomenon as "attention" in a neurophysiological preparation and make a good case for the role of the colliculus in shifts of attention. Their discussion of difficulties in operationalizing "attention" will prove useful to psychologists who have in general only begun to deal with the implications of such phenomena for spatial vision (68, 170).

Some of Gordon's intriguing observations on the superficial layers of cat superior colliculus (86) are worth mentioning in detail despite the fact that some of those observations are yet to be confirmed in higher species (Goldberg & Wurtz 84). One of the striking characteristics of those superior colliculus cells that exhibit directional sensitivity is the anisotropic character of that sensitivity. In general, such cells tend to be more responsive to movement outward from the center of the field (centrifugal) than to movement inward from the periphery (centripetal). This direction preference, Gordon has suggested, helps the colliculus determine " 'where the stimulus is and where it is going' in order to bring the stimulus into the center of the visual field and keep it there." Recording from deeper layers of the cat superior colliculus, Gordon found striking evidence that a cell, which could be driven either by visual stimuli or by auditory stimuli, had its two receptive fields (auditory and visual) in the same area of perceptual space. The colliculus then has not only a topographic map of visual space, but also a topographic map of auditory space and a given cell monitors roughly the same area of space in both modalities. Moreover, directionally selective cells in these deeper collicular layers tended to have the same direction preference in both input modalities. Such cells, with analogous preferences in each input modality, might explain a variety of puzzling phenomena. For example, Wertheimer (209) noted that within minutes after birth a human infant seemed to have a workable, crude common map of visual and auditory space. While there might not be a direct causal relationship between the bimodal superior colliculus cells which Gordon described and any human behavioral phenomena, it is clear that there is increasing interest in bimodal effects in spatial vision (Engel & Dougherty 69, Day 65, Morrell 134, Dougherty, Jones & Engel 66). We may be approaching the point where it will no longer be premature (Stent 182) to explore bimodal effects in spatial vision. While engaging in this wild speculation, it might be appropriate to suggest that the psychophysical literature already contains reports of differential centrifugal and centripetal motion sensitivity (Scott, Lavender, McWhirt & Powell 165), not unlike that which Gordon describes for collicular cells. These data are consistent with Richards' controversial claim that certain aspects of human motion perception are mediated by the superior colliculus (Richards 155). Even though such cells may actually play no role whatever in human spatial vision, they do provide a framework within which certain experimental manipulations make sense and without which they would be unthinkable.

Psychophysical Linking Hypotheses

Clearly, one of the recurrent themes in the study of spatial vision has been an interest in correlating observations made at different levels of analysis. Whether these correlations are attempted at the level of the inner plexiform layer of the retina or at the level of the hypercomplex cells (Nakayama & Roberts 140), some rules of translation between the levels must be assumed. The rules that relate visual or perceptual events to their physiological correlates are psychophysical linking hypotheses. Brindley (36) has written of the need and difficulty involved in making such rules or assumptions explicit. As one goes through the literature on spatial vision one is struck time and again by the failure to make and test explicit and well formed psychophysical linking hypotheses. Since such hypotheses are critical for the advancement of spatial vision, it may be worthwhile to consider them and their implications.

Brindley proposed that there may at present be only one generally accepted psychophysical linking hypothesis: "Whenever two stimuli cause physically indistinguishable signals to be sent from the sense organs to the brain, the sensations produced by these stimuli, as reported by the subject in words, symbols or actions, must also be indistinguishable" (p. 133). By accepting this argument we can make statements about the indistinguishability of stimuli *a* and *b* under conditions *x* and *y*. Brindley also proposed that we may adopt without question the converse of this proposition: physiological events which are distinguishable from one another give rise to different perceptual effects. Observations which contain statements about the distinguishability or indistinguishability of sensations are the constituents of Class A experiments. Such experiments include matching and threshold experiments of all kinds. Observations that cannot be expressed as the identity or nonidentity of sensations are Class B observations. These include descriptions of entoptic phenomena, response time experiments, scaling experiments, etc.

Because Brindley recognizes the validity of only the one general psychophysical linking hypothesis described above, he has proposed that Class A experiments must necessarily be more informative of the underlying physiology than are Class B experiments. Other people have from time to time proposed sets of linking hypotheses, including Boynton & Onley's (31) useful elaboration of Brindley's scheme. Some time ago, Boring (29) presented an operational form of G. E. Mueller's psychophysical axioms which have considerable merit and provide a good companion to Brindley's argument. Among the points which Boring made is that the possibility of finite "just noticeable differences" on the sensory continuum make it somewhat risky to accept without question the proposition that different physiological events necessarily give rise to behaviorally defined just noticeable differences.

Brindley has proposed that it is possible to convert many Type B observations (e.g. the Purkinje shift) into equivalent Type A observations (e.g. thresholds for light of various wavelengths as a function of adaptation level, photopic through scotopic). While this may very well be true, the rules by which one translates from Class B to Class A are not always clear. For example, Brindley suggested (36, p. 146) the waterfall illusion (motion aftereffect) is a Class B counterpart of observations made by Pantle & Sekuler (145) at threshold level. Pantle & Sekuler, extending the earlier observations of Sekuler & Ganz, found that viewing contours which move in one direction selectively raises the luminance threshold for contours which move in that same direction. Brindley's assertion that these threshold observations are Class A equivalents of the waterfall illusion is probably wrong. Sekuler, Lehr, Stone & Wolf (168) showed that the threshold effect of viewing moving contours behaves quite differently from the suprathreshold effect (waterfall illusion) under certain conditions of stimulation.

This implies that we must be careful in extrapolating from threshold observations to suprathreshold ones, and that it is not always possible in an a priori fashion to specify the Class A counterpart of any given Class B observation. The following example might give additional insight into why this is so. Consider a single, simple cortical cell of the kind described by Hubel & Wiesel. Its response is determined by several stimulus dimensions. Such cells cannot singly signal unequivocally the orientation of a stimulus in its receptive field (or, for that matter, any of the other properties to which it is sensitive). A given response level from one of these simple cells could be produced by any of an infinite number of combinations of stimulus orientation, length, width, etc. This means that the suprathreshold appearance of stimuli, insofar as simple cells contribute at all, must be determined by the pattern of cross-cell activity (cf. Erickson 72), by the pooled or summed activity levels of very many cells. On the other hand, it is possible to assume that the detection threshold for a given target is controlled by one, or very few, cells—the one or ones that would be optimally stimulated by the particular combination of stimulus properties possessed by the target. This conception owes an obvious debt to the domain of color vision. While the suprathreshold appearance (color) of a stimulus is the product of the pooled, weighted response of several wavelength sensitive channels, the detection threshold for a given target is determined by that channel which is most sensitive, given the prevailing combination of test wavelength, background wavelength and luminance (70). In this vein, then, Sekuler, Lehr, Stone & Wolf (168) have argued that while the detection threshold for contours moving downward through the field is determined exclusively by mechanisms sensitive to downward motion, the suprathreshold appearance of a target's direction of motion is jointly controlled by several mechanisms, each sensitive to a different range of directions. One of the key unsettled questions of spatial vision then is the relationship between threshold and suprathreshold observations. Before we can establish clear rules for psychophysical linking hypotheses, we must be in a position to make some general statements about the relationship between the levels of psychophysical observations. This question is critical for any attempt to make predictions of psychophysical observations from the often scant data at the physiological level. Almost alone among neurophysiologists, Hirsch (98) has considered this problem.

ANALYSIS OF SPATIAL FREQUENCY RESPONSES

A promising new approach to spatial vision is one that makes use of spatial frequency analysis. Westheimer (213) paints an amusing, but highly accurate portrait of subjects across the world being exposed to a staggering variety of spatial, temporal, and even spatio-temporal sinusoidal modulations. Sinusoidal luminance distributions (gratings) have gained great popularity. Two questions clearly need answering: why are such odd stimuli being used and what sort of information does their use give us about spatial vision?

As we will see, not all experiments which use these sinusoidal stimuli make the same level of theoretical commitment to those stimuli. The spatial response of the visual system is sometimes measured with sinusoidal inputs because the experimenter assumes the visual system to be linear, at least near threshold. This means that the response is proportional to the input. More formally, linearity implies a system that obeys the principle of superposition—if the response of the system to stimulus $f_i(x)$ is $f_o(x)$ and the response of the system to stimulus $g_i(x)$ is $g_o(x)$, then the response to the combination of $f_i(x) + g_i(x)$ is $f_o(x) + g_o(x)$ for all pairs of $f_i(x)$ and $g_i(x)$, where i subscripts an input function defined over space and o subscripts an output function defined over space. A second assumption made implicity in most studies of spatial frequency response is that the system is space-invariant or homogeneous. This means simply that regardless of where on the input surface the input function is directed, the relationship between output and input will be invariant. Symbolically, we may state that a system is homogeneous if for all pairs of input positions, x_1 and x_2, $f_o(x_1) = f_o(x_2)$ whenever $f_i(x_1) = f_i(x_2)$. A third related assumption, isotropy, is discussed by Cornsweet (58). Since, of the three assumptions just described, isotropy is the one best met by the visual system it will be ignored in what follows.

If the visual system's spatial response can be considered linear and homogeneous, sinusoidal inputs are *eigenfunctions* for the system, i.e. the response of the system to a sinusoidal input will be a sinusoid of the same frequency but, perhaps, of different amplitude or phase or both (177). While many experiments have shown this assumption of linearity to be not unreasonable, for small signals at least, it must always be remembered that in reality the visual system is strongly nonlinear—possessed as it is of both threshold and saturation points.

Sinusoids defined over space are useful in the direct, empirical generation of contrast sensitivity functions. These functions characterize the ability of the visual system to transfer information at various spatial frequencies from stimulus input to output. Similar plots are often found in popular photography or hi-fi magazines. The plot for an amplifier may relate output to input with input frequency, in the time domain, as a variable. In vision, the analogous plots display sensitivity as a function of input frequency in the space time, i.e. spatial frequency expressed usually as cycles/degree. Sensitivity is defined as the reciprocal of percent threshold modulation—difference between peaks and troughs—required for the observer to distinguish the stimulus from a uniform field of equivalent space-average luminance.

There are two main uses for this spatial contrast sensitivity function, and they differ very much in their underlying theoretical assumptions. First, the function may be a quick and useful summary of the overall response of the visual system. As we'll see in a moment it is often important to have such a summary—much as it may be important to have the analogous information on a loudspeaker before purchasing it. Second, if the visual system were truly linear we could use the contrast sensitivity function to predict the response of that system to any arbitrarily chosen spatial input—including, perhaps, the Union Jack (213). As we will also see, experiments have been done which attempt to predict, from the contrast sensitivity function, how the visual system will respond to nonsinusoidal, small signal stimuli. To the extent that they are successful, we may consider the assumption of linearity not to be too far off. Useful descriptions of the process involved in these predictions are available (75, 216).

Descriptive Uses of Contrast Sensitivity Functions

Recent years have seen the increasing use of contrast sensitivity functions to summarize not only the response of the whole eye-brain system, but of selected portions of that system as well. Campbell & Green (45) produced separate contrast sensitivity functions for (*a*) the optics of the eye (*b*) the remainder of the visual system, including neural structures. Ohzu & Enoch (141) produced similar functions for the retina of the human eye. Later, the use of the contrast sensitivity function in clinical contexts will be discussed (28, 92). Three examples here will provide some indication of the diversity of possible uses for this function. Berkley & Watkins (15, 16) used evoked potentials to estimate the acuity limits of the cat. Data relating magnitude of evoked potential to the spatial frequency of the evoking stimulus are of great importance in bridging the gap between single cell recording and behavior in the cat. Related data on the human evoked potential were reported by Campbell & Kulikowski (47). Finally, Shlaer (173) gave an elegant description of the optical transfer characteristics of the eye of the eagle, arguing that some of the incredible feats of acuity claimed by eagleophiles are really impossible.

Linear Systems Uses of Contrast Sensitivity Functions

This may be the appropriate place to repeat Kelly's cautionary note on the role of Fourier analysis in the study of flicker (109), observing simply that the same *caveat* certainly holds for the case of spatial vision and spatial frequency analysis. Kelly pointed out that "Despite its importance, mathematical analysis of the stimulus alone does not constitute a theory. Some current investigators seem to regard Fourier analysis itself as a model of the visual process (which they call 'the Fourier model'), but this is erroneous. Fourier analysis has the same status as vector analysis, matrix analysis, or any other branch of mathematics; it is one of many tools that are useful for constructing models. But there is usually more to constructing a good theory than just using the right tools" (109, p. 274). While Kelly's point is well taken, it should be made stronger by a reminder that *any* application of Fourier methods necessarily involves assumptions about the system being analyzed.

One particularly good example of Kelly's argument is the study by Campbell, Carpenter & Levinson (43), using the techniques of linear systems analysis to predict the visibility of various aperiodic stimuli from knowledge of the overall, system contrast sensitivity function. The contrast sensitivity function was used to predict the visibility of a single bar (one-half cycle of a sinusoidal grating), of a double bar (a full cycle of the grating) and of a target in which the grating was restricted to one half the field while the other half was uniform and at the equivalent space average luminance. If we assume that the visual system, at least near threshold, is a linear system, one which obeys the principle of superposition, we can determine its response to any arbitrary stimulus by summing its responses to appropriately chosen components of that arbitrary stimulus.

The line spread function is the image of a line object. This spread function, in the distance domain, and the contrast sensitivity function, in the frequency domain, are related by a Fourier transform (152). Campbell, Carpenter & Levinson (43) computed the line spread function from the Fourier cosine transform of the contrast sensitivity function. Since both variables are defined on the spatial domain, we may convolve the line spread function with the luminance profile of the stimulus, yielding the response of the system, also in the spatial domain. The response of the detector is assumed to be a function of the maximum peak-to-trough amplitude difference in the output of the convolution. This operation is repeated for various frequencies of the aperiodic stimulus. It is then possible to determine, for any aperiodic stimulus used, the expected output of the visual system as a function of the input frequency. After completing these computations, Campbell et al had only two emendation ("fudge") factors available for fitting the experimental observations—one a constant associated with a given subject's sensitivity as a detector of peak-to-trough amplitudes, and the other a constant which slid the predictions for a given subject along the *x*, spatial frequency axis. This study is one in which both the failures and successes of the theoretical predictions are informative. The predictions were quite good when two conditions were met: first, the data from the double bar conditions were excluded, and second, data primarily for higher spatial frequencies, i.e. greater than 10 c/degrees were considered. The failure in the case of the double bar stimulus (one full cycle of a grating) means that linear theory has to be "false in the extreme case of two single bars of opposite contrast, separated by considerable distance" (43, p. 296). At low spatial frequencies, with large distances between peaks and troughs of the convolution output, the assumptions of the model would be up against the obvious fact that the human retina is functionally organized into isoplanatism patches, finite regions each characterized by a somewhat different spread function (cf. Harvey & Pöppel 95, Van Doorn, Koenderink & Bouman 195). Westheimer has put this especially well in his arguments that "the heterogeneity of retinal structure makes the analysis of spatial visual function with extended sinusoidal targets somewhat risky" (212, p. 183). The spatial grain of the retina varies perhaps by as much as a factor of 10 as one goes from the fovea to the point only 10° peripheral (Westheimer 213).

Even if the retina were not heterogeneous with respect to characteristic local spread functions, the visual system may lack the mechanisms required to detect differences between widely separated peaks and troughs in the retinal image. To sum up, while these experiments (43) make elegant use of some of the tools of Fourier analysis and linear systems analysis, they do not test, in the study under consideration, the possibility that the visual system operates on the Fourier components of the aperiodic targets (cf. Sullivan, Georgeson & Oatley 190). Paraphrasing Kelly rather imperfectly, this study uses the tools of Fourier analysis but does not constitute evidence for a Fourier theory.

Multiple-Channel Models

What sorts of theoretical interpretations can be given to the human spatial sensitivity function? What sorts of mechanisms could give rise to it? Westheimer points out that this standard, human contrast sensitivity function can be derived from the convolution of sinusoidal spatial inputs with the standard "Mexican hat" receptive field model profile with an excitatory center diameter of about 3 minutes (212, p. 182). Under a variety of conditions the curve shows that the visual system has peak sensitivity at intermediate spatial frequencies, with decreasing sensitivity for either higher or lower frequencies. There are two general classes of models proposed to explain the function. The first, a single-channel model, considers the information from receptive field profiles of all sizes to be pooled prior to mechanisms which detect the target, say a grating. Evidence from selective adaptation experiments (e.g. 144) supports quite a different interpretation, a multiple-channel model. This model assumes the contrast sensitivity function to be the envelope of sensitivities for a whole series (number unspecified) of separate channels, each sensitive to a limited region of the spectrum. If the outputs of these various channels were detected or measured in a relatively independent fashion, we would have one generic form of a multiple-channel model of spatial vision. An analogy to color vision might be useful. The overall sensitivity envelope of the photopic system coexists with—and presumably is produced by—some combination of three color sensitive channels. The operation of the individual channels can be measured if one goes to certain experimental lengths, using, for example, Stiles' increment threshold procedure (70). Let us note one final point before going on to consider the multiple-channel model as it has developed over the past few years in spatial vision. A multiple-channel model does not necessarily imply that under all stimulus levels and for all tasks the visual system behaves as though composed of totally independent spatial frequency channels. To anticipate somewhat a point made at length later, independence of spatial frequency channels seems to hold only near threshold (with low contrast inputs) and there is increasing evidence of theoretically interesting inhibitory cross-talk between channels sensitive to somewhat different frequency bands as the responses of those individual channels increase. Moreover, the importance of task variables in spatial frequency analysis is just beginning to be examined (50).

What is the likely neural origin of these spatial frequency selective channels? This is a question that has recently been reopened. It has been commonly assumed that the first major stage of spatial contrast analysis was carried by the outputs of retinal ganglion cells. Several observations reported during the review period seem to raise questions about this assumption. From a study of connections between retinal ganglion cells and their target cells in the lateral geniculate nucleus, Maffei & Fiorentini (125) have suggested that retinal ganglion cells, at least in cat, are not passing contrast information along to the geniculate cells. Moreover, two psychophysical studies indicated that scotopic spatial adaptation levels do not affect sensitivity, as one would expect from current ideas about the reduction in retinal ganglion cell surround inhibition with scotopic conditions (90). As Fiorentini & Maffei put it, "To whatever extent perceptual contrast effects can be explained in terms of receptive field organization, they cannot be accounted for by the properties of *retinal* receptive fields. The properties of more central visual receptive fields such as those of the lateral geniculate body or cortex seem to account better for the observed scotopic contrast phenomena" (80, p. 78–79).

A model of the visual system, if it is to be of much use, has to deal with more than the response to simple sinusoidal gratings. How does a multiple-channel model deal with more complicated stimuli—real world scenes for example? The model postulates that the visual system decomposes any scene into its spatial frequency components. Each component is then detected in a manner that is independent of the others (159). The general finding, at threshold, is that components of a stimulus which differ by as much as a factor of two in spatial frequency are detected quite independently of one another. For example, a complex grating (one consisting of more than one spatial frequency component) is detected—discriminated from a homogeneous field—when the contrast of one of its spatial frequency components is above threshold. Imagine that we measure the threshold for a simple sinusoidal grating of frequency F and then measure the threshold for another simple sinusoidal grating of $2F$ frequency. Suppose further that because of their relative positions on the contrast sensitivity function the F grating had the lower threshold of the two. If we then create a compound grating with both F and $2F$ components, regardless of their phase relationships, and measure the contrast threshold for the compound (again, the contrast at which the grating is discriminably different from a homogeneous field of equivalent mean luminance) that threshold is numerically identical with the point at which the contrast of the F component itself reached threshold.

In summary, it is important to recognize that models of spatial vision differ along a number of relatively independent dimensions. For example, a model may make assumptions about the linearity of the system being described. A model can be defined as multiple channel or single channel. Multiple-channel models can incorporate various degrees of cross-talk among channels; the channels, as well as the cross-talk, may be either linear or nonlinear.

Fourier Models

An important distinction needs to be made between the multiple-channel model and a stronger version of that model, which claims not only a spatial frequency analysis by independent channels each sensitive to particular spatial frequency band, but which claims that the visual system uses a particular kind of spatial analysis in this operation, an analysis into its Fourier components (Pollen, Lee & Taylor 151). This strong Fourier version of the multiple-channel model is not logically mandated by the findings concerned with the independence of various spatial frequency channels. The multiple-channel model or some version of it could be correct even if the visual system did not perform a set of operations isomorphic with Fourier analysis. Still there are many reasons for using this outlandish notion of a Fourier model as a working assumption.

Fourier theory states simply that any arbitrary waveform can be analyzed into appropriate sine and cosine components and that the reverse process is also possible: that any arbitrary waveform can be approximated or synthesized from appropriate components. In spatial vision it is commonly assumed that retinal ganglion cells or cells such as simple cortical cells perform a hardware analysis whose output can be thought of as giving the power in each of a number of spatial frequency bands. Although a single-channel Fourier model of spatial frequency is logically possible it is easily shown to be false (Pantle & Sekuler 144). Consequently the only Fourier model we'll consider is the standard, multiple-channel Fourier model.

Regardless of its ultimate correctness, this point of view does have several attractive aspects: first, it serves to emphasize what may be heuristically significant similarities between spatial vision and audition (Carterette, Friedman & Lovell 52, Kay & Matthews 108, Stromeyer & Julesz 189, Carter & Henning 51). Second, it implies a useful way of quantifying certain kinds of stimuli, particularly spatially complex ones. The addition of certain auxiliary assumptions permits prediction of independence, additivity or masking interaction among stimuli. It is these auxiliary assumptions that constitute a theory, not the manner in which the stimuli are described (109). Third, the idea of multiple and independent channels for the analysis of various bands of spatial frequency information fits nicely with the work of Enroth-Cugell and her collaborators on the sensitivity profiles of cat retinal ganglion cells, lateral geniculate, and cortical receptive fields (e.g. Campbell, Cleland, Cooper & Enroth-Cugell 44). Since the contrast sensitivity function is central to so many experiments testing a Fourier model it is nice that the function is easily derivable from first principles. Fourth, the assumption that the visual system performs some kind of Fourier analysis of its retinal image input provides a convenient way of explaining certain sticky perceptual phenomena. For example, if only the distribution of power in various spatial frequency channels is considered, the representations of the stimulus patterns would be invariant over shifts in phase or with translational changes (Rybicki, Tracy & Pollen 158, Armstrong & Sekuler 4). This would also provide a ready-made explanation for the fact that we can recognize objects despite changes in their location in the visual field from presentation to presentation. Finally, the Fourier version of the multiple-channel model permits the prediction of a variety of nonintuitive visual phenomena (Blakemore, Nachmias & Sutton 25). These successful predictions represent the major achievements of the model and some can be profitably summarized here, followed by an indication of possible problems with the formulation.

Campbell & Robson (49) gave an explicit statement of the Fourier multiple-channel model. While not all their findings unambiguously require such a model, some being well handled by a single-channel model, other of the data do. From the Fourier representation of various nonsinusoidal gratings (e.g. square wave grating), Campbell & Robson could predict the detectability of the grating; these predictions required only knowledge of the contrast sensitivity function. These results merely show that the system is approximately linear and do not mandate the independent detection of various spatial frequency components, a key part of a multiple-channel model. By Fourier theory, a square wave grating may be treated as a combination of a fundamental frequency F and modulation $4/\pi$, a third harmonic, $3F$, with modulation $4/3\pi$, a fifth harmonic, $5F$ with modulation $4/5\pi$, etc. When such a square wave grating was just detectable it appeared sinusoidal. Additional contrast was needed for it to appear square. Campbell & Robson found that from data on the detectability of simple sinusoidal gratings of F and $3F$, they could predict the contrast of the square wave grating at which it would first appear square rather than sinusoidal. This finding does seem to require the independent detection of various frequency components, supporting a multiple-channel model.

As further evidence for the model, Blakemore & Campbell (20) showed that exposure to a high contrast square wave grating of frequency F raises the threshold for sinusoidal gratings of frequency F and that for gratings of $3F$ as well (although to a lesser degree, as predicted). This latter finding is expected if the visual system were doing a Fourier analysis on the square wave grating, decomposing it into its fundamental and odd harmonics. Of the odd harmonics only $3F$ would have adequate power to produce detectable adaptation. It should be noted that many papers that support a multiple-channel model (e.g. 144) find that predictions from the Fourier position fail at low spatial frequencies. It may well be that while the Fourier multiple-channel model is fine for higher frequencies, the visual system has adapted an alternative approach to the analysis of low frequency components of the retinal image.

More recent papers have been aimed directly at the Fourier multiple-channel model. Sullivan, Georgeson & Oatley (190) measured the contrast threshold for single bars, of varying width, as well as for sinusoidal gratings of various spatial frequencies. Measurements were made with and without prior adaptation to gratings (sinusoidal of 5.5 c/deg or 16 c/deg) or bars (7.5 or 1.25 minutes wide). As expected, test gratings in the vicinity of 5.5 c/deg had elevated thresholds after exposure to an adaptation grating of 5.5 c/deg and a similar, localized elevation near the adapting frequency following exposure to 16 c/deg. The power spectrum for a single bar, in Fourier terms, is quite different from what one expects by simply treating the bar as a half-cycle of the appropriate width grating. The spectra are of the form $(\sin bx/x)^2$ where b is one half the bar width. This means that a single bar of width 1.25 min will have a fairly uniform distribution of spectral power from 1 c/deg through 20 c/deg. Most important for the Sullivan et al experiment is the fact that both adapting bars have approximately the same power in the spectral region where the contrast sensitivity function is at its most sensitive—between 2 and 4 c/deg. Adapting to a sinusoidal grating of 5.5 c/deg raises the threshold for all test bar widths in a fairly uniform fashion without evidence of selective adaptation. This is presumably dependent upon the fact that all the test bars have approximately the same power in the region of the adapting spatial frequency, 5.5 c/deg. Correspondingly, exposure to a grating of 16 c/deg has virtually no effect on the thresholds for bars of various widths, since all of the test bar spectra have considerable power at other, lower frequency regions (e.g. 5 c/deg) upon which we would expect the 16 c/deg sinusoidal grating to be ineffective. In the same way exposure to either bar width is sufficient to elevate the threshold in a uniform fashion for any test bar width. This too is predictable from (*a*) the spectrum of adapting stimulus (*b*) the spectrum of the test stimulus (*c*) the contrast sensitivity function and (*d*) the assumption that threshold, for any target whatever, is reached as soon as any one of its frequency components exceeds its own threshold power. Note that this final assumption is central to the multiple-channel model (Graham & Nachmias 91, Sachs, Nachmias & Robson, 159) and is the standard assumption for interpreting data from any threshold type experiment (e.g. Stiles' two-color increment threshold experiments, Enoch 70). The nonselective character of bar–bar interactions raises questions about the assumption (Pantle & Sekuler 144) that as far as the visual system is concerned spatial frequency and width are simply and reciprocally related. Certainly, the findings of Sullivan et al are inconsistent with that assumption.

Carter & Henning (51) gave an elegant translation of some auditory experiments into the domain of spatial vision. This exercise was designed to show that "in representing visual spatial frequencies the behaviour of the eye can be considered as similar to the behaviour of the Helmholtz's model of the ear" (p. 356). Visibility was measured using a forced-choice procedure for two kinds of test targets as a function of the contrast of the test targets. One target was 160 cycles of a grating of 5.9 c/deg while the other was a single cycle of the same frequency grating. The power spectra of these two targets are quite different, with nearly all of the power in the multi-cycle grating lying right around 5.9 c/deg while the power of the single cycle grating has a more nearly uniform distribution. In the main part of their experiment Carter & Henning used veiling visual noise which was either narrow-band and limited to the region around 5.9 c/deg or was broad-band noise. The narrow-band noise, as expected from the relation of its spectrum to the spectra of the two test targets, elevated the threshold only for the full grating (here both veiling noise and test target had power restricted to the same portion of the spectrum). Again, the Fourier spectra of the targets, along with the assumptions of the multiple-channel model permit the prediction of the data. A related experiment was reported for suprathreshold visibility (apparent contrast) measurements by Weisstein & Bisaha (206).

Another study, by Stromeyer & Julesz (189), tested the usefulness of the Fourier multiple-channel model while reminding us of the growing debt researchers in spatial vision owe their brethren in auditory research. In a design much like classic masking designs in audition (160), Stromeyer & Julesz measured the masking of sinusoidal gratings veiled by filtered, dynamic noise of various spatial frequency content. Virtually all of their data converge on one simple proposition: only masking noise in the immediate vicinity of the test spatial frequency is effective in elevating the threshold. In one experiment, for example, masking was measured as a function of the width of the noise band. This band was kept centered on the test frequency. Masking increased with the width of the masking band up to about ±1 octave (an octave change in spatial frequency is a twofold change). Beyond this critical band, further noise had no effect. Stromeyer & Julesz devoted considerable time to comparing the critical bands in audition (frequency) and in vision (spatial frequency). Among the striking parallels is the observation that in both modalities there are approximately 25–35 difference thresholds within a critical band.

Before turning to some of the flies in the otherwise soothing ointment, the study by Maffei & Fiorentini (124) on Fourier synthesis in vision should be considered. Recall that just as any arbitrary luminance distribution can be represented (analyzed) in terms of appropriate frequency sine and cosine components, the components can be chosen to construct (synthesize) any arbitrary luminance distribution. This reversibility of the Fourier transform was tested by Maffei & Fiorentini in a most unusual experiment. Assume that there is a mechanism in the brain, at or beyond the point of binocular combination, capable of Fourier synthesis. If we present a sinusoidal grating of frequency F to one eye and a sinusoidal grating of frequency $3F$ to the other and if the phases of the two gratings are correct and their relative contrasts appropriate, the Fourier synthesizer will be receiving inputs identical to what it would get if we presented a square wave grating just to a single eye. Subjects confirm the perceptual similarity of the dichoptically presented Fourier components to the monoptically presented square wave grating. Quantitative measurements were made by asking subjects to adjust the contrast of the dichoptic components until a square wave grating was seen. For five different fundamental frequencies, a grating appeared to be square wave when the third harmonic amplitude was 1/3 that of the fundamental. This, of course, is what we'd expect from Fourier synthesis. Similarly good agreement was found for the synthesis of a dichoptic rectangular wave grating from sinusoidal components to each eye. It should be noted that presenting a high contrast (ten times threshold) fundamental produced an unsatisfactory fit to the theory. Low contrast fundamental frequency gratings seem to be critical for these experiments.

Anomalous Observations

Despite the growing acceptance of the idea that the human visual system may indeed be performing a hardware Fourier-like analysis and, at threshold, be detecting the power in various spatial frequency bands with independent mechanisms, there are several observations that will clearly require changes in the basic model. Many of the difficulties fall into two logical classes: one set of observations demonstrates interactions between channels postulated to be "independent"; the second set of observations is inconsistent with the strong proposition that human spatial vision is exclusively the product of Fourier analysis performed by the visual system. Both sets of observations suggest the excessive simplicity of the Fourier version of the multiple-channel model. The observations which will be described in this section identify how the theories need to be modified; they do *not* show the theories to be without considerable value.[1]

One difficulty seems to be with the variability in the estimate of channel width in the spatial frequency domain. Generally, adaptation experiments suggest broader spatial frequency channels than are suggested by threshold or additivity experiments (Graham 90). Ultimately these estimates can only be reconciled by a better understanding of what we are doing to the visual system in the various "adaptation" paradigms.

Tolhurst (192) has reported some observations that can be explained most easily if we postulate that, above threshold, spatial frequency channels inhibit one another. Tolhurst has found, for example, that both the fundamental and third harmonic in a compound adapting stimulus are less effective in their threshold raising effects then they would be if presented singly. Although this effect is small (about .10 log units) it does seem to be genuine, growing systematically with the contrast of the adapting stimuli. Tolhurst points out that this inhibition between spatial frequency channels would be analogous to the inhibition between orientation channels postulated by Blakemore, Carpenter & Georgeson (21) to explain some psychophysical observations. While this suggestion of inhibition between orientation analyzers was originally disputed (Coltheart 55, 56, Blakemore, Carpenter & Georgeson 22) it has received support in the studies by Sekuler & Littlejohn (169), Benevento, Creutzfeldt & Kuhnt (14), and Blakemore & Tobin (26). The physiological observations of Benevento et al present a model for inhibitory cross-talk between cortical columns of cells tuned to differing orientations and direction of motion. This means that the concept of a cell's "trigger feature" (Barlow, Narasimhan & Rosenfeld 10) will have to be extended to take into account those features which inhibit a cell as well as those which are excitatory. Stecher, Sigel & Lange (180) have described other psychophysical observations which seem to require the concept of inhibition between spatial frequency channels. Unlike Tolhurst, Stecher et al found inhibition between spatial frequencies usually considered to be within a single spatial frequency band (e.g. 8c/deg and 10.7 c/deg).

[1]Again it may be useful to consider the parallel situation in audition. Ohm's Acoustic Law, which is essentially the auditory version of what we have been calling the multiple-channel Fourier model, is only partially correct. Various phenomena of periodicity, pitch, and masking are at variance with Ohm's Acoustic Law. W. D. Ward considers the law in his chapter on music perception in Tobias' *Foundations of Modern Auditory Theory:* "For years musicians have been told that the ear is able to separate any complex signals into a series of sinusoidal signals—that it acts as a Fourier analyzer. This quarter-truth, known as Ohm's Other Law, has served to increase the distrust with which perceptive musicians regard scientists, since it is readily apparent to them that the ear acts in this way only under very restricted conditions. . . ." (p. 438). My suspicion is that the multiple-channel Fourier model in vision will rapidly approach the status of Ohm's Other Law—a quarter truth. But, lest this be taken as a cause for despair, it should be remembered that a quarter is far greater than no truth at all. We should not lose sight of the fact that at least under certain ideal conditions the eye, like the ear, may be describable as a multiple-channel Fourier analyzer.

Campbell & Howell (46) described an intriguing demonstration of a kind of monocular rivalry suitable for classroom or laboratory, which testifies strongly to the existence of inhibitory interactions of some kind between channels sensitive to (*a*) different orientations or (*b*) different spatial frequencies or both. The basic phenomenon is a kind of rivalry or perceptual alternation between overlapping sinusoidal gratings at right angles to one another. Variation in several of the parameters led Campbell & Howell to conclude the phenomenon is consistent with the idea "that orientations and spatial frequencies are processed in independent channels which are highly selective (± 15° and ± 1 octave). At the same time, these channels are interdependent, for the alternation must mean they interact" (46, p. 21). A closely related effect, alternating monocular rivalry between orthogonal contours in an afterimage, was reported by Sindermann & Lüddeke (174). It is certain that both these phenomena will receive a good deal of attention in coming years. Finally, Pantle (143) demonstrated that translation of a complex grating causes its components to interact at threshold while for a nonmoving grating the same components are quite independent.

One thing seems certain, regardless of the impact these anomalous findings may have, any adequate model will have to be able to account not only for independence of channels at threshold, but also for the possibility of inhibitory interactions when they are suprathreshold. Similar problems are being faced in color vision and it may be instructive to researchers in spatial vision to examine the conceptual models proposed for such phenomena (Boynton, Das & Gardiner 30). There are precedents, in the Limulus retina and in the case of brightness contrast in humans (96), for supposing that the spatial interaction between adjacent elements grows as their respective response levels grow. This means that elements that show no evidence of inhibitory interactions at or near their own thresholds may show strong inhibition when stimulation is suprathreshold.

Greenwood (93) compared the contrast sensitivity functions obtained with two kinds of targets—structured, sinusoidal gratings and unstructured, grain images. The large difference between sensitivity to the two kinds of stimuli (a factor of 25) led Greenwood to suggest that the structure of the target—quite apart from its spatial frequency characteristics—controls its detectability. This experiment is strong proof that the visual system cannot be totally described as a Fourier analyzing system. If such a description were appropriate, there would have been no difference between the sensitivity to Greenwood's two kinds of targets, taking their spectral characteristics into account.

Armstrong & Sekuler (4) found Fourier theory inadequate for predicting the extent to which a small, 1° square target containing a grating of 3 cycles/deg would be masked by two larger gratings of the same frequency. Their enabling assumption was that masking would be a function of the similarity of the spectra for test and masking gratings. The spectrum of the masking field was manipulated by variation in the vertical separation between its upper and lower halves. As the gap between the two halves went from zero to nonzero values, the spectrum of the masking target lost power at the fundamental and gained it at lower frequencies, corresponding roughly to the width of the gap. The test target remained centered in the field, with masking gratings positioned symmetrically about the center. A two-position forced-choice procedure was used to measure luminance thresholds. The spectra led to the prediction that considerable masking would occur even when the masking and test targets were fairly widely separated in space (when the gap between the two halves of the masking grating was large). Contrary to the predictions from Fourier theory, masking fell virtually to zero as soon as the spatial overlap between masking and test targets went to zero.

One final set of findings raises some difficulties for the Fourier multiple-channel model and, indeed represents a great challenge to any explanatory scheme. There is a variety of contours which for want of better name we may term "anomalous contours." From the Fourier point of view such contours are anomalous because they have no representation in the stimulus' power spectrum. They can be observed under several different kinds of conditions and may in fact not all be ultimately amenable to a uniform explanation. When a section of a random dot stereogram is actually empty of dots, it may appear to contain contours (57, 106). Similar anomalous contours are the sharp edges that surround depth planes in various of the random dot stereograms—there are regions which seem, for example, to float as sharply defined and outlined squares above the background. The anomaly is that the edges of the planes are so strikingly contoured, when in actuality such contours and sharp edges have no physical basis. Gregory (94) has described related anomalous contours in patterns with none of the complexities of random dot stereograms. Moreover such anomalous contours seem, according to Gregory, to be able to produce the standard geometric illusions, much as real contours can. While I doubt the usefulness of the kind of theory that Gregory advances to "explain" his observations (he says that the visual system "postulates" the existence of the contours and, voilà they are there), the phenomena are a challenge. Similar anomalous edges and contours can be seen in a computer driven display of spatial random dots. If the dots in a central horizontal strip are held stationary while upper and lower sections are caused to drift across the screen, the center section will appear to have a sharply defined edge which has no physical basis (P. Tynan, personal communication).

A final kind of anomalous contour is related to the phenomenon in audition of periodicity pitch (108, 176). E. Levinson (personal communication) created a complex grating by amplitude modulating a 5 c/deg sinusoidal carrier with a 1 c/deg sinusoid. The resultant complex grating has a spectrum with power at 4, 5 and 6 c/deg (half the power at 4 and 6 as at 5 c/deg). There was a distinct 1 c/deg periodicity in the complex grating. This perceptually obvious component can be shown to have no representation in the energy spectrum of the amplitude modulated grating. Moreover, the complex grating, used as an adapting stimulus, produced no threshold elevation for simple test gratings of 1 c/deg.

With few exceptions, recent work with various forms of linear systems approach has largely ignored the question of the appearance of suprathreshold targets. One obvious difficulty is that as we move away from threshold signals, the obvious nonlinearity of the visual system intrudes (Westheimer 213). Thus as a sinusoidal grating is raised in contrast it takes on an increasingly nonsinusoidal appearance, with the "brighter" bars seeming wider than the "darker" regions. One hypothesis to deal with this observation is that some nonlinear transform occurs quite early in the visual system (59).

While much research on the detection of simple and compound gratings is consistent with a multiple-channel model of the kind outlined by Sachs, Nachmias & Robson (159), such a model requires added psychophysical linking hypotheses to predict how things will look. Westheimer (213) reminds us that these threshold experiments only tell us when a grating will be seen as different from a uniform field but not how it will appear. If one postulates that the appearance of the world is even in part produced by a synthesis of information in various spatial frequency channels (Maffei & Fiorentini 124), there ought to be a whole set of unexplored perceptual phenomena which are produced by shifting balances among the responses of various spatial frequency channels. Among the few explorations of this possibility is the study by Blakemore, Nachmias & Sutton (25) of the shift in apparent spatial frequency of a suprathreshold grating as a function of adaptation to various frequencies. But how, for example, does the apparent frequency of a grating vary with exposure duration? Several studies have shown that the sensitivity of various spatial frequency channels is differentially affected by short exposures (137, 138). If the balance of activity in various spatial frequency channels shifts with exposure duration, we might expect an illusion of altered apparent spatial frequency with short exposures of suprathreshold gratings (cf 194a).

Feature Detectors

In parallel with the advances in the development of multiple-channel models for the analysis of spatial frequency, there has been an accelerated growth in studies which purport to demonstrate the existence of feature detecting mechanisms by which "the brain decomposes the physical image of the external world into a great multitude of anatomic channels each of which is processed independently before being ultimately synthesized into a subjective global impression" (88, p. 2). If this approach is ultimately to fulfill its promise, several problems will have to be resolved. First, we will have to consider what the relationship of these mechanisms is to other dimensions of spatial visual sensitivity, including spatial frequency. Does, for example, the analysis of spatial frequency information proceed in parallel with that of orientation? If not, can we make supported statements about the sequence in which features are analyzed? Two studies related to this question will suffice here. Campbell & Maffei (48) claimed to show that the tilt after-effect was not related to the spatial frequency of the adaptation and test targets. A similar finding has been reported by Parker (146). If these claims are taken at face value, the tilt induced on a test grating is independent of the spatial frequency relationship between it and the spatial frequency of the adapting grating. Campbell & Maffei used this datum to support the idea that "the mechanism responsible for orientational selectivity occurs before the processes leading to spatial selectivity" (48, p. 838). These theoretically significant findings require a more secure experimental basis since (*a*) they are inconsistent with other work in the literature, notably on the McCollough effect, (*b*) the data themselves are not very convincing, and (*c*) at least one investigator (M. Sullivan personal communication) did find evidence of spatial selectivity in the tilt after-effect using forced-choice procedures.

Tolhurst & Hart (194) found that thresholds for moving contours were elevated equally by prior retinal image movement whether it was produced by (*a*) eye movement with a stationary field, or by (*b*) a moving field with no tracking eye movements. This suggests that the site of direction specific adaptation in the human visual system is prior to point of operation of the corollary discharge which discounts eye movements. Other studies of direction specific adaptation have been reported by May (131), Erke & Gräser (73), Breitmeyer (33), Luria & Ryan (120), and Beck & Stevens (13). Related to the issue of the corollary dischage (Skavenski 175) are reports of cells in cat visual cortex which respond differentially to uniform and relative motion in the field (Burns, Gassanov & Webb 42, Bridgeman 35). Such cells would facilitate the discrimination of retinal image motion which was due to motion of objects from retinal image motion components produced by eye-movements. The implications of the analysis of relative motion for the perception of movement are discussed elsewhere (167).

There is an often ignored danger inherent in the assumptions behind experiments which try to identify the relationship between the neural sites at which various information is extracted and used (Tolhurst & Hart, 194), i.e., it is possible that any phenomenon can be generated in more than one site in the visual system. Julesz (106) has argued, for example, that there are several sites at which information about visual motion is extracted. This possibility needs to be taken into account in all studies where an attempt is made to identify the locus of some phenomenon of spatial vision or to identify the relationship between the loci for two different phenomena.

The family of effects related to the McCollough effect (121) continued to grow at an alarming rate during this review period, with a number of new observations (34, 76, 117, 131, 132, 135, 136, 188). While work continues on these challenging long-lived phenomena, there seems to be a growing sophistication in the uses to which after-images and stabilized retinal images are put in the service of the examination of feature analyzers. The papers by D. Brown and his associates (39, 40, 60, 164) and those of Atkinson (5, 6) testify to this point. The experiments by Atkinson suggest that after-images may bear stronger functional resemblance to the characteristics of their "real" predecessors than had hitherto been suspected. Not only does Atkinson show that after-images of line exhibit the same meridional anistropies that real lines do (see also 201), but she describes rather complex inhibitory interactions between pairs of lines in an afterimage. Such interactions are reminiscent of Parlee's (147) measurements of masking of one line by another. Because of Atkinson's observations and those on alternating monocular rivalry in after-images (174) one wonders about the extent to which after-image of contours, for example, behaves like "real" contours in a variety of paradigms. Perhaps good use can be made of the concept "equivalent contour," in analogy with "equivalent background" for spatially uniform fields (12).

Finally, Bagrash (8) and Kerr & Thomas (110) extended a non-Fourier multiple-channel model measuring selective adaptation with radially symmetric stimuli which cannot be dismissed as candidates for visual system *eigenfunctions.* There were two new studies of feature detectors from the Cambridge Laboratory. Tolhurst (193) gave us the first good evidence of edge detectors (as opposed to bar or grating detectors or what have you) and proposed a new, tenative explanation of both Mach bands and the Craik-Cornsweet-O'Brien illusion. See also references 153, 161, 171, and 198 for additional discussion of this illusion. Sharpe (171) used temporal modulation to make visible the shadows of the retinal blood vessels. He reports that the shadows, being essentially stabilized retinal images, fade and require increasingly higher contrast over time to remain visible. Most relevant to the issue of feature detectors is the finding that the fading which transfers binocularly and may have a central component, exhibits remarkable specificity for orientation and direction of movement. Having mentioned interocular transfer, I would be remiss if I did not cite Andrews' (2) brief and provocative observation about the possible information to be gained from such measurements. These observations are well complemented by those of Julesz (106) on the same subject.

OBSERVATIONS WITH CLINICAL IMPACT

As indicated in the preamble to this review, one of the trends which has grown during the review period is the cooperation between clinicians and nonclinicians with a mutual interest in spatial vision. As evidence for this claim, consider the following sample of observations.

The spatial contrast sensitivity function, discussed earlier, is both a descriptive and normative tool and has proven important in several clinical contexts recently. Bodis-Wollner (28) found changes in the contrast sensitivity functions of patients with cerebral lesions. While most patients showed a relatively greater loss at the high frequency end of the function, at least one showed a deficit in the midfrequency portion of the range (2–10 c/deg). While one must exercise great care in interpreting these results, several things are clear. First, it is important, as Bodis-Wollner reminds us forcefully, to distinguish between acuity, as normally defined, and the information represented in the contrast sensitivity function, since acuity measures the resolvability of small details presented at very high (1.0) contrast. One could argue that the contrast sensitivity function is a more ecologically valid measure of ability to resolve details, since only rarely are we presented with 1.0 contrast objects in the real world. Second, Bodis-Wollner makes the following fascinating suggestion: "Assuming that the brain does use a harmonic analysis for pattern recognition, then in suprathreshold stimulus conditions a proper balance of independent signals is required to account for an invariant neural representation of the retinal image. In this case a nonuniformly altered contrast sensitivity would pose a greater difficulty in pattern recognition than a simple drop in visual acuity" (28, p. 770). One can see in Bodis-Wollner's data the recovery of normal contrast sensitivity over the period of six weeks testing, paralleling the patient's own recovery. Data on one of his patients, showing a depression mid-range in the contrast sensitivity function, suggests a loss in one channel of a multiple-channel system. If we did, in fact, have good solid normative data against which to judge a given subject's function, Bodis-Wollner's idea of plotting a "visuogram"—the ratio, at each spatial frequency, of normal contrast sensitivity to that of a given patient—would be a good one. But clearly the normative data are needed first.

Another clinical use of the contrast sensitivity function was reported by Green (92). Taking advantage of laser produced interference fringes to bypass the optics of the eye, Green was able to estimate the likely postoperative acuity of cataract patients. Such information, of course, provides an important guide to the likely value of the cataract removal.

Mitchell, Freeman, Millodot & Haegerstrom (81, 133) used various sorts of grating targets to measure the neural consequences of early selective contour deprivation in human vision. There is a growing literature on the visual effects of rearing neonatal animals under various conditions of stimulus deprivation (Blakemore & Cooper 23, Hirsch 98, Spinelli, Hirsch, Phelps & Metzler 178, Ganz, Hirsch, & Tieman 83) or rearrangement (Shaler 172). In a brief summary statement on this literature, Barlow & Pettigrew (11) offered the provocative comment that in kittens only two stimulus analyzing functions emerge without requiring appropriate environmental inputs: functions sensitive to direction of motion through the field and a kind of primitive sensitivity to binocular disparity.

Kittens reared under normal, nondeprived conditions have simple cortical cells "tuned" to contours of various orientations, with orientation preferences distributed uniformly about polar coordinates. Hirsch & Spinelli (99) and Blakemore & Cooper (23) showed that if kittens were reared for several months, from birth onward, in a manner that kept them from seeing contours of a particular orientation (e.g. horizontal) there would be a paucity of simple cells tuned at or near that deprived orientation. Moreover, the kittens would appear to be behaviorally blind to contours oriented at or near the deprived orientation. Mitchell et al reasoned that similar neural alterations might occur in humans whose visual systems were selectively deprived of exposure to certain stimulus orientations. In astigmatism there is an inequality in sharpness with which contours of different orientations are imaged. Astigmatic subjects might then show the neural consequences of this partial and selective contour deprivation. Using laser produced interference fringes on the retina as well as conventional gratings, Mitchell et al found clear evidence for a neural (as opposed to optical) meridional amblyopia—loss of acuity for certain stimulus orientations. Moreover, the degree of meridional amblyopia was strongly related to the degree of astigmatism. This work implies that unless astigmatism is detected and corrected very early in life it may very well produce lasting changes in the development and organization of the visual nervous system. Mitchell et al offered some speculation on the relevance of their results to possible cross-cultural differences in perception. It is well-known that a variety of visual functions exhibit what might be termed the Meridional Effect (Appelle 3). Acuity, detection and other visual functions seem to be better when the targets are oriented at vertical and horizontal, and poorest at orientations between (obliques). Mitchell et al proposed that such adult deficits at oblique orientations might arise from the relative paucity of oblique contours in the environments of children raised in the highly technological societies filled with man-made horizontal and vertical contours.

The speculations of Mitchell and his associates are made even more intriguing by the recent demonstration by Fiorentini, Ghez & Maffei (78, 79) that the Meridional Effect depend in adults upon experience. Fiorentini et al had human subjects wear Dove prisms, which rotated the visual field by 30° or 45°. The prisms were worn for periods of 4 to 7 days, during which time the subjects experienced a decrease in apparent tilt (i.e. adaptation to the sensory rearrangement). In rough parallel with this phenomenal adaptation there were changes in two measures of the Meridional Effect. First, there was a decrease in the usual difference between contrast threshold for a vertical grating and the threshold for an oblique grating. Second, there was a decrease in the difference in the averaged evoked potential produced by an oscillating vertical grating and an oscillating oblique grating. Fiorentini et al observed "The findings suggest that during prisms adaptation plastic changes occur in the postretinal mechanisms responsive to target orientation." (78, p. 545).

The relationship of Mitchell et al's findings to certain common clinical problems is worth noting. In particular, amblyopia *ex anopsia* (amblyopia of disuse) may occur when, in early life, one or both eyes is deprived of normal visual stimulation by corneal opacities, congenital cataracts, or other obstacles (von Noorden 200). Clearly, amblyopia of all forms, including strabismic amblyopia, is a disorder that researchers in spatial vision are going to have important input to. Since amblyopia is estimated to effect some seven million Americans (32) such research efforts ought to be strongly encouraged.

In order to help identify the neural locus of functional amblyopia in one of their patients, Lawwill and his colleagues (112) used the Westheimer effect (211) to compare receptive field sizes in the amblyopic and normal eyes. With the visual evoked potential as a dependent measure, Lawwill et al found the critical sizes of the surround, in the Westheimer paradigm, to be substantially enlarged in the amblyopic eye. This led them to conclude that the locus of the functional amblyopia is peripheral to the cortex, the site of the evoked response.

Work is continuing on various attempts to use the visual evoked potential as the basis for an objective, automatic, and sensitive refraction (Ludlam & Meyers 118, Dawson et al 63). Finally, Pöppel, Held & Frost (149) reported some rather remarkable observations on residual visual function in areas of the field which are quite blind by standard definitions. Although the residual function is exceedingly slight, its existence is of considerable importance for theories which implicate midbrain structures in vision. Moreover, and most relevant here, the unusual stimuli required to demonstrate the effect remind us of the importance of perimetry with moving targets (7, 74).

METHODOLOGICAL ISSUES

Regardless of the brilliance of its insights, a research area can only be as good as the tools it uses. In spatial vision, most experiments depend strongly on the integrity and replicability of earlier findings. Several of the experiments discussed here require the observer to make judgments that can only be described as "difficult." Especially when dealing with small effects (e.g. 0.3 log units or less), it is important to establish that criterion shifts of one kind or another are not distorting the results. It is ironic that while the field of spatial vision has grown more sophisticated in the techniques of stimulus generation and in theory-building, there has not been a corresponding increase in the sophistication of psychophysical procedures. While all data do not have to be collected using forced-choice procedures, in experiments requiring difficult judgments it would be useful to check some of them using more objective procedures. Consider but two examples of this point. Weitzman, Smith & Karasik (207) using a signal detection analysis, found that at least a part of the Meridional Effect may be due to criterion rather than pure sensitivity differences. Pollack (150) found that "subjectively" subthreshold stimuli were quite detectable if forced-choice testing was used.

One advantage of a forced-choice procedure is that the observer is presented with a null stimulus on each trial, aiding him to discriminate the presence from the absence of the target whose threshold value is being sought. Particularly in experiments where it may be difficult for the observer to discriminate the test target from some after-image of the adaptation stimulus, a clearly defined null stimulus would be invaluable. As a kind of compromise between the time consuming psychophysics of signal detection theory (Nachmias 139) and the very quick, but very dirty, psychophysical method of adjustment, experimenters might consider the use of an "implicit null stimulus." This would entail restricting the test target to a previously specified portion of the field, leaving the rest of the field uniform at the same space average luminance. The ability to compare the top and bottom of the field with the knowledge that the test target will only appear in the top half, would make even difficult judgments easier, i.e. less absolute. The cost of this procedure is the possibility that edges will complicate the spectrum and affect the visibility of the test target (43).

The evidence of interaction between spatial and temporal aspects of visual stimulation suggests that theories of spatial vision cannot completely ignore the temporal characteristics of that stimulation. Some of the interactions with temporal variables may, in fact, provide good insight into the nature of the spatial response itself (e.g. 137, 138, Watanabe et al 203). If, to take a conservative position, there is any interaction whatever between the spatial and temporal selectivities of various mechanisms in the human visual system, care must be taken in generalizing from experiments on spatial vision in which only a single value of temporal stimulation has been used. The pattern of spatial responses to stimuli that are temporal impulses may be quite different from those to stimuli with extended step functions. These possibilities need to be investigated. A paradigm that is of potential use in such investigations has been introduced by Matin, Matin, Hirsch & Kornheiser (129). Their adaptation of Crawford's (61) rapid dark and light adaptation procedure measured the apparent tilt of a line presented for 10 msec at various temporal positions before, during and after an inducing line of 3 sec duration. Large transient effects at onset and offset of the inducing stimulus were strikingly similar to those which Crawford reported for early light and dark adaptation. Related to this paradigm is the fact that we must always be alert to the possible effects of the temporal rise and fall rates of spatially defined stimuli, particularly when their total duration is short. At the very least, information about this variable ought to be reported if not properly controlled (e.g. Carter & Henning 51).

Selective adaptation has often been used to "isolate" mechanisms sensitive to one or another aspect of stimulation. In this work, temporal variables have largely been ignored. As we shall see, this fact seriously jeopardizes the value of the data so far accumulated. Orientational selectivity, attributed by most workers to the characterisitcs of orientation analyzers like those described by Hubel & Wiesel, has been studied with three different temporal conditions: test target preceding the adaptation field, test target following the adaptation field, and the two targets overlapping temporally. Kulikowski, Abadi & King-Smith (111) showed convincingly that these temporal conditions do not yield equivalent estimates of orientational selectivity, though the first procedure just described, in which test precedes adaptation, was not examined. Additional complications are introduced into this messy picture when we consider the implications of the observations of Matin et al (discussed above). Those observations suggest that not only might the three different temporal arrangements give different data on orientational selectivity, but, moreover, temporal variation *within* any of the three procedures might give still other answers. For example, would selectivity vary, using temporally overlapping test and adaptation fields, with their onset asynchrony? The observations by Matin et al and related data on orientation selectivity in backward masking (166) make one suspect that it would. All of this has rather disquieting implications not only for the invariance of psychophysical estimates of orientation selectivity, but also for the invariance of other measures as well. For example, temporal variables have largely been ignored in experiments which measure the width of spatial frequency channels. Part of the discrepancy among estimates of channel width may in fact be related to just such differences between the temporal aspects of the relevant experiments.

So far the methodological suggestions have been largely directed toward threshold measurements. What about measurements of suprathreshold phenomena? There seems to be an increasing willingness to use the kind of dependent measure advocated so forcefully by S. S. Stevens. Stevens, who passed away during this review period, argued for the use of direct scaling procedures, magnitude estimation among others. While there is nothing logically "wrong" with these procedures, one would hope that in the future such dependent measures will be calibrated at the very least. For example, numerical estimates of the apparent contrast of *constant* contrast targets (206) should be calibrated with similar estimates made to targets of various contrast. Such calibration data would very much enhance the interpretability of the subject's verbal responses. Working on a somewhat different problem, Sindermann & Lüddeke (174) did provide the kind of calibration advocated here.

In two papers published posthumously (198, 199), von Békésy described the use of a novel procedure by which suprathreshold spatial effects such as Mach bands could be measured objectively. In the von Békésy compensation procedure a subject is given control over the spatial distribution of luminance and adjusts it until the

Mach band is just cancelled. The luminance required to compensate for the Mach band measures the band's strength. This procedure is one that lends itself to creative implementation with online computer driven cathode ray displays.

The brief, but important, note of Williams & Williams (217) should remind us to make sure subjects do not hum while observing. Humming while watching television produces horizontal lines on the screen whose frequency and other characteristics are a function of the hum's qualities. Rushton had earlier given a theoretical basis for these observations. While humming might improve the interest of many television programs, it might also wreak havoc with data from experiments using cathode ray displays of various kinds.

Finally, useful developments in areas just peripheral to spatial vision ought to be briefly mentioned. Barlow, Narasimhan & Rosenfeld (10) have argued convincingly for strong cooperation among psychologists, physiologists, and computer scientists in a common attack on the problems of spatial vision and pattern recognition. This sort of interaction has already produced some computer programs constructed to mimic the hierarchical feature analyzing operations described by some physiologists (Wallingford 202, Fukushima 82). While the present state of the art in all three disciplines—psychology, physiology, and computer science—limits the real informativeness of hardware models, there is hope that computer models will develop to the point where the idiosyncracies of their operation suggest new insight into spatial vision just as the idiosyncracies of psychophysical and physiological observations now do.

Acknowledgments

Preparation of this chapter was supported by grants EY-00321 and NS-10094 from the Institutes of Health. Several students, most notably Robert Armstrong, were of great assistance in helping me to organize material and ideas for the chapter.

Literature Cited

1. Alpern, M. 1972. Eye movements. In *Visual Psychophysics,* ed. D. Jameson, L. M. Hurvich, 303–30. Berlin: Springer. 812 pp.
2. Andrews, D. P. 1972. The site of adaptation shown in figural aftereffects. *Vision Res.* 12:1065–67
3. Appelle, S. 1972. Perception and discrimination as a function of stimulus orientation: The "Oblique Effect" in man and animals. *Psychol. Bull.* 78: 266–78
4. Armstrong, R., Sekuler, R. 1972. *Spatial spread of orientation-specific masking.* Presented at Psychonomic Soc. Meet., St. Louis
5. Atkinson, J. 1972. The effect of size, retinal locus, and orientation on visibility of a single afterimage. *Percept. Psychophys.* 12:213–17
6. Atkinson, J. 1972. Visibility of an afterimage in the presence of a second afterimage. *Percept. Psychophys.* 12:257–62
7. Aulhorn, E., Harms, H. 1972. Visual perimetry. In *Visual Psychophysics,* ed. D. Jameson, L. M. Hurvich, 102–45. Berlin: Springer. 812 pp.
8. Bagrash, F. M. 1973. Size-selective adaptation: psychophysical evidence for size-tuning and the effects of stimulus contour and adapting flux. *Vision Res.* 13:575–98
9. Barlow, H. B. 1972. Dark and light adaptation: Psychophysics. In *Visual Psychophysics,* ed. D. Jameson, L. M. Hurvich, 1–28. Berlin: Springer. 812 pp.
10. Barlow, H. B., Narasimhan, R., Rosenfeld, A. 1972. Visual pattern analysis in

machines and animals. *Science* 177: 567–75
11. Barlow, H. B., Pettigrew, J. D. 1971. Lack of specificity of neurones in the visual cortex of young kittens. *J. Physiol. London* 218:98–100
12. Barlow, H. B., Sparrock, J. M. B. 1964. The role of afterimages in dark adaptation. *Science* 144:1309–14
13. Beck, J., Stevens, A. 1972. An aftereffect to discrete stimuli producing apparent movement and succession. *Percept. Psychophys.* 12:482–86
14. Benevento, L. A., Creutzfeldt, O. D., Kuhnt, U. 1972. Significance of intracortical inhibition in visual-cortex. *Nature* 238:124–26
15. Berkley, M. A., Watkins, D. W. 1971. Visual acuity of the cat estimated from evoked cerebral potentials. *Nature New Biol.* 234:91–92
16. Berkley, M. A., Watkins, D. W. 1973. Grating resolution and refraction in the cat estimated from evoked cerebral potential. *Vision Res.* 13:403–16
17. Bishop, P. O., Henry, G. H. 1971. Spatial vision. *Ann. Rev. Psychol.* 22: 119–60
18. Bishop, P. O., Henry, G. H. 1972. Striate neurons–receptive field concepts. *Invest. Ophthalmol.* 11:346–54
19. Blackwell, H. R. 1972. Luminance difference thresholds. In *Visual Psychophysics,* ed. D. Jameson, L. M. Hurvich, 78–101. Berlin: Springer. 812 pp.
20. Blakemore, C., Campbell, F. W. 1969. On the existence of neurons in the human visual system selectively sensitive to the orientation and size of retinal images. *J. Physiol. London* 203:237–60
21. Blakemore, C., Carpenter, R. H. S., Georgeson, M. A. 1970. Lateral inhibition between orientation detectors in the human visual system. *Nature* 228: 37–39
22. Blakemore, C., Carpenter, R. H. S., Georgeson, M. A. 1971. Lateral thinking about lateral inhibition. *Nature* 234:418–19
23. Blakemore, C., Cooper, G. F. 1970. Development of the brain depends on the visual environment. *Nature* 228:477–78
24. Blakemore, C., Iversen, S. D., Zangwill, O. L. 1972. Brain functions. *Ann. Rev. Psychol.* 23:413–56
25. Blakemore, C., Nachmias, J., Sutton, P. 1970. The perceived spatial frequency shift: Evidence for frequency selective neurones in the human brain. *J. Physiol. London* 210:727–50
26. Blakemore, C., Tobin, E. A. 1972. Lateral inhibition between orientation detectors in cat's visual cortex. *Exp. Brain Res.* 15:439–40
27. Bliss, J. 1971. A reading machine with tactile display. In *Visual Prosthesis,* ed. T. D. Sterling, E. A. Bering, S. V. Vaughan Jr., 259–63. New York: Academic. 382 pp.
28. Bodis-Wollner, I. 1972. Visual-acuity and contrast sensitivity in patients with cerebral lesions. *Science* 178:769–71
29. Boring, E. G. 1941. An operational restatement of G. E. Muller's psychophysical axioms. *Psychol. Rev.* 48: 457–64
30. Boynton, R. M., Das, S. R., Gardiner, J. 1966. Interactions between photopic visual mechanisms revealed by mixing conditioning fields. *J. Opt. Soc. Am.* 56:1775–80
31. Boynton, R. M., Onley, J. W. 1962. A critique of the special status assigned by Brindley to "psychophysical linking hypotheses" of "Class A". *Vision Res.* 2: 383–90
32. Breinin, G. M. 1967. Research in strabismus. In *Vision and Its Disorders,* 50–64. Washington, D.C.: GPO. 225 pp.
33. Breitmeyer, B. G. 1973. A relationship between the detection of size, rate, orientation and direction in the human visual system. *Vision Res.* 13:41–58
34. Breitmeyer, B. G., Cooper, L. A. 1972. Frequency-specific color adaptation in the human visual system. *Percept. Psychophys.* 11:95–96
35. Bridgeman, B. 1972. Visual receptive fields sensitive to absolute and relative motion during tracking. *Science* 178: 1106–8
36. Brindley, G. S. 1970. *Physiology of the Retinal and Visual Pathway.* Baltimore: Williams & Wilkins. 2nd ed. 315 pp.
37. Brindley, G. S. 1971. Report to the Conference on Visual Prosthesis. In *Visual Prosthesis,* ed. T. D. Sterling, E. A. Bering, S. V. Pollack, H. G. Vaughan Jr., 41–48. New York: Academic. 382 pp.
38. Brindley, G. S., Lewin, W. S. 1968. The sensations produced by electrical stimulation of the visual cortex. *J. Physiol. London* 196:479–93
39. Brown, D. R., Schmidt, M. J., Cosgrove, M. P., Zuber, J. J. 1972. Stabilized images: Further evidence for central pattern processing. *Psychon. Sci.* 29:106–108

40. Brown, D. R., Schmidt, M. J., Fulgham, D. D., Cosgrove, M. P. 1973. Human receptive field characteristics: Probe analysis of stabilized images. *Vision Res.* 13:231–44
41. Brown, J. L. 1973. Visual sensitivity. *Ann. Rev. Psychol.* 24:151–86
42. Burns, B. D., Gassanov, U., Webb, A. C. 1972. Responses of neurons in cat's visual cerebral-cortex to relative movement of patterns. *J. Physiol. London* 226:133–51
43. Campbell, F. W., Carpenter, R. H. S., Levinson, J. Z. 1969. Visibility of aperiodic patterns compared with that of sinusoidal gratings. *J. Physiol. London* 204:283–98
44. Campbell, F. W., Cleland, B. G., Cooper, G. F., Enroth-Cugell, C. 1968. The angular selectivity of visual cortical cells to moving gratings. *J. Physiol. London* 198:237–50
45. Campbell, F. W., Green, D. G. 1965. Optical and retinal factors affecting visual resolution. *J. Physiol. London* 181:576–93
46. Campbell, F. W., Howell, E. R. 1972. Monocular alternation: Method for investigation of pattern vision. *J. Physiol. London* 225:19–21P
47. Campbell, F. W., Kulikowski, J. J. 1972. The visual evoked potential as a function of contrast of a grating pattern. *J. Physiol. London* 222:345–56
48. Campbell, F. W., Maffei, L. 1971. The tilt aftereffect: A fresh look. *Vision Res.* 11:833–40
49. Campbell, F. W., Robson, J. G. 1968. Application of Fourier analysis to the visibility of gratings. *J. Physiol. London* 197:551–66
50. Carpenter, P. A., Ganz, L. 1972. An attentional mechanism in analysis of spatial frequency. *Percept. Psychophys.* 12:57–60
51. Carter, B. E., Henning, G. B. 1971. Detection of gratings in narrow-band visual noise. *J. Physiol. London* 219:355–65
52. Carterette, E. C., Friedman, M. P., Lovell, J. D. 1969. Mach bands in hearing. *J. Acoust. Soc. Am.* 45:986–98
53. Cleland, B. G., Levick, W. R. 1972. Physiology of cat retinal ganglion cells. *Invest. Ophthalmol.* 11:285–91
54. Cleland, B. G., Dubin, M. W., Levick, W. R. 1971. Sustained and transient neurones in the cat's retina and lateral geniculate nucleus. *J. Physiol. London* 217:473–96
55. Coltheart, M. 1971. Visual feature-analyzers and aftereffects of tilt and curvature. *Psychol. Rev.* 78:114–21
56. Coltheart, M. 1971. Is there lateral inhibition in the visual cortex? *Nature* 231: 256
57. Coren, S. 1972. Subjective contours and apparent depth. *Psychol. Rev.* 79: 359–67
58. Cornsweet, T. N. 1970. *Visual Perception.* New York: Academic. 475 pp.
59. Corwin, T. R. 1971. Effect of masking of light on the apparent contrast of flashed gratings. *J. Opt. Soc. Am.* 61: 1172–76
60. Cosgrove, M. P., Schmidt, M. J., Fulgham, D. S., Brown, D. R. 1972. Stabilized images: Dependent variable specificity of pattern-specific effects with prolonged viewing. *Percept. Psychophys.* 11:398–402
61. Crawford, B. H. 1947. Visual adaptation in relation to brief conditioning stimuli. *Proc. Roy. Soc. Ser. B* 134: 283–302
62. Cunningham, W. R., Galbraith, G. C. 1972. Age differences in perception of Julesz patterns. *Gerontologist* 12: 57
63. Dawson, W. W., Perry, N. W. Jr., Childers, D. G. 1972. Variations in human cortical response to patterns and image quality. *Invest. Ophthalmol.* 11: 789–99
64. Day, R. H. 1972. Basis of perceptual constancy and perceptual illusion. *Invest. Ophthalmol.* 11: 525–32
65. Day, R. H. 1972. Visual-auditory distance constancy. *Nature* 238:227–28
66. Dougherty, W. G., Jones, G. B., Engel, G. R. 1971. Sensory integration of auditory and visual information. *Can. J. Psychol.* 25:476–85
67. Dreher, B. 1972. Hypercomplex cells in the cat's striate cortex. *Invest. Ophthalmol.* 11:355–56
68. Engel, F. L. 1971. Visual conspicuity, directed attention and retinal locus. *Vision Res.* 11:563–76
69. Engel, G. R., Dougherty, W. G. 1971. Visual-auditory distance constancy. *Nature* 234:308
70. Enoch, J. M. 1972. The two-color threshold technique of Stiles and derived component color mechanisms. In *Visual Psychophysics,* ed. D. Jameson, L. M. Hurvich, 537–67. Berlin: Springer. 812 pp.
71. Enroth-Cugell, C., Robson, J. G. 1966. The contrast sensitivity of retinal ganglion cells of the cat. *J. Physiol. London* 187:517–52

72. Erickson, R. P. 1968. Stimulus coding in topographic and non-topographic afferent modalities: on the significance of the activity of individual sensory neurons. *Psychol. Rev.* 75:447–65
73. Erke, H., Gräser, H. 1972. Reversibility of perceived motion: Selective adaptation of the human vision system to speed, size and orientation. *Vision Res.* 12:69–87
74. Fankhauser, F. 1969. Kinetic perimetry. *Ophthalmologica* 158:406–18
75. Faulkner, E. A. 1969. *Introduction to the Theory of Linear Systems,* 24–43. London: Chapman & Hall. 89 pp.
76. Favreau, O. E., Emerson, V. F., Corballis, M. C. 1972. Motion perception: color-contingent aftereffect. *Science* 176:78–79
77. Fiorentini, A. 1972. Mach band phenomena. In *Visual Psychophysics,* ed. D. Jameson, L. M. Hurvich, 188–201. Berlin: Springer. 812 pp.
78. Fiorentini, A., Ghez, C., Maffei, L. 1972. Physiological correlates of adaptation to a rotated visual field. *Brain Res.* 42:544–45
79. Fiorentini, A., Ghez, C., Maffei, L. 1972. Physiological correlates of adaptation to a rotated visual field. *J. Physiol. London* 227:313–22
80. Fiorentini, A., Maffei, L. 1973. Contrast in night vision. *Vision Res.* 13: 73–80
81. Freeman, R. D., Mitchell, D. E., Millodot, M. 1972. Neural effect of partial visual deprivation in humans. *Science* 175:1384–86
82. Fukushima, K. 1970. A feature extractor for curvilinear patterns: A design suggested by the mammalian visual system. *Kybernetik* 7:153–60
83. Ganz, L., Hirsch, H. V. B., Tieman, S. B. 1972. Nature of perceptual deficits in visually deprived cats. *Brain Res.* 44: 547–68
84. Goldberg, M. E., Wurtz, R. H. 1972. Activity of superior colliculus in behaving monkey. I. Visual receptive fields of single neurons. *J. Neurophysiol.* 35: 542–59
85. Ibid. Activity of superior colliculus in behaving monkey. II. Effect of attention on neuronal responses, 560–74
86. Gordon, B. 1972. The superior colliculus of the brain. *Sci. Am.* 227:72–83
87. Gorian, I. S., Meyerson, J. A., Tonkonogii, I. M., Tsukkerman, I. I. 1972. On the perception of patterns with statistical characteristics. *Neuropsychologia* 10:97–102
88. Gouras, P. 1973. Visual neurophysiology: Feature-detecting channels. *Invest. Ophthalmol.* 12:2–3
89. Graham, C. G. et al, Eds. 1965. *Vision and Visual Perception.* New York: Wiley. 637 pp.
90. Graham, N. 1972. Spatial frequency channels in the human visual system: Effects of luminance and pattern drift rate. *Vision Res.* 12:53–68
91. Graham, N., Nachmias, J. 1971. Detection of grating patterns containing two spatial frequencies: A comparison of single-channel and multiple-channel models. *Vision Res.* 11:251–59
92. Green, D. G. 1970. Testing the vision of cataract patients by means of laser-generated interference fringes. *Science* 168:1240–42
93. Greenwood, R. E. 1973. Visibility of structured and unstructured images. *J. Opt. Soc. Am.* 63:226–31
94. Gregory, R. L. 1972. Cognitive contours. *Nature* 238:51–52
95. Harvey, L. O., Pöppel, E. 1972. Contrast sensitivity of human retina. *Am. J. Optom.* 49:748–53
96. Heinemann, E. G. 1972. Simultaneous brightness induction. In *Visual Psychophysics,* ed. D. Jameson, L. M. Hurvich, 146–69. Berlin: Springer. 812 pp.
97. Henry, G. H., Bishop, P. O. 1972. Striate neurons–receptive field organization. *Invest. Ophthalmol.* 11:357–68
98. Hirsch, H. V. B. 1972. Visual perception in cats after environmental surgery. *Exp. Brain Res.* 15:405–23
99. Hirsch, H. V. B., Spinelli, D. N. 1970. Visual experience modifies distribution of horizontally and vertically oriented receptive fields in cats. *Science* 168: 869–71
100. Hoffman, K.-P. 1972. The retinal input to the superior colliculus in the cat. *Invest. Ophthalmol.* 11:467–73
101. Hubel, D. H., Wiesel, T. N. 1962. Receptive fields, binocular interaction and functional architecture in the cat's visual cortex. *J. Physiol. London* 160: 106–54
102. Hubel, D. H., Wiesel, T. N. 1965. Receptive fields and functional architecture in two non-striate visual areas (18 and 19) of the cat. *J. Neurophysiol.* 28: 229–89
103. Ibid 1967. Cortical and callosal connections concerned with the vertical meridian of visual fields in the cat. 30: 1561–73
104. Hubel, D. H., Wiesel, T. N. 1968. Receptive fields and functional architec-

ture of monkey striate cortex. *J. Physiol. London* 195:215–43
105. Jameson, D., Hurvich, L. M., Eds. 1972. *Visual Psychophysics.* Berlin: Springer. 812 pp.
106. Julesz, B. 1971. *Foundations of Cyclopean Perception.* Chicago: Univ. Chicago Press. 406 pp.
107. Julesz, B. 1972. Cyclopean perception and neurophysiology. *Invest. Ophthalmol.* 11:540–48
108. Kay, R. H., Matthews, D. R. 1972. Existence in human auditory pathways of channels selectively tuned to modulation present in frequency-modulated tones. *J. Physiol. London* 225:657–77
109. Kelly, D. H. 1972. Flicker. In *Visual Psychophysics,* ed. D. Jameson, L. M. Hurvich, 273–302. Berlin: Springer. 812 pp.
110. Kerr, L. G., Thomas, J. P. 1972. Effect of selective adaptation on detection of simple and compound parafoveal stimuli. *Vision Res.* 12:1367
111. Kulikowski, J. J., Abadi, R., King-Smith, P. E. 1973. Orientational selectivity of grating and line detectors in human vision. *Vision Res.* 13:1479–86
112. Lawwill, T., Cox, W. E., Tuttle, D., Meur, G., Burian, H. M. 1973. Lateral inhibition and the VER in the central field of an amblyopic subject. *Invest. Ophthalmol.* 12:154–56
113. LeGrand, Y. 1968. *Light, Colour and Vision.* London: Chapman & Hall. 2nd ed. 564 pp.
114. Leibowitz, H. W., Harvey, L. O. Jr. 1973. Perception. *Ann. Rev. Psychol.* 24:207–40
115. Levick, W. R., Cleland, B. G., Dubin, M. W. 1972. Lateral geniculate neurons of cat: Retinal inputs and physiology. *Invest. Ophthalmol.* 11:302–11
116. Lindsay, P. H., Norman, D. A. 1972. *Human Information Processing.* New York: Academic. 737 pp.
117. Lovegrove, W. J., Over, R. 1972. Color adaptation of spatial frequency detectors in human visual system. *Science* 176:541–43
118. Ludlam, W. M., Meyers, R. R. 1972. The use of visual evoked responses in objective refraction. *Trans. NY Acad. Sci.* 34:154–70
119. Lund, R. D. 1972. Anatomic studies on the superior colliculus. *Invest. Ophthalmol.* 11:434–41
120. Luria, S. M., Ryan, A. 1973. Adaptation to a masking stimulus. *J. Opt. Soc. Am.* 63:201–204
121. McCollough, C. 1965. Color adaptation of edge detectors in the human visual system. *Science* 148:1115–16
122. McIlwain, J. T. 1972. Central vision: Visual cortex and superior colliculus. *Ann. Rev. Physiol.* 34:291–314
123. MacKay, D. M. 1972. Visual stability. *Invest. Ophthalmol.* 11:518–24.
124. Maffei, L., Fiorentini, A. 1972. Processes of synthesis in visual perception. *Nature* 240:479–81
125. Maffei, L., Fiorentini, A. 1972. Retinogeniculate convergence and analysis of contrast. *J. Neurophysiol.* 35:65–72
126. Marg, E. 1971. Some design aspects of a visual prosthetic system. In *Visual Prosthesis,* ed. T. D. Sterling, E. A. Bering, S. V. Pollack, H. G. Vaughan Jr., 241–43. New York: Academic. 382 pp.
127. Marg, E., Adams, J. E., Rutkin, B. 1968. Receptive fields of cells in the human visual cortex. *Experientia* 24: 348–50
128. Marg, E., Adams, J. E. 1970. Evidence for a neurological zoom system in vision from angular changes in some receptive fields of single neurons with changes in fixation distance in the human visual cortex. *Experientia* 26:270–72
129. Matin, E., Matin, L., Hirsch, J., Kornheiser, A. 1972. *The Dynamics of Induced Tilt.* Presented at Am. Acad. Optom. Meet., New York
130. Matin, L. 1972. Eye movements and perceived visual direction. In *Visual Psychophysics,* ed. D. Jameson, L. M. Hurvich, 331–380. Berlin: Springer. 812 pp.
131. May, J. G. 1972. Chromatic adaptation of orientation-specific and size-specific visual processes in man. *Vision Res.* 12:1509–17
132. Mayhew, J. E. W., Anstis, S. M. 1972. Movement aftereffects contingent on color, intensity, and pattern. *Percept. Psychophys.* 12:77–85
133. Mitchell, D. E., Freeman, R. D., Millodot, M., Haegerstrom, G. 1973. Meridional amblyopia: Evidence for modification of the human visual system by early visual experience. *Vision Res.* 13:535–58
134. Morrell, F. 1972. Visual systems' view of acoustic space. *Nature* 238:44–46
135. Murch, G. M. 1972. Binocular relationships in a size and color orientation specific aftereffect. *J. Exp. Psychol.* 93:30–34
136. Murch, G. M., Hirsch, J. 1972. McCollough effect created by complementary afterimages. *Am. J. Psychol.* 85:241–47

137. Nachmias, J. 1967. Effect of exposure duration on visual contrast sensitivity with square wave gratings. *J. Opt. Soc. Am.* 57:421–27
138. Nachmias, J. 1968. Visual resolution of two-bar patterns and square-wave gratings. *J. Opt. Soc. Am.* 58:9–13
139. Nachmias, J. 1972. Signal detection theory and its application to problems in vision. In *Visual Psychophysics,* ed. D. Jameson, L. M. Hurvich, 56–77. Berlin: Springer. 812 pp.
140. Nakayama, K., Roberts, D. J. 1972. Line length detectors in human visual system: Evidence from selective adaptation. *Vision Res.* 12:1709–14
141. Ohzu, H., Enoch, J. M. 1972. Optical modulation by the isolated human fovea. *Vision Res.* 12:245–51
142. Over, R. 1972. Spatial aftereffects. *Invest. Ophthalmol.* 11:533–40
143. Pantle, A. 1972. *Effect of Stimulus Movement on the Detection Thresholds for Simple and Complex Gratings.* Presented at Assoc. Res. Vision Ophthalmol. Meet., Sarasota, Fla.
144. Pantle, A., Sekuler, R. 1968. Size detecting mechanisms in human vision. *Science* 162:1146–48
145. Pantle, A., Sekuler, R. 1969. Contrast response of human visual mechanisms sensitive to orientation and direction of motion. *Vision Res.* 9:397–406
146. Parker, D. M. 1972. Contrast and size variables and tilt aftereffect. *Quart. J. Exp. Psychol.* 24:1–7
147. Parlee, M. B. 1969. Visual backward masking of a single line by a single line. *Vision Res.* 9:199–205
148. Pettigrew, J. D. 1972. The neurophysiology of binocular vision. *Sci. Am.* 227:84–95
149. Pöppel, E., Held, R., Frost, D. 1973. Residual visual function after brain wounds involving the central visual pathways in man. *Nature* 243:295–96
150. Pollack, I. 1972. Visual discrimination of "unseen objects": Forced choice testing of Mayzner-Tresselt blanking effects. *Percept. Psychophys.* 11:121–28
151. Pollen, D. A., Lee, J. R., Taylor, J. H. 1971. How does the striate cortex begin the reconstruction of the visual world? *Science* 173:74–77
152. Ratliff, F. 1965. *Mach bands: Quantitative Studies on Neural Networks in the Retina,* 143–59. San Francisco: Holden-Day. 365 pp.
153. Ratliff, F. 1972. Contour and contrast. *Sci. Am.* 226:90–101
154. Regan, D. 1972. *Evoked Potentials in Psychology, Sensory Physiology and Clinical Medicine.* New York: Wiley-Interscience. 328 pp.
155. Richards, W. 1971. Motion detection in man and other animals. *Brain Behav. Evol.* 4:162–81
156. Riggs, L. A., Wooten, B. R. 1972. Electrical measures and psychophysical data on human vision. In *Visual Psychophysics,* ed. D. Jameson, L. M. Hurvich, 690–731. Berlin: Springer. 812 pp.
157. Rushton, W. A. H. 1972. Light and dark adaptation. *Invest. Ophthalmol.* 11:503–17
158. Rybicki, G. B., Tracy, D. M., Pollen, D. A. 1972. Complex cells response depends on interslit spacing. *Nature New Biol.* 240:77–78
159. Sachs, M., Nachmias, J., Robson, J. G. 1971. Spatial frequency channels in human vision. *J. Opt. Soc. Am.* 61:1176–86
160. Scharf, B. 1970. Critical bands. In *Foundations of Modern Auditory Theory,* ed. J. V. Tobias, 157–202. New York: Academic. 466 pp.
161. Schiffman, H., Crovitz, H. F. 1972. A two-stage model for brightness. *Vision Res.* 12:2121–31
162. Schiller, P. H. 1972. Role of monkey superior colliculus in eye movement and vision. *Invest. Ophthalmol.* 11:451–60
163. Schimmel, H., Vaughan, H. G. Jr. 1971. Design of a prosthetic system. In *Visual Prosthesis,* ed. T. D. Sterling, E. A. Bering, S. V. Pollack, Vaughan, H. G. Jr., 216–40. New York: Academic. 382 pp.
164. Schmidt, M. J., Cosgrove, M. P., Brown, D. R. 1972. Stabilized images: Functional relationships among populations of orientation-specific mechanisms in the human visual system. *Percept. Psychophys.* 11:389–92
165. Scott, T. R., Lavender, A. A., McWhirt, R. A., Powell, D. A. 1966. Directional asymmetry of motion aftereffect. *J. Exp. Psychol.* 71:806–15
166. Sekuler, R. 1965. Spatial and temporal determinants of visual backward masking. *J. Exp. Psychol.* 70:401–406
167. Sekuler, R. 1974. Motion perception. In *Handbook of Perception,* ed. E. Carterette, M. Friedman. New York: Academic
168. Sekuler, R., Lehr, D., Stone, W., Wolf, M. 1971. Human visual motion sensitivity: Evidence against a ratio theory

of sensory coding. *Percept. Psychophys.* 9:483–84

169. Sekuler, R., Littlejohn, J. 1974. Tilt aftereffect following very brief exposures. *Vision Res.* 14. In press
170. Sekuler, R., Tynan, P., Levinson, E. 1973. Visual temporal order: A new illusion. *Science* 180:210–12
171. Sharpe, C. R. 1972. Visibility and fading on thin lines visualized by their controlled movement across retina. *J. Physiol. London* 222:113–34
172. Shlaer, R. 1971. Shift in binocular disparity causes compensatory change in the cortical structure of kittens. *Science* 173:638–41
173. Shlaer, R. 1972. Eagle's eye: Quality of retinal image. *Science* 176:920–22
174. Sindermann, F., Lüddeke, H. 1972. Monocular analogues to binocular contour rivalry. *Vision Res.* 12:763–72
175. Skavenski, A. A. 1972. Inflow as a source of extraretinal eye position information. *Vision Res.* 12:221–29
176. Small, A. M. 1970. Periodicity pitch. In *Foundations of Modern Auditory Theory,* ed. J. V. Tobias, 3–54. New York: Academic. 466 pp.
177. Sperling, G. 1964. Linear theory and the psychophysics of flicker. *Doc. Ophthalmol.* 18:3–15
178. Spinelli, D. N., Hirsch, H. V. B., Phelps, R. W., Metzler, J. 1972. Visual experience as a determinant of response characteristics of cortical receptive fields in cats. *Exp. Brain Res.* 15:289–304
179. Sprague, J. M. 1972. Superior colliculus and pretectum in visual behavior. *Invest. Ophthalmol.* 11:473–82
180. Stecher, S., Sigel, C., Lange, R. V. 1974. Composite adaptation and spatial frequency interactions. *Vision Res.* 14. In press
181. Stent, G. S. 1972. Cellular communication. *Sci. Am.* 227:42–51
182. Stent, G. S. 1972. Prematurity and uniqueness in scientific discovery. *Sci. Am.* 227:84–93
183. Sterling, T. D., Bering, E. A., Pollack, S. V., Vaughan, H. G. Jr. 1971. *Visual Prosthesis.* New York: Academic. 382 pp.
184. Sterling, T. D., Vaughan, H. G. Jr. 1971. An overview: What makes a visual prosthesis possible. In *Visual Prosthesis,* ed. T. D. Sterling, E. A. Bering, S. V. Pollack, H. G. Vaughan Jr., 1–17. New York: Academic. 382 pp.
185. Sterling, T. D., Weinkam, J. J. 1971. Preprocessing of sensed information for analysis and display. In *Visual Prosthesis,* ed. T. D. Sterling, E. A. Bering, S. V. Pollack, H. G. Vaughan Jr., 145–50. New York: Academic. 382 pp.
186. Stone, J. 1972. Morphology and physiology of the geniculocortical synapse in the cat: The question of parallel input to the striate cortex. *Invest. Ophthalmol.* 11:338–46
187. Stone, J., Hoffman, K.-P. 1971. Conduction velocity as a parameter in the organisation of the afferent relay in the cat's lateral geniculate nucleus. *Brain Res.* 32:454–59
188. Stromeyer, C. F. III. 1972. Edge-contingent color aftereffects: Spatial frequency specificity. *Vision Res.* 12:717–33
189. Stromeyer, C. F. III., Julesz, B. 1972. Spatial-frequency masking in vision: Critical bands and spread of masking. *J. Opt. Soc. Am.* 62:1221–32
190. Sullivan, G. D., Georgeson, M. A., Oatley, K. 1972. Channels for spatial frequency selection and the detection of single bars by the human visual system. *Vision Res.* 12:383–94
191. Thompson, R. F. 1967. *Foundations of Physiological Psychology.* New York: Harper & Row. 688 pp.
192. Tolhurst, D. J. 1972. Adaptation to square-wave gratings: Inhibition between spatial frequency channels in human visual system. *J. Physiol. London* 226:231–48
193. Tolhurst, D. J. 1972. On the possible existence of edge detector neurones in the human visual system. *Vision Res.* 12:797–804
194. Tolhurst, D. J., Hart, G. 1972. Psychophysical investigation of effects of controlled eye-movements on movement detectors of human visual system. *Vision Res.* 12:1441–46

194a. Tynan, P., Sekuler, R. 1973. *Temporal Determinants of Perceived Spatial Frequency.* Presented at Opt. Soc. Am. Meet., Rochester, NY

195. Van Doorn, A. J., Koenderink, J. J., Bouman, M. A. 1972. The influence of retinal inhomogeneity on the perception of spatial patterns. *Kybernetik* 10:223–30
196. Vaughan, H. G. Jr., Schimmel, H. 1971. Feasibility of electrocortical visual prosthesis. In *Visual Prosthesis,* ed. T. D. Sterling, E. A. Bering, S. V. Pollack, H. G. Vaughan Jr., 65–79. New York: Academic. 382 pp.

197. von Békésy, G. 1967. *Sensory Inhibition.* Princeton: Princeton Univ. Press. 265 pp.

198. von Békésy, G. 1972. Mach bands measured by a compensation method. *Vision Res.* 12:1485–97

199. von Békésy, G. 1972. Compensation method to measure the contrast produced by contours. *J. Opt. Soc. Am.* 62:1247–51

200. von Noorden, G. K. 1972. Classification, diagnosis and natural history of amblyopia. *Isr. J. Med. Sci.* 8:1465–68

201. Wade, N. J. 1972. Orientation effects on line afterimage. *Percept. Psychophys.* 12:409–16

202. Wallingford, E. G. Jr. 1972. A visual pattern recognizing computer program based on neurophysiological data. *Behav. Sci.* 17:241–48

203. Watanabe, A., Mori, T., Nagata, S., Hiwatashi, K. 1968. Spatial sine-wave response of the human visual system. *Vision Res.* 8:1245–65

204. Weinstein, G. W., Hobson, R. R., Baker, F. H. 1971. Extracellular recordings from human retinal ganglion cells. *Science* 171:1021–22

205. Weisstein, N. 1969. What the frog's eye tells the human brain: Single cell analyzers in the human visual system. *Psychol. Bull.* 72:157–76

206. Weisstein, N., Bisaha, J. 1972. Gratings mask bars and bars mask gratings: Visual frequency response to aperiodic stimuli. *Science* 176:1047–49

207. Weitzman, D. O., Smith, J. M., Karask, R. 1972. Signal detection analysis of meridional variations to vertical and horizontal gratings. *Vision Res.* 12: 1755–58

208. Werblin, F. S. 1973. The control of sensitivity in the retina. *Sci. Am.* 228: 71–79

209. Wertheimer, M. 1961. Psychomotor coordination of auditory and visual space at birth. *Science* 134:1692

210. Westheimer, G. 1965. Visual acuity. *Ann. Rev. Psychol.* 16:359–80

211. Westheimer, G. 1967. Spatial interaction in human cone vision. *J. Physiol. London* 190:139–54

212. Westheimer, G. 1972. Visual acuity and spatial modulation thresholds. In *Visual Psychophysics,* ed. D. Jameson, L. M. Hurvich, 170–87. Berlin: Springer. 812 pp.

213. Westheimer, G. 1973. Fourier analysis of vision. *Invest. Ophthalmol.* 12:86–87

214. Wickelgren, B. G. 1971. Superior colliculus: Some receptive field properties of bimodally responsive cells. *Science* 173:69–72

215. Wickelgren, B. G., Sterling, P. 1969. Influence of visual cortex on receptive fields in the superior colliculus of the cat. *J. Neurophysiol.* 32:16–23

216. Williams, C. A., Becklund, O. A. 1972. *Optics: A Short Course for Engineers and Scientists,* 196–230. New York: Wiley-Interscience. 397 pp.

217. Williams, P. C., Williams, T. P. 1972. Effect of humming on watching television. *Nature* 239:407

218. Wurtz, R. H., Goldberg, M. E. 1972. Activity of superior colliculus in behaving monkey. IV. Effects of lesions on eye movements. *J. Neurophysiol.* 35: 587–96

SOMESTHESIS ❖216

J. F. Hahn
Psychology Department, University of Virginia, Charlottesville

This review focuses on single-unit recording data from mammalian first-order afferent fibers and from cerebral cortex and, where possible, on the relationships between these data and psychophysical data. It is largely confined to research reports appearing in archival literature from 1965 through 1972, except that only the latter half of the period is included for the vestibular senses, because they were the exclusive topic of the preceding review of somesthesis.

Every reviewer for the Annual Reviews must become a firm believer in the statement that most of the scientists who ever lived are alive and publishing today. It is a source of real regret that it is practically possible to review only selected topics within a research area, and that it is not possible to discuss every paper that may have some bearing on a topic.

TACTILE SENSITIVITY

Recording single nerve fiber activity in awake human subjects while simultaneously making psychophysical measurements and obtaining the subjects' verbal reports would be a powerful research tool for the correlation of electrophysiological and psychological data, provided that man had been considerate enough to develop only one homogeneous class of receptors and afferent nerve fibers. Then, even though the electrophysiological data were obtained from only one or two nerve fibers at a time, while the subject's responses were based on the whole set of fibers that were activated by the stimulus, the investigator could proceed with his correlations knowing that the fibers from which he recorded reflected accurately the behavior of the whole set of fibers. Inasmuch as there are several classes of mechanoreceptors in human skin, only when stimuli are restricted in locus and limited to threshold values can one sometimes be reasonably sure of the correlation between the subject's verbal report and the unitary nerve-fiber activity picked up by the investigator's microelectrode. At suprathreshold levels, although subjective reports are likely to reflect the activity of more than one class of receptor, it is still possible to examine the single-unit responses to various kinds of stimulation and to relate these to comparable data obtained from other species as a check on the validity of extrapolating the data from the other species to humans.

Data of this sort are becoming available. It is possible to obtain single-unit recordings from the large nerve fibers in the median nerve of awake man (73), but it is difficult to avoid injury to the nerve fiber (72). "Spontaneous" activity in these large-fiber mechanoreceptors was not accompanied by sensation. "Rapidly adapting" and "slowly adapting" receptors were found in the hand, as one would expect from the data on monkey (43, 44, 58, 68), with the receptive field sizes for both being about half the diameter of a finger tip (22). A stimulus just strong enough to elicit one or two action potentials in the fiber from a rapidly adapting receptor is at threshold for a verbal report of sensation; this report extends the finding by Hensel & Boman (27) some years ago that a single action potential from a human hair receptor sufficed to elicit sensation. Many of the slowly adapting units were less sensitive than the rapidly adapting ones, responding only to indentation sufficient to yield a steady pressure sensation. In a survey of over 60 mechanoreceptive units in human glabrous skin (40), slowly adapting units were three times more numerous than were rapidly adapting units. The authors recognized that their technique was biased for large fibers, but felt that humans have a relatively higher proportion of slowly adapting units than monkeys do.

An alternative approach to the correlation of electrophysiological data and human psychophysical data is to obtain the electrophysiological data from conventional preparations in another species, being careful to use the same experimental paradigms, apparatus, and procedures that are used in obtaining the human psychophysical data. A survey of the afferent populations involved enables one to reconstruct what the response of the population must be to the same stimulus parameters that were employed in the human psychophysical study. One can then test the assumption that a similar population of afferents was involved in the human response by seeing how well the human response can be predicted from the electrophysiological data.

This has been done for a precisely controlled vibrating stimulus applied to the hand (68). Single-unit recordings were obtained from the median nerve of macaque, and thresholds and magnitude estimates were obtained from human observers. Single-unit recordings were obtained from quickly adapting mechanoreceptors, slowly adapting receptors, and Pacinian receptors. Their threshold and suprathreshold responses were measured in response to a number of variations in the vibratory stimulus parameters. The human response to the same stimuli was obtained. One aspect of the human response was that the sensations resulting from stimuli in the frequency range 5–40 Hz differed from those resulting from frequencies above 60–80 Hz. The sensation corresponding to the lower frequency stimulus was one of flutter or oscillation, while the sensation corresponding to the higher frequency stimulus was one of buzz or hum. There were thus two categories of sensation to be accounted for, and three categories of mechanoreceptor that might have been involved. Because of the similarity in the experimental paradigms and stimulus parameters that had been involved in both the electrophysiological and psychophysical data, it was possible to conclude that the slowly adapting mechanoreceptors had "no essential role" in the sensations of flutter or of vibration, because the receptors disagreed in their behavior with the psychophysical findings; on the basis of the agreement between electrophysiological and psychophysical data it was reasonable to presume that the quickly adapting receptors were involved in the sensation of flutter, and the Pacinian receptors in the sensation of vibration. Several other correlations between the neural and psychophysical data were shown as well. In subsequent experiments (53), these data were confirmed and were extended by showing parallelism between monkey and human psychophysical data.

An analogous set of experiments was carried out to extend the findings to receptors of hairy skin (52). Here the flutter sensation was found to depend upon activity in rapidly adapting alpha fibers that end in or about hair follicles, while the high frequency vibration sensation was again signalled by Pacinian afferents. In this case there were three other classes of mechanoreceptors that might have been involved in carrying information about stimulus periodicity, but as was the case in glabrous skin, it could be shown that their threshold and suprathreshold behavior in response to variation of stimulus parameters did not match the psychophysical data. It is worth noting that in all cases the different classes of mechanoreceptive afferents were in fact carrying information about the periodicity of the stimulus, as evidenced by the time locking of their discharges to the cycles of the stimulus. The question of what use, if any, the nervous system makes of this information is like the question that will come up in a later section of this review: what use, if any, does the nervous system make of the temperature information that is present in the output of some populations of temperature-responsive mechanoreceptors? It is therefore worth noting here that the question of how the stimulus-periodicity information is used by the several classes of receptors in the three studies just cited was answered, not by comparing the electrophysiological data from the various classes of mechanoreceptors with respect to their dynamic range, differential sensitivity, or degree of time locking, in an effort to decide which were the most versatile and faithful reporters of vibratory stimuli, but was answered by directly comparing the human psychophysical data with what one might call the electrophysiological psychophysical data.

In the period under review there have appeared a number of experiments on single-unit first-order afferent fibers in which careful attention has been paid to the control and variation of stimulus parameters, although comparisons with human psychophysical data have been limited largely to published reports from other laboratories. Probably the most extensively studied class of receptor during the period was the *Pincus Haarscheibe,* or tactile pad, which now is commonly called the Type I receptor. Its characteristics have been studied in many creatures, including sheep, mice, rats, rabbits, guinea pigs, opossums, cats, monkeys, and humans (45, 46, 49, 50, 63, 64, 66, 69, 71). Together with studies cited in the survey of somesthesis in the 1966 *Annual Review of Psychology,* these studies have documented in detail the microscopic and ultramicroscopic structure of the receptor, the quantitative details of its displacement sensitivity and displacement-rate sensitivity, as well as its response to various frequencies of sinusoidal stimulation, and the way in which the discharges from several such receptors are integrated as they converge upon the stem axon. Unfortunately, the literature is contradictory on whether these receptors have anything to do with sensation. On the one hand, Tapper (70) has reported establishing in cat a conditioned avoidance to weak tactile stimuli to Type I receptors. On the other hand, Harrington & Merzenich (25) did not obtain positive reports of sensation in response to stimulation of Type I receptors in human subjects. Some investigators believe that they have experienced sensations resulting from stimuli confined to their own Type I receptors; other investigators are convinced that stimulation of their Type I receptors produces no sensation. Part of the problem may be that Type I receptors are often not as easy to identify unambiguously in humans as they are in some of our favorite laboratory animals. Smith (64), in eight samples of human abdominal skin, found Type I receptors easy to identify in two samples, hard to identify in four samples, and impossible to identify in two samples; moreover, some presumed Type I receptors on sectioning turned out to be skin, not Type I receptors at all. Perhaps more convincing evidence will become available from experiments in which Type I receptors in humans are identified on the basis of electrophysiological characteristics as well as visual ones.

Several other functional types of mechanoreceptor have been characterized during the period under review. Two types of phasic receptor in cat's foot (47), and a slowly adapting receptor in glabrous skin of raccoon (54) have been described. The Type II receptor of hairy skin (11) has small punctiform receptive fields easily excited by stretching the skin as well as by indenting the skin, a low discharge rate in the absence of an experimenter-imposed stimulation, and a discharge rate with fairly uniform interspike intervals in response to steady stimulation. Three types of hair receptor have been described in cat and rabbit (6). They are all rapidly adapting receptors, sensitive to velocity of displacement. Tylotrich hair receptors (50) and down hair receptors respond with a stream of discharges during movement of the hair; the guard hair receptors respond with not more than three or four impulses. Another laboratory confirmed these classifications (9, 59), but divided the guard hair receptors into two types—G_1 with higher velocity thresholds, and G_2 with lower velocity thresholds—and in addition announced the existence of yet another receptor type in hairy skin, the field receptor, with rather large, stretch-sensitive receptive fields not associated with hairs. In fact, the investigators suggested that there might be two functional types of field receptor, but felt that their data did not support this hypothesis with sufficient strength to make that assertion.

Response characteristics have also been examined for the receptors associated with the carpal hairs on the leg of cat (56, 57) and for the receptors of the mystacial vibrissae of rat (80) and cat (21, 23, 55). Each vibrissa is innervated by several nerve fibers that serve only that vibrissa, and each is sensitive only to certain directions of vibrissa movement. The inference is made that the vibrissae do not serve merely as obstacle detectors, but are well suited to serving as active "feelers" of the animal's oral environment. The number of functional classifications of receptor types serving the vibrissae has been hypothesized to be at least two (23), four (21), or four plus a miscellaneous category (80).

As the number of functional receptor classifications grows, one cannot help wondering to what extent history is repeating itself. A similar proliferation of groupings took place in the cytoarchitectonic classification of cerebral cortical areas, and in the anatomical classification of sensory nerve endings in the skin, before it was accepted that not every observable difference among cells meant that they belonged to different populations. Perhaps these doubts arise only because it is hard to imagine why the cat needs in his hairy skin half a dozen different types of mechanoreceptors, including a separate type for each type of hair, in addition to the somewhat more deeply lying Pacinian type and to the low-threshold mechanoreceptors served by C-fibers. More likely the problem is that there is still much to be learned before we know which of the observed response differences are important. For example, if it were to be found that a single anatomical type of ending had two modes of termination in the tissues, in one of which its thresholds were lower than in the other, should it be said that there are two types of receptors? There are problems, of course, in deciding what defines a single ending (36, 48). The variety of anatomical classification criteria, the variety of names that have been attached to what may be a single ending, and the fact that we need to know more about variability within and between receptors in different tissues and in different species, all mean that the correlation of structure with function is complicated by uncertainties on both sides.

THERMAL SENSITIVITY

Warm

Temperature receptors continue to be slow to yield their secrets, but progress is being made. Recordings from multifiber preparations do show increasing activity with skin warming (51, 65), and single-unit recordings have been obtained from receptors that are specifically sensitive to warming and that show little or no responsiveness to mechanical stimuli. Data have been obtained from such units in monkey (26, 29) and in the nasal region of cat (28, 30). The axons appear to be in the C- and small A-fiber range. They have regular discharges that increase in rate with increases in the temperature of the stimulus above the temperature of the skin; to a sudden temperature rise they may show a dynamic response of as high as 200 impulses per second, but the rates signaling steady temperatures are much lower, ranging about 10 to 20 impulses per second. There is some suggestion, from a sample of eight fibers, that two populations of response characteristics may exist (29), although a much larger sample will be required to verify this.

Relating the electrophysiological findings to the behavioral findings regarding warmth sensitivity continues to be difficult. Based on avoidance conditioning data in the cat (38), the inference has been made that cats cannot feel warm stimulation on the back or thigh unless the warmth reaches noxious intensities. Nevertheless, new findings (4, 51, 65) continue to add support to the earlier literature showing the existence in these areas of receptors sensitive to only moderate degrees of warming. On the other hand, behavioral measurements (5) of the sensitivity of the cat's upper lip to warming show a sensitivity here to as little as 1°C of warming, although the electrophysiological data from infraorbital nerve serving the same area (37) show no neural acitivty resulting from this warming, but only a diminution of the already ongoing activity. The investigators raised the old question of whether such diminution of activity could itself be the warmth signal. Our present state of knowledge seems to be this: In some body loci there are skin receptors that signal the presence of a warm stimulus, but this information appears to be without behavioral consequence to the animal; there are other body loci in which warm stimuli are of behavioral consequence to the animal, but in which specific warmth receptors have been sought and not found.

Cool

Cool receptors are not as hard to find as warm receptors are. As more data accumulate on cool receptors in different body areas (2, 31, 32, 39) it appears that cool receptors have in common an inverted U-shaped function relating both their static and dynamic firing rates to skin temperature. The maximum firing rate is typically found in the range 21°C–34°C, with an average around 27° or 28°. Some units are still firing at 10°C or 40°C. Maximum firing rates at static temperature levels are low, in the vicinity of 5–15 impulses per second, although firing rates rise to over 100 per sec for more rapid temperature changes.

The inverted U-shaped function relating firing rate to temperature means that it is often ambiguous which temperature is being signaled by a given firing rate. One of the mechanisms that has been proposed for resolving this ambiguity will be described later in this review, in the discussion of receptors that respond both to mechanical and to thermal stimulation. Another proposed mechanism for dealing with the ambiguity (33, 34) makes use of the following observation: As the temperature applied to cold receptors drops, the initially uniform firing rate gives way to a "bursting" pattern of activity in the region of 33°C; as the temperature further decreases to the general vicinity of 24°C, the impulses tend to cluster into groups of two up to six action potentials. Receptor temperature thus could be encoded either in terms of the number of impulses per burst, or in terms of the mean inter-spike interval within each burst, because both of these parameters are monotonically related to temperature within this roughly 10° range. (Below the lower temperature the bursting pattern turns into an irregular train of impulses.) Clearly the temperature information is there in either one of these parameters of the spike train; it remains to be ascertained whether it is used in this form.

Mechanical Plus Thermal Sensitivity

Several types of mechanoreceptors are also responsive to cooling. Action potentials are initiated at the onset of cooling, and if the unit is already discharging to a mechanical stimulus, cooling will increase the steady discharge rate. During the period under review, two interpretations of these well-established findings have been discussed. One view (35), and probably the prevailing one, is that the temperature effect is merely "noise" in the system, and has nothing to do with temperature sensation. The fact that these mechanoreceptors are notably less sensitive to temperature change than are true temperature receptors, and the fact that these mechanoreceptors can be made to produce much higher discharge rates to mechanical than to thermal stimuli, are offered as evidence to support the inference that these receptors play no part in temperature sensation. Since the firing rate to a given mechanical stimulus is increased when that stimulus is cooled, one would predict that a coin resting on one's forehead would feel heavier if it were cool than it would feel at skin temperature; almost a century ago Weber shows this to be true (75). It was shown (67) however that a coin also feels heavier when its temperature is raised above skin temperature, which is hard to reconcile with the fact that the temperature-responsive mechanoreceptors fire at lower rates when the temperature of a mechanical stimulus is raised.

An alternative interpretation has been suggested: the temperature responsiveness of these mechanoreceptors does play a part in temperature discrimination, but it does so only in conjunction with a quantitatively different temperature characteristic of another class of receptor. If there were two classes of receptors that differed systematically from each other in their thermal and mechanical responsiveness, their outputs would then in effect present the central nervous system with a pair of simultaneous equations that it could solve to recover the information about either the thermal or the mechanical stimuli, or both, that were producing the discharges in two sets of afferent fibers. In the oral-lingual regions of monkeys, for example, two classes of temperature-responsive neurons have been described by Poulos & Lende (60, 61). The class of unit that responded to thermal but not to mechanical stimulation showed the typical inverted U function relating firing rate to temperature that has been found in other units responsive to cooling. A second class of unit, responsive both to thermal and to mechanical stimulation, showed a dynamic response whose magnitude increased monotonically as the degree of cooling was increased. The purely temperature sensitive units, therefore, showed the type of ambiguity with respect to temperature that led to the hypothesis, mentioned earlier in this review, that the "bursting" activity observed in cold fibers may be an additional code that serves to remove this ambiguity. In the reports just cited, the alternative "simultaneous equation" hypothesis is proposed: smaller temperature changes near skin temperature are signaled by the units responsive only to temperature, while larger increases in cooling could be signaled by the units that are sensitive both to mechanical and to thermal stimulation. The information that the signals in these units refer to temperature would be given by the presence of simultaneous activity in the temperature-only units. Presumably when the temperature-only units were silent, the central nervous system would interpret activity in the thermally-sensitive mechanoreceptors as representing mechanical stimulus information.

The evidence that the Type I receptor takes part in such a scheme is negative. Its temperature sensitivity in the cat and monkey (15) does not predict the facts of temperature discrimination. The Type I population in the cat is not subdivided into the two or more sets of sensitivities that would be necessary under a "simultaneous-equation" hypothesis (10). The other classes of thermally responsive mechanoreceptors have not been studied in this regard.

Recently reported thermal thresholds obtained by behavioral methods in humans and monkeys (41) have been interpreted to support Poulos & Lende's hypothesis that thermal-mechanical units may participate in temperature sensation in monkeys and in humans. It was suggested that in human subjects the proportion of thermal-only units involved is probably greater than that in monkeys. The electrophysiological and behavioral studies differed in several aspects of stimulation; for instance, the quantitative electrophysiological data were obtained from oral-lingual regions, whereas the behavioral data were obtained from the glabrous skin of the hand. As already noted in this review, electrophysiological and behavioral data can be compared with much more confidence when they are obtained either simultaneously from the same subjects, or at least with a serious effort made to have identical paradigms, parameters, and procedures in both cases.

C-FIBERS

During the review period there appeared a systematic survey in cat of the responsiveness of receptors with unmyelinated afferents to a variety of graded stimuli (4). From previous reports it was known that this population includes mechanoreceptors, temperature receptors, and receptors that respond only to noxious levels of stimulation. In the present study on the posterior femoral nerve about half of the sample consisted of receptors that respond either to weak mechanical stimuli or to temperature changes of less than 2°C, with the great majority being mechanoreceptors. Only the temperature receptors ever showed background activity in the absence of skin damage.

About a third of the sample were polymodal nociceptors, a class of high threshold units; these responded to temperatures in the 42–56°C range, to moderately intense mechanical stimulation, and to irritating chemicals. These characteristics differ from those of the A-fiber nociceptors that respond only to damaging levels of mechanical stimulation (8). Another group of C-fiber receptors, not as large, had rather varied characteristics but had in common moderately high mechanical thresholds, and were possibly responsive to intense cold. Roughly half of the entire sample was thus found to require noxious levels of stimulation, while the majority of the remaining units responded to weak tactile stimuli, and a few responded to cooling or to warming.

The C-fiber mechanoreceptors, although sensitive, are notably less capable than A-fiber receptors of reporting rapid stimulus changes (3). They respond preferentially to slowly moving stimuli, they fatigue with remarkable rapidity and recover with remarkable slowness, and are considered to be skin receptors, not hair receptors (although they do respond to hair movement, and to stretching of the skin). They also respond to being cooled, although not as vigorously as they do to mechanical stimulation. The response to cooling is similarly sluggish, fatigues rapidly, and recovers slowly; the fairly small degree of cross-adaptation between the two modes of stimulation suggests that there is a moderate degree of independence of the mechanisms involved (24).

VESTIBULAR SENSITIVITY

Vestibular sensitivity was the sole topic of the somesthesis chapter in the 1970 *Annual Review of Psychology*. Much of the important literature in the field appears in technical reports, which were extensively surveyed in that review. The present review is confined to some of the single-cell and psychophysical studies that have appeared in the archival literature since then.

It has been shown that adaptation of nystagmus to prolonged constant angular acceleration does indeed occur (7). With the use of accelerations higher than those used in previous studies, 3–24°/sec^2, it was found that adaptation sets in after half a minute, regardless of stimulus intensity. This agrees with the previous literature regarding subjective estimates of acceleration.

Recently published data provide lower estimates of the absolute thresholds for angular acceleration in male human subjects (12, 13). Thresholds of the oculogyral illusion in 32 normal men for rotation about the yaw (swivel-chair) axis had a mean value of 0.11°/sec^2 with a range from 0.04 to 0.28. Thresholds of perception in 53 normal men had a mean value of 0.41°/sec^2 with a range from 0.05 to 2.20. The correlation among thresholds was not statistically significantly different from zero. In a study of 18 normal men, the same mean threshold was obtained for the yaw axis, a similar threshold value for the roll (cartwheel) axis, and a mean value of 0.67°/sec^2 for the threshold of the rotation about the pitch (somersault) axis. (This last value was not statistically significantly larger than the values for the other two axes.) There was little correlation among the thresholds, so that measurement of thresholds for one axis is not a useful predictor of thresholds for the other axes of rotation.

Single-cell data have been reported that suggest that semicircular canal receptors can respond to rotation of a linear acceleration vector around the head without angular acceleration, such as when one is on a platform that is hung from four parallel cables and is swung in a circle (1). The investigators are careful to point out that they were probably recording from second-order afferent fibers, and therefore they cannot exclude the possibility of modulation by a signal dependent on sequential activation of macular receptors.

Centrifuge data have been reported that qualitatively support the idea that a man's perception of his body position depends primarily on utricular shear forces only up to 1 g, because the predicted effect on perception of body position at greater g values is greater than the obtained effects (62, 74). The investigators are not inclined to believe that vestibularly deficient men can perceive their body position in the absence of nonvestibular cues.

Our understanding of vestibular sensitivity in mammals has been considerably extended by studies in first-order afferent fibers of the squirrel monkey (19). The neurons have resting discharges ranging from a few to over 200 impulses/ sec, with a mean value of 90. Rotation of the horizontal canal in the direction that deflects the cupula toward the utriculus increases the discharge rate; for the vertical canals deflection of the cupula toward the utriculus decreases the discharge rate; rotation in the reverse directions decreases the discharge rate below the resting level. The effect is asymmetric: the decreases tend to be smaller than the corresponding increases. A number of the units gave no evidence of sensory adaptation, so that their response to constant angular acceleration was that to be expected as the cupula's elasticity returned it to its resting position. There were other neurons that did give evidence of sensory adaptation. The mean sensitivity to angular acceleration was about two impulses per second per degree per second squared, but ranged from a quarter to double this figure. The changes in firing rate at threshold must be quite small.

Sinusoidal stimulation showed that the dynamics of the system are more complex than those of a simple torsion pendulum (16). Four time constants, rather than two, are required in the transfer function for a linear system that will approximate the obtained data reasonably well. Sensory adaptation, and receptor sensitivity both to cupular displacement and to the velocity of the displacement, are believed to be among the factors involved. Neurons tended to differ in the regularity of their discharge (20), but although certain other response characteristics such as sensitivity and response dynamics tended to be correlated with discharge regularity, the frequency distributions for these characteristics did not provide any clear evidence for the existence of more than one receptor population.

The responses to static tilt of peripheral neurons innervating otolith organs in the squirrel monkey have also been reported (17). Neurons believed to innervate the sacculus had a resting discharge around 45 impulses/sec, those serving the utriculus, about 80 impulses/sec. The neurons responded either to pitch or to roll, and the response was approximately a linear function of the calculated shear force on the end organs. There was a slight nonlinearity of response, the increase above resting discharge being slightly larger than the corresponding decrease.

CEREBRAL CORTEX

The third somatotopically organized projection area in cat, in the dorsal part of the anterior suprasylvian gyrus, has single neurons with static characteristics similar to those in the first and second areas. They are modality-specific, with restricted, mainly contralateral receptive fields (14). Microelectrode exploration of somatosensory area I of unanesthetized monkey has produced the mapping principle of the "dermatomal trajectory" (76, 77). The principle explains why, for example, two adjacent peripheral receptive fields often have adjacent cortical projections, but also explains why they need not be neighbors on the cortical map. It lies beyond this reviewer's powers to present a verbal explanation of the principle. The interested reader is referred to the illustrations and accompanying descriptions in the original papers.

Single-cell recordings in somatosensory area II of unanesthetized monkey show this area also to be organized in terms of dermatomal trajectories, although somatosensory area II is served by distinctly different pathways (78). Neurons in posterior portions of the area are polysensory (cutaneous, auditory, visual), respond to deep hard pressure, and possess wide, discontinuous, frequently asymmetric receptive fields. Cells more anterior respond to gentle cutaneous stimuli; ipsilateral and contralateral body halves are superimposed—a given cortical neuron has precisely matched and symmetric body areas in its receptive fields.

The vertical columnar organization that one has come to expect of cortical sensory projection areas has been reported for somatosensory area I of anesthetized cat. A vertical column was often found to consist of cells responding to manual touch, or to tap, or to hair receptors (42). In the middle and deep layers of the hand areas in Brodmann's areas 1 and 3 of macaque, columnar segregation of slowly adapting and quickly adapting units tended to be further segregated by area, with most of the slowly adapting units being found in area 3 (58).

Not to be outdone by visual cortex, somatosensory area I has yielded evidence in unanesthetized monkey of directionally sensitive cells (79). About one third of the sample of cortical cells were at least twice as responsive to precisely controlled stroking of the receptive field in certain preferred directions relative to other directions. The necessary control procedure showed that this was not a characteristic of the responses in first-order afferent fibers, thus denying the possibility of differential stimulus effectiveness for different directions of stroking.

The experiments on sensations of flutter and of vibration, and the peripheral receptors involved in them, have been followed up with studies of the responses of cortical neurons in unanesthetized monkeys (53). Cortical neurons served by the quickly adapting receptors that are involved in the sensation of flutter have background discharge rates of 5–20 impulses/sec. As amplitude of a sinusoidal mechanical stimulus increases, the discharge rate increases in a smooth, monotonically and negatively accelerating function that is not substantially different for stimulus frequencies between 30 and 200 Hz. The fact that the plateaus of one-to-one time locking with the cycles of the stimulus which are seen in the first-order afferent fibers are not seen in cortical neurons suggests that several of the latter with different sensitivities converge upon the cortical neuron. There is, however, a probabalistic time locking of the cortical discharges to cycles of the stimulus, interspike interval histograms showing an increased time locking with increasing stimulus amplitude.

The cortical neurons activated by the stimuli that entrain the Pacinian receptor types show very rapid increases in their discharge rates with increasing stimulus amplitudes, but do not show a temporal ordering of discharges corresponding to the frequency of the stimulus. This might lead one to expect that one could discriminate between frequencies of sinusoidal stimulation applied to the skin only in the frequency range to which the first of these two classes of cortical neurons respond. Psychophysical data obtained in the present study, as well as in an earlier study by Goff (18), show that frequency discrimination is possible in the frequency range to which the second class of cortical neurons responds. The investigators therefore suggested that the discrimination of the frequency of a flutter stimulus is based on the periodicity of the cortical neural discharge; they proposed that labeled lines—a somatosensory analog of auditory place theory—are the basis of differential perception of vibratory frequency.

IN RETROSPECT

In reading papers for this chapter, your reviewer has been impressed by how often investigators in psychophysical studies are forced to try to relate their data to electrophysiological data that were obtained under experimental conditions not well designed for the comparison, and how often the comparable problem exists when one tries to relate single-cell data to psychophysical findings. The few exceptions encountered in which the psychophysical and electrophysiological experiments were planned to be complementary make clear that this is a much more efficient way to proceed.

Literature Cited

1. Benson, A. J., Guedry, F. E., Jones, G. M. 1970. Responses of semicircular canal dependent units in vestibular nuclei to rotation of a linear acceleration vector without angular acceleration. *J. Physiol. London* 210:475–94
2. Benzing, H., Hensel, H., Wurster, R. 1969. Integrated static activity of lingual cold receptors. *Pfluegers Arch.* 311: 50–54
3. Bessou, P., Burgess, P. R., Perl, E. R., Taylor, C. B. 1971. Dynamic properties of mechanoreceptors with unmyelinated (C) fibers. *J. Neurophysiol.* 34:116–31
4. Bessou, P., Perl, E. R. 1969. Response of cutaneous sensory units with unmyelinated fibers to noxious stimuli. *J. Neurophysiol.* 32:1025–43
5. Brearley, E. A., Kenshalo, D. R. 1970. Behavioral measurements of the sensitivity of cat's upper lip to warm and cool stimuli. *J. Comp. Physiol. Psychol.* 70:1–4
6. Brown, A. G., Iggo, A. 1967. A quantitative study of cutaneous receptors and afferent fibres in the cat and rabbit. *J. Physiol. London* 193:707–33
7. Brown, J. H., Wolfe, J. W. 1969. Adaptation to prolonged constant angular acceleration. *Acta Otolaryngol.* 67:389–98
8. Burgess, P. R., Perl, E. R. 1967. Myelinated afferent fibres responding specifically to noxious stimulation of skin. *J. Physiol. London* 190:541–62
9. Burgess, P. R., Petit, D., Warren, R. M. 1968. Receptor types in cat hairy skin supplied by myelinated fibers. *J. Neurophysiol.* 31:833–48
10. Casey, D. E., Hahn, J. F. 1970. Thermal effects on response of cat touch corpuscle. *Exp. Neurol.* 28:35–45
11. Chambers, M. R., Iggo, A. 1967. Slowly-adapting cutaneous mechanoreceptors. *J. Physiol. London* 192:26P
12. Clark, B., Stewart, J. D. 1969. Effects of angular acceleration on man: thresholds for perception of rotation and the oculogyral illusion. *Aerospace Med.* 40: 952–56
13. Clark, B., Stewart, J. D. 1970. Thresholds for the perception of angular acceleration about the three major body axes. *Acta Otolaryngol.* 69:231–38
14. Darian-Smith, I., Isbister, J., Mok, H., Yokata, T. 1966. Somatic sensory cortical projection areas excited by tactile stimulation of the cat: a triple representation. *J. Physiol. London* 182:671–89
15. DuClaux, R., Kenshalo, D. R. 1972. The temperature sensitivity of the type I slowly adapting mechanoreceptors in cats and monkeys. *J. Physiol. London* 224:647–64
16. Fernandez, C., Goldberg, J. M. 1971. Physiology of peripheral neurons innervating semicircular canals of the squirrel monkey. II. Response to sinusoidal stimulation and dynamics of peripheral vestibular system. *J. Neurophysiol.* 34: 661–75
17. Fernandez, C., Goldberg, J. M., Abend, W. K. 1972. Response to static tilts of peripheral neurons innervating otolith organs of the squirrel monkey. *J. Neurophysiol.* 6:978–97
18. Goff, G. D. 1967. Differential discrimination of frequency of cutaneous mechanical vibration. *J. Exp. Psychol.* 74:294–99
19. Goldberg, J. M., Fernandez, C. 1971. Physiology of peripheral neurons innervating semicircular canals of the squirrel monkey I. Resting discharge and response to constant angular accelerations. *J. Neurophysiol.* 34:635–60
20. Ibid. Physiology of peripheral neurons innervating semicircular canals of the squirrel monkey. III. Variations among units in their discharge properties, 676–84
21. Gottschaldt, K. M., Iggo, A., Young, D. W. 1972. Electrophysiology of the afferent innervation of sinus hairs, including vibrissae, of the cat. *J. Physiol. London* 222:60P–61P
22. Hagbarth, K. E., Hongell, A., Hallin, R. G., Torebjörk, H. E. 1970. Afferent impulses in median nerve fascicles evoked by tactile stimulation of the human hand. *Brain Res.* 24:423–42
23. Hahn, J. F. 1971. Stimulus-response relations in first-order sensory fibres from cat vibrissae. *J. Physiol. London* 213:215–26
24. Hahn, J. F. 1971. Thermal-mechanical stimulus interactions in low-threshold C-

fiber mechanoreceptors of cat. *Exp. Neurol.* 33:607–17
25. Harrington, T., Merzenich, M. M. 1970. Neural coding in the sense of touch: human sensations of skin indentation compared with the responses of slowly adapting mechanoreceptive afferents innervating the hairy skin of monkeys. *Exp. Brain Res.* 10:251–64
26. Hensel, H. 1969. Cutane Wärmereceptoren bei Primaten. *Pfluegers Arch.* 313: 150–52
27. Hensel, H., Boman, K. K. A. 1960. Afferent impulses in cutaneous sensory nerves in human subjects. *J. Neurophysiol.* 23:564–78
28. Hensel, H., Huopaniemi, T. 1969. Static & dynamic properties of warm fibers in the infraorbital nerve. *Pfluegers Arch.* 309:1–10
29. Hensel, H., Iggo, A. 1971. Analysis of cutaneous warm and cold fibres in primates. *Pfluegers Arch.* 329:1–8
30. Hensel, H., Kenshalo, D. R. 1969. Warm receptors in the nasal region of cats. *J. Physiol. London* 204:99–112
31. Hensel, H., Wurster, R. D. 1969. Static behavior of cold receptors in the trigeminal area. *Pfluegers Arch.* 313:153–54
32. Hensel, H., Wurster, R. D. 1970. Static properties of cold receptors in nasal area of cats. *J. Neurophysiol.* 33:271–75
33. Iggo, A. 1969. Cutaneous thermoreceptors in primates and sub-primates. *J. Physiol. London* 200:403–30
34. Iggo, A., Iggo, B. J. 1971. Impulse coding in primate cutaneous thermoreceptors in dynamic thermal conditions. *J. Physiol. Paris* 63:287–90
35. Iggo, A., Muir, A. R. 1969. Structure and function of a slowly adapting touch corpuscle in hairy skin. *J. Physiol. London* 200:763–96
36. Kantner, M. 1965. La Morphologie des recepteurs dans la peau. *Acta Anat.* 60: 463–78
37. Kenshalo, D. R., Brearley, E. A. 1970. Electrophysiological measurements of the sensitivity of cat's upper lip to warm and cool stimuli. *J. Comp. Physiol. Psychol.* 70:5–14
38. Kenshalo, D. R., Duncan, D. G., Weymark, C. 1967. Thresholds for stimulation of the inner thigh, footpad, and face of cats. *J. Comp. Physiol. Psychol.* 63: 133–38
39. Kenshalo, D. R., Gallegos, E. S. 1967. Multiple temperature-sensitive spots innervated by single nerve fibers. *Science* 158:1064–65
40. Knibestöl, M., Vallbo, A. B. 1970. Single unit analysis of mechanoreceptor activity from the human glabrous skin. *Acta Physiol. Scand.* 80:178–95
41. Laursen, A. M. 1972. Thermal thresholds in man and monkey. *Exp. Neurol.* 34:25–32
42. Levitt, J., Levitt, M. 1968. Sensory hindlimb representation in SMI cortex of cat —a unit analysis. *Exp. Neurol.* 22: 259–75
43. Lindblom, U. 1965. Properties of touch receptors in distal glabrous skin of the monkey. *J. Neurophysiol.* 28:966–85
44. Lindblom, U., Lund, L. 1966. The discharge from vibration-sensitive receptors in the monkey foot. *Exp. Neurol.* 15: 401–17
45. Lindblom, U., Tapper, D. N. 1966. Integration of impulse activity in a peripheral sensory unit. *Exp. Neurol.* 15:63–69
46. Ibid 1967. Terminal properties of a vibro-tactile receptor. 17:1–15
47. Lynn, B. 1969. The nature and location of certain phasic mechanoreceptors in the cat's foot. *J. Physiol. London* 201: 765–73
48. Malinovsky, L. 1966. Variability of sensory nerve endings in foot pads of a domestic cat. *Acta Anat.* 64:82–106
49. Mann, S. J. 1965. Haarscheiben in the skin of sheep. *Nature* 502:1228–29
50. Mann, S. J. 1968. The tylotrich (hair) follicle of the American oppossum. *Anat. Rec.* 160:171–79
51. Martin, H. F., Manning, J. W. 1969. Rapid thermal cutaneous stimulation: peripheral nerve responses. *Brain Res.* 16:524–26
52. Merzenich, M. M., Harrington, T. 1969. The sense of flutter-vibration evoked by stimulation of the hairy skin of primates: comparison of human sensory capacity with the responses of mechanoreceptive afferents innervating the hairy skin of monkeys. *Exp. Brain Res.* 9:236–60
53. Mountcastle, V. B., Talbot, W. H., Sakata, H., Hyvärinen, J. 1969. Cortical neuronal mechanisms in flutter-vibration studied in unanesthetized monkeys. Neuronal periodicity and frequency discrimination. *J. Neurophysiol.* 32:452–84
54. Munger, B. L., Pubols, L. M., Pubols, B. H. 1971. The Merkel rete papilla: a slowly adapting sensory receptor in mammalian glabrous skin. *Brain Res.* 29:47–61
55. Nier, K. 1972. Phasenfrequenzgang neuraler Impulsmuster von Vibrissenreceptoren. *Pfluegers Arch.* 334:357–66

56. Nilsson, B. Y. 1969. Structure and function of the tactile hair receptors on the cat's foreleg. *Acta Physiol. Scand.* 77: 396–416
57. Ibid. Hair discs and Pacinian corpuscles functionally associated with the carpal tactile hairs in the cat, 417–28
58. Paul, R. L., Merzenich, M., Goodman, H. 1972. Representation of slowly and rapidly adapting cutaneous mechanoreceptors of the hand in Brodmann's areas 3 and 1 of *macaca mulatta. Brain Res.* 36:229–49
59. Perl, E. R. 1968. Myelinated afferent fibres innervating primate skin and their response to noxious stimuli. *J. Physiol. London* 197:593–615
60. Poulos, D. A., Lende, R. A. 1970. Responses of trigeminal ganglion neurons to thermal stimulation of oral-facial regions. I. Steady-state response. *J. Neurophysiol.* 33:508–17
61. Ibid. Response of trigeminal ganglion neurons to thermal stimulation of oral-facial regions. II. Temperature change response, 518–26
62. Schöne, H., Wade, N. J. 1971. The influence of force magnitude on the perception of body position: II. Effect of body posture. *Brit. J. Psychol.* 62:347–52
63. Smith, K. R. 1967. The structure and function of the Haarscheibe. *J. Comp. Neurol.* 131:459–74
64. Smith, K. R. 1970. The ultrastructure of the human Haarscheibe and Merkel cell. *J. Invest. Dermatol.* 54:150–59
65. Stolwijk, J. A., Wexler, I. 1971. Peripheral nerve activity in response to heating the cat's skin. *J. Physiol. London* 214: 377–92
66. Straile, W. E. 1969. Encapsulated end-organs in the rabbit, mouse, sheep, and man. *J. Comp. Neurol.* 136:317–36
67. Szabadföldi, M. 1865. Beiträge zur Physiologie des Tastsinnes. Cited in *Sensation and Perception in the History of Experimental Psychology,* E. G. Boring, 1942. New York: Appleton-Century-Crofts. 466 pp.
68. Talbot, W. H., Darian-Smith, I., Kornhuber, H. H., Mountcastle, V. B. 1968. The sense of flutter-vibration: Comparison of the human capacity with response patterns of mechanoreceptive afferents from the monkey hand. *J. Neurophysiol.* 31:301–34
69. Tapper, D. N. 1965. Stimulus-response relationships in the cutaneous slowly-adapting mechanoreceptor in hairy skin of the cat. *Exp. Neurol.* 13:364–85
70. Ibid 1970. Behavioral evaluation of the tactile pad receptor system in hairy skin of the cat. 26:447–59
71. Tapper, D. N., Galera-Garcia, C., Brown, P. B. 1972. Sinusoidal mechanical stimulation of the tactile pad receptor: tuning curves. *Brain Res.* 36:223–27
72. Torebjörk, H. E., Hallin, R. G., Hongell, A., Hagbarth, K. E. 1970. Single unit potentials with complex waveform seen in microelectrode recordings from the human median nerve. *Brain Res.* 24: 443–50
73. Vallbo, A. B., Hagbarth, K. E. 1968. Activity from skin mechanoreceptors recorded percutaneously in awake human subjects. *Exp. Neurol.* 21:270–89
74. Wade, N. J., Schöne, H., 1971. The influence of force magnitude on the perception of body position. I. Effect of head posture. *Brit. J. Psychol.* 62:157–63
75. Weber, E. H. 1846. Der Tastsinn und das Gemeingefühl. Cited in *Sensation and Perception in the History of Experimental Psychology,* E. G. Boring, 1942. New York: Appleton-Century-Crofts. 466 pp.
76. Werner, G., Whitsel, B. L. 1968. Topology of the body representation in Somatosensory Area I of primates. *J. Neurophysiol.* 31:856–69
77. Whitsel, B. L., Dreyer, D. A., Roppolo, J. R. 1971. Determinants of body representation in postcentral gyrus of macaques. *J. Neurophysiol.* 34:1018–34
78. Whitsel, B. L., Petrucelli, L. M., Werner, G. 1969. Symmetry and connectivity in the map of the body surface in Somatosensory Area II of primates. *J. Neurophysiol.* 32:170–83
79. Whitsel, B. L., Roppolo, J. R., Werner, G. 1972. Cortical information processing of stimulus motion on primate skin. *J. Neurophysiol.* 35:691–717
80. Zucker, E., Welker, W. I. 1969. Coding of somatic sensory input by vibrissae neurons in rat's trigeminal ganglion. *Brain Res.* 12:138–56

PERSONALITY

❖217

Philip S. Holzman[1]
Department of Psychiatry and Department of Psychology, University of Chicago

INTRODUCTION

If the human organism is indeed, as Gardner Murphy (99) wrote, a region of perpetual interaction, a structured locus of change whose boundaries are fragile and indefinite, then constant change and perpetual *becoming* claim title to man's essence and to his personality. Yet many personality studies have focused on the organism at one particular moment in time to fix his qualitative and quantitative distinctions. While they are necessary and important, such cross-sectional studies of traits, attitudes, or motives have slighted the continuous instability of the organism, for personality never *is,* it is always *becoming.* This hyperbole highlights an apparent paradox: although persons are continuously changing, they are also recognizable over time and thus to some extent stable. Previous reviews in this series have reflected a concern with structure and its measurement. This review, however, will focus on issues of change, on the adaptive tasks posed by growth, on changing oneself to fit into a changing ecology or changing the environment to fit oneself; in short, on the longitudinal perspective of personality.

Personologists, for the most part, have shied away from longitudinal studies for well-known methodological reasons, some of which are: the investigation may outlive the investigator; new methods of observation and measurement may render obsolete those decided upon earlier; measuring instruments adopted for one age range may be unsuitable for another; and the characteristics studied at one age may no longer be present at a later age. Yet there have been a few intrepid investigators who, defying both these inherent difficulties and the *Zeitgeist,* have presented data on personality development, on the constant *becoming.* These studies receive more than cursory mention in this chapter. Issues of theory have clamored for a hearing, and arguments over the essential nature of man—as automaton or as responsible regulator of his own fate—have appeared in several books and papers. This chapter

[1]The preparation of this survey was supported in part by research grant MH-19477 from the National Institute of Mental Health. The author is indebted to Randall Rowlett, who assisted most skillfully at all phases of this survey, and to Gardner Murphy, Robert Holt, and Herbert Schlesinger for their always helpful comments.

will review some of these arguments. Finally, some theorists have implicated environmental factors in personality change, but some obvious exogenous factors like chemical compounds have received only scant attention by personologists. The relationship of these substances to personality change will also be considered.

Broadly speaking, information about human personality comes from four different sources of study. The first is that of biochemical and physiological dispositions, conceived to have genetic as well as environmental origins. The second is studies of morphology, of body type. The third is that of the societal realm, including the impact of social forces upon the growing child and the differentiated personal responses—motives, traits, behaviors, attitudes—which derive from societal sources. The fourth is the examination of clinical contacts with people who have suffered adaptive and adjustive failures and from such observations—they are generally observations in depth and over time—we have obtained most of our knowledge about the dynamics of adaptation.

Current psychoanalytic thinking exemplifies the clinical source; role theory and group dynamics stem from the societal realm. Although in the past the morphological body-build concepts have had significant impact on personality theorists (e.g. 136), there has been a noteworthy decline in interest in such concerns. There is visible increase in the numbers of biochemical and physiological approaches; these include not only such early studies as Schachter's (131), but the growing literature on behavior genetics (46, 124), biochemical aspects of psychopathology (e.g. 112) and the short-term and long-term chemical alteration of moods, cognition, and general adaptation. From the perspective of the societal approaches as well as from the clinical, lively debates have occurred concerning the nature of man—whether he is to be conceived of as dominant over his surround, relatively autonomous of his social context (27, 86, 153), or a reactive organism whose general behavior can be programmed or at least controlled or predicted by careful manipulation of environmental contingencies (97, 137). A further but related debate within this realm concerns the issue of the developmental continuity of behavior and traits. The most striking development emerging from the clinical and the societal approaches within the last few years has been the appearance of so-called humanistic personologies, with a concern for such qualities as "fulfillment," "ideal values," and "self-actualization" (88, 121). This development shares the quasi-utopian vision of the more behavioristic approaches, either by "actualizing" man's inner potentials (the humanistic approach) or by programming the environment (the behavioristic approach). In contrast the clinical enterprise emphasizes the limits, inner and outer, on ultimate achievement, the ubiquitous presence of conflict and ambivalence, and a reliance on pathology to give clues to normal personality development. Efforts to reduce the complexities of personality theory and to simplify the classification of points of view within and between personality theories led Maslow to suggest that the study of personality can be approached from three vantage points: 1. behavior-centered, learning-dominated, stimulus-response oriented, or "behavioristic," represented by Skinner; 2. psychoanalytic, represented by Freud and Erikson; and 3. the existential, humanistic, or "third force" view, represented by Maslow, Rogers, or May (88, 89, 121).

Each of these "schools" can generate research strategies, and these reflect their (*a*) implicit view of the nature of man, (*b*) order of priorities for the phenomena to investigate about personality, and (*c*) preference for methods suitable to bring out the effects they deem important. It would seem that the task ahead requires a unified field approach that will combine the viable techniques of all three views so that investigations can examine all the visible modalities of human personality in ways that do not slight any of the aspects of the person. Something like this amalgam has already occurred in the field of experimental psychopathology—which this reviewer regards as a branch of personology—whose investigators use operant tenchiques on animals to observe the behavioral effects of chemical compounds and then speculate about the genetic, biochemical, and learned basis for the behavior (cf. 112, 134).

THEORY

A major theoretical statement on personality—metatheoretical is probably the better description—appears in Chein's *The Science of Behavior and the Image of Man* (27). Chein challenges both the positivistic position as represented in behavioristic approaches and the existential positions. While accepting the main features of both these approaches, Chein views them from an organismic-motivational-transactional perspective. He does not deny that highly predictable stimulus-response relationships can be seen when cognitive, affective, and motivational factors are ignored, but believes that the simplicity of the behaviorists' scheme is achieved at the expense of arbitrarily eliminating the complexity of human behavior. The view of man as a helpless pawn either of environmental contingencies or of biological constraints rests on what Chein believes is a dubious assumption—that all the determinants of behavior are included in man's constitution and in the environment.

Chein's central integrating concept is motivation, whose paradigmatic definition is "behavior is a motive of the behaviors it includes." Thus, driving a car is a motive for turning on the ignition; and studying for an examination is a motive for going to the library. In this view the person is an active agent and not a passive medium for the interplay of constitution and environment. Since man's own activities affect that interplay, motivation is a coequal determinant of *behavior* and along with constitution and environment, one of the three sufficient conditions. Behavior is thus free, according to Chein, to the extent that environment and constitution do not dictate or preclude a particular action.

While modifiable, motives become interrelated with and interdependent on other motives. They become part of a complex network of relationships and the effect of this motivational complex is a relatively stable, quasi-self-sustaining system of motives "commonly referred to as character and personality." Chein elaborates this statement of the subject matter not only of personality but of most of psychology, and makes a compelling case for his view that man plays an active role not only in the "causal complex of the world about him but also plays a part in shaping himself both as psychological being and as biological organism." Chein's view of the personologist's task is to investigate the manifold behaviors possible when the purely constitutional and environmental factors have been minimized—that is, to investigate the conditions and consequences of motivation. The phenomena that the radical behaviorists and the biological determinists view as the sole legitimate object in the study of man Chein relegates to a subsidiary and supporting role.

The issue of purpose, which Tolman (148) alone among the behaviorists confronted as a knotty problem, Chein embraces as a necessary part of understanding behavior: if a *motive* emphasizes the dynamic effect of the superordinate on the subordinate act, *purpose* refers to the service or function of the subordinate with respect to the superordinate act.

Although the enduring motivational structure seems to be bound to the body—for it moves with the body and cannot survive the body—it is not identical with the body nor is it contained in the body. Chein's is a transactional view of motives and thus of behavior and personality. In contrast, Gordon Allport regarded the personality as being bound within a physical body; Chein argues that just as abilities cannot be conceived of without the objects to be manipulated when the ability is activated, so motives cannot be conceived of as independent of their behaviors which involve objects.

Chein also denies that the *trait* should be regarded as the ultimate unit of personality. Rather there are six basic concepts of personality: spontaneity, directedness, the environmental conditions for the fulfillment of action, the interrelationship of one act with another, the distressing character of drive states (arising from the unavailability of a course of action suitable to eliminate the drive state, "or in other words, the diffuse random discharge of neural energy into motor outlets of the body is per se distressing and that this is an ultimate psychological given"), and finally, the concept of the self as a feeling of the "hereness in the thereness," a locus in space and time. In contrast, a trait is simply a regularity of an abstracted aspect of behavior, the regularity depending on specifiable kinds of conditions of motive and situation.

These strong positions vie with those of B. F. Skinner, whose views of the image of man have been stated in several places and again powerfully in *Beyond Freedom and Dignity* (137). The concept of "autonomous man," Skinner avers, is an error. Environmental contingencies are everywhere and they produce behavior. Intention, purpose, choice, decision, and desire are all replaced by the idea of an active and shaping environment. "The environment not only prods or lashes, it *selects* . . . It is now clear that we must take into account what the environment does to an organism not only before but after it responds. Behavior is shaped and maintained by its consequences."

In a text that views sympathetically a social behavioristic position, Mischel (97) defines personality as a field of study rather than as a property of people. The subdisciplines or related areas of human development, cognition, creativity, learning, and behavior observation should all claim the personologist's attention. Mischel vigorously and cogently criticizes psychodynamic approaches to personology but is not equally critical of the social behavioristic view—that a person is what he does. Mischel's point of departure is behavioral specificity; since predictions of manifest behavior from presumed traits, dispositions, or motives are significantly less accurate than from a knowledge of the stimulus conditions, the proper object of study is not the inner world of the person but the social context, the stimulus conditions which control the person's behavior. This reasoning, of course, assumes that the principal task of the personologist is to predict actual behavior in a molecular sense. Thus, Chein's and Mischel's view of what personology is all about differ radically.

White's new text (154) continues his eclectic but essentially psychodynamic approach, written in the tradition established by H. A. Murray. White observes that we are considerably more skilled in explaining and understanding how people become bogged down by pathology (although these explanations are generally post hoc), than in understanding natural and often successful adaptive maturation and growth.

Clinicians study lives in trouble at close range and over long periods of time, thus accumulating much more data about lives that become bogged down than do the experimentalists about adaptive behavior from their comparatively brief contacts with their subjects. White attempts to describe general principles of growth and development and also to understand the way individuals are organized for their adaptive tasks, incorporating his ideas of competence and effectence motivation, and integrating family, the group, and the social as central dynamic systems.

Dahlstrom (29) attempted to answer the perplexing issue of whether behavioral consistencies and inconsistencies—such as they exist—may properly be ascribed either to personality structure or to environmental contingencies. Dahlstrom proposes the construction of a typology in which a species type need not be identical with any individual member of the species. The requirements for a sophisticated typology—in fact, of personality structure—would include (*a*) *flexibility* so that shifts in classifications could be made if a personality pattern changes, as it may in the course of maturation (17, 81, 82, 111); and (*b*) the development of a *taxonomy of syndromes of dysfunction* which recognizes that the dysfunctions and not the individuals are classified in syndromes. Dahlstrom rejects the conception of personality traits proposed by Allport, Cattell, or Diamond as the ideal structural variables in this system, for such conceptions of traits do not allow for intra-individual change and are not responsive to intra-organismic or environmental challenges in analogy to physical systems such as the cardiovascular system. Dahlstrom has no ready candidate for the component variables in this dynamic system to replace *traits,* but he does suggest that ideas such as the distinction between trait anxiety and state anxiety are promising (140), as is the concept of social "roles" (23). Personality studies have only attempted to measure the more enduring "quasi-stationary" (113) features of human personality, for instance the efforts of Gough, Cattell, or of those investigating moral character (74), perceptual and cognitive styles (41, 68, 157), or Piagetian stages (111). We do not yet possess the metrics for assessing intra-individual variation over short and long periods of time including those that can be interpreted as attempts to maintain stability in the face of internal and external pressures. In order to identify and refine attributes of personological types, Dahlstrom argues for methods that combine formal testing procedures and scaling techniques. These possibly mechanical techniques are to be tempered by the human observer who must check on the "reasonableness" of the personality taxonomy—the coherences—yielded by statistical techniques.

Mischel's observation (97) seems valid that prediction of behavior from traits is poor and that discontinuity and inconsistency in behavior are as frequent as are apparent continuities. Block (16) has offered an explanation of such apparent discontinuities. The preferred method, he notes, for isolating regularities has been the correlation of behaviors presumed to be related, and results have indeed been disappointing. Four reasons for these disappointments are cited: 1. The behaviors under study may be insignificant or not salient. 2. The context must be considered. 3. The behaviors being studied (the phenotypes) may be mediated by different underlying variables (genotypes). 4. Whatever behavioral consistency exists may break down when a person has reached a personal limit of strain.

Loevinger (80) approached the issue of stability and change in personality from the vantage point of "ego development." Just as the upright position of a gyroscope is maintained by its rotation, she wrote, and thrusts and counter-thrusts maintain the shape of an arch, so the structure of the ego and its functioning in interaction with other people is maintained by its activity. A comparable point of view is found in Piaget's idea of "mobile equilibrium"—the more mobile the structure, the more stable it is. The essence of ego functioning, in Loevinger's view, is a striving to master, to integrate, and to make sense of experience. The development of ego functioning consists in a progressive differentiation of parts and a simultaneous and continuous hierarchization, in which the parts are subordinated to the organic whole and organized and regulated by laws of the whole organism. Thus, empirical studies which demonstrate that people change or do not change with respect to some behaviors do not become proof or disproof of an ontology. Rather they highlight questions of what remains stable and what becomes transformed. Like a variation on a musical theme, the new version emerges from its earlier form, resembles it, and yet is different from it.

Loevinger observes that most theories of personality view development dialectically, and view growth not as linear and continuous but as involving turning points or stages. Growth of a set of qualities increases up to a point and then either declines or is eclipsed by the growth of another set of qualities. The new set may not only oppose the previous one but also incorporate aspects of it, and in this process may replace it and itself be changed by it. This process of dialectic epigenetic development is characteristic of the theories of Piaget, Freud, Kohlberg, as well as Loevinger. She refers to this kind of theory as "a milestone process" in contrast to the "polar conceptions" of development. Milestone theories tend to be typological and allow for manifold arrangements of characteristics, as well as for descriptions of persons who do not advance beyond certain stages. Loevinger's own theory of personality or ego epigenesis (79–82) is strongly influenced by the holistic orientation and dialectic stance of Piaget, Freud, Werner, Baldwin, and G. H. Mead. Her labels for the successive stages she has distinguished are "autistic" (in which the infant is oblivious to everything except physical needs), "impulsive" (in which the infant is a creature of impulses and is concerned with self-demands and the demands of others in order to secure satisfaction), "self-protective" (which in small children is ritualistic and in older children may be opportunistic, manipulative and exploitative), "conformist" (in which rules are obeyed because they are rules and in which the overwhelming concern is being loved and approved, but in which the conception that others have an inner life is extremely limited), "conscientious" (in which others are now seen as differentiated in terms of feelings and thoughts), and "autonomous" (where tolerance for the ironies of life are realized). Her descriptions of these stages emphasize the common elements that all persons either experience in passing through or in arresting at a particular stage. Each of the stages is both a normal developmental period and a point at which a particular individual may be "located." Among adults there are representative examples of any particular stage. No age boundaries have yet been described for children. This theory—as well as those on which it is modeled—contrasts with the "polar theories" which view personality development in terms of a single motive, striving, or quality such as that of "self-actualization" (45) or "competence" (153). In Loevinger's view "polar theories" illustrate "the ontological fallacy" in that they assert that all people, however phenotypically different they seem, are basically driven by the same motive. These theories assume that the motive that may characterize one late stage of development can explain behavior at "all previous stages and of the transitions from stage to stage" (80, p. 117). Thus, in the "polar theories," transformations of motivations are either denied or ignored, while such transformations are taken as given and indeed are *the* problem for explanation in the "milestone theories."

Loevinger and her co-workers (81, 82) have constructed a test and a set of scales for measuring the successive stages of ego development. These scales are in widespread use as a research tool in studies of personality development and functioning. The test involves the completion of 36 sentence stems, and is designed for either group or individual administration. Almost all of the published research involving this test has been with women and girls 12 years and older, but work on the standardization of the sentence stems for males and younger people is in progress. Reliability was satisfactorily high (between .75 and .85) as estimated by median interrater correlations for single items and for total protocols. Validity of the test as measured against clinical interviews was about .60.

THE LIFE CYCLE

The problem of continuity in development is of central concern in the major theoretical statements of the past year. It would therefore seem helpful to marshall the evidence for and against them. The remainder of this chapter will allocate studies to two broad categories: those dealing with adaptation in the course of the life cycle, and those dealing with adaptation in the face of exogenous factors. In the former, we will consider evidence of stability and change in the course of growth and maturation; in the latter, the stability of personality under the impact of such factors as drugs.

Early Childhood

An abiding concern of developmental personologists has been that of continuity in various traits and abilities, not the least of which is those behaviors loosely subsumed under "intelligence." A significant review of this area by McCall, Hogarty & Hurlburt (90) made use of the longitudinal data gathered at the Fels Research Institute. The authors noted that Bayley's assessment of early studies of mental growth of infants failed to establish predictive validity of scores earned in the first year or two of life, although these scores may have been a valid index of cognitive ability at the time of testing. These poor predictions, it is assumed, were not the outcome of the unreliability of the tests, and McCall et al, using the Fels' data, determined that at 6 months and at 12 months parental education alone is the best predictor of childhood IQ. There is almost no predictive advantage in considering infant test results until about 18 months, when incorporating results of infant testing with parental education and socioeconomic status in a multiple regression equation slightly improves prediction of childhood IQ. Early vocalization is the subtest that predicts later IQ best, a finding that is more reliable for girls than for boys. The uneven predictive power of infant tests and the instability of correlations across ages supports neither the concept of a *g* factor of mental development, nor a conception of a skill-specific, age-specific factor. The authors suggest that

> within any age (or developmental level), one could discern subsets of skills that would be highly related within a set but the subsets would be independent from one another. Some of these skill sets might possess relationships with similar or qualitatively different skill sets at a future age; others might lead to a 'dead-end' in terms of their developmental significance.

Such an interpretation resembles the Piagetian and Eriksonian epigenetic schemes of development. McCall et al suggest that

> However, there are alternative interpretations of the content of this developmental trend. The exploration of objects, imitation of adult behavior, and displays of verbal fluency all require the infant to possess a type of social extraversion that permits him to interact freely with a strange examiner. Thus, the major dimension underlying normal infant mental test performance may not be 'mental' at all but rather a social inhibition versus extraverted personality style. Another alternative is that the developmental trend observed in the infant behavior may actually reflect trends and consistencies in parental behavior that are then reflected in the child. A mother who plays contingently or provides toys for potential contingent effects during the first few months of her child's life may be the same parent who plays imitation games a few months later, and provides an adequate and encouraging language model for her child during the second year (90, pp. 742–43).

Clearly related to the above findings and formulations are those of L. B. Murphy (100) who, with her colleagues A. Moriarty and G. Heider, over a number of years has been reporting longitudinal studies of 60 children. Her observations and tests of 32 of these 60 children focused on the ways the children dealt with problems of living at various ages, and the nature of the transitions and leaps in their development. Her emphasis is upon the development of individual styles of adaptation.

> Many of the children surprised us in certain ways, even while exhibiting much continuity. For example, a stoical and strong preschooler considered to be one of the 'best copers' in many ways became discouraged, embittered, and poorly controlled at the prepuberty stage; a very vulnerable infant became an unusually competent, understanding and well-functioning teenager; a forthright, and at times aggressive, preschool girl became a

> sympathetic and a nurturant child at home and at school. These highlights suggest the range of areas in which change occurred, and the traumatic degree of these changes (100, pp. 96, 97).

Changes in IQ ranged from 10 to 30 points; there were frequent spurts in growth, in temperament, and in response zones. As sources of change Murphy proposed genic differences, exogenous and endogenous traumata such as deprivations and illnesses, the idiosyncratic patterning of relationships between child and environment, special vulnerabilities, and the special learning or reinforcement history.

The concept of "coping" is central in Murphy's theorizing about personality development and functioning. In her view the human organism actively strives to come to terms with endogenous and exogenous factors in his life-space. The relationship between the repertoire of a child's coping techniques—in Murphy's terms—and the psychoanalytic conception of "defenses" receives some clarification in one of her recent papers (101). Murphy notes that both defense mechanisms and coping mechanisms are a part of the repertoire of the normal child and have a common source in the early behaviors of the infant. Yet coping is the more inclusive concept. There is a continuum between the earlier methods of active coping and the later methods of defense, some of which become patterned into defense mechanisms. By the age of 3 or 4 most children have already developed a repertoire of such mechanisms and these form a part of their normal coping resources.

Normal children use defense mechanisms with considerable flexibility, and these appear neither as substitutes for active efforts nor as results of failures of active efforts. Murphy insists that defense mechanisms or specific coping devices neither inevitably lead to pathology nor guarantee normal development, the latter being a complex outcome of interactions between the balance of child's vulnerabilities and strengths and their interaction with the expected and adventitious patterns of stress and support from the environment.

D. G. Freedman (37) reported on an 8-month longitudinal twin study rating their filmed behavior. This study showed that the identical twins were substantially more alike than same-sex fraternal twins on several of Bayley's scales. Freedman's study eliminated the factor of mutual imitation inevitable in studies of older twins. While monozygotic twins are more similar than dizygotic twins on early interpersonal measures, the concordance is not maintained in later life. A second study using the Bayley weekly "Social Interest Scale" over the first 5 months replicated the earlier findings. These results provide further evidence for a significant genetic component in the basic behavior of social interaction. An empirical study of neonates from six different ethnic groups found each group unique in some way—generally in temperament. Similarities, however, were more apparent than differences. Another empirical study found that female neonates smile more than do males and at 6 months they stare more at social objects.

Thomas et al reported in 1963 (146) on 80 children studied in terms of nine behavioral variables: activity level, rhythmicity, approach-withdrawal, adaptability, intensity of reaction, threshold responsiveness, quality of mood, attention span, and persistence. The authors determined that initially identifiable characteristics of reactivity are persistent features of the child's behavior throughout the first 2 years of life. The category of adaptability showed an especially high level of interperiod correlation of stability.

In order to measure stability, the authors divided the data into five 6-month time periods and employed three different forms of statistical analysis. The stability of "preponderance ratings" for each of the 80 children in all nine categories through the first 2 years showed interperiod agreement to be statistically significant for each child with 35.8% of the preponderant ratings being identical in all five periods (versus chance of 1.2%). Seventy-eight of the 80 children maintained a statistically reliable rank pattern in four or more categories over the first 2 years.

The data were collected by means of parental interviews at 3-month intervals during the first year and at 6 months thereafter. The parents were questioned about concrete descriptive details, although the central concept of this group of investigators is "temperament," by which they mean a style of reaction rather than a specific kind of behavior or specific motives for behavior. The only category of temperament which did not show stability over time in this initial study was "activity."

Although later studies by this group (147), following up 136 children into the latency age, report that the originally noted characteristics of temperament of most children tended to persist into the latency years, the authors do not conclude that temperament is unchangeable. A factor analysis of the children's behavioral profiles yielded three general kinds of temperament. A first factor, which included 40% of the children, was described as "an easy group," characterized by positive mood, regularity in body functions, low to moderate intensity reaction, adaptability, and positive approach to new situations. Ten percent of the children formed a "difficult" group, characterized by irregular bodily functions, intensity of reaction, withdrawal in the face of new stimuli, slow adaptation, and negative mood. Fifteen percent of the children were included in a group that was "slow to warm up," characterized by low activity level, initial withdrawal to new stimuli, slow adaptation, somewhat negative mood, and low intensity of reaction. Thirty-five percent of the sample could not be classified into any of the three factors. Forty-two of the children showed behavior problems severe enough to require psychiatric attention, and about 75% of this group came from the "difficult" cluster, while only 18% came from the "easy group." The authors observed that different temperaments require different kinds of parental and educational handling. If a child's characteristics and his environment are in harmony, healthy development can be expected [cf. Escalona's concept of stable patterns of experience (32)]. In regard to adaptation, this study considers both the effects of adaptability as a characteristic of the child and the necessity for the parenting adults to adapt to the child's specific temperament.

Havighurst (54) reported that knowledge of a child's socioeconomic status is the best predictor of later behaviors and attributes including: IQ, level of education and occupation to be achieved, work attitudes, age at marriage, number of children, sexual behavior, and type of neurosis if any. Only during prenatal life and the first 6 months after birth is the predictive value of social class inconsequential. If, indeed, socioeconomic status does predict neonatal characteristics, the prediction is probably based on the superior nutrition and mental care afforded by higher status. Social class differences in social behavior by the age of 6 months were attributed to mother-infant interactions characteristic of different classes.

Somatic and psychological factors were also integrated in a series of studies on the effects of enriched or impoverished experiences on brain cell anatomical structure and chemistry of rats. Increases in number and size of synaptic junctions, in thickness of cerebral cortex, in activity of acetylcholinesterase, and in number of glial cells, were attributed to enriched environment for the first 4 to 10 weeks of life. These changes were not a function of increased handling, stress, or of hormonal variations (126–128). In a parallel set of studies, Sackett (130) was able to show that social responsiveness of monkeys was related to early social isolation, with males showing the effect to a greater extent than females. For humans, however, a study by Hertzig & Birch (58) suggests that a socially impoverished environment does not produce an inevitable and progressive decline in IQ. These investigators measured the IQs of 45 working class Puerto Ricans and 94 middle-class white boys and girls at age 3 and again at age 6. Both groups increased in IQ, with the white children increasing more. The issue of stability versus continuity remains unsettled by these studies.

Another follow-up study of intelligence (69) reported on 24 men and 24 women of the original standardization populations of the Stanford-Binet and WAIS tests. Test scores were available from 1931, 1941, 1956, and 1969 for the Stanford-Binet and from 1956 and 1969 for the WAIS. For both tests stability in adulthood was rather high (.77 and .73). Correlations from preschool age to adulthood were low (.41 and .39). The mean IQs continued to rise over the years 39 to 44, with those men who had initially higher levels continuing to gain the most. Women, on the other hand, who had the highest preadult IQs gained the least in the adult years, suggesting that bright women tend not to fulfill their intellectual potential, a finding consistent with that reported in Block (19).

Late Childhood

A report by Kagan (67) may help clarify the problem of stability, continuity, and change in personality development. He, like others, noted that behavior in the first 2 years of life is not a good predictor of later functioning in all environmental contexts. Kagan observed children in two Guatemalan Indian cultures and concluded that stimulus deprivation in early childhood resulted in only temporary cognitive lags; by preadolescence the children were demonstrating vigorous growth in cognitive skills. Thus, "separate maturational factors seem to set the time of emergence of basic functions, and experience can slow down or speed up that emergence by several months or three to four years, but nature will win in the end. The capacity for perceptual analysis, imitation, inference, language, deduction, symbolism, and memory will eventually appear in sturdy form." Whatever retardation deprivation produces is not as immutable as has been supposed. A parallel finding is the demonstration (141) that "depressed" monkeys—those reared in isolation and who show retarded and deviant social behavior—can be "cured" of their "depression" by being placed with younger female monkeys for a 26-week period. The forces of growth and maturation seem to have their own pace and momentum; the organism is not totally the product of a tyranny of environmental shocks, praises, reinforcements, and other contingencies.

Two interesting cross-sectional studies addressed themselves to the development of moral sense. One study involved 5000 children aged 10 to 14 from seven cultures, including U.S. blacks and whites, matched for socioeconomic status and sex and representing equal samples from each culture and grade level (143). The second study involved 115 American whites from kindergarten through the first year of college (144). The investigators report that notions of rules and laws are surprisingly similar across cultures. In six of seven cultures, the parents appear as the most powerful authorities, those able to make one follow a rule. The authors regard this finding as evidence that affiliative, nurturant strategies—prescriptive in nature—are more effective than punitive strategies—prohibitive—in inducing behavioral compliance. Tapp and Kohlberg described the children as progressing from a preconventional stage where rules are obeyed to a conventional stage where rules are maintained to a postconventional stage where rules are created. The modal stage for even the college youth was clearly conventional. These studies reflect an image of man that is less antisocial, uncontrolled, evil-spreading than generally conventional, rule-seeking, and social.

Block (17) reported a longitudinal study of development utilizing data originally gathered for two earlier studies of adolescence and childhood: the "Guidance Study," (84) and the "Oakland Growth Study" (65). Longitudinal data on these subjects continued to be accumulated, but there was no systematic attempt to organize, codify, and interpret them until Block's investigation. From these two studies 171 subjects returned for further intensive testing in adulthood. A variety of data was available through adolescence for both groups of subjects, including school grades, teacher reports, ratings of social behavior, interviews, IQ scores, Rorschach protocols, TAT protocols, subjective reports, peer reports, and newspaper clippings concerning the subjects. New follow-up data from adulthood was derived from interviews totaling an average of 12 hours each in which the subject's life, career, marriage, early life experiences, and family interactions were examined. Also administered, but kept separate from the later analysis, were the Rorschach, TAT, California Psychological Inventory, MMPI interview data with the spouse, free play ratings, early family ratings, and interviews with the subjects' mothers. All these data were not available for each subject, however, and Q-technique was used to evaluate the large mass of data. The task was to describe 171 adults as examined by a number of psychologists over a number of years including during their adolescence, and over about 3 days when they were in their 30s. Correlations between the composite Q-sorts at junior high school age, senior high school age, and at adulthood measured global personality change in the subjects. Mean correlations between junior high school and senior high school ages were .77 and .75 for males and females respectively. Between senior high school and adulthood they were .56 and .54 for males and females respectively. But the wide range of correlations indicates that a number of subjects changed a good deal while others remained relatively stable. The male "nonchangers" for both transition periods seem to be self-confident, quick, resourceful, and vigorous, in contrast to the "changers" who seem to be dependent, unsure of themselves, tense and guarded. For the females, however, this finding is reversed with the changers eager to chart their own destinies, competent and full of confidence. Yet even in the most extreme changers continuity is evident. From a factor analysis of the adult Q-sorts, Block derived six female and five male types, and then traced the subjects' lives back to the earlier years to come up with composite developmental profiles and types. As a general finding, by adulthood children fused the characteristics of their parents, favoring the more active parent. A child's maladjustment tended to be correlated with maladjustment of the opposite-sex parent rather than with that of the same-sex parent. Patterns of impulse control were related to the way in which the parents handled the child's impulsive behavior. Father seemed to be equally as important as mother in the child's character development. Low intelligence seemed to be more predictive of life outcome than was higher intelligence.

Jeanne Block studied socialization of sex roles in several samples of American children and of children from six Northern European countries (19). The results showed a surprising cross-national consistency in sex-role socialization. Little boys were encouraged to achieve and compete, to become independent, control their feelings and restrict expressions of emotion, to follow the masculine "agentic" ideal (6). Little girls were encouraged to develop and maintain close and interpersonal relationships, to talk about their troubles, to reflect upon life, and were given comfort and reassurance, to follow the feminine "communal" ideal (6).

Adolescence and Young Adulthood

A study by Block, Van der Lippe & Block (18) explored in some depth the interaction of high and low sex role with high and low socialization for men and women. High and low masculinity and femininity show marked differences when moderated by different levels of socialization. Each sex role, in western culture, has associated with it certain positive and negative qualities. Thus the female role implies conservation and nurturance, but also inhibition of impulse, submission, anxiety, and the capacity for guilt. The male role implies initiation and instrumentality, but also domination, aggression, impulsivity, and egocentrism. For men, socialization has a broadening effect in that it joins the allegedly masculine quality of competence and instrumentality to the allegedly feminine quality of interdependence. For women, on the other hand, socialization has a more restricting effect and necessitates the renunication of achievement and autonomy. Thus low feminine-low socialized women were actively assertive and engaged in cognitive pursuits. It appears that socialization allows men to reap the positive aspects of both sex roles and encourages the disavowal of negative masculine components. For women, on the other hand, socialization reinforces sex-role identification and denies them the positive masculine attributes.

An extended discussion of sex-role aspects of femininity appears in Bardwick's excellent text (7). She reviews and comments on studies of sex-role behaviors and arrives at conclusions similar to those of Block et al (18). Bardwick's concerns, however, range across issues of feminine identity, self-esteem, motivation for achievement, and motivational change.

In an empirical study of 1051 student radicals and conservatives and their parents, Block (20) sought to determine whether student protest was the result of unresolved oedipal conflicts, as suggested by Feuer (35) and Bettelheim (14), or the outcome of socialization patterns within families politically active and liberal, as suggested by Flacks (36), Keniston (70, 71), and Smith, Haan & Block (139). The data were collected in 1964 and in 1967 when student protest was considerably more prevalent than today. Many students held values similar to their parents' while rejecting societal values. Yet a significant number were both activists and held attitudes discordant with those of their parents. The authors concluded that student protest can stem from a variety of sources, including oedipal rebellion and congruent socialization patterns.

In 1965 Heath (55) attempted to validate a construct of maturity which involves five developmental lines: increased stability, integration, allocentrism, autonomy, and the availability of experiences to awareness. He examined the 10 most and 10 least mature juniors and seniors at Haverford College as selected by members of the faculty, administration, and student body. The subjects were interviewed and given tests including the Rorschach, TAT, Adjective Checklist, the author's own Self-Image Questionnaire, the California F-Scale, the Stroop Color-Word Test, and the MMPI. Predictions derived directly from Heath's model of maturing were generally confirmed by test results: mature men were shown to be significantly more stable, congruent, allocentric, and accurate in their self-image. Interview data generally supported the maturing construct, that is, immature men reported more incidents of parental emotional instability and tended to be more critical of their families, had fewer and less important achievements to report and described themselves in less positive and goal-oriented terms. Mature men surpassed the immature men in academic achievement although the two groups did not differ in intelligence. The mature men participated more fully in all phases of the extracurricular and athletic programs, appeared to have many more affectionate and close relationships, and made fewer visits to the infirmary. Of considerable interest is the finding that both the mature and the immature men experienced regressive periods of disorganization, and Heath concluded that effective adaptation does not preclude temporarily regressing to more autocentric modes of behavior. A more mature person can permit himself to become temporarily unstable, disintegrated, and autocentric if adaptation requires such regression [cf. Kris' concept of "regression in the service of the ego" (75), and Schafer's elaboration of that idea (133)]. In a later study, Heath (56) followed up the personality changes of the Haverford students over a period of several years to test his model of maturity in the developmental process, to study various types of maturing effects, and to explore in a longitudinal fashion the fate of the students. He judged that the most important maturational change in college was the progressive integration of students as influenced by their interpersonal relationships. A follow-up study found that the maturing effects of college persisted and sometimes was even more evident after graduation. The foremost change reported was the resolution of the "identity crisis" and stabilization of the self-concept around central determining and integrative values rather than around interpersonal relationships as predicted from the undergraduate data. Heath stresses the role of "supportive disorganization" in the development of mature values and intellective skills. Freshmen tend to become unstable and disorganized when first confromted with the new environment of college but they eventually become more stable and autonomous. Heath's studies, like Neugarten's formulations (see below), document development as a continuing process, taking place over a long time span, and not as a mere endogenous unfolding maturation. Personal relationships and experiences have powerful leveling and shaping effects. It is important to note, moreover, that the same environment that had a positive effect on the more mature students had a retarding effect on the immature sample.

Adulthood

Most studies of personality development consider adaptation and maturation from the early years up to early adulthood. Even as late as 1968, in a book devoted to the development of personality (78), the author devoted 9/10 of his book to the years from birth to young adulthood, thus giving only 1/10 of the space for the rest of the life cycle. Neugarten (102) commented, "One cannot help but wonder why we have had such a long prologue and first act, only to find that we have no play to watch. What happens in that period of life, that is—at least for most middle-class people—a great second act? And what happens in the third act, which the author himself describes as the climax of middle age? And is there—surely not—no movement in the final act . . ."

The central idea of a collection of papers devoted completely to parenthood (4), and strongly oriented toward psychoanalytic theory, is that the parental role is a changing one that follows an epigenetic sequence. Not only has the parental role evolved phylogenetically, but it continues to evolve for each parent in interaction with the growth of the child. Jessner, Weigert & Foy (63) examined women's conflicting motivations about pregnancy and the attitudes and unconscious fantasies that are experienced prior to the birth of the child. A number of transformations are observed, especially during the first pregnancy that correspond to the physiological changes of each trimester. A study of the effect of pregnancy on 29 husbands was undertaken by McCorkel (92), whose major interest was to define the nature of the crisis in becoming a father and the adaptive responses to it. He distinguished three groups of husbands: romantically oriented, career oriented, and family oriented. As with the expectant mother, the husband's attitudes changed during pregnancy, depending significantly on his dominant orientation toward marriage and pregnancy. Anthony (2) examined both normal and pathological parental responses to children in the oedipal phase. He observed that the great majority of parents are unaware of their involvement in their child's oedipal transition, though reactions may range from amused awareness to a revival of the oedipal crisis in the parent. Kestenberg (72) studied the effects on parents of having to share their latency-age child with the community. She states that in this transitional phase the child threatens the parents by making demands that they change their attitudes to suit his needs. A major measure of the parents' acceptance of their child's latency is their willingness to surrender the child to the teacher. The child's own widening social contacts also guides the parents' socialization. Anthony (3) proposed five contemporary stereotypic reactions of parents to adolescents: the adolescent as a dangerous and endangered object, as a sexual object, as an object of envy, as lost object, and as a maladjusted individual. He argues that the response of any parent to an adolescent may be dictated by three factors: a collective reaction based on stereotypes, an idiosyncratic reaction based on the personalities and the experiences involved, and a "transference" reaction based on pre-existing factors from an earlier stage of the parents' life.

According to Neugarten (104–108), in the middle and older years chronological age as a variable changes in significance. It is the use of one's experiences which prove to be significant markers in the development of adult personality functions: the ways one confronts work, love, time, and death; the changes in self-feeling as a function of marriage, parenthood, retirement, widowhood, and illness. Mere specification of chronological age in personality studies without reference to such intervening experiences and their mastery contributes little to the study of lives and is a poor predictor of life outcome. Thus Neugarten's explanation (103) for the ineffectiveness of long-range predictions from childhood or adolescence into adulthood rests on a failure to acknowledge the importance of such intervening variables as marriage, parenthood, job failure, or widowhood. The salient issues of childhood are no longer salient during adulthood, and it is inappropriate to predict vocational success from school success, adult pathology from childhood withdrawal, or adult attainment from early retardation.

Rosen & Neugarten (122) found that "ego energy" as measured by the TAT—and defined as the ability to integrate wide ranges of stimuli, to perceive and deal with complicated or conflictual situations, to perceive affects as important in life, and to be actively assertive—shows a decrease with increased age. Neugarten refers to this change as increased *interiority* (104). No relationships, however, were found between ego energy and sex or socioeconomic status. In a cross-cultural longitudinal study, Gutmann (50, and 105) confirmed his earlier finding that with increased age there is a trend—as measured by TAT stories—away from active realistic mastery styles to regressive, passive, and magical styles of dealing with conflict. This finding probably reflects an increasing difficulty to manage one's inner life and to think logically in old age.

Havighurst (53) noted that the psychological response to retirement depends on one's attitude toward work. Data indicate that retirement does not cause ill health, rather ill health is a critical factor in many decisions to retire. Busse (22) noted the serious impact on personality of the loss of hearing, a primary means of maintaining contact with environment: there is a tendency to become suspicious and paranoid. Misunderstanding by others of a partially deaf person's hesitation to respond can precipitate or speed major disruptions in interpersonal relations. Significant differences between the Rorschach protocols of older persons with and without hearing loss have been found. Busse also suggests that those who survive well in old age are self-centered individuals, less involved with other people and better able to accept the loss of a spouse or child.

EXOGENOUS FACTORS

Although personologists have considered culture, environment, and family atmosphere in personality growth and development, they have generally neglected a number of other exogenous factors such as nutrition and drugs.

The effects of chronic malnutrition can be seen in stunted growth and in developmental lags in intellectual functioning. Physically there is a relationship between chronic malnutrition and the reduction in number and size of brain cells, extent of myelinization, structural changes in the brain and spinal cord, and a number of pathological central nervous system lesions (15). In rhesus monkeys a protein-deficient diet produced behavioral deficits (158). Thus effects of malnutrition on personality development and functioning would seem to be considerable, although these effects have not been precisely catalogued as yet.

Public attention has recently focused on the use and abuse of pharmacologic agents, and scientific interest in the personality predispositions to drug abuse and the short- and long-term effects on personality functioning of a number of these substances has also increased.

Predispositions

ALCOHOL The most familiar toxic substance abused by man is alcohol. There is wide agreement that young people—adolescents—are introduced to alcoholic beverages in their own homes (87) and that adolescent problem drinkers come from homes in which one or both of the parents are heavy drinkers (49). Peer experiences also influence the development of drinking patterns (64). Of considerable importance as well are religious sanctions—proscription or prescription—concerning drinking. Jewish customs prescribe consumption of alcohol and indeed regulate its intake even to the extent of prescribing periods of excess, thus controlling its intake. In Protestant usage alcohol is either forbidden or unregulated and thus uncontrolled. It is therefore understandable that studies have shown that heavy drinkers among young adults or adolescents come from homes in which the parents are heavy drinkers, have friends who drink heavily, and either have weak religious affiliations or belong to a religious group that proscribes drinking.

There have been many attempts to describe the personality qualities of heavy drinkers. The clinical literature has emphasized qualities of the "essential alcoholic" which include "low anxiety tolerance, generalized avoidant tendencies, egocentricity, weak introspection, and demanding, dependent relations" (132). Only a few studies of this pattern have yielded findings statistically valid. Williams (156), on the basis of an adjective checklist, described the male college student heavy drinker as anxious, impulsive, aggressive, with little concern for others and with a low opinion of himself. Competence and achievement are generally lower in the adolescent drinker than in the abstainer. Jones (66) reports a similar constellation for female students who are heavy drinkers. McClelland (91), using the TAT, concluded that the young alcohol abuser is highly concerned with his sense of potency and that drinking seems to increase the subjective feeling of power. Mogar et al (98) studied 101 male and 100 female alcoholic patients using the MMPI. The authors identified five distinct types among the female sample (normal manic, normal depressive, hysterical, psychopathic, and passive-aggressive) and six distinct types among the male sample (passive-aggressive, depressive, compulsive, schizoid, prepsychotic, and passive-dependent). Each type, the authors conclude, needs different therapeutic intervention.

NARCOTIC DRUGS Most studies report that the users of heavy narcotics such as heroin come from broken families (123, 149) and are members of ethnic minorities (13, 25, 149), living in a densely populated urban area with significant impoverishment and disorganization in the environment. Personality correlates of narcotic abusers include immaturity, low frustration tolerance, a tendency to avoid anxiety rather than to cope actively with frustration, superficial interpersonal relationships, and a lack of clear goals and healthy resources (43, 76, 118), qualities which clinicians have recognized on the basis of less systematic observations. Recent studies have proposed a contagious disease model for the spread of some narcotic addictions such as heroin use (62). Such a model would require alignment with the findings about specific personality predispositions to addiction. It may be that contagion is of greater importance in certain highly disorganized areas of the inner city, while in less deprived sections of a metropolis personality disposition is a principal determinant.

Farnsworth (34) distinguished between students who are curious about drugs, experiment with them, and then abandon them, and those who are seeking to solve their problems with drugs. The latter group is characterized by feelings of inadequacy, disillusionment, and fear of intimacy. Freedman (39) also suggests that many of these drugs offer "a lure from the acquisition of competence," a way of shortcircuiting personal growth and avoiding confronting the complexity of reality. Hinckley et al (60) studied 451 students attending a university psychiatric facility and, using the MMPI, compared a number of characteristics of drug users and nonusers. Drug users came predominantly from the college of liberal arts and the graduate school. Students with active religious affiliations had a lower percentage of use. Thirty-seven percent of the students rating their mental health as poor were users. The users tended to be nonconformists with antisocial feelings and barely suppressed feelings of anger. Robbins et al (120) reported that drug users at two colleges described themselves as moody and unhappy.

BARBITURATES Anumonye (5) studied 20 barbiturate-dependent subjects and 20 nondrug-dependent controls. Self-administered questionnaires, psychological tests, structured interviews, and an examination of case records show that the addict group was psychiatrically ill in ways similar to the control group, with a common personality type and no definable psychological characteristics which would distinguish the addicts from the nonaddicts.

MARIHUANA Brill et al (21) report that greater use of marihuana is related to higher scores on stimulus-seeking scales and the psychopathic deviate scale of the MMPI. More males than females report daily use. While users of marihuana manifest greater psychopathology than do nonusers, those who used marihuana as well as other drugs show even more impairment (51, 52). Yet with marihuana smoking increasing, it is not clear whether these trends will persist.

PSYCHOTOMIMETIC AND ANALEPTIC DRUGS McGlothlin & Arnold (93) reported the result of a 10-year follow-up study of 247 persons who had taken LSD in either a therapeutic or experimental setting. They were reinterviewed 10 years later, and comparisons were made between subjects who used LSD only under the direction of a therapist or experimenter and those who had continued to use LSD on their own. The authors concluded that LSD attracts persons who have a tendency to experience naturally occurring mind-alerting experiences and to value intuition and a casual, spontaneous style of life. Smart & Fejer (138) concluded that among the users of LSD, behavior disorders and psychoses were more frequent than would be expected by chance. There were strong indications, however, that much of the psychopathology predated the use of LSD. The LSD users were also underachievers, though their IQs and ages were similar to those of the nonusers. Welpton (151) studied 10 chronic LSD users by means of psychiatric interviews and psychological tests. Eight subjects also had extensive experience with amphetamines. The author concluded that the subjects used LSD to relieve their chronic despair and to find some meaning in life. They hoped to be open to all sensations, to find what was true and genuine in life, to be more aware of things around them, and to become more creative. By temporarily breaking down self-object boundaries with the drug, they sought to achieve intense intimacy with others. Their use of LSD supplied a group identity, made them feel cared about, and also provided a purpose to life: to proselytize for psychedelic experience. A significant characteristic of the users of hallucinogenics is their clannishness and cultist behavior. Another investigator found that the personality dispositions of these users include poor modulation of hostility, intropunitiveness, low self-confidence, excessive passivity, and poor cognitive organization (38, 40).

Bell (9) obtained histories from 34 of a group of 40 amphetamine addicts and determined that one or both of two classes of stressful events preceded the addictions: the rejection by or separation from a person on whom the patient was emotionally dependent, and a transition to a more demanding adult role (independence, heterosexual intercourse, marriage, parenthood). The addicts themselves, however, denied the importance of these events. The population of users and abusers of psychotomimetic drugs in contrast to the users of narcotics is predominantly middle and upper-middle class (52, 73). A high proportion of users have had parent losses early in life (44). One study reports that in the families of high users there is a prevalent atmosphere of emotional instability, with inadequate setting of limits on children, poor tolerance for anger, and generally unempathic relationships among family members (73).

In a study of the relationship between personality and addiction, Chein (26) concluded that neither maladjustment nor personality structure per se is sufficient to account for addiction. Two other sets of determinants are involved: influences of social climate, attitudes, values, stresses, and gratification current in the community. Addiction is most probable if the use of opiate drugs is adaptive, functional, or ego syntonic. These changes operate at four levels within the individual: the level of conscious experience, of certain defenses, of unconscious processes, and of psychophysiological reactions.

Acute Effects of Drug Ingestion

There are numerous reports that narcotic, stimulant and hallucinogenic drugs inhibit productivity, creativity, and meaningful interpersonal relationships. Once vulnerable students begin taking such drugs, their entire lives revolve around them (34). Barbiturate intoxication dedifferentiates mental structure and has significant effects on memory. Six normal subjects were trained on a series of tasks involving different aspects of memory and attention and their individual sensitivity to secobarbital was determined. They were tested at several levels of the drug on a double-blind basis, and replicable dose-response curves were produced. When the test demand was great, even high doses had no apparent effect. When the demand load was moderate or mild, a dose-related drug effect was obtained. One investigator proposed that barbiturate addiction is far more destructive to personality structure than is opiate addiction (77).

MARIHUANA The studies of marihuana thus far are limited to acute effects, and the results are not as consistent as are those dealing with the narcotics, the barbiturates, and the psychotomimetic drugs. Brill et al (21) report that marihuana is considerably safer than alcohol or barbiturates. It causes no physical dependence or tolerance, although it may produce psychic dependence and habituation. Some clinical studies, using an average of 2 grams of marihuana containing one percent delta-9-tetrahydrocannabinol (THC) found little if any impairment on simple psychological and perceptual-motor tests. Renault et al (117), however, in a study of the development of tolerance to marihuana, reported a dose-response effect on heart rate and a decrement in time estimation, although there was some improvement in performance over time. After repeated administration, five of seven subjects believed incorrectly that the potency of the drug increased over time, providing some evidence of an accumulation effect. Some toxicity was evident in four of the subjects who complained of perceptual distortions and a tendency toward disorientation and confusion. One subject underwent a psychotic reaction and became confused about his identity. The level of toxicity seems to have been related both to dosage and emotional susceptibility, for the subjects receiving the strongest dosage (2.8% THC twice a day), and the one subject with a history of depression "were those who displayed the most abnormal behavior." Marihuana, however, displays no clinically obvious withdrawal symptoms, and all drug effects were reversed immediately with a return to placebo.

LSD A study of 30 experimental subjects and 20 controls had subjects perform a variety of psychological tasks while under LSD and placebo. Typical LSD effects included difficulty in thinking and in controlling thoughts, especially in directing attention, loss of control over emotions and behavior, a feeling of numbness in the body, nausea, perceptual changes in size, shape, weight and proportions of the body image, loss of contact between self and environment, and difficulty in speaking. Generalized slowing up appears to be one of the reliable effects of the drug (8).

AMPHETAMINES Cox & Smart (28) report that the acute effects of amphetamine ingestion are rapidly felt. The subjective experiences include an initial sharp arousal of intense pleasure and immediate physiological changes in blood pressure, pulse, and pupil size, and blurred vision. Symptoms such as insomnia, appetite loss, micturition difficulties, thirst, and increased energy are accompanied by heightened activity and alertness and a feeling of euphoria. These writers report that chronic ingestion of amphetamines can lead to memory impairment, severe gastrointestinal symptoms, lethargy, depression, and paranoid psychosis. Griffith & Oates (48) administered 10 mg of amphetamine every 4 hours to four healthy male volunteers for as long as the subjects could tolerate that amount. All developed a brief paranoid psychosis within 5 days, and one subject developed a psychotic reaction within 24 hours. Euphoria was a common response to early administration but disappeared when the cumulative dose reached 50 mg. A 1972 study (47) attempted to replicate this finding by eliminating possible confounding variables such as prolonged sleep deprivation, combined drug effects, or latent psychosis. Nine adult male volunteers with previous high-dose amphetamine experience were used. Psychological testing showed no indication of borderline psychosis, schizoid personality, or organic brain damage, but some sociopathic tendencies were noted. A 6-week drug-free hospitalization and a one-week control period preceded the intravenous administration of 10 mg of dextro-amphetamine sulfate (D-amphetamine is 10 times more potent than L-amphetamine) and subsequent hourly oral doses of 5 to 10 mg when they could be tolerated. Four subjects were kept on the drug until a clearly defined psychosis was observed. One of the two subjects who received the 5 mg hourly doses experienced a brief paranoid reaction. Of three subjects withdrawn from the drug during the prepsychotic phase, one subject nevertheless developed an acute psychotic reaction. As in the 1968 study, all subjects appeared depressed when the cumulative dose exceeded 50 mg. Paranoid delusions were common in all subjects developing a psychosis, but there was no evidence of auditory or visual hallucinations. Psychotic behavior ceased when the drug was discontinued, in most cases within 8 hours, although in one case suspiciousness persisted for several days. Ellinwood (31) reported similar symptoms including hypersexuality and visual illusions.

PHENCYCLIDINE Meltzer et al (96) reported that phencyclidine (Sernyl) produced in all subjects a proprioceptive disturbance, followed by a disorder in thinking like that seen in schizophrenic psychoses, thus confirming an observation made by Luby et al (83). Neither the thought disorder nor the observed rise in plasma creatine phosphokinase (a muscle enzyme reported increased in acute psychoses) in some of the subjects was observed in the toxic conditions resulting from other drugs such as amphetamines.

MALNUTRITION The lack of critical nutritional substances has been shown to have profound effects on personality and behavior. Birch & Gussow (15) reported that the single most common behavioral finding in malnourished children is apathy, accompanied by irritability. The child's ability to respond appropriately to significant stimuli in his environment is reduced during the period of chronic malnutrition, and continued malnutrition is accompanied by progressive behavioral regression.

Individual Differences in Response to Drugs

Most investigators report differential responsiveness to drugs. Anderson (1) noted marked variation in the ability of different individuals to develop tolerance to barbiturates. Renault et al (117) reported marked individual variations in subjects' response to marihuana. The most extensive controlled investigation of individual responsiveness to drug use, however, has been the study by Barr et al (8), which demonstrated that each person reacted in ways that were highly congruent with an independent assessment of his defenses, coping resources, cognitive styles, and other aspects of personality structure. Changes occurring under drug intoxication state were related to personality dispositions in the predrug state. The subjective reports and statistical analysis of behavioral and psychological test data distinguished several patterns of personality organization and associated drug response. The descriptions of these patterns are full, rich, informative, and represent a model for integrating objective test data with clinical material. Another team of investigators (95) noted that subjects who placed strong emphasis on structure and control, used extremes for self-description, had high scores on scales of severity of judgment and dogmatism, and high scores on the active-aggression and achievement-competition scales of the TAT, and who had high GSR tended to respond minimally to an LSD experience. On the other hand, subjects who scored high on a hypnotic susceptibility test, preferred an unstructured life style, and displayed greater esthetic sensitivity, imaginativeness, passivity, and noncompetitiveness, responded most intensely to LSD. The latter group also tended to report more enduring effects. Widrow (155) also reported that LSD effects are determined by pre-existing character structure, personality state, and circumstances associated with drug taking. Ellinwood (30) observed that although there is a dose-response relationship with amphetamine, amphetamine psychosis occurred more often in schizoid than in antisocial subjects.

There seems little doubt that the effects of drugs is a complex interaction between the pharmacological activity of the drug, the dosage, the physical stamina, and personality characteristics of the subject, and the situation in which the drug is taken.

Long-Term Effects of Drugs and Malnutrition

No scientific studies have reported on long-term effects of marihuana or hashish (e.g. 145), although there are anecdotal reports of personality changes occurring with chronic marihuana use (21). Indeed, the aggregate of evidence overwhelmingly suggests that just as excessive, long-term use of alcohol has deleterious physical, social, and psychological effects, so might marihuana (and any other drug). To extend the comparison, marihuana seems to be no more eroding of personality stability than is the temperate or occasional use of alcohol (159). Yet the effects of long-term heavy use have not been sufficiently studied so that antecedent and consequent factors can be clearly distinguished. But the subtle behavioral effects of marihuana intoxication moved Freedman (39) to comment, pending further study of chronic use:

> Marihuana does produce a disinhibition which can affect motor skill and judgment. A person high on marihuana does not, however, show ataxia; this means he does not signal others about his potentially poor judgment . . . Nor does marihuana signal the user with gastritis, nausea, and hangover to restrain his input . . . Accordingly, daily trips—escapes from reality—*could* readily occur as a habit leading to disregard for reality.

Barr et al (8) report no lasting effects, either positive or negative, from their experiment with LSD. The most systematic follow-up study of drug use is that of McGlothlin et al (95). Of 72 male graduate students who were followed up at 6 months, 24 had received 200 micrograms of LSD in each of three sessions. Fifty-eight percent of the experimental group subjectively reported some lasting effects after 6 months. This was consistent with a finding that in that group GSR in response to stress situations dropped. However, psychological changes were not impressive. Since the subjects who reacted most strongly to the drug experience were also those who were most likely to report enduring effects, it is difficult to separate motivation to change from enduring drug effects. Another study (94) found evidence of minimal brain damage in heavy LSD users. Significant impairment on the Halstead Category Test followed heavy ingestion of LSD, although clinical examination did not reveal significant signs of organic impairment. In this study also it was not possible to separate antecedent from consequent conditions, nor was it possible to separate the effect of a persisting toxic effect from a more enduring chronic brain syndrome. In McGlothlin & Arnold's 1971 study (93), the majority of those subjects who took LSD under medical advice felt that their LSD experience had resulted in some lasting effects, but the proportion reporting change on individual variables over time did not exceed that of the control group. Those who continued to take LSD without medical advice, in comparison to the control group, demonstrated large and consistent differences on subjective and objective measures, a finding that suggests that LSD does not so much produce change as attract a particular kind of person—evidence again for a significant interaction of drug effects and motivation.

OTHER EXOGENOUS FACTORS

The measurement of aggressive behavior and aggressive inhibitory tendencies, described in a set of experiments by Olweus, took account of the social context, personality of the aggressor, and stimulus conditions (109). The author devised an "aggression inventory" which may be found useful by personologists. Holzman &

Rousey (61) demonstrated that preventing a person from hearing his own voice while he speaks has a disinhibiting effect, particularly in those people who manifest a leveling-repressive cognitive-control disposition. Their experiment suggested that different personality structures require a different quality and quantity of stimulus input for smooth development and functioning, a "psychoecology of everyday life," as it were.

THE HIGH-RISK METHOD

The persistence of strong circumstantial evidence for the genetic transmission of a vulnerability to many forms of psychopathology (46, 59, 124, 125) has stimulated the use of the "high-risk" method of research. This method seeks first to identify those who are assumed to be vulnerable to a disease, disposition, or defect, and then to observe which ones of this population actually develop the pathology. Measures taken prior to the manifest appearance of the pathology, and which distinguish those who do and do not succumb, can yield important information on the nature of vulnerability. Garmezy (42) has succinctly described several strategies for selecting subjects for vulnerability research: genetic (on the basis of a parent's history of disease), psychogenic (on the basis of manifest symptomatology already present in the child), sociogenic (on the basis of presumed noxious social conditions), and early neglect (e.g. birth complications, nutritional defects). The mere presence of a mentally ill parent in the home has pathogenic effects on the child. Whether this vulnerability is a function of genetic or family-interaction factors or interactions of both is a question posed but not definitively answered by a study of 253 families with 652 children. The authors (119) reported that the mental illness of mothers has more of an effect on children than does the mental illness of fathers. Preschool children escaped the effect of the ill parents more easily than did older children. In children of patients hospitalized with tuberculosis there was virtually no serious upset. High-risk methods will be used increasingly and will become major tools in personality and psychopathology research. Their effective use, however, depends upon the observation of meaningful variables.

NEW TEXTS

A number of new personality textbooks appeared in 1972. Maddi's *Personality Theories* (85) has been revised with expanded treatments of Angyal, Murray, Maslow, and McClelland. Maddi & Costa (86) have written an illuminating source book on Allport, Maslow, and Murray as representatives of a "humanistic" tradition in personality theory. B. Weiner (150) has contributed a thoughtful treatment of motivation. It is indeed more than a text on motivation and can vie for a place in personality courses. Wenar's (152) book views personality from a developmental vantage point and gives strong emphasis to the early years. Rotter, Chance & Phares (129) have written a text emphasizing the social learning view associated with Rotter. It contains copious experimental applications of the "internalizer-externalizer" typology. A small but meaty text on personality theorists—particularly role theorists—is that by Heine (57). L. Rappoport (114) has offered an interesting developmental personality text which spans the life cycle although it devotes only 17% of its pages to the years after 25. Razran (116), by expanding his classic paper on Soviet psychophysiology (115), provides us with a valuable key to the literature emerging from the post-Pavlovians. A major test by Cattell (24) gives the reader an in-depth survey of the psychology of abilities and general intelligence from a physiological, phylogenetic, and ontogenetic view, with explanatory psychometric schemata.

CONCLUSION

Resolution of prominent issues in personality studies requires methods adapted to the problems. Changes, development, emergence, stability—these are some of the areas whose elucidation is limited by cross-sectional studies. Until recently, however, the shortcomings of longitudinal techniques have hindered use of prospective studies. New developments in method—perhaps incorporating the suggestions of Bell (11) and of Schaie & Strother (135) to combine cross-sectional studies with scheduled reappraisals to yield information about age-related changes—no doubt will spur increased usage of longitudinal techniques in the near future. More personologists may show a willingness to grapple with the complexities of longitudinal methods rather than content themselves with neat but time- and significance-limited reports. Separation of antecedent from consequent events, the understanding of effects of environmental contingencies, and of adventitious and self-administered endogenous factors, await the wider adoption of the longitudinal view of persons. Some speculative statements about man as free agent may not be sustained by the new data. It might well turn out that environmental factors will affect different persons differently, depending upon their genic endowment, constitutional factors, the meaning of particular adventitious factors to them, their coping and defensive repertoire, and the social context to which they adapt.

Literature Cited

1. Anderson, G. 1969. Sedative abuse. In *Drug Addiction and Drug Abuse,* ed. R. Feldman. Boulder, Colo.: Wiche
2. Anthony, E. J. 1970. The reactions of parents to the oedipal child. See Ref. 4, 275–88
3. Ibid. The reactions of parents to adolescents and to their behavior, 307–24
4. Anthony, E. J., Benedek, T., Eds. 1970. *Parenthood: Its Psychology and Psychopathology.* Boston: Little, Brown
5. Anumonye, A. 1970. Personality factors and barbiturate dependence. *Brit. J. Addict.* 64:365–70
6. Bakan, D. 1966. *The Duality of Human Existence.* Chicago: Rand McNally
7. Bardwick, J. M. 1971. *Psychology of Women: A Study of Bio-cultural Conflicts.* New York: Harper & Row
8. Barr, H., Langs, R., Holt, R. R., Goldberger, L., Klein, G. S. 1972. *LSD: Personality and Experience.* New York: Wiley
9. Bell, D. S. 1971. The precipitants of amphetamine addiction. *Brit. J. Psychiat.* 119:171–77
10. Bell, R. Q. 1953. Convergence: An accelerated longitudinal approach. *Child Develop.* 24:145–52
11. Ibid 1954. An experimental test of the accelerated longitudinal approach. 25: 281–86
12. Bell, R. Q. 1959. Retrospective and prospective views of early personality development. *Merrill-Palmer Quart. Behav. Develop.* 6:131–44
13. Bender, L. 1963. Drug addiction in adolescence. *Comp. Psychiat.* 4:131–34
14. Bettelheim, B. 1969. Obsolete youth. *Encounter* 23:29–42
15. Birch, H. G., Gussow, J. D. 1970. *Disadvantaged Children—Health, Nutri-*

tion, and School Failure. New York: Harcourt, Brace & World
16. Block, J. 1968. Some reasons for the apparent inconsistency of personality. *Psychol. Bull.* 70:210–12
17. Block, J. 1971. *Lives Through Time.* Berkeley, Calif.: Bancroft
18. Block, J., Van der Lippe, A., Block, J. H. Sex-role and socialization patterns: Some personality concomitants and environmental antecedents. In press
19. Block, J. H. 1972. *Conceptions of sex role: Some cross-cultural and longitudinal perspectives.* Presented at Bernard Moses Mem. Lect., Univ. California, Berkeley
20. Block, J. H. 1972. Generational continuity and discontinuity in the understanding of societal rejection. *J. Pers. Soc. Psychol.* 22:333–45
21. Brill, N. Q. et al 1970. The marihuana problem. *Ann. Intern. Med.* 73:449–65
22. Busse, E. W. 1960. Aging and personal relations. In *Aging: Some Social Biological Aspects,* ed. N. W. Shock, 225–34. Washington, D.C.: Am. Assoc. Advan. Sci.
23. Carson, R. C. 1969. *Interaction Concepts of Personality.* Chicago: Aldine
24. Cattell, R. B. 1971. *Abilities: Their Structure, Growth and Action.* Boston: Houghton-Mifflin
25. Chein, I. 1959. The status of sociological and social psychological knowledge concerning narcotics. In *Narcotic Drug Addiction Problems.* Washington, D.C.: U.S. Dep. HEW
26. Chein, I. 1964. *The Road to H: Narcotics, Delinquency, and Social Policy.* New York: Basic Books
27. Chein, I. 1972. *The Science of Behavior and the Image of Man.* New York: Basic Books
28. Cox, C., Smart, R. 1970. The nature and extent of speed use in North America. *J. Can. Med. Assoc.* 102:724–29
29. Dahlstrom, W. G. 1972. *Personality Systematics and the Problem of Types.* Morristown, N.J.: General Learning Press
30. Ellinwood, E. H. 1967. Amphetamine psychosis: I. Description of the individuals and process. *J. Nerv. Ment. Dis.* 144:273–83
31. Ellinwood, E. H. 1969. Amphetamine psychosis: II. Theoretical implications. *J. Psychedelic Drugs* 2:121–40
32. Escalona, S. K. 1968. *The Roots of Individuality.* Chicago: Aldine
33. Escalona, S. K. 1971. Impact of the mother's presence upon behavior: The first year. *Hum. Develop.* 14:2–15
34. Farnsworth, D. 1969. Drugs: Their use and abuse by college students. In *Psychiatry, Education, and the Young Adult.* Springfield, Ill.: Thomas
35. Feuer, L. 1969. *The Conflict of Generations: The Character and Significance of Student Movements.* New York: Basic Books
36. Flacks, R. 1967. The liberated generation: An exploration of the roots of student protest. *J. Soc. Issues* 23:52–75
37. Freedman, D. G. 1971. An evolutionary approach to research on the life cycle. *Hum. Develop.* 14:87–99
38. Freedman, D. X. 1968. On the use and abuse of LSD. *Arch. Gen. Psychiat.* 18:330–47
39. Freedman, D. X. 1969. Drug abuse: Comments on the current scene. In *Drugs and Youth,* ed. J. R. Wittenborn. Springfield: Thomas
40. Freedman, D. X. 1972. Non-pharmacological factors in drug dependence. In *Drug Abuse,* ed. S. Btesh. New York: Plenum
41. Gardner, R. W., Holzman, P. S., Klein, G. S., Linton, H., Spence, D. P. 1959. Cognitive control. *Psychol. Issues* 1: 1–186
42. Garmezy, N. 1972. Models of etiology for the study of children at risk for schizophrenia. In *Life History Research in Psychopathology,* Vol. 2, ed. M. Roff, L. N. Robins, M. Pollack. Minneapolis: Univ. Minnesota Press
43. Gilbert, J. G., Lombardi, D. N. 1967. Personality characteristics of young male narcotic addicts. *J. Consult. Psychol.* 31:536–38
44. Gillie, O. 1969. Drug addiction: Facts and folklore. *Sci. J.* 5A:75–80
45. Goldstein, K. 1939. *The Organism.* New York: American Book
46. Gottesman, I. I., Shields, J. 1972. *Schizophrenia and Genetics: A Twin Study Vantage Point* (with a contribution by Paul E. Meehl). New York: Academic
47. Griffith, J. D., Cavanaugh, J., Held, J., Oates, J. A. 1972. Dextroamphetamine: Evaluation of psychomimetic properties in man. *Arch. Gen. Psychiat.* 27:97–100
48. Griffith, J. D., Oates, J. A. 1968. Paranoid episodes induced by drug. *J. Am. Med. Assoc.* 205:39–46
49. Gusfield, J. 1970. The structural context of college drinking. See Ref. 87
50. Gutmann, D. L. 1964. An exploration of ego configurations in middle and later life. See Ref. 107, 114–48

51. Harmatz, J. S., Shader, R. I., Salzman, C. 1972. Marihuana users and nonusers. *Arch. Gen. Psychiat.* 26:108–12
52. Harris, E. M. 1971. Measurement of alienation in college students: Marihuana users and nonusers. *J. Sch. Health* 41:130–33
53. Havighurst, R. J. 1960. Work and retirement. See Ref. 22, 41–50
54. Havighurst, R. J. 1971. Social-class perspectives on the life cycle. *Hum. Develop.* 14:110–24
55. Heath, D. 1965. *Explorations in Maturity.* New York: Appleton-Century-Crofts
56. Heath, D. 1968. *Growing Up in College: Liberal Education and Maturity.* San Francisco: Jossey-Bass
57. Heine, P. J. 1971. *Personality in Social Theory.* Chicago: Aldine
58. Hertzig, M. E., Birch, H. G. 1971. Longitudinal course of measured intelligence in preschool children of different social and ethnic backgrounds. *Am. J. Orthopsychiat.* 41:416–26
59. Heston, L. L. 1966. Psychiatric disorders in foster-home reared children of schizophrenic mothers. *Brit. J. Psychiat.* 112:819–25
60. Hinckley, R. G. et al 1970. Nonmedical drug use among college student psychiatric patients. *J. Am. Coll. Health Assoc.* 18:333–41
61. Holzman, P. S., Rousey, C. 1971. Disinhibition of communicated thought: Generality and role of cognitive style. *J. Abnorm. Psychol.* 77:275–81
62. Hughes, P. H., Crawford, G. A. 1972. A contagious disease model for researching and intervening in heroin epidemics. *Arch. Gen. Psychiat.* 27:149–58
63. Jessner, L., Weigert, E., Foy, J. L. 1970. The development of parental attitudes during pregnancy. See Ref. 4, 209–44
64. Jessor, R., Collins, M. I., Jessor, S. L. 1972. On becoming a drinker: Social-psychological aspects of an adolescent transition. *Ann. NY Acad. Sci.* 197: 199–213
65. Jones, H. E. 1938. The California adolescent growth study. *J. Educ. Res.* 31:561–67
66. Jones, M. C. 1971. Personality antecedents and correlates of drinking patterns in women. *J. Consult. Clin. Psychol.* 36:61–69
67. Kagan, J. 1972. *Cross-cultural perspectives on early development.* Presented at Am. Assoc. Advan. Sci. Meet., Washington, D.C.
68. Kagan, J., Moss, H. A., Sigel, I. E. 1963. Psychological significance of styles of conceptualization. *Monogr. Soc. Res. Child Develop.* 28:73–112
69. Kangas, J., Bradway, K. 1971. Intelligence at middle age: A 38-year follow-up. *Develop. Psychol.* 5:333–37
70. Keniston, K. 1968. *Young Radicals: Notes on Committed Youth.* New York: Harcourt, Brace & World
71. Keniston, K. 1969. *The other end of the oedipus complex.* Presented at Am. Orthopsychiat. Assoc. Meet., New York
72. Kestenberg, J. S. 1970. The effect on parents of the child's transition into and out of latency. See Ref. 4, 289–306
73. Keuhn, J. L. 1970. Student drug user and his family. *J. Coll. Stud. Personnel* 11:404–13
74. Kohlberg, L. 1964. Development of moral character and moral ideology. In *Review of Child Development Research* ed. M. Hoffman, L. W. Hoffman, 1: 383–431. New York: Russell-Sage Found.
75. Kris, E. 1952. *Psychoanalytic Explorations in Art.* New York: Int. Univ. Press
76. Laskowitz, D. 1961. The adolescent drug addict: An Adlerian view. *J. Individ. Psychol.* 17:68–79
77. Laurie, P. 1967. *Drugs: Medical, Psychological and Social Facts.* Baltimore: Penguin
78. Lidz, T. 1968. *The Person.* New York: Basic Books
79. Loevinger, J. 1966. The meaning and measurement of ego development. *Am. Psychol.* 21:195–206
80. Loevinger, J. 1969. Theories of ego development. In *Clinical Cognitive Psychology,* ed. L. Breger. Englewood Cliffs, N.J.: Prentice Hall
81. Loevinger, J., Wessler, R. 1970. *Measuring Ego Development,* Vol. 1. San Francisco: Jossey-Bass
82. Loevinger, J., Wessler, R., Redmore, C. 1970. *Measuring Ego Development,* Vol. 2. San Francisco: Jossey-Bass
83. Luby, E. D., Cohen, B. D., Rosenbaum, G., Gottlieb, J. S., Kelley, R. 1959. Study of a new schizophrenomimetic drug—Sernyl. *Arch. Neurol. Psychiat.* 81:363–69
84. MacFarlane, J. W. 1938. Some findings from a 10-year guidance research program. *Progr. Educ.* 7:527–35
85. Maddi, S. 1972. *Personality Theories: A Comparative Analysis.* Homewood, Ill.: Dorsey
86. Maddi, S., Costa, P. T. 1972. *Humanism in Personology: Allport, Maslow & Murray.* Chicago: Aldine-Atherton
87. Maddox, G. L., Ed. 1970. Drinking prior to college. In *The Domesticated*

Drug: Drinking Among Collegians. New Haven: Coll. & Univ. Press
88. Maslow, A. H. 1968. *Toward a Psychology of Being.* Princeton: VanNostrand. 2nd ed.
89. May, R. 1972. *Power and Innocence: A Search for the Sources of Violence.* New York: Norton
90. McCall, R. B., Hogarty, P. S., Hurlburt, N. 1972. Transitions in infant sensorimotor development and the prediction of childhood I.Q. *Am. Psychol.* 27:728–48
91. McClelland, D. C. 1971. The power of positive drinking. *Psychol. Today* 4:40–41, 78–79
92. McCorkel, R. J. Jr. 1964. *Husbands and pregnancy: An exploratory study.* MA Thesis. Univ. of North Carolina
93. McGlothlin, W., Arnold, D. O. 1971. LSD revisited: A 10-year follow-up of medical LSD use. *Arch. Gen. Psychiat.* 24:35–49
94. McGlothlin, W., Arnold, D. O., Freedman, D. X. 1969. Organicity measures following repeated LSD ingestion. *Arch. Gen. Psychiat.* 21:704–9
95. McGlothlin, W., Cohen, S., McGlothlin, M. S. 1967. Long lasting effects of LSD on normals. *Arch. Gen. Psychiat.* 17:521–32
96. Meltzer, H. Y., Holzman, P. S., Hassan, S. Z., Guschwan, A. 1972. Effects of phencyclidine and stress on plasma creatine phosphokinase (CPK) and aldolase activities in man. *Psychopharmacologia* 26:44–53
97. Mischel, W. 1971. *Introduction to Personality.* New York: Holt, Rinehart & Winston
98. Mogar, R. E., Wilson, W. M., Helm, S. T. 1970. Personality subtypes of male and female alcoholic patients. *Int. J. Addict.* 5:99–113
99. Murphy, G. 1947. *Personality: A Biosocial Approach to Origin and Structure.* New York: Harper & Row
100. Murphy, L. B. 1964. Factors in continuity and change in the development of adaptational styles in children. *Vita Hum.* 7:96–114
101. Murphy, L. B. 1970. The problem of defense and the concept of coping. In *The Child in His Family,* ed. E. J. Anthony, Koupernik. New York: Wiley
102. Neugarten, B. L. 1969. A truncated view of the life cycle; review of Lidz, *The Person. Contemp. Psychol.* 14: 409–11
103. Neugarten, B. L. 1969. Continuities and discontinuities of psychological issues into adult life. *Hum. Develop.* 12: 121–30
104. Neugarten, B. L. 1970. Dynamics of transition of middle age to old age: Adaptation and the life cycle. *J. Geriat. Psychiat.* 4:71–87
105. Neugarten, B. L. Personality change in late life: A development perspective. In press
106. Neugarten, B. L., Ed. 1968. *Middle Age and Aging.* Univ. Chicago Press
107. Neugarten, B. L. et al, Eds. 1964. *Personality in Middle and Late Life.* New York: Atherton
108. Neugarten, B. L., Dowty, N. The middle years. In *American Handbook of Psychiatry,* Vol. 1, Part 3, ed. S. Arieti. In press
109. Olweus, D. 1972. *Personality in aggression.* Rep. No. 1, Inst. Psychol., Univ. Bergen, Norway
110. Piaget, J. 1956. The general problems of the psychobiological development of the child. In *Discussions on Child Development,* Vol. 4, ed. J. M. Tanner, B. Inhelder. New York: Int. Univ. Press
111. Piaget, J. 1963. *The Origins of Intelligence in Children.* New York: Norton
112. Pollin, W. 1972. The pathogenesis of schizophrenia. *Arch. Gen. Psychiat.* 27:29–39
113. Rapaport, D. 1967. The theory of attention cathexis. In *Collected Papers of David Rapaport,* ed. M. M. Gill. New York: Basic Books
114. Rappoport, L. 1972. *Personality Development: The Chronology of Experience.* Glenview, Ill.: Scott, Foresman
115. Razran, G. 1961. The observable unconscious and the inferable conscious in current Soviet psychophysiology: Intrioceptive conditioning, somantic conditioning, and the orienting reflex. *Psychol. Rev.* 68:81–147
116. Razran, G. 1971. *Mind in Evolution: An East-West Synthesis of Learned Behavior and Cognition.* Boston: Houghton-Mifflin
117. Renault, P. F. et al. Repeated administration of marihuana smoke to humans. In press
118. Rettig, S., Pasamanick, B. 1964. Subcultural identification of hospitalized male drug addicts: A further examination. *J. Nerv. Ment. Dis.* 139:83–86
119. Rice, E., Ekdahl, M. C., Miller, L. 1971. *Children of Mentally Ill Parents.* New York: Behavioral Publ.
120. Robbins, E., Robbins, L., Frosch, W. A., Stern, M. 1970. College student drug use. *Am. J. Psychiat.* 126:1743–51

121. Rogers, C. 1963. The actualizing tendency in relation to "motives" and to consciousness. In *Nebraska Symposium on Motivation,* ed. M. R. Jones, 1–24. Lincoln: Univ. Nebraska Press
122. Rosen, J. L., Neugarten, B. L. 1964. Ego functions in the middle and later years: A thematic apperception test study. See Ref. 107, 90–104
123. Rosenberg, C. M. 1968. Young drug addicts: Addiction and its consequences. *Med. J. Aust.* 1:1031–33
124. Rosenthal, D. 1971. *Genetics of Psychopathology.* New York: McGraw-Hill
125. Rosenthal, D. et al 1968. Schizophrenics' offspring reared in adoptive homes. In *The Transmission of Schizophrenia,* ed. D. Rosenthal, S. S. Kety, 377–91. Oxford: Pergamon
126. Rosenzweig, M. R. 1972. Brain changes in response to experience. *Sci. Am.* 2026:22–29
127. Rosenzweig, M. R., Bennett, E. L., Diamond, M. C. 1972. Cerebral effects of differential experience in hypophysectomized rats. *J. Comp. Physiol. Psychol.* 79:56–66
128. Rosenzweig, M. R., Mollgaard, K., Diamond, M. C., Bennett, E. L. 1972. Negative as well as positive synaptic changes may store memory. *Psychol. Rev.* 79:93–96
129. Rotter, J., Chance, J. E., Phares, E. J. 1972. *Applications of a Social Learning Theory of Personality.* New York: Holt, Rinehart & Winston
130. Sackett, G. P. 1972. Exploratory behavior of rhesus monkeys as a function of rearing experience and sex. *Develop. Psychol.* 6:260–70
131. Schachter, S., Singer, J. E. 1962. Cognitive, social, and physiological determinants of emotional state. *Psychol. Rev.* 69:379–99
132. Schafer, R. 1948. *Clinical Applications of Psychological Tests.* New York: Int. Univ. Press
133. Schafer, R. 1958. Regression in the service of the ego: The relevance of a psychoanalytic concept for personality assessment. In *Assessment of Human Motives,* ed. G. Lindzey, 119–48. New York: Holt, Rinehart & Winston
134. Schuster, C. R. 1972. The use of animal models for the study of drug abuse. In *Research Advances in Alcohol and Drug Problems,* Vol. 1, ed. R. J. Gibbins et al. New York: Wiley
135. Schaie, K. W., Strother, C. 1968. A cross-sequential study of age changes in cognitive behavior. *Psychol. Bull.* 70: 671–80
136. Sheldon, W. H., Stevens, S. S. 1942. *The Varieties of Temperament: A Psychology of Constitutional Differences.* New York: Harper
137. Skinner, B. F. 1971. *Beyond Freedom and Dignity.* New York: Bantam
138. Smart, R., Fejer, D. 1969. Illicit LSD users: Their social backgrounds, drug use and psychopathology. *J. Health Soc. Behav.* 10:297–308
139. Smith, M. B., Haan, N., Block, J. H. 1970. Social psychological aspects of student activism. *Youth & Society* 1: 261–88
140. Spielberger, C. D., Lushene, R. E., McAdoo, W. G. 1970. *Theory and measurement of anxiety states.* Florida State Univ. (Mimeo)
141. Suomi, S. J., Harlow, H. F. 1972. Social rehabilitation of isolate-reared monkeys. *Develop. Psychol.* 6:487–96
142. Tapp, J. The psychological limits of legality. In *The Limits of Law, Nomos XV,* ed. J. R. Pennock, J. W. Chapman. New York: Atherton. In press
143. Tapp, J., Levine, F. 1970. Persuasion to virtue: A preliminary statement. *Law & Soc. Rev.* 4:565–82
144. Tapp, J., Kohlberg, L. 1971. Developing senses of law and legal justice: Socialization, the law, and society. *J. Soc. Issues* 27:65–91
145. Tennant, F. S. Jr., Groesbeck, C. J. 1972. Psychiatric effects of hashish. *Arch. Gen. Psychiat.* 27:133–36
146. Thomas, A., Birch, H. G., Chess, S., Hertzig, M. E., Korn, S. 1963. *Behavioral Individuality in Early Childhood.* New York Univ. Press
147. Thomas, A., Chess, S., Birch H. G. 1970. The origin of personality. *Sci. Am.* 223:102–9
148. Tolman, E. C. 1949. *Purpose of Behavior in Animals and Men.* Berkeley: Univ. California Press (1932)
149. Vaillant, G. E. 1966. A 12-year follow-up of New York narcotic addicts and the natural history of a chronic disease. *New Engl. J. Med.* 275:1283–88
150. Weiner, B. 1972. *Theories of Motivation: From Mechanism to Cognition.* Chicago: Markham
151. Welpton, C. 1968. Psychodynamics of chronic lysergic acid diethylamide use. *J. Nerv. Ment. Dis.* 147:377–85
152. Wenar, C. 1971. *Personality Development from Infancy to Adulthood.* Boston: Houghton-Mifflin

153. White, R. W. 1959. Motivation reconsidered: The concept of competence. *Psychol. Rev.* 66:297–333
154. White, R. W. 1972. *The Enterprise of Living: Growth and Organization in Personality.* New York: Holt, Rinehart & Winston
155. Widroe, H. J. 1968. A treatment-oriented scheme of LSD-induced psychopathology. *Clin. Toxico.* 1:179–85
156. Williams, A. 1970. College problem drinkers: A personality profile. See Ref. 87
157. Witkin, H., Dyk, R. B., Faterson, H. F., Goodenough, D. R., Karp, S. A. 1962. *Psychological Differentiation.* New York: Wiley
158. Zimmerman, R. R., Sture, P. L., Strobel, D. A., Hom, H. L. 1972. Abnormal social development of protein-malnourished rhesus monkeys. *J. Abnorm. Psychol.* 80:125–31
159. *Marihuana: A signal of misunderstanding.* 1972. First rep. Nat. Comm. Marihuana and Drug Abuse. Washington, D.C.: GPO

BRAIN FUNCTION: Changing Ideas on the Role of Sensory, Motor, and Association Cortex in Behavior ❖218

R. B. Masterton and M. A. Berkley
Department of Psychology, Florida State University, Tallahassee

INTRODUCTION

The classical three-way subdivision of cerebral neocortex into sensory, motor, and association areas is the product of a convergence of experimental and clinical evidence over almost a century (cf. 203). However, in the last 20 years, evidence difficult to reconcile with this idea has begun to accumulate. For example, we now know that neural activity in sensory cortex does not just mirror receptor activity, nor is motor cortex the "keyboard of the mind." Furthermore, we know that association takes place both in animals with little or no association cortex and in animals in which the normal complement of association cortex has been surgically removed (e.g. 235, 236, 333, 334).

Because of these obvious difficulties with the classical view, it seemed worthwhile to review the main lines of inquiry that have tended to demand a more sophisticated view of the contribution of the various areas of cerebral neocortex. However, to provide a format that is easy to follow, we have retained the classical distinctions as the basis for subdividing the review itself. Therefore, there are six main sections dealing respectively with visual, auditory, and somatosensory cortex, motor cortex, and finally posterior and frontal association cortex. Each of these sections has been further divided along methodological lines (i.e. anatomy, physiology, and behavior).

VISUAL CORTEX

Research on visual cortex has always played a dominant part in theories of the role of cortical sensory areas, and certainly the recent past is no exception. Along with the invention of new techniques, this dominance has brought about a virtual explosion of research on visual cortex ranging from its anatomy and physiology through ablation-behavior experiments. Specific reviews of this vast literature can be found in Bishop (27) and in Weiskrantz & Cowey (425).

Anatomy

The cat and the monkey continue to be the most popular animals for anatomical investigations of "visual cortex." In the cat, Otsuka & Hassler (306) have delineated the major cortical areas related to vision on cytoarchitectonic grounds, and have, in addition, related these areas to the varied fissural patterns found in cat brains. A more recent study by Sanides & Hoffmann (353) has confirmed previous descriptions and added some new details regarding subdivisions within visual and visually related cortex. These two studies provide the current anatomical touchstones for electrophysiologists and behaviorists working with cats. Relatively little recent work along these lines has been done on the already well-studied monkey striate cortex.

A number of other animals [the tree shrew (95), hedgehog (214), and grey squirrel (167, 215)] have now been examined to determine the locus of the visual cortex on the basis of cytoarchitecture. In general, these studies have found that the largest area of representation is for the binocular visual field and that anatomical boundaries and functional boundaries (as derived from electrophysiological mapping experiments) coincide very well (167, 214).

Classical descriptions of the thalamic projections to cortex have held that the cortical target area of the dorsal lateral geniculate (*DGL*) is exclusively striate cortex (321). While no evidence to the contrary has thus far developed for primates, a number of investigators have described extrastriate projections from DGL in the cat (23, 44, 125, 137, 293). Although past studies had suggested that area 19 and a lateral suprasylvian area also received DGL projections (124, 137), recent studies by Burrows & Hayhow (44) have shown that these projections are limited to areas 17 and 18.

Since the knowledge of the evolutionary development of the geniculostriate system can be expected to reveal some wide ranging organizational principles of the visual system, several investigators have studied the thalamocortical projections in the visual system in such animals as the guinea pig (77), grey squirrel (215), tree shrew (95), opossum (17–19), platypus (62), and echidna (61). These studies have shown a remarkable consistency in the retino-geniculo-cortical scheme. Thus, the cat continues to be the only animal in which an enigmatic extrastriate geniculate projection has been identified.

The observation of an anomaly found in the DGL of the Siamese cat (162) has led to a number of investigations demonstrating that the projection from the eye to lateral geniculate nucleus is also abnormal in this animal. As will be discussed in a later section, this abnormality is also reflected in the projections to visual cortex.

Beyond the geniculocortical projections, an entirely new picture is emerging regarding visual projections to cortex. A number of investigators have shown that the pulvinar and lateralis posterior nuclei of the thalamus project extensively to a belt of cortex surrounding striate cortex (95, 153, 175, 290). These thalamic nuclei receive their visual input from the tectum (95, 153). Thus, there seem to be at least two pathways from eye to cortex, one from retina to geniculate to cortex and the other from retina to tectum to posterior thalamus to cortex. The consequences of these new anatomical findings are already being felt in the interpretation of ablation-behavior experiments and may provide the key to understanding the mechanisms underlying residual vision in animals in which area 17 has been completely ablated.

Although a number of workers have searched for extrageniculate input to the striate cortex, only one study reports such an input (19). At the time of this review, except for the cat (44) and the opossum (19), no anatomical studies have reported a thalamic input to striate cortex other than from the lateral geniculate.

Application of the new silver stains continues to reveal details of neuronal organization that are producing reevaluations of electrophysiological and behavioral studies. Special attention is being paid to the laminar distribution of inputs (18, 67, 194, 213, 231) and the internal connections within cortex (357).

In a further effort to characterize "visual cortex," recent anatomical studies have also been focused on the distribution of efferents from striate cortex. It has been shown that fibers originating in the superficial three layers of cortex project downward to terminate in cortical layer 5 (377) and also in the adjacent area 18 (376, 404). Deeper layers in area 17 project to the superior temporal sulcus and the pulvinar nucleus of the thalamus. Another subcortical target of obvious significance is the tectum, which receives afferents from areas 17 and 18 in the cat. There is evidence that area 18, in addition to sending fibers across the corpus callosum (195) and to tectum (129), also sends a small bundle of fibers to the pons (138). In the cat, area 17 sends efferents to 18, 18 back to 17, and both areas to the Bishop-Clare area and to area 19 (124, 443). Several studies report species differences in the cortical recipient zone of efferents from area 17 (376, 461). Thus, in Rhesus monkeys, areas 18 and 19 receive area 17 input while in Saimiri only area 18 receives such input (376).

Considerable interest has been shown in the projections of striate cortex to the thalamus as a possible feedback pathway (130, 173, 183, 184, 291, 292), especially since there is scant evidence for an efferent pathway to retina in mammals. Although it first appeared that only area 18 projected to the lateral geniculate nucleus (183), autoradiographic methods have now confirmed an efferent projection from area 17 to the lateral geniculate in the cat (184, 291).

Physiology

Mapping of the visual world onto visual cortex in various animals has continued and now includes, for example, the hedgehog (165) and tree shrew (216). Since the cytoarchitectonic borders of area 17 have been found to coincide closely with the borders of the visual fields determined electrophysiologically in these animals as well as others (167, 214, 216), it now appears that the anatomical borders of area 17 can be used as a guide to determine the extent of the field projection, and conversely, that the visual field map determined by electrophysiological methods can be used to delineate the extent of striate cortex.

The investigation of response characteristics in single neurons of visual cortex continues unabated (e.g. 64, 255, 297, 380, 382). In addition to making some modifications of Hubel & Wiesel's (188) classification scheme (e.g. simple, complex, hypercomplex), numerous investigators have been making quantitative measurements of still other properties of single units (28, 255, 297). For example, Bishop and his colleagues (28, 177) in a series of papers have manipulated such parameters as the velocity of the stimulus, and the size, the orientation, and the extent of binocular input. Among the significant contributions made by this group is the introduction of a new technique called the "activated discharge" method (27). While the technique utilizes existing technology and some old ideas in neurophysiology, it has proved a valuable method in revealing new properties of cortical neurons. The activated discharge is produced by continuously stimulating a cell through one eye and attempting to influence it by another eye. This method has succeeded in demonstrating inhibitory inputs even in single units that have little or no spontaneous activity and thus, has revealed that a much greater percentage of cortical cells are binocular than was once thought on the basis of stimulation of each eye alone (177).

Many of the cells respond in a very specific way to binocular input. Several investigators (e.g. 9) have described cells in striate cortex of the cat that give a maximal response when the two monocular receptive fields are in correspondence. Furthermore, it was found that some receptive fields are in correspondence even though they are slightly disparate on each retina. These results provide a firm neurophysiological substrate for stereopsis, e.g. depth perception through the use of retinal disparity (9, 27, 30, 318).

The evidence for columnar organization in visual cortex derived from electrophysiological studies continues to accumulate and now appears to be overwhelming. For example, in addition to the columnar organization of preferred orientations shown by Hubel & Wiesel (188), Blakemore (30) has demonstrated columnar organization for retinal disparity and visual direction and, as mentioned previously, Hubel & Wiesel have shown binocularity columns as well using anatomical methods (194). The extent of functional interactions between these columns is now a subject of considerable interest (32).

While a great many details of cortical organization have been worked out using extracellular methods, the capability for describing excitatory and inhibitory interactions that intracellular recording provides is yet to be extensively explored. Creutzfeldt and his colleagues (16, 78, 296) have been the most active investigators using this methodology, but progress has been slow and the technical difficulties currently appear to mitigate widespread use of this method.

Given the tools of electrophysiology and the considerable backlog of quantitative findings on single cell properties in visual cortex, a number of investigators have turned their attention to problems of perception in an attempt to ascertain if single cells can code some fundamental perceptual properties, such as masking (294) or stability of the visual world (86). One possible mechanism to account for perceptual stability would be changes in cell properties related to changes in head, body, or eye positions. Although such a mechanism may be difficult to reconcile with current theories of neural processing in visual cortex, there have been a number of reports (86, 186) in which receptive field orientation selectivity seems to be modified by a change in body position.

To determine how receptive fields of cortical neurons are built up, the receptive field properties of cells in the several cortical laminae have been compared. For example, the electrophysiological finding that some cells in layer 4 have receptive fields more like geniculate cells has been taken as evidence that these cells receive input from the lateral geniculate nucleus more directly than do cells with dissimilar fields (27, 28).

Another line directed toward understanding the synthesis of receptive field properties in visual cortex has been followed by the Australian group. These investigators have confirmed that two classes of neurons, termed transient and steady-state cells, project from the retina to the lateral geniculate nucleus, and they were able to follow this dichotomy of cell types from the lateral geniculate to cortex (182, 394). In general, the steady-state cells appear to project primarily to simple cells while the transient cells project primarily to complex cells. The functional significance of these findings has yet to be realized but it may be a large step forward in understanding the bifurcated input to cortex from DGL in the cat.

How cells come to have the receptive field properties that they do is a question of great interest to all neuroscientists. One popular approach to the study of this problem is investigating the ontogeny of the properties of visual cortex neurons (11). The early experiments by Hubel & Wiesel (189–192, 441) have shown the development of functional amblyopia in monocularly deprived (65, 88, 298, 342) animals and a lack of binocularly activated cells in the visual cortex of monocularly deprived animals when tested as adults (189, 190, 365). These experiments have been extended using a different method, induced squint, produced by sectioning one of the extraocular muscles. With this procedure, it has been found both in cats (190) and monkeys (299) that there is a reduction in the number of binocular cells in visual cortex (68), and an amblyopia results. The question of recovery from this defect with subsequent correction is still a matter of some controversy (299), but because of these findings, the normal development of interocular alignment has enjoyed renewed interest (363, 364).

Probably the most exciting finding in recent years has been the demonstration that selective visual experience can modify the receptive field properties of cells in the visual system of cats. For example, Hirsch & Spinelli (178–180, 381) and Blakemore & Cooper (31) have shown that young kittens exposed for a few hours a day to only one contour (e.g. either horizontal or vertical edges or lines) show a preponderance of cells sensitive to that contour as adults, and a dearth of cells responsive to contours of other orientations. Just as in the induced-squint and visual deprivation experiments, a rather clear behavioral deficit has been demonstrated (122, 178). These effects appear to be irreversible if the animal is not given normal visual experience during the critical period. These findings provide a firm experimental base for demonstrating the plasticity of the nervous system and susceptibility to environmental influences (350). It is not unreasonable to assume that a similar plasticity will be found in other systems as well when appropriate selective-experience methods are applied.

Coincident with the experiments on squint and monocular/binocular deprivation is an observation on the Siamese cat (162) mentioned previously. For many years it has been widely known that Siamese cats have a naturally occurring squint. This squint now appears to be due to a genetic anatomical anomaly in the visual system which consists of a misrouting of the fibers at the optic chiasma (68, 76, 162, 193). This defect results in an intrusion of ipsilateral fibers in the contralateral field. Because the anatomical projections of the visual system in the normal cat are so well understood, it has been possible to predict the field defect in the Siamese cat due to its anomalous projection. Several investigators using single cell recording techniques in lateral geniculate nucleus and cortex have demonstrated the field intrusion that was predicted by the anatomical investigations (68, 163, 193). These findings raise a fundamental question regarding the treatment of squint in humans. Treatment has often consisted of surgical correction, yet these findings in the Siamese cat suggest that rather than a muscular imbalance producing a squint, a neuroanatomical peculiarity within the visual system may be producing the abnormal eye position. If this is true, the value of surgical correction of squint is questionable.

Recent anatomical demonstrations of efferents from visual cortex to superior colliculus have provided impetus for a number of electrophysiological studies which have evaluated the role of these efferents in determining the receptive field properties of tectal cells (272, 349, 393, 440). These studies suggest that many tectal cells lose their orientation specificity after removal of striate cortex.

On the afferent side, while there is scant evidence for extrageniculate input to visual cortex, numerous investigators have demonstrated inputs to the geniculocortical system from mesencephalic structures (117, 181, 253, 305, 371, 372), The exact route of these inputs has not yet been established anatomically, however.

In light of these diverse approaches to the visual system and the plethora of published findings on visual system properties, it is not surprising that a number of workers have attempted to generate pattern perception theories utilizing visual neuron properties already known to exist (10, 79, 277, 319, 320). While the predictive validity of these sophisticated theories has yet to be demonstrated, they encourage one to think that a fundamental understanding of the neural basis for some facets of visual perception may not be too far off.

Behavior

Ablation experiments in which visual cortex is removed and residual visual abilities are measured continue to be the major source of information regarding the functional role of visual cortex. Although the early observations by Kluver (223) of a loss of pattern vision in monkeys deprived of visual cortex have been confirmed numerous times, his findings of virtually complete pattern blindness must now be tempered. There appears to be a greater capacity for vision in monkeys without striate cortex than previously realized (196, 311), and in the cat, primate-like visual defects can only be produced if several cortical areas outside striate cortex are included in the ablation (82, 100, 379).

Humphreys & Weiskrantz (196) have reported that monkeys deprived of striate cortex are capable of accurate spatial localization, e.g. normal orientation in space and a considerable amount of eye-hand coordination for grasping objects. Other residual visual capacities have also been described in striatectomized monkeys (311, 356, 357). Since these results suggest some kind of parallel processing of visual information, it is satisfying to note that anatomists have now provided several extrageniculate pathways that could participate in vision not mediated by striate cortex (e.g. 95, 153, 276). Thus, a number of investigators have suggested that a considerable amount of geniculocortical-like visual discrimination is possible at subcortical levels, e.g. superior colliculus (7, 205) and accessory optic system (311). Alternatively, the retinal-tectal-pulvinar-cortex pathway has been suggested as the route mediating these discriminations (95, 374).

When striate cortex is ablated in other animals such as cats (100), rabbits (462), hedgehogs (166), rats (69, 73, 136, 378), and tree shrews (205, 418, 419), the deficits on pattern vision are not quite as clear cut. These animals, all nonprimates, appear to be capable of nearly normal visual behavior without striate cortex. Whether these animals are processing visual information in alternate pathways in the same way as it is processed in striate cortex, or are utilizing alternate mechanisms as well as alternate pathways is a subject of continuing controversy (222, 418). For example, it is not impossible that an animal deprived of striate cortex solves certain pattern discrimination problems on the basis of other cues (such as temporal intensity) that can be derived by scanning the visual display.

While it may be possible for an animal to discriminate patterns through the use of a variety of visual cues, it has been thought his capacity to resolve fine detail is a unique property of striate cortex (22, 71, 223). Numerous investigators have demonstrated a dramatic reduction in visual acuity in animals deprived of visual cortex and have also shown that small lesions confined to known projection areas of cortex will produce reductions in acuity predictable from the field position of the defect (71, 345). One troubling finding is this regard has been reported by Diamond and his group: they found no reduction in the tree shrew's capacity to resolve fine gratings after the complete removal of striate cortex (419). The tectal-pulvinar-cortex pathway could mediate this capability (418, 419).

The exciting findings by Barlow, Blakemore & Pettigrew (9) and Bishop (27) on the processing of binocular information in cat cortex (cf. physiology section) has led a number of investigators to analyze the role of striate cortex in depth perception. While there are yet very few reports on this question, it appears that the cat can use retinal disparity to make depth judgements (119) and that removal of striate cortex results in deficits in depth perception in cats (271), but may not in rats (39).

The purely visual function of striate cortex has been little challenged by the findings of the last few years. There are, however, a few studies which indicate that striate cortex may also participate in a number of other activities that are not obviously visual [e.g. avoidance behavior (128, 249–251, 259, 313), audition (383)]. But because reports of nonvisual functions of visual cortex are still rare, their significance relative to the total role of striate cortex in behavior is difficult to evaluate at this time.

The role of the corpus callosum in the integration of the two visual hemifields (126, 362, 412, 413) and hemisphere differences (344, 422) in visual behavior are subjects of great interest as are the effects of training and interoperative experience on postoperative performance on visual discriminations (33, 34, 136, 317).

AUDITORY CORTEX

The idea that auditory cortex is necessary for auditory sensation is now all but buried in the past. Useful reviews of the anatomical, physiological, and behavioral experimentation leading to this conclusion can be found in Neff (284, 285, 288), Erulkar (110), Sachs (352), Elliott & Trahiotis (107), and Masterton & Diamond (268).

Anatomy

The locus and extent of auditory cortex has now been delineated in a variety of animals other than cat (e.g. 239, 241, 243), but information on some important cases is still apparently lacking. For example, cytoarchitectonic, electrophysiological, and thalamic projection techniques still disagree in their conclusions on the extent of auditory cortex in monkeys (cf. 37, 423).

The search for tonotopic maps within auditory cortex, so typical of the 50s and early 60s, has now dwindled with the conclusion that although tonotopicity exists, it is neither as precise nor as prevalent as it is in lower auditory centers [e.g. see the contributions and bibliographies in Woolsey (455), Goldstein et al (152), Miller (273), and Purser & Whitfield (331), and the discussion in Sachs (352)]. Anatomical experimentation, whether electrophysiological or histological, has turned instead to the identification of subareas within auditory cortex and to particulars of their input and output.

On the afferent side, it is already reasonably safe to conclude that there are at least two thalamocortical auditory systems, one projecting from the medial geniculate to an auditory "core" area of cortex and another projecting from part of the posterior group of thalamic nuclei to a "belt" of cortex surrounding the core (96, 154, 433). Whether there exist further important subdivisions within these areas in all mammals (as there certainly is in cats) or clear physiological and behavioral differences in the contribution of these two afferent auditory systems has not been determined.

The efferents from auditory cortex have also been investigated with the new silver stains. In addition to showing intrahemispheric (91) and interhemispheric (92) projections, recent studies have found tracts descending from auditory cortex to basal ganglia, ventral thalamus, midbrain tegmentum, and pontine nuclei, as well as reciprocating pathways to the major auditory structures in thalamus and midbrain (93). The latter pathways can be thought of as part of the descending auditory system (87, 332); but the pathways to basal ganglia, ventral thalamus, and tegmentum are hard to reconcile with the classical view of sensory cortex.

Physiology

The electrophysiological analysis of auditory cortex has begun to advance rapidly. Brugge (42, 43), Goldstein (149, 151, 152, 164), Whitfield (397, 432, 433), and their respective colleagues have gone far beyond questions of tonotopicity, regularly including monaural and binaural sounds, clicks, tone ramps, etc., in their battery of test stimuli. Others have included specific vocalizations (120, 395, 448, 449) or have recorded activity in awake or behaving subjects evoked by a variety of stimuli

(12, 208, 209, 354, 355). This expansion of test stimuli and experimental conditions reflects the fact that many cortical neurons are not responsive to tones of any frequency and also reflects an undercurrent of thinking that the passive neural responses to tones and their simple combinations may have been overemphasized in physiological experimentation in the past (268, 456). The argument has been made that auditory cortex is concerned more with the features of sound sources than it is with the physical features of sounds themselves (268, 456). This physical vs biological (or sounds vs sounds sources) dichotomy of auditory features has been prompted as much by the results of ablation-behavior experiments as it has by electrophysiological experimentation itself.

Goldstein and his colleagues have explored the possible functional significance of the columnar organization of auditory cortex (1, 150), and also have succeeded in making intracellular recordings (336). The variety of response characteristics of single units ("on," "off," "on-off," "through," "groupers," "lockers"), and the variety of "best stimuli" (clicks, noise bursts, swept tones, etc.) seem to be very individualistic characteristics of cortical neurons that currently defy quantification (336). But it has been shown that most of these characteristics are the result of convergent interaction somewhere in the pathway from ear to cortex rather than in cortex itself. Therefore, it can be concluded that some features of the stimulation are being extracted at successive synapses in the auditory pathway. However, the best way to characterize these "features" is far from settled, and no one theoretical viewpoint has yet begun to predominate.

Behavior

A number of ablation-behavior experiments on auditory cortex have been performed recently. Neff's reviews (285–288) of this literature through the late 60s reveal the reasons why research has drifted away from strictly psychophysical experimentation on tones. Summarizing the earlier work, it is reasonably safe to state that ablation of auditory cortex does *not* affect the capacity to discriminate sound vs silence, nor the intensity or frequency of tones in any mammal. Only sound localization and lateralization and certain complex (tonal patterns) or naturalistic discriminations (voice sounds) seem to be permanently and severely disrupted by cortical ablation (e.g. 70, 89, 90, 94, 267, 341).

The lack of involvement of auditory cortex in the discrimination of the physical elements of sound (intensity, frequency) and its clear involvement in the biological elements (sound localization, species-specific calls, etc.) has been demonstrated in a variety of mammals ranging from the primitive opossums (334, 335) to the highly specialized cats (e.g. 45, 75, 220, 303, 434) and monkeys (266, 398). But the results of the most recent of these experiments seem to show that even with these discriminations, the deficit resulting from auditory cortex ablation is more "audito-motor" than "auditory." That is, even though the deficit is confined to strictly auditory discriminations, the particular behavioral response required of the animal may be a crucial factor in determining whether or not the discrimination is disrupted after ablation (176, 268).

SOMATOSENSORY CORTEX

Since Woolsey (454) showed that potentials evoked by somatosensory stimuli could be recorded from motor cortex and that movements could be evoked by stimulation of somatosensory cortex, the classic distinction between somatosensory cortex and motor cortex has been blurred. This fact is now often alluded to by use of the terms "Sm" and "Ms" in referring to what was once called somatosensory and motor cortex, respectively—the lower case letters reminding the reader that somatosensory cortex is motor too, and vice versa. Recently, research has been directed to discovering and describing features that distinguish the two areas and indeed, such features have been found. However, the idea of two relatively independent homunculi, one representing the dermatomes, the other controlling the myotomes, is probably buried forever. Therefore, the studies cited here and those cited under "Motor cortex" should be grouped together in any consideration of the subject.

Anatomy

The mapping of somatosensory cortex in mammals has almost come to an end with the conclusion that in primitive and advanced mammals alike, the body surface is represented at the cortex in an order-preserving map with more cortical surface given over to body areas that are heavily innervated. Therefore, in this most basic sense, the pioneering conclusions of Adrian have been verified, and the topology of the somatosensory projection has been satisfactorily explained (2, 270, 329, 330, 427, 429, 430, 435–438). Of the many strictly anatomical questions still remaining, the significance of the columnar and laminar arrangements (426) and of the fine structure within the cortex itself (314), and the question of which peripheral fiber populations do and which do not gain cortical representation are now in the forefront (e.g. 20, 80, 81, 121, 168, 169, 302, 312). Luckily, most recent discoveries have tended to simplify rather than to complicate the anatomical picture (eg. 155). Landgren & Silfvenius' (232–234, 367–369) elaborate verifications that some peripheral Group Ia afferents (afferents from muscle spindles) gain cortical representation has shattered the old rule that proprioceptive activity does not reach the cortex directly. Similarly, the localization of a cortical area activated by stimulation of taste fibers has removed still another exception from the discussion (121, 351).

But one discovery in particular will probably have far reaching consequences for future research into somatosensory cortex. It is now known that the dorsal column and the anterolateral spinothalamic systems are not the only spinal somatosensory pathways. There is at least one other system (spinocervical) which is as direct a pathway from body to cortex as the others and possibly more so (e.g. 106, 123, 359, 417). This discovery may go a long way in explaining the persistence of fine discrimination after lesions of dorsal column, medial lemniscus, or somatosensory cortex (359).

Physiology

The electrophysiological investigation of somatosensory cortex is just beginning to become concerned with "feature extraction" as that term has been popularized by vision research (439). More usual as topics are its interactions with motor and association cortex (36, 197, 281, 343) and the relation of neural activity to conscious experience (verbal report) in humans.

This latter line of research has been reviewed by Libet et al (246–248) who have uncovered several striking features of somatosensory sensation in humans including the facts that stimulation in somatosensory cortex must be persistent to evoke consciousness, that different patterns of cortical stimulation evoke different qualities of sensation, and that cortical stimulation is about equally likely to evoke natural qualities as paresthesia. Other physiological reviews of somatosensation can be found in Hyvärinen (197, 198) and in the books edited by Kenshalo (221), by Kornhuber (see 248), and by Somjen & Nashold (see 247).

Behavior

The difficulty in controlling somatosensory and kinesthetic stimuli in moving animals continues to plague behavioral research on somatosensory cortex. Unlike vision or audition, most behavioral experiments on the somatosensory system are forced to rely on qualitative judgments of abnormalities, or on measurable deficits in relatively complex motor activities, with the result that progress has been slow and painstaking. Among the more informative series of recent experiments are those by Semmes & Mishkin (396a) in monkeys, by Berkley (21) and Glassman in cats (131–134), and by Finger in rats (118). Perhaps most revealing for the present topic, however, is the fact that most authors continue to describe the deficits, or the lesions, as sensorimotor instead of either sensory or motor. This choice of terms clearly reflects the difficulty in segregating the two systems in the traditional fashion.

MOTOR CORTEX (AREAS 4, 6, AND 8)

The classical view of motor cortex holds that area 4 is the origin of a precisely somatotopic corticospinal or pyramidal tract and gains most of its input from area 6, while area 6, in turn, gains its input from the association cortex surrounding it. It follows from this view that unilateral excision of area 4 should result in perfect hemiplegia, and, further, that because of the clear motor homunculus in area 4, a punctate lesion should result in paralysis for voluntary movement in one small muscle group. Perhaps more than others, the early work of Tower (405), of Travis & Woolsey (409), and especially of Glees & Cole (135) foreshadowed the difficulties that the old view would meet. But where research into motor cortex was once confined mostly to electrophysiological mapping and gross ablation-behavior experiments, it now includes highly sophisticated electrophysiological, neuroanatomical, and behavioral techniques and their several combinations. It will be seen that these more refined techniques have now rendered the classical view almost untenable in all animals except, possibly, humans.

Anatomy

The experimental silver-staining techniques have shown that area 4 gains a great deal of input not only from area 6 but also from the adjacent somatosensory cortex (areas 1, 2, 3, and 5), and from the ventrolateral nucleus of the dorsal thalamus. Area 6 gains input from almost all other areas of cortex and also from the thalamus (e.g. 116, 340, 389–392). Perhaps more surprising are the demonstrations by electrophysiological recording of short-latency potentials evoked in motor cortex neurons by stimuli in almost every modality (8, 35, 66, 105, 147, 148, 210, 245, 264, 265, 347, 399, 415, 428, 431). In most mammals, therefore, the projections to areas 4 and 6 do not serve well to differentiate them from each other or to differentiate them from association, or even sensory, cortex.

The output of areas 4 and 6, long known to include the corticospinal tract, also includes recurrent fibers to the sources of their input, fibers to the basal ganglia, and longer fibers to the brainstem motor and sensory nuclei (227, 229, 263, 278, 279). It is these last fibers, those projecting from "motor cortex" to *sensory* neurons at lower levels that have come as a surprise and have opened the possibility that the cortical motor system might have been derived from, and maybe still is, a descending somatosensory system with a strictly motor component only recently acquired in a few specialized mammals.

In a long line of neuroanatomical studies Kuypers and his colleagues (226–230) have shown that the corticospinal tract, once considered the chief output of cortex, and thought to extend from cortex directly to motor neuron in the spinal cord, is a rare exception, not the rule, among mammals. In most mammals, the corticospinal tract hardly exists, in the sense that it does not extend further than the uppermost segments of the spinal cord and synapses almost entirely on somatosensory and internuncial neurons rather than on motor neurons. Only in mammals that have the ability to move their digits independently, (e.g. anthropoids, racoons, phalangers) does the corticospinal tract penetrate deeply into the cord or synapse on motor neurons (230, 261, 262, 316, 337).

Woolsey and his colleagues have shown repeatedly that both motor cortex and somatosensory cortex have both motor and somatosensory characteristics (454). This overlap of function seems to have an obvious evolutionary history since, in primitive mammals, sensory and motor maps are nearly perfectly overlapped (240, 242) while in anthropoids they are much more segregated.

If the converse question is raised—what is the extent of the cortical area of origin of the pyramidal (or peduncular) tract?—a similar conclusion is reached. In primitive mammals, almost the entire neocortex (excepting possibly area 17) must be ablated before the fiber degeneration in the peduncles or pyramids is complete, while in man the degeneration is almost complete after excision of area 4 alone (204, 206, 207). Therefore, a definition of motor cortex based on its efferents is little better than the one based on its afferents. In most mammals either definition is much too inclusive and certainly more inclusive than a cytoarchitectonic definition.

Because of the dense fiber connections of areas 4 and 6 with the basal ganglia and the thalamus (which in turn receives cerebellar imput via the red nucleus), even the distinction between pyramidal and extrapyramidal motor systems has begun to blur (e.g. 116). Certainly the heavy connections between cortex and basal ganglia permits motor cortex to be thought of as the origin of the extrapyramidal system as properly as it is the origin of the pyramidal system.

Physiology

Although the mapping of motor cortex in a variety of mammals continues to be useful for comparative purposes, the greatest advance in the physiology of motor cortex, and the pyramidal tract, specifically, has come from the laboratories of Evarts (112–115) and of Porter (185, 187, 322–326). Evarts recorded from single neurons in the motor cortex of awake monkeys while they were performing a conditioned movement of the wrist. By this means the activity of the cortical neurons could be correlated with the overt movements of the animal and the timing and coding of the neural activity analyzed in behavioral terms. It is satisfying to note that this line of research has shown clear and important differences in the pyramidal tract cells of motor cortex as opposed to nonpyramidal tract cells and cells in other areas (113, 115). Activity in the neurons in motor cortex precede movements (by up to 100 msec), while activity in cells in either somatosensory cortex or in the frontal eye fields (area 8) follow movements (29, 115). Furthermore, the activity in the motor neurons is correlated with the displacement or position of limb or eye (113).

Porter and his colleagues (185, 187, 322, 325, 326) have verified Evarts' conclusions and have also described the effect of motor cortex activity on spinal motor neurons (185, 324). Still others have come to the same conclusion as Evarts using other responses (225, 252) or other techniques (83, 84). Thus, it would seem that some neurons in motor cortex do indeed play a special role in the initiation of some movements. However, because these characteristics are observed only in neurons whose axons traverse the pyramids and we have already noted that anthropoids are among the very few mammalian varieties that possess a corticospinal tract in the strict sense, it would not be surprising if such a marked difference between motor and sensory cortex does not prevail among mammals in general.

Particularly interesting for the present purpose, however, are the studies of O'Brien & Fox (300, 301) and by Woody and his colleagues (109, 450–453) who have investigated neural activity in motor cortex during conditioning. This work has suggested that conditioning produces a relatively permanent change in the response characteristics of some motor cortex neurons as well as in behavior. By stimulating the same neurons directly, it appears that the motor neurons themselves are changed as a result of conditioning and are not just reflecting changes that have taken place in neurons elsewhere.

Behavior

The most recent ablation-behavior experiments on motor cortex or the pyramidal system have been confined with three exceptions (13, 204, 337) to cats and monkeys. In each case, as it has been in the past, the behavioral observations are broad-ranging and almost completely qualitative (e.g. "unnatural posture," "subnormal tone," etc.). But the one common result of this line of inquiry is the surprising number of actions that are *not* lost to an animal as a result of massive cortical removals. In general the degree of effect of a cortical or pyramidal lesion varies from what appears to be little or nothing in primitive mammals to sharply defined contralateral paralysis in humans (204, 206, 207, 411) with intermediate effects in monkeys (14, 40, 237, 238, 416). Whether this gradient of effect parallels the differences in the development of the pyramidal tract or whether the loss just seems to be greater in anthropoids because they have more to lose to begin with, is far from decided. What is clear, however, is that the contribution of motor cortex can no longer be discussed for mammals in general—so far, the differences in its role obscure the similarities.

POSTERIOR ASSOCIATION CORTEX

Of the posterior cortical areas classified as "association," those concerned with vision in the temporal and occipital lobes have been the most extensively studied and have undergone the most significant change in the conceptualization of their function; while those located in the parietal lobe have attracted only scant attention (54, 55, 58, 59). Three excellent reviews have appeared in recent years, one anatomical (459), one functional (276), and one a comprehensive review of all aspects of visual association cortex (157).

Anatomy

The cortical areas most often included in the visual "association" category are: (*a*) inferotemporal cortex (area 20); (*b*) prestriate cortex (including areas 18 and 19); and *(c)* a transition zone between these two regions in the occipital-temporal junction (157). Relatively little recent work has been done on the cytoarchitecture of these areas in primates; most workers rely on the classical studies by von Bonin & Bailey (37), and the older literature. However, several recent studies have been done in nonprimates, e.g. cat (174, 175, 353), tree shrew (95), and hedgehog (165, 166, 214). These studies indicate that it has not been possible to distinguish homologs of all of the primate areas on the basis of cytoarchitecture alone: many workers rely on similarities in other anatomical features (e.g. efferent and afferents) to make cross-species comparisons. It is interesting that some current boundaries of visual association cortex in monkeys have been established primarily through ablation studies (276) (cf. last section).

Numerous studies of the afferents to visual association cortex have confirmed the existence of cortico-cortical inputs from striate cortex via circumstriate belt or prestriate cortex (74, 460, 461). These studies have revealed a characteristic of prestriate cortex hitherto unknown: the ventrolateral prestriate area has at least three separate foveal projections (74, 458). The only other major cortico-cortical inputs to this area yet known are from the contralateral inferotemporal cortex and the ventral potion of dorsolateral frontal granular cortex (157).

The subcortical inputs to inferotemporal cortex consist of a major input from the lateral pulvinar nucleus of the thalamus (72, 157, 159, 339) while the subcortical input to prestriate cortex derives primarily from the inferior pulvinar (6, 157, 200, 201). Studies of visual association cortex in the cat describe essentially the same pattern of inputs with the major exception that prestriate cortex also receives an input from DGL (44, 124, 137, 290, 291, 293).

Efferents from these prestriate areas have also been described (174, 366), and, on the basis of these efferents, a cortical region in the cat anatomically comparable to inferotemporal cortex in the monkey has been discovered (353). Efferents from inferotemporal cortex project to circumstriate belt cortex, the frontal lobe, basal ganglia, dorsal medial, and pulvinar nuclei of the thalamus, and the superior colliculus (157, 375). Prestriate cortex sends efferents to contralateral prestriate cortex (275), pulvinar, inferotemporal cortex (276), and in the cat, to the lateral pontine nucleus (41, 138).

Physiology

Because of its anatomical distance from visual receptors, it has been very difficult to study visual association cortex with electrophysiological methods (282), but topographic maps have been made (4, 5). Several evoked potential studies have attempted to relate electrical changes to behavioral changes, e.g. during visual discriminations (127, 146), or under various arousal states (157), etc. The recorded potentials are extremely labile and, thus far, have not been found to be consistently related to any one particular stage of visual learning (157).

Single cell recording has been more successful. Recordings have been made in areas 18, 19, and the Bishop-Clare area (304, 406, 457), and in the middle suprasylvian gyrus in the cat (101, 102, 407, 408). In general, the receptive fields of cells in these areas appear to have more complex properties than cells in striate cortex. This finding has been interpreted by some as representing a still higher stage in the theoretical hierarchy of receptive fields as proposed by Hubel & Wiesel, but the usefulness of this idea is yet to be demonstrated. Similar recordings have been made in area 18 of the monkey, but unlike the cat, cells sensitive to retinal disparity are found only in area 18 (191).

Recordings made in inferotemporal cortex of monkeys (15, 104, 158, 160, 161) have demonstrated the existence of extremely complex and surprisingly specific receptive fields. So specific are these receptive fields that Gross et al (160) were never certain that they had found the unique properties of these cells. Another unusual feature of inferotemporal cells is the large size of the receptive fields and the invariable inclusion of the fovea. Bender et al (15) have also found that cells in inferotemporal cortex depend heavily on the striate-prestriate pathway for their activation. These results have been taken as evidence for still further hierarchical elaboration of receptive fields as suggested by the Hubel & Wiesel model. In addition, these results have clearly established a role for the visual "association" areas much more closely related to sensory function than had been earlier imagined.

Behavior

Ever since the classic studies of Kluver and Bucy on the effects of bilateral removal of temporal lobes in monkeys, it has been known that visual information is somehow processed there. Later studies showed that it was inferotemporal cortex (rather than structures lying under it) that produced the visual deficits (e.g. 201, 275). In general, these deficits have been described as deficits in the retention and learning of complex visual discriminations (47, 48, 50, 51, 111, 328, 338, 443–445, 447). No deficits have been found on any fundamental visual dimension, e.g. absolute threshold, visual acuity, flicker thresholds, nor in visuo-motor behavior following inferotemporal cortex ablations (157, 360).

The question of whether inferotemporal deficits can also be produced by ablation of a major input area (prestriate cortex) has only recently been resolved (275). Whereas earlier papers had reported little or no change in visual discrimination performance following prestriate lesions (e.g. 328, 459), recent studies in monkeys in which the newly discovered ventrolateral prestriate areas (foveal prestriate areas) were ablated produced dramatic deficits comparable to, if not more severe than, inferotemporal lesions themselves (72, 159, 219, 257, 258).

In contrast, destruction of the pulvinar, another major input to this cortical region, does not produce a significant behavioral deficit (276).

Even though the deficits resulting from inferotemporal ablation are purely visual, there are several conditions which vitiate the defect. The defect is reduced (*a*) if the lesions are made in young animals; (*b*) if the animals are preoperatively overtrained (157); and *(c)* if shock is used to punish errors (256).

Similar experiments in cats have not been performed partly because the locus of a homologous or at least analogous cortical zone is unknown. Nevertheless, in the few experimental animals with ablated extrastriate areas, only mild deficits have been found (e.g. 170). Ablations of area 20 in the cat have yet to be done.

FRONTAL CORTEX

Despite 40 years of careful and ingenious experimentation on the role of prefrontal or granular frontal cortex, this area of the brain continues to be one of the most puzzling. The starting point of most recent research can be found in the comprehensive volume edited by Warren & Akert (420) published in 1964, and contributions to a 1971 symposium in Poland on the same subject are beginning to appear in *Acta Neurobiologiae Experimentalis.* But because of the large amount and diversity of research activity in this area, many papers and certainly most reviews are out of date by the time they are finally published.

Anatomy

Great strides toward the description of the myriad connections of prefrontal cortex have been made with the Nauta-Gygax and Fink-Heimer silver stains. Where once the afferents to prefrontal cortex were thought to be adequately described after mention of the projections from the medial dorsal nucleus (MD) of the thalamus and a general reference to cortico-cortical projections from temporal and parietal lobes, it is now known that most of the subareas of prefrontal cortex (areas 9, 10, 11, 12, etc) have a unique combination of afferents and efferents, most of which are order-preserving (24–26, 98, 212, 218, 244, 283, 307, 308, 310, 315, 370, 410, 414). Thus, the idea that prefrontal cortex is a large field relatively homogeneous in cytoarchitecture or afferent and efferent connections can no longer be retained (346).

Of the many newly discovered afferents perhaps the most surprising are those that project to orbital prefrontal cortex (via MD) from olfactory cortex (108, 283, 327,

361) or from cells near the gustatory nucleus solitarius of the hindbrain (63). The presence of these fibers means that a part of the prefrontal cortex is much closer to the nose (in terms of the number of intervening synapses) and, possibly, to the taste buds, than was ever suspected before. Perhaps even more startling, prefrontal cortex is closer to the nose than auditory cortex is to the ear. Although no one has yet suggested that orbital frontal cortex be called olfactory sensory neocortex, these facts certainly suggest that prefrontal cortex as a whole may fall somewhat short of being the human "organ of civilization."

On the efferent side, similarly important discoveries have been made. Again depending on the subarea of origin within prefrontal cortex, studies have demonstrated heavy projections to the striatum, to cingulate cortex, and to as far as the tegmentum in the medulla, in addition to pathways reciprocating the heavy afferent pathways from the thalamus and the parietal and temporal lobes (e.g. 41, 98, 211, 212, 217, 260, 283, 289, 307, 310, 327, 361, 410, 414). Thus, prefrontal cortex discharges directly into the extrapyramidal system (suggesting a somatic motor role) and into Papez' circuit (suggesting a visceral motor role). When this array of outputs is considered along with the olfactory and gustatory input and the temporal and parietal lobe input, it is difficult to discover a single term that might properly convey the range of possible functions of this area. Certainly, the term "association" does not help.

Physiology

Because it was long thought that prefrontal cortex was synaptically remote from either sensory or motor neurons (and therefore electrically "silent"), few of the usual electrophysiological recording or stimulation experiments have been done for purposes other than anatomy (103). Instead, electrophysiological and behavioral techniques have been combined so that either neural activity is recorded while an animal is performing one or another task known to depend on prefrontal cortex (224, 295), or electrical stimulation is used to disrupt or facilitate the same behavioral activities (348, 384, 386). It is encouraging to note that some single units have been found whose activity is correlated with various stages of performance of prefrontal tasks and that stimulation certainly disrupts and, in some cases, possibly facilitates the same tasks.

Behavior

A relatively large number of essentially behavioral experiments on prefrontal cortex continue to appear each year. With a few exceptions (e.g. 358) they are derived more or less directly from the deficit in spatial delayed response known to result from prefrontal damage (202). In general, these experiments follow at least one of three directions: either they attempt to localize the subsystem within the prefrontal system (MD-prefrontal-caudate) whose damage is responsible for the classic delayed-response deficit, or they attempt to find other tasks that are disrupted, or they attempt to catalog the similarities and differences in prefrontal function between primates and nonprimates.

Perhaps the most fundamental functional subdivision within prefrontal cortex appears to be between the dorsolateral convexity on one hand and the orbital or ventrolateral convexity on the other. Recent studies converge on the idea that delayed-response tasks are more sensitive to dorsolateral lesions than to orbital lesions, while response reversal and other diverse tasks are more sensitive to orbital lesions than to dorsolateral lesions (cf. 46, 49, 52, 141, 145, 156, 172, 199, 254, 274, 387, 388). In addition, monkeys with orbital lesions suffer deficits in social behavior not suffered by monkeys with dorsolateral lesions (38, 53, 85, 373, 396). There is some evidence that the orbital region can be further subdivided into lateral vs posteromedial with lesions in the former resulting in the response reversal deficit and lesions in the latter resulting in the deficit in social behavior.

Similarly, spatial delayed-response seems to be most sensitive to lesions in the vicinity of sulcus principalis and within this region possibly to lesions surrounding the middle third of the sulcus (e.g. 56, 57, 385). Furthermore, both the spatial and delay factors, in combination, must be present in the task before a deficit can be seen (145).

This dorsolateral vs orbital subdivision of anthropoid prefrontal cortex may also help to explain the differences between primate and nonprimate deficits after prefrontal lesions. Tissue homologous to prefrontal cortex (i.e. projection area of the thalamic nucleus, or medialis dorsalis), has begun to be located in nonprimates, usually on the ventral and medial surfaces of the frontal pole instead of the lateral surface (49, 244). In terms of connections and MD cytoarchitecture, nonprimate prefrontal cortex seems to be more like the orbital frontal cortex and less like the dorsolateral cortex of primates (3, 283). In parallel, the symptoms resulting from lesions in nonprimates may be more like those resulting from orbital lesions and less like those resulting from dorsolateral lesions in primates (60, 97, 99, 420, 421, 442).

The possibility that nonprimate prefrontal cortex is homologous to only part of primate frontal cortex seems to be upheld by ontogenetic studies (139, 140, 142–144, 156, 171, 172, 400, 424), which have begun to describe the limits of plasticity in this region, and by phylogenetic (269) studies. The expansion of prefrontal cortex in the primate line began only after the primate lineage separated from the other mammalian lineages and a large part of its total expansion seems to have been due to the appearance of what is now identified as the parvocellular MD-dorsolateral division. If this proves to be the case, it follows that dorsolateral cortex almost certainly does not play the same role in nonprimates as it does in primates and might well be unique to primates; more consistency among mammals, primate or not, might be found in the anatomy and functions of the orbital division.

SUMMARY

In the context of this review we have attempted to illustrate that the three-way division of cerebral neocortex into areas labelled "sensory," "motor," or "association" has lost most of its original usefulness. Almost every report cited here either demonstrates, suggests, or refers to, nonsensory functions in sensory areas, nonmotor functions in motor areas, or nonassociative functions in association areas; and some reports refer to this issue explicitly (e.g. 401–403).

In surveying the reports, one gains the impression that very few workers in the field still use the classical terms to imply function; rather, they have been progressively restricted in their usage such that now they are little more than an anatomical shorthand. It can be anticipated that because of their anatomical usefulness the terms will continue to be employed at least until research has suggested an alternative of comparable generality. Until then, it can only be hoped that these outmoded terms will not be taken seriously by those outside the field, nor, especially, by new generations of students.

Literature Cited

1. Abeles, M., Goldstein, M. H. Jr. 1970. Functional architecture in cat primary auditory cortex: Columnar organization and organization according to depth. *J. Neurophysiol.* 33:172–87
2. Adrian, E. D. 1941. Afferent discharges to the cerebral cortex from peripheral sense organs. *J. Physiol.* 100:159–91
3. Akert, K. 1964. Comparative anatomy of frontal cortex and thalamo-frontal connections. In *The Frontal Granular Cortex and Behavior,* ed. J. M. Warren, K. Akert, 372–96. New York: McGraw-Hill
4. Allman, J. M., Kaas, J. H. 1971. A representation of the visual field in the caudal third of the middle temporal gyrus of the owl monkey *(Aotus trivirgatus). Brain Res.* 31:85–105
5. Ibid. Representation of the visual field in striate and adjoining cortex of the owl monkey *(Aotus trivirgatus).* 35:89–106
6. Allman, J. M., Kaas, J. H., Lane, R. H., Miezin, F. M. 1972. A representation of the visual field in the inferior nucleus of the pulvinar in the owl monkey. *Brain Res.* 40:291–302
7. Anderson, K. V., Symmes, D. 1969. The superior colliculus and higher visual functions in the monkey. *Brain Res.* 13:37–52
8. Asanuma, H., Rosen, I. 1972. Functional role of afferent inputs to the monkey motor cortex. *Brain Res.* 40:3–5
9. Barlow, H. B., Blakemore, C., Pettigrew, J. D. 1967. The neural mechanism of binocular depth discrimination. *J. Physiol.* 193:327–42
10. Barlow, H. B., Narasimhan, R., Rosenfeld, A. 1972. Visual pattern analysis in machines and animals. *Science* 177: 567–75
11. Barlow, H. B., Pettigrew, J. D. 1971. Lack of specificity of neurones in the visual cortex of young kittens. *J. Physiol.* 218:98–100
12. Barrett, T. W. 1971. Cortical wavefront movements to a changing sound source. *Brain Res.* 27:271–80
13. Bautista, N. S., Matzke, H. A. 1965. A degeneration study of the pyramidal tract of the opossum. *J. Comp. Neurol.* 124:367–75
14. Beck, C. H., Chambers, W. W. 1970. Speed, accuracy, and strength of forelimb movement after unilateral pyramidotomy in rhesus monkeys. *J. Comp. Physiol. Psychol. Monogr.* 70:1–22
15. Bender, D. B., Rocha-Miranda, C. E., Gross, C. G., Volman, S., Mishkin, M. 1972. Effects of striate lesions and commissure section on the visual response of neurons in inferotemporal cortex. *Physiologist* 15:84
16. Benevento, L. A., Creutzfeldt, O. D., Kuhnt, U. 1972. Significance of intracortical inhibition in the visual cortex. *Nature* 238:124–26
17. Benevento, L. A., Ebner, F. 1969. Lateral geniculate nucleus projections to neocortex in the opossum. *Anat. Res.* 163:294
18. Benevento, L. A., Ebner, F. 1971. The areas and layers of corticocortical terminations in the visual cortex of the Virginia opossum. *J. Comp. Neurol.* 141:157–90
19. Ibid. The contribution of the dorsal lateral geniculate nucleus to the total pattern of thalamic terminations in striate cortex of the Virginia opossum. 143: 243–60
20. Benjamin, R. M., Emmers, R., Blomquist, A. J. 1968. Projection of tongue nerve afferents to somatic sensory Area I in squirrel monkey *(Saimiri sciureus). Brain Res.* 7:208–20
21. Berkley, K. J., Kenshalo, D. R. 1972. Evidence for cortical function in pain sensation in the cat. *Fed. Proc.* In press

22. Berkley, M. A., Watkins, D. W. 1973. Grating resolution and refraction in the cat estimated from evoked cerebral potentials. *Vision Res.* 13:403–15
23. Berkley, M. A., Wolf, E., Glickstein, M. 1967. Photic evoked potentials in the cat: Evidence for a direct geniculate input to visual II. *Exp. Neurol.* 19:188–98
24. Bignall, K. E. 1969. Bilateral temprofrontal projections in the squirrel monkey: Origin distribution and pathways. *Brain Res.* 13:319–27
25. Ibid. 1970. Auditory input to frontal polysensory cortex of the squirrel monkey: Possible pathways. 19:77–86
26. Bignall, K. E., Imbert, M. 1969. Polysensory and corticocortical projections to frontal lobe of squirrel and rhesus monkeys. *Electroencephalogr. Clin. Neurophysiol.* 26:206–15
27. Bishop, P. O. 1970. Beginning of form vision and binocular depth discrimination in cortex. In *The Neurosciences,* ed. F. O. Schmitt, 471–85. New York: Rockefeller Univ. Press. 1068 pp.
28. Bishop, P. O., Dreher, B., Henry, G. H. 1971. Stimulus specificities of the discharge centre in the receptive field of simple striate neurones in the cat. *J. Physiol.* 218:53–55
29. Bizzi, E. 1968. Discharge of frontal eye field neurons during saccadic and following eye movements in unanesthetized monkeys. *Exp. Brain Res.* 6:69–80
30. Blakemore, C. 1970. The representation of three-dimensional visual space in the cat's striate cortex. *J. Physiol.* 209:155
31. Blakemore, C., Cooper, G. F. 1970. Development of the brain depends on the visual environment. *Nature* 228:477–78
32. Blakemore, C., Fobin, E. A. 1972. Lateral inhibition between orientation detectors in the cat's visual cortex. *Exp. Brain Res.* 15:439–40
33. Bland, B. H., Cooper, R. M. 1969. Posterior neodecortication in the rat: Age at operation and experience. *J. Comp. Physiol. Psychol.* 69:345–54
34. Bland, B. H., Cooper, R. M. 1970. Experience and vision of the posterior neodecorticate rat. *Physiol. & Behav.* 5:211–14
35. Blomquist, A. J., Lorenzini, C. A. 1965. Projection of dorsal roots and sensory nerves to cortical sensory motor regions of squirrel monkey. *J. Neurophysiol.* 28:1195–1205
36. Boisacq-Schepens, N. 1971. *Etude microphysiologique de l'organisation fonctionnelle du cortex sensori-motor.* Louvain: Vander. 279 pp.
37. Bonin, G. von, Bailey, P. 1947. The neocortex of *Macaca mulatta.* Illinois monographs in the medical sciences. Urbana: Univ. Illinois. 163 pp.
38. Bowden, D. M., Goldman, P. S., Rosvold, H. E., Greenstreet, R. L. 1971. Free behavior or rhesus monkeys following lesions of the dorsolateral and orbital prefrontal cortex in infancy. *Exp. Brain Res.* 12:265–74
39. Braun, J., Lundy, E., McCarthy, F. 1970. Depth discrimination in rats following removal of visual neocortex. *Brain Res.* 20:283
40. Brinkman, J., Kuypers, H. G. J. M. 1972. Splitbrain monkeys: Cerebral control of ipsilateral and contralateral arm, hand, and finger movements. *Science* 176:536–39
41. Brodal, P. 1971. Corticopontine projection in cat. 1. Projection from proreate gyrus. *J. Comp. Neurol.* 142:127–34
42. Brugge, J. F., Dubrovsky, N. A., Aitkin, L. M., Anderson, D. J. 1969. Sensitivity of single neurons in auditory cortex of cat to binaural tonal stimulation; Effects of varying interaural time and intensity. *J. Neurophysiol.* 32:1005–24
43. Brugge, J. F., Merzenich, M. M. 1971. Representation of frequency in auditory cortex in the macaque monkey. In *Physiology of the Auditory System,* ed. M. B. Sachs, 283–88. Baltimore: Nat. Educ. Consult. 384 pp.
44. Burrows, G., Hayhow, W. R. 1971. The organization of the thalamocortical visual pathways in the cat. *Brain, Behav. Evol.* 4:220–72
45. Butler, R. A., Diamond, I. T., Neff, W. D. 1957. Role of auditory cortex in discrimination of changes of frequency. *J. Neurophysiol.* 20:108–20
46. Butter, C. M. 1964. Habituation of responses to novel stimuli in monkeys with selective frontal lesions. *Science* 144:313–15
47. Butter, C. M. 1968. The effect of discrimination training on pattern equivalence in monkeys with inferotemporal and lateral striate lesions. *Neuropsychologia* 6:27–40
48. Butter, C. M. 1969. Impairments in selective attention to visual stimuli in monkeys with inferotemporal and lateral striate lesions. *Brain Res.* 12:374–383
49. Butter, C. M. 1969. Perseveration in extinction and in discrimination reversal tasks following selective frontal abla-

tions in *Macaca mulatta. Physiol. & Behav.* 4:163–71

50. Butter, C. M., Doehrman, S. R. 1968. Size discrimination and transposition in monkeys with striate and temporal lesions. *Cortex* 4:35–46
51. Butter, C. M., Hirtzel, M. 1970. Impairment in sampling visual stimuli in monkeys with inferotemporal lesions. *Physiol. & Behav.* 5:369–70
52. Butter, C. M., McDonald, J. A. 1969. Orality, preference behavior, and reinforcement value of nonfood object in monkeys with orbital frontal lesions. *Science* 164:1306–7
53. Butter, C. M., Snyder, D. R., McDonald, J. A. 1970. Effects of orbital frontal lesions on aversive and aggressive behavior in rhesus monkeys. *J. Comp. Physiol. Psychol.* 72:132–44
54. Butters, N., Barton, M. 1970. Effect of parietal lobe damage on the performance of reversible operations in space. *Neuropsychologia* 8:205–14
55. Butters, N., Barton, M., Brody, B. A. 1970. Role of the right parietal lobe in the mediation of crossmodal associations and reversible operations in space. *Cortex* 6:174–90
56. Butters, N., Pandya, D. 1969. Retention of delayed-alternation: Effect of selective lesions of sulcus principalis. *Science* 165:1271–73
57. Butters, N., Pandya, D., Sanders, K., Dye, P. 1971. Behavioral deficits in monkeys after selective lesions within the middle third of sulcus principalis. *J. Comp. Physiol. Psychol.* 76:8–14
58. Butters, N., Samuels, I., Goodglass, H., Brody, B. 1970. Short-term visual and auditory memory disorders after parietal and frontal lobe damage. *Cortex* 6:440–59
59. Butters, N., Soeldner, C., Fedio, P. 1972. Comparison of parietal and frontal lobe spatial deficits in man: extrapersonal vs. personal (egocentric) space. *Percept. Motor Skills* 34:27–34
60. Campbell, B. A., Ballantine, P. II, Lynch, G. 1971. Hippocampal control of behavioral arousal: Duration of lesion effects and possible interactions with recovery after frontal cortical damage. *Exp. Neurol.* 33:159–70
61. Campbell, C. B. G., Hayhow, W. R. 1971. Primary optic pathways in the echidna, *Tachyglossus aculeatus:* An experimental degeneration study. *J. Comp. Neurol.* 143:119–36
62. Ibid 1972. Primary optic pathways in the duckbill platypus *Ornithorynchus anatmus:* An experimental degeneration study. 145:195–208
63. Chi, C. C. 1970. An experimental silver study of the ascending projections of the central gray substance and adjacent tegmentum in the rat, with observations in the cat. *J. Comp. Neurol.* 130:259–76
64. Chow, K. L., Masland, R. H., Stewart, D. L. 1971. Receptive field characteristics of striate cortical neurons in the rabbit. *Brain Res.* 33:337–52
65. Chow, K. L., Stewart, D. L. 1972. Reversal of structural and functional effects of long-term visual deprivation in cats. *Exp. Neurol.* 34:409–33
66. Chu, N., Rutledge, L. T. 1971. Multisensory activation of pyramidal tract neurons in the cat. *Exp. Neurol.* 30: 352–61
67. Colonnier, M. 1968. Synaptic patterns on the different cell types in the different laminae of the cat visual cortex: An electron microscope study. *Brain Res.* 9:268–87
68. Cool, S. J., Crawford, M. L. J. 1972. Absence of binocular coding in striate cortex units of Siamese cats. *Vision Res.* 12:1809–14
69. Cooper, R. M., Bland, B. H., Gillespie, L. A., Whitaker, R. H. 1970. Unilateral posterior cortical and unilateral collicular lesions and visually guided behavior in the rat. *J. Comp. Physiol. Psychol.* 72:286–95
70. Cornwell, P. 1967. Loss of auditory pattern discrimination following insular-temporal lesion in cats. *J. Comp. Physiol. Psychol.* 63:165–68
71. Cowey, A., Ellis, C. M. 1969. The cortical representation of the retina in squirrel and rhesus monkeys and its relation to visual acuity. *J. Exp. Neurol.* 24: 374–85
72. Cowey, A., Gross, C. G. 1970. Effects of foveal prestriate and inferotemporal lesions on visual discrimination by rhesus monkeys. *Exp. Brain Res.* 11:128–44
73. Craft, L. H., Butler, C. M. 1968. Effect of striate cortex removal on wavelength discrimination in rats. *Psychol. Rec.* 18:311–16
74. Cragg, B., Ainsworth, A. 1969. The topography of the afferent projections in the circumstriate visual cortex of the monkey studies by the Nauta method. *Vision Res.* 9:733–47
75. Cranford, J., Diamond, I. T., Ravizza, R. J., Whitfield, I. C. 1970. Unilateral lesions of the auditory cortex and the "precedence effect." *J. Physiol.* 213: 18–19

76. Creel, D. J. 1971. Visual system anomaly associated with albinism in the cat. *Nature* 231: 465–66
77. Creel, D. J., Giolli, R. A. 1972. Retinogeniculostriate projections in guinea pigs: Albino and pigmented strains compared. *Exp. Neurol.* 36: 411–25
78. Creutzfeldt, O. D. 1970. Some principles of synaptic organization in the visual system. In *The Neurosciences: Second Study Program,* ed. F. O. Schmitt, 630–47. New York: Rockefeller Univ. Press
79. Creutzfeldt, O. D., Poppel, E., Singer, W. 1971. Quantitativer ansatz zur analyse der funktionellen organisation des visuellen cortex (Untersuchungen an Primaten). In *Zeichenerkennug durch biologische und technische Systeme,* 81–95. Berlin: Springer
80. Curry, M. J. 1972. The effects of stimulating the somatic sensory cortex on single neurones in the posterior group (PO) of the cat. *Brain Res.* 44:463–81
81. Ibid. The exteroceptive properties of neurones in the somatic part of the posterior group (PO). 44:439–62
82. Dalby, D. A., Meyer, D. R., Meyer, P. M. 1970. Effects of occipital neocortical lesions upon visual discrimination in the cat. *Physiol. & Behav.* 5:727–34
83. Deecke, L., Becker, W., Grozinger, B., Scheid, P., Kornhuber, H. 1972. Human brain potentials preceding voluntary limb movements. *Electroencephalogr. Clin. Neurophysiol.* 33:97–104
84. Deecke, L., Scheid, P., Kornhuber, H. H. 1969. Distribution of readiness potential, premotion positivity, and motor potential of the human cerebral cortex preceding voluntary finger movements. *Exp. Brain Res.* 7:158–68
85. Deets, A. C., Harlow, H. F., Singh, S. D., Blomquist, A. J. 1970. Effects of bilateral lesions of the frontal granular cortex on the social behavior of rhesus monkeys. *J. Comp. Physiol. Psychol.* 72:452–61
86. Denney, D., Adoijani, C. 1972. Orientation specificity of visual cortical neurons after head tilt. *Exp. Brain Res.* 14: 312–17
87. Desmedt, J. E., Mechelse, K. 1959. Corticofugal projections from temporal lobe in cat and their possible role in acoustic discrimination. *J. Physiol.* 147:17–18
88. Dews, P. B., Wiesel, T. N. 1970. Consequences of monocular deprivation on visual behavior in kittens. *J. Physiol.* 206:437–55
89. Dewson, J. H. III. 1964. Speech sound discrimination by cats. *Science* 144: 555–56
90. Dewson, J. H. III, Pribram, K. H., Lynch, J. C. 1969. Effects of ablations of temporal cortex upon speech sound discrimination in the monkey. *Exp. Neurol.* 24:579–91
91. Diamond, I. T., Jones, E. G., Powell, T. P. S. 1968. The association connections of the auditory cortex of the cat. *Brain Res.* 11:560–79
92. Ibid. Interhemispheric fiber connections of the auditory cortex of the cat. 11:177–93
93. Ibid 1969. The projection of the auditory cortex upon the diencephalon and brain stem in the cat. 15:305–40
94. Diamond, I. T., Neff, W. D. 1957. Ablation of temporal cortex and discrimination of auditory patterns. *J. Neurophysiol.* 20:300–15
95. Diamond, I. T., Snyder, M., Killackey, H., Jane, J. A., Hall, W. C. 1970. Thalamo-cortical projections in the tree shrew *(Tupaia glis). J. Comp. Neurol.* 139:273–306
96. Diamond, I. T., Utley, J. D. 1963. Thalamic retrograde degeneration study of sensory cortex in opossum. *J. Comp. Neurol.* 120:129–60
97. Divac, I. 1971. Frontal lobe system and spatial reversal in the rat. *Neuropsychologia* 9:175–83
98. Divac, I. 1972. Neostriatum and functions of prefrontal cortex. *Acta Neurobiol. Exp.* 32:461–77
99. Divac, I., Warren, J. M. 1971. Delayed response by frontal monkeys in the nencki testing situation. *Neuropsychologia* 9:209–17
100. Doty, R. W. 1971. Survival of pattern vision after removal of striate cortex in the adult cat. *J. Comp. Neurol.* 143: 341–70
101. Dow, B. M., Dubner, R. 1969. Visual receptive fields and responses to movement in an association area of cat cerebral cortex. *J. Neurophysiol.* 32:773–84
102. Ibid 1971. Single unit responses to moving visual stimuli in middle suprasylvian gyrus of the cat. 34:47–55
103. Dua, S., MacLean, P. D. 1964. Localization for penile erection in medial frontal lobe. *Am. J. Physiol.* 207: 1425–34
104. Dubner, R., Zeki, S. M. 1971. Response properties and receptive fields of cells in an anatomically defined region of the

superior temporal sulcus in the monkey. *Brain Res.* 35:528–32
105. Dubrovsky, B., Garcia-Rill, E. 1971. Convergence of tectal and visual cortex input to pericruciate neurons. *Exp. Neurol.* 33:475–84
106. Eidelberg, E., Woodbury, C. M. 1972. Apparent redundancy in the somatosensory system in monkeys. *Exp. Neurol.* 37:573–81
107. Elliott, D. N., Trahiotis, C. 1972. Cortical lesions and auditory discrimination. *Psychol. Bull.* 77:198–222
108. Encabo, H., Bekerman, A. J. 1971. Responses evoked in nucleus medalis dorsalis of the thalamus by subcortical stimulation. A microelectrode study. *Brain Res.* 28:35–46
109. Engel, J. Jr., Woody, C. D. 1972. Effects of character and significance of stimulus on unit activity at coronal-pericruciate cortex of cat during performance of conditioned motor response. *J. Neurophysiol.* 35:220–29
110. Erulkar, S. D. 1972. Comparative aspects of spatial localization of sound. *Physiol. Rev.* 52:237–347
111. Ettlinger, G., Gautrin D. 1971. Visual discrimination performance in the monkey: The effect of unilateral removals of temporal cortex. *Cortex* 7:317–31
112. Evarts, E. V. 1969. Activity of pyramidal tract neurons during postural fixation. *J. Neurophysiol.* 32:375–85
113. Evarts. E. V. 1971. Unit studies of the organization of the motor system in unanesthetized monkeys. *Proc. Int. Union Physiol. Sci.* 8
114. Evarts, E. V. 1972. Activity of motor cortex neurons in association with learned movement. *Int. J. Neurosci.* 3: 113–24
115. Evarts, E. V. 1972. Contrasts between activity of precentral and postcentral neurons of cerebral cortex during movement in the monkey. *Brain Res.* 40: 25–31
116. Evarts, E. V., Thach, W. T. 1969. Motor mechanisms of the CNS: Cerebrocerebellar interrelations. *Ann. Rev. Physiol.* 31:451–98
117. Feeney, D. M., Orem, J. M. 1972. Modulation of visual cortex inhibition during reticular evoked arousal. *Physiol. & Behav.* 9:805–8
118. Finger, S. 1972. Lemniscal and extralemniscal thalamic lesions and tactile discrimination in the rat. *Exp. Brain Res.* 15:532–42
119. Fox, R., Blake, R. R. 1971. Stereoscopic vision in the cat. *Nature* 233:55–56
120. Funkenstein, H. H., Nelson, P. G., Winter, P., Wollberg, Z., Newman, J. D. 1971. Unit responses in auditory cortex of awake squirrel monkeys to vocal stimulation. In *Physiology of the Auditory System,* ed. M. B. Sachs, 307–16. Baltimore: Nat. Educ. Consult. 384 pp.
121. Ganchrow, D., Erickson, R. P. 1972. Thalamocortical relations in gustation. *Brain Res.* 36:289–305
122. Ganz, L., Hirsch, H. V. B., Tieman, S. B. 1972. The nature of perceptual deficits in visually deprived cats. *Brain Res.* 44:547–68
123. Gardner, E., Morin, F. 1957. Projection of fast afferents to the cerebral cortex of monkey. *Am. J. Physiol.* 189:152–58
124. Garey, L. J., Jones, E. G., Powell, T. P. S. 1968. Interrelationships of striate and extrastriate cortex with the primary relay sites of the visual pathway. *J. Neurol. Neurosurg. Psychiat.* 31:135–57
125. Garey, L. J., Powell, T. P. S. 1971. An experimental study of the termination of the lateral geniculo-cortical pathway in the cat and monkey. *Proc. Roy. Soc. B.* 179:41–63
126. Gavalas, R. J., Sperry, R. W. 1969. Central integration of visual half-fields in split-brain monkeys. *Brain Res.* 15: 97–106
127. Gerbrandt, L. K., Spinelli, D. N., Pribram, K. H. 1970. The interaction of visual attention and temporal cortex stimulation on electrical activity evoked in the striate cortex. *Electroencephalogr. Clin. Neurophysiol.* 29:146–55
128. Gillespie, L. A., Cooper, R. M. 1973. Visual cortical lesions in the rat and a conditioned emotional response (CER). *J. Comp. Physiol. Psychol.* 83:76–91
129. Giolli, R. A., Guthrie, M. 1967. Organization of projections of visual areas I and II upon the superior colliculus and pretectal nuclei in the rabbit. *Brain Res.* 6:388–90
130. Giolli, R. A., Guthrie, M. 1971. Organization of subcortical projections of visual areas I and II in the rabbit. An experimental degeneration study. *J. Comp. Neurol.* 142:351–76
131. Glassman, R. B. 1970. Contralateral and ipsilateral transfer of a cutaneous discrimination in normal and callosum-sectioned cats. *J. Comp. Physiol. Psychol.* 70:470–75
132. Glassman, R. B. 1970. Cutaneous discrimination and motor control following somatosensory cortical ablations. *Physiol. & Behav.* 5:1009–19

133. Ibid 1971. Discrimination of passively received kinesthetic stimuli following sensorimotor cortical ablation in cats. 7:239–43
134. Glassman, R. B. 1971. Recovery following sensorimotor cortical damage: Evoked potentials, brain stimulation, and motor control. *Exp. Neurol.* 33: 16–29
135. Glees, P., Cole, J. 1950. Recovery of skilled motor functions after small repeated lesions in motor cortex in macaque. *J. Neurophysiol.* 13:137–48
136. Glendenning, R. L. 1972. Effects of training between two unilateral lesions of visual cortex upon ultimate retention of black-white discrimination habits by rats. *J. Comp. Physiol. Psychol.* 80: 216–29
137. Glickstein, M., King, R. A., Miller, J., Berkley, M. 1967. Cortical projections from the dorsal lateral geniculate nucleus of cats. *J. Comp. Neurol.* 130: 55–75
138. Glickstein, M., Stein, J., King, R. A. 1972. Visual input to the pontine nuclei. *Science* 178:1110–11
139. Goldman, P. S. 1971. Functional development of the prefrontal cortex in early life and the problem of neuronal plasticity. *Exp. Neurol.* 32:366–87
140. Goldman, P. S. 1972. Developmental determinants of cortical plasticity. *Acta Neurobiol. Exp.* 32:495–511
141. Goldman, P. S., Rosvold, H. E. 1970. Localization of function within the dorsolateral prefrontal cortex of the rhesus monkey. *Exp. Neurol.* 27:291–304
142. Goldman, P. S., Rosvold, H. E. 1972. The effects of selective caudate lesions in infant and juvenile rhesus monkeys. *Brain Res.* 43:53–66
143. Goldman, P. S., Rosvold, H. E., Mishkin, M. 1970. Evidence for behavioral impairment following prefrontal lobectomy in the infant monkey. *J. Comp. Physiol. Psychol.* 70:454–63
144. Goldman, P. S., Rosvold, H. E., Mishkin, M. 1970. Selective sparing of function following prefrontal lobectomy in infant monkeys. *Exp. Neurol.* 29: 221–26
145. Goldman, P. S., Rosvold, H. E., Vest, B., Galkin, T. W. 1971. Analysis of the delayed-alternation deficit produced by dorsolateral prefrontal lesions in the rhesus monkey. *J. Comp. Physiol. Psychol.* 77:212–20
146. Goldrich, S. G., Stamm, J. S. 1971. Electrical stimulation of inferotemporal and occipital cortex in monkeys: Effects on visual discrimination and spatial reversal performance. *J. Comp. Physiol. Psychol.* 74:448–58
147. Goldring, S., Aras, E., Weber, P. C. 1970. Comparative study of sensory input to motor cortex in animals and man. *Electroencephalogr. Clin. Neurophysiol.* 29:537–50
148. Goldring, S., Ratcheson, R. 1972. Human motor cortex: Sensory input data from single neuron recordings. *Science* 175:1493–95
149. Goldstein, M. H. Jr. 1968. Single unit studies of cortical coding of simple acoustic stimuli. In *Physiological and Biochemical Aspects of Nervous Integration,* ed. F. D. Carlson, 132–51. Englewood Cliffs, New Jersey: Prentice-Hall. 391 pp.
150. Goldstein, M. H. Jr., Abeles, M., Daly, R. L., McIntosh, J. 1970. Functional architecture in cat primary auditory cortex: Tonotopic organization. *J. Neurophysiol.* 33:188–97
151. Goldstein, M. H. Jr., Hall, J. L. II, Butterfield, B. O. 1968. Single-unit activity in the primary auditory cortex of unanesthetized cats. *J. Acoust. Soc. Am.* 43:444–55
152. Goldstein, M. H. Jr., Rebaupierre, F. de, Yeni-Komshian, G. H. 1971. Cortical coding of periodicity pitch. In *Physiology of the Auditory System,* ed. M. B. Sachs, 299–306. Baltimore: Nat. Educ. Consult. 384 pp.
153. Graybiel, A. M. 1972. Some ascending connections of the pulvinar and nucleus lateralis posterior of the thalamus in the cat. *Brain Res.* 44:99–125
154. Graybiel, A. M. 1973. Some fiber pathways related to the posterior thalamic region in the cat. *Brain, Behav. Evol.* In press
155. Graybiel, A. M. 1973. The thalamo-cortical projection of the so-called posterior nuclear group: A study with anterograde degeneration methods in the cat. *Brain Res.* 49:229–44
156. Greenstreet, R. L. 1971. Free behavior of rhesus monkeys following lesions of the dorsolateral and orbital prefrontal cortex in infancy. *Exp. Brain Res.* 12: 265–74
157. Gross, C. G. 1973. Visual functions of inferotemporal cortex. In *Handbook of Sensory Physiology,* ed. R. Jung. Berlin: Springer. In press
158. Gross, C. G., Bender, D. B., Rocha-Miranda, C. E. 1969. Visual receptive fields of neurons in inferotemporal cortex of the monkey. *Science* 166:1303–6

159. Gross, C. G., Cowey, A., Manning, F. J. 1971. Further analysis of visual discrimination deficits following foveal prestriate and inferotemporal lesions in rhesus monkeys. *J. Comp. Physiol. Psychol.* 76:1–7
160. Gross, C. G., Rocha-Miranda, C. E., Bender, D. B. 1972. Visual properties of neurons in inferotemporal cortex of the Macaque. *J. Neurophysiol* 35:96–111
161. Gross, C. G., Schiller, P. H., Wells, C., Gerstein, G. L. 1967. Single-unit activity in temporal association cortex of the monkey. *J. Neurophysiol.* 30:833–43
162. Guillery, R. W. 1969. An abnormal retinogeniculate projection in Siamese cats. *Brain Res.* 14:739–41
163. Guillery, R. W., Kaas, J. H. 1971. A study of normal and congenitally abnormal retinogeniculate projections in cats. *J. Comp. Neurol.* 143:73–100
164. Hall, J. L. II, Goldstein, M. H. Jr. 1968. Representation of binaural stimuli by single units in primary auditory cortex of unanesthetized cats. *J. Acoust. Soc. Am.* 43:456–61
165. Hall, W. C., Diamond, I. T. 1968. Organization and function of the visual cortex in hedgehog. I. Cortical cytoarchitecture and thalamic retrograde degeneration. *Brain, Behav. Evol.* 1:181–214
166. Ibid. Organization and function of the visual cortex in hedgehog. II. An ablation study of pattern discriminations. 1:215–43
167. Hall, W. C., Kaas, J., Killackey, H., Diamond, I. T. 1971. Cortical visual areas in the grey squirrel *(Sciurus carolinesis):* A correlation between cortical evoked potential maps and architectonic subdivisions. *J. Neurophysiol.* 34:437–52
168. Handwerker, H. O., Sassen, M. 1972. Contribution of naturally stimulated D- and G-Hair receptors to the excitation of cortical SI-neurons. *Pflügers Arch.* 334:310–26
169. Handwerker, H. O., Zimmermann, M. 1972. Cortical evoked responses upon selective stimulations of cutaneous group III fibers and the mediating spinal pathways. *Brain Res.* 36:437–40
170. Hara, K. 1962. Visual defects resulting from prestriate cortical lesions in cats. *J. Comp. Physiol. Psychol.* 55:293–98
171. Harlow, H. F., Blomquist, A. J., Thompson, C. I., Schlitz, K. A., Harlow, M. K. 1968. Effects of induction age and size of frontal lobe lesions on learning in rhesus monkeys. In *Neuropsychology of Development,* ed. R. L. Isaacson, 79–120. New York: Wiley
172. Harlow, H. F., Thompson, C. I., Blomquist, A. J., Schlitz, K. A. 1970. Learning in rhesus monkeys after varying amounts of prefrontal lobe destruction during infancy and adolescence. *Brain Res.* 18:343–53
173. Harting, J., Noback, C. R. 1971. Subcortical projections from the visual cortex in the tree shrew *(Tupaia glis). Brain Res.* 25:21–33
174. Heath, C. J., Jones, E. G. 1970. Connexions of area 19 and the lateral suprasylvian area of the visual cortex of the cat. *Brain Res.* 19:302–5
175. Heath, C. J., Jones, E. G. 1971. The anatomical organization of the suprasylvian gyrus of the cat. *Ergeb. Anat. Entwicklungsgesch.* 45:3–64
176. Heffner, H. H. Unpublished observations
177. Henry, G. H., Bishop, P. O., Coombs, J. S. 1969. Inhibitory and sub-liminal excitatory receptive fields of simple units in cat striate cortex. *Vision Res.* 9: 1289–96
178. Hirsch, H. V. B. 1972. Visual perception in cats after environmental surgery. *Exp. Brain Res.* 15:405–23
179. Hirsch, H. V. B., Spinelli, D. N. 1970. Visual experience modifies distribution of horizontally and vertically oriented receptive fields in cats. *Science* 168: 869–71
180. Hirsch, H. V. B., Spinelli, D. N. 1971. Modification of the distributes of receptive field orientation in cats by selective visual exposure during development. *Exp. Brain Res.* 13:509–27
181. Hobson, J. A., McCarley, R. W. 1971. Cortical unit activity in sleeping and waking. *Electroencephalogr. Clin. Neurophysiol.* 30:97–112
182. Hoffman, K-P. Stone, J. 1971. Conduction velocity of afferents to cat visual cortex: A correlation with cortical receptive field properties. *Brain Res.* 32:460–66
183. Hollander, H. 1970. The projection from the visual cortex to the lateral geniculate body (LGB). An experimental study with silver impregnation methods in the cat. *Exp. Brain Res.* 10: 219–35
184. Hollander, H. 1972. Autoradiographic evidence for a projection from the striate cortex to the dorsal part of the lateral geniculate nucleus in the cat. *Brain Res.* 41:464–66

185. Hore, J., Porter, R. 1972. Pyramidal and extrapyramidal influences on some hindlimb motoneuron population of the arboreal brush-tailed possum *Trichosurus vulpecula*. *J. Neurophysiol.* 35:112–21
186. Horn, G., Hill, R. M. 1969. Modifications of receptive fields of cells in the visual cortex occurring spontaneously and associated with bodily tilt. *Nature* 221:186–88
187. Horne, M., Porter, R. 1971. The effects of prolonged cortical stimulation on the natural activity of neurones in the precentral gyrus of conscious monkeys. *Brain Res.* 34:115–26
188. Hubel, D. H., Wiesel, T. N. 1962. Receptive fields, binocular interaction and functional architecture in the cat's visual cortex. *J. Physiol.* 160:106–54
189. Hubel, D., Wiesel, T. N. 1964. Effects of monocular deprivation in kittens. *Arch. Exp. Pathol. Pharmakol.* 248:492–97
190. Hubel, D. H., Wiesel, T. N. 1965. Binocular interaction in striate cortex of kittens reared with artificial squint. *J. Neurophysiol.* 28:1041–59
191. Hubel, D. H., Wiesel, T. N. 1970. Stereoscopic vision in macaque monkey. Cells sensitive to binocular depth in area 18 of the macaque monkey cortex. *Nature* 225:41–42
192. Hubel, D. H., Wiesel, T. N. 1970. The period of susceptibility to the physiological effects of unilateral eye closure in kittens. *J. Physiol.* 206:419–36
193. Ibid 1971. Aberrant visual projections in the Siamese cat. 218:33–62
194. Hubel, D. H., Wiesel, T. N. 1972. Laminar and columnar distribution of geniculo-cortical fibers in the macaque monkey. *J. Comp. Neurol.* 146:421–50
195. Hughes, A., Wilson, M. E. 1969. Callosal terminations along the boundary between visual areas I and II in the rabbit. *Brain Res.* 12:19–25
196. Humphrey, N. K., Weiskrantz, L. 1967. Vision in monkeys after removal of the striate cortex. *Nature* 215:595–97
197. Hyvärinen, J. 1973. CNS: Afferent mechanisms with emphasis on physiological and behavioral correlations. *Ann. Rev. Physiol.* 35:243–72
198. Hyvärinen, J., Poranen, A., Jokinen, Y. 1973. Central sensory activities between sensory input and motor output. In *The Neurosciences: Third Study Program,* ed. F. O. Schmitt. Cambridge: MIT Press. In press
199. Iversen, S. D., Mishkin, M. 1970. Perseverative interference in monkeys following selective lesions of the inferior prefrontal convexity. *Exp. Brain Res.* 11:376–86
200. Iwai, E., Mishkin, M. 1968. Two visual foci in the temporal lobe of monkeys. In *Neurophysiological Basis of Fear and Behavior,* ed. N. Yoshii, N. Buchwald, Japan: Osaka Univ. Press
201 Iwai, E., Mishkin, M. 1969. Further evidence on the locus of the visual area in the temporal lobe of the monkey. *Exp. Neurol.* 25:585–94
202. Jacobsen, C. F., Nissen, H. W. 1937. Studies of cerebral function in primates. IV. The effects of frontal lobe lesions on the delayed laternation habit in monkey. *J. Comp. Psychol.* 23:101–12
203. James, W. 1890. *The Principles of Psychology* 1:12–80. Reprinted 1950. New York: Dover. 689 pp.
204. Jane, J. A., Campbell, C. B. G., Yashon, D. 1969. The origin of the corticospinal tract of the tree shrew *(Tupaia glis)* with observations of its brainstem and spinal terminations. *Brain, Behav. Evol.* 2:160–82
205. Jane, J. A., Levey, N., Carlson, N. J. 1972. Tectal and cortical function in vision. *Exp. Neurol.* 35:61–77
206. Jane, J. A., Yashon, D., Becker, D. P., Beatty, R., Sugar, O. 1968. The effect of destruction of the corticospinal tract in the human cerebral peduncle upon motor function and involuntary movements: Report of 11 cases. *J. Neurosurg.* 28:581–85
207. Jane, J. A., Yashon, D., DeMeyer, W., Bucy, P. C. 1967. The contribution of the precentral gyrus to the pyramidal tract of man. *J. Neurosurg.* 26:244–48
208. Jewett, D. L., Romano, M. N. 1972. Neonatal development of auditory system potentials averaged from the scalp of rat and cat. *Brain Res.* 36:101–15
209. Jewett, D. L., Williston, J. S. 1971. Auditory-evoked far fields averaged from the scalp of humans. *Brain* 94:681–96
210. Johnson, R. N., Hanna, G. R. 1972. Modulation of the thalamocortical motor system by sensory information. *Brain Res.* 38:35–47
211. Johnson, T. N., Rosvold, H. E. 1971. Topographic projections on the globus pallidus and the substantia nigra of selectively placed lesions in the precommissural caudate nucleus and putamen in the monkey. *Exp. Neurol.* 33: 584–96
212. Johnson, T. N., Rosvold, H. E., Mishkin, M. 1968. Projections from behaviorally defined sectors of the prefrontal cortex to the basal ganglia, septum, and

diencephalon of the monkey. *Exp. Neurol.* 21:20–34

213. Jones, E. G., Powell, T. P. S. 1970. An anatomical study of converging sensory pathways within the cerebral cortex of the monkey. *Brain* 93:793–820
214. Kaas, J. H., Hall, W. C., Diamond, I. T. 1970. Cortical visual areas I and II in the hedgehog: Relation between evoked potential maps and architectonic subdivisions. *J. Neurophysiol.* 33:595–615
215. Kaas, J. H., Hall, W. C., Diamond, I. T. 1972. Visual cortex of the grey squirrel *(Sciureus carolinesis):* Architectonic subdivisions and connections from the visual thalamus. *J. Comp. Neurol.* 145: 273–306
216. Kaas, J. H., Hall, W. C., Killackey, H., Diamond, I. T. 1972. Visual cortex of the tree shrew *(Tupaia glis):* Architectonic subdivisions and representations of the visual field. *Brain Res.* 42:491–96
217. Karol, E. A., Pandya, D. M. 1971. The distribution of the corpus callosum in the rhesus monkey. *Brain* 94:471–86
218. Kawamura, K., Otani, K. 1970. Corticocortical fiber connections in the cat cerebrum: The frontal regions. *J. Comp. Neurol.* 139:423–48
219. Keating, E. G., Horel, J. A. 1972. Effects of prestriate and striate lesions of performance of simple visual tasks. *Exp. Neurol.* 35:322–36
220. Kelley, J. B., Whitfield, I. C. 1971. Effects of auditory cortical lesions on discriminations of rising and falling frequency-modulated tones. *J. Neurophysiol.* 34:802–16
221. Kenshalo, D. R., Ed. 1968. *The Skin Senses.* Springfield, Ill.: Thomas. 636 pp.
222. Killackey, H., Wilson, M., Diamond, I. T. 1972. Further studies of the striate and extrastriate visual cortex in the tree shrew. *J. Comp. Physiol. Psychol.* 81: 45–63
223. Kluver, H. 1941. Visual functions after removal of the occipital lobes. *J. Psychol.* 11:23–45
224. Kubota, K., Niki, H. 1971. Prefrontal cortical unit activity and delayed alternation performance in monkeys. *J. Neurophysiol.* 34:337–47
225. Kubota, K., Niki, H. 1971. Precentral cortical unit activity and jaw movement in chronic monkeys. In *Oral-Facial Sensory and Motor Mechanisms,* ed. R. Dubner, Y. Kawamura, 365–79. New York: Appleton. 379 pp.
226. Kuypers, H. G. J. M. 1958. Pericentral cortical projections to motor and sensory nuclei. *Science* 128:662–63
227. Kuypers, H. G. J. M. 1958. Some projections from the pericentral cortex to the pons and lower brainstem in monkey and chimpanzee. *J. Comp. Neurol.* 110:221–56
228. Kuypers, H. G. J. M. 1960. Central cortical projections to motor, somatosensory and reticular cell groups. In *Structure and Function of the Cerebral Cortex,* ed. D. Tower, J. Schade, 138–43. Amsterdam: Elsevier. 384 pp.
229. Kuypers, H. G. J. M. 1960. Central cortical projects to motor and somotosensory cell groups. *Brain* 83:161–84
230. Kuypers, H. G. J. M. 1964. The descending pathways to the spinal cord, their anatomy and function. Progress in Brain Research. In *Organization of the Spinal Cord,* ed. J. C. Eccles, J. P. Schade, 178–202. Amsterdam: Elsevier. 285 pp.
231. Laemle, L., Benhamida, C., Purpura, D. P. 1972. Laminar distribution of geniculo-cortical afferents in visual cortex of the postnatal kitten. *Brain Res.* 41:25–37
232. Landgren, S., Silfvenius, H. 1968. Projections of the eye and the neck region on the anterior suprasylvian cerebral cortex of the cat. *Acta Physiol. Scand.* 80:196–214
233. Landgren, S., Silfvenius, H. 1969. Projection to cerebral cortex of Group I muscle afferents from the cat's hind limb. *J. Physiol.* 200:353–72
234. Landgren, S., Silfvenius, H., Wolsk, D. 1967. Somato-sensory paths to the second cortical projection area of the Group I muscle afferents. *J. Physiol.* 191:543–59
235. Lashley, K. S. 1944. Studies of cerebral function in learning: XIII. Apparent absence of transcortical association in maze learning. *J. Comp. Neurol.* 80:505
236. Lashley, K. S. 1948. The mechanism of vision: XVIII. Effects of destroying the visual "associative areas" of the monkey. *Genet. Psychol. Monogr.* 37: 107–66
237. Lawrence, D. G., Kuypers, H. G. J. M. 1968. Functional organization of the motor system in the monkey: I. The effects of bilateral pyramidal lesions. *Brain* 91:1–14
238. Ibid. The functional organization of the motor system in the monkey: II. The effect of lesions of the descending brainstem pathways. 91:15–36
239. Lende, R. A. 1963. Cerebral cortex: A sensorimotor amalgam in the marsupialia. *Science* 141:730–32

240. Lende, R. A. 1963. Motor representation in the cerebral cortex of the opossum *(Didelphis virginianus). J. Comp Neurol.* 121:405–15
241. Ibid. Sensory representation in the cerebral cortex of the opossum *(Didelphis virginiana).* 121:395–403
242. Lende, R. A. 1964. Representation in the cerebral cortex of a primitive mammal: sensorimotor, visual, and auditory fields in the echidna *(Tachyglossus aculeatus). J. Neurophysiol.* 27:37–48
243. Lende, R. A., Sadler, K. M. 1967. Sensory and motor areas in neocortex of hedgehog *(Erinaceus). Brain Res.* 5: 390–405
244. Leonard, C. M. 1969. The prefrontal cortex of the rat. I. Cortical projection of the mediodorsal nucleus. II. Efferent connections. *Brain Res.* 12:321–43
245. Lewis, M. McD., Porter, R., Horne, M. 1971. The effects of impairment of afferent feedback from the moving limb on the natural activities of neurones in the precentral gyrus of conscious monkeys: A preliminary investigation. *Brain Res.* 32:467–73
246. Libet, B., Alberts, W. W., Wright, E. W. Jr., Feinstein, B. 1967. Responses of human somatosensory cortex to stimuli below threshold for conscious sensation. *Science* 158:1597–1600
247. Libet, B., Alberts, W. W., Wright, E. W. Jr., Feinstein, B. 1973. Cortical and thalamic activation in conscious sensory experience. In *Proceedings of International Symposium on Neurophysiology in Man,* ed. G. Somjen, B. Nashold. Amsterdam: Excerpta Med. In press
248. Libet, B., Alberts, W. W., Wright, E. W. Jr., Lewis, M., Feinstein, B. 1973. Some cortical mechanisms mediating conscious sensory responses and the somatosensory qualities in man. In *Somatosensory System,* ed. H. Kornhuber. Stuttgart: Georg Thieme. In press
249. Lubar, J. F., Middaugh, L. D. 1971. Avoidance conditioning in cats with striate and auditory cortex lesions and contrasting effects of peripheral blindness. *J. Comp. Physiol. Psychol.* 76: 26–30
250. Lubar, J. F., Perachio, A. A., Kavanaugh, A. J. 1966. Deficits in active avoidance behavior following lesions of the lateral and posterolateral gyrus of the cat. *J. Comp. Physiol. Psychol.* 62: 263–69
251. Lubar, J. F., Schostal, C. J., Perachio, A. A. 1967. Non-visual functions of visual cortex in the cat. *Physiol. and Behav.* 2:179–84
252. Luschei, E. S., Garthwaite, C. R., Armstrong, M. E. 1971. Relationship of firing patterns of units in face area of monkey precentral cortex to conditioned jaw movements. *J. Neurophysiol.* 34:552–61
253. McCarley, R. W., Hobson, J. A. 1970. Cortical unit activity in desynchronized sleep. *Science* 167:901–3
254. McEnaney, K. W., Butter, C. M. 1969. Perseveration of responding and non-responding in monkeys with orbital frontal ablations. *J. Comp. Physiol. Psychol.* 68:558–61
255. Mandl, G. 1970. Localization of visual patterns by neurons in cerebral cortex of the cat. *J. Neurophysiol.* 33:812–26
256. Manning, F. J. 1971. Punishment for errors and visual discrimination learning by monkeys with inferotemporal cortex lesions. *J. Comp. Physiol. Psychol.* 75:146–52
257. Manning, F. J. 1971. The selective attention "deficit" of monkeys with ablations of foveal prestriate cortex. *Psychon. Sci.* 25:291–92
258. Manning, F. J. 1972. Serial reversal learning by monkeys with inferotemporal or foveal prestriate lesions. *Physiol. & Behav.* 8:177–81
259. Manning, F. J., Gross, C. G. 1971. Partial reinforcement: Effects on visual learning after foveal prestriate and inferotemporal lesions. *Physiol. & Behav.* 6:61–64
260. Martin, G. F. 1968. The pattern of neocortical projections to the mesencephalon of the opossum *(Didelphis virginiana). Brain Res.* 11:593–610
261. Martin, G. F., Fisher, A. M. A. 1972. A further evaluation of the origin, the course and the termination of opossum corticospinal tract. *J. Neurol. Sci.* 7: 177–87
262. Martin, G. F., Megirian, D., Roebuck, A. 1970. The corticospinal tract of the marsupial phalanger *(Trichosurus vulpecula). J. Comp. Neurol.* 139:245–57
263. Martin, G. F., West, H. J. 1967. Efferent neocortical projections to sensory nuclei in the brainstem of the opossum *(Didelphis virginiana). J. Neurol. Sci.* 5:287–302
264. Massion, J., Angaut, P., Albe-Fessard, D. 1965. Activités évoquées chez le chat dans la région du nucleus ventralis lateralis par diverses stimulations sensorielles. I. Etude macro-physiol-

ogique. *Electroencephalogr. Clin. Neurophysiol.* 19:433–51

265. Ibid. Activités évoquées chez le chat dans la région du nucleus ventralis lateralis par diverses stimulations sensorielles. II. Etude macrophysiologique. 19:452–69
266. Massopust, L. C. Jr., Wolin L. R., Frost, V. 1970. Increase in auditory middle frequency discrimination thresholds after cortical ablation. *Exp. Neurol.* 28:299–307
267. Masterton, R. B., Diamond, I. T. 1964. Effects of auditory cortex ablation on discrimination of small binaural time differences. *J. Neurophysiol.* 27:15–36
268. Masterton, R. B., Diamond, I. T. 1973. Hearing: Central neural mechanisms. *Handbook of Perception, Vol. 3.* Academic. In press
269. Masterton, R. B., Skeen, L. C. 1972. The evolution of intelligence: I. Delayed alternation in primitive mammals. *J. Comp. Physiol. Psychol.* 81:423–33
270. Meulders, M., Gybels, J., Bergmans, J., Gerebtzoff, M. A., Goffart, M. 1966. Sensory projections of somatic, auditory and visual origin to the cerebral cortex of the sloth *(Cholepus hoffmanni Peters). J. Comp. Neurol.* 126:535–45
271. Meyer, P. M., Anderson, R. A., Braun, M. G. 1966. Visual cliff preferences following lesions of the visual neocortex in cats and rats. *Psychon. Sci.* 4:269–70
272. Michael, C. R. 1970. Integration of retinal and cortical information in the superior colliculus of the ground squirrel. *Brain, Behav. Evol.* 3:1–4
273. Miller, J. M. 1971. Single unit discharges in behaving monkeys. In *Physiology of the Auditory System,* ed. M. B. Sachs, 317–26. Baltimore: Nat. Educ. Consult. 347 pp.
274. Mishkin, M. 1964. Perseveration of central sets after frontal lesions in monkeys. In *The Frontal Granular Cortex and Behavior,* ed. J. M. Warren, K. Akert, 219–41. New York: McGraw-Hill
275. Mishkin, M. 1966. Visual mechanisms beyond striate cortex. In *Frontiers in Physiological Psychology,* ed. R. Russell, 93–116. New York: Academic
276. Mishkin, M. 1972. Cortical visual areas and their interaction. In *Brain and Human Behavior,* ed. A. G. Karcgmar, J. C. Eccles, 187–208. Berlin: Springer
277. Mittenthal, J. E., Kristan, W. B., Tatton, W. G. 1972. Does the striate cortex begin reconstruction of the visual world? *Science* 176:316–17
278. Mizuno, N., Clemente, C. D., Sauerland, E. K. 1969. Projections from the orbital gyrus in the cat. II. To telencephalic and diencephalic structures. *J. Comp. Neurol.* 136:127–42
279. Mizuno, N., Sauerland, E. K., Clemente, C. D. 1968. Projections from the orbital gyrus in the cat. I. To brain stem structures. *J. Comp. Neurol* 133: 463–76
280. Myers, R. E. 1972. Cortical mechanisms involved in social behavior. *Acta Neurobiol. Exp.* 32:567–79
281. Narikashvili, S. P., Arutyunov, V. S., Guma, E., Moniava, E. S. 1968. Interaction between the primary sensory and association areas of the cerebral cortex in the cat. *Physiol. & Behav.* 3: 761–71
282. Narikashvili, S. P., Kajaia, D. V., Timchenko, A. S. 1969. On the origin of cortical association responses to visual stimulation in the cat. *Brain Res.* 14: 417–25
283. Nauta, W. J. H. 1971. Problem of frontal lobe-reinterpretation. *J. Psychiat. Res.* 8:167–83
284. Neff, W. D. 1960. Role of the auditory cortex in sound discrimination. In *Neural Mechanisms of the Auditory and Vestibular Systems,* ed. G. L. Rasmussen, W. F. Windle, 211–16. Springfield, Ill.: Thomas. 422 pp.
285. Neff, W. D. 1961. Neural mechanisms of auditory discrimination. In *Sensory Communication,* ed. W. A. Rosenblith, 259–78. Cambridge: MIT Press. 844 pp.
286. Neff, W. D. 1962. Neural structures concerned in localization of sound in space. *Psychol. Beitr.* 6:492–500
287. Neff, W. D. 1965. Auditory discrimination affected by cortical ablations. Presented at *International Symposium on Sensorineural Hearing Processes and Disorders, Detroit, Michigan.* Unpublished
288. Neff, W. D. 1968. Localization and lateralization of sound in space. Presented at *Ciba Foundation Symposium on Hearing Mechanisms in Vertebrates,* 207–31. London: Churchill. 320 pp.
289. Newman, P. P., Wolstencroft, J. H. 1959. Medullary responses to stimulation of orbital cortex. *J. Neurophysiol.* 22:516–23
290. Niimi, K., Inoshita, H. 1971. Cortical projections of the lateral thalamic nuclei in the cat. *Proc. Jap. Acad.* 47: 664–69
291. Niimi, K., Kawamura, S., Ishimaru, S. 1970. Anatomical organization of cor-

ticogeniculate projections in the cat. *Proc. Jap. Acad.* 46:878–83
292. Niimi, K., Kawamura, S., Ishimaru, S. 1971. Projections of the visual cortex to the lateral geniculate and posterior thalamic nuclei in the cat. *J. Comp. Neurol.* 143:279–312
293. Niimi, K., Sprague, J. 1970. Thalamocortical organization of the visual system in the cat. *J. Comp. Neurol.* 138:219–50
294. Nikara, T. 1971. Visual masking effects in single units of the cat striate cortex. *Japan J. Physiol.* 21:119–32
295. Niki, H., Sakai, M., Kubota, K. 1972. Delayed alternation performance and unit activity of the caudate head and medial orbitofrontal gyrus in the monkey. *Brain Res.* 38:343–53
296. Noda, H., Creutzfeldt, O. D., Freeman, R. B. 1971. Binocular interaction in the visual cortex of awake cats. *Exp. Brain Res.* 12:406–21
297. Noda, H., Freeman, R. B., Gies, B., Creutzfeldt, O. D. 1971. Neuronal responses in the visual cortex of awake cats to stationary and moving targets. *Exp. Brain Res.* 12:389–405
298. Noorden, G. K. von, Dowling, J. E., Ferguson, D. C. 1970. Experimental amblyopia in monkeys. I. Behavioral studies of stimulus deprivation amblyopia. *Arch. Ophthal.* 84:206–14
299. Noorden, G. K. von, Dowling, J. E. 1970. Experimental amblyopia in monkeys. II. Behavioral studies in strabismic amblyopia. *Arch. Ophthalmol.* 84:215–20
300. O'Brien, J. H., Fox S. S. 1969. Single-cell activity in cat motor cortex. I. Modifications during classical conditioning procedures. *J. Neurophysiol.* 32:267–84
301. Ibid. Single-cell activity in cat motor cortex. II. Functional characteristics of the cell related to conditioning changes. 32:285–96
302. O'Brien, J. H., Pimpaneau, A., Albe-Fessard, D. 1971. Evoked cortical responses to vagal, laryngeal and facial afferents in monkeys under chloralose anesthesia. *Electroencephalogr. Clin. Neurophysiol.* 31:7–20
303. Oesterreich, R. E., Strominger, N. L., Neff, W. D. 1971. Neural structures mediating differential sound intensity discrimination in the cat. *Brain Res.* 27:251–70
304. Ohno, T., Kiyohara, T., Simpson, J. I. 1970. Postsynaptic potentials evoked in cells of area 19 and its lateral zone during stimulation of the visual pathway in cat. *Brain Res.* 20:453–56
305. Orem, J., Feeney, D. M. 1971. Reciprocal reticular influences on cells in rostral and caudal visual cortex of the cat. *Brain Res.* 30:200–3
306. Otsuka, R., Hassler, R. 1962. Uber anfbau und gliederung der corticalen sehsphare bei der katze. *Arch. Psychiat. Zeitsche Neurol.* 203:212–34
307. Pandya, D. N., Dye, P., Butters, N. 1971. Efferent corticocortical projections of the prefrontal cortex in the rhesus monkey. *Brain Res.* 31:35–46
308. Pandya, D. N., Kuypers, H. G. J. M. 1969. Corticocortical connections in the rhesus monkey. *Brain Res.* 13:13–36
310. Pandya, D. N., Vignolo, L. A. 1971. Intrahemispheric and interhemispheric projections of the precentral, premotor and arcuate areas in the rhesus monkey. *Brain Res.* 26:217–33
311. Pasik, T., Pasik, P. 1971. The visual world of monkeys deprived of striate cortex: effective stimulus parameters and the importance of the accessory optic system. *Vision Res.* 3:419–35
312. Paul, R. L., Goodman, H., Merzenich, M. 1972. Alternations in mechanoreceptor input to Brodmann's areas 1 and 3 of the postcentral hand area of *Macaca mulatta* after nerve section and regeneration. *Brain Res.* 39:1–19
313. Perachio, A. A., Lubar, J. F. 1970. Striate cortex ablation and deficits in conditioned avoidance response. *Physiol. & Behav.* 5:1063–67
314. Peters, A., Walsh, T. M. 1972. A study of the organization of apical dendrites in the somatic sensory cortex of the rat. *J. Comp. Neurol.* 144:253–68
315. Petras, J. M. 1971. Connections of parietal lobe. *J. Psychiat. Res.* 8:71–94
316. Petras, J. M., Lehman, R. A. W. 1966. Corticospinal fibers in the raccoon. *Brain Res.* 3:195–97
317. Petrinovitch, L., Carew, T. J. 1969. Interaction of neocortical lesion size and interoperative experience in retention of a learned brightness discrimination. *J. Comp. Physiol. Psychol.* 68:451–54
318. Pettigrew, J. D., Nikara, T., Bishop, P. O. 1968. Binocular interactor in single units in cat striate cortex: Simultaneous stimulation by a single moving slit with receptive fields in correspondence. *Exp. Brain Res.* 6:391–406
319. Pollen, D. A., Lee, J. R., Taylor, J. H. 1971. How does the striate cortex begin the reconstruction of the visual world. *Science* 173:74–77
320. Pollen, D. A., Taylor, J. H., Lee, J. R. 1972. Does the striate cortex begin re-

construction of the visual world. *Science* 176:317–19
321. Polyak, S. 1957. *The Vertebrate Visual System,* ed. H. Kluver, Chicago: Univ. Chicago Press. 1390 pp.
322. Porter, R. 1970. Early facilitation at corticomotoneuronal synapses. *J. Physiol.* 207:733–45
323. Porter, R. 1972. Relationship of the discharges of cortical neurones to movement in free-to-move monkeys. *Brain Res.* 40:39–43
324. Porter, R., Hore, J. 1969. Time course of minimal corticomotoneuronal excitatory postsynaptic potentials in lumbar motoneurons of the monkey. *J. Neurophysiol.* 32:443–51
325. Porter, R., Lewis, M. McD., Horne, M. 1971. Analysis of patterns of natural activity of neurones in the precentral gyrus of conscious monkeys. *Brain Res.* 34:99–113
326. Porter, R., Muir, R. B. 1971. The meaning for motoneurones of the temporal pattern of neural activity in pyramidal tract neurones of conscious monkeys. *Brain Res.* 34:127–42
327. Powell, T. P. S., Cowan, W. M., Raisman, G. 1965. The central olfactory connections. *J. Anat.* 99:791–99
328. Pribram, K. H., Spinelli, D. N., Reitz, S. L. 1969. The effects of radical disconnexion of occipital and temporal cortex on visual behavior of monkeys. *Brain* 92:301–12
329. Pubols, B. H. Jr., Pubols, L. M. 1971. Somatotopic organization of spider monkey somatic sensory cerebral cortex. *J. Comp. Neurol.* 141:63–76
330. Pubols, B. H. Jr., Pubols, L. M. 1972. Neural organization of somatic sensory representation in the spider monkey. *Brain, Behav. Evol.* 5:312–66
331. Purser, D., Whitfield, I. C. 1972. Thalamocortical connexions and tonotopicity in the cat medial geniculate body. *J. Physiol.* 222:161–62
332. Rasmussen, G. L. 1964. Anatomic relationships of the ascending and descending auditory systems. In *Neurological Aspects of Auditory and Vestibular Disorders,* ed. W. S. Fields, B. R. Alford, 5–23. Springfield, Ill.: Thomas. 383 pp.
333. Ravizza, R. J., Heffner, H. E., Masterton, R. B. 1969. Hearing in primitive mammals, II: Hedgehog. *J. Aud. Res.* 9:8–11
334. Ravizza, R. J., Masterton, R. B. 1971. The habituation of auditory reflexes in the decorticate opossum *(Didelphis virginiana). Physiol. & Behav.* 6:717–22
335. Ravizza, R. J., Masterton, R. B. 1972. Contribution of neocortex to sound localization in opossum *(Didelphis virginiana). J. Neurophysiol.* 35:344–56
336. Rebaupierre, F. de, Goldstein, M. H. Jr., Yeni-Komshian, G. 1972. Intracellular study of the cat's primary auditory cortex. *Brain Res.* 48:185–204
337. Rees, S., Hore, J. 1970. The motor cortex of the Brush-tailed possum *(Trichosurus vulpecula):* Motor representation, motor function and the pyramidal tract. *Brain Res.* 20:439–51
338. Reitz, S. L. 1969. Effects of serial disconnection of striate and temporal cortex on visual discrimination performance in monkeys. *J. Comp. Physiol. Psychol.* 68:139–46
339. Reitz, S. L., Pribram, K. H. 1969. Some subcortical connections of the inferotemporal gyrus of monkey. *Exp. Neurol.* 25:623–45
340. Rispal-Padel, L., Massion, J. 1970. Relations between the ventrolateral nucleus and the motor cortex in the cat. *Exp. Brain Res.* 10:331–39
341. Riss, W. 1959. Effect of bilateral temporal cortical ablation on discrimination of sound direction. *J. Neurophysiol.* 22:374–84
342. Rizzolatti, G., Tradardi, V. 1971. Pattern discrimination in monocularly reared cats. *Exp. Neurol.* 33:181–94
343. Robinson, D. L., Doty, R. W. 1972. Transcollosal effects on single units in second somatosensory area (SII) of the cat. *Fed. Proc.* 31:303
344. Robinson, J. S., Voneida, T. J. 1970. Quantitative differences in performance on abstract discrimination using one or both hemispheres. *Exp. Neurol.* 26:72–83
345. Rolls, E. T., Cowey, A. 1970. Topography of the retina and striate cortex and its relationship to visual acuity in rhesus monkeys and squirrel monkeys. *Exp. Brain Res.* 10:298–310
346. Rosabal, F. 1967. Cytoarchitecture of the frontal lobe of the squirrel monkey. *J. Comp. Neurol.* 130:87–108
347. Rosen, I., Asanuma, H. 1972. Peripheral afferent inputs to the forelimb area of the monkey motor cortex: Input-output relations. *Exp. Brain Res.* 14:257–73
348. Rosen, S. C., Stamm, J. S. 1972. Transcortical polarization: Facilitation of delayed response performance by monkeys. *Exp. Neurol.* 35:282–89

349. Rosenquist, A. C., Palmer, L. A. 1971. Visual receptive field properties of cells of the superior colliculus after cortical lesions in the cat. *Exp. Neurol.* 33: 629–52

350. Rosenzweig, M. R. et al 1969. Influences of environmental complexity and visual stimulation on development of occipital cortex in rat. *Brain Res.* 14: 427–45

351. Ruderman, M. I., Morrison, A. R., Hand, P. J. 1972. A solution to the problem of cerebral cortical localization of taste in the cat. *Exp. Neurol.* 37: 522–37

352. Sachs, M. B., Ed. 1971. *Physiology of the Auditory System.* Baltimore: Nat. Educ. Consult. 347 pp.

353. Sanides, F., Hoffmann, J. 1969. Cyto- and myeloarchitecture of the visual cortex of the cat and of the surrounding integration cortices. *J. Hirnforsch.* 11: 79–104

354. Saunders, J. C. 1971. Cochlear nucleus and auditory cortex activity during threshold discriminations in cats. *Electroencephalogr. Clin. Neurophysiol.* 30:73–78

355. Saunders, J. C. 1971. Selective facilitation and inhibition of auditory and visual evoked response during avoidance conditioning in cats. *J. Comp. Physiol. Psychol.* 76:15–25

356. Schilder, P., Pasik, P., Pasik, T. 1972. Extrageniculostriate vision in the monkey. III. Circle vs. triangle and "red vs. green" discrimination. *Exp. Brain Res.* 14:436–48

357. Schilder, P., Pasik, T., Pasik, P. 1971. Extrageniculostriate vision in the monkey. II. Demonstration of brightness discrimination. *Brain Res.* 32:383–98

358. Schlag-Rey, M., Lindsley, D. B. 1970. Effect of prefrontal lesions on trained anticipatory visual attending in cats. *Physiol. & Behav.* 5:1033–41

359. Schwartz, A. S., Eidelberg, E., Marchok, P., Azulay, A. 1972. Tactile discrimination in the monkey after section of the dorsal funiculus and lateral lemniscus. *Exp. Neurol.* 37:582–96

360. Schwartzkroin, P. A., Cowey, A., Gross, C. G. 1969. A test of an "efferent model" of the function of inferotemporal cortex in visual discrimination. *Electroencephalogr. Clin. Neurophysiol.* 27:594–600

361. Scott, J. W., Leonard, C. M. 1971. The olfactory connections of the lateral hypothalamus in the rat, mouse, and hamster. *J. Comp. Neurol.* 141:331–44

362. Sherman, S. M. 1971. Role of visual cortex in interocular transfer in the cat. *Exp. Neurol.* 30:34–45

363. Sherman, S. M. 1972. Development of interocular alignment in cats. *Brain Res.* 37:187–203

364. Sherman, S. M. 1972. Visual development in cats. *Invest. Ophthalmol.* 11: 394–401

365. Sherman, S. M., Hoffman, K-P., Stone, J. 1972. Loss of a specific cell type from dorsal lateral geniculate in visually deprived cats. *J. Neurophysiol.* 35:532–41

366. Shoumura, K., Itoh, K. 1972. Intercortical projections from the lateral wall of the suprasylvian gyrus, the Clare-Bishop area, of the cat. *Brain Res.* 39: 536–39

367. Silfvenius, H. 1970. Projections to the cerebral cortex from afferants of the interosseous nerves of the cat. *Acta Physiol. Scand.* 80:196–214

368. Silfvenius, H. 1972. Projections to the cat cerebral cortex from fore-and hind limb group I muscle afferents. *Umea Univ. Med. Diss.* Umea, Sweden: Univ. Umea. 46 pp.

369. Silfvenius, H. 1972. Properties of cortical Group I neurones located in the lower bank of the anterior suprasylvian sulcus of the cat. *Acta Physiol. Scand.* 84:555–76

370. Singer, P., Bignall, K. E. 1970. Multiple somatic projections to frontal lobe of squirrel monkey. *Exp. Neurol.* 27: 438–53

371. Skrebitsky, V. G. 1969. Nonspecific influences on neuronal firing in the central visual pathway. *Exp. Brain Res.* 9: 269–83

372. Skrebitsky, V. G. 1969. Postsynaptic inhibition in photically evoked responses and its change during distraction of the animal. *Brain Res.* 14:510–12

373. Snyder, D. 1970. Fall from social dominance following orbital frontal ablations in monkeys. *Proc. Ann. Conv. Am. Psychol. Assoc., 78th,* 235–36

374. Snyder, M., Diamond, I. T. 1968. The organization and function of the visual cortex in the tree shrew. *Brain, Behav. Evol.* 1:244–88

375. Spatz, W. B., Tigges, J. 1972. Experimental-anatomical studies on the "middle temporal visual area" in primates. *J. Comp. Neurol.* 146:451–64

376. Spatz, W. B., Tigges, J. 1972. Species difference between Old World and New World monkeys in the organization of the striate-prestriate association. *Brain Res.* 43:591–94

377. Spatz, W. B., Tigges, J., Tigges, M. 1970. Subcortical projections, cortical associations, and some intrinsic interlaminar connections of the striate cortex in the squirrel monkey (Saimiri). *J. Comp. Neurol.* 140:155–74
378. Spear, P. D., Braun, J. J. 1969. Nonequivalence of normal and posteriorly neodecorticate rats on two brightness discrimination problems. *J. Comp. Physiol. Psychol.* 67: 225–39
379. Spear, P. D., Braun, J. J. 1969. Pattern discrimination following removal of visual neocortex in the cat. *Exp. Neurol.* 25:331–48
380. Spinelli, D. N., Barrett, T. W. 1969. Visual receptive field organization of single units in the cat's visual cortex. *Exp. Neurol.* 24:76–98
381. Spinelli, D. N., Hirsch, H. V. B., Phelps, R. W., Metzler, J. 1972. Visual experience as a determinant of the response characteristics of cortical receptive fields in cats. *Exp. Brain Res.* 15:289–304
382. Spinelli, D. N., Pribram, K. H., Bridgeman, B. 1970. Visual receptive field organization of single units in the visual cortex of monkey. *Int. J. Neurosci.* 1:-67–74
383. Spinelli, D. N., Starr, A., Barrett, T. W. 1968. Auditory specificity in unit recordings from cat's visual cortex. *Exp. Neurol.* 22:75–84
384. Stamm, J. S. 1969. Electrical stimulation of monkeys' prefrontal cortex during delayed-response performance. *J. Comp. Physiol. Psychol.* 67:535–46
385. Stamm, J. S. 1970. Dorsolateral frontal ablations and response process in monkeys. *J. Comp. Physiol. Psychol.* 70: 437–67
386. Stamm, J. S., Rosen, S. C. 1969. Electrical stimulation and steady potential shifts in prefrontal cortex during delayed response performance by monkeys. *Acta Biol. Exp.* 29:385–99
387. Stepien, I., Stamm, J. S. 1970. Impairments on locomotor task involving spatial opposition between cue and reward in frontally ablated monkeys. *Acta Neurobiol. Exp.* 30:1–12
388. Ibid. Locomotor delayed response in frontally ablated monkeys. 30:13–18
389. Steriade, M. 1969. Alterations of evoked neuronal discharges in motor and somesthetic cortices during the sleep-wakefulness cycles in the monkey. *Electroencephalogr. Clin. Neurophysiol.* 27:641–735
390. Ibid. Ascending control of motor cortex responsiveness. 26:25–40
391. Steriade, M. 1970. The cerebello-thalamocortical pathway: Ascending (specific and unspecific) and corticofugal controls. *Int. J. Neurol.* 7:177–200
392. Steriade, M., Iosif, G., Apostol, V. 1969. Responsiveness of thalamic and cortical motor relays during arousal and various stages of sleep. *J. Neurophysiol.* 32:251–65
393. Sterling, P., Wickelgren, B. 1970. Function of the projection from the visual cortex to the superior colliculus. *Brain, Behav. Evol.* 3:210–15
394. Stone, J. 1972. Morphology and physiology of the geniculo-cortical synpase in the cat: The question of parallel input to the striate cortex. *Invest. Ophthalmol.* 11:338–46
395. Suga, N. 1972. Analysis of information-bearing elements in complex sounds by auditory neurons of bats. *Audiology* 11:58–72
396. Suomi, S. J., Harlow, H. F., Lewis, J. K. 1970. Effect of bilateral frontal lobectomy of social preferences of rhesus monkeys. *J. Comp. Physiol. Psychol.* 70:448–53
396a. Semmes, J., Mishkin, M. 1965. Somatosensory loss in monkeys after ipsilateral cortical ablation. *J. Neurophysiol.* 28:473–86
397. Swarbrick, L., Whitfield, I. C. 1972. Auditory cortical units selectively responsive to stimulus "shape". *J. Physiol.* 224:68–69
398. Symmes, D. 1967. Discrimination of intermittent noise by Macaques following lesions of the temporal lobe. *Exp. Neurol.* 16:201–14
399. Teyler, T. J., Shaw, C., Thompson, R. F. 1972. Unit responses to moving visual stimuli in the motor cortex of the cat. *Science* 176:811–13
400. Thompson, C. I., Harlow, H. F., Blomquist, A. J., Schlitz, K. A. 1971. Recovery of function following prefrontal lobe damage in rhesus monkeys. *Brain Res.* 35:37–48
401. Thompson, R. F., Bettinger, L. A., Birch, H., Groves, P. M. 1969. Comparison of evoked gross and unit responses in association cortex of waking cat. *Electroencephalogr. Clin. Neurophysiol.* 27:146–51
402. Thompson, R. F., Johnson, R. H., Hoopes, J. J. 1963. Organization of auditory, somatic sensory, and visual projection fields of cerebral cortex in the cat. *J. Neurophysiol.* 26:343–64

403. Thompson, R. F., Smith, H. E., Bliss, D. 1963. Auditory, somatic sensory and visual response interactions and interrelations in association and primary cortical fields of the cat. *J. Neurophysiol.* 26:365–77
404. Tigges, J., Tigges, M., Kalaha, C. S. 1972. Efferent connections of area 17 in *Galago. Am. J. Phys. Anthro.* In press
405. Tower, S. S. 1940. Pyramidal lesion in the monkey. *Brain* 63:36–90
406. Toyama, K., Matsunami, K. 1968. Synaptic action of specific visual impulses upon cat's parastriate cortex. *Brain Res.* 10:473–76
407. Toyama, K., Matsunami, K., Ohno, T. 1969. Antidromic identification of association commissural and corticofugal efferent, cells in cat visual cortex. *Brain Res.* 14:513–17
408. Toyama, K., Tokashiki, S., Matsunami, K. 1969. Synaptic action of the commissural impulses upon association efferent cells in cat visual cortex. *Brain Res.* 14: 518–20
409. Travis, M., Woolsey, C. N. 1956. Motor performance of monkeys after bilateral partial and total cerebral decortications. *Am. J. Phys. Med.* 35:273–310
410. Van Hoesen, G. W., Pandya, D. N., Butters, N. 1972. Cortical afferents to the entorhinal cortex of the rhesus monkey. *Science* 175:1471–73
411. Voneida, T. J. 1967. The effect of pyramidal lesions on the performance of a conditioned avoidance response in cats. *Exp. Neurol.* 19:483–93
412. Voneida, T. J., Robinson, J. S. 1970. Effect of brain bisection on capacity for gross comparison of patterned visual input. *Exp. Neurol.* 26:60–71
413. Ibid 1971. Visual processing in the split-brain cat: one versus two hemispheres. 33:420–31
414. Voneida, T. J., Trevarthen, C. B. 1969. An experimental study of transcallosal connections between the proreus gyri of the cat. *Brain Res.* 12:384–95
415. Vonronin, L. L., Tanengol'ts, L. I. 1969. Postsynaptic reactions in neurons in motor cortex of cat cerebrum to stimuli of different modalities. *Zh. Vyssh. Nerv. Deyatel. im. I. P. Pavlova* 19:1, 71–82
416. Walker, A. E. 1970. The role of the cerebral peduncle in movements. In *Neurosciences Research,* ed. S. Ehrenpreis, O. Solnitzky, 175–207. New York: Academic
417. Wall, P. D., Dubner, R. 1972. Somatosensory pathways. *Ann. Rev. Physiol.* 34:315–36
418. Ward, J. P., Masterton, M. 1970. Encephalization and visual cortex in the tree shrew. *Brain, Behav. Evol.* 3:421–69
419. Ware, C. B., Casagrande, V., Diamond, I. T. 1972. Does the acuity of the tree shrew suffer from removal of striate cortex? *Brain, Behav. Evol.* 5:18–29
420. Warren, J. M., Akert, K., Ed. 1964. *The Frontal Granular Cortex and Behavior.* New York: McGraw-Hill. 477 pp.
421. Warren, J. M., Cornwell, P. R., Warren, H. B. 1969. Unilateral frontal lesions and learning by rhesus monkeys. *J. Comp. Physiol. Psychol.* 69:498–505
422. Webster, W. G. 1972. Functional asymmetry between the cerebral hemispheres of the cat. *Neuropsychologia* 10:75–87
423. Wegener, J. G. 1964. Auditory discrimination behavior of brain damaged monkeys. *J. Aud. Res.* 4:227–57
424. Wegener, J. G., Stamm, J. S. 1966. Behavior flexibility and the frontal lobes. *Cortex* 2:188–201
425. Weiskrantz, L., Cowey, A. 1970. Filling in the scotoma: A study of residual vision after striate cortex lesions in monkeys. In *Progress in Physiological Psychology,* ed. E. Stellar, J. Sprague, 237–58. New York: Academic
426. Welker, C. 1971. Microelectrode delineation of fine grain somatotopic organization of SmI cerebral neocortex in albino rat. *Brain Res.* 26:259–75
427. Welker, C., Shinha, M. M. 1972. Somatotopic organization of SmII cerebral neocortex in albino rat. *Brain Res.* 37:132–36
428. Welt, C., Aschoff, J. C., Kameda, K., Brooks, V. B. Intracortical organization of cat's motorsensory neurons. In *Neurophysiological Basis of Normal and Abnormal Motor Activities,* ed. M. D. Yahr, D. P. Purpura, 255–93. Hewlett, NY: Raven Press. 500 pp.
429. Werner, G. 1970. The topology of the body representation in the somatic afferent pathway. In *The Neurosciences: Second Study Program,* ed. F. O. Schmitt, 605–17. New York: Rockefeller Univ. Press.
430. Werner, G., Whitsel, B. L., Petrucelli, L. M. 1972. Data structure and algorithms in the primate somatosensory cortex. *Brain & Hum. Behav.* 5:164–86
431. Wettstein, A., Handwerker, H. O. 1970. Afferente Verbindungen zu schnell-und

langsamleitenden Pyramidenbahnneuronen der Katze. *Pflügers Arch.* 320: 247–60

432. Whitfield, I. C. 1969. Response of the auditory nervous system to simple time-dependent acoustic stimuli. *Ann. NY Acad. Sci.* 156:671–77
433. Whitfield, I. C. 1971. Auditory Cortex: Tonal, temporal, or topical? In *Physiology of the Auditory System,* ed. M. B. Sachs, 289–98. Baltimore: Nat. Educ. Consult. 347 pp.
434. Whitfield, I. C. 1971. Mechanisms of sound localization. *Nature* 233:95–97
435. Whitsel, B. L., Dreyer, D. A., Roppolo, J. R. 1971. Determinants of body representation in postcentral gyrus of macaques. *J. Neurophysiol.* 34:1018–34
436. Whitsel, B. L., Petrucelli, L. M., Ha, H., Dreyer, D. A. 1972. The resorting of spinal afferents as antecedent to the body representation in the post-central gyrus. *Brain, Behav. Evol.* 5:303–41
437. Whitsel, B. L., Petrucelli, L. M. Sapiro, G., Ha, H. 1970. Fiber sorting in the fasciculus gracilis of squirrel monkeys. *Exp. Neurol.* 29:227–42
438. Whitsel, B. L., Petrucelli, L. M., Werner G. 1969. Symmetry and connectivity in the map of the body surface in somatosensory Area II of primates. *J. Neurophysiol.* 32:170–83
439. Whitsel, B. L., Roppolo, J. R., Werner, G. 1972. Cortical information processing of stimulus motion on primate skin. *J. Neurophysiol.* 35:691–717
440. Wickelgren, B., Sterling, P. 1969. Influence of visual cortex on receptive fields in the superior colliculus of the cat. *J. Neurophysiol.* 32:16–23
441. Wiesel, T. N., Hubel, D. H. 1965. Comparison of the effects of unilateral and bilateral eye closure on cortical unit responses in kittens. *J. Neurophysiol.* 28: 1029–40
442. Wikmark, G., Warren, J. M. 1972. Delayed response learning by cage-reared normal and prefrontal cats. *Psychon. Sci.* 26:243–45
443. Wilson, M. 1968. Inferotemporal cortex and the processing of visual information in monkeys. *Neuropsychologia* 6: 135–40
444. Wilson, M., Kaufman, H. M. 1969. Effect of inferotemporal lesions upon processing of visual information in monkeys. *J. Comp. Physiol. Psychol.* 69:44–48
445. Wilson, M., Kaufman, H. M., Zieler, R. E., Lieb, J. P. 1972. Visual identification and memory in monkeys with circumscribed inferotemporal lesions. *J. Comp. Physiol. Psychol.* 78:173–83
447. Wilson, M., Wilson, W. A. Jr., Sunenshine, H. S. 1968. Perception, learning, and retention of visual stimuli by monkeys with inferotemporal lesions. *J. Comp. Physiol. Psychol.* 65:404–12
448. Winter, P., Funkenstein, H. H. 1970. The auditory cortex of the squirrel monkey: neuronal discharge patterns to auditory stimuli. *Proc. 3rd Int. Congr. Primatol.* 2:24–28
449. Wollberg, Z., Newman, J. D. 1972. Auditory cortex of squirrel monkey: response patterns of single cells to species-specific vocalizations. *Science* 175:212–14
450. Woody, C. D. 1970. Conditioned eye blink: Gross potential activity at coronal-precruciate cortex of the cat. *J. Neurophysiol.* 33:838–50
451. Woody, C. D., Engel, J. Jr. 1972. Changes in unit activity and thresholds to electrical microstimulation at coronal-pericruciate cortex of cat with classical conditioning of different facial movements. *J. Neurophysiol.* 35: 230–41
452. Woody, C. D., Vassilevsky, N. N., Engel, J. Jr. 1970. Conditioned eye blink: Unit activity at coronal-precruciate cortex of the cat. *J. Neurophysiol.* 33: 851–64
453. Woody, C. D., Yarowsky, P. J. Conditioned eye blink using electrical stimulation of coronal-precruciate cortex as conditional stimulus. *J. Neurophysiol.* 35:242–52
454. Woolsey, C. N. 1958. Organization of somatic sensory and motor area of the cerebral cortex. In *Biological and Biochemical Bases of Behavior,* ed. H. F. Harlow, C. N. Woolsey, 63–83. Madison: Univ. Wisconson Press. 476 pp.
455. Woolsey, C. N. 1971. Tonotopic organization of the auditory cortex. In *Physiology of the Auditory System,* ed. M. B. Sachs, 271–82. Baltimore: Nat. Educ. Consult. 347 pp.
456. Worden, F. G., Galambos, R. 1972. Auditory processing of biologically significant sounds. *Neurosci. Res. Program Bull.* 10:7–98
457. Wright, M. J. 1969. Visual receptive fields of cells in a cortical area remote from the striate cortex in the cat. *Nature* 223:973–75

458. Zeki, S. M. 1969. Representation of central visual fields in prestriate cortex of monkey. *Brain Res.* 14:271–91
459. Zeki, S. M. 1969. The secondary visual areas of the monkey. *Brain Res.* 13: 197–226
460. Zeki, S. M. 1971. Convergent input from the striate cortex (area 17) to the cortex of the superior temporal sulcus in the rhesus monkey. *Brain Res.* 28: 338–40
461. Zeki, S. M. 1971. Cortical projections from two prestriate areas in the monkey. *Brain Res.* 34:19–35
462. Zilbert, D. E., Riesen, A. H. 1971. A comparison of the effects of infant and adult retinal lesions upon visual acuity in the rabbit. *Exp. Neurol.* 33:445–58

ORGANIZATION DEVELOPMENT

❖219

Frank Friedlander and L. Dave Brown[1]
Department of Organization and Administration, Case Western Reserve University
Cleveland, Ohio

INTRODUCTION

Organization development (OD) has emerged both from the demands of a changing environment and from knowledge provided by the evolution of the applied behavioral sciences. Rapid changes within organizational environments have demanded organizational processes and structures which are far more flexible and responsive than traditional bureaucratic structures (22, 112). There have also been dramatic shifts in the social environment—in the life styles, needs, and values of the human working force. Increase in professionalization, educational level, and ease of mobility have decreased organizational loyalty and dependency. There have been efforts to challenge authority, a gradual shift from organizational relevance to personal relevance (66), and a trend toward preference for collaborative rather than hierarchical roles (131). Much of the alienation and disenchantment in our current society is attributed to the institution of work (139). Work is seen as an arena in which considerable leverage can be exerted to improve the quality of life.

Concurrent with and in partial response to these changes in the environment, a number of developments have occurred in the behavioral science disciplines. These include the realization that a variety of social and psychological factors affect work performance (127); the discovery that group decision-making affects personal involvement, motivation, and commitment (118); findings that participation increases ownership of change (56); and the use of groups as agents of change in organizations (48). T-groups and sensitivity training began in the late 1940s as an educational method which focused upon group processes and group dynamics (37). Approaches to sociotechnical systems (162) and work motivation (98, 99) have more recently incorporated the organizational tasks and social structures as important dimensions of organizational change. With a few major exceptions (15, 112, 113), contemporary organization theory has not yet contributed heavily to the field of organization

[1]This review was supported in part by the National Institute of Mental Health, U.S. Public Health Service (Research Grant 5 RO1 MH 20719).

development. Its prime concern is in describing, analyzing, and theorizing about the status quo of the organization rather than the planned change processes which might improve its condition.

Today OD is emerging as a field of interdisciplinary academic study and as a recognized profession. Increasing numbers of practitioners are employed by organizations. There is an accrediting agency for OD practitioners[2] plus several professional organizations with OD divisions. Although research and theory have seriously lagged behind the practice of OD, a number of original books devoted primarily to OD have appeared in the past 5 years: Argyris (15, 16); Golembiewski (86); French & Bell (75); Beckhard (20); Bennis (23); Blake & Mouton (27); Lawrence & Lorsch (113); Schein (145); Walton (168); Fordyce & Weil (73); Lippitt (119). In addition, several edited collections on OD have appeared: Bennis, Benne & Chin (24); Hornstein et al (101); Burke (41); Burke & Hornstein (42); Margulies & Raia (124); Schmuck & Miles (147). Review chapters and papers are now in progress which attempt to review a number of studies and to suggest frameworks for understanding organizational change (5, 21, 84, 159).

The framework we shall use in reviewing OD views organizations as composed of people with different sets of values, styles, and skills; technologies with different characteristics; and processes and structures which reflect different kinds of relationships between people or between people and their work (114). Processes and structures are the integrating mechanisms for (*a*) applying human resources to technological processes for task accomplishment, and *(b)* facilitating the utilization of technological processes for human fulfillment. From this perspective OD is a method for facilitating change and development in people (e.g. styles, values, skills), in technology (e.g. greater simplicity, complexity), and in organizational processes and structures (e.g. relationships, roles) (80). The objectives of OD generally can be classified as those optimizing human and social improvement or as those optimizing task accomplishment or more likely as some (often confused) blend of the two.

Our concept of organization development calls for change in technology and structure (technostructural) or change in individuals and their interaction processes (human-processual), rather than efforts to change only the people, only the structure/process, or only the technology of the organization. The rationale behind this decision is twofold. First, the organizational processes and structures are the major linkage between the human and technological inputs into the organization; process and structure are thus core concepts of the organization as a system. Second, much of the literature on change indicates the relative impotence of efforts to change only technology (e.g. industrial engineering, operations research, and scientific management approaches), only people (e.g. selection methods, sensitivity groups, and most training), or only the structure (e.g. rearrangements and reorganizations based only on structural elements). For example, strong resistance or failure is often encountered in efforts to change only the organization structure (59), only the technology of the organization (163), or only the individual (46, 47, 71, 81).

[2]The International Association for Applied Social Scientists.

The framework for our discussion of OD is pictured in Figure 1. An organization includes people, technology, and process/structure. These components interact in the technostructural and human-processual systems on behalf of the objectives of human fulfillment and task accomplishment. Although we have not pictured it in Figure 1, the environment obviously interacts with all of these components in terms of input to and output from the organization.

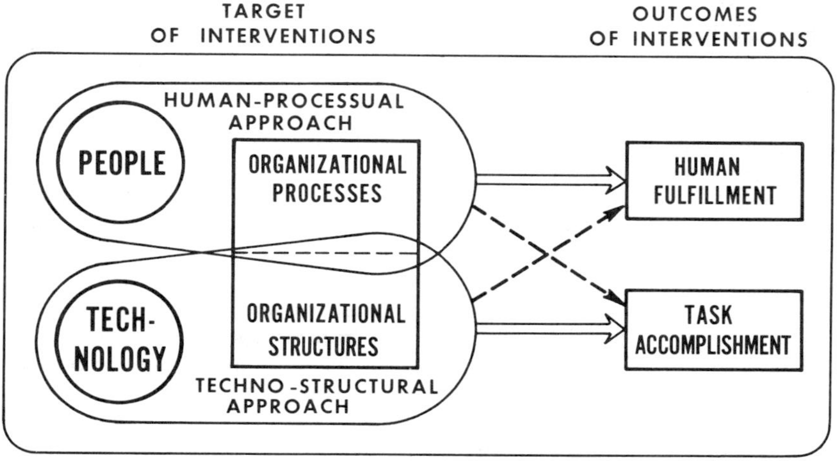

Figure 1 Approaches to organization development

As indicated in Figure 1, the human-processual and technostructural change approaches converge at the interface of the organization process and structure. Both process and structure are concerned with authority, communication, decision making, goal setting, and conflict resolution. But process implies the implementation of these as dynamic behavioral events and interactions, whereas structure describes these as ongoing sets of durable roles and relationships. Attitudes and behavior are clearly affected by both process (130) and structure (137). Over time, structures can be changed by processes that are inconsistent with them and processes are constrained and facilitated by organizational structures. Since process and structure are embedded in each other, it is almost impossible to create lasting change in one without modification of the other. Yet there are those who focus on changing organizational structures with no involvement in the behavioral processes in which these structures are embedded, and those who are totally concerned with changing processes, oblivious of the ongoing structures which underlie these processes.

If organizations can be viewed as composed of three components (people, technologies, and structures), so also can OD itself be understood by this model. It is at once a set of personal values, a set of change technologies, and a set of processes or structures through which the change agent relates to the organizational system. Thus OD interventions can be described in terms of the degree to which they incorporate values of humanism, democracy, economics, and science; the degree to which they utilize such technologies as team building, job design, and survey feedback; the degree to which they incorporate collaborative or unilateral relationships between change agent and organization; and the degree to which they are intended to optimize human/social benefit or productivity/performance objectives.

The values of the more humanistic and democratic approaches to OD are stated rather explicitly in the literature. Many of these stem from the Theory Y assumptions of McGregor (128). Tannenbaum & Davis (160), for example, clearly state these as values in transition in society: toward a positive and confirming view of man as a whole person, in process; toward encouraging the effective expression of feelings, authenticity, risk, confrontation, and collaboration. These values are similar to the humanistic-democratic values expressed by others (22, 86, 124).

The objectives of OD are obviously colored by these values. They include creating an open problem-solving climate, supplementing the authority of role and status with the authority of knowledge and competence, locating decision-making and problem-solving as close to information sources as possible, building trust and collaboration, developing a reward system which recognizes the organizational mission and the growth of people, helping managers to manage according to relevant objectives rather than past practices, and increasing self-control and self-direction for people within the organization (42, 155). Others see OD objectives as increased problem-solving capacity (15, 155), cultural change (42), or re-education (86, 174).

The relationships of OD practitioners to organizational systems vary from facilitative-collaborative to unilateral-directive. In the latter, the change agent gathers data, analyzes it, reports his findings to senior management, and recommends changes. In the more facilitative role, the change agent helps others engage in exploration, diagnosis, and development. Phases in the facilitative-collaborative process include helping the organization identify problems, set priorities, develop data, plan action strategy, test and implement alternatives, and evaluate the change effort (20, 109, 120, 124).

The main body of this review is divided into these two sections: technostructural and human-processual change approaches. We exclude studies and conceptualizations not encompassed in one of these two approaches. We omit studies which were not concerned with change per se, or which were not field studies in organizational settings. We have also not considered some approaches because of space limitations or inclusion in previous reviews: e.g. management by objectives, pay and incentive systems, staffing systems.

RESEARCH ISSUES IN ORGANIZATION DEVELOPMENT

As in most of the applied behavioral sciences, research and theory on OD follow practice. This may reflect either the difficulties of doing research on OD or the impotence of research in creating practical theory and contributing to improved practice. The first explanation locates responsibility in organizational systems for lack of cooperation and appreciation of research; the second locates responsibility in research for lack of relevance and applicability to the organization.

Research on organizations, even stable organizations, presents a host of difficulties. Organizations are complex systems, with many relevant variables that combine in intricate interactions. The student of organizations must cope with size, complexity, and sluggish responses to events. Controlled comparisons are difficult, and the costs of developing a large sample of organizations can be astronomical. Behavioral science is just beginning to grapple with the social psychology of research, and organizational researchers must cope with issues like the attitude toward the research of the respondent's boss (2) and the obvious need by respondents to benefit from the research (78).

On the other hand, issues of complexity, reactivity to research, and extraneous variation to research interventions reflect human and social realities. If reactivity, for example, is considered a "research finding," it has as much validity as those the researcher expected.

Much recent energy has been directed toward issues of reactivity, complexity, and extraneous variation. In one approach, the researcher attempts to avoid making his presence known in the research situation through unobtrusive, experimental, or statistical designs. The assumptions behind these methods are similar to those in the physical sciences—that reactivity and complexity can be successfully reduced or eliminated by reducing or eliminating the intrusion of the researcher. "Objectivity" can thereby be increased. A second approach takes the opposite stance. It attempts to incorporate the researcher and his data-gathering methods into the OD situation. The assumption is not only that the researcher-client relationship cannot be avoided, but that it sets a climate and structure which has clear repercussions on the research outcomes. This approach focuses upon the researcher-client relationship as one to be openly explored and implemented rather than avoided.

Webb et al (171) have developed a host of "unobtrusive measures" that are collected without respondent awareness and so "uncontaminated" by his reactions (though their use raises some thorny ethical problems that have pragmatic consequences for the consultant). One of the risks here is that the basic value system implied in unobtrusiveness contradicts the values of openness and involvement underlying OD. Planned change interventions are necessarily active and influencing, not unobtrusive. A second risk is that the choice of variables which can be unobtrusively collected may well preclude those which maximize relevance to understanding the OD process.

A second approach to the issue of extraneous variation and human reactivity is to utilize experimental design. D. T. Campbell & Stanley (45) describe "quasi-experimental" designs that allow relatively unambiguous results from field investigations. D. T. Campbell (43) has applied such designs to conceptualize "reforms as experiments," and has shown that it is possible to develop relatively undistorted estimates of the impact of social reform.

The concept of "convergence" also offers a third hope for dealing with the chaotic complexity in OD research. Convergence of flawed research designs can lead to relatively unambiguous conclusions when the flaws cancel each other (45). Convergence of methodologies for measuring a single variable lead to more reliable measures (44). Convergence of diagnostic interpretations by feedback and discussion of preliminary results can lead to elaborated and validated understandings of a specific situation (97). Convergence of different information sources on events (e.g. consultant, different groups in the organization, outsiders) can lead to increased validity of perceptions. Temporal convergence can be obtained by examining patterns over time. All these approaches lead to clearer specification of the important phenomena in the complex interweaving of organizational events.

A fourth strategy is to develop data collection methods that are clearly relevant to organizational problem solving and so have high "face validity" to respondents: Blake et al's (29) intergroup workshop, Beckhard's (19) "confrontation meeting," Jenks' (107) "organizational Q-sort," Argyris' (13) content analysis of tape recordings of management decision making, and Alderfer & Brown's (6) "empathic questionnaire" are all methodologies that rely in part for their effectiveness on their obvious relevance to respondents' organizational lives.

A fifth approach is to improve the relationship between researcher/consultant and respondent. Argyris (14, 15) has suggested that the quality of information obtained is a function of the relationships between researcher and respondent, and there is some evidence to support this argument. Alderfer (1) found that relationships established in interviews prior to answering a questionnaire led to franker questionnaire responses; Brown (38) found evidence that relationships between researcher/consultants and clients were improved by interaction in feedback meetings; Clark (52) noted that failure to strengthen and broaden organizational "sanction" of research led to research termination.

OD research can produce a range of outcomes, not all of them expected. One obvious product is evaluation of various types of OD intervention (e.g. Marrow, Bowers & Seashore 126; Bowers 35). Another expected outcome is the generation of new theories grounded in organizational experience (e.g. Jaques 106). OD research may also serve to guide further activities: Alderfer's (2) study of division manager reactions to the researcher/consultant had implications for further work with the organization; survey feedback can serve as a tool for organizational development (123) or as a means of increasing understanding (97); Culbert (58) has reported an intriguing use of research to persuade a client that his preferred interventions were not going to solve the problem. OD research may also be an intervention in and of itself: Sanford (144) describes change in students and faculty in response to interviews; Hunt & Lichtman (104) report a study in which pretest effects outweighed the effects of training—a disturbing result for both trainers and pretesters. All four functions—intervention evaluation, theory generation, activity guide, intervention per se—are highly relevant to both researchers and consultants.

Current research on OD is much like action research of the 1940s and 1950s (50, 75). Like action research, OD research has tensions built into it that are likely to lead either to "action" (OD consulting) or to "research" (development of organization theory), but not to both.

The concept of action research as originally advanced had two sets of goals built into it (117): both "the study of general laws" and the "diagnosis of a specific situation." But Rapoport (138) suggests that action researchers have come to subordinate research goals to action goals. Note, for example, the lack of mention of any development of new *theories* of change in French & Bell's definition of action research for OD: ". . . action research is the application of the scientific method of fact finding and experimentation to practical problems requiring action solutions and involving the collaboration of scientists, practitioners, and laymen" (75, p. 87).

The divergence between research-theory perspectives and action-change perspectives is sometimes attributed to contradictory postures vis-à-vis organizational problems: the researcher's *descriptive* stance, required for understanding the problem, contradicts the consultant's *prescriptive* stance, required for developing problem solutions. Alternating hats requires much self-awareness and strength of purpose (see Argyris 15). Furthermore, researcher/consultants serve two client systems whose requirements and criteria for evaluation are at least superficially incompatible: consumers of research want "general laws" and sneer at "applied research," and consumers of consultants want "specific diagnoses" and scoff at "abstract theorizing." Reputation with one client system may be purchased at the cost of reputation with the other.

Although these pressures create tensions for researcher/consultants, the separation of roles is not inevitable, or even desirable. Developing teams of specialists is one response to the problem (e.g. Blake et al 28, Miles et al 130). But in the long run, greater integration of the two perspectives within a single theorist-researcher-practitioner person is necessary.

The processes which researchers and consultants utilize seem similar in a number of ways. Consultants tend to build a data base from their previous experiences, develop theory of practice inductively, apply this practice-theory, note the repercussions, and revise their practice-theory accordingly. Researchers utilize a similar method. The researcher's inductive process draws more upon external data (previous research studies and literature) rather than previous personal experience; he tends to test his theory deductively in a more external sense through instruments and observational methods rather than through direct experience and involvement. But there is much that each can learn from the other. The consultant may need help in building a systematic method for learning and practice, and researchers might learn much from investigating the action implications and impact of their findings. If science is knowledge-getting (as its Latin derivation indicates), both researchers and practitioners can use as much of it as they can get. There is evidence that more OD research is being done and that interest in trying to combine action and research is on the rise (144). Ultimately, the field needs a metatheory of research and practice that clarifies and integrates the choices confronting the researcher/consultant. Some of the groundwork for that theory has already been laid.

In one sense the very dilemmas that OD research faces are its opportunities to create a new approach to knowledge-getting and knowledge-giving. It faces these dilemmas because, unlike many disciplines, it is a humanistic, change-oriented, professionally practiced field. Its current research methods are based on traditions that knowledge-getting and knowledge-giving are separate; that evaluation and validation of change lead to understanding development processes; that external rigor, control, and standardization are ideal methodological characteristics; that knowledge necessarily produces change.

Most research reported in this review, for example, has taken an evaluative stance, utilizing reliable pre- and post-measures selected and administered by the researcher to increase his knowledge of change and development in the "other" (e.g. the person, group, organization, etc). Pre-post measures provide for the practitioner and the client systems data at only two points in time, rather than a continuous picture of the interactive developmental process. Continuous documentation (e.g. a detailed case study) provides data on the ongoing interactive processes which occurred, but does not provide immediate feedback to guide subsequent action steps. The issue is somewhat similar to suggesting to a person about to shave his face to look at yesterday's photographs of his preshave and postshave face instead of looking in the mirror. A moving picture would provide continuous data, but still not the immediate feedback or client control that shaving in a mirror provides. Thus for consultant and client relevance, research is most useful if it provides immediate continuous feedback of the process and progress of intervention and development. OD theory based on this kind of research would provide the greatest validity on change processes and might also provide the most relevance to practitioners.

This calls for collaboration between researcher and organization members well beyond current unilateral research relationships (77a). It calls for more open communication on the conflicting interests between the two parties as a mutual problem to be solved collaboratively, a recognition of the legitimacy of each other's interests, and a search for solutions which are responsive to both sets of needs.

TECHNOSTRUCTURAL APPROACHES

Technostructural approaches to OD refer to theories of and interventions into the technology (e.g. task methods and processes) and the structure (e.g. the relationships, roles, arrangements) of the organization. Technostructural approaches are rooted in the fields of engineering, sociology, psychology, economics, and open systems theory. Change interventions are intended to affect the work content and method and to affect the sets of relationships among workers. Within the broad heading of technostructural development are included sociotechnical systems perspectives, job design and enlargement, and job enrichment. These methods are easier to separate in theory than in practice, but the conceptual distinction among them has implications that are important enough to warrant their preservation in this discussion.

Sociotechnical systems and job design are, in part, a reaction to and an emergence from two earlier and still current perspectives of change: (*a*) scientific management and industrial engineering which focus upon the physical environment and physiological requirements of workers; and (*b*) psychology and social psychology, which focus on the social relationships and personal needs of the workers. Proponents of sociotechnical systems and job design criticize the physical approach for treating social groups and individuals mechanistically, and criticize the psychological approach for ignoring the technology of the organization or treating it as unchangeable. Further criticism is that both approaches treat the organization as a closed system, dealing with intraorganizational issues in piecemeal fashion and ignoring the important linkages between the organization and its environment (60).

The concept of sociotechnical systems has been applied to the work initiated in England, particularly at the Tavistock Institute. Sociotechnical interventions are directed at the fit between the technological configurations and the social structure of work units. The term "job design" until recently has been applied to developments in the U.S., particularly those initiated at the University of California at Berkeley. Job design studies have sought to manipulate the configuration of technology, as in task designs and assignments making up jobs, and to explore the effects of these changes on personal, social, and organizational phenomena (60). We have grouped job design studies together with job enlargement studies since the methodologies are similar. Job design and enlargement are concerned with increasing satisfaction and performance, although there seems to be greater concern in job design to enhance performance, and greater concern in job enlargement to enhance job satisfaction. Job enrichment is derived from theories of motivation, whereas job enlargement is based on industrial engineering principles. In job enrichment, work functions from a vertical slice of the unit are brought together into a single job to increase the challenge of that job (and therefore the motivation of the jobholder); in job enlargement, work functions from horizontal slices of the work unit are consolidated to provide greater variety and a sense of the whole task.

There are also differences in scope among these three approaches. Sociotechnical systems take into account the entire system, job design focuses upon sets of interrelated functions, and job enrichment is concerned primarily with single jobs. Successful job enrichment, for example, may enrich a single job at the expense of other jobs in that unit. Sociotechnical systems, on the other hand, frequently rearrange relationships among roles or tasks or the sequence of activities.

Sociotechnical Systems

In one of the earliest studies in sociotechnical systems, Trist & Bamforth (163) found that two different social systems in British coal mining were associated with very different levels of productivity, absenteeism, and accidents. Traditional coal mining utilized small, cohesive work groups working as autonomous teams, each establishing its own system of work with each worker performing a variety of tasks. Technological advances led to a change in which work groups of about 40 men in three shifts were formed, with their activities spread over a wide area. The task requirements prohibited close interpersonal relations and group identification; workers were assigned to narrow tasks and paid on an individual rather than a team basis. The longwall method resulted in lowered performance, higher absenteeism, feelings of passivity and indifference and emotional strain. When many of the social and group relationships were reintroduced into a "composite longwall method," productivity, attendance, safety, and morale were substantially improved (70, 164).

Rice (140), another member of the Tavistock group, applied similar concepts in an Indian weaving mill. Installation of automatic looms and task specialization led to a decline in the quantity and quality of woven products. Rice introduced a number of changes: the number of job levels was reduced from nine to three, tasks were made interchangeable, and semiautonomous work groups were created and placed in charge of a set of looms. During the following 2 years, productivity rose, wasted-cloth rate declined, and morale rose dramatically.

More recently, Tavistock group members have worked with the employee relations group of Shell UK Limited to develop and diffuse throughout the organization a philosophy of management that explicitly emphasizes the maintenance and development of human resources as well as productivity as corporate goals (100). Originally conceived as the initial step in a company-wide effort to decrease worker alienation and apathy, the diffusion of the new philosophy and the subsequent changes in procedures and productivity bargains presage major changes in the quality of life and levels of productivity in the organization.

On a larger scale, the Tavistock group is now heavily involved in experiments in "industrial democracy" being carried out at the national level in Norway. In collaboration with workers, employers, and the Norwegian government, a number of field experiments in the effects of different work philosophies and sociotechnical arrangements have been carried out. Though the results available are only preliminary, there is evidence (70a, 160a, 162a) that the changes do indeed have important effects on both productivity and alienation.

Job Design and Job Enlargement

Like the sociotechnical systems approach, job design and enlargement focus upon both the technical aspects of the job and the social structures which support it. They also attempt to increase satisfaction and performance by building in greater variety, discretion, feedback, identity, and responsibility for whole task completion.

In one of the earliest studies in job design, Marks (125), as reported in Davis & Canter (61), conducted an experiment on the shop floor to change the configuration of technology through task design and job assignments. For example, operations, inspection, and securing of materials were combined into one job and performed at individual work stations. This design resulted in improvements in output, quality, production flexibility, and job attitude. In a similar study (57) in which assembly jobs were changed over to more independent bench jobs, production time decreased and quality increased. Preference for self-pacing was found as the reason for preferring bench jobs, but social interaction and work interaction showed sharp reductions. Similar results have been found for enlargement of maintenance jobs (63). Job enlargement for supervisors has resulted in a greater orientation to the technical problems of production and to worker training. Although no changes were observed in production, costs, absenteeism, grievances, or transfers, there were significant increases in quality (62). In a summary of a number of job enlargement projects, Stewart (158) found that quality of product improved, labor costs decreased, operators generally preferred job enlargement in a short time, and problems inherent in paced groups largely disappeared.

Alderfer (3) concludes in a review that job enlargement results in increased overall job satisfaction and greater meaningfulness of work. Lawler (111) reviewed ten studies and found quality improvements in all, but productivity increases in only four. Davis (60) explains such improvements as a consequence of increased number and variety of tasks, self-determination of pacing, increased responsibility for quality, increased discretion of work methods, and sense of work completion. Alderfer (3) found that enlarged jobs are judged by non-jobholder experts as requiring more technical competence and opportunity for innovation, more variety of duties, and more need to deal with people. Incumbents of enlarged jobs reported increased satisfaction with opportunities to use their skills and abilities and decreased satisfaction with their relations with superiors. Friedman (82) reports a study in which interaction and communication between foremen and workers increased, resulting in increased prestige for workers. However, at least two studies report negative effects of job enlargement on interpersonal work relationships. Conant & Kilbridge (57) note that social interaction opportunities and work interaction showed sharp reductions in bench work. Alderfer (3) reports that job enlargement resulted in lower satisfaction with respect from superiors.

Alderfer (3) suggests that differing results of job enlargement on interpersonal relations is contingent upon the technology. In continuous process technology, where there is a high demand for interdependency among employees, job enlargement may place greater stress on these interdependencies, resulting in lowered satisfaction.

Job Enrichment

Job enrichment is the restructuring of the content of a set of jobs or functions which are vertically related to enhance the employee's opportunity for responsibility, achievement, challenge, and growth. It generally involves collapsing various vertical functions into a single more responsible function. Proponents of job enrichment are somewhat critical of job enlargement, claiming that job enlargement condenses the boredom and monotony of several jobs into one job. Job enrichment as an organizational process evolved from the two-factor motivation theory developed by Herzberg, Mausner & Snyderman (99); the theory stresses that man's needs at work are met essentially by the nature of his work. The major motivators that can be built into work are increased achievement, recognition, responsibility, advancement, task capability, and knowledge. Herzberg's research and theory (98, 99) have focused upon individual motivation rather than upon the implementation of organizational change processes which might increase motivation. It is essentially a theory of motivation rather than a theory of change.

The most widely known study in the implementation of job enrichment was done by Ford (72) at American Telephone. Underlying these efforts has been the assumption that increased motivation cannot result from training or other attempts to instill in workers greater energy and involvement. Rather, all one can do is provide the employee a task which offers greater challenge; he will then become intrinsically motivated. The initial target of change is job content, not the employee. Ford (72) studied a number of job enrichment programs at American Telephone in a variety of departments with different tasks, utilizing several different methods to introduce the job enrichment intervention. An effort was made to keep the environment of the job constant so that results could be attributed solely to change in the job content.

Results indicated that turnover and absenteeism were reduced, quality of service was increased, and employee attitudes toward work improved in work units which received job enrichment.

There are a number of reviews of job enrichment applications (10, 122, 143) and several additional accounts of application findings (129, 135). Although the number of well-designed studies is too few to make broad generalizations, there are indications that job enrichment has positive effects on satisfaction and motivation (72). There is reason to believe that the quality of production increases more than the quantity (10, 111), although this applies to applications which combine job enrichment and enlargement. In much of the literature, the concept of "motivation" is used as a convenient device to explain increased performance or satisfaction. The direct effect on motivation of job enrichment programs is unexplored.

There are a number of questions regarding the relative impact of the process through which changes are introduced and implemented and the impact of the restructured job. In some studies employees participated in decisions, while in others only supervisors influenced the restructuring. The assumption which underlies directive implementation is that task related experiences lead to changes in attitudes and needs (89, 121); changed work experience will result in attitude change, rather than vice versa. In connection with this, Hackman & Lawler (92) and Alderfer (3) suggest that experiencing higher order need satisfaction will result in the development of higher order needs.

Job enrichment and job enlargement generally ignore individual and technological differences; most proponents assume that job enrichment or enlargement are applicable and relevant regardless of the individual concerned and regardless of the technology of the organization. But Turner & Lawrence (165) found that enriched jobs resulted in greater satisfaction and less absenteeism for small-town workers but not for urban employees. Similarly, Hulin & Blood (103) and Blood & Hulin (33) found that workers who hold traditional values about work and achievement respond positively to complex jobs, but more alienated (urban, blue-collar) workers respond negatively to complex jobs. Hackman & Lawler (92) report positive correlations between job complexity (variety, autonomy, task identity, feedback) and motivation, satisfaction and performance *only* for employees with higher order need strength (e.g. for accomplishment, growth, challenge, variety, participation). Wanous (170) found that higher order need strength accounted for more of the relationships between job complexity and positive outcomes than either the blue-collar, urban distinction made by Hulin & Blood (103) or the Protestant ethic values distinction made by Blood (32). Standing (156) found that the degree of satisfaction within a single set of jobs varied as a function of the cognitive complexity of the employee. The degree of satisfaction with the work itself was an inverted U-shaped function of cognitive complexity. These studies suggest a contingency theory in which the probability of job enrichment and enlargement resulting in increased performance or satisfaction is contingent upon the needs of the employee, his cognitive complexity, and his cultural milieu.

Similarly, increases in performance and satisfaction resulting from these changes may be contingent upon the technology of the organization. Task identity, for example, may be difficult to establish in a continuous process technology, but autonomy and feedback seem easier to implement in an automated process technology than in heavy assembly work (31). Several organizations are finding job enrichment and enlargement simply impossible given their huge investments in stationary equipment. Other contingencies which the organization may face include lack of sufficient skills to take on more demanding work, short-term lowered performance which frequently accompanies organizational change, union resistance or disinterest (143).

The sociotechnical studies reviewed in this section consistently indicate increased performance and productivity—a finding that is less clear for job design/enlargement or job enrichment. The evidence on job enrichment is too sparse as yet to make unqualified claims as to its effectiveness; more research is needed. All three approaches seem to result in quality increases, lowered absenteeism, and lowered turnover. The evidence for production time decreases and cost savings is mixed for job enlargement and job enrichment. In terms of attitudinal change, job satisfaction tends to increase as a result of job enlargement and job enrichment. Job enlargement, however, tends to result in a more socially isolated role for the workers, which increases both the need and difficulty in relating to others with whom their tasks are interdependent. Sociotechnical systems avoid this issue by social restructuring of the work group, resulting in clear increases in group morale.

Changes in job design have typically incorporated many simultaneous changes in task variety, self-determination and discretion, responsibility, challenge, and wholeness; in the degree to which the task requires hierarchical, collaborative, or autonomous behavior; and in different technologies. Research has generally not attempted to isolate these as independent variables, nor has it explored relative changes in different kinds of motivation, satisfaction, and performance. We need to explore the relative effects of participative and nonparticipative change processes upon the implementation and success of job design changes. At this point, much of what we can say is: given these employees, this technology, this change process, and this job design structure, this happened in terms of satisfaction and performance. We need more specificity of the complex interactions of independent, dependent, moderator, and process variables to specify cause, effect, and contingency.

HUMAN PROCESSUAL APPROACHES

Human process intervention focuses on the human participants and the organization processes (e.g. communication, problem solving, decision making) through which they accomplish their own and the organization's goals. This orientation to OD is rooted in the academic fields of psychology, social psychology, and anthropology and in the applied disciplines of group dynamics and the human relations movement. Human process-orientation change agents tend to value human fulfillment highly and to expect improved organizational performance to follow on improved human functioning and processes (152). These two don't necessarily go hand in hand, even though it may be more comfortable to assume this.

Process-oriented consultants typically have been sensitive to the nature of the consultant role (145, 157). A good deal of thought has been given to some of the dilemmas experienced by consultants (11, 15), the problems of developing a valid organizational diagnosis (15), and the risks of alternative interventions (94).

Although practitioners have developed a number of alternative interventions concerned with human processes in organizations (cf. Beckhard 20, Fordyce & Weil 73, Burke & Hornstein 42, French & Bell 75), most research efforts focus on three general areas of process-oriented intervention: survey feedback, group development, and intergroup development.

These three intervention strategies are founded on some common assumptions: sharing information can be valuable, particularly when it hitherto has remained unshared but has influenced organizational processes (like some covert feelings); confronting and working through differences among people who must work together can enhance collaboration; participation in decision making can lead to increased commitment. Survey feedback involves organizational groups in discussing diagnostic data and planning action steps. Group development activities emphasize improving group abilities to accomplish their tasks. Intergroup development interventions press for improved management of the interfaces between groups. These three forms of intervention are at least potentially compatible, and often are used in sequence, beginning with survey feedback and moving to group and intergroup development activities.

Survey Feedback

Survey feedback is a process in which data is systematically collected (usually by questionnaires) from members of an organization, analyzed in summary fashion, and fed back selectively to organization members. To varying degrees, outside staff and organization members collaboratively design the questions to be asked, jointly analyze and interpret the data, and feed back in meetings to organization units from which the data was collected for purposes of diagnosis and potential change. The intervention has developed from traditional attitude surveys which were administered to employees and fed back to management; in recent years findings have been presented to employee respondents as well, partly to gain their cooperation in future studies. Such feedback has now taken on clear organizational development purposes as well (36, 130), on the assumption that discrepancies between organizational ideals and actual responses to the survey will generate motivation for change (136).

Early participation of organization members in the design and collection of data is likely to increase the relevance of the feedback (123, 130, 132). Organization members may be asked to develop questions for the survey, or they may be interviewed to determine what issues are relevant (130). Early involvement in one study increased awareness of interpersonal problems between supervisors and subordinates (7).

The part played by organizational superiors in the feedback meetings is critical. Baumgartel (17) found that perception of supervisory behavior changed as a consequence of increased information flow and problem confrontation between hierarchical levels after feedback. Chase (49) reports that the feedback process tended to equalize power even in a highly threatening environment, and Klein, Kraut & Wolfson (108) report that use of line managers rather than personnel representatives to feed back data resulted in more satisfaction and greater perceived utilization of the data. Participation of superiors in discussion of the feedback may facilitate effective use of the information. On the other hand, a resistant or antagonistic superior can undermine the process; Alderfer & Ferris (7) suggest that managers meet in peer groups to prepare for feedback of potentially threatening results before meeting with their subordinates in family groups.

External consultants can play an important role in the survey feedback process; they may design instruments, analyze, present and interpret the data, plan for action steps, and analyze the process of the feedback meetings (cf. Miles et al 130). Alderfer & Ferriss (7) found that participants reacted more favorably to feedback by outsider-insider consultant teams than to insiders alone, and Chase (49) reports better problem-solving and meeting outputs with an outside consultant present.

Processes which occur during the feedback meetings also appear to influence the outcomes of those meetings. In the Detroit Edison studies, groups which had more intensive feedback sessions (aided by a consultant) showed more positive attitude change than groups with less intensive sessions (17). Brown (38) found evidence that participants were more receptive to feedback after the meetings, and Klein, Kraut & Wolfson (108) found that face-to-face feedback meetings were more effective than written reports. Participation in feedback meetings can effect the group's perceptions of problems (49), its expectations of improvement (7), and the quality of its interaction (130).

It seems clear that survey feedback meetings can lead to attitudinal changes by participants. Miles et al (130) report improved satisfaction with decisions (even though they were not implemented); Mann (123) found improvement in attitudes toward work, supervisors, progress, and group ability to get the job done; Bowers (35) reports improvement in organizational climate, managerial task and interpersonal leadership, and satisfaction; Brown (38) found increased participant involvement in the organization.

But the longer term changes in individual behavior or organizational performance appear to be contingent on more than just survey feedback. Despite highly successful meetings and increased satisfaction, Miles et al (130) found that few action steps or structural changes emerged from the meeting and so little change occurred. Brown (38) notes that the higher involvement did not persist without follow-up, and Frohman (83) found that more change occurred with consultant follow-up than without it.

The research literature suggests that the effectiveness of survey feedback can be increased by collaborative involvement of the participants, participation of unit management, facilitation by an outside consultant, and specific decisions about follow-up and action steps. There is evidence that survey feedback can be an effective "bridge" between diagnostic activities (e.g. interviewing or questionnaire administration) and active intervention, since its primary effects seem to be on attitudes and perceptions of the situation. But there is little evidence that survey feedback alone leads to changes in individual behavior or organizational performance.

Group Development Intervention

OD practitioners have emphasized the importance of the work group rather than the individual (40, 102). Group development interventions like "team-building," according to French & Bell, are "probably the most important single group of (OD) interventions" (75, p. 112).

Descriptions of different forms of team-building technology are easily obtained (e.g. Clark 53, 54; French & Bell 75; Fordyce & Weil 73; Golembiewski 86; Burke & Hornstein 42). Beer (21) classifies the different approaches to group development according to the primary issues they treat: (*a*) goal-setting activities (18, 20) that establish clear goals for the team to achieve; (*b*) interpersonal relations development (12, 13, 152) to improve the quality of interaction among team members; (*c*) role analysis work (65, 95) for increased clarity about each member's role and responsibilities; and (*d*) "Managerial Grid" group development (26) to prepare the group for later phases in the grid OD program.

The literature contains a number of case studies of group development activities from the vantage point of the consultant (69, 110). But these case studies offer little more than the flavor of the experience.

The impact of team-building activities has been explored systematically by several investigators. Argyris (12) and Harrison (93) report interview, observation, and questionnaire data from three groups of managers, two of which experienced T-group training and a comparison group. The study was frankly exploratory and suffers from methodological problems, but the data suggested changes in values and behavior of participants occurred. In a subsequent study, Argyris (13) trained an executive group to be more "interpersonally competent"; time series analysis of tape recordings suggested that the training affected executive meeting behavior, though only anecdotal evidence for the relationship between the changed behavior and increased effectiveness was available. In a larger study, Friedlander (76) found that four trained teams reported significantly higher levels of group effectiveness, mutual influence, and personal involvement and participation than did the eight control groups. Schmuck, Runkel & Langmeyer (148) trained the faculty of a junior high school and compared the experimental faculty with the faculties of several similar schools. The experimental faculty reported more positive perceptions of the principal, the staff meetings, and the level of innovations in teaching, and they espoused more norms consistent with laboratory values than the controls; the authors also report anecdotal data about positive changes.

The critical elements of the team-building process remain only partially explored. Friedlander further analyzed the data from his field experiment (76) and found that the impact of the team building varied greatly across the four participant groups (77). Comparison of the most positively affected group with the two least positively affected led to the discovery that the context in which the team building took place was very important: ". . . the quality of integrated prework and postwork processes surrounding the laboratory is a far more potent determiner of developmental impact than are variations in trainer role and behavior or differences in climate and content of laboratory training session" (77, p. 395). Another analysis of the same data (79) revealed that the impact of team-building activities was also influenced by the level of intragroup trust at the outset. Initial intragroup trust was a better predictor of subsequent perceptions of group effectiveness and the worth of group meetings than the initial ratings on the same dimensions. But intragroup trust itself was not increased by the training except when pre- and postwork with the consultant occurred. Harvey & Boettger (96) found that a brief "experiment" involving member confrontation of the group leader led to behavior change. They also found that the four participants who confronted the leader during the "experiment" were significantly more positive about him a year later than the eight participants who did not. Since those who confronted the leader selected themselves, we cannot be sure that the confrontation alone accounted for the differing perceptions, but the finding is consistent with the theory that confrontation is a critical element of successful team building, even if it cannot be considered unambiguous.

There remains a dearth of evidence for the effects of team building external to the group developed. Harrison (93) noted that the changed interpersonal perceptions of Argyris' T-group participants did not generalize to the participants' subordinates. Bigelow (25), on the other hand, found that participation in group development activities affected teachers in the classroom, even though the group development activities were not designed to change classroom behavior. Analysis of tapes of teacher classroom behavior indicated that participants became more integrative and less dominative than controls, and that student perception of relationships with their peers improved in the classrooms with trained teachers. Fosmire, Keutzer & Diller (74) report the results of group development with the entire faculty of a new high school. Their intervention led to increased interpersonal openness and acceptance of conflict among the faculty and to increased perceptions by students of the faculty as responsive and themselves as responsible.

Though none of the research designs is flawless, there is convergent evidence that group development activities affect participant attitudes and sometimes their behavior as well. These effects may also "spill over" in some fashion to other organization members. It remains unclear, however, what mechanisms operate in successful team development activities, or what critical conditions must be satisfied for successful generalization of learnings outside the team, or what effects group development has on actual task performance.

Intergroup Relations Development

Problems at the interfaces between groups in an organization are endemic in modern organizations, and they are a matter of central concern to OD practititioners (23, 75). Lawrence & Lorsch (113) suggest that intergroup relations problems are an inevitable correlate of the differentiation of organizational subsystems to meet and deal with environmental complexity. Important conflict has been reported between different departments in business organizations (68, 151), between headquarters and field teams (30), between field and administrative officers of the State Department (23), between a management development program and other subsystems in a bank (4), between union and management representatives (29, 30), among different occupational specialties in coal mines (164), and between potential merger partners (34).

There is no shortage of ideas for managing intergroup conflict. Some theories have been developed in social psychological research (154), others from work with organizations (141). Neilsen (133) describes seven strategies for intervening in intergroup conflict that vary in the degree to which they deal with behavior alone or with both behavior and attitudes. Walton (167) has suggested four interventions for third parties to help manage intergroup conflict: 1. reduce the potential for conflict (e.g. change structure or personnel); 2. resolve substantive issues (e.g. make the decisions); 3. help manage manifest conflict (e.g. be a referee); 4. facilitate a change in the relationships.

The first two alternatives require power over the combatants, an option that some technostructural consultants have used to great effect. Trist et al (164), for example, eliminated counterproductive intergroup conflict among coal miners by changing the sociotechnical system. But most human process consultants have no such power or they decline to use it. They have preferred the latter two interventions: helping manage manifest conflict and facilitating relationship changes. Walton (168) offers some provocative insights into the complexities of the third party role; his approach involves improving intergroup relations by improving relations between their representatives.

A more common approach has been to foster a general "problem-solving" approach to the relations between groups. Blake, Shepard & Mouton (30) argue for problem solving in the context of a nine-cell typology of intergroup conflicts based on the degree of inevitability of the conflict, the size of the stakes, and the possibility of agreement. Schmidt & Tannenbaum (146) suggest four different approaches, culminating with problem solving. "Problem solving" is the preferred outcome for both if the groups are interdependent.

Intergroup development interventions to change relationships and manage conflict in practice are based on information sharing, confrontation of differences, and working through to new understandings. The prototype design requires groups to develop lists of their perceptions of themselves, the other group, and their views of the other group's perceptions of them, and then to use the lists as input to developing better understanding of each other and to creating future action plans. This design was developed by Blake and his colleagues (29, 30), but it has been used and recommended by many others (e.g. Beckhard 20; French & Bell 75).

There is very little systematic research on the effectiveness of such interventions in the field. Case studies abound (e.g. Blake, Mouton & Sloma 29), but they leave many questions about the efficacy of the intervention unresolved. Golembiewski & Blumberg (87, 88) report attitudinal changes after a workshop that included confrontation among several groups from the same organization, but while participant attitudes changed in the ways predicted by the investigators, no data were collected on the consequences of the intervention for individual behavior or organizational performance. Further, effects of the intergroup intervention may have been confounded by a simultaneous confrontation between the participants and the consultants (who, after all, constituted an extra-organizational group that was potentially a unifying "external enemy" for all participants).

It is painfully evident that more research is needed before much can be said about the utility of the present process-oriented technology for managing intergroup relations. There is a good deal of activity going on, but relatively little in the way of unambiguous findings available. We simply do not know much about whether OD interventions lead to better management of intergroup relations or not.

A related area that demands further investigation is the role of the consultant in the management of intergroup relations. The consultant's impact as representative of a group—a group external to and possibly a threat to his client—is not often considered. Lewicki & Alderfer (116) have explored some of the dilemmas encountered by researcher/consultants to intergroup conflicts, but further investigation of this aspect of OD research/consultation is needed.

COMPARATIVE STUDIES OF OD INTERVENTIONS

One approach to comparison of OD interventions has been to examine successful and unsuccessful interventions reported in the literature. Greiner (91) compared 18 studies of organization change (technostructural, human-processual, multifaceted, and non-OD approaches) and found three features that distinguished successes: (*a*) successes consistently arose from strong internal and external pressures for change; (*b*) successes followed a consistent pattern from initial pressures to the gradual involvement of many levels including top management in diagnosis and change activities; and (*c*) successes were characterized by shared decision making rather than unilateral or delegated decisions.

Buchanan (39) derived three OD "crucial issues" that separated the successful from unsuccessful from the study of ten cases of human process interventions: (*a*) successes introduced a new model of operation to guide changes; (*b*) successes established linkages with others *inside* the target system; and (*c*) successes established linkages with others *outside* the target system.

But Greiner's (91) and Buchanan's (39) studies do not evaluate alternative interventions. Bowers (35) has compared empirically the impacts over time of four interventions—interpersonal process consultation, task process consultation, laboratory training (group development), and survey feedback—and two control conditions—data handback and no treatment—on a host of attitudinal variables. Survey feedback, interpersonal process consultation, and data handback led to positive changes on a majority of the dependent measures, while task process consultation led to no change, and laboratory training and no treatment led to negative changes. Further analysis indicated that changes in perceived organizational climate (human resources primacy, communication flow, motivational climate, decision-making practices, technological readiness, and lower-level influence) influenced the impacts of the interventions; without positive climate changes no interventions had very positive effects, and with them even laboratory training helped. The only intervention that directly improved organizational climate, however, was survey feedback.

Bowers' (35) findings about the impact of survey feedback may reflect the importance of developing a shared conception of problems and appropriate action steps, an interpretation that is consistent with Buchanan's (39) emphasis on a "new model" to organize change efforts, Greiner's (91) "shared" decision making about diagnoses and solutions, and our earlier description of survey feedback as an apprropriate "bridge" between diagnosis and subsequent interventions.

MULTIFACETED ORGANIZATION DEVELOPMENT

There are a number of reports of organization development activities with organizations as a whole. Some are anecdotal case studies (e.g. Beckhard 18; Davis 64; Alschuler 9), and some evaluations of interventions based on attempts to collect "harder" data, albeit with design problems (e.g. Blake et al 28; Huse & Beer 105; Zand, Steele & Zalkind 175). Relatively few reports, however, combine interventions into both technostructure and human processes with systematic efforts to evaluate the interventions' effects or to account theoretically for the phenomena observed.

Whyte & Hamilton (173) report work that predates the term "OD," but that fits under the OD rubric. With only a hazy theory of organizational change, the authors began an avowedly exploratory project with the "Tremont Hotel" in 1945. They observed and interviewed people in five departments and top management, and developed solutions to problems through group meetings of those involved. The organizational changes that resulted included redefined roles, improved productivity and safety records, decreased turnover, and improved interpersonal relations.

Another pioneering study was reported by Jaques (106), who began work in the late 1940s with the Glacier Metal Company in England. He reports five cases of work with company subsystems that requested the help of the research team, whose task was: ". . . developing methods of offering technical assistance to groups that requested the help of the team in exploring underlying and concealed forces—whether psychological, cultural, structural, or technological—that were impeding their progress or otherwise reducing their efficiency" (106, p. 306). The team observed and interviewed members at work, and offered their impressions and interpretations at group meetings to help clarify underlying issues. Although Jaques claims no responsibility for organizational changes, it is clear from his descriptions that the interventions of the research team often influenced discussion and decisions taken.

Seashore & Bowers (149) studied an explicit attempt to change three of an organization's five departments through several interventions including problem-solving meetings, seminars, survey feedback, and personal coaching and counseling. Results supported the hypothesis that the interventions contributed to positive change on pre-established dimensions, and that the experimental groups changed more positively than the controls.

In a subsequent study, the same authors collaborated with Marrow to study the changes in the Weldon Manufacturing Corporation after its acquisition by a competitor (126). The new owners launched a change program that included technical system changes, widespread training, more careful selection, revised payment systems, and increased participation in decision making and problem solving at all levels. Results included positive attitude changes, increased return on capital and production efficiency, and decreased turnover and absenteeism relative both to past performance and to the company's major competitor. Follow-up research 7 years later (150) indicated that many changes were durable over that period.

Hill (100) studied a major sociotechnical change process in the Tavistock tradition of OD at Shell UK Limited. Carefully orchestrated interventions to clarify company objectives and values, share them with all levels, and then to share responsibility for increasing profitability and for meeting community needs led to positive changes in understanding, levels of individual skill, and organizational climate. Of 23 departments, 15 reported organizational or procedural changes, 10 reported job design changes, 10 reported changes in responsibility and commitment, and 5 reported improved performance. There were also changes in plant design, staff appraisal systems, manpower planning, and job enrichment programs.

Finally, Lawrence & Lorsch (112) have developed a "contingency theory" of organization that describes organizational structure and process contingent on the environmental uncertainty. They have explored the implications of contingency theory for OD and reported change efforts in a variety of organizations that seek to take into account the interfaces between individuals, groups, the organization, and its environment. Although only crude efforts at evaluation have been made, the theory is one of the most promising yet available in OD, in that it attempts to account systematically for both structural and processual variables and interventions at various levels in the organization.

More recently, Clark & Krone (55) have developed a framework for open systems design and planning which encompasses the individual, his group process and structure, and the realities of his perceived organizational environment.

Of the six cases, three—Whyte & Hamilton (173), Jaques (106), and Lawrence & Lorsch (112)—emphasize exploration of the processes of organizational change, and their primary contribution is to conceptual formulations of those processes. The others—Seashore & Bowers (149), Marrow, Bowers & Seashore (126), and Hill (100)—emphasize careful evaluation of explicit interventions into organizational structures and processes on behalf of planned change. The evidence suggests that such projects can lead to changes in organizational performance as well as changes in individual attitudes and behavior.

Examination of the six reports also suggests some other observations. First, OD is not a short-term process; on the contrary, these cases took years to bear fruit. Second, it is important to have the support and active involvement of top management in the project; without that support it is difficult to gain commitment from lower levels. Third, in these projects interventions were made at several levels of the organizational hierarchy; support of top management by itself is not a sufficient condition for success. Finally, unambiguous evaluation of OD interventions is exceedingly difficult to arrange even with professional researchers involved as in these cases.

CONCLUSIONS

We have described OD as a planned change effort where the intervention is at the individual and process (human-processual) levels or the technological and structural (technostructural) levels. Excluded from our concept of OD are change efforts which deal only with individuals and do not make parallel efforts to change the structures and processes in which these individuals live and work, change efforts which focus entirely upon the technological factors and do not consider the structures and processes needed to support these changed technologies, and change efforts which impose structural reorganization without considering human or technological needs and demands. We have therefore reviewed studies of change which deal with the technostructural or human-processual aspects of the organization, and have found these to be reasonably effective beginnings for organizational change.

In general, human-processual approaches (survey feedback, group, and intergroup methods) have a number of positive effects on the attitudes of those involved. There is little evidence, however, that organizational processes actually change, or that performance or effectiveness is increased. Of the technostructural approaches, sociotechnical systems has the clearest effect on performance, while all three methods (sociotechnical, job design and enlargement, job enrichment) tend to increase satisfaction with work. These findings, however, may be colored by the fact that almost all technostructural interventions have been done with blue-collar or lower level white-collar workers, whereas most human-processual interventions were done with white-collar management groups. In blue-collar jobs, where more concrete criteria of performance are available, increased effectiveness may be easily measured. On the other hand, higher level white-collar jobs deal increasingly with abstract performance criteria that make measurement difficult. Little is reported in the literature about using human-processual approaches with blue-collar workers, or about using technostructural approaches with management level employees. This may be due to the inapplicability of different methods to different levels, or it may reflect the difficulty in measuring abstract criteria as noted above.

In one sense, sociotechnical systems, job design/enlargement, and job enrichment are theories about the appropriateness of certain social and technological structures rather than change methods. They have emerged from theories which attempt to understand and explain the currrent condition of personal, social, and technical systems. On the other hand, survey feedback, group, and intergroup methods have emerged from efforts to invent processes for development, influence, and movement. They may be methods for getting a change process moving, but it is never clear what their structural implications are. Increased integration of the two approaches, we think, will increase the present capacity of OD to influence organizational effectiveness toward both human fulfillment and task accomplishment.

We believe that OD needs to explore various technologies, different sorts of change agent-client relationships, and alternative values currently emerging in our society. OD needs a framework to encompass this diversity that would encompass different values, different technologies, and different relationships contingent on different planned outcomes of intervention.

Some of the potential richness and diversity of OD are represented in its application to wider planned social change activities. Goodstein & Boyer (90) intervened on behalf of the community in a municipal agency; Walton (169) tried to develop solutions to international border questions in an intergroup workshop with country representatives; Wedge (172) describes an effort to intercede between antagonists in international conflict; Levin & Stein (115) and Duhl & Steetle (67) report interventions or attempts to intervene in community conflicts. These efforts have been marginally successful at best, and they may represent only the publishable tip of an iceberg of complete failures. OD today is a long way from being the general theory and technology of planned social system change we would like to see it become.

Why so? If we are to develop a more general theory of planned change, what is necessary? OD has been developed within and for an extremely narrow range of organizations: by far the most common consumer of OD to date has been business and industry. A more general theory of planned change must come to grips with a number of issues that OD at present ignores.

The future of OD rests in part on its values and the degree to which its practice, theory, and research are congruent with those values. Thus far, most OD is initiated by the organization—for the purpose of furthering such organizational goals as increased performance. We seldom question the merits of these goals as part of the OD process. Though most OD practitioners and researchers in some degree value both organizational task accomplishment *and* human fulfillment, there is an organizational press in favor of the former. OD as a field runs the risk of encouraging and implementing subtle but persuasive forms of exploitation, curtailment of freedom, control of personality, violation of dignity, intrusion of privacy—all in the name of science and of economic and technological efficiency. Within the hierarchical fabric of everyday organizational power struggles, OD researcher/consultants typically represent the control needs of management. The needs of those lower in the organization for a higher quality of life, for an expanded range of occupational and life choices may seldom be known or acted upon by the consultant. The only choice for many such employees is to remain in or leave their organization. Ross (142) points out that many value discussions in the field at the moment skate over some fundamental questions about present societal arrangements: OD may well be another organizational palliative, engaged in "making some people happier at the job of making other people richer" (142, p. 583). We need to consider in more depth what values are central to planned change and what implications those values have for client selection (or creation), permissible strategies and tactics, appropriate use of fees and other compensation. OD as a field is faced with decisions about the balance it can and will strike between changing institutions to increase human development and changing people to promote institutional development. The two goals are rarely consistent with each other.

Theoretically most of OD has adopted what Walton (166) has called the "attitude change strategy" for social change, which is based on shared information, trust among the parties, collaboration, and free choice. Less attention has been paid to the "power strategy" for social change, which is based on information management, distrust, conflict, and coercion (though many OD interventions borrow the power of the establishment to enact changes). More effective OD will require more elaboration of the theory of power from the points of view of both the powerful and the powerless (e.g. Gamson 85), and so will a broader theory of planned change.

Finally, broader applications of a theory of planned change will require expanded intervention technologies. Such technologies might include techniques for training advocates (51), tactics for organizing a power base and a client system where none existed before (8), technologies for information management and control for social ends (161), or rational strategies for the management of violence (134).

We are saying that current OD theory and practice may be a small part of a rich, broad, far-reaching, relevant field of planned change. As the wider field is legitimized and developed, and as broader technologies and theories are developed, these will feed back into and enrich the field of OD.

If the practice and theory of OD is to merge into a broader field of planned change, what role will research play in this transformation? We believe that research will either play a far more crucial role in the advancement of this field, or become an increasingly irrelevant appendage to it. Thus far it has utilized its techniques primarily for evaluation and validation, and its current techniques are well adapted to this. Thus far it has chosen to play a relatively uninvolved and distant role in the change-practice situation. Thus far it has focused on producing data for research needs rather than practice needs. As a result, we have theory from an external research prespective only. We have generally failed to produce a theory of change which emerges from the change process itself. We need a way of enriching our understanding and our action synergistically rather than at one or the other's expense—to become a science in which knowledge-getting and knowledge-giving are an integrated process, and one that is valuable to all parties involved. We believe that a theory of planned change must be a theory of practice, which emerges from practice data and is of the practice situation, not merely about it.

Literature Cited

1. Alderfer, C. P. 1968. Comparison of questionnaire responses with and without preceding interviews. *J. Appl. Psychol.* 52:335–40
2. Alderfer, C. P. 1968. Organizational diagnosis from initial client reactions to a researcher. *Hum. Organ.* 27: 260–65
3. Alderfer, C. P. 1969. Job enlargement and the organizational context. *Personnel Psychol.* 22:418–26
4. Alderfer, C. P. 1971. Effect of individual, group and intergroup relations on attitudes toward a management development program. *J. Appl. Psychol.* 55:302–11
5. Alderfer, C. P. 1974. Change processes in organizations. In *Handbook of Industrial and Organizational Psychology,* ed. M. D. Dunnette. Chicago: Rand McNally
6. Alderfer, C. P., Brown, L. D. 1972. Designing an empathic questionnaire for organizational research. *J. Appl. Psychol.* 56:456–60
7. Alderfer, C. P., Ferriss, R. 1972. Understanding the impact of survey feedback. See Ref. 42, 234–43
8. Alinksy, S. D. 1972. *Rules for Radicals.* New York: Vintage
9. Alschuler, A. 1972. Toward a self-renewing school. *J. Appl. Psychol.* 8: 577–600
10. Anderson, J. W. 1970. The impact of technology on job enrichment. *Personnel* 47:29–37
11. Argyris, C. 1961. Explorations in consulting-client relationships. *Hum. Organ.* 20:121–33
12. Argyris, C. 1962. *Interpersonal Competence and Organizational Effectiveness.* Homewood, Ill.: Dorsey
13. Argyris, C. 1965. *Organization and Innovation.* Homewood, Ill.: Irwin-Dorsey
14. Argyris, C. 1968. Unintended consequences of rigorous research. *Psychol. Bull.* 70:185–97
15. Argyris, C. 1970. *Intervention Theory and Method.* Reading, Mass.: Addison-Wesley
16. Argyris, C. 1971. *Management and Organizational Development: The Path from Xa to Yb.* New York: McGraw-Hill
17. Baumgartel, H. 1959. Using employee questionnaire results for improving organizations. *Kans. Bus. Rev.* 2–6
18. Beckhard, R. 1966. An organization improvement program in a decentralized organization. *J. Appl. Behav. Sci.* 2:3–25
19. Beckhard, R. 1967. The confrontation meeting. *Harvard Bus. Rev.* 45: 149–55

20. Beckhard, R. 1969. *Strategies of Organizational Development*. Reading, Mass.: Addison-Wesley
21. Beer, M. 1974. The technology of organization development. See Ref. 5
22. Bennis, W. G. 1966. *Changing Organizations*. New York: McGraw-Hill
23. Bennis, W. G. 1969. *The Nature of Organization Development*. Reading, Mass.: Addison-Wesley
24. Bennis, W. G., Benne, K. D., Chin, R., Eds. 1969. *The Planning of Change*. New York: Holt, Rinehart & Winston. 2nd ed.
25. Bigelow, R. C. 1971. Changing classroom interaction through OD. See Ref. 147, 71–85
26. Blake, R. R., Mouton, J. S. 1968. *Corporate Excellence Through Grid Organizational Development*. Houston: Gulf Publ.
27. Blake, R. R., Mouton, J. S. 1969. *Building a Dynamic Organization Through Grid Organization Development*. Reading, Mass.: Addison-Wesley
28. Blake, R. R., Mouton, J. S., Barnes, L. B., Greiner, L. E. 1964. Breakthrough in organizational development. *Harvard Bus. Rev.* 42:37–59
29. Blake, R. R., Mouton, J. S., Sloma, R. L. 1965. The union-management intergroup laboratory: strategy for resolving intergroup conflict. *J. Appl. Behav. Sci.* 1:25–57
30. Blake, R. R., Shepard, H. A., Mouton, J. S. 1964. *Managing Intergroup Conflict in Industry*. Ann Arbor: Found. Res. Hum. Behav.
31. Blauner, R. 1964. *Alienation and Freedom*. Univ. Chicago Press
32. Blood, M. R. 1969. Work values and job satisfaction. *J. Appl. Psychol.* 53: 456–59
33. Blood, M. R., Hulin, C. L. 1969. Alienation, environmental characteristics, and worker responses. *J. Appl. Psychol.* 51:284–90
34. Blumberg, A., Wiener, W. 1971. One from two: facilitating an organizational merger. *J. Appl. Behav. Sci.* 7: 87–102
35. Bowers, D. G. 1973. OD techniques and their results in 23 organizations: the Michigan ICL Study. *J. Appl. Behav. Sci.* 9:21–43
36. Bowers, D. G., Franklin, J. F. 1972. Survey-guided development: using human resources measurement in organizational change. *J. Contemp. Bus.* 1:43–55
37. Bradford, L. P., Gibb, J. R., Benne, K. D. 1964. *T-Group Theory and Laboratory Method*. New York: Wiley
38. Brown, L. D. 1972. Research action: organizational feedback, understanding, and change. *J. Appl. Behav. Sci.* 8:697–74
39. Buchanan, P. C. 1971. Crucial issues in OD. See Ref. 101, 386–400
40. Burke, W. W. 1971. A comparison of management development and organization development. *J. Appl. Behav. Sci.* 7:569–79
41. Burke, W. W. 1972. *Contemporary Organization Development: Conceptual Orientation and Interventions*. Washington: NTL/IABS
42. Burke, W. W., Hornstein, H. A., Eds. 1972. *The Social Technology of Organization Development*. Fairfax, Va.: NTL Learning Resources Corp.
43. Campbell, D. T. 1969. Reforms as experiments. *Am. Psychol.* 24:409–29
44. Campbell, D. T., Fiske, D. W. 1959. Convergent and discriminant validation by the multitrait-multimethod matrix. *Pyschol. Bull.* 56:81–105
45. Campbell, D. T., Stanley, J. C. 1963. *Experimental and Quasi-Experimental Designs for Research*. Chicago: Rand-McNally
46. Campbell, J. P. 1971. Personnel training and development. *Ann. Rev. Psychol.* 22:291–306
47. Campbell, J. P., Dunnette, M. D. 1968. Effectiveness of T-group experiences in managerial training and development. *Psychol. Bull.* 70:73–104
48. Cartwright, D. 1951. Achieving change in people: some applications of group dynamics theory. *Hum. Relat.* 4:381–92
49. Chase, P. 1968. A survey feedback approach to organization development. In *Proceedings of the Executive Study Conference*. Princeton: Educ. Test. Serv.
50. Chein, I., Cook, S. W., Harding, J. 1948. The field of action research. *Am. Psychol.* 3:43–50
51. Chesler, M. A., Lohman, J. E. 1971. Changing schools through student advocacy. See Ref. 147, 185–211
52. Clark, A. W. 1972. Sanction: a critical element in action research. *J. Appl. Behav. Sci.* 8:713–31
53. Clark, J. V. 1970. Task group therapy 1: goals and the client system. *Hum. Relat.* 23:263–77
54. Ibid. Task group therapy 2: intervention and problems of practice, 383–403

55. Clark, J. V., Krone, C. G. 1972. Towards an overall view of organizational development in the early seventies. In *Management of Change and Conflict,* ed. J. M. Thomas, W. G. Bennis. Baltimore: Penguin Books
56. Coch, L., French, J. R. P. 1948. Overcoming resistance to change. *Hum. Relat.* 1:512–32
57. Conant, E. H., Kilbridge, M. D. 1965. An interdisciplinary analysis of job enlargement: technology, costs and behavioral implications. *Ind. Labor Relat. Rev.* 18:377–95
58. Culbert, S. A. 1972. Using research to guide an OD project. *J. Appl. Behav. Sci.* 8:203–36
59. Dalton, M. 1965. Managing the managers. *Hum. Organ.* 14:4–10
60. Davis, L. E. 1966. The design of jobs. *Ind. Relat.* 6:21–45
61. Davis, L. E., Canter, R. R. 1956. Job design research. *J. Ind. Eng. 7:275*
62. Davis, L. E., Volfer, E. S. 1965. Intervening responses to changes in supervisor job designs. *Occup. Psychol.* 34: 171
63. Davis, L. E., Werling, R. 1960. Job design factors. *Occup. Psychol.* 34:-109–32
64. Davis, S. A. 1967. An organic problem-solving method of organizational change. *J. Appl. Behav. Sci.* 3:3–21
65. Dayal, I., Thomas, J. M. 1968. Operations KDE: developing a new organization. *J. Appl. Behav. Sci.* 4:473–586
66. DeSalvia, D. N., Gemmill, G. R. 1971. An exploratory study of the personal value system of college students and managers. *Acad. Manage. J.* 14: 227–38
67. Duhl, L. J., Steetle, N. J. 1969. Newark: community or chaos, a case study of the medical school controversy. *J. Appl. Behav. Sci.* 5:537–72
68. Dutton,. J. M., Walton, R. E. 1972. Interdepartmental conflict and cooperation: two contrastive studies. In *Managing Group and Intergroup Relations,* ed. J. W. Lorsch, P. R. Lawrence, 285–309. Homewood, Ill.: Irwin-Dorsey
69. Dyer, W. G., Maddocks, R. F., Moffitt, J. W., Underwood, W. J. 1970. A laboratory-consultation model for organization change. *J. Appl. Behav. Sci.* 6:211–27
70. Emery, F. E., Trist, E. L. 1960. Sociotechnical systems. In *Management Sciences: Models and Techniques,* ed. C. W. Churchman, M. Verhulst. New York: Pergamon
70a. Emery, F. E., Thorsrud, E. 1969. *Form and Content in Industrial Democracy.* London: Tavistock
71. Fleishman, E. A. 1953. Leadership climate, human relations training, and supervisory behavior. *Personnel Psychol.* 6:205–22
72. Ford, R. N. 1969. *Motivation Through Work Itself.* New York: Amenaan Manage. Assoc.
73. Fordyce, J. K., Weil, R. 1971. *Managing with People.* Reading, Mass.: Addison-Wesley
74. Fosmire, F., Keutzer, C., Diller, R. 1971. Starting up a new senior high school. See Ref. 147, 87–112
75. French, W. L., Bell, C. H. 1973. *Organization Development.* Englewood Cliffs, N.J.: Prentice-Hall
76. Friedlander, F. 1967. The impact of organizational training laboratories upon effectiveness and intervention of ongoing work groups. *Personnel Psychol.* 20:289–308
77. Friedlander, F. 1968. A comparative study of consulting processes and group development. *J. Appl. Behav. Sci.* 4:377–99
77a. Friedlander, F. 1968. Behavioral research as a transactional process. *Hum. Organ.* 27:369–79
78. Friedlander, F. 1970. Emerging blackness in a white research world. *Hum. Organ.* 29:239–50
79. Friedlander, F. 1970. The primacy of trust as a facilitator of further group accomplishment. *J. Appl. Behav. Sci.* 6:387–400
80. Friedlander, F. 1972. Congruence in organization development. *Proc. 31st Ann. Meet. Acad. Manage. 1971,* 153–60
81. Friedlander, F., Greenberg, S. 1971. The effect of job attitudes, training and organization climate upon performance of the hard-core unemployed. *J. Appl. Psychol.* 55:287–95
82. Friedman, G. 1961. *The Anatomy of Work.* Glencoe, Ill: Free Press
83. Frohman, M. A. 1970. *An empirical study of a model and strategies for planned organizational change.* PhD thesis. Univ. Michigan
84. Frohman, M. A., Sashkin, M. 1970. *The practice of organization development: a selective review.* Unpublished data
85. Gamson, W. 1968. *Power and Discontent.* Homewood, Ill.: Dorsey

86. Golembiewski, R. T. 1972. *Renewing Organizations.* Itasca, Ill.: Peacock Publ.
87. Golembiewski, R. T., Blumberg, A. 1967. Confrontation as a training design in complex organizations: attitudinal changes in a diversified population of managers. *J. Appl. Behav. Sci.* 3:525–47
88. Golembiewski, R. T., Blumberg, A. 1968. The laboratory approach to organization change: confrontation design. *Acad. Manage. J.* 11:199–210
89. Goodman, P., Baloff, N. 1968. Task experience and attitudes toward decision making. *Organ. Behav. Hum. Perform.* 3:202–16
90. Goodstein, L. D., Boyer, R. K. 1972. Crisis intervention in municipal agency: a conceptual case history. *J. Appl. Behav. Sci.* 8:318–40
91. Greiner, L. E. 1967. Patterns of organizational change. *Harvard Bus. Rev.* 45:119–28
92. Hackman, J. R., Lawler, E. E. 1971. Employee reactions to job characteristics. *J. Appl. Psychol.* 55:259–86
93. Harrison, R. 1962. Impact of the laboratory on perceptions of others by the experimental group. See Ref. 12, 261–71
94. Harrison, R. 1970. Choosing the depth of organizational intervention. *J. Appl. Behav. Sci.* 6:181–202
95. Harrison, R. 1972. Role negotiation: a tough minded approach to team development. See Ref. 42, 84–96
96. Harvey, J. B., Boettger, C. R. 1971. Improving communication within a managerial workgroup. *J. Appl. Behav. Sci.* 7:164–74
97. Heller, F. A. 1969. Group feedback analysis: a method of field research. *Psychol. Bull.* 72:108–17
98. Herzberg, F. 1966. *Work and the Nature of Man.* Cleveland: World Publ.
99. Herzberg, F., Mausner, B., Snyderman, B. B. 1959. *The Motivation to Work.* New York: Wiley
100. Hill, P. 1971. *Towards a New Philosophy of Management.* New York: Barnes and Noble
101. Hornstein, H. A., Bunker, B. B., Burke, W. W., Gindes, M., Lewicki, R. J. 1971. *Social Intervention: A Behavioral Science Approach.* New York: Free Press
102. Hornstein, H. A., Bunker, B. B., Hornstein, M. G. 1971. Some conceptual issues in individual and group oriented strategies of intervention into organizations. *J. Appl. Behav. Sci.* 7: 557–67
103. Hulin, C. L., Blood, M. R. 1968. Job enlargement, individual differences, and workers responses. *Psychol. Bull.* 69:41–55
104. Hunt, R. G., Lichtman, C. M. 1972. Pretest influences in evaluating the organizational effects of a supervisory counseling training program. *J. Appl. Behav. Sci.* 8:503–6
105. Huse, E. F., Beer, M. 1971. Eclectic approach to OD. *Harvard Bus. Rev.* 49:103–12
106. Jaques, E. 1952. *The Changing Culture of a Factory.* New York: Dayden
107. Jenks, R. S. 1970. An action-research approach to organizational change. *J. Appl. Behav. Sci.* 6:131–50
108. Klein, S. M., Kraut, A. I., Wolfson, A. 1971. Employee reactions to attitude survey feedback: study of the impact of structure and process. *Admin. Sci. Quart.* 16:497–514
109. Kolb, D. A., Frohman, A. L. 1970. An organization development approach to consulting. *Sloan Manage. Rev.*
110. Kuriloff, A. H., Atkins, S. 1966. T-group for a work team. *J. Appl. Behav. Sci.* 2:63–93
111. Lawler, E. E. 1969. Job design and employee motivation. *Personnel Psychol.* 22:426–35
112. Lawrence, P. R., Lorsch, J. W. 1967. *Organization and Environment.* Boston: Div. Res., Harvard Bus. Sch.
113. Lawrence, P. R., Lorsch, J. W. 1969. *Developing Organizations: Diagnosis and Action.* Reading: Addison-Wesley
114. Leavitt, H. J. 1965. Applied organizational change in industry: structural, technological, and humanistic approaches. In *Handbook of Organizations,* ed. J. G. March. Chicago: Rand McNally
115. Levin, G., Stein, D. D. 1970. System intervention in a school community conflict. *J. Appl. Behav. Sci.* 6:337–52
116. Lewicki, R. J., Alderfer, C. P. 1972. *"Researchers" dilemmas in studying intergroup conflict.* Yale Univ. working paper
117. Lewin, K. 1946. Action research and minority problems. *J. Soc. Issues.* 2: 34–46
118. Lewin, K. 1947. Group decision and social change. In *Readings in Social Psychology,* ed. T. Newcomb, E. Hartley. New York: Holt. Rev. ed.

119. Lippitt, G. L. 1969. *Organization Renewal.* New York: Appleton-Century-Crofts
120. Lippitt, R., Watson, J., Westley, B. 1958. *The Dynamics of Planned Change.* New York: Harcourt, Brace
121. Locke, E. A. 1968. Toward a theory of task motivation and incentives. *Organ. Behav. Hum. Perform.* 3:157–89
122. Maher, J. R. 1971. *New Perspectives in Job Enrichment.* New York: Van Nostrand-Reinhold
123. Mann, F. C. 1961. Studying and creating change. See Ref. 24, 605–15. 1st ed.
124. Margulies, N., Raia, A. P. 1972. *Organization Development: Values, Process, and Technology.* New York: McGraw-Hill
125. Marks, A. R. N. 1954. *An investigation of modifications of job design in an industrial situation and their effects on some measures of economic productivity.* PhD thesis. Univ. California, Berkeley
126. Marrow, A. J., Bowers, D. G., Seashore, S. E. 1967. *Management by Participation.* New York: Harper and Row
127. Mayo, E. 1933. *The Human Problems of an Industrial Civilization.* New York: Macmillan
128. McGregor, D. 1960. *The Human Side of Enterprise.* New York: McGraw-Hill
129. Meyers, S. M. 1964. Who are your motivated workers? *Harvard Bus. Rev.* 42:73–88
130. Miles, M. G., Hornstein, H. A., Callahan, D. M., Calder, P. H., Schiavo, R. S. 1969. The consequences of survey feedback: theory and evaluation. See Ref. 24, 456–68
131. Miner, J. B. 1971. Changes in student attitudes toward bureaucratic role prescriptions during the 1960's. *Admin. Sci. Quart.* 16:227–38
132. Neff, F. W. 1965. Survey research: a tool for problem diagnosis and improvement in organizations. In *Applied Sociology,* ed. S. M. Miller, A. W. Gouldner. New York: Free Press
133. Neilsen, E. H. 1972. Understanding and managing intergroup conflict. See Ref. 68, 329–43
134. Oppenheimer, M. 1969. *The Urban Guerilla.* Chicago: Quadrangle
135. Paul, W. J., Robertson, K. B., Herzberg, F. 1969. Job enrichment pays off. *Harvard Bus. Rev.* 47:61–78
136. Peak, H. 1955. Attitude and motivation. In *Nebraska Symposium on Motivation,* ed. M. R. Jones. Lincoln: Univ. Nebraska
137. Porter, L. W., Lawler, E. E. 1965. Properties of organization structure in relation to job attitudes and job behavior. *Psychol. Bull.* 64:23–51
138. Rapoport, R. N. 1970. Three dilemmas in action research. *Hum. Relat.* 23:499–513
139. Report of a Special Task Force to the Secretary of Health, Education and Welfare, 1973. *Work in America.* Cambridge, Mass: MIT Press
140. Rice, A. K. 1958. *Productivity and Social Organization: The Ahmedabad Experiment.* London: Tavistock
141. Rice, A. K. 1969. Individual, group and intergroup processes. *Hum. Relat.* 22:565–84
142. Ross, R. 1971. OD for whom. *J. Appl. Behav. Sci.* 7:58–85
143. Rush, H. M. F. 1971. *Job Design for Motivation.* New York: Conf. Board Rep. 515
144. Sanford, N. 1970. Whatever happened to action research? *J. Soc. Issues* 26: 3–23
145. Schein, E. H. 1969. *Process Consultation: Its Role in Organization Development.* Reading, Mass.: Addison-Wesley
146. Schmidt, W. H., Tannenbaum, R. 1972. Management of differences. See Ref. 42, 127–40
147. Schmuck, R. A., Miles, M. B., Eds. 1971. *OD in Schools.* Palo Alto: National Press
148. Schmuck, R. A., Runkel, P. J., Langmeyer, D. 1969. Improving organizational problem solving in a school faculty. *J. Appl. Behav. Sci.* 5:455–90
149. Seashore, S. E., Bowers, D. G. 1963. *Changing the structure and functioning of an organization.* Monogr. 33, Univ. Michigan Survey Res. Center
150. Seashore, S. E., Bowers, D. G. 1970. Durability of organizational change. *Am. Psychol.* 25:227–23
151. Seller, J. A. 1963. Diagnosing interdepartmental conflict. *Harvard Bus. Rev.* 41:121–32
152. Shepard, H. A. 1965. Changing interpersonal and intergroup relations in organizations. See Ref. 114, 1115–43
154. Sherif, M., Harvey, O. J., White, B. J., Hood, W. R., Sherif, C. 1961. *Conflict and Cooperation: the Robbers' Cave Experiment.* Norman, Okla.: Univ. Book Exch.
155. Sherwood, J. J. 1971. An introduction to organization development. *Exp. Publ. Syst. APA* 11

156. Standing, T. E. 1973. Satisfaction with the work itself as a function of cognitive complexity. *Proc. 81st Ann. Conv. APA*
157. Steele, F. I. 1969. Consultants and detectives. *J. Appl. Behav. Sci.* 5:187–202
158. Stewart, P. A. 1967. *Job Enlargement.* Iowa City: Univ. Iowa Coll. Bus. Admin.
159. Strauss, G. 1973. Organization development. In *Handbook of Work Organization in Society,* ed. R. Dubin. Chicago: Rand McNally
160. Tannenbaum, R., Davis, S. A. 1969. Values, man and organizations. *Ind. Manage. Rev.* 10:67–86
160a. Thorsrud, E. 1969. A strategy for research and social change in industry: a report on the industrial democracy project in Norway. *Soc. Sci. Inform.* 9 (5): 65–90
161. Torezyner, J. 1972. The political conflict of social change: a case study of innovation in adversity in Jerusalum. *J. Appl. Behav. Sci.* 8:287–317
162. Trist, E. L. 1969. On socio-technical systems. See Ref. 24, 269–82
162a. Trist, E. 1970. A socio-technical critique of scientific management. Presented at Edinburgh Conf. Impact Sci. Technol. Edinburgh Univ.
163. Trist, E. L., Bamforth, K. W. 1951. Some social and psychological consequences of the longwall method of coal getting. *Hum. Relat.* 4:3–38
164. Trist, E. L., Higgin, G. W., Murray, H., Pollock, A. B. 1963. *Organizational Choice.* London: Tavistock
165. Turner, A. N., Lawrence, P. R. 1968. *Industrial Jobs and the Worker.* Cambridge, Mass.: Harvard Univ. Grad. Sch. Bus. Admin.
166. Walton, R. E. 1965. Two strategies of social change and their dilemmas. *J. Appl. Behav.* Sci. 1:167–79
167. Walton, R. E. 1967. Third party role in interdepartmental conflict. *Ind. Relat.* 7:29–43
168. Walton, R. E. 1969. *Interpersonal Peacemaking: Confrontations and Third Party Consultation.* Reading, Mass.: Addison-Wesley
169. Walton, R. E. 1970. A problem-solving workshop on border conflicts in Eastern Africa. *J. Appl. Behav. Sci.* 6:453–89
170. Wanous, J. P. 1973. Individual differences and employee reactions to job characteristics. *Proc. 81st Ann. Conv. APA*
171. Webb, E. J., Campbell, D. T., Schwartz, R. D., Sechrest, L. 1965. *Unobtrusive Measures: Nonreactive Research in the Social Sciences.* Chicago: Rand McNally
172. Wedge, B. 1971. A psychiatric model for intercession in intergroup conflict. *J. Appl. Behav. Sci.* 7:733–61
173. Whyte, W. F., Hamilton, E. L. 1964. *Action Research for Management.* Homewood, Ill.: Irwin-Dorsey
174. Winn, A. 1969. The laboratory approach to organization development: a tentative model of planned change. *J. Manage. Stud.* 6:157
175. Zand, D. E., Steele, F. I., Zalkind, S. S. 1969. The impact of an organizational development program on perceptions of interpersonal, group, and organizational functioning. *J. Appl. Behav. Sci.* 5:393–410

❖220

OBJECTIVE DIAGNOSTIC TESTS AND MEASURES

Lewis R. Goldberg[1]
University of Oregon and Oregon Research Institute, Eugene, Oregon

In a previous chapter in the *Annual Review of Psychology* covering a quite different topic, Tulving & Madigan succumbed to the torment of the *Annual Review* author and wished aloud that ". . . at least some writers, faced with the decision of whether to publish or perish, should have seriously considered the latter alternative" (149, p. 442). If this final solution to the problems faced by reviewers seems at all unappreciative, consider the following dilemma: (*a*) the present chapter, the first on a topic that will now be reviewed once every 3 years, must be held to approximately 25 printed pages; (*b*) in 25 *Annual Review* pages, if one avoided all text whatsoever, one could include a bibliography of about 675 titles; (*c*) during the 3 year period 1970–1972, the period chosen for this review, there appeared over 750 titles on one instrument, the MMPI, alone (12), and thus it would not be possible even to list merely a bibliography of MMPI reports; (*d*) each year there are over 3000 titles (including books, chapters in edited books, and journal articles) of some relevance to this topic (12), or close to 10,000 for the entire period. So, clearly, this review must be ruthlessly selective, hacking away most of this bloat with machete-like abandon.

Towards this end, efforts have been made to avoid duplicating the material covered in chapters on assessment, human abilities, personality, attitudes and opinions, personnel selection, scaling, and test theory in previous *Annual Review* volumes, and in chapters on personality, genetics of behavior, social and cultural

[1]The author wishes to acknowledge the contributions of Endel Tulving and Stephen Madigan (149), who, while never having met the author nor having seen a draft of this chapter, have provided quite substantial guidance by previous example. Any errors in the manuscript, therefore, are clearly their fault. Kudos, on the other hand, might be sent to the author, who is always most appreciative. As he is for the financial support which permitted him to undertake this adventure, support provided by Grant MH-12972 from the National Institute of Mental Health, U.S. Public Health Service. Investigators who feel neglected or misunderstood are encouraged to seek relief from the Public Health Service.

influences on psychopathology, human information processing, and statistics in the present volume. However, any such review shares a problem with the zone defense in professional football: namely that excellent scientific reports, like talented tight ends, can often slip through the cracks between the zones. Readers who feel that their favorite instrument was given short shrift, or no shrift, are encouraged to write the author, who may be able to provide them with an extensive specialized bibliography.

In the current *Annual Review of Psychology* master plan, this chapter is part of the genus *Abnormal and Clinical Psychology,* and the species *Assessment of Psychopathology.* The "objective" in the title is meant to contrast with "projective" (whatever that may convey), not necessarily with "subjective," as one might have guessed. The chapter itself is arranged as a diagnostic instrument. Since the material becomes increasingly more technical as one proceeds through it, one can assess his degree of involvement with the field simply by noting the page on which he moves to potentially greener pastures.

FOR THOSE WHO HAVE WANDERED INTO THIS CHAPTER FROM ACROSS THE BORDERS . . .

If you read only one book in this field every 10 years, the choice for you has now been made easy: read Jerry Wiggins' *Personality and Prediction: Principles of Personality Assessment* (155). A magisterial integration of the concepts and the research from a field whose complex sprawl had easily bested all previous attempts, this textbook is the most important single volume written about assessment since 1957 and the original edition of Cronbach & Gleser's *Psychological Tests and Personnel Decisions.* From the opening chapter on correlation and multiple regression to the penetrating analyses of five milestone assessment projects at the end, Wiggins presents an even-handed account of the conflicts and convergences of this inchoate field. Along the way, the reader will encounter such topics as moderator variables and the prediction of predictability, contingency tables and actuarial prediction, clinical prediction and its automation, decision theory and personnel assignment, observational techniques (including reliability theory, trait attribution, and behavioral analysis), structured techniques, and the role of theoretical models in assessment science and practice. Buy it; you'll like it.

At a considerably more technical level, one other book published during this period stands out as a signal achievement. Cronbach & Gleser (23) have returned again, now with two collaborators, Nanda & Rajaratnam, to produce a second methodological landmark. Their multifaceted generalization of classical reliability theory, entitled *The Dependability of Behavioral Measurements* (24), is an evolutionary reconceptualization of the fundamental measurement base for objective diagnostic procedures. Warning: This is not a book for the mathematically fragile or the conceptually timid. Translation: I found it hard sledding.

Not so with two excellent compendia from the period, McReynolds' *Advances in Psychological Assessment, Volume 2* (94) and Butcher's *Objective Personality Assessment* (13). The former includes chapters on the assessment of places, of children, of managerial talent, of aggression, of intrinsic motivation, of therapy outcomes, and of psychotic behavior, plus a mercilessly long mother by the present author surveying the history of personality scales and inventories (54). The latter book, which focuses primarily on the MMPI, includes two absolutely superb chapters, one by Paul Meehl (98) and the other by Warren Norman (107). Meehl has returned to writing about assessment again, albeit in some obscure places (96, 97, 99, 100). His writing style has changed over the years since that bodacious flurry of extraordinarily influential papers published between 1945 and 1960, and his papers now read as exquisite rambles through a tortuously labyrinthine phenomenology. As a consequence, one leaves Meehl's writing today with a sense of awe, rather than, as before, with a new point of view. Norman (107) is something else again. If Wiggins wins the literary prize for best novel-length work, Norman is the clear winner in the short-story-length class. Word for word, his Psychometric Considerations for a Revision of the MMPI contains more measurement wisdom than anything else published during the decade.

This was the period of the revised test handbook, with five old friends of the practitioner-on-the-street spawning new ones. These mighty tomes, all rich sources of material on the merits and demerits of their respective tests, include Matarazzo's comprehensively revised WAIS handbook, *Wechsler's Measurement and Appraisal of Adult Intelligence* (91); Campbell's *Handbook for the Strong Vocational Interest Blank* (14); the first volume of Dahlstrom, Welsh & Dahlstrom's two-volume revision of their *MMPI Handbook* (26); Megargee's *California Psychological Inventory Handbook* (101); and Cattell, Eber & Tatsuoka's *Handbook for the Sixteen Personality Factor Questionnaire* (18). All five volumes are real handbooks in today's sense of that term, which means that none of them is small enough to be held with one hand. Though, to be fair, they look puny when compared to the gargantuan products of O. K. Buros (11, 12). His two latest works, which might logically be called handsbooks since neither is small enough to be held with both hands, include the monumental *Seventh Mental Measurements Yearbook* (covering the period 1964–1970 and 1157 tests) and *Personality Tests and Reviews* (which, among many other significant things, reprints all reviews of personality measures from the first six Yearbooks). Most psychologists know that if they need information about a particular test, they should consult Buros' latest Yearbook. Less widely known is the fact that virtually all books about assessment are listed there, each followed by lengthy excerpts from most of the reviews these books received in professional journals. For information about published tests and related books, there is simply no better source.

The key word in that last sentence was "published," obviously only the tip of the assessment ice. Tailor-made instruments are often used in psychological research, and reports of their psychometric properties are sometimes included in journal articles. No one systematically reviews that stuff (other than *Psychological Abstracts,* which catalogs everything—and, thus, nothing). Now there is such a survey, at least for measures used with children: Johnson & Bommarito's *Tests and Measurements in Child Development* (71) includes 309 instruments, well classified and well described. If you wandered in here from developmental psychology, you'll want to order this one at the same time you order the Wiggins volume.

FOR THOSE WHOSE INTEREST IN THIS CHAPTER IS AT LEAST PARTIALLY PRACTICAL OR APPLIED . . .

If you are into the practice of psychodiagnosis these days, many authors will teach you how to do it right (meaning *their* way), while many more will urge you to jump ship and give up the enterprise altogether. By and large, the former write or edit books, while the latter write chapters and journal articles. Exceptions to this general law are Raymond B. Cattell and Hans J. Eysenck, who do both things—and often. Eysenck alone had 60 publications during this 3-year period, including 6 books (actually 8, since one edited work was in three volumes [43–45]). For Eysenck's approach to diagnosis, see (40, 42). For Cattell's position, see (16). For the views of others, try another chapter or two in the edited book by Mahrer (88)—particularly that of Lorr (82)—or pick up the short booklet by Dahlstrom (25).

Of those critics who fight to make you switch, one of the best is Albee (1). Such pugnacious types, in turn, are opposed by some highly muscled hardhats with a heavy biological emphasis, among them Meehl (97, 99), Rimland (125), Rosenthal (128), and Gottesman & Shields (61). If there's anyone around who hasn't yet read Rimland's audacious argument against psychogenesis, run—do not walk—to the nearest library and start reading it. Rimland is doubtless wrong, as are we all, but after you have read his piece, you will never think *quite* the same way again. Which means that you may be ready to compromise. If so, read Begelman (5), Gough (62), and Draguns & Phillips (33).

Pecking away at people who use traditional diagnostic syndromes has been a preoccupation among psychologists with a behavior-modification or social-learning orientation towards psychochange (120). Much of the time spent in this business has been devoted to exorcising such hobgoblins as traits, diagnoses, medical models, and similar demons. Apparently most of this dangerous work has now been accomplished, and some authors can turn their attention to other pursuits. For recent perspectives on the role of assessment in behavior modification, see the reviews by Kanfer (72) and by Goldfried & Kent (58), as well as the important theoretical article by Mischel (104). And for an assessment book that behaviorists will find congenial and informative, see the volume edited by Costello, entitled *Symptoms of Psychopathology* (21). This handbook includes chapters on the assessment and treatment of such "symptoms" as depression, anxiety, phobias, obsessions and compulsions, tics, stuttering, thumbsucking, enuresis, hyperactivity, sleeplessness, alcoholism, drug addiction, academic underachievement, exhibitionism, homosexuality, asthma, headaches, and other horrors—only a smattering of the ailments of any graduate student.

Indeed, students can often convince themselves that their brains are turning mushy. If this is your own hypothesis, it might be wise to consult one of the recent volumes on the assessment of brain damage, either Goodglass & Kaplan's *Assessment of Aphasia and Related Disorders* (60), a test manual for the *Boston Diagnostic Aphasia Test,* or Russell, Neuringer & Goldstein's *Assessment of Brain Damage: A Neuropsychological Key Approach* (130), essentially a test manual for the *Halstead-Reitan Impairment Index.* Three related volumes are focused primarily on children: (*a*) a report of a superb empirical study, Deutsch & Schumer's *Brain-Damaged Children: A Modality-Oriented Exploration of Performance* (29); (*b*) another monograph reporting a study of cognitive perceptual motor dysfunction (Rubin et al 129); and finally (*c*) Wender's new textbook, *Minimal Brain Dysfunction in Children* (152).

Disturbed children tend to maintain a low profile in the eyes of the community at large, at least until one of them begins to steal things or to assault others, when he becomes a part of that national epidemic called "crime in the streets." Among the many publications which relate at least tangentially to the prediction of criminal behaviors are the theoretically exquisite volume by Schachter, *Emotion, Obesity, and Crime* (132); a revised edition of Eysenck's *Crime and Personality* (41); a monograph on underachievement by Kipnis called *Character Structure and Impulsiveness* (74); and two new books by the high priests of this field, Sheldon and Eleanor Glueck (49, 50). One of their volumes, *Toward a Typology of Juvenile Offenders* (49), reports the results of an empirical study in which three types of delinquents were discovered. The other book, an edited volume on the identification of predelinquents (50), should be read by everyone in assessment—at least by everyone who is willing to be exasperated, provoked, and stimulated at one and the same time. Some of the contributors to this short book discuss the empirical evidence on the validity of the Glueck five-factor table (based on interviewer ratings of (*a*) kind of paternal discipline, (*b*) type of maternal supervision (*c*) degree of paternal and (*d*) maternal affection, and (*e*) cohesiveness of the family) in predicting —or, unfortunately, most often postdicting—delinquency. The great mass of "evidence" from retrospective studies indicating that the system correctly identifies (I kid you not!) 91%, 81%, 91%, 89%, 90%, 90%, 91%, 92%, 100%, 100%, 82%, 81%, 86% of various delinquent samples in the U.S. and 92%, 92%, 85%, 88%, 90%, 80%, 91%, 90%, 98%, and 92% of various delinquent samples in Japan, Puerto Rico, England, France, and West Germany is clearly not scientific evidence at all, since these studies included data from only two cells in the overall fourfold table, always omitting the proportion of *nondelinquents* who would have been correctly and incorrectly diagnosed. On the other hand, that rising righteous indignation of yours may be wrongeous, if one is to believe the results of a few genuinely predictive studies reported in later chapters of this book; the apparent validity of the Gluecks' prediction scheme is uncanny—in fact, it seems better than reliability theory would suggest is possible. Clearly, there is something funny going on here, and it's about time that somebody takes a highly critical peek at it all.

If delinquency is a phenomenon which is quite predictable, at least by some standards, then suicide is near the other pole of this continuum. Two reviews of the scientific literature on suicide prediction were published during this period, one by Lester (78) and the other by Brown & Sheran (10). Neither is very encouraging. Nor are Bloch & Goodstein (7), who have reviewed the empirical evidence on the links between personality measures and various speech disorders, including stuttering. Their verdict: no links.

Diagnosis Based on Naturalistic Observation or Life History Data

A two-volume potpourri of conference papers, entitled *Life History Research in Psychopathology* (126, 127), provides brief reports of some recent longitudinal investigations. The first volume is focused largely on studies of schizophrenia, while the second includes a wider sampling of problems (e.g. delinquency, alcoholism, narcotic addiction, and suicide). In an important related paper, not included in these compendia, Overall (109) discussed a 2000-patient exploration of the relationship between marital history and psychopathology (the more previous marriages, the less present pathology, regardless of present marital status). Moral: It's not what you're doing, but what you've done, that counts. This conclusion is hard to assimilate with those from a series of investigations (Myers et al 106, Rahe et al 121) which suggest that the number of life changes one experiences is positively related to the incidence of physical and emotional problems. (Ostensibly, having many marriages and divorces means having a lot of life changes.) However, the life-change findings have come mainly from military samples, where the incidence of extreme psychopathology must be rather low, while Overall's conclusion stems exclusively from a study of psychiatric patients, where the incidence of nondeviancy is definitionally near zero. Investigators looking for something fun to do might try combining the methodology of both approaches, using a heterogeneous sample of subjects.

Back in the old days (meaning right now at most traditional psychiatric settings), diagnosis was a single-stage, global, completely intuitive process: patients were interviewed by a clinician, who then assigned the patient to a diagnostic class or type. Nowadays (meaning at some research-oriented settings), these traditional diagnoses are supplemented by others which stem from a multistage process that combines more molecular intuitive judgments with empirical classification procedures. Specifically, the clinician, at the end of his diagnostic interview (142), now may complete one or more standardized rating scales, recording forms, or behavioral checklists. The clinician's responses to these precoded forms are then combined, by clerk or computer, to provide a set of syndrome scores. The profile of scores, in turn, is then used, again by clerk or computer, to assign the patient to a particular diagnostic cluster or type. The classification system (i.e. the entire set of types) may originally have been developed either intuitively or empirically via previous cluster analyses of large samples of score profiles. An example of the former is Spitzer & Endicott's DIAGNO system (140), while examples of the latter include the taxonomies devised by Lorr (82, 83, 87) and by Overall (110, 112).

These attempts to standardize, to fractionate, and thus to objectify the process of clinical decision making have been among the most significant achievements in psychodiagnosis during the past decade. Yet, since most reports of these developments have been published in psychiatric journals, this work may not be as familiar to psychologists as it should be. For this reason, the present chapter will provide more detail about these procedures than about most others, for which extensive reviews are already available (12).

The standardized report forms, which provide the initial data for all of the semiautomatic diagnostic systems, differ from each other in length, in focus, in the degree of structure they impose on the clinical interview from which the clinician's observations and judgments are derived, and—of most importance—in the level of inference required of the clinician (159). At one extreme of this continuum are the most abstract types of depth interpretations found in some psychoanalytic interviews; at the other extreme are the behavior frequency counts favored by investigators with a social-learning viewpoint.

The widely used *Brief Psychiatric Rating Scale* (BPRS), developed by Overall and Gorham, lies on the abstract side of this continuum (115). A 7-category scale (not present, very mild, mild, moderate, moderately severe, severe, extremely severe) is used for rating 18 symptoms.[2] In addition, the BPRS can be scored for four higher-order factor scores (thinking disturbance, anxious depression, hostile-suspiciousness, and withdrawal-retardation), each the sum of three separate ratings; for two syndrome contrasts (schizophrenic/depressive and coping/resignation); and for a total pathology composite (the sum of all 18 ratings). Recently, Overall has developed the *Factor Construct Rating Scale* (FCRS), which uses the same type of 7-category scales for rating 17 symptoms.[3] Cluster analyses of FCRS profiles have suggested 5 major patient types, which Overall has labeled depression, thinking disorder, extrapunitiveness, neuroticism, and agitation-excitement (110, 112).

Lorr & Klett's popular *Inpatient Multidimensional Psychiatric Scale* (IMPS) demands somewhat less abstract judgments than those required for the BPRS or the FCRS. Its 75 items include 45 symptom intensity ratings (each on a 9-category scale), 13 symptom frequency ratings (each on a 5-category scale), and 17 dichotomous items. Newly hospitalized psychotic patients were interviewed and rated independently by two raters using the IMPS; factor analyses of such data from a number of separate samples provide the data base for 10 IMPS syndrome scores.[4] Cluster analyses of IMPS profiles in various samples have led Lorr to conclude that about 60% of psychotics can be categorized into 11 types, 7 of which are the same for men and women (excited, excited-hostile, hostile paranoid, hallucinated paranoid, grandiose paranoid, and anxious-depressed), 2 are unique to men (disoriented and anxious-disorganized) and 2 to women (excited-disorganized and retarded-disorganized) (82, 83, 87).

In contrast to the rather global taxonomic efforts of Overall and of Lorr, a team of investigators at the New York State Psychiatric Institute has been attempting to map the activities and behaviors of psychiatric patients in a far more articulated manner. Led by Spitzer & Endicott, this interdisciplinary group has produced three major rating schedules and a half dozen recording forms during the period of this review. The *Psychiatric Status Schedule* (PSS) was designed to provide multifaceted coverage of psychiatric signs and symptoms (including the use of drugs and alcohol, plus antisocial and illegal activities), as well as to evaluate impairment in diverse life

[2]Conceptual disorganization, hallucinatory behavior, unusual thought content; anxiety, guilt feelings, depressive mood; hostility, suspiciousness, uncooperativeness; emotional withdrawal, motor retardation, blunted affect; somatic concern, tension, mannerisms and posturing, grandiosity, excitement, and disorientation.

[3]Mental disorganization, mental distortion, affective impoverishment, bizarre motor manifestations, psychomotor retardation, agitation-excitement, extrapunitiveness, intropunitiveness, depressive mood, elevated mood, passive dependence, dominant control, denial, intellectualization, over-responsiveness, neuroticism (obsessive, compulsive, or phobic symptoms), and anxiety-tension.

[4]Excitement, hostile belligerence, paranoid projection, grandiose expansiveness, perceptual distortions, anxious intropunitiveness, retardation and apathy, disorientation, motor disturbances, and conceptual disorganization.

roles (143). The 21-page PSS booklet includes both a standardized interview guide and an interrelated inventory of 321 precoded items, most of which are brief nontechnical descriptions of small samples of verbal behavior (e.g. *Query:* "What kinds of things do you worry about?" *Item 15:* "Mentions he worries a lot or that he can't stop worrying"). Factor analyses of item responses from an earlier version led to the development of 17 PSS symptom scales,[5] a denial of illness scale, plus five role impairment scales (for the roles of wage earner, housekeeper, student or trainee, mate, and parent). In addition, as with the BPRS, the symptom scales can be summarized by four higher-order composite scores (subjective distress, behavioral disturbance, impulse control disturbance, and reality testing disturbance), as well as an index of overall role impairment.

A close relative of the PSS is the new *Psychiatric Evaluation Form* (PEF), an attempt to cover much the same ground using far more global ratings (38). The PEF is housed in a 9-page booklet, which contains 27 rating scales and 2 checklists. Nineteen symptom scales are scored,[6] plus the same 5 types of role impairment as in the PSS. Another new instrument in this series is the *Current and Past Psychopathology Scales* (CAPPS), which includes 28 items from the PEF, 13 others of some incremental diagnostic significance, and 130 life history items (37). CAPPS scoring keys, again based upon factor analyses of previous protocols, include 8 indices of current pathology,[7] plus 18 life history scales.[8] In addition, the 171 CAPPS responses can be used to provide a computer-based psychiatric diagnosis, via the DIAGNO-II program (140).

PSS, PEF, and CAPPS, which were designed primarily as research instruments, are multipage booklets with separate scoresheets which must be keypunched prior to computer processing. Such instruments are hard to sell to busy practitioners, whose devotion to paperwork may not be so fueled by scientific ambition. Nonetheless, clinicians must be inveigled into cooperation if the diagnostic scientists are to achieve their dream: a large-scale systematic research project in which standardized observational data are collected on all patients admitted to every hospital in a state,

[5]Depression-anxiety, daily routine or leisure time impairment, social isolation, suicide or self-mutilation, somatic concern; speech disorganization, inappropriate affect or appearance or behavior, agitation-excitement, interview belligerence or negativeness, disorientation or memory impairment, retardation or lack of emotion; antisocial impulses or acts, drug abuse, reported overt anger; grandiosity, suspicion-persecution-hallucinations; and alcohol abuse.

[6]Depression, anxiety, suicide or self-mutilation, somatic concerns; speech disorganization, agitation-excitement, hallucinations, inappropriateness, disorientation or memory loss; belligerence-negativism, denial of illness, grandiosity, suspicion-persecution; retardation or lack of emotion, social isolation, impairment in daily routine or leisure time; narcotics-drugs, antisocial; and alcohol abuse.

[7]Reality testing, depression-anxiety, impulse control, somatic concern, disorganization, obsessive-guilt-phobic, elation-grandiosity, and overall role impairment.

[8]Depression-anxiety, impulse control, social and sexual relations, reality testing, dependency, somatic concern, obsessive-compulsive symptoms, anger-excitability, mania, sexual disturbance, memory and orientation, disorganization, organicity, neurotic childhood, phobia, retardation, hysteria, and intellectual performance.

or better yet, in a multistate region. As a compromise between the scientists' need for data standardization and response completeness and the practitioners' need for brevity and simplicity, a number of new recording forms have been developed. Among the most impressive of these is an integrated set of six psychiatric record forms developed by the Spitzer & Endicott team (141). These forms, which were developed for a collaborative project involving 7 states and the District of Columbia (the *Multi-State Information System for Psychiatric Patients*), were designed for recording psychiatric status and history within a computerized record-keeping system. All are 8 1/2 by 11 inch forms which can be automatically processed by an optical reader for transmission directly into a computer and/or for storage on computer punchcards. The *Problem Appraisal Scales* (PAS), a one-page summary of the patient's presenting problems upon admission to the hospital, includes 38 5-category rating scales covering physical, intellectual, and social symptoms. The *Psychiatric Diagnosis Recording Form* (PDRF) is a single-page checklist for recording one, two, or three diagnoses from the "official" list provided, plus the diagnostic stage (admission, provisional, reevaluation, or final). The *Mental Status Examination Record* (MSER) is a 4-page condensation of the PSS, which includes 156 symptom rating scales and 101 checklist items. A hospital (PER) and a community (PER-C) form of the *Periodic Evaluation Record* permit a brief evaluation of patient functioning during the past week; each of these single-page forms includes 28 scales and 45 checklist items from the MSER, thus permitting analyses of patient change. Finally, the *Psychiatric Anamnestic Record* (PAR), a 4-page form with 152 rating scales and 266 checklist items, covers the information typically included in a complete psychiatric case history.

Another enterprising effort to standardize and automate clinical records is being carried out by Sletten, Ulett, and their associates at the State of Missouri's Division of Mental Health (34, 138, 151). This team has been developing a computer-based network called the *Missouri Automated Standard System of Psychiatry,* which now serves 10 hospitals and 9 clinics within the state. Virtually everything normally collected from and about each patient is fed into the computer's hungry maw, mostly via single-page checklists which substitute for the transcribed records of yesteryear. The *Missouri Automated Mental Status Examination* (136) includes 111 symptom-descriptive items which are scored on two dozen or so factor analytically based scales. These scales plus another couple of dozen demographic variables have been used in stepwise multiple-discriminant analyses to predict the final psychiatric diagnoses for 12 types of patients (139). Studies using large samples and a cross-validation design have suggested the utility of these linear functions for purposes of diagnosis, as well as for predicting length of stay in the hospital, likelihood of running away, and potential for committing suicide and for assaulting others (134).

Other single-page Missouri checklists include: (*a*) the *Missouri Inpatient Behavior Scale,* 90 items relating to ward behavior; (*b*) the *Community Adjustment Profile System,* 100 items about social functioning obtained from the patient's relatives or friends, which provides 10 scale scores; (*c*) a form to record demographic data plus all movements between installations; (*d*) a checklist for the emergency room or admissions desk; (*e*) one to record the findings from a physical examination; (*f*) a form for the social worker to record information about social functioning; (*g*) an alcohol questionnaire; (*h*) a medicaid report; (*i*) an outpatient contact sheet; (*j*) a form for recording all medication data; (*k*) another for recording blood chemistry; (*l*) yet another for information about any nursing home care; and (*m*) various forms for business records. Even the Missouri psychometrician is in the act. While the *Peabody Picture Vocabulary Test* (a standard instrument in the system) is not yet administered by robots, patients sort the 550 MMPI items, each printed on a prepunched IBM card, into two piles (True vs False), which are then fed to the computer for scoring. With such a system it becomes possible to check a clinical hunch with a flick of the programmer. Want to know what sort of patients committed suicide in the state during the past few years? Just ask the computer to search its files, find them all, and list their combined characteristics. Voila (135)!

The Institute of Living in Hartford, Connecticut, is another institution that has attempted to computerize evaluations. Their new instruments include: (*a*) a 650-item mental status examination which can be completed by the clinician via a television monitor integrated with a modified typewriter keyboard (Donnelly et al 32); (*b*) a one-page machine-readable form for recording nursing notes, thus permitting an automated sequential analysis of patient change (Stroebel & Glueck 144); and (*c*) a single-page machine-readable interview schedule that provides delinquency predictions in a more objective manner than has been possible in the past (Glueck 48). All of these efforts, however, are based on the use of prespecified coding categories (e.g. multiple-choice questions). Wouldn't it be nifty, some have suggested, if the clinician or the patient could respond to the computer in their natural language, in narrative essay style? That day hasn't *quite* arrived, but it may be on the way. Eiduson & Ramsey-Klee (35) at the Reiss-Davis Child Study Center in Los Angeles have been designing a general information processor, called the *Psychiatric Case History Event System* (PsyCHES), which represents a step in this direction. And Benfari et al (6) at Harvard have been developing another such sophisticated system, called *Computer Assigned Symptom Evaluation* (CASE).

If the reader hasn't fallen asleep by this point, news of some additional L-data measures may serve to do the trick. A short symptom checklist for the diagnosis of schizophrenia, the *New Haven Schizophrenic Index* (NHSI), can be scored from hospital records; intuitively derived item weights are used to produce a total score, which purportedly is highly related to clinical diagnosis (3). Also working from patient records, Hautaluoma (67) has reported a methodologically sophisticated analysis of psychiatric syndromes and their relation to antecedent behaviors and treatment prognoses. In a similar vein, Martorano & Nathan (90) factor analyzed the 100-item *Boston City Hospital Behavioral Checklist* and related these factors to those from the IMPS and to traditional diagnoses. Similar types of analyses have been undertaken to compare the data from American versus English patients (Everitt et al 39) and to identify and/or classify depressed patients (Paykel 117, Zung 160). And when a 64-symptom instrument, the *Symptom Distress Checklist,* was factor analyzed, items in the resulting four factors were found to be highly related to the clusters obtained when 20 clinicians were instructed to group the 64 symptoms intuitively (Derogatis et al 28). Two overviews of this scene are now available, one by Ulett & Sletten (150) and the other by Stroebel & Glueck (145).

Although the vast majority of these investigations have been focused exclusively on adult psychiatric patients, there have been a few studies of children. Among the most intriguing new child measures is the *Personality Inventory for Children* (PIC), which consists of 600 true-false items to be completed by the mothers of children between the ages of 6 and 16 (Wirt et al 158). PIC scales, which are still under development, include 11 constructed by the intuitive strategy,[9] plus at least 8 constructed by the external (empirical) approach.[10] Far more restricted in content is the *Louisville Fear Survey for Children,* an 81-item inventory that can be completed by parents or teachers on the one hand, and by children or their peers on the other (Miller et al 103); a factor analysis of parents' ratings of their children suggested three major kinds of fears: physical injury, natural events, and psychic stress. Teachers' ratings of the problem behaviors of elementary school children have been factor analyzed by Miller (102) and by Dielman & Cattell (30, 31). Miller's analyses have led to the development of his *School Behavior Check List,* which includes 6 subscales (low need for achievement, aggression, anxiety, academic disability, hostile isolation, and extraversion), plus a total disability score. Dielman & Cattell found 5 replicated oblique factors from a 62-item problem behavior checklist (hyperactivity, sluggishness, suspiciousness, withdrawal, and acting out). Modern kids must be turning soft; there were far more ways of getting into trouble back in the good old days.

Diagnosis Based on Questionnaire or Self-Report Data

Life history data normally must be encoded by human observers before being processed for assessment purposes, and we human observers have been known to have less than perfect fidelity for this transmission task. Various biases, context effects, and stereotypes plague us; our channel capacity is severely limited; and we get disrupted by boredom, fatigue, illness, as well as a host of situational and interpersonal distractions. In short, since humans are expensive middlemen, psychometricians often opt for self-report measures, which attempt to deal direct. However, an individual's social stimulus value is a mighty significant aspect of his personality, and individuals may not always see themselves exactly as others see them. So personality assessors pays their money and takes their choice: between L-data, smudged, warped, or otherwise distended by gliches in the transmission system; or Q-data, with its own full share of foibles and frailties. If we are wealthy enough, we can buy both products. And when we can figure out how best to meld them together, we will have achieved a scientific breakthrough of the highest magnitude (57).

[9]Withdrawal, excitement, reality distortion, aggression, somatic concern, anxiety, social skills, family relations, physical development, intellectual development, and asocial tendencies.

[10]General maladjustment, delinquency, learning disability, sexual identification, cerebral dysfunction, intelligence, somatization, and defensiveness.

For the nonce, however, let us consider Q-data as a codified form of interpersonal communication used by one person to evaluate, assess, classify or diagnose another. The content domain of the communication, which is specified by the assessor, can include perceptions of observable past events (9), symptoms of emotional disturbance (51, 92, 131), transitory moods (93), or any other beliefs, opinions, or attitudes of interest to the nosiest of snoops. For example, the *Minnesota-Briggs History Record* is an attempt to measure via questionnaire some of the variables typically obtained from L-data (9). Indeed, the inventory was initially developed for use by relatives of patients hospitalized for psychiatric problems, and only recently has it been converted to a self-report format. The new version, which contains 127 items, provides 7 scales (family disunity, conflict with parents, health awareness, introversion, school or job failure, social misfit, and breakdowns or addictions). While the Minnesota-Briggs was designed to measure enduring life history patterns, a new *Profile of Mood States* (POMS) was built to assess highly transient and fluctuating affective states (93). The POMS consists of 65 items, mostly state-descriptive adjectives (e.g. "shaky"), each to be rated on a 5-category scale (not at all, a little, moderately, quite a bit, extremely). Factor analyses of a larger set of items led to the development of 6 highly homogeneous scales, measuring the moods of tension, depression, anger, vigor, fatigue, and confusion. For a fascinating methodological footnote on the measurement of moods, see the report by Meddis (95).

Psychodiagnostic intervews, for all their potential utility (142), have one clear liability, namely their extraordinary cost in professional time. The desire for an inexpensive substitute for a diagnostic examination led to the development of the very first personality scales (54) and subsequently the need seems to have continued unabated. Maultsby & Slack (92) have developed a computer-based system for obtaining case histories directly from the patient, the output being a report to the clinician. However, computers themselves are not all that cheap, and they are awkward to truck around on house calls. Clearly, a self-administered questionnaire would be the cheapest way out. D. P. Goldberg (a distant relative of the author, on the O'Hallahan side of the family) has recently attempted to construct another one, this to identify individuals with nonpsychotic psychiatric disorders and to assess the severity of their problems. The research monograph that reports his efforts (51) includes the response proportions from each of three types of subjects (psychiatric hospital inpatients, clinic outpatients, and a normal community sample) to each of 140 symptom-descriptive items, the overwhelming majority of which differentiated significantly among the three samples. The results of a factor analysis of the 93 most differentiating items are also provided, along with data on the characteristics of a revised 59-item scale. Schachter (131) has been trying much the same trick, with the hope of identifying the schizophrenics among those pregnant women who register for prenatal care. And Selzer (133) has developed a 25-item *Michigan Alcoholism Screening Test* (MAST), which appears to work wonders at detecting those who admit drinking a good deal (105).

Two multiscale psychopathology inventories have appeared of late, one of which has been published in the scientific literature and is thus free to the user, while the other has been published commercially and is indeed quite expensive. However, unlike fast automobiles and fine wine, in this case the cheaper is also the better. Specifically, Lanyon (77) has given away his *Psychological Screening Inventory* (PSI), a carefully constructed 130-item instrument that provides scores on 5 scales: (*a*) alienation (similarity to psychiatric patients); (*b*) social nonconformity (similarity to incarcerated criminals); (*c*) discomfort or anxiety; (*d*) expression (extraversion or undercontrol); and (*e*) test-taking defensiveness. In contrast, one writes to a post office box in New York's Grand Central Station to find out about the new *Experiential World Inventory* (EWI), a 400-item wonder that is supposed to provide scores on 8 scales: (*a*) sensory perception; (*b*) time perception; (*c*) body perception; (*d*) self-perception; (*e*) perception of others; (*f*) ideation; (*g*) dysphoria; and (*h*) impulse regulation (36). For those who must see it to believe it, Table 1 lists some EWI items, along with a few concocted by the famous humorist, Art Buchwald. Actually, Buchwald's items are included simply for comic relief; every *Annual Review* chapter needs some comic relief. But the tabled EWI items are not all that unrepresentative of the entire set, a fact that makes the EWI manual a gold mine to item buffs. For in that manual are all 400 item endorsement proportions, separately computed within various samples of college students, neurotics, schizophrenics, alcoholics, and prisoners. As an example, take that subtle item for vampire detection (312: "I would like to drink blood"). Roughly 1 or 2 percent of the individuals in normal samples endorse that item, while between 5 and 10 percent of those in schizophrenic samples do so. Happily, however, roughly the same endorsement proportions apply to EWI item 48 ("I cannot fully open my mouth"). Lest you get complacent, however, I must pass on the dire findings for item 102 ("I sometimes feel an urge to bite somebody"): 25% of male college students endorse that one, while only 1% of the coeds do so. Add one more problem for Women's Lib.

AND THEN THERE'S THE MMPI As alert readers may have remembered, there is always a lot going on in this arena, far too much to write about here. However, a few major developments probably should be mentioned, if only briefly. Among the most significant recent MMPI studies are three by Overall and his associates. Two of these were on alcohol abuse (116, 153), and the third was a match race between the MMPI and the 16 PF, comparing their ability at differentiating among 13 different types of psychiatric diagnoses; the winner was the MMPI, by many lengths (157). In another excellent study, Lorr & Gilberstadt (84) joined forces to assess the relationships between Lorr's IMPS rating types (L-data) and Gilberstadt's MMPI profile types (Q-data); the verdict: very little overlap. Nonetheless, the development of new profile types continues (63), as does research on the characteristics of persons in each type (66, 80, 119). Hopefully these findings will be incorporated into the computer programs that are used to provide those automated interpretive reports, but don't hold your breath. O'Dell (108) has shown that, at least for the products of one of these services, individuals are unable to distinguish between the accuracy of a flattering universal report and one prepared specifically from their MMPI responses. Three overviews of this business, by Fowler (47), by Kleinmuntz (75), and Manning (89) are now available, thus sparing me the pleasure.

Table 1 Would the *real* set of items please step forward?

Set 1[a]	Set 2[b]
The sight of blood no longer excites me.	Animals often try to fool me.
It makes me furious to see an innocent man escape the chair.	I feel like killing untidy people.
When I was a child, I was an imaginary playmate.	I sometimes taste sound.
I am bored by thoughts of death.	Someone is making copies of me.
I become homicidal when people try to reason with me.	I sometimes think other people's thoughts.
I don't like it when somebody is rotten.	I am afraid somebody may cut off my nose.
Most of the time I go to sleep without saying goodby.	Old men are indecent.
Frantic screams make me nervous.	I am someone else.
	I would like to drink blood.
	I feel that my ideas may turn into insects.

[a]Written by Art Buchwald, the noted humorist.
[b]Included in the *Experiential World Inventory.*

Many users have complained that the MMPI is too long. Since a good many items, especially those towards the end of the booklet, are not scored on the standard clinical scales, there have been numerous attempts to expunge them. Various expurgated versions of the MMPI have been devised, the most popular being editions of 399, 373, and 366 items. A recent trend is to whittle down this item pool even more, to the first 168 items, or to a selected 86 (the Midi-Mult), or even to 71 (the Mini-Mult) (65). Since the direction of this movement is evident, the future should see the MMPI reduced to bare bones, namely a few single-item scales. For detecting latent obesity, one needs only the lone item: "I can't believe I ate the w-h-o-l-e thing." The masculinity-femininity scale can be replaced by one true-false item: "I am a male" (54). And the neurotic scales can all coalesce into the single item: "I am a jerk."

Whatever one thinks of the present status of the MMPI, virtually no one will deny its extraordinary historical influence upon assessment research and upon psychodiagnostic practice. Eventually, however, old inventories, like old soldiers, must slowly fade away. Hopefully the next decade will bring the MMPI's successor, perhaps the new *Differential Personality Inventory* (15, 147) if it can be lured out of hiding. In the interim, since the MMPI will continue to be used and used heavily, it should be employed as sagely as possible. At present it is used anachronistically: the original clinical scales (each developed empirically to differentiate a particular small sample of psychiatric patients from a larger nonpsychiatric sample) are now employed as the structural elements in fairly elaborate quasiconfigural profile typologies, and an individual's responses are interpreted in reference to the attributes that tend to characterize others with similar score profiles. However, as Norman (107) has argued so articulately:

> Whatever one thinks of the desirability of the original construction of the basic clinical scales (granting the purposes for which they were intended), it is abundantly clear that they are about as inappropriate and maladapted a set as one could imagine for their current uses in profile analysis and interpretation and typal class definition [p. 64].

Specifically, the original clinical scales have at least three major liabilities for the task for which they are now being employed: (*a*) each scale is highly heterogeneous in manifest content, and consequently it is next to impossible to attribute any unambiguous and/or content-coherent message to a particular scale score; (*b*) the set of scales is both substantively and structurally redundant, a problem that is severely exacerbated by items keyed on two or more scales; and (*c*) a sizable amount of potentially significant information from the initial item pool is not even available, either because it stems from the many items that are never scored or because sets of negatively correlated items are included in the same scale, thus effectively eliminating their effects. While these psychometric facts of life were not obvious in the late 1930s when the MMPI was being constructed, they are today. Consequently, until the MMPI item pool is replaced, it is time to move from the old clinical scales to a new set of content-coherent and structurally independent ones.

Over the years there have been numerous attempts to factor various sets of MMPI items. In contrast to similar analyses of MMPI scale scores which typically extract around three factors, the various analyses at the item level have produced little agreement about the number of factors in the MMPI pool; the estimates have ranged from around three, when the late Robert Tryon tried his hand at this game (148), to some unspecified but far larger number in the rotoplots of Raymond B. Cattell (27). Barker, Fowler & Peterson (4) extracted nine factors, but then they only used 373 of the MMPI's 550 items. In any case, given a few dozen extra pages, I would argue the heresy that factor analysis of items is as risky an enterprise as is empirical item analysis using criterion groups. What is needed for the construction of new MMPI scales is a multistrategy approach that is maximally sensitive to item content.

Wiggins (154) has used precisely such tactics in the development of his 13 new MMPI content scales. Always with a sharp eye on manifest content, while simultaneously keeping his sights aligned by means of empirical homogeneity analyses, Wiggins has fashioned a set of MMPI scales that are far better suited for use in profile typologies than are the original clinical scales. Unfortunately, since the content scales haven't been around as long, there are far fewer data available about them (118, 146, 156). As a result, the practitioner should be encouraged to employ both the clinical and the content scales, just as with the *Strong Vocational Interest Blank* he can now employ the statistically homogeneous and content-coherent Basic Interest Scales along with the classic occupational ones (8, 14). And, to past MMPI investigators, an urgent request: rescore those old answer sheets on Wiggins' content scales, and run that vintage study once again. Two publications for the price of one! If anyone should object, tell them you obtained your authorization on these very pages.

Diagnosis Based on Test Data

Inventories are often loosely referred to as personality tests, but they aren't, and thus they shouldn't be. One cannot be too sticky about this, however, since over the years the term "objective test" has been defined in extraordinarily diverse ways. As this chapter is not the place to resolve the arcane semantic issues involved, tests will be defined, quite dogmatically, by right of adverse possession if you will (or if you won't, by right of eminent domain): an objective test is one in which the examinee, without gross cheating, can alter his score in one direction at most; this definition is roughly equivalent to that proposed long ago by Cronbach for a "maximum performance" task. By this definition, most standardized measures of physiological activity and physical proficiency, as well as most aptitude and achievement examinations, qualify as objective tests.

Within clinical psychology these instruments have rarely been used for differential diagnosis, with the notable exception of those used for the detection of brain damage. The latter measures really should be reviewed by someone whose knowledge of neurophysiology is a light year or two beyond that of your reporter; consequently, the wary are hereby advised to skip immediately to the next paragraph. For you unwary, however, five excellent studies of the *Halstead Neuropsychological Test Battery* have recently appeared (59, 76, 79, 123, 124). Overall & Gorham (111) used the WAIS and a group-administered and computer-scored version of the *Holtzman Inkblot Test* to check the hypothesis that performance differences between brain-damaged patients and those with no such damage are similar to the differences that normally occur as a function of aging; for the two tests employed, that hypothesis proved dead wrong. In another report on brain damage in old age, Kendrick (73) discussed his *Digit Copying* and *Synonym Learning* tests. Finally, Lewinsohn and his students (81) have tested patients' short-term memory via visual, auditory, and kinesthetic modalities, showing that the test performance of those with anterior damage is worse than those with posterior. Moral: Fall backwards.

Welcome back, wary. As you probably know, the outstanding, and longstanding, advocate of the use of objective tests in clinical diagnosis is Raymond B. Cattell. Over the years, Cattell has been collating existing tests, devising new ones, and factor analyzing various subsets of his resulting collection. He has published two major volumes dealing with these efforts, as well as two versions of his *Objective-Analytic Personality Test Battery.* For so energetic a sales campaign, customer response has been sluggish. The problem has been to convince clinicians that objective tests are more valid predictors of significant clinical behaviors than are other types of measures commonly available. Fabian & Comrey (46) made such a comparison and reached the opposite conclusion. Most of Cattell's efforts, however, always go into yet another factor analysis (17); this ploy, while unlikely to convert the heathen, is certain to stir up someone who enjoys the same bead game (Howarth 69). Finally, however, Cattell has published a report on the relationships between objective tests and clinical diagnoses (19). It should have been a corker. Instead, it must go down as one of the most amorphous and prolix of a long line of publications not always noted for their crispness. The tragedy is that there probably *is* something important going on here, since Lorr and Hamlin (64, 85, 86) carried out reasonably similar types of analyses and found gold.

FOR THOSE ASSESSMENT SCIENTISTS WHO HAVE BEEN HANGING IN HERE ALL THIS LONG . . .

As usual, there is both good news and bad news. First let me acknowledge the bad news, which you already discovered for yourself before reading word one of this chapter: your best work (your entire production?) has been overlooked in the author's pigheaded scramble to conform to page limitations. The good news: you get another chance 3 years from now. In the interim, what are the scientific problems on which we should all be working? The author has attempted to answer this question, for the broader discipline of which this is a part, in a paper published only a short while ago (57). In capsule summary, these problems include: (*a*) discovering the most important individual differences from the host observable; (*b*) measuring those attributes as precisely as possible; and (*c*) finding optimal methods for employing these measures in both basic and applied endeavors. No wishy-washy character, the author stands 1000% behind his previous choice. In the space remaining, let us look at some recent research on the last two of these three problems.

Measurement normally begins with the presentation of a stimulus (e.g. an item or a question) to a subject, in order to elicit a precodified (e.g. multiple choice), or potentially codifiable, response. Such a response is rarely considered a measure in and of itself; a lone response may be both unreliable (in that future responses to the exact same stimulus would not all be identical) and unrepresentative of responses to closely related stimuli (generalization from single instances, like generalizations from single subjects, can be hazardous to your health). Consequently, the responses to a set of stimuli are typically accumulated and then averaged in some manner before reliable measurement is thought to have occurred. The basic problem in scale construction is selecting the particular set of stimuli, the accumulated responses to which are used to produce a score. There are three general approaches to this task; callously disregarding older terminology, I refer to these as the Intuitive, Internal, and External strategies of scale construction (56). Many test constructors have used a combination of two strategies—typically the Intuitive and the Internal (70) or more rarely the Intuitive and the External (62)—and Meehl (98) now advocates a combination of all three. Jackson (70) has provocatively challenged the alleged superiority of the External over the Intuitive strategies, and Ashton & Goldberg (2) have risen to his bait. For two other such empirical comparisons, see Fabian & Comrey (46) and Goldberg (56).

After measures have been constructed, they really ought to be used. For most purposes more than one measure will be used at the same time, so that the measures —like the items before them—typically must be combined in some fashion. Long ago two broad integration possibilities were distinguished: actuarial (or statistical) and subjective (or "clinical"). When they are pitted against each other repeatedly, as in a cockfight, neither manages to kill off the other in a clean enough manner so that all of the betting money changes hands. Most psychologists have come to agree with Meehl (96), who long ago set up the gaming regulations. On the other hand, Holt (68) has always objected to those very rules, and thus he sporadically confesses his refusal to pay up. The major unresolved problems today (other than persuading Holt to do some research instead of exhorting others to do it for him) include, on the actuarial side, a specification of the sort of prediction functions that are most appropriate for today's measures, and on the subjective side, a specification of the optimal meld of empirical data with informed intuition.

The first problem has been formulated as a comparison between linear and configural prediction models (22, 52, 55, 98). As the arch-linearist on these battle lines at present, the author hereby asserts his belief that virtually all psychological relationships are going to turn out to be nonlinear and configural in nature. When measures of individual differences become precise enough, then the various nonlinear prediction models will become useful. At the moment, however, our measures are still too gross to expect nonlinear models to outperform linear ones, given the clear statistical problems involved in the former's selection and use. These problems are particularly poignant at the moment, since so much effort is presently going into the development of complex profile typologies and into the search for trait-by-treatment interactions; the latter include not only the traditional patient-by-drug interactions, but also some patient-by-therapist ones (20, 122).

And finally there's human intuition—much exalted, much maligned, often grossly misused, but typically all that's around. Most sorts of clinical decisions are made subjectively if for no other reason than that at this primitive state of our science the appropriate actuarial data have not yet been analyzed. Ostensibly, practitioners who are called upon to make such decisions on a daily basis come to learn a bit about how to make them. Nonetheless, professionals are still only human and, as noted before, humans have their days: good and bad, up and down, topsy and turvy. A few years ago I pondered whether the practitioner's inherent unreliability might not be separated from his—hopefully somewhat valid—judgmental policies (53). Since a simple linear regression model can often be constructed to capture critical aspects of many judgmental strategies, what would happen if one substituted one of the judgmental models for the expert himself? An empirical study of 29 clinical psychologists attempting to differentiate the MMPI profiles of psychotic from neurotic patients suggested that models tended to function at least as well as the humans that were modeled (53).

Happily, this finding has now been replicated in a number of subsequent studies, and various investigators seem to have arrived independently at much the same conclusion, albeit by somewhat different routes. For example, investigative teams in Texas (113, 114) and in Missouri (137) have begun to model the decisions of psychiatrists selecting the most appropriate drug for different types of patients. Since diagnosis has already been automated in some settings, this consequent automation of treatment decision making could serve to eliminate the clinician altogether. If you find yourself being tickled by this fantasy, just remember: *you* could be the very next to go . . .

Literature Cited

1. Albee, G. W. 1970. Notes toward a position paper opposing psychodiagnosis. See Ref. 88, 385–95
2. Ashton, S. G., Goldberg, L. R. 1973. In response to Jackson's challenge: The comparative validity of personality scales constructed by the external (empirical) strategy and scales developed intuitively by experts, novices, and laymen. *J. Res. Pers.* 7:1–20
3. Astrachan, B. M. et al 1972. A checklist for the diagnosis of schizophrenia. *Brit. J. Psychiat.* 121:529–39
4. Barker, H. R., Fowler, R. D., Peterson, L. P. 1971. Factor analytic structure of the short form MMPI items in a VA Hospital population. *J. Clin. Psychol.* 27:228–33
5. Begelman, D. A. 1971. Misnaming, metaphors, the medical model, and some muddles. *Psychiatry* 34:38–58
6. Benfari, R. C., Leighton, A. H., Beiser, M., Coen, K. 1972. CASE: Computer assigned symptom evaluation. *J. Nerv. Ment. Dis.* 154:115–24
7. Bloch, E. L., Goodstein, L. D. 1971. Functional speech disorders and personality: A decade of research. *J. Speech Hearing Dis.* 36:295–314
8. Borgen, F. H. 1972. Predicting career choices of able college men from occupational and basic interest scales of the Strong Vocational Interest Blank. *J. Couns. Psychol.* 19:202–11
9. Briggs, P. F., Rouzer, D. L., Hamberg, R. L., Holman, T. R. 1972. Seven scales for the Minnesota-Briggs History Record with reference group data. *J. Clin. Psychol.* 28:431–48
10. Brown, T. R., Sheran, T. J. 1972. Suicide prediction: A review. *Life-Threatening Behav.* 2:67–98
11. Buros, O. K., Ed. 1970. *Personality Tests and Reviews.* Highland Park, N.J.: Gryphon
12. Buros, O. K., Ed. 1972. *Seventh Mental Measurements Yearbook,* Vols. 1 and 2. Highland Park, N.J.: Gryphon
13. Butcher, J. N., Ed. 1972. *Objective Personality Assessment.* New York: Academic
14. Campbell, D. P. 1971. *Handbook for the Strong Vocational Interest Blank.* Stanford Univ. Press
15. Carlson, K. A. 1972. Classes of adult offenders: A multivariate approach. *J. Abnorm. Psychol.* 79:84–93
16. Cattell, R. B. 1970. The integration of functional and psychometric requirements in a quantitative and computerized diagnostic system. See Ref. 88, 9–52
17. Cattell, R. B., Delhees, K. H., Tatro, D. F., Nesselroade, J. R. 1971. Personality structure checked in primary objective test factors, for a mixed normal and psychotic sample. *Multivar. Behav. Res.* 6:187–214
18. Cattell, R. B., Eber, H. W., Tatsuoka, M. M. 1970. *Handbook for the Sixteen Personality Factor Questionnaire (16PF).* Champaign, Ill.: IPAT
19. Cattell, R. B., Schmidt, L. R., Bjerstedt, A. 1972. Clinical diagnosis by the Objective-Analytic Personality Batteries. *J. Clin. Psychol.* 28:239–312
20. Chartier, G. M. 1971. A-B therapist variable: Real or imagined? *Psychol. Bull.* 75:22–23
21. Costello, C. G., Ed. 1970. *Symptoms of Psychopathology: A Handbook.* New York: Wiley
22. Croft, D. J. 1972. Is computerized diagnosis possible? *Comput. Biomed. Res.* 5:351–67
23. Cronbach, L. J., Gleser, G. C. 1965. *Psychological Tests and Personnel Decisions.* Urbana: Univ. Illinois Press. 2nd ed.
24. Cronbach, L. J., Gleser, G. C., Nanda, H., Rajaratnam, N. 1972. *The Dependability of Behavioral Measurements: Theory of Generalizability for Scores and Profiles.* New York: Wiley
25. Dahlstrom, W. G. 1972. *Personality Systematics and the Problem of Types.* Morristown, N.J.: General Learning Press
26. Dahlstrom, W. G., Welsh, G. S., Dahlstrom, L. E. 1972. *An MMPI Handbook. Vol. 1—Clinical Interpretation.* Minneapolis: Univ. Minnesota Press. Rev. ed.
27. Delhees, K. H., Cattell, R. B. 1971. The dimensions of pathology: Proof of their projection beyond the normal 16 PF source traits. *Personality* 2:149–73
28. Derogatis, L. R., Lipman, R. S., Covi, L., Rickels, K., Uhlenhuth, E. H. 1970. Dimensions of outpatient neurotic pathology: Comparison of a clinical versus an empirical assessment. *J. Consult. Clin. Psychol.* 34:164–71
29. Deutsch, C. P., Schumer, F. 1970. *Brain-damaged Children: A Modality-Oriented Exploration of Performance.* New York: Brunner/Mazel

30. Dielman, T. E., Cattell, R. B., Lepper, C. 1971. Dimensions of problem behavior in the early grades. *J. Consult. Clin. Psychol.* 37:243–49
31. Dielman, T. E., Cattell, R. B., Rhoades, P. A. 1972. Cross-validational evidence on the dimensions of problem behavior in the early grades. *Multivar. Behav. Res.* 7:33–40
32. Donnelly, J., Rosenberg, M., Fleeson, W. P. 1970. The evolution of the mental status—past and future. *Am. J. Psychiat.* 126:997–1002
33. Draguns, J. G., Phillips, L. 1971. *Psychiatric Classification and Diagnosis: An Overview and Critique.* New York: General Learning Press
34. Eaton, M. E., Altman, H., Schuff, S., Sletten, I. 1970. Missouri Automated Psychiatric History for relatives and other informants. *Dis. Nerv. Syst.* 31: 198–202
35. Eiduson, B. T., Ramsey-Klee, D. M. 1970. A strategy for life history research using computer-based information processing techniques. See Ref. 126, 127–46
36. El-Meligi, A. M., Osmond, H. 1970. *Manual for the Clinical Use of the Experiential World Inventory.* New York: Mens Sana
37. Endicott, J., Spitzer, R. L. 1972. Current and Past Psychopathology Scales (CAPPS): Rationale, reliability, and validity. *Arch. Gen. Psychiat.* 27:678–87
38. Endicott, J., Spitzer, R. L. 1972. What! Another rating scale? The Psychiatric Evaluation Form. *J. Nerv. Ment. Dis.* 154:88–104
39. Everitt, B. S., Gourlay, A. J., Kendell, R. E. 1971. An attempt at validation of traditional psychiatric syndromes by cluster analysis. *Brit. J. Psychiat.* 119: 399–412
40. Eysenck, H. J. 1970. The classification of depressive illnesses. *Brit. J. Psychiat.* 117:241–50
41. Eysenck, H. J. 1970. *Crime and Personality.* London: Granada. Rev. ed.
42. Eysenck, H. J. 1970. A dimensional system of psychodiagnostics. See Ref. 88, 169–207
43. Eysenck, H. J., Ed. 1970. *Readings in Extraversion-Introversion. Vol. 1: Theoretical and Methodological Issues.* London: Staples Press
44. Eysenck, H. J., Ed. 1971. *Readings in Extraversion-Introversion. Vol. 2: Fields of Application.* London: Staples Press
45. Eysenck, H. J., Ed. 1971. *Readings in Extraversion-Introversion. Vol. 3: Bearings on Basic Psychological Processes.* London: Staples Press
46. Fabian, J. J., Comrey, A. L. 1971. Construct validation of factored neuroticism scales. *Multivar. Behav. Res.* 6:287–99
47. Fowler, R. D. Jr. 1972. Automated psychological test interpretation: The status in 1972. *Psychiat. Ann.* 2:10–28
48. Glueck, B. C. Jr. 1972. Automation in the prediction of delinquency. See Ref. 50, 115–21
49. Glueck, S., Glueck, E. 1970. *Toward a Typology of Juvenile Offenders: Implications for Therapy and Prevention.* New York: Grune & Stratton
50. Glueck, S., Glueck, E., Eds. 1972. *Identification of Predelinquents: Validation Studies and Some Suggested Uses of Glueck Table.* New York: Intercontinental Medical Book Corp.
51. Goldberg, D. P. 1972. *The Detection of Psychiatric Illness by Questionnaire: A Technique for the Identification and Assessment of Non-Psychotic Psychiatric Illness.* London: Oxford Univ. Press
52. Goldberg, L. R. 1969. The search for configural relationships in personality assessment: The diagnosis of psychosis vs. neurosis from the MMPI. *Multivar. Behav. Res.* 4:523–36
53. Goldberg, L. R. 1970. Man versus model of man: A rationale, plus some evidence, for a method of improving on clinical inferences. *Psychol. Bull.* 73: 422–32
54. Goldberg, L. R. 1971. A historical survey of personality scales and inventories. See Ref. 94, 293–336
55. Goldberg, L. R. 1972. Man versus mean: The exploitation of group profiles for the construction of diagnostic classification systems. *J. Abnorm. Psychol.* 79:121–31
56. Goldberg, L. R. 1972. Parameters of personality inventory construction and utilization: A comparison of prediction strategies and tactics. *Multivar. Behav. Res. Monogr.* No. 72–2
57. Goldberg, L. R. 1972. Some recent trends in personality assessment. *J. Pers. Assess.* 36:547–60
58. Goldfried, M. R., Kent, R. N. 1972. Traditional versus behavioral personality assessment: A comparison of methodological and theoretical assumptions. *Psychol. Bull.* 77:409–20
59. Goldstein, G., Shelly, C. H. 1972. Statistical and normative studies of the Halstead Neuropsychological Test Bat-

tery relevant to a neuropsychiatric hospital setting. *Percept. Mot. Skills* 34:603–20
60. Goodglass, H., Kaplan, E. 1972. *The Assessment of Aphasia and Related Disorders.* Philadelphia: Lea & Febiger
61. Gottesman, I. I., Shields, J. 1972. *Schizophrenia and Genetics: A Twin Study Vantage Point.* New York: Academic
62. Gough, H. 1971. Some reflections on the meaning of psychodiagnosis. *Am. Psychol.* 26:160–67
63. Gynther, M. D., Altman, H., Warbin, R. W., Sletten, I. W. 1972. A new actuarial system for MMPI interpretation: Rationale and methodology. *J. Clin. Psychol.* 28:173–79
64. Hamlin, R. M., Lorr, M. 1971. Differentiation of normals, neurotics, paranoids, and nonparanoids. *J. Abnorm. Psychol.* 77:90–96
65. Harford, T., Lubetkin, B., Alpert, G. 1972. Comparison of the standard MMPI and the Mini-Mult in a psychiatric outpatient clinic. *J. Consult. Clin. Psychol.* 39:243–45
66. Hathaway, S. R., Monachesi, E., Salasin, S. 1970. A follow-up study of MMPI high 8, schizoid, children. See Ref. 126, 171–88
67. Hautaluoma, J. 1971. Syndromes, antecedents, and outcomes of psychosis: A cluster-analytic study. *J. Consult. Clin. Psychol.* 37:332–44
68. Holt, R. R. 1970. Yet another look at clinical and statistical prediction: Or, is clinical psychology worthwhile? *Am. Psychol.* 25:337–49
69. Howarth, E. 1972. A factor analysis of selected markers for objective personality factors. *Multivar. Behav. Res.* 7: 451–76
70. Jackson, D. N. 1971. The dynamics of structured personality tests: 1971. *Psychol. Rev.* 78:229–48
71. Johnson, O. G., Bommarito, J. W. 1971. *Tests and Measurements in Child Development: A Handbook.* San Francisco: Jossey-Bass
72. Kanfer, F. H. 1972. Assessment for behavior modification. *J. Pers. Assess.* 36:418–23
73. Kendrick, D. C. 1972. The Kendrick battery of tests: Theoretical assumptions and clinical uses. *Brit. J. Soc. Clin. Psychol.* 11:373–86
74. Kipnis, D. 1971. *Character Structure and Impulsiveness.* New York: Academic
75. Kleinmuntz, B. 1972. *Computers in Personality Assessment.* Morristown, NY: General Learning Press
76. Klonoff, H., Fibiger, C. H., Hutton, G. H. 1970. Neuropsychological patterns in chronic schizophrenia. *J. Nerv. Ment. Dis.* 150:291–300
77. Lanyon, R. I. 1970. Development and validation of a Psychological Screening Inventory. *J. Consult. Clin. Psychol. Monogr.* 35:No. 1, Part 2
78. Lester, D. 1970. Attempts to predict suicidal risk using psychological tests. *Psychol. Bull.* 74:1–17
79. Levine, J., Feirstein, A. 1972. Differences in test performance between brain-damaged, schizophrenic, and medical patients. *J. Consult. Clin. Psychol.* 39:508–11
80. Lewandowski, D., Graham, J. R. 1972. Empirical correlates of frequently occurring two-point MMPI code types: A replicated study. *J. Consult. Clin. Psychol.* 39:467–72
81. Lewinsohn, P. M., Zieler, R. E., Libet, J., Eyeberg, S., Nielson, G. 1972. Short-term memory: A comparison between frontal and nonfrontal right- and left-hemisphere brain-damaged patients. *J. Comp. Physiol. Psychol.* 81:248–55
82. Lorr, M. 1970. A typological conception of the behavior disorders. See Ref. 88, 101–16
83. Lorr, M. 1971. Dimensions and categories for assessment of psychotics. See Ref. 94, 198–215
84. Lorr, M., Gilberstadt, H. 1972. A comparison of two typologies for psychotics. *J. Nerv. Ment. Dis.* 155: 144–48
85. Lorr, M., Hamlin, R. M. 1970. Estimation of the major psychotic disorders by objective test scores. *J. Nerv. Ment. Dis.* 151:219–24
86. Lorr, M., Hamlin, R. M. 1971. A multimethod factor analysis of behavioral and objective measures of psychopathology. *J. Consult. Clin. Psychol.* 36: 136–41
87. Lorr, M., Klett, C. J. 1970. Life history differentia of five acute psychotic types. See Ref. 126, 147–57
88. Mahrer, A. R., Ed. 1970. *New Approaches to Personality Classification.* New York: Columbia Univ. Press
89. Manning, H. M. 1971. Programmed interpretation of the MMPI. *J. Pers. Assess.* 35:162–76
90. Martorano, R. D., Nathan, P. E. 1972. Syndromes of psychosis and nonpsy-

chosis: Factor analysis of a systems analysis. *J. Abnorm. Psychol.* 80:1–10
91. Matarazzo, J. D. 1972. *Wechsler's Measurement and Appraisal of Adult Intelligence.* Baltimore: Williams and Wilkins. 5th ed.
92. Maultsby, M. C. Jr., Slack, W. V. 1971. A computer-based psychiatry history system. *Arch. Gen. Psychiat.* 25: 570–72
93. McNair, D. M., Lorr, M., Droppleman, L. F. 1971. *Manual for the Profile of Mood States.* San Diego, Calif.: Educational and Industrial Testing Service
94. McReynolds, P., Ed. 1971. *Advances in Psychological Assessment, Vol. 2.* Palo Alto, Calif.: Science and Behavior Books
95. Meddis, R. 1972. Bipolar factors in mood adjective checklists. *Brit. J. Soc. Clin. Psychol.* 11:178–84
96. Meehl, P. E. 1971. Law and the fireside inductions: Some reflections of a clinical psychologist. *J. Soc. Issues* 27:65–100
97. Meehl, P. E. 1972. A critical afterword. See Ref. 61, 367–415
98. Meehl, P. E. 1972. Reactions, reflections, projections. See Ref. 13, 131–89
99. Meehl, P. E. 1972. Specific genetic etiology, psychodynamics, and therapeutic nihilism. *Int. J. Ment. Health* 1:10–27
100. Meehl, P. E. 1973. *Psychodiagnosis: Selected Papers.* Minneapolis: Univ. Minnesota Press
101. Megargee, E. I. 1972. *The California Psychological Inventory Handbook.* San Francisco: Jossey-Bass
102. Miller, L. C. 1972. School Behavior Check List: An inventory of deviant behavior for elementary school children. *J. Consult. Clin. Psychol.* 38:134–44
103. Miller, L. C., Barrett, C. L., Hampe, E., Noble, H. 1972. Factor structure of childhood fears. *J. Consult. Clin. Psychol.* 39:264–68
104. Mischel, W. 1973. Towards a cognitive social learning reconceptualization of personality. *Psychol. Rev.* 80:252–83
105. Moore, R. A. 1972. The diagnosis of alcoholism in a psychiatric hospital: A trial of the Michigan Alcoholism Screening Test (MAST). *Am. J. Psychiat.* 128:1565–69
106. Myers, J. K., Lindenthal, J. J., Pepper, M. P. 1971. Life events and psychiatric impairment. *J. Nerv. Ment. Dis.* 152: 149–57
107. Norman, W. T. 1972. Psychometric considerations for a revision of the MMPI. See Ref. 13, 59–83
108. O'Dell, J. W. 1972. P. T. Barnum explores the computer. *J. Consult. Clin. Psychol.* 38:270–73
109. Overall, J. E. 1971. Associations between marital history and the nature of manifest psychopathology. *J. Abnorm. Psychol.* 78:213–21
110. Overall, J. E. 1971. Major phenomenological sub-types in a general psychiatric population. *Dis. Nerv. Syst.* 32:383–87
111. Overall, J. E., Gorham, D. R. 1972. Organicity versus old age in objective and projective test performance. *J. Consult. Clin. Psychol.* 39:98–105
112. Overall, J. E., Henry, B. W., Markett, J. R. 1972. Validity of an empirically derived phenomenological typology. *J. Psychiat. Res.* 9:87–99
113. Overall, J. E., Henry, B. W., Markett, J. R., Emken, R. L. 1972. Decisions about drug therapy: I. Prescriptions for adult psychiatric outpatients. *Arch. Gen. Psychiat.* 26:140–45
114. Overall, J. E., Hollister, L. E. 1972. Decisions about drug therapy: II. Expert opinion in a hypothetical situation. *Behav. Sci.* 17:349–60
115. Overall, J. E., Klett, C. J. 1972. *Applied Multivariate Analysis,* 4–23. New York: McGraw-Hill
116. Overall, J. E., Patrick, J. H. 1972. Unitary alcoholism factor and its personality correlates. *J. Abnorm. Psychol.* 79:303–9
117. Paykel, E. S. 1971. Classification of depressed patients: A cluster analysis derived grouping. *Brit. J. Psychiat.* 118:275–88
118. Payne, F. D., Wiggins, J. S. 1972. MMPI profile types and the self-report of psychiatric patients. *J. Abnorm. Psychol.* 79:1–8
119. Persons, R. W., Marks, P. A. 1971. The violent 4–3 MMPI personality type. *J. Consult. Clin. Psychol.* 36: 189–96
120. Phillips, L., Draguns, J. G. 1971. Classification of the behavior disorders. *Ann. Rev. Psychol.* 22:447–82
121. Rahe, R. H., Mahan, J. L., Arthur, R. J., Gunderson, E. K. E. 1970. The epidemiology of illness in naval environments. I. Illness types, distribution, severities, and relationship to life change. *Mil. Med.* 135:443–52

122. Razin, A. M. 1971. A-B variable in psychotherapy: A critical review. *Psychol. Bull.* 75:1–21
123. Reitan, R. M., Boll, T. J. 1971. Intellectual and cognitive functions in Parkinson's disease. *J. Consult. Clin. Psychol.* 37:364–69
124. Reitan, R. M., Fitzhugh, K. B. 1971. Behavioral deficits in groups with cerebral vascular lesions. *J. Consult. Clin. Psychol.* 37:215–23
125. Rimland, B. 1969. Psychogenesis versus biogenesis: The issues and the evidence. In *Changing Perspectives in Mental Illness,* ed. S. C. Plog, R. B. Edgerton, 702–35. New York: Holt, Rinehart & Winston
126. Roff, M., Ricks, D. F., Eds. 1970. *Life History Research in Psychopathology.* Minneapolis: Univ. Minnesota Press
127. Roff, M., Robins, L. N., Pollack, M., Eds. 1972. *Life History Research in Psychopathology, Vol. 2.* Minneapolis: Univ. Minnesota Press
128. Rosenthal, D. 1971. *Genetics of Psychopathology.* New York: McGraw-Hill
129. Rubin, E. Z., Braun, J. S., Beck, G. R., Llorens, L. A. 1972. *Cognitive Perceptual Motor Dysfunction: From Research to Practice.* Detroit: Wayne State Univ. Press
130. Russell, E. W., Neuringer, C., Goldstein, G. 1970. *Assessment of Brain Damage: A Neuropsychological Key Approach.* New York: Wiley-Interscience
131. Schachter, J. 1970. Development of a screening questionnaire for schizophrenia: A pilot study. *Arch. Gen. Psychiat.* 23:30–34
132. Schachter, S. 1971. *Emotion, Obesity, and Crime.* New York: Academic
133. Selzer, M. L. 1971. The Michigan Alcoholism Screening Test: The quest for a new diagnostic instrument. *Am. J. Psychiat.* 127:1653–58
134. Sletten, I. W., Altman, H., Ulett, G. A. 1971. Routine diagnosis by computer. *Am. J. Psychiat.* 127:1147–52
135. Sletten, I. W., Brown, M. L., Evenson, R. C., Altman, H. 1972. Suicide in mental hospital patients. *Dis. Nerv. Syst.* 33:328–35
136. Sletten, I. W., Ernhart, C. B., Ulett, G. A. 1970. The Missouri Automated Mental Status Examination: Development, use and reliability. *Compr. Psychiat.* 11:315–27
137. Sletten, I. W., Osborn, R. W., Cho, D. W., Altman, H. 1971. Agreement on specificity of psychotropic drugs. *Curr. Ther. Res.* 13:292–97
138. Sletten, I. W., Ulett, G. A. 1972. The present status of automation in a state psychiatric system. *Psychiat. Ann.* 2: 42–57
139. Sletten, I. W., Ulett, G. A., Altman, H., Sundland, D. 1970. The Missouri Standard System of Psychiatry (SSOP): Computer generated diagnosis. *Arch. Gen. Psychiat.* 23:73–79
140. Spitzer, R. L., Endicott, J. 1969. DIAGNO II: Further developments in a computer program for psychiatric diagnosis. *Am. J. Psychiat.* 125:12–21
141. Spitzer, R. L., Endicott, J. 1971. An integrated group of forms for automated psychiatric case records: A progress report. *Arch. Gen. Psychiat.* 24:540–47
142. Spitzer, R. L., Endicott, J. 1973. The value of the interview for the evaluation of psychopathology. In *Psychopathology: Contributions from the Social, Behavioral, and Biological Sciences,* ed. M. Hammer, K. Salzinger, S. Sutton, 397–408. New York: Wiley
143. Spitzer, R. L., Endicott, J., Fleiss, J. L., Cohen, J. 1970. The Psychiatric Status Schedule: A technique for evaluating psychopathology and impairment in role functioning. *Arch. Gen. Psychiat.* 23:41–55
144. Stroebel, C. F., Glueck, B. C. Jr. 1970. Computer derived global judgments in psychiatry. *Am. J. Psychiat.* 126: 1057–66
145. Stroebel, C. F., Glueck, B. C. Jr. 1972. The diagnostic process in psychiatry: Computer approaches. *Psychiat. Ann.* 2:58–77
146. Taylor, J. B., Ptacek, M., Carithers, M., Griffin, C., Coyne, L. 1972. Rating scales as measures of clinical judgment III: Judgments of the self on personality inventory scales and direct ratings. *Educ. Psychol. Meas.* 32:543–57
147. Trott, D. M., Morf, M. E. 1972. A multimethod factor analysis of the Differential Personality Inventory, Personality Research Form, and Minnesota Multiphasic Personality Inventory. *J. Couns. Psychol.* 19:94–103
148. Tryon, R. C., Bailey, D. E. 1970. *Cluster Analysis.* New York: McGraw-Hill
149. Tulving, E., Madigan, S. A. 1970. Memory and verbal learning. *Ann. Rev. Psychol.* 21:437–84
150. Ulett, G. A., Sletten, I. W. 1971. Computers and psychiatric case records. *Brit. J. Hosp. Med.* 6:291–300

151. Ulett, G. A., Sletten, I. W., Ameiss, A., Thompson, W. A. 1973. Realities and prospects for the use of computers in psychiatric hospital management. *Psychiat. Ann.* 3:27–53
152. Wender, P. H. 1971. *Minimal Brain Dysfunction in Children.* New York: Wiley-Interscience
153. Whitelock, P. R., Overall, J. E., Patrick, J. H. 1971. Personality patterns and alcohol abuse in a state hospital population. *J. Abnorm. Psychol.* 78:9–16
154. Wiggins, J. S. 1969. Content dimensions in the MMPI. In *MMPI: Research Developments and Clinical Applications,* ed. J. N. Butcher, 127–80. New York: McGraw-Hill
155. Wiggins, J. S. 1973. *Personality and Prediction: Principles of Personality Assessment.* Reading, Mass.: Addison-Wesley
156. Wiggins, J. S., Goldberg, L. R., Appelbaum, M. 1971. MMPI content scales: Interpretative norms and correlations with other scales. *J. Consult. Clin. Psychol.* 37:403–10
157. Williams, J. D., Dudley, H. K. Jr., Overall, J. E. 1972. Validity of the 16 PF and the MMPI in a mental hospital setting. *J. Abnorm. Psychol.* 80:261–70
158. Wirt, R. D., Hampton, A. C., Seat, P. D. 1972. The psychometric prediction of delinquency. See Ref. 127, 66–76
159. Wittenborn, J. R. 1972. Reliability, validity, and objectivity of symptom-rating scales. *J. Nerv. Ment. Dis.* 154:79–87
160. Zung, W. W. K. 1972. The Depression Status Inventory: An adjunct to the Self-Rating Depression Scale. *J. Clin. Psychol.* 28:539–43

INTERVENTION TECHNIQUES: SMALL GROUPS

❖221

Kurt W. Back[1]
Duke University, Durham, North Carolina

Research in the field of small group intervention is more than a simple application of social psychological techniques. Although the techniques of group intervention are analogous to those explored in social psychological experiments, the whole context of the intervention movement makes other considerations important.

NOT A TECHNIQUE BUT A MOVEMENT

Working with small groups, either ongoing or selected for the specific purpose of intervention, is possible in many different ways. Groups have been used for religious, ideological, and political indoctrination, and there has been concern with the functioning of family, work, and community groups for a long time. The current interest in intervention derives, however, from a particular constellation of developments in behavioral science without any societal goals. Nevertheless, we are looking here not at a development purely within psychology, but at a social movement with its sects, ideologies, and polemics. A knowledge of historical conditions is thus important in understanding the movement. We shall present, therefore, the historical background of current group intervention techniques, especially those connected with sensitivity training and encounter groups. After this orientation we can then discuss methodological and theoretical issues.

Two reasons are usually given for using small groups as a direct entry point to a change process: (*a*) specific features of group interaction can be utilized to produce the desired effect; and (*b*) a small group may be a strategic point of attack in an attempt either to solve large organizational problems or to effect change in individuals.

Small groups have been important tools in many contexts, especially in religious ritual and some of the dramatic performances which came out of it. In these cases, however, it is apparent that the group action was embedded in the whole system

[1]The editorial assistance of Mrs. Joanna D. Morris is gratefully acknowledged.

of beliefs, ulterior aims, and rules which tended to justify it. Thus the religious system and ritual lent themselves little to direct concern with group intervention by itself, though some of the ritual revealed shrewd insight into group processes. The shift toward open interest in the technique for its own sake was adumbrated by Aldous Huxley in 1932 in his novel *Brave New World* (42). Here, describing a society which has rejected all ultimate values in favor of instrumental values related to immediate functioning, he realizes that group actions in the society remain important but have to be pursued for their own sake. Thus a bishop becomes a community songster and the people romp together in weekly group sessions. We shall return eventually to the important role of religion and peak experiences in small group techniques.

HISTORY OF SMALL GROUP INTERVENTION

Discussion

Small group intervention proper may be said to have started with the concentration of effort on the group process itself rather than using it as an adjunct to another kind of procedure. Its earliest embodiments came from efforts in psychotherapy on the one side and personnel management on the other. Some additional developments in social psychology and education were also important.

The earliest use of group process in psychotherapy can be credited to Jacob Moreno. Moreno combined psychotherapy and dramatic techniques in his creation of psychodrama (75). He felt that the two-person situation of the therapist and patient could not be used effectively to recreate all the interpersonal situations in which the patient was enmeshed and which may have led to his difficulties. He therefore created scenes in which the patient was able to act out important events in his life with a variety of other people representing significant figures in his environment (alters), being helped by people representing himself who could act out better or more strongly what he would like to do (auxiliary egos). Moreno externalized the personal topography of mind by setting the stage in three circles, the highest and innermost of which represented the most private, intimate, and dominating thoughts, with more and more superficial parts of the personality represented by the outer circles. We find in Moreno's early work the seeds of many of the later small group techniques. However, one of the great differences from later work is that the whole scene was staged for the benefit of only one patient. All the other members of the group were therapists or their helpers. Thus Moreno did not create group psychotherapy in today's sense, but he coined some of the important concepts used in later times, among them the ideas of encounter and here-and-now.

Moreno stayed quite apart from the mainstream of psychotherapeutic development. Orthodox psychoanalysis was unfriendly to any radical changes in therapy techniques, and Moreno's own work occupied a niche somewhere between psychological therapy and dramatic training. Although his work was transported from Vienna to Washington at Saint Elizabeths Hospital, it remained for a long time an isolated phenomenon. One of the reasons might have been that he represented himself from time to time as a divinely inspired leader (74).

Another impetus toward small group intervention came through psychotherapy from the Tavistock Institute in London, where psychiatric work was influenced by a theory developed by Melanie Klein, a psychoanalyst (48–50, 85). This theory, which sees in group and therapeutic processes a reenactment of age-old myths and is quite willing to spell out the connection between these myths and the therapy process, is more hospitable to group therapy than is orthodox Freudianism. Several of the psychiatrists at Tavistock Institute as far back as the 1930s used groups in psychotherapeutic endeavors, even taking over and familiarizing the term "here-and-now" (31, 97).

Psychotherapeutic groups were also started in the United States, especially in institutional settings where the groups persisted through time, and where therapists, social workers, and psychiatrists could see how the group interaction could influence the therapy process and could be used to help it. Slavson (90, 91) at the Jewish Board of Guardians, Redl (78) in Detroit, and Bettelheim (18, 19) at the Orthogenic School in Chicago put patients in group situations for therapeutic purposes and in this way advanced some ideas of group psychotherapy.

Another route for group methods to become influential was through the developing interest in personnel management. Following the reaction against Taylor's (93) theory of scientific management which concentrated mainly on man-machine relationships, some industrial psychologists turned their interest toward the informal groups among the workers. The existence of these groups must have been noticed before, but their importance and possible use for management purposes can be traced primarily to one set of studies, the Westinghouse Studies by Mayo (72) and Roethlisberger & Dickson (79). These studies originated in a desire to investigate pure man-machine relationships, in this case the relationship between lighting and performance. The investigators found, to their surprise, that lighting was less important than purely human factors; they later directed their attention toward the actions of informal groups within the company. Their detailed observations of the informal joking relationships in a small work group are still used as the major illustration for theories of small group development in industry.

At the same time a counseling program at Westinghouse was started which tried to improve the efficiency of the relationships within the plant by concentrating on tensions arising from personal problems of the workers as well as problems within the group organization. This program, probably the origin of group programs in industry, has since been discontinued; the discontinuance has given rise to controversy about the importance of the whole experiment and of small groups in industry (38, 53). At that time, however, different industries started similar programs of group orientation, among them the Harwood Manufacturing Corporation in Virginia (14, 71) and Dewey and Almy in Cambridge (68). In both these cases the initiation of the programs was mainly due to the individual efforts of the personnel managers, Bavelas and French at Harwood and Douglas McGregor at Dewey and Almy. These men were later able, through their positions and financial help, to influence the development of the group intervention technique.

Another impetus for the group movement came through the New Deal programs of the 1930s. Some of these programs involved large-scale efforts to change systems using minimum personnel, and some even dealt with the founding of new communities. For several of these projects, apparently independently, it was decided almost by necessity to use groups as targets for change and education. This was necessary because the needed amount of professional help was not available. Such was the case in the development of literacy programs, the creation of new communities, and the farm settlement programs. The last of these involved an application of Moreno's techniques of sociometry and sociodrama on a large scale (67). The literacy programs are important because they involved some of the future leaders of the sensitivity training movement.

Development in the theory of sociology and social psychology also prepared the ground for the emergence of small group techniques. In sociology, the works of Simmel, Cooley, and Park were rediscovered and with them the importance of the small group (46). In social psychology the application of experimental methods to the study of groups made it possible to use the traditional laboratory methods of psychologists to investigate social problems. The work of Lewin, Sherif, Bales, Allport, Asch, and their students stimulated the interest of other social psychologists in the study of small groups, and also provided examples of the use of observation and manipulation of groups. In addition, these studies aided theoretical development by showing the influence of small groups on individual behavior. Such notions and concepts as Sherif's (87) "frames of reference," Hyman's (43) "reference groups," Lewin's (59) "group standards," and Asch's (6) "conformity pressure" contributed to the formation of a conceptual framework for understanding and manipulating small groups.

Events surrounding World War II and its aftermath furthered the development of all these trends and also helped to bring them together. Programs aimed at forming crews of soldiers, such as air crews, into functioning groups as rapidly as possible led to the refinement of group formation techniques and helped, for instance, the Tavistock Institute to develop many of its methods (31). This made psychiatrists more accepting of group procedures and led them to develop therapy groups which could be run by less highly trained professionals and where different patients could help each other. Wartime dislocation necessitated a high premium being placed on efficient personnel management and cultural integration of new workers. An additional effect of the war was that many social psychologists in academic life were thrown into contact with the everyday programs of nonacademic organizations, especially the armed forces. Training in an actually functioning operation illustrated for them the importance of group methods to assess individual performance. Studies of combat effectiveness showed the importance of loyalty to small groups in the U.S. Army (92).

Postwar problems also seemed amenable to small group techniques. These problems included the readaptation of prisoners of war to home conditions (28, 29), the reduction of intergroup tensions (95), and the improvement of labor relations (36, 45). Thus the immediate postwar years saw a great flowering of group intervention techniques and the foundation both of places where small group techniques were studied in an academic way and also of institutes whose members applied techniques of direct group intervention.

Start of the Movement

At this time academic, theoretical, social psychology laboratory experimentation, and the development of group intervention techniques were strongly allied, encompassing a field known as group dynamics. Within a few years, however, these two wings separated and consequently it is possible to discuss group intervention as a topic in itself, although many of those in the field have retained overlapping interest in the two branches.

The development of the group intervention movement was precipitated by some events which occurred in the immediate postwar period when the first group training laboratories developed a vehicle of small group intervention which has given the field its center and strength. This is a technique which has at various times been called T-group, sensitivity training, and encounter group. The impetus came from the almost fortuitous discovery that group techniques become more impressive and important for the members if the content of the group discussion is turned upon itself. That is, efficient group techniques are those in which members discuss what happens in the group, and the main content of the group work is the relationships within the group. Thus the main function of the group technique becomes the meeting or encounter, and the interest is on the here-and-now, the two concepts foreshadowed by Moreno. The technique, which was originally discovered in a laboratory on intergroup relationships at New Britain, Connecticut, in 1946, was consciously expanded in the first set of laboratories organized by the National Training Laboratory at Bethel, Maine (26, 52, 66).

The NTL program, which was initiated under the guidance and theoretical orientation of Kurt Lewin and carried on after his death by his associates and students, was also aided by some people who had worked on group development in its earliest stages, including Leland Bradford and Kenneth Benne. It was also aided by association with the Tavistock Institute in England. The history of the movement can be summarized by division into four periods: the Heroic Period from 1946 to 1950, the Dormant Period of the 1950s, the Explosion of the 1960s, and the Crisis which developed toward the end of the 1960s (8).

The Heroic Period

The first 5 years were almost completely concentrated at the Bethel laboratory, and different techniques were being used every year. There were questions on how to adapt this new method to different kinds of applications in the behavioral sciences; whether, for instance, to give it a somewhat psychiatric content and make it a sort of therapy for normals. The format, length, and content of the sessions, and the degree of emphasis on applicability were experimented with; different people with different backgrounds were attracted and invited. Other problems were faced: the question of group composition—whether they should be strangers or people working together; the question of location of the laboratory—whether or not it should be away from the general habitat of the group members, a sort of cultural island; and other problems. Different kinds of research were tried and abandoned in attempts to evaluate the program, and the laboratory became, in consequence, a training ground for new types of research.

Finally, by about 1950–1952, the program jelled. This coincided with a change of leadership in that the people who were originally leading the groups were kicked upstairs to be consultants and leaders of the NTL, and a new group took over as the actual group leaders. The format of the whole program stabilized and the T-group or training group, which became for a long time the mainstay of the movement, was created and developed.

A parallel development occurred in England at the same time. The Tavistock Institute had been functioning as a psychiatric institution with interests in group therapy and group processes (31, 44). Some of their ideas were similar to group dynamics. Following experiences with the British armed forces, a group at Tavistock evolved large-scale intervention techniques for use in industry and rehabilitation centers. Tavistock initiated a special brand of group intervention techniques, still following the psychiatric model, which looked at the client organization as a patient. There was some contact and mutual influence between this group and the group at Bethel; in the late 1940s W. R. Bion wrote a series of articles on group intervention which influenced many practices on both sides of the Atlantic (later collected in Bion 20).

The Dormant Period

At this time the National Training Laboratory had settled down to a routine, though it was still novel for many. It trained people from different countries and different environments, and in this way increased its influence. In addition, many of the trainees and associates at Bethel went to other places and started innovative and different kinds of centers. On the West coast some centers were started which were more interested in individual training than in making people more efficient in groups. There the term "sensitivity training" was coined. One of the more remarkable events during this time was the dissemination of the technique to other countries in the Caribbean and in Europe where the technique was taken up in several different contexts. Europeans, especially the French (54) and Scandinavians (39), adopted group intervention techniques as part of political reconstruction and have remained much more conscious of the general social implications of the movement than their American counterparts. In the meantime, the original center of the movement at Bethel tended to stagnate and needed a new impetus.

Explosion

In the 1960s several events occurred which led to a sudden expansion of the movement. The National Training Laboratory reorganized itself and, like its European counterparts, sought to influence the seats of power. They did this by organizing programs for leaders such as special presidents' laboratories where industrial leaders were invited for training. These laboratories were successful and helped to pull many industries, businesses, community organizers, and government agencies into the Bethel orbit. The whole institutional structure was reorganized by having training programs for people who later could become members or associates of the program and be given assignments to lead workshops in various parts of the country with the stamp of approval of the NTL itself. In the workshops at NTL, programs were adapted for different kinds of consumers, such as community or recreational leaders.

A different influence came with the foundation of the Esalen Institute in California (8, 41). Esalen tried to serve several purposes, including at first giving seminars on new ideas for changing behavior and controlling the mind. These ideas were often inspired by Oriental philosophy and religion. Perhaps the somewhat pragmatic influence of the earlier years, especially in the National Training Laboratory, had run its course and group intervention needed some new religious infusion. The Esalen Institute used group techniques but called them encounters, and was more directed toward individual development than toward group action. The encounter group became popular, Esalen was quickly publicized in many national magazines, and group encounters or T-groups became a symbol of the life-style of the upper middle class. The popularity of this new branch contrasted with the more conservative Eastern approach. However, there was some contact between the two centers, and some of the new Esalen techniques were tried at Bethel and the labs which Bethel influenced. It was clear to some in the mid-1960s that the approach used in the mid-1940s would not have to be followed slavishly, just as the innovators of the 1940s were not bound by the techniques of experimental social psychology of the 1920s.

By the end of the decade three distinctly different centers had developed. One was the old National Training Laboratory, which by that time was part of the National Education Association. The NTL retained its original emphasis on group efficiency and group progress, although it tried to use some of the human relations approaches from the West. It was very much concerned with establishing consulting relationships with government and business agencies, and also with keeping its respectability by avoiding extreme experimentation and keeping a moderate position.

By contrast, Esalen and the human potential centers which followed it encouraged experimentation of all sorts. They kept the encounter technique as the central attraction while incorporating new ideas from Indian, Japanese, and Chinese philosophy, and later from Persian Sufism, astrology, mysticism, and various massage techniques. This was the movement which caught the popular imagination. One of Esalen's allies was the Western Behavioral Science Institute, headed by Carl Rogers, which took some of Rogers' ideas on counseling and adapted them to group counseling (80, 81). Ideologically the WBSI was probably close to Esalen, but it stayed more within the psychology framework from which its leaders came.

The third center was the Tavistock Institute in London. Here intervention techniques, in the medical sense, were applied to factories, housing projects, and delinquent groups, diagnosing the problem and trying to adopt remedies specific to the situation. In addition, the Institute held general group sessions, but the clientele were restricted to professionals in human relations, and the content was directed toward general understanding of interpersonal processes.

Crisis

By the end of the 1960s, the bulk of the movement had overexpanded and felt financial and organizational strain. At the National Training Laboratory this was brought to a head by the fact that the long-time director, Leland Bradford, retired in 1970 and a successor had to be found. In addition, various financial problems had to be solved. One attempt at getting a new director failed because the candidate, Warren Bennis, tried to redirect the whole laboratory back to some of its original, socially imaginative programs and also combine it with a graduate university where these new skills could be taught. A new director was finally agreed on, and he made some fiscal changes, including division of the NTL into different organizations depending on the kind of client population (8).

At the Western Behavioral Science Institute a direct split occurred with the more humanistic members leaving and founding the Center for the Study of the Person, while the more conventional group remained at the Institute. At first the WBSI not only lost many of its people but also all of its contracts, while the new center attracted some research and promotional work. However, at a later time, the Institute recovered although it did less encounter work and more work, often very imaginative, in the education and poverty areas.

Esalen and its centers changed their technique too, deemphasizing the approach of attracting masses of people for weekend and week-long encounters and trying instead to train a kind of dedicated follower by having longer sessions where people were inducted into communal living. In Esalen's urban center in San Francisco, however, they found that encounter had stopped drawing people; the big drawing cards now were occult sessions on the one side and physical kinds of manipulation and training on the other. Thus in the personal growth centers, the percentage of the time devoted to encounter groups has probably decreased, and it may soon be that this field cannot be called small group intervention techniques any longer but instead a sort of personal therapy and influence.

THEORY

Reality of Groups

With this heterogeneous background and current development, it is easy to see why there is no codified theory to which all group interveners subscribe. However, there is a surprising amount of agreement on general principles. The first article of faith is the principle of the importance of the small group as a carrier of change, its influence on the individuals who are its members, and its influence on the organizations to which it may belong. The prime area of agreement here is that the group exists as a meaningful and real unit. General theories of social psychology and group dynamics are neutral on the reality of groups. They claim that the group can be considered as a unit, but also that the structure of and the interpersonal relationships within the group must be considered. In the theories of group intervention, the group is more of a real unit, while in the general field of social psychology a nominalistic point of view, considering the group as a collection of individuals, exists side by side with a consideration of the group as a whole, as more than the sum of its parts.

The basic idea of group intervention came from aspects of Lewin's work (56, 60). The group is looked on as a kind of spatial, structured unit similar to personality constructs in Lewin's other work. Each of the places within the group is then filled by a role which is necessary for the survival of the group, even if at the moment there is no individual to fill it. Therefore, a group is a collection of positions and roles, and not of individuals. This point of view was developed originally by Morton Deutsch (30) and taken up by Benne & Sheats (16) in describing the first National Training Lab. The nature of the functional roles within the group is differently defined by different theories, but the idea has persisted in spite of periodic neglect.

The unity of the group is expressed most clearly in the work of the Tavistock Institute, where the group is taken as an actual unit and treated almost like a patient who is hurting because certain of the group functions are not being fulfilled. The basic Tavistock technique is then to diagnose the hurt or the symptoms as they relate to the actual working group, and to retrain the people to fulfill the functions of the group better.

The theory on which most of the Tavistock work has been based derives mainly from W. R. Bion (20). He saw the main task of a group as doing productive work, but that this is inhibited by "derived functions"—interpersonal relationships which consist of dependency, fight-flight, and pairing. Only if these three functions are worked through and are in balance can real, productive work be accomplished. Bion believed also that the same relationships hold true in individuals, and that the imbalance of derived functions leads to illness. Thus the Tavistock theory, originally the most clinically and psychoanalytically based approach of all the intervention theories, takes the group most seriously as a real unit.

Change Technique

The group dynamics theory, which prevails in the mainstream of the intervention movement at NTL, looks at the process differently. Lewin's legacy is shown in his last two articles on quasi-stationary equilibrium (57) and on feedback (58). The first term was introduced to describe how attitudes or behaviors of individuals are anchored within group norms, conceptualized as a force field with a gradient dependent on the attitudes of the people in the person's immediate environment, his immediate group membership (57). Pushing a person away from the place where he is and away from the mean of the group pushes him, in effect, against stronger and stronger forces, and hence the moment that the push stops, he will slide back to the original position. The only effective ways of changing a person are either to change the whole group or to unfreeze the person who wants to change by abolishing the forces which anchored him in the group and making him choose a new group as anchor.

This theory illustrates the two techniques which are used in application to small group intervention. Persons are being changed as part of the whole group during the workshop which effects the change. The second technique is used when the person faces the problem of coming back to the old environment. In this case, he is like the person who is suddenly removed from the force field which has changed him, so that he slides back to his old equilibrium. To counteract that, several devices are used. One consists of treating the whole back-home group in the workshop. This is the technique used by the Tavistock Institute and by industrial consultants such as Blake & Mouton (21). It is not, however, the technique of the more orthodox group laboratory trainers. A compromise is to take several people from the same organization into a training group so that a small, independent subgroup can be formed in the new environment which may relieve the pressures of the larger back-home group. In general, however, great pessimism exists about the possibility of long-range change. One popular theory is that carryover is only possible under conditions where the trainee has power. Therefore, it is probably easier to change a person's behavior in his family than in his work situation.

Feedback

The second concept introduced by Lewin is that of feedback (58). Viewing the output of a group as a topic of conversation or as input into the group action, the group may discuss for a long time a fight which has broken out, how many important incidents have occurred, or their feelings toward the leader. These are topics which have occurred "right now" in the group, and are also those in which people have been recently emotionally involved. Discussion of these issues brings out people's defenses, emotions, justifications for what they did, and possible understanding of why they did it. Thus this kind of reinforcing feedback might make for either a benign circle or a vicious circle, depending on one's point of view.

Utopian Theories

Thus intervention theory is based, in part, on theories of social psychology, personality, and psychiatry. However, it would be wrong to suppose that this theory has remained completely within the framework of experimental social psychology and theoretical group dynamics. Many people involved with the movement, although well versed in traditional theories, would object that most of them are too flat, too mechanistic, and view the person too much as an object of social forces (4). The key points in this objection are a need to look at the individual as an emotional and active being and an aversion to the use of single variables and the experimental kinds of manipulation which characterize current social psychology. The model which such theorists as Schutz (83, 84), Argyris (1, 2), and Aronson (5) produce would use interventions and the affect they arouse as the most effective way to understand behavior. But they would also admit in general that a world outside the group does exist and, perhaps to their sorrow, accept the similarity between present circumstances and some of the current textbook theories. They have to propose an alternative model of human behavior and use this model for their consulting work.

All the theories on group intervention have a certain ambiguity in common. They are not so much theories of what is, of how groups function, as of what could be, of how groups *should* function. They are not theories of how people adjust to their world, especially to their social world, but of an alternative way of behaving. They are less an application of a psychological theory than a vision of a new world and a new social movement. We shall see later how this utopian orientation affects research in the field.

RESEARCH

Normally, the procedure in discussing an applied field like small group intervention would be to start from the small group theories, going through the experimental evidence which has been cited by the theories, and then deal with the problems of application and research directed toward that field. The historical context of the present discussion, however, makes this procedure unfeasible and unrealistic. Much of the theory of small group intervention has common origins with the sensitivity group movement. Their history has since diverged, in fact has diverged so much that many proponents from either side have doubted the relevance of the one for the other. Thus, there are some joint interests found only in the earlier times and only a few fragments of linkage between the two can be used in discussing the research evidence for small group intervention in more recent times.

Early Laboratory Studies

The early development of experimental social psychology dealt primarily with groups in the laboratory. But even the first study, a study of authoritarian, democratic, and laissez-faire groups in the laboratory by Lewin, Lippitt & White (61), dealt with a problem which was based on small group intervention. It was a question of which way groups should be formed, which way groups would function more effectively, in terms both of outcome and of effects on their members. This study may be methodologically questionable; by today's standards the independent variables are somewhat complex and vaguely defined, and some of the experimental controls were difficult to execute in such a way as to render the results unambiguous. However, for a while this line of research was followed by Lippitt in the assessment and training programs of the Office of Strategic Services (76) and by Lewin and others in studies on group decisions (59).

In all these studies there was an effort to make the group the aim of the study and also to show how the group actions would be more productive under some conditions of participation by the members, especially under conditions in which the members themselves could feel that they were part of the decision-making process. In the meantime the first sensitivity group programs in Connecticut and Bethel had started, and they were influential in initiating a line of basic research. One of the more ambitious offshoots of this research effort was the so-called Conference Research Project by Marquis, Guetzkow & Heyns (70).

The common core of these studies showed a contrast between the traditional theories of organization and management and psychological theories. The idea of a complete line and staff organization, where decisions arrive from the top power levels, may be passed in conference with relevant staff members, and then are passed on to the line for execution, seemed to be contraindicated by psychological factors. Although this method might lead to quick and efficient organization and be necessary in emergency situations, it had a negative effect on the morale and performance of the participants. However, none of these studies was very conclusive about the gains and losses of either type of system or how they could be combined. It may be that this inconclusiveness was the root cause of the split into the work with group intervention on the one hand and social psychological research on the other. The results of working with different types of groups in a realistic setting were never clear enough to justify any definite conclusion related to social psychological theory. On the other hand, the confusion of factors inherent in such situations, such as the personality of either the leader or the members or the particular techniques used, led the experimental social psychologists to pursue more simplified situations which involved a retreat from dealing with groups.

Network Studies

In the first decade after the group dynamics movement started, the split was not very deep. Several research trends appeared which influenced the group intervention techniques and provided a theoretical underpinning for the movement. One was an attempt to distinguish more clearly between organization for task requiredness and concern for the morale of the participants. Bavelas (15) and Leavitt (55) developed a technique of restricting communication between members of a group through artificial channels and then studying the efficiency of group performance by the subjects. Thus a group could be put together where everybody could communicate with everybody else, or communication could be restricted by having one person control all channels. Between these two extremes were various combined and hierarchical situations. This kind of research has continued to be a good way to test many hypotheses about group structure.

In general, the studies found that the hierarchical structure was most efficient in quickly finding a solution to simple problems, but it led to low morale in those people who were not involved in the decision process. The complete communication structure, which corresponded to the most democratic and participatory situation, led to high morale in the participants but frequently to low efficiency. However, the more complicated the problem was, the smaller was the advantage of the more hierarchical system. After these initial findings, this line of research went more and more into detailed questions about the relation between ability, task complexity, and organization, and finally into questions which were not relevant to group process (86).

Group Observation

A second research approach developed at that time concerned the direct observation of group process, especially of decision-making groups. This technique was evolved by Bales in cooperation with his colleagues and students, and consisted, at least at the start, mainly of two parts. One was the development of a system of observation categories by which groups could be described in a standardized manner and different groups and techniques compared. The ideal product would have been a sensitive instrument for group measurement and evaluation which would be analogous to the Stanford-Binet for individual testing. This hope was not quite realized. However, although norms have never really been established, Bales's final system of 12 categories divided into task-related and emotional ones has been used in later group research (10).

Bales's second contribution was to use these categories to establish a model for the normal progress of groups and the regularity of certain phenomena within groups. Bales used as models certain decision-making and problem-solving groups including case studies, conferences in a clinic, and discussions of organizational problems. He found a regular course of progress in these kinds of situations in which emotional and task-related categories assumed differential importance. The emotional categories were dominant at the beginning and at the end of each problem discussed, while the task-related categories predominated during the discussion itself. He also found that, over the course of a group, two kinds of leaders tended to emerge—one, the task leader, assumed leadership during the task-related discussion, and the other, the play leader, assumed leadership during the emotional discussion. These two leadership roles were quite distinct, were never filled by the same person, and were sometimes even antagonistic toward each other (13).

One would have thought that the availability of this kind of method and the number of hypotheses which could be derived through its use would have resulted in both a theoretical and an applied interest in pursuing the technique. However, the early interest in the observation of groups which led to small group laboratories being built in the 1950s has petered out (12). It is strange to see on how little evidence these theories, which are still basic in social psychology, are really founded. The original few studies by Bales & Slater (13) and Bennis & Shepard (17) have been praised, doubted, or attacked, but little replication or further research has been done. Contentions have also been made that some of the regularities observed were more a function of the fact that the participants knew they were being observed and thus showed their normative behavior, how they should act and not how they normally would act in a group (96). There has been little systematic study of groups since Bales, and most of the laboratories built for this purpose are used today for individual or two-person experiments. Bales himself continued his work more in the direction of classifying personalities than of building a theory of group development (11).

Conformity

A third approach that could have been relevant was a study of group-induced conformity. Based on Asch's (6) original studies of conformity pressures, a set of experiments by Festinger and his associates showed the conditions under which group pressure is related to conformity, the conditions under which deviation occurs, how deviates are dealt with in the groups, and in general how the power of groups is used to keep them together and to influence their members (7, 9, 34, 35, 47, 82). Here again, the first studies used groups, usually whole groups, to create the conditions of cohesion and group influence. What emerged was the obverse of the dangers of complete line management, namely the terror and power of the group itself and its ability to distort individual judgment. Although these studies are recognized by the group interventionists, their relation to actual group settings has not been investigated, and they represent today more a classical field in group dynamics than a subject of current research interest.

The Split in Research

The influence of these studies on directing research in the setting of group intervention itself has been limited for several reasons. One is the declining importance of group studies in experimental social psychology. It is clear that if several people in a group are allowed to behave as they want, each of them can behave in very many different ways, and therefore a tremendous amount of variables will be put into play. In order to tease out the effects of different conditions, of the different personalities of the people involved, the interaction patterns, the situation, and so on, more and more different conditions have to be controlled. That is, the participation of the other people in the group may be simulated instead of real, the possible interactions may become more and more limited, and the time span of development of the group may become too small to imitate the real progression of a 3-week laboratory. As soon as the unwieldiness of groups in these respects was recognized, most researchers in social psychology turned their interest instead toward individual behavior. In 1954 Borgatta (25) forecast, in a half-serious parody, the emergence of the no-person groups where everybody will just be simulated; today, research has almost caught up with his prediction.

Thus the development of social psychological research led to findings of less and less relevance to the study of group intervention. In turn, this might have been the basis of the interventionists' mistrust, which grew larger and larger, of scientific methods and traditional research. Here the history went in the opposite direction. Faced with the difficulties of having such a complex situation, the interveners accepted these difficulties and became less and less interested in testable hypotheses. For a while the human relations training labs were used as sources for research data. Some studies came out of the early Bethel laboratories dealing with, for instance, roles within groups, influence, and group leadership. Some group experiments were also done by people who had been participants at Bethel, such as the study by Coch & French (27) on changing work habits in industry. An early study by Lippitt (66) followed up group members after they left the centers and investigated their later effectiveness in their work. These kinds of studies were done at the time when social psychologists still worked with groups and there were many researchers present at the labs. Some of the studies done at Bethel were used for doctoral dissertations in social psychology (40, 62, 94).

It became hard to justify studies done in a group setting. Should the group laboratories be mainly used as settings where social processes could be observed and studied, or should the technique of intervention be studied, evaluated, and improved through research? The first alternative reached its climax in classes in which social psychology was taught by means of sensitivity groups, especially one class in the

Harvard Social Relations Department. Out of this class three books (69, 73, 89) and a great number of articles have come forth, all of them describing the group process, the relationships between different interactions, and the progress of the class. The amount of data the class provided also made it possible to develop new measurement techniques. Some of the development of Bales's own scales was a result of this course (11), and some intricate content analysis techniques were worked out using data from it (33). However, the interest in the classes came more from the emotional impact that they had on the members at the time, and found expression in intense narratives such as Slater's (89) more than in quantitative studies.

These studies form a convenient dividing line between the early interest in sensitivity groups as a convenient site for psychological experiments and the later interest in their emotional impact for its own sake. Many of these later studies are mainly descriptions of the process involving some use of data, but never arriving at or testing general hypotheses. In general, they adopt the stance of the advocate who is trying to show that something does happen and that some effect can occur.

Evaluation Studies

It would indeed be surprising if these intense experiences occurring over a period of several weeks did not have any effect at all on the participants, considering that the much weaker influences which are exerted in social psychological laboratory experiments produce measurable effects. The question in all research is not whether anything occurs at all, but under what conditions it occurs and how it can be controlled. From the point of view of research it is much more important to show how the production of even a small effect occurs than it is to demonstrate changes in some people without knowing what caused them and what kind of people they are. Of course, in order to publicize the programs and to impress people that something is happening, the former approach is sufficient, but it can hardly be considered what is conventionally called research.

The fate of evaluation research in this field shows the difficulties with which research on intervention is faced. As mentioned previously, there was an attempt in the first laboratories to evaluate the effects on the participants through follow-up and later reports. However, not enough conclusive results were obtained to make this kind of procedure attractive to most investigators. An analysis of 149 evaluation and process studies done in the 25 years since the beginning of sensitivity groups shows that very few used any behavioral measures taken after the laboratory ended, even fewer used reports from others than the participants themselves, and hardly any used control groups (8). The worst studies in these respects were done during the Dormant and Explosion Periods of the 1950s and early 1960s. During this time we find either reports that changes of any kind have occurred, or narrative descriptions of the process which give the reader a feeling of what is happening in the group, at least as far as the author-observer sees it. Similar studies are also reported involving applications of the technique to therapy and industrial situations and to situations aimed at the resolution of group conflicts (32, 51). Some of the most recent studies in the survey showed an improvement in methodology, which may be a hopeful sign.

The procedural inadequacies of most of the evaluation studies may represent a general reaction against the scientific method or at least against the methods which the experimental social psychologists use. The lack of findings forced the interveners to make a virtue of necessity. Many people in the sensitivity training movement reject the way most social psychological research, or psychological research in general, is being performed and proclaim that not only do they have a better way of changing and educating people but also a better way of doing research (3, 4). This is partly a counterattack against the flight of many social psychologists away from working with groups, and partly an attempt to show that the group process which is being advocated is also a process of research. Thus, articles on intervention techniques spend most of their time attacking traditional research methods and promoting new methods which supposedly correspond to the new kinds of groups which they are advocating. It might come to pass that only those social psychologists who are indoctrinated with a belief in the higher value of the techniques which are promoted through group intervention will be recognized as being able to do research on these techniques.

New Trends

However, there are indications of a new trend in research. There is some interest among psychologists in examining some of the tenets of the encounter group movement. Although they are starting with some of the more primitive propositions, they eventually may find some way of going more deeply into the process itself. Some studies are now being done to explore the effects of nonverbal communication, touching, and closeness on group cohesion (24, 37). These are not necessarily studies of group intervention, but studies of some of the suppositions about how groups are formed. Another development has been at least one study, by Lieberman, Yalom & Miles (63), which is trying to evaluate encounter groups in a more overarching design by comparing several techniques, using two groups to represent each technique, and also employing adequate controls. This study has yielded valuable information about the importance of the leader in the group, the problems of measuring danger to the participants, the high rate of casualties in certain kinds of groups, and the possibility of classifying the processes which occur.

Finally, there have been some attempts to look at the groups from outside as social phenomena, to assess their function from a different perspective than that of the group interventionist. For instance, a hypothesis has been put forth that sensitivity groups, with their unstructured procedures and all-powerful leaders, tend to induce great anxiety, and that many of the techniques used in the training laboratories are ways of coping with this anxiety (22, 23). The current crisis period in the movement may lead to a decision within the movement itself to take a new course and may spur a new kind of research approach which will use different techniques than those previously envisaged by either the experimental social psychologist or the people in the movement itself.

Some of the general concepts underlying group intervention techniques are based on theories in social psychology. However, the approach used in the development of the group intervention techniques is different from that of traditional social psychology. Many of the earlier experiments, such as the Westinghouse and Harwood studies, really laid the foundations of some of current social psychological theory. However, the later development of this theory is held by many of the people engaged in intervention techniques to be too one-sided.

Utopian Research

The ideas at the base of intervention techniques are not so much a theory corresponding to the world as it is as they are a theory of the world as it could be, itself transformed through these intervention techniques. This point of view becomes particularly apparent among the leaders in the group intervention movement who are themselves social psychologists and have in a way worked on both sides of the street. Thus Argyris (3) has practically defined two worlds, A and B. Society A is the world in which the general laws of current social psychology and experimental work hold but which is controlled by norms, goal directedness, instrumental activities, and passivity of the observed object. On the other hand, society B is characterized by openness, absence of norms, the possibility of expressing emotion, and an emphasis on interpersonal relations. Argyris admits that this kind of society is rare and at the present time is practically only found in the world of T-groups. What he does neglect is, of course, the fact that T-groups have their own norms, norms of expressing emotions and so on, which exert as much influence on the group members as societal norms, but in a different direction.

Argyris's two types correspond to similar divisions in other theories such as McGregor's (68) X and Y and Likert's (64, 65) authoritative and participative systems. It might be safe to say that these theorists are proposing two different kinds of societies or groups, two different kinds of norms by which it is possible for groups to function. The new set of norms, the Y or B or participative (system 4), whatever the new group is called, might be easier than the old to set up as an ideal and a goal for certain kinds of changes in group functioning.

Even when theory is discussed purely in the abstract we can see the relation between description and analysis on the one side and action and utopian goals on the other. Where the social psychological tradition persists in treating current circumstances as invariable facts of human nature, the extreme on the other side is to treat goals and utopias as proven characteristics of viable and existing systems. The theory underlying intervention, therefore, is intimately tied up with its application to particular settings and purposes.

MEANS AND ENDS

We can now see more clearly the functions of group intervention. Small groups are the locus of intensive emotional interaction and are also a vehicle for achieving many aims in society. Intervention by group process can be used to make the group more efficient in pursuing its purpose, but intervention at this level and under these emotional conditions gives the process an added meaning beyond the group's ostensive purpose. We recall in this connection the original function of group intervention as part of religious ritual.

We can start with the ostensive goals of the intervention. These goals may be directed toward some influence on the individual members of the group, on the functioning of the group itself, or on the larger organization of which it is a member. In the first case the aim may be teaching skills to the members; it can be a technique to introduce new methods in schools or professional training. Or it may aim to induce a deeper personality change, in which case it becomes an adjunct or even principal feature of psychotherapy. The last case is exemplified in the use of groups in personnel management. The group intervention method is used as a way of increasing the efficiency of a business, industry, or governmental or voluntary organization. In the extreme, of course, it might be used as a method of reconstituting society, which is probably the approach some of the European, more politically oriented leaders are using.

There remains the second case, the movement of the group into itself. Here, in a way, the emphasis on group process is shown in its purest condition. When the effects on the participants are relatively weak, the groups serve a kind of recreational function, which has given the "psych-resorts" such great popularity and mass recognition. When a stronger effect is sought, the groups may actually aim at becoming a reconstructed society or alternate life-style, such as was proposed by Argyris, Likert, and McGregor. It is here that the original connection of small groups with religious efforts becomes most prominent and most ominous.

In all these situations, except perhaps the last one, there is a certain incongruity between means and ends. Strong emotions and attempts at involvement of the members are used for ends which are, after all, usually quite pedestrian or trivial. In fact, this incongruity is one of the principal difficulties in any evaluation of intervention techniques. It seems obvious that something happens to people during these intense emotional sessions and the immediate reaction of most people seems to confirm this. However, detailed investigation of long-range changes or effects which are congruent with the ostensive purposes of the intervention leads to extremely ambiguous results. The more adequate measurement techniques are often used in studies which find the smallest changes (8).

Scientists have also been concerned about the negative effects or the dangers of the group intervention techniques. Here again, little research has been done to define the dangers. As a matter of fact, the definition of danger within the groups has become a pointed issue. Perhaps following the religious model of the soul going through darkness to light, some encounter leaders do not take evidence of nervous breakdowns, psychotic episodes, and the like as evidence of bad effects of the program, but say instead that this is part of the development of the person toward a higher level (77, 88). In the same way, the group intervention programs in industry can lead some managers who are participants in the groups not to become better managers but to decide that work in industry is not for them. It can be argued whether this is really a deleterious effect; it cannot be argued, of course, that it is not what the particular industry paid for when it sent its workers to attend the group.

Research on casualties will have to be done in a carefully controlled fashion, and consideration must be given to casualties other than merely those designated by the group leader. In fact, it has been shown that group leaders in general are the least qualified persons to identify casualties (63). This, incidentally, is an interesting sidelight on the sensitivity which the leaders of sensitivity training have. Intensive follow-up studies of the kind used to look for positive effects are even more needed for assessing negative effects. However, most of the data on casualties as well as on positive effects are mainly anecdotal and difficult to evaluate.

Going beyond the questions of the effectiveness and danger of intervention groups, these groups provide an interesting site for studies of interaction, since in many of them the purely interpersonal aspects of interaction are heightened to a tremendous extent. Thus, much of the research on group intervention really has very little to do with the groups themselves, but uses them more as a real-life, real-time experimental situation for studying social interactions.

Another kind of research which has not been sufficiently pursued involves looking at the intervention technique as a social phenomenon of our time. The existence of small intervention groups for their own sake is probably one of the more unique characteristics of our society. They have not prospered because they have been successful in achieving their stated aims, as evaluation research has shown, nor have they revolutionized methodology or brought about a new era of understanding of human behavior. Therefore, we have to look more at the social conditions surrounding the people who lead and participate in groups of this kind. Little research has been done on this, but ideas for such research might include studying the recruitment of participants and leaders and assessing the importance of the group techniques in the general working of society.

Thus from every point of view, from the history of development of the technique, from evaluation, research, and application, we are led to the relationship between small group intervention and the values of society. The change from the original use of the technique in early religious ritual to the secular, instrumental method of today; the experimentation with a new, explosive, important force within human relations and the tentative efforts to control it; the new search for peak experiences through group action—all these can be studied by investigating the group procedures, but they are also important in their relation to lasting cultural trends. The best way to understand the group intervention movement is to look at it simultaneously as a psychological technique and a social problem.

Literature Cited

1. Argyris, C. 1962. *Interpersonal Competence and Organizational Effectiveness.* Homewood, Ill.: Dorsey
2. Argyris, C. 1965. *Organization and Innovation.* Homewood, Ill.: Dorsey
3. Argyris, C. 1969. The incompleteness of social-psychological theory: examples from small group, cognitive consistency, and attribution research. *Am. Psychol.* 24:893–908
4. Argyris, C. 1970. *Intervention Theory and Method.* Reading, Mass.: Addison-Wesley
5. Aronson, E. 1972. *The Social Animal.* San Francisco: Freeman
6. Asch, S. E. 1956. Studies of independence and conformity: a minority of one against a unanimous majority. *Psychol. Monogr.* 70, no. 9 (whole no. 416)
7. Back, K. W. 1951. Influence through social communication. *J. Abnorm. Soc. Psychol.* 46:9–23
8. Back, K. W. 1972. *Beyond Words.* New York: Russell Sage
9. Back, K. W. et al 1950. The methodology of studying rumor transmission. *Hum. Relat.* 3:307–12
10. Bales, R. F. 1950. *Interaction Process Analysis: A Method for the Study of*

Small Groups. Cambridge, Mass.: Addison-Wesley
11. Bales, R. F. 1970. *Personality and Interpersonal Behavior.* New York: Holt
12. Bales, R. F., Flanders, N. A. 1954. Planning an observation room and group laboratory. *Am. Sociol. Rev.* 19:771–81
13. Bales, R. F., Slater, P. E. 1955. Role differentiation in small decision-making groups. In *Family Socialization and Interaction Process,* ed. T. Parsons, R. F. Bales, J. Olds, M. Zelditch Jr., P. E. Slater, 259–306. Glencoe, Ill.: Free Press
14. Bavelas, A. 1947. Role playing and management training. *Sociatry* 2:183–91
15. Bavelas, A. 1950. Communication patterns in task-oriented groups. *J. Acoust. Soc. Am.* 22:725–30
16. Benne, K. D., Sheats, P. 1948. Functional roles of group members. *J. Soc. Issues* 4, 2:41–49
17. Bennis, W., Shepard, H. 1956. A theory of group development. *Hum. Relat.* 9: 415–37
18. Bettelheim, B. 1955. *Love is Not Enough —The Treatment of Emotionally Disturbed Children.* New York: Free Press
19. Bettelheim, B. 1955. *Truants From Life —The Rehabilitation of Emotionally Disturbed Children.* New York: Free Press
20. Bion, W. R. 1961. *Experiences in Groups.* New York: Basic Books
21. Blake, R., Mouton, J. 1968. *Corporate Excellence through Grid Organizational Development.* Houston: Gulf Publ.
22. Blumenstiel, A. D. 1970. An ethos of intimacy: constructing and using a situational morality. In *Deviance and Respectability: The Social Construction of Moral Meanings,* ed. J. D. Douglas, 435–53. New York: Basic Books
23. Blumenstiel, A. D. 1971. *Structure and legitimacy: participant observation research on laboratory training.* Presented at AAAS, Philadelphia
24. Boderman, A., Freed, D. W., Kinnucan, M. T. 1972. "Touch me, like me": testing an encounter group assumption. *J. Appl. Behav. Sci.* 8:527–33
25. Borgatta, E. F. 1954. Sidesteps toward a nonspecial theory. *Psychol. Rev.* 61: 343–52
26. Bradford, L., Gibb, J., Benne, K. 1964. *T-Group Theory and Laboratory Method.* New York: Wiley
27. Coch, L., French, J. 1948. Overcoming resistance to change. *Hum. Relat.* 1: 512–32
28. Curle, A. 1947/48. Transitional communities and social reconnection. A follow-up study of the civil resettlement of British prisoners of war. Part I. *Hum. Relat.* 1:42–68
29. Curle, A., Trist, E. L. 1947/48. Transitional communities and social reconnection. A follow-up study of the civil resettlement of British prisoners of war. Part II. *Hum. Relat.* 1:240–88
30. Deutsch, M. 1949. The effect of cooperation and competition upon group process. *Hum. Relat.* 2:124–52, 190–231
31. Dicks, H. V. 1970. *50 Years of the Tavistock Clinic.* London: Routledge and Kegan Paul
32. Doob, L. W. 1970. *Resolving Conflict in Africa.* New Haven: Yale Univ. Press
33. Dunphy, D. C. 1968. Phases, roles, and myths in self-analytic groups. *J. Appl. Behav. Sci.* 4:195–225
34. Festinger, L. 1950. Informal social communication. *Psychol. Rev.* 57:271–82
35. Festinger, L., Thibaut, J. 1951. Interpersonal communication in small groups. *J. Abnorm. Soc. Psychol.* 46:92–100
36. French, J., Kornhauser, A., Marrow, A. J., Eds. 1946. Conflict and cooperation in industry. *J. Soc. Issues* 2, no. 1 (whole issue)
37. Gergen, K. J., Gergen, M. K. 1971. *Encounter: research catalyst for general theories of social behavior.* Presented at AAAS, Philadelphia
38. Hampden-Turner, A. 1970. *Radical Man.* Cambridge, Mass.: Schenkman
39. Higgin, G. 1972. The Scandinavians rehearse the liberation. *J. Appl. Behav. Sci.* 8:643–63
40. Horowitz, M. W., Lyons, J., Perlmutter, H. V. 1951. Induction of forces in discussion groups. *Hum. Relat.* 4:57–76
41. Howard, J. 1970. *Please Touch.* New York: McGraw-Hill
42. Huxley, A. 1932. *Brave New World.* Garden City, N. J.: Doubleday
43. Hyman, H. H. 1942. The psychology of status. *Arch. Psychol. NY* 269
44. Jaques, E., Ed. 1947. Social therapy. *J. Soc. Issues* 3, no. 2 (whole issue)
45. Jaques, E. 1951. *The Changing Culture of a Factory.* London: Tavistock
46. Katz, E., Lazarsfeld, P. F. 1955. *Personal Influence.* Glencoe, Ill.: Free Press
47. Kelley, H. H. 1951. Communication in experimentally created hierarchies. *Hum. Relat.* 4:39–56
48. Klein, M. 1948. *Contributions to Psycho-analysis, 1921–1945.* London: Hogarth
49. Klein, M. 1952. *Developments in Psycho-analysis.* London: Hogarth
50. Klein, M. 1963. *Our Adult World, and other Essays.* London: Heinemann
51. Lakin, M. 1970. *Arab and Jew in Israel.* Washington, D.C.: NTL Publications

52. "Landmarks." 1967. *J. Appl. Behav. Sci.* 3, no. 2 (whole issue)
53. Landsberger, H. 1965. *Hawthorne Revisited.* Ithaca: New York School of Industrial and Labor Relations
54. Lapassade, G. 1970. *Groupes, Organizations, et Institutions.* Paris: Gauthier-Villars
55. Leavitt, H. J. 1951. Some effects of certain communication patterns on group performance. *J. Abnorm. Soc. Psychol.* 46:38–50
56. Lewin, K. 1935. *Dynamic Theory of Personality.* New York: McGraw-Hill
57. Lewin, K. 1947. Frontiers in group dynamics I: concept, method and theory in social science; social equilibrium. *Hum. Relat.* 1:5–40
58. Ibid. Frontiers in group dynamics II: channels of group life and social planning and action research, 143–53
59. Lewin, K. 1948. *Resolving Social Conflicts.* New York: Harper
60. Lewin, K. 1951. *Field Theory in Social Science.* New York: Harper
61. Lewin, K., Lippitt, R., White, R. 1939. Patterns of aggressive behavior in experimentally created "social climates." *J. Soc. Psychol.* 10:271–99
62. Lieberman, M. 1958. *The relationship of group climate to individual change.* PhD thesis. Univ. Chicago
63. Lieberman, M., Yalom, I., Miles, M. 1973. *Encounter Groups: First Facts.* New York: Basic Books
64. Likert, R. 1961. *New Patterns in Management.* New York: McGraw-Hill
65. Likert, R. 1967. *The Human Organization.* New York: McGraw-Hill
66. Lippitt, R. 1949. *Training in Community Relations.* New York: Harper
67. Loomis, C. 1939. Sociometrics and the study of new rural communities. *Sociometry* 2:56–76
68. McGregor, D. 1960. *The Human Side of Enterprise.* New York: McGraw-Hill
69. Mann, R. 1967. *Interpersonal Styles and Group Development.* New York: Wiley
70. Marquis, D. G., Guetzkow, H., Heyns, R. W. 1951. A social psychological study of the decision-making conference. In *Groups, Leadership and Men: Research in Human Relations,* ed. H. Guetzkow, 55–67. Pittsburgh: Carnegie Press
71. Marrow, A. J. 1957. *Making Management Human.* New York: McGraw-Hill
72. Mayo, E. 1933. *The Human Problems of an Industrial Civilization.* New York: Macmillan
73. Mills, T. 1964. *Group Transformation.* Englewood Cliffs, N. J.: Prentice-Hall
74. Moreno, J. 1941. *The Words of the Fa ther.* Beacon, N. Y.: Beacon House
75. Moreno, J. 1946, 1959. *Psychodrama,* Vols. I and II. Beacon, N.Y.: Beacon House
76. Office of Strategic Services Assessment Staff 1948. *Assessment of Men.* New York: Rinehart
77. Perls, F. 1969. *Gestalt Therapy Verbatim.* Lafayette, Calif.: Real People Press
78. Redl, F. 1942. Group emotion and leadership. *Psychiatry* 5:573–96
79. Roethlisberger, F., Dickson, W. 1939. *Management and the Worker.* Cambridge, Mass.: Harvard Univ. Press
80. Rogers, C. 1951. *Client-Centered Therapy in Current Practice, Implications and Theory.* Boston: Houghton Mifflin
81. Rogers, C. 1961. *On Becoming a Person.* Boston: Houghton Mifflin
82. Schachter, S. 1951. Deviation, rejection and communication. *J. Abnorm. Soc. Psychol.* 46:190–207
83. Schutz, W. 1968. *Joy.* New York: Grove
84. Schutz, W. 1971. *Here Comes Everybody.* New York: Harper
85. Segal, H. 1964. *Introduction to the Work of Melanie Klein.* New York: Basic Books
86. Shaw, M. E. 1964. Communication networks. In *Advances in Experimental Social Psychology,* ed. L. Berkowitz, 1:111–47. New York: Academic
87. Sherif, M. 1936. *The Psychology of Social Norms.* New York: Harper and Row
88. Silverman, J. 1970. When schizophrenia helps. *Psychology Today* 4, Sept.: 63–65
89. Slater, P. 1966. *Microcosm.* New York: Wiley
90. Slavson, S. R. 1940. Group therapy. *Ment. Hyg.* 24:36–49
91. Slavson, S. R. 1964. *A Textbook in Analytic Group Psychotherapy.* New York: Int. Univ. Press
92. Stouffer, S. A. et al 1949. *The American Soldier,* Vols I and II. Princeton Univ. Press
93. Taylor, F. W. 1911. *The Principles of Scientific Management.* New York: Harper
94. Watson, J. 1952. *Some social-psychological correlates of personality: a study of the usefulness of psychoanalytic theory in predicting behavior.* PhD thesis. Univ. Michigan
95. Weltfish, G., Ed. 1945. Racial and religious prejudice in everyday living. Parts I and II. *J. Soc. Issues* 1, no. 1 and 2 (whole issues)
96. Wilson, S. R. 1969. The effect of the laboratory situation on experimental discussion groups. *Sociometry* 32:220–36
97. Yalom, I. 1970. *The Theory and Practice of Group Psychotherapy.* New York: Basic Books

BEHAVIORAL GENETICS[1] ❖222

P. L. Broadhurst and D. W. Fulker
University of Birmingham, England

John Wilcock
University College, Cardiff, Wales

The history of the area known as behavioral genetics (psychological genetics, sometimes shortened to psychogenetics) is, as mirrored in the pages of earlier volumes of the *Annual Review of Psychology,* but a short one. Fuller's 1960 review (88), covering the period from 1955, showed that activity in the late 1950s was directed to practical human problems such as mental illness. A major technique in work with humans was the twin study; most animal work aimed simply to demonstrate genetic control, comparing strain, as the independent variable, with behavior, as the dependent. Crossbreeding of strains was done largely in the Mendelian tradition of trying to isolate single genes. Attempts to find gene-behavior pathways emphasized audiogenic seizures. Such work continues, but now a major part of psychogenetic research is biometric and quantitative.

McClearn & Meredith in 1966 (161) observed that strain differences were commonplace and to be regarded only as a starting point. Of major interest were advances in human cytogenetics which continue to provide insights. There were also some biochemical and single-gene studies. Most of the rat and mouse work reported were studies on strain differences, although selective and crossbreeding studies were more plentiful.

In 1970 McClearn wrote a distinguished review for a sister volume, the *Annual Review of Genetics* (157), with a useful historical introduction, but the purely psychological story was not resumed until 1971 with Lindzey, Loehlin, Manosevitz

[1]We are indebted to all those who sent us reprints and preprints, both individuals and journal editors, for their timely assistance in extending the coverage of this review. Its preparation was indirectly supported by the (British) Medical Research Council's programme grant for work on psychogenetics to Professors P. L. Broadhurst and J. L. Jinks, FRS, at the University of Birmingham, and by the Office of Scientific and Technical Information's project on library information services. We gratefully acknowledge the assistance of Mr. E. F. Gouthwaite in bibliographic matters and the comments of Dr. J. Angus on insect behavior.

& Thiessen's long and comprehensive review (150), which chronicled the further decline of simple strain comparisons and the increase of quantitative genetic analyses. The growth of studies using physiological analyses and the increasing interest in evolution were stressed. Meanwhile Childs (38) reviewed behavioral genetics from a viewpoint appropriate to the *Annual Review of Medicine.*

The growing importance of the field is reflected in the increasing frequency of reviews which, according to the 1971 "master plan" of the *Annual Review of Psychology,* should appear at 3-year intervals. But increasing frequency means decreasing size, and the present review must be shorter than many of those mentioned. Hence, in addition to maintaining an enforced selectivity, we have relied much more on previous reviews for background references than did our predecessors, using the five cited above to the exclusion of other earlier sources unless absolutely necessary. But their total of 1213 citations, with surprisingly little overlap, makes them a valuable repository of information on which to base our current progress report, which reviews the literature from approximately late 1969 to early 1973.

Our organization is simple: the first section deals with work using infra-human animals as subjects, the second with work with humans. The animal section is organized broadly by methodology, progressing from relatively simple to more complex situations and designs, with a detour through a single phenotype, that relating to alcohol preference, as befits a topic putatively concerned more directly with real-life problems. This approach also governs the organization of the section on humans in terms of the traditional categorization of behavioral phenotypes, but it necessitates a terminal discussion of methodology.

ANIMAL RESEARCH

Reviews

Topics include developmental problems (94), learning (257), audiogenic seizures (90), alcoholism (159), aggression (160), genetic homeostasis (120), and evolutionary contexts (240, 269); a general review by Thiessen (239) provides a history of mouse strains.

Major Genes

Interest in major-gene analysis continues. Studies of neurological mutants in *Drosophila* by Benzer and his co-workers have reached an exciting stage (see 150, p. 73; 38, p. 380). By producing flies which are structural mosaics for genes controlling various abnormal behavior traits, including one named "drop dead," they have succeeded in mapping gene location with reference to known marker structures, on the two-dimensional surface provided by the egg, with such precision that the origin of the defect can be pin-pointed (118). Thus in the case mentioned it has been shown that it is the brain and not any other part of the fly that must be involved. Analysis by this powerful genetic mosaic technique of other more complex behavior is promised and will be eagerly awaited.

In mice a study of the effects of four alleles differing in respect to tyrosinase activity at the albino locus showed that behavioral differences were unrelated to either eye pigmentation or tyrosinase activity (241). When pigmented and albino segregants were tested for descent from a visual cliff using different lighting and platform heights, albinos were slower under all conditions (187). To discuss these findings, simply in terms of acrophobia added to a postulated photophobia is to minimize developmental history. A major gene which affects sensory receptors from birth must express itself in behavioral differences at maturity. Debate continues (23, 268) over the efforts at conceptual clarification in this area (see 150, p. 72).

Using a developmental approach, van Abeelen & Kalkoven (1) compared normal and Nijmegen waltzer mice on reflex and behavioral measures at several ages. Unlike major reflex differences which disappeared by weaning, behavioral differences persisted into adulthood. The deficient performance of retinal degenerate segregants on jump-out and one-way avoidance learning was shown to be a function of poor visual capacity, (259) whereas albino mice, if tested in dim red light, were not deficient. Albino segregants were progressively inferior to pigmented mice in a water-escape task (78). Since initial scores were identical, light intensity is unlikely to have been important. Mutations producing obesity in mice were detailed in relation to food-intake regulation by Fuller (89).

Major-gene analysis has been approached through study of behavioral differences rather than mutation. Whitney (266) measured the tendency to vocalize among randomly bred mice, finding frequencies expected for a single locus with complete dominance. Collins (43) has now mapped the position of the audiogenic seizure-prone gene using this approach.

Selection

Progress in ongoing behavioral selection studies as well as new selections for behavioral characteristics, continues to be reported. The sophisticated selection experiment of DeFries and co-workers, in which mice were bidirectionally selected for open-field activity, exceeds ten generations (50). Realized heritability was reliably estimated at 13%. Because the selection lines (as well as controls) were replicated, it could be shown that the negative correlation between defecation and activity was not a fortuitously correlated response. Tests at S_{10} checked the situational generality of the selection response. Differentiation of strains by activity in boxlike and illuminated apparatus had elements in common with that in the open field. Activity in wheels did not differentiate the strains.

Mouse strains bidirectionally selected for rearing did not differ systematically in adrenal or thyroid activity (2). However, Blizard & Chai (16), selecting for release of radioactively labeled iodine from the thyroid, found their strains differed in open-field defecation and water-maze learning. The results complement work on the Maudsley strains of rats selected for open-field differences and found to differ in thyroid funtion (see 161, p. 536).

Lagerspetz & Lagerspetz (141) now report results to S_{19} of their bidirectional selection for aggression in mice, noting no change since S_7, though strain differences in aggressiveness may be reversed by social experiences. Mice were selected over seven generations for learning activity in a T-maze (119). The authors' analysis showed a small genetic component. In four generations of selection of mice for rapid water-escape learning, realized heritability was found to be low (78).

Roubicek et al (209) selected rats for high and low water intake for eight generations at an ambient temperature of 22°C and for nine at 35°C. Selections for high intake at high temperature and low intake at the low were successful, but selections for increased intake at the low temperature and for decreased at the high were much less so. However, transfer of animals selected for increased intake at low temperature to the hot environment produced an intake similar to that of the rats selected at that temperature, though the relationship between the two low intake lines under comparable conditions was less marked. This difference is reflected in the higher genetic correlation of intake in the two environments for the high lines compared with the low. No abnormalities in urine concentration, adrenals, pituitaries, or kidneys were found in these strains, which consequently should make good material for behavioral studies.

A preliminary communication (26), which nevertheless reported 19 generations of bidirectional selection for shuttle-box avoidance in the rat, indicated an asymmetry comparable to that found previously in a similar experiment (see 150, p. 55).

Imprinting is widely regarded as a biologically important behavior. Graves & Siegel (98) bidirectionally selected chicks over five generations and found asymmetry for response to selection favoring rapid approach, but not for slow approach. Three lines of domestic chickens, bidirectionally selected for mating behavior, were studied for the effects of androgen therapy on sexual behavior (162). Level of restored mating behavior depended on genotype.

Alcohol Preference

In an ongoing study, Eriksson (67, 69) bidirectionally selected for voluntary ethanol consumption in the rat. At S_{17} the low strain was more active in the open field. Examination of the metabolic differences between the strains (81) showed that the high alcohol strain had a higher brain serotonin content; the difference was more extreme after exposure to alcohol (6). This strain voluntarily drank to intoxication (68).

Whitney, McClearn & DeFries (267) reconsidered earlier reports and presented new data on alcohol preference in rats and mice. They calculated various heritabilities, all consistently low, and questioned the assumption that heritabilities must be population specific. A study using two mouse strains and their filial and backcross generations has reported slightly higher heritability indices and considerable directional dominance for nondrinking behavior (66). A similar analysis of morphine intake in the same strains encountered severe scalar problems (70). Good agreement with a two-gene model was found for preference and consumption in two strains and their filial and backcrosses, without demonstrated involvement of coat-color genes (91). Inter- and intra-strain differences in preferences in mice were also reported (71, 194).

Pursuing his search for underlying mechanisms, McClearn proposed a negative feedback model (158) and, with co-workers (223), reported that intraperitoneal injections of ethanol produced higher accumulations of blood acetaldehyde in a nonpreference strain. Odor has been implicated in ethanol aversion in BALB/c mice (178).

Three studies relate alcohol consumption to other behaviors in mice and rats. A factor analytic study related alcohol consumption to two factors, audiogenic reactivity and disorganized behavior (195). An analysis using filial and backcrosses found alcohol preference in mice to be negatively related to open-field defecation and urination (265). Higher voluntary intake, however, was found in strains of rats selected for high emotionality and high avoidance (212). At two symposia (80, 222) material on the value of animals in alcoholism research was presented.

Simple Strain Differences

Despite previous caveats, strain differences continue to be reported and some merit brief attention. However, the practice of using laboratory rodents "bought in," i.e. reared somewhere other than in the home laboratory, must raise doubts about the validity of the findings reported, depending, of course, on what is known about the phenotype investigated.

Interest has arisen in measurements of brain biochemistry. Comparisons among rat strains have included telencephalic serotonin metabolism (207), acetylcholinesterase (230), and tyrosinehydroxylase—a rate-limiting enzyme in the biosynthesis of brain amines—which was found to relate inversely to activity (221). Rick et al (204) found a similar association between activity and GABA. Studies using drugs affecting the cholinergic system supported the existence of a genetically controlled brain cholinergic mechanism which facilitates exploration in mice (3, 4).

Several studies have been based on rat strains selected for behavioral characteristics including derivations of the Maudsley and Roman strains (see 161, p. 535, 150, p. 55 respectively). The most recent of a series (102) has confirmed strain differences; emotionality, as measured by suppression of drinking by unsignaled shock, was unrelated to defecation (121), as was spontaneous activity and avoidance conditioning (211, 213).

In further reports from Schlesinger and co-workers (see 150, p. 41, and 157, p. 454), a heterogeneous and an inbred mouse strain were both found to be susceptible to audiogenic seizure priming, though optimum stimulus exposure varied between them (20). Substances known to affect levels of biogenic amines reduced susceptibility to seizure after priming without affecting priming itself.

Simple Genetic Analyses

By this rubric, we mean analyses uncomplicated by environmental variables, though genetic designs may be quite complex. When three mouse strains and their first filials were compared on water-escape learning, the filials performed as well as the fastest inbred strain (77); in another study two strains and their first filials were compared for activity by means of two types of automatic recorders (191). When saccharine preference was compared in four inbred mouse strains, broad heritabilities were found to be high (192). Comparisons involving filial and backcrosses showed extreme heterosis for nest building in mice, in a study which also presented a diallel analysis (143). The pattern of differences between the broad and narrow heritabilities supports the adaptive significance of this character, interesting for its a priori relationship to biological fitness.

Van Oortmerssen (183), from an ethological analysis based on extensive filial crosses, has suggested that some laboratory strains of mice arise from surface-nesting wild progenitors while others derive from hole-nesters. Developmental differences in passive avoidance in two strains of mice and their F_1s were shown to depend on shock level (233), and Hegmann (110) found strain differences in nerve conduction velocities which were faster in reciprocal F_1s obtained between two of the six strains. Wahlsten (258) "bought in" strains for an interesting attempt to study mechanisms underlying response to shock and avoidance learning by equating shock level eliciting jumping. Multivariate analyses of behavioral sequences in two mouse strains and their filial and backcrosses showed evidence of segregation of sequence elements (148).

Of two mouse studies based on parent-offspring covariation, one (245) demonstrated the absence of change in a measure of narrow heritability for runway learning, while the other (181) showed high narrow heritability for avoidance learning.

Studies with an Environmental Dimension

Of more interest than simple demonstrations of strain differences are recent attempts to show the limits of generality by utilizing more than one environment. For example, interstrain fighting in mice was shown to be dependent on infantile stimulation (198), and when male mice from two "bought in" strains were kept at five different temperatures and three different population densities to study the effects of these factors on aggression (100), the strain differences did not interact with environmental variables. An interesting limitation of generality arising from strain-measurement interaction was reported by Goodrick (95), who compared automatic and direct observations of open-field activity which varied differentially in two mouse strains. Differences in the effect of a companion on exploratory behavior were found in two strains of mice (227). Another social variable, litter size, was similarly studied (62). Factor analysis revealed dimensions interpreted as territorial marking, autonomic balance, acrophobia, and motor discharge. Although litter size directly affected the first two, the only interaction of litter size with genotype was in respect of motor discharge.

Vale et al (251) "bought in" male mice of five inbred strains that displayed differences in population density effects for number of aggressive attacks and for adrenal weight. Genotype-density interactions were also found, but the relationship between behavioral and physiological measures was unsystematic. Scott et al (219) linked the effects of amphetamine on fighting in mice to differences in its effect on body temperature in two strains. Their findings relate to explanations of the aggregation-toxicity effect of this drug which invoke body temperature.

Investigation of nest building at two ambient temperatures (152) showed for one strain a negative correlation with food consumption at the lower temperature. Vocalization in infant mice was shown to depend on strain and ambient temperature as well as age (14, 180).

Complex Processes, Including Genotype-Environment Interaction

With this section we begin the consideration of what we see as the central problem in behavioral genetics. Psychologists quite rightly regard their discipline as having analytical difficulties; geneticists view their area similarly. The intersection of interests in behavioral genetics must therefore raise problems of considerable complexity, on either the genetic or the environmental side and often on both (25). Erlenmeyer-Kimling (72), deploring the lack of effort directed to the solution of these problems, blames the daunting nature of the task. We have necessarily concentrated on studies that emphasized these complexities, but we do not, of course, undervalue those that attempted to provide a framework on which to build further. Some of what has preceded may be regarded as falling into this latter category.

Vale and collaborators, who recognize the importance of such a positive approach (see 150, p. 76), have presented a series of intriguing sex X strain X hormone interaction studies of aggressive and sexual behavior in mice (248–250). Their results have led them to suggest that sexual behavior may in fact be less dimorphic than aggressive behavior.

Fulker (84) reanalyzed three studies—one on rats and two on mice—of prenatal and shock stress (244). Patterns of reciprocal F_1 differences yielded to a model in which the additive genetic effects were buffered by contribution from the maternal environment.

Henderson has continued his systematic attack on problems in this area (see 150). In a 6 X 6 diallel study of mice, additive genetic variation in a complex food-seeking task was released by environmental enrichment, although the underlying genetic pattern remained essentially the same under both environmental treatments (113). A similar finding emerged for spontaneous alternation (111). Brain weight showed greater heterosis in the environmentally enriched group (112). In another diallel study on enrichment, Henderson found that it led to only small changes in discrimination learning (114). These studies can be contrasted since aversive motivation was used in the second study.

In attempting the analysis of gene-action in relation to environmental determinants, the various approaches adopted by Broadhurst & Jinks (24) open several possibilities. Their implications have been reviewed by Fulker et al (87), who presented a preliminary multivariate analysis of an 8 X 8 diallel cross of rat strains, with infantile stimulation as an imposed environmental treatment. Genotype-environment interaction was considerable in the additive components of variation in open-field measures, but minimal in avoidance conditioning. As in Henderson's work with mice, directional dominance not interacting with treatment was found. More detailed analyses have revealed the subtlety of the interaction within avoidance acquisition (271) in that a progressive change in genetic control has indicated the possibility of two distinct behavioral processes underlying learning. Since they correspond to the two factors of Mowrer's theory, it might be argued that behavioral genetics is beginning to have something of direct interest to say to one of its parent disciplines.

Less systematic effects suggestive of similar mechanisms in mouse avoidance conditioning were found by Royce et al (210) in a 6 X 6 diallel, which also showed clear evidence of directional dominance for high avoidance.

Genetic analysis of factor scores confirmed the different genetic substrates for those two frequently combined measures of emotionality in the mouse, urination and defecation. The results of two studies (171, 182) using mouse diallels and concerned with conditioning, maze learning, and activity were interpreted in part in terms of dominance relationships dependent on the particular crosses involved. But this epistasis (nonallelic interaction), evident in extensive biometric analyses, may be a function of the choice of extreme parental lines in relatively small diallel crosses.

Several other small diallels in mice have been reported (30, 44, 83, 206, 247). The use of the variance-covariance diagram of Jinks for the proper presentation of the results is a welcome sign of an increasing awareness of the power of this method.

As we have seen, *Drosophila* lend themselves to powerful analyses. The quantitative approach employs such behaviors as geotaxis (279) and locomotor activity, which Hay (107) used in a design employing all possible filial and backcrosses (14 in all) to establish directional dominance for high activity in *D. melanogaster.* This study also incorporated an environmental variable (culture) and provided the first unambiguous demonstration of duplicate gene interaction and dispersed gene distribution for a behavioral trait. Such genetic architecture is typical of fitness traits which determine uniformly high levels in free-mating populations. For a measure of preening, additive and dominance maternal effects were found among females, whereas among males maternal and progeny genotype interactions occurred. Diallels gave supporting evidence. In further work (109) genetic factors were implicated in social interactions in flies. Manning & Hirsch (153) investigated genetic mechanisms in a strain of *D. stimulans* selected for slow mating.

Population considerations often involve complex behavioral processes (see 150, p. 69); Ehrmann has now implicated olfactory cues in density dependent selection in *D. pseudoobscura* (63). In other *Drosophila* species similar effects are observed (64, 108), but frequency-dependent selection was not found in house flies (37). Using mice, Yanai & McClearn showed that females determine mating preference (282). In some strains they prefer to mate with males of different strains (281), and early exposure to adult males may play a part (283). An interstrain comparison of sexual performance in pairings forming a "diallel" pattern showed male rats' success to be inversely related to success in the female (164), whereas in a study of mouse aggression using filial and backcrosses, restriction to pairing within generations only made interpretation difficult (264). In a true diallel cross of mouse sexual behavior, Vale & Ray (246) reduced the problem by pairing uniformly with only one of the strains. Models for dyadic social interaction measurment in psychogenetics have been discussed (237).

As we have seen, many of these quantitative studies make inferences from their results that bear on natural selection and evolutionary processes. It may be necessary to use behavior putatively related to fitness to substantiate such inferences (238, 270).

Study of the relevance of laboratory populations to wild populations is likely to be enhanced by biometric (85) and other (49, 177) techniques for investigating the genetic architecture and gene flow of the latter. Meanwhile, comparisons of wild and domesticated rodent species have been made (93, 199, 226), with some results suggesting that laboratory strains compare more favorably than previous reports have indicated (21, 22, 154, 200, 232).

HUMAN RESEARCH

Reviews

A comprehensive account edited by Kaplan (134), one on twins (172), and others on abnormal psychology (136, 224, 228) have appeared.

Normal Cognitive Abilities

General intelligence continues to receive most attention. Because early work in this area set high standards, many publications attempt reinterpretation and synthesis of already existing data. Burt (28), Jensen (126), and Vandenberg (253) have drawn extensively on earlier studies to conclude that differences in IQ in the populations surveyed are largely under genetic control: broad heritability was found to account for 70 to 80% of the variation, family environmental variation for about half that remaining, and random environment for the rest. Jinks & Fulker (131) reanalyzed data from five major studies using biometric methods (155) to investigate the genetic architecture of IQ. Distortions due to sampling and to both gene-environment correlations and interactions were judged absent; they therefore concluded that at least 22–100 genes controlled IQ, that narrow heritability was 71% (assortative mating accounting for 14% of this), and that dominance variation was 15%. The average level of dominance was 0.74 or more, dominance being for high IQ, and increaser and decreaser genes were found on the average to be equally frequent. A simple account of this analysis may be found elsewhere (86). Substantial dominance variation detected by three different methods tends to confirm Burt & Howard's earlier finding (see 88, p. 56), while its direction conforms to the expectation that components of IQ have been of adaptive advantage during evolution. The influence of assortative mating was expected since the IQs of spouses correlate more than any other human behavioral trait (254). However, its influence has been most strikingly demonstrated by Eaves (56), who used the Reeds' extensive pedigree data from five generations (see 150, p. 51) and showed that only genetic models incorporating assortative mating fitted the data successfully.

Additional evidence (127) supports a fairly simple genetic model: genotype-environment interaction and genetic threshold effects were found to be absent, and all three fundamental components—phenotypic, genotypic, and environmental—were found to be normally distributed.

Maternal effects may complicate any simple model: such effects, probably of intrauterine origin, are clearly indicated by the association between birth weight and IQ, recently confirmed for multiple births (201, 214). Willerman and associates (274) suggested postnatal maternal effects on the measured IQ of children of interracial marriage, but the results rest on weakly supported assumptions. A further study employing a similar approach with white subjects presented more convincing evidence (273). Children resembled their high- and low-scoring mothers more than their high- and low-scoring fathers. However, the failure of maternal effects to influence parent-offspring correlations differentially indicates their probably minor importance as a systematic source of variation.

Fascinating evidence is emerging concerning the developmental stability of a genetic component in intelligence. Wilson & Harpring (275, 276) report impressive results from administering the Bayley scales to 261 pairs of MZ and DZ twins at frequent intervals during their first 2 years. The profiles of the developmental lags and spurts, responsible for the typically low correlations at different ages, were very similar, especially for MZ twins. The figures suggest that heritable factors account for about half the variation in profile similarity and demonstrate that even the fine detail of some aspects of mental development as measured by the Bayley scale is under relatively tight genetic control. In a study of development of IQ from 3 to 12 years using sibling-sibling and parent-offspring correlations, the average level of intelligence also appeared highly heritable, but not the pattern of development (156). However, these methods must be less powerful than the use of MZ twins. The design has also been criticized on other grounds (262). At the other extreme of age, a continuing study of senescent twins suggested that the genetic component in IQ remains high well into the eighth decade of life (124). Unfortunately, numbers were insufficient to warrant profile analysis.

A large genetic component in IQ variation extending over a wide age range may have important consequences for human population structure. One possible consequence is that natural selection may be acting on IQ through differential fertility. Previous studies (see 157, p. 458) and a later follow-up (261) suggest that selection differentials are positive, tending to increase IQ. Selection may not be acting uniformly throughout the full range of IQ (60, 76), however, and the possibility of dysgenic trends in some subpopulations should be noted (130). However, since there is good reason to believe, on both general evolutionary grounds and recent evidence (122), that the narrow heritability of fertility is low in some populations, there may be no long-term effects, whatever the size of the heritability of IQ and its correlation with family size.

Another consequence of a large genetic component in IQ is its possible influence on class structure and mobility (58, 242). Differences in IQ between father and son correlate +.37 with differences in social position (260). Partial and multiple correlations were used to unravel the interrelated factors of educational level, social class, and IQ. Eckland (59) sees these intergenerational consequences of IQ as most important.

Yet a third possible consequence is that genetic endowment might explain part of the 15 points average difference in measured IQ between white and black Americans. This claim by Jensen (125) provoked more debate than any other psychogenetic issue of our times; timely press releases by the journal's editorial staff ensured an instant controversy. Jensen's is a thorough account of the genetics of IQ and scholastic achievement which he related to the results of compensatory education. These, he claimed, were inconsistent with existing environmental explanations. The paper was soon reprinted (126) with invited criticism and a reply (104, see also 105). A fascinating blow-by-blow account of the original publication and its early aftermath can be found in *Genetics and Education* (129), which again reprints the article together with others and bibliographies relevant to the debate. Jensen's considered reply (130) argues that no plausible combination of environmental factors known to influence IQ, and which differentiate blacks from whites, seems capable of producing a mean difference as large as 15 points. He finds most consistent with the evidence the hypothesis that from one half to three quarters of the difference is attributable to genetic factors. While he convincingly demolishes most current environmentalist explanations, we may be simply suffering from a dearth of good research into environmental variables. None so far for which there is evidence available is deemed adequate, but that is a far cry from proving that none exist. Moreover, we rely on a weak form of proof when we rely on the mere consistency of a genetic model with the data. Whereas the model for IQ based on white populations has been thoroughly tested, such is not the case here. We must avoid what Willerman (272) in a book review (73) calls "premature closure" (216). Diverse views on race and IQ may be found in (29, 188, 203), but for balanced views in small compass, we recommend Thoday & Gibson (243) and Cavalli-Sforza (33).

The need for more research is seen by many; the question is, of what kind? A major difficulty is that inferences about the relative contribution of heredity and environment to differences between groups are not possible simply from a knowledge of their relative contributions within them. DeFries (48) has formulated the problem showing the unknown parameters involved. What other (less indirect) evidence could be gathered?

Fostering studies have been suggested (19, 272). Certainly they produce most convincing direct evidence for the relative importance of genetic and environmental influences within subpopulations. The problem is that fostered children must carry their color across populations, unlike the class origins of such children within populations. But comparisons involving very young foster children would have merit. The study of interracial marriages is a related approach (274).

A second direct method, which employs blood groups as a covert means of identifying the extent of mixtures of genes which typically differentiate blacks and whites, and correlates these differences with IQ, has been elaborated by Heston et al (see 130, p. 224). Using simpler methods, it was found (184) that such blood groups correlate with a measure of mental ability in blacks, though not in whites; a Monte Carlo simulation (185) showed that problems of statistical inference involved in stepwise multiple regression were responsible for the high correlation and new data failed to show the relationship. Loehlin, Vandenberg & Osborne (151a) reanalyzed the original data together with new, calculating separate correlations for black and white subjects between composite mental test scores and the presence of blood group genes. Rank correlation between these correlations themselves and the rank order of decreasing frequency among blacks of the 16 genes studied indicated no association between the extent of white ancestry and mental ability. Before concluding that there was no evidence for a genetic component in the black-white difference, they tested the efficiency of their method and found that genes in one blood group system, known to have relatively greater frequency in Europe, failed to predict the presence of genes of greater European frequency in other systems. They observed that genes that themselves are no longer associated cannot be expected to be associated with other genes affecting IQ. Larger samples might help, but the method does not look promising, especially in view of the very large overlap in the interracial frequencies.

A third direct line of research is to seek genotype-environment interactions to explain the difference. Scarr-Salapatek (215) carried out a twin study involving black and white children using aptitude and achievement tests. She compared heritabilities in the different races and social class combinations, and suggested that heritability was low in groups disadvantaged by either race or class, thus supporting the idea that disadvantaged children do not reach their full potential. While this may be true, her data cannot support the conclusion. Eaves & Jinks (57) showed that the study suffered from methodological weakness: the conclusions do not even suggest a genetic component within races, let alone any interaction with race or social class. Barker's rejoinder (12), insofar as can be judged, suggests that something may yet be salvaged! While Vandenberg (252) has reported a small twin study on black subjects' IQ, we clearly do not know enough to suggest genotype-environment interaction in black populations. Again the prospect is not promising, for Jensen (128) failed to find convincing interaction between race, class, and sex, and evidence from white populations suggests no genotype-environment interactions for IQ (127, 131).

Turning from general intelligence to other congitive abilities, available evidence on school achievement (104, 130) implies that genetic components account for only about 40% of variation, half that for IQ. This is partly because common family environment accounts for some 50% compared to about 10% for IQ. Such differences could explain why compensatory education affects attainment more than IQ.

Does sex-linkage underlie observed sex differences (99) in many special cognitive abilities (144)? Polygenic sex-linkage is indicated by parent-offspring and sibling correlations, the pattern depending on sex of parent and of offspring, as originally worked out by Mather & Jinks (see 155, p. 291). Stafford, who reported this pattern for spatial ability (see 161, p. 526), found a similar pattern for mathematical ability and suggested a major recessive gene (236). Further data relating to spatial abilities have been reported (103), and Bock & Kolakowski (17) demonstrated a possible single recessive sex-linked gene operating against a background of environmental and autosomal variation. Combining a variety of spatial test items to score 727 boys and girls on a normal ogive model of the test, they decomposed the distributions of scores for each sex separately into the two equal-variance normal distributions best fitting the data, equal variation being expected once allowance has been made for the effect of the major gene. They showed that their model strikingly fitted the data and applied equally well to parent-offspring correlations from their own and previous studies. Finally they noted that such a recessive gene might be more associated with fitness (rather than the more usual expectation of dominance), if natural selection acted primarily through the male. Evidence suggesting an autosomal linkage between a major gene for verbal ability and blood-group genes depends on the greater within-pair variance found for DZ twins discordant for blood groups (18).

Other investigated phenotypes of interest include musical ability, which showed (235) genotype × instruction interaction; number estimation (101); and laterality

(146), for which a model postulating one locus for cerebral dominance and one for relative hand control was shown to fit a variety of data (178a). Cultural and genetic factors could not be distinguished (140) for sensitivity to flickering light in part of a study of racial differences in Hawaii (40).

Mental Retardation

Given a large genetic component in cognitive abilities, it follows that much retardation, other than extreme forms attributable to major genes or traumata, will result from normal polygenic segregation. Thus, using a narrow heritability of 70% for IQ and allowing for assortative mating, it has been shown (86) that a polygenic model predicts within 1% the frequency of subnormality from subnormal matings in the Reeds' data. Combining the two approaches, Berman & Ford (15) predicted phenylketonurics' IQ from those of their parents and siblings. Discrepancies were related to phenylalanine levels in the blood. The complexity of genotype-environment interaction in this area is illustrated by a study which manipulated these levels by dietary regimens to find the optimal effect on IQ amelioration (92).

Among other factors of possible methodological importance in the genetics of subnormality are sex-linkage and inherited maternal effects, already mentioned as additional complications of the polygenic model of normal variation. Lehrke (144) proposed that sex-linkage for several cognitive abilities might explain the greater variability of males, resulting in their greater contribution to the retarded as well as to the gifted. His arguments have been criticized mainly on statistical grounds (see 145), but the possibility remains. Maternal effects, probably mediated via inherited intrauterine inadequacy, were detected by Ahern & Johnson (5) in the Reeds' data on IQ. Probably the best evidence for directional dominance for high IQ has come from Schull & Neel (see 150, p. 45), who, in their continued study of inbreeding in Japan (218), have shown effects of parental consanguinity on IQ and achievement (179), which, while nonsignificant, reproduced those previously found. Retardation should thus result from severe inbreeding. Seemanova (220) writing on incest among first-degree relatives, who have a very high inbreeding coefficient (¼), described an impressive series of 161 such relatives plus 95 half-sibling controls. Among the former, 40 showed moderate to severe retardation; among the latter, none.

Kessler & Moos, reviewing chromosomal abnormalities (137), concluded that, with the possible exception of space-form deficit in Turner's (XO) syndrome, such abnormalities are only associated with a general retardation, as in Down's syndrome (10). Concerning major-gene effects, for those who curled up with McKusick after the last annual review, the third edition is a must (163).

Normal Personality

It is well established that most aspects of personality are at least under some genetic control. Eysenck (74), Vandenberg (255), and Shields (224) have reviewed the area.

A methodologically elegant study is that reported by Hill & Hill (115, 116). It involved 97 married couples who had been tested with the Minnesota Multiphasic

Personality Inventory at school, thus ensuring no postmarriage biases. Twenty-eight of their children were then tested at the same age their parents had been, thus ensuring no age bias. Despite these small numbers, the results were judged free of common artifacts. Positive assortative mating was indicated for three psychoticism scales. A cross-correlation matrix yielded intriguing relationships such as the correlation (+0.3, on the average) of depression in wives with psychoticism in husbands, whereas the reciprocal correlations were essentially zero. Parent-offspring correlations for psychoticism scales, together with those for mania, showed greatest narrow heritability when corrected for assortative mating, as this design allows.

The multivariate methods developed by Vandenberg and collaborators (see 150, p. 50) in the cognitive domain have been adapted by Eaves (55) to analyze genetic and environmental covariance among MZ twins tested on Eysenck's PEN questionnaire. The structure of the within-pair matrix, assessed using principal components, indicated environmental covariance structure. Genetic covariance was also investigated using a kind of canonical analysis. He concluded that environmental influences determined variation in neuroticism and introversion-extraversion in a unitary manner, but several genetic variables determined psychoticism. A well-defined genotypic factor also emerged for neuroticism, but not for introversion-extraversion. Another study employing a dimensional approach has been reported (41).

The co-twin control method allows a control for genotype to permit a more accurate assessment of environmental influences. Developmental studies have used this method to relate personality differences to possible causal influences (8, 42). Babies better endowed became more secure and trusting infants and better coping, assertive toddlers. Wilson et al (277) found MZ twins were more alike than DZ twins in temper frequency, demands for attention, and crying; this difference between MZ and DZ twins was larger among babies than at later ages up to 6 years. Some of these findings were related to motor performance (276). Van den Daele (46) reported evidence of a genetically controlled regulation of infant responses to rocking and soothing sound; hypnotic susceptibility may be controlled similarly (174). In an extensive and massive series of twin studies in Sweden by Cederlöf and co-workers (see 35, 36), which previously attracted little attention, research is now focused (82) on twins discordant for mortality but concordant for smoking. Present evidence implicates factors other than smoking, such as accidents and suicide, in the greater morbidity found among smokers. Another co-twin control study (149) related dissatisfaction with life to incidence of heart disease.

In a small twin study of sexual behavior, Chilton (39) produced evidence that the age at which masturbation, orgasm, and other sexual activity began is heritable. Difficulties inherent in research into sexuality are apparent, but the study points to an important, neglected area.

Abnormal Personality

Some progress is being made in our understanding of schizophrenia, affective disorders, alcoholism, and the XYY syndrome; discussion here will be restricted to these topics. Two major books have appeared on schizophrenia: Kaplan's work (133) brings together some 30 contributors on a variety of topics related to the genetics of schizophrenia, and Gottesman & Shields' study (96) is based on the Maudsley twin sample. Meehl's afterword (167) appraises this as a "definitive work, a magnum opus, a beautiful book indeed." It is also a gold mine, since it provides case histroies and diagnoses of all 24 MZ and 33 DZ twin pairs originally identified through an index case. These diagnoses were investigated in a cross-national study (225). Six diagnosticians, differing widely in their training and outlook, not surprisingly produced different concordance rates. But consensus diagnosis maximized the heritability, restoring some faith in the diagnosis of schizophrenia. Psychometric implications have been discussed (96, 132, 167). While concordance rates for MZ and DZ twins have been falling recently, perhaps due to better sampling procedures (see 150, p. 64), consensus diagnosis restores concordance values to the region of 46% for MZ and 14% for DZ (97), much closer to those in the older studies. Allen et al (7) also found more searching diagnostic methods increased concordance rates.

New data from Iceland (135), based on public records, gave typically low concordance rates for many kinds of relatives (but not twins), and preliminary findings (13), have suggested that among children of two psychotic parents, the incidence of psychosis is about half that previously suggested. Inouye's data on MZ twins separated before the age of 5 years (123) yield the same incidence as that for twins reared together, suggesting that between family environmental influences are small in determining schizophrenia (see 150, p. 63), but Kety, Rosenthal & Wender and co-workers (138, 208) confirmed earlier findings (see 38, p. 386) that incidence of broad-spectrum schizophrenia among adopted children of schizophrenic parents was as high as that among home-reared children, though the incidence of severe cases was much less. Perhaps severity is modified by home environment while disposition is not. The same research program produced evidence (263) that it is the downward social mobility of schizophrenics rather than prevailing cultural influences, that produces the high incidence in low socioeconomic groups.

Fischer (79) used an ingenious design to investigate the importance of home environment to children of parents themselves MZ twins discordant for schizophrenia. The age-corrected risk for children of schizophrenic parents (9.5%) is not significantly different from the nonschizophrenic (12.3%), suggesting no obvious parental effects. However, the nonschizophrenic parents could hardly be regarded as a normal control group.

Attempts to fit genetic models to data on concordance rates continue (see 150, p. 65). But recent attention has been directed to threshold models of liability developed by Falconer (75) and others (61, 231) and used by Gottesman & Sheilds (see 157, p. 439), who later point out the difficulty of distinguishing a one-gene from a polygenic threshold model (97). Kidd & Cavalli-Sforza (139) encountered the same difficulty, not surprisingly, since the polygenic model includes the case of a single gene as an approximate special case. However, Reich et al's method (202) of multiple thresholds based on different degrees of severity should resolve the issue, provided that reliable population base rates for each threshold can be obtained, since this method has effectively distinguished between one-gene and polygenic models of animal phenotypes. Fulker (86) assessed gene action for liability, using a simple biometric extension of the threshold model, and detected additive variation but little or no variation due to dominance or between-family environment.

As others have pointed out (e.g. 150, p. 64), environmental factors in schizophrenia must be very important, since MZ discordance is about 50%. But the absence of a strong between-family environmental effect and the marked discordance point to physiological differences, possibly arising early in life. Mednick's prospective study (165, 166) of children at risk is one investigating this possibility. A distinctive premorbid condition is found in those adolescents who have suffered breakdowns, with birth anoxia implicated.

In a study of discordant twins (234), biochemical variables have recently received most attention. Interpretation was complicated by long-standing drug treatments, but the lactate-pyruvic ratio involved in brain oxygen metabolism differed within discordant pairs. Pollin (196) discussed evidence bearing on his suggestion that catecholamine levels may be important in a physiological predisposition to schizophrenia. From the same major study, another possible predisposing marker in discordant pairs was reported (280) in the form of reduced platelet monoamine oxidase activity. Findings from a new, prospective high-risk study by Anthony (9) delineate five premorbid syndromes.

Interest in population aspects of schizophrenia continues. Moran (173) discussed the role of heterozygote advantage and mutation in maintaining a high level of schizophrenia in the population. Lane (142) discussed the possibility that fertility may be even greater than previously supposed, especially among female schizophrenics.

Research on affective psychoses continues to be dominated by Perris's (see 38, p. 388) suggestion that unipolar (depression only) and bipolar (depression with mania) disorders are under two distinct forms of genetic control. Winokur (278) showed that when only bipolar cases were considered, evidence of a dominant sex-linked gene was striking, a father-son concordance of zero completing the expected familial pattern exactly. Mendlewicz et al (168) associated bipolar depression with color blindness in the pedigrees of seven families, again suggesting sex-linkage, but unipolar depression (11) more clearly followed a polygenic pattern of inheritance, since the disorder occurred with equal frequency in male and female lines. Perris, who originally favored a dominant sex-linked model for the unipolar disorder, now favors polygenic inheritance for both (193), as do Slater et al (229); thus Winokur's findings supporting sex-linkage for the bipolar disorder are atypical. Some bipolar fathers have bipolar sons which cannot happen with sex-linkage alone. Evidence of either heterogeneity of gentic control or a threshold mechanism for both bi- and unipolar depression has been presented (169, 197).

Questionnaire studies have established a genetic component in alcohol use (151, 190), but Schuckit et al (217) have presented the first clear evidence of a genetic factor in its abuse. Half-siblings were used together with objective criteria of alcoholism and other psychiatric disturbances were avoided. The frequency of alcoholism in half-sibs with an alcoholic parent who lived with the child was 46%, compared with 50% if they did not. When there was no alcoholic parentage, but the child was reared with an alcoholic step-father or mother, the figure was 14% compared with 8% where the step parent was not alcoholic. The appropriate comparisons clearly indicate that genetic factors are important and that the mere presence of an alcoholic in the home unimportant. Good evidence of assortative mating for alcoholism and associated psychiatric disorders has been found (205).

The effects of sex chromosome aberrations on personality continue to be discussed (see 38, p. 394; 137), but most attention is focused on the XYY syndrome and its possible link with aggressive and criminal behavior. Two excellent reviews (117, 186) summarize and evaluate available data, the latter review covering a wealth of material on physical and developmental abnormalities. The controversy concerning the high frequency of XYY individuals in mental and penal institutions is far from resolved. Owen concluded that rates in the majority of either mental hospitals or prisons are no higher than reliable population rates. But Hook found that for institutions of a kind reserved for the criminally insane, rates are from 5 to 20 times higher than those in the general population. This discrepancy is partly due to the different population rates used and partly to Hook's rejection of lower rates in samples previously screened for abnormal height, but mainly to the different institutions selected for comparison. Some association between XYY and such special institutionalization remains a distinct possibility, although Hook suggests the risk is slight. Moreover, both reviews, in line with Kessler & Moos' earlier review of this area (see 150, p. 68), failed to reveal any consistent association with personality and behavior. Hook plans a study of 11,000 young males whose sex chromosome compositions are to be ascertained at birth.

Methodology

This final section will review briefly some methodological developments. Three texts on statistical genetics are noteworthy in this connection (34, 45, 155), and some work already discussed will be cited again.

The study of twins will continue to form an important part of most research designs. Their uses and limitations have been ably described by Vandenberg (255), who also has provided new evidence on intrapair attitudes. Bulmer's (27) excellent book is indispensable to understanding the biology of twinning.

A general approach to partitioning variation in individual differences in behavior has, it is argued (131), certain advantages over others. Assumptions are tested and components of the model used are estimated with simple but efficient methods. Components can then be validly used to explore genetic control, using conventional methods of biometric genetics. The approach is flexible and can be extended to the multivariate case (54). Eaves has also discussed the requirements of genetic design in terms of the relationships–twins, siblings, and other family constellations–involved (51, 52) and the sample sizes needed (53) if significant results are to be expected. Morton (175) described a number of powerful biometric methods applicable to psychogenetic problems and noted that forms of multiple regression are the obvious ways to identify behavioral patterns associated with single genes. With many genes and many sets of behavioral phenotypes, the natural extention is generalized canonical correlation, for which satisfactory methods now exist (31).

Haseman & Elston (106) have described a powerful method for detecting linkage between a major marker gene and either major-gene or polygenic variation by using siblings and regressing the square of the sib difference onto the estimated likelihood of carrying the marker. Pakstis et al (189) used this method to detect linkage between activity measures in children and blood-group markers. Elston & Stewart (65) extended the model to cover more complex genetic situations in which extensive pedigree data are available (see also 176). The threshold models (231) which have been used in schizophrenia research may be extended to the biometric analysis of polygenic inheritance (86) or treated as special cases of complex segregation analysis (175). In the latter case the multiple threshold model of Reich et al (202) should help distinguish single-gene from polygenic models and thus resolve the protracted debate about the genetic determination of schizophrenia.

Morton (175) is skeptical about genetic analysis where genetic and environmental influences are correlated, whereas Cattell developed MAVA, multiple abstract variance analysis, for just such situations (see 88, p. 55). However, it seems likely that certain limited models may be possible (131, 170). Cattell's (32) major recent contribution has been a heroic extension of MAVA attempting to separate the genetic and environmental effects of both maturation and learning. To accomplish this would require employing MAVA to partition both independent and dependent variables within a number of subpopulations. Correlating appropriate pairs of components across such subsets would lead to a regression equation for estimating genetic and environmental scores for individual subjects, which could then be examined for the effects of maturation and learning.

The opportunity to test more complex and specific genetic hypotheses is now within reach. Methodology is now well worked out and theory is far ahead of experimental endeavor. We foresee a period of concentration on gathering empirical data which can then be consolidated into a comprehensive structure of knowledge.

We cannot conclude this review without mentioning Darlington's book (47), which, in the opinion of at least one of us, may prove to have been the most important citation of all.

Literature Cited

1. Abeelen, J. H. F. van, Kalkhoven, J. T. R. 1970. Behavioural ontogeny of the Nijmegen waltzer, a neurological mutant in the mouse. *Anim. Behav.* 18: 711–18
2. Abeelen, J. H. F. van, Kroon, P. H. W. van der, Bekkers, M. F. J. 1973. Mice selected for rearing behavior: some physiological variables. *Behav. Genet.* 3:85–90
3. Abeelen, J. H. F. van, Smits, A. J. M., Raaijmakers, W. G. M. 1971. Central location of a genotype-dependent cholinergic mechanism controlling exploratory behaviour in mice. *Psychopharmacologia* 19:324–28
4. Abeelen, J. H. F. van, Gilissen, L., Hanssen, T., Lenders, A. 1972. Effects of intrahippocampal injections with methylscopolamine and neostigmine upon exploratory behaviour in two inbred mouse strains. *Psychopharmacologia* 24:470–75
5. Ahern, F. M., Johnson, R. C. 1973. Inherited uterine inadequacy: An alternate explanation for a portion of cases of defect. *Behav. Genet.* 3:1–12
6. Ahtee, L., Eriksson, K. 1972. 5-hydroxytryptamine and 5-hydroxyindolylacetic acid content in brain of rat strains selected for their alcohol intake. *Physiol. Behav.* 8:123–26
7. Allen, M. G., Cohen, S., Pollin, W. 1972. Schizophrenia in veteran twins: A diagnostic review. *Am. J. Psychiat.* 128:939–45
8. Allen, M. G., Pollin, W., Hoffer, A. 1971. Parental, birth, and infancy factors in infant twin development. *Am. J. Psychiat.* 127:1597–1603
9. Anthony, E. J. 1972. A clinical and experimental study of high-risk children

and their schizophrenic parents. In *Genetic Factors in "Schizophrenia,"* ed. A. R. Kaplan, 380–406. Springfield, Ill.: Thomas. 698 pp.
10. Apgar, V., Ed. 1970. Down's syndrome (Mongolism). *Ann. NY Acad. Sci.* 171:303–688
11. Baker, M., Dorzab, J., Winokur, G., Cadoret, R. 1972. Depressive disease: evidence favoring polygenic inheritance based on an analysis of ancestral cases. *Arch. Gen. Psychiat.* 27:320–29
12. Barker, W. F. 1973. *The Relationship between Sample Size, Power and Heritability Estimates.* Presented at 3rd Ann. Meet. Behav. Genet. Assoc., Chapel Hill, N. Carolina
13. Bastiansen, S., Kringlen, E. 1972. Children of two psychotic parents: a preliminary report. *Proc. 4th Int. Symp. Psychother. Schizophrenia, Turku, Finland, 1971.* Amsterdam: Excerpta Med.
14. Bell, R. W., Nitschke, W., Zachman, T. A. 1972. Ultra-sounds in three inbred strains of young mice. *Behav. Biol.* 7: 805–14
15. Berman, J. L., Ford, R. 1970. Intelligence quotients and intelligence loss in patients with phenylketonuria and some variant states. *J. Pediat.* 77:764–69
16. Blizard, D. A., Chai, C. K. 1972. Behavioral studies in mice selectively bred for differences in thyroid function. *Behav. Genet.* 2:301–9
17. Bock, R. D., Kolakowski, D. 1973. Further evidence of sex-linked major-gene influence on human spatial visualizing ability. *Am. J. Hum. Genet.* 25:1–14
18. Bock, R. D., Vandenberg, S. G., Bramble, W., Pearson, W. 1970. A behavioral correlate of blood-group discordance in dizygotic twins. *Behav. Genet.* 1:89–98
19. Bodmer, W. F. 1972. Race and I.Q.: the genetic background. In *Race, Culture and Intelligence,* ed. K. Richardon, D. Spears, M. Richards, 83–113. Harmondsworth, Middlesex: Penguin. 205 pp.
20. Boggan, W. O., Freedman, D. X., Lovell, R. A., Schlesinger, K. 1971. Studies in audiogenic seizure susceptibility. *Psychopharmacologia* 20:48–56
21. Boice, R. 1972. Some behavioral tests of domestication in Norway rats. *Behaviour* 42:198–231
22. Boreman, J., Price, E. 1972. Social dominance in wild and domestic Norway rats (Rattus norvegicus). *Anim. Behav.* 20:534–42
23. Bovet, D., Bovet-Nitti, F., Oliverio, A. 1972. Gene action and behavior of C3H and DBA mice: a reply to Wilcock and Thiessen. *Psychol. Bull.* 78:351–52
24. Broadhurst, P. L., Jinks, J. L. 1966. Stability and change in the inheritance of behaviour in rats: a further analysis of statistics from a diallel cross. *Proc. Roy. Soc. London* 165:450–72
25. Broadhurst, P. L., Jinks, J. L. 1974. Psychological genetics, from the study of animal behavior. In *Handbook of Modern Personality Theory,* ed. R. B. Cattell, R. M. Dreger. New York: Appleton-Century-Crofts
26. Brush, F. R., Sakellaris, P. C. 1973. *Bidirectional Genetic Selection for Shuttlebox Avoidance Learning in the Rat.* See Ref. 12
27. Bulmer, M. G. 1970. *The Biology of Twinning in Man.* Oxford: Clarendon. 205 pp.
28. Burt, C. 1972. Inheritance of general intelligence. *Am. Psychol.* 27:175–90
29. Cancro, R., Ed. 1971. *Intelligence: Genetic and Environmental Influences.* New York: Grune and Stratton. 312 pp.
30. Carran, A. B. 1972. Biometrics of reversal learning in mice: II. Diallel cross. *J. Comp. Physiol. Psychol.* 78:466–70
31. Carroll, J. D. 1968. Generalization of canonical correlation analysis to three or more sets of variables. *Proc. 76th Ann. Conv. APA,* 227-28
32. Cattell, R. B. 1973. Unraveling maturational and learning developments by the Comparative MAVA and structural learning approaches. In *Life-Span Developmental Psychology: Methodological Issues,* ed. J. R. Nesselroade, H. W. Reese. New York: Academic. In press
33. Cavalli-Sforza, L. L. 1970. Problems and prospects of genetic analysis of intelligence at the intra- and inter-racial level. In *Disadvantaged Child, Vol. 3. Compensatory Education: A National Debate,* ed. J. Hellmuth, 111-23. New York:Brunner Mazel. 460 pp.
34. Cavalli-Sforza, L. L., Bodmer, W. F. 1971. *The Genetics of Human Populations.* San Franscisco: Freeman. 965 pp.
35. Cederlöf, R. 1966. Urban factor and prevalence of respiratory symptoms and "angina pectoris": a study on 9,168 twin pairs with the aid of mailed questionnaires. *Arch. Environ. Health* 13: 743–48
36. Cederlöf, R., Friberg, L., Jonsson, E., Kaij, L. 1961. Studies on similarity diagnosis in twins with the aid of mailed questionnaires. *Acta Genet.* 11:338–62
37. Childress, D., McDonald, I. C. 1973. Test for frequency-dependent mating success in the house fly. *Behav. Genet.* 3:217–24

38. Childs, B. 1972. Genetic analysis of human behavior. *Ann. Rev. Med.* 23:373–406
39. Chilton, B. 1972. Psychosexual development in twins. *J. Biosoc. Sci.* 4: 277–86
40. Chung, C. S., Morton, N. E., Yasuda, N. 1966. Genetics of interracial crosses. *Ann. NY Acad. Sci.* 134: 666–87
41. Claridge, G., Canter, S., Hume, W. I. 1973. *Personality Differences and Biological Variations: A study of twins.* Oxford: Pergamon. 175 pp.
42. Cohen, D. J. et al 1972. Personality development in twins: competence in the newborn and preschool periods. *J. Am. Acad. Child Psychiat.* 11:625–44
43. Collins, R. L. 1970. A new genetic locus mapped from behavioral variation in mice: audiogenic seizure prone (ASF). *Behav. Genet.* 1:99–109
44. Connor, J. L., Winston, H. 1972. Genetic analysis of conditioned emotional responses in the mouse *(Mus musculus L). J. Comp. Physiol. Psychol.* 81: 37–44
45. Crow, J. F., Kimura, M. 1970. *An Introduction to Population Genetics Theory.* New York: Harper & Row. 591 pp.
46. Daele, L. D. van den 1971. Infant reactivity to redundant propioceptive and auditory stimulation: a twin study. *J. Psychol.* 78:269–76
47. Darlington, C. D. 1969. *The Evolution of Man and Society.* London: Allen & Unwin. 753 pp.
48. DeFries, J. C. 1972. Quantitative aspects of genetics and environment in the determination of behavior. In *Genetics, Environment and Behavior. Implications for Educational Policy,* ed. L. Ehrmann, G. S. Omenn, E. Caspari, 5–16. New York: Academic. 324 pp.
49. DeFries, J. C., McClearn, G. E. 1970. Social dominance and Darwinian fitness in the laboratory mouse. *Am. Natur.* 104:408–11
50. DeFries, J. C., Wilson, J. R., McClearn, G. E. 1970. Open-field behavior in mice: selection response and situational generality. *Behav. Genet.* 1:195–211
51. Eaves, L. J. 1969. The genetic analysis of continuous variation: a comparison of experimental designs applicable to human data. *Brit. J. Math. Statist. Psychol.* 22:131–47
52. Ibid 1970. The genetic analysis of continuous variation: a comparison of experimental designs applicable to human data. II. Estimation of heritability and comparison of environmental components. 23:189–98
53. Eaves, L. J. 1972. Computer simulation of sample size and experimental design in human psychogenetics. *Psychol. Bull.* 77:144–52
54. Eaves, L. J. 1972. The multivariate analysis of certain genotype-environment interactions. *Behav. Genet.* 2: 241–44
55. Eaves, L. J. 1973. The structure of genotypic and environmental covariation for personality measurements: an analysis of the PEN. *Brit. J. Soc. Clin. Psychol.* 12:275–82
56. Eaves, L. J. 1973. Assortative mating and intelligence: an analysis of pedigree data. *Heredity* 30:199–210
57. Eaves, L. J., Jinks, J. L. 1972. Insignificance of evidence for differences in heritability of IQ between races and social classes. *Nature* 240:84–88
58. Eckland, B. K. 1971. Social class structure and the genetic basis of intelligence. See Ref. 29, 65–76
59. Eckland, B. K. 1972. Comments on school effects, gene-environment covariance and the heritability of intelligence. See Ref. 48, 297–306
60. Eckland, B. K. 1972. Trends in the intensity and direction of natural selection. *Soc. Biol.* 19:215–23
61. Edwards, J. H. 1969. Familial predisposition in man. *Brit. Med. Bull.* 25:58–64
62. Egan, O., Royce, J. R. 1973. Litter size and emotionality in two strains of mice. *J. Comp. Physiol. Psychol.* 82:55–59
63. Ehrmann, L. 1972. A factor influencing the rare male mating advantage in *Drosophila. Behav. Genet.* 2:69–78
64. Ibid. Rare male advantages and sexual isolation in *Drosophila immigrans,* 79–84
65. Elston, R. C., Stewart, J. 1971. A general model for the genetic analysis of pedigree data. *Hum. Hered.* 21:523–42
66. Eriksson, K. 1971. Inheritance of behaviour towards alcohol in normal and motivated choice situations in mice. *Ann. Zool. Fennici* 8:400–5
67. Eriksson, K. 1971. Rat strains specially selected for their voluntary alcohol consumption. *Ann. Med. Exp. Biol. Fenn.* 49:67–72
68. Eriksson, K. 1972. Alcohol consumption and blood alcohol in rat strains selected for their behavior towards alcohol. See Ref. 80, 121–25
69. Eriksson, K. 1972. Behavioral and physiological differences among rat strains specially selected for their alcohol consumption. *Ann. NY Acad. Sci.* 197:32–41

70. Eriksson, K., Kiianmaa, K. 1971. Genetic analysis of susceptibility to morphine addiction in inbred mice. *Ann. Med. Exp. Biol. Fenn.* 49:73–78
71. Eriksson, K., Pikkarainen, P. H. 1968. Differences between the sexes in voluntary alcohol consumption and liver ADH-activity in inbred strains of mice. *Metabolism* 17:1037–42
72. Erlenmeyer-Kimling, L. 1972. Gene-environment interactions and the variability of behavior. See Ref. 48, 181–208
73. Eysenck, H. J. 1971. *The IQ Argument, Race, Intelligence and Education.* New York: Library Press. 156 pp.
74. Eysenck, H. J. 1974. Genetic factors in personality development. In *Human Behavior Genetics,* ed. A. R. Kaplan. Springfield, Ill.: Thomas. In press
75. Falconer, D. S. 1967. The inheritance of liability to diseases with variable age of onset, with particular reference to diabetes mellitus. *Ann. Hum. Genet.* 31: 1–20
76. Falek, A. 1971. Differential fertility and intelligence: current status of the problem. *Soc. Biol.* 18:S50–S59
77. Festing, M. F. W. 1973. Water escape learning in mice I. Strain differences and biometrical considerations. *Behav. Genet.* 3:13–24
78. Ibid. Water escape learning in mice II. Replicated selection for increased learning speed, 25–36
79. Fischer, M. 1971. Psychoses in the offspring of schizophrenic monozygotic twins and their normal co-twins. *Brit. J. Psychiat.* 118:43–52
80. Forsander, O., Eriksson, K., Eds. 1972. *Biological Aspects of Alcohol Consumption. International Symposium 1971,* Helsinki. Finnish Found. Alcohol Stud. No. 20. 293 pp.
81. Forsander, O. A., Eriksson, C. J. P. 1972. Metabolic characteristics of rat strains consuming different amounts of alcohol. See Ref. 80, 43–49
82. Friberg, L., Cederlöf, R., Lundman, T., Olsson, H. 1970. Mortality in smoking discordant monozygotic and dizygotic twins: a study on the Swedish twin registry. *Arch. Environ. Health* 21:508–13
83. Friedmann, J. K. 1973. A diallel analysis of the genetic underpinnings of mouse sleep. *Physiol. Behav.* In press
84. Fulker, D. W. 1970. Maternal buffering of rodent genotypic responses to stress: a complex genotype-environment interaction. *Behav. Genet.* 1: 119–24
85. Ibid 1972. Applications of a simplified triple-test cross. 2:185–98
86. Fulker, D. W. 1973. A biometrical genetic approach to intelligence and schizophrenia. *Soc. Biol.* 20:266–75
87. Fulker, D. W., Wilcock, J., Broadhurst, P. L. 1972. Studies in genotype-environment interaction. I. Methodology and preliminary multivariate analysis of a diallel cross of eight strains of rat. *Behav. Genet.* 2:261–87
88. Fuller, J. L. 1960. Behavior genetics. *Ann. Rev. Psychol.* 11:41–70
89. Fuller, J. L. 1972. Genetic aspects of regulation of food intake. *Advan. Psychosom. Med.* 7:2–24
90. Fuller, J. L., Collins. R. L. 1970. Genetics of audiogenic seizures in mice: a parable for psychiatrists. *Sem. Psychiat.* 2:75–88
91. Fuller, J. L., Collins, R. L. 1972. Ethanol consumption and preference in mice: a genetic analysis. *Ann. NY Acad. Sci.* 197:42–48
92. Fuller, R., Shuman, J. 1971. Treated phenylketonuria: intelligence and blood phenylalanine levels. *Am. J. Ment. Defic.* 75:539–45
93. Galef, B. G. Jr., Clark, M. M. 1971. Social factors in the poison avoidance and feeding behavior of wild and domesticated rat pups. *J. Comp. Physiol. Psychol.* 75:341–57
94. Ginsburg, B. E. 1971. Developmental genetics of behavioral capacities: the nature-nurture problem re-evaluated. *Merrill-Palmer Quart. Behav. Develop.* 17:187–202
95. Goodrick, C. L. 1971. Direct observation and automated scoring of the activity of active and inactive inbred mouse strains. *Behav. Res. Methods Instrum.* 3:255–56
96. Gottesman, I. I., Shields, J. 1972. *Schizophrenia and Genetics: A Twin Study Vantage Point.* New York: Academic. 433 pp.
97. Gottesman, I. I., Shields, J. 1973. Genetic theorising and schizophrenia. *Brit. J. Psychiat.* 122:15–30
98. Graves, H. B., Siegel, P. B. 1969. Bidirectional selection for responses of *Gallus domesticus* chicks to an imprinting situation. *Anim. Behav.* 17:683–91
99. Gray, J. A., Drewett, R. F. 1974. The genetics and development of sex differences. See Ref. 25
100. Greenberg, G. 1972. The effects of ambient temperature and population density on aggression in two inbred strains of mice, *Mus musculus. Behaviour* 42: 119–30

101. Guttman, R. 1970. Parent-offspring correlations in the judgement of visual number. *Hum. Hered.* 20:57–65
102. Harrington, G. M. 1972. Strain differences in open-field behavior of the rat. *Psychon. Sci.* 27:51–53
103. Hartlage, L. C. 1970. Sex-linked inheritance of spatial ability. *Percept.. Mot. Skills* 31:610
104. Harvard Educ. Rev. 1969. *Environment, Heredity and Intelligence.* Reprint Ser. 2. 246 pp.
105. Harvard Educ. Rev. 1969. *Science, Heritability and I.Q.* Reprint Ser. 4. 97 pp.
106. Haseman, J. K., Elston, R. C. 1972. The investigation of linkage between a quantitative trait and a marker locus. *Behav. Genet.* 2:3–19
107. Hay, D. A. 1972. Genetical and maternal determinants of the activity and preening behaviour of *Drosophila melanogaster* reared in different environments. *Heredity* 28:311–36
108. Hay, D. A. 1972. Recognition by *Drosophila melanogaster* of individuals from other strains or cultures: support for the role of olfactory cues in selective mating? *Evolution* 26:171–76
109. Hay, D. A. 1973. Effects of genetic variation and culture conditions on the social behavior of *Drosophila melanogaster. Behav. Genet.* 3:107–19
110. Hegmann, J. P. 1972. Physiological function and behavioral genetics. I. Genetic variance for peripheral conduction velocity in mice. *Behav. Genet.* 2:55–67
111. Henderson, N. D. 1970. A genetic analysis of spontaneous alternation in mice. *Behav. Genet.* 1:125–32
112. Henderson, N. D. 1970. Brain weight increases resulting from environmental enrichment: a directional dominance in mice. *Science* 169:776–78
113. Henderson, N. D. 1970. Genetic influences on the behavior of mice can be obscured by laboratory rearing. *J. Comp. Physiol. Psychol.* 72:505–11
114. Ibid 1972. Relative effects of early rearing environment and genotype on discrimination learning in house mice. 79:243–53
115. Hill, M. S. 1973. Hereditary influence on the normal personality using the MMPI. II. Prospective assortative mating. *Behav. Genet.* 3:225–32
116. Hill, M. S., Hill, R. N. 1973. Hereditary influences on the normal personality using the MMPI. I. Age corrected parent-offspring resemblances. *Behav. Genet.* 3:133–44
117. Hook, E. B. 1973. Behavioral implications of the human XYY genotype. *Science* 179:139–50
118. Hotta, Y., Benzer, S. 1972. Mapping of behaviour in *Drosophila* mosaics. *Nature* 240:527–35
119. Hurnik, J. F., Bailey, E. D., Jerome, F. N. 1973. Selection for divergent lines of mice based on their performance in a T-maze. *Behav. Genet.* 3:45–55
120. Hyde, J. S. 1973. Genetic homeostasis and behavior: analysis, data, and theory. *Behav. Genet.* 3:233–46
121. Imada, H. 1972. Emotional reactivity and conditionability in four strains of rats. *J. Comp. Physiol. Psychol.* 79: 474–80
122. Imaizumi, Y., Nei, M., Furusho, T. 1970. Variability and heritability of human fertility. *Ann. Hum. Genet.* 33: 251–59
123. Inouye, E. 1972. Monozygotic twins with schizophrenia reared apart in infancy. *Jap. J. Hum. Genet.* 16:182–90
124. Jarvik, L. F., Blum, J. E., Varma, A. O. 1972. Genetic components and intellectual functioning during senescence: a 20-year study of aging twins. *Behav. Genet.* 2:159–71
125. Jensen, A. R. 1969. How much can we boost IQ and scholastic achievement? *Harvard Educ. Rev.* 39:1–123
126. Jensen, A. R. 1969. How much can we boost IQ and scholastic achievement? See Ref. 104, 1-123
127. Jensen, A. R. 1970. IQ's of identical twins reared apart. *Behav. Genet.* 1: 133–48
128. Jensen, A. R. 1971. The race X sex X ability interaction. See Ref. 29, 107–61
129. Jensen, A. R. 1972. *Genetics and Education.* London: Methuen. 379 pp.
130. Jensen, A. R. 1973. *Educability and Group Differences.* London: Methuen. 407 pp.
131. Jinks, J. L., Fulker, D. W. 1970. Comparison of the biometrical genetical, MAVA, and classical approaches to the analysis of human behavior. *Psychol. Bull.* 73:311–49
132. Jones, M. B. 1971. Heritability as a criterion in the construction of psychological tests. *Psychol. Bull.* 75:92–96
133. Kaplan, A. R., Ed. 1972. *Genetic Factors in "Schizophrenia."* Springfield, Ill.: Thomas. 698 pp.
134. Kaplan, A. R., Ed. 1974. *Human Behavior Genetics.* Springfield, Ill.: Thomas. In press
135. Karlsson, J. L. 1971. Rates of the schizophrenic genotype in relatives of psychotic persons. *Hereditas* 69:223–31

136. Kessler, S. 1974. Psychiatric genetics. In *American Handbook of Psychiatry,* ed. D. A. Hamburg, H. K. H. Brodie, 6, "New Psychiatric Frontiers." New York: Basic Books. 2nd ed. In press
137. Kessler, S., Moos, R. H. 1973. Behavioral aspects of chromosomal disorders. *Ann. Rev. Med.* 24:89–102
138. Kety, S. S., Rosenthal, D., Wender, P. H., Schulsinger, F. 1971. Mental illness in the biological and adoptive families of adopted schizophrenics. *Am. J. Psychiat.* 128:302–6
139. Kidd, K. K., Cavalli-Sforza, L. L. 1973. An analysis of the genetics of schizophrenia. *Soc. Biol.* 20:254–65
140. Klein, T. W., DeFries, J. C. 1973. Racial and cultural differences in sensitivity to flickering light. *Soc. Biol.* 20: In press
141. Lagerspetz, K. M. J., Lagerspetz, K. Y. H. 1971. Changes in the aggressiveness of mice resulting from selective breeding, learning and social isolation. *Scand. J. Psychol.* 12:241–48
142. Lane, E. 1971. Biasing factors affecting estimates of fertility rates of schizophrenics. *J. Psychol.* 78:49–63
143. Lee, C. T. 1973. Genetic analyses of nest-building behavior in laboratory mice *(Mus musculus). Behav. Genet.* 3:247–56
144. Lehrke, R. 1972. A theory of X-linkage of major intellectual traits. *Am. J. Ment. Defic.* 76:611–19
145. Ibid. Response to Dr. Anastasi and to the Drs. Nance and Engel, 626–31
146. Levy, J., Nagylaki, T. 1972. A model for the genetics of handedness. *Genetics* 72:117–28
148. Lieblich, I., Guttman, R., Naftali, G. 1973. Genotypic control of time-sample behavior patterns in mice. *Behav. Genet.* 3:257–62
149. Liljefors, I., Rahe, R. H. 1970. An identical twin study of psychosocial factors in coronary heart disease in Sweden. *Psychosom. Med.* 32:523–42
150. Lindzey, G., Loehlin, J., Manosevitz, M., Thiessen, D. 1971. Behavioral genetics. *Ann. Rev. Psychol.* 22:39–94
151. Loehlin, J. C. 1972. An analysis of alcohol-related questionnaire items from the National Merit twin study. *Ann. NY Acad. Sci.* 197:117–20
151a. Loehlin, J. C., Vandenberg, S. G., Osborne, R. T. 1973. Blood group genes and Negro-White ability differences. *Behav. Genet.* 3:263–70
152. Lynch, C. B., Hegmann, J. P. 1973. Genetic differences influencing behavioral temperature regulation in small mammals. II. Genotype-environment interactions. *Behav. Genet.* 3:145–54
153. Manning, A., Hirsch, J. 1971. The effects of artificial selection for slow mating in *Drosophila simulans.* II. Genetic analysis of the slow mating line. *Anim. Behav.* 19:448–53
154. Mason, J. J., Price, E. O. 1973. Escape conditioning in wild and domestic Norway rats. *J. Comp. Physiol. Psychol.* 84:403–7
155. Mather, K., Jinks J. L. 1971. *Biometrical Genetics: The Study of Continuous Variation.* London: Chapman & Hall. 2nd ed. 382 pp.
156. McCall, R. B. 1970. Intelligence quotient pattern over age: comparisons among siblings and parent-child pairs. *Science* 170:644–47
157. McClearn, G. E. 1970. Behavioral genetics. *Ann. Rev. Genet.* 4:437–68
158. McClearn, G. E. 1972. The genetics of alcohol preference. See Ref. 80, 113–19
159. McClearn, G. E. 1973. The genetic aspects of alcoholism. In *Alcoholism: Progress in Research and Treatment.* ed. P. Bourne, R. Fox, 337–58. New York: Academic. 452 pp.
160. McClearn, G. E., DeFries, J. C. 1973. Genetics and mouse aggression. In *The Control of Aggression: Implications from Basic Research,* ed. J. F. Knutson, 59–77. Chicago: Aldine. 310 pp.
161. McClearn, G. E., Meredith, W. 1966. Behavioral genetics. *Ann. Rev. Psychol.* 17:515–50
162. McCollom, R. E., Siegel, P. B., van Krey, H. P. 1971. Responses to androgen in lines of chickens selected for mating behavior. *Hormones & Behavior* 2:31–42
163. McKusick, V. A. 1971. *Mendelian Inheritance in Man.* Baltimore: Johns Hopkins Press. 3rd ed. 738 pp.
164. McLean, J. H., Dupeire, W. A. III, Elder, S. T. 1972. Strain differences in the mating behavior of Sprague-Dawley, Long-Evans, and Wistar male rats. *Psychon. Sci.* 29:175–76
165. Mednick, S. A. 1970. Breakdown in individuals at high risk for schizophrenia: possible predispositional perinatal factors. *Ment. Hyg.* 54:50–63
166. Mednick, S. A., Mura, E., Schulsinger, F., Mednick, B. 1971. Perinatal conditions and infant development in children with schizophrenic parents. *Soc. Biol.* 18:S103–13
167. Meehl, P. E. 1972. A critical afterword. See Ref. 96, 367–415
168. Mendlewicz, J., Fleiss, J. L., Fieve, R. R. 1972. Evidence for X-linkage in the

transmission of manic-depressive illness. *J. Am. Med. Assoc.* 222:1624–27
169. Mendlewicz, J., Fieve, R. R., Rainer, J. D., Fleiss, J. L. 1972. Manic-depressive illness: a comparative study of patients with and without a family history. *Brit. J. Psychiat.* 120:523–30
170. Meredith, W. 1973. A model for analyzing heritability in the presence of correlated genetic and environmental effects. *Behav. Genet.* 3:271–78
171. Messeri, P., Oliverio, A., Bovet, D. 1972. Relations between avoidance and activity: a diallel study in mice. *Behav. Biol.* 7:733–42
172. Mittler, P. 1971. *The Study of Twins.* Harmondsworth, Middlesex: Penguin. 192 pp.
173. Moran, P. A. P. 1972. Theoretical considerations on schizophrenia genetics. See Ref. 133, 294–309
174. Morgan, A. H., Hilgard, E. R., Davert, E. C. 1970. The heritability of hypnotic susceptibility of twins: a preliminary report. *Behav. Genet.* 1:213–24
175. Morton, N. E. 1972. Human behavioral genetics. See Ref. 48, 247–65
176. Morton, N. E., Yee, S., Lew, R. 1971. Complex segregation analysis. *Am. J. Hum. Genet.* 23:602–11
177. Myers, J. H., Krebs, C. J. 1971. Genetic, behavioral, and reproductive attributes of dispersing field voles *Microtus pennsylvanicus* and *Microtus ochrogaster. Ecol. Monogr.* 41:53–78
178. Nachman, M., Larue, C., Le Magnen, J. 1971. The role of olfactory and orosensory factors in the alcohol preference of inbred strains of mice. *Physiol. Behav.* 6:53–59
178a. Nagylaki, T., Levy, J. 1973. "The sound of one paw clapping" isn't sound. *Behav. Genet.* 3:279–92
179. Neel, J. V. et al 1970. The effects of parental consanguinity and inbreeding in Hirado, Japan. II. Physical development, tapping rate, blood pressure, intelligence quotient, and school performance. *Am. J. Hum. Genet.* 22: 263–86
180. Nitschke, W., Bell, R. W., Zachman, T. 1972. Distress vocalizations of young in three inbred strains of mice. *Develop. Psychobiol.* 5:363–70
181. Oliverio, A. 1971. Genetic variations and heritability in a measure of avoidance learning in mice. *J. Comp. Physiol. Psychol.* 74:390–97
182. Oliverio, A., Castellano, C., Messeri, P. 1972. Genetic analysis of avoidance, maze, and wheel-running behaviors in the mouse. *J. Comp. Physiol. Psychol.* 79:459–73
183. Oortmerssen, G. A. van 1971. Biological significance, genetics and evolutionary origin of variability in behavior within and between inbred strains of mice *(Mus musculus):* a behaviour genetic study. *Behaviour* 38:1–92
184. Osborne, R. T., Suddick, D. E. 1971. Blood type gene frequency and mental ability. *Psychol. Rep.* 29:1243–49
185. Owen, D. R. 1972. Blood type gene frequency and mental ability: premature conclusions? *Psychol. Rep.* 31:835–39
186. Owen, D. R. 1972. The 47, XYY male: a review. *Psychol. Bull.* 78:209–33
187. Owen, K., Thiessen, D. D., Lindzey, G. 1970. Acrophobic and photophobic responses associated with the albino locus in mice. *Behav. Genet.* 1:249–55
188. Page, E. B. 1972. Behavior and heredity. *Am. Psychol.* 27:660–61
189. Pakstis, A., Scarr-Salapatek, S., Elston, R. C., Siervogel, R. 1972. Genetic contributions to morphologic and behavioral similarities among sibs and dizygotic twins: linkages and allelic differences. *Soc. Biol.* 19:185–92
190. Partanen, J., Bruun, K., Markkanen, T. 1966. *Inheritance of drinking behavior: a study on intelligence, personality, and use of alcohol of adult twins.* Helsinki: Finnish Found. Alcohol Stud. No. 14. 159 pp.
191. Peeler, D. F. Jr. 1972. Activity as a function of genetic variables and opportunity for exploration. *Psychon. Sci.* 27:176–78
192. Pelz, W. E., Whitney, G., Smith, J. C. 1973. Genetic influences on saccharin preference of mice. *Physiol. Behav.* 10: 263–66
193. Perris, C. 1971. Abnormality on paternal and maternal sides: observations in bipolar (manic-depressive) and unipolar depressive psychoses. *Brit. J. Psychiat.* 118:207–10
194. Poley, W. 1972. Alcohol-preferring and alcohol-avoiding C57BL mice. *Behav. Genet.* 2:245–48
195. Poley, W., Yeudall, L. T., Royce, J. R. 1970. Factors of emotionality related to alcohol consumption in laboratory mice. *Multivar. Behav. Res.* 5:203–8
196. Pollin, W. 1971. A possible genetic factor related to psychosis. *Am. J. Psychiat.* 128:311–17
197. Pollitt, J. 1972. The relationship between genetic and precipitating factors in depressive illness. *Brit. J. Psychiat.* 121:67–70
198. Porter, R. H. 1972. Infantile handling differentially effects (sic) inter-strain

dominance interaction in mice. *Behav. Biol.* 7:415–20
199. Price, E. 1970. Differential reactivity of wild and semi-domestic deermice *(Peromyscus maniculatus). Anim. Behav.* 18:747–52
200. Price, E. O., Loomis, S. 1973. Maternal influence on the response of wild and domestic Norway rats to a novel environment. *Develop. Psychobiol.* 6:203–8
201. Record, R. G., McKeown, T., Edwards, J. H. 1970. An investigation of the difference in measured intelligence between twins and single births. *Ann. Hum. Genet.* 34:11–20
202. Reich, T., James, J. W., Morris, C. A. 1972. The use of multiple thresholds in determining the mode of transmission of semi-continuous traits. *Ann. Hum. Genet.* 36:162–83
203. Richardson, K., Spears, D., Richards, M., Eds. 1972. *Race, Culture and Intelligence.* Harmondsworth, Middlesex: Penguin. 205 pp.
204. Rick, J. T. et al 1971. GABA production in brain cortex related to activity and avoidance behaviour in eight strains of rat. *Brain Res.* 32:234–38
205. Rimmer, J., Winokur, G. 1972. The spouses of alcoholics: an example of assortative mating. *Dis. Nerv. Syst.* 33: 509–11
206. Rose, A., Parsons, P. A. 1970. Behavioural studies in different strains of mice and the problem of heterosis. *Genetica* 41:65–87
207. Rosecrans, J. A., Schechter, M. D. 1972. Brain 5-hydroxytryptamine correlates of behavior in rats: strain and sex variability. *Physiol. Behav.* 8:503–10
208. Rosenthal, D., Wender, P. H., Kety, S. S., Welner, J., Schulsinger, F. 1971. The adopted-away offspring of schizophrenics. *Am. J. Psychiat.* 128:307–11
209. Roubicek, C. B., Ray, D. E., Douglas, M. E. 1972. Genetic regulation of water intake in the rat. *Physiol. Behav.* 8: 1107–12
210. Royce, J. R., Yeudall, L. T., Poley, W. 1971. Diallel analysis of avoidance conditioning in inbred strains of mice. *J. Comp. Physiol. Psychol.* 76:353–58
211. Satinder, K. P. 1971. Genotype-dependent effects of D-amphetamine sulphate and caffeine on escape-avoidance behavior of rats. *J. Comp. Physiol. Psychol.* 76:359–64
212. Ibid 1972. Behavior-genetic-dependent self-selection of alcohol in rats. 80: 422–34
213. Satinder, K. P. 1972. Effects of intertrial crossing punishment and D-amphetamine sulfate on avoidance and activity in four selectively bred rat strains. *Psychon. Sci.* 29:291–93
214. Scarr, S. 1969. Effects of birth weight on later intelligence. *Soc. Biol.* 16:249–56
215. Scarr-Salapatek, S. 1971. Race, social class, and IQ. *Science* 174:1285–95
216. Ibid. Unknowns in the IQ equation, 1223–28
217. Schuckit, M. A., Goodwin, D. A., Winokur, G. 1972. A study of alcoholism in half siblings. *Am. J. Psychiat.* 128:1132–36
218. Schull, W. J., Nagano, H., Yamamoto, M., Komatsu, I. 1970. The effects of parental consanguinity and inbreeding in Hirado, Japan. I. Stillbirths and prereproductive mortality. *Am. J. Hum. Genet.* 22:239–62
219. Scott, J. P., Lee, C., Ho, J. E. 1971. Effects of fighting, genotype, and amphetamine sulfate on body temperature of mice. *J. Comp. Physiol. Psychol.* 76: 349–52
220. Seemanova, E. 1971. A study of children of incestuous matings. *Hum. Hered.* 21:108–28
221. Segal, D. S., Kuczenski, R. T., Mandell, A. J. 1972. Strain differences in behavior and brain tyrosine hydroxylase activity. *Behav. Biol.* 7:75–81
222. Seixas, F. A., Omenn, G. S., Burk, D., Eggleston, S., Eds. 1972. Nature and nurture in alcoholism. *Ann. NY Acad. Sci.* 197:1–229
223. Sheppard, J. R., Albersheim, P., McClearn, G. 1970. Aldehyde dehydrogenase and ethanol preference in mice. *J. Biol. Chem.* 245:2876–82
224. Shields, J. 1973. Heredity and psychological abnormality. In *Handbook of Abnormal Psychology,* ed. H. J. Eysenck, 540–603. London: Pitman. 2nd ed. 906 pp.
225. Shields, J., Gottesman, I. I. 1972. Cross-national diagnosis of schizophrenia in twins: the heritability and specificity of schizophrenia. *Arch. Gen. Psychiat.* 27:725–30
226. Shumake, S. A., Thompson, R. D., Caudill, C. J. 1971. Taste preference behavior of laboratory versus wild Norway rats. *J. Comp. Physiol. Psychol.* 77:489–94
227. Simmel, E. C., Walker, D. A. 1972. The effects of a companion on exploratory behavior in two strains of inbred laboratory mice. *Behav. Genet.* 2:249–54

228. Slater, E., Cowie, V. 1971. *The Genetics of Mental Disorders.* London: Oxford Univ. Press. 413 pp.
229. Slater, E., Maxwell, J., Price, J. S. 1971. Distribution of ancestral secondary cases of bipolar affective disorders. *Brit. J. Psychiat.* 118:215–18
230. Smissaert, H. R., Hitman, K. T. 1971. Acetylcholinesterase from Tryon maze-bright and Tryon maze-dull rat strains is identical. *Physiol. Behav.* 6:729–30
231. Smith, C. 1970. Heritability of liability and concordance in monozygous twins. *Ann. Hum. Genet.* 34:85–91
232. Smith, R. H. 1972. Wildness and domestication in *Mus musculus:* a behavioral analysis. *J. Comp. Physiol. Psychol.* 79:22–29
233. Sprott, R. L. 1972. Passive-avoidance conditioning in inbred mice: effects of shock intensity, age, and genotype. *J. Comp. Physiol. Psychol.* 80:327–34
234. Stabenau, J. R. et al 1969. Study of monozygotic twins discordant for schizophrenia. Some biologic variables (lactate-pyruvic ratio; 3, 4-dimethoxy-phenlethylamine (sic); S_{19} macroglobulin; antirabbit red cell hemagglutin; protein bound iodine). *Arch. Gen. Psychiat.* 20:145–58
235. Stafford, R. E. 1970. Estimation of the interaction between heredity and environment for musical aptitude of twins. *Hum. Hered.* 20:356–60
236. Stafford, R. E. 1972. Hereditary and environmental components of quantitative reasoning. *Rev. Educ. Res.* 42:183–201
237. Stewart, J. M., Curtsinger, J. W., Collins, R. L. 1973. *Genetic models for social interaction: I. Agonistic behavior in mice.* Presented at 3rd Ann. Meet. Behav. Genet. Assoc., Chapel Hill, N. Carolina
238. St. John, R. D. 1973. Genetic analysis of tail rattling in the mouse. *Nature* 241:549–51
239. Thiessen, D. D. 1970. Philosophy and methods in behavior genetics: its relation to biology. In *Contemporary Scientific Psychology,* ed. A. R. Gilgen, 71–114. New York: Academic. 328 pp.
240. Thiessen, D. D. 1972. A move toward species-specific analyses in behavior genetics. *Behav. Genet.* 2:115–26
241. Thiessen, D. D., Lindzey, G., Owen, K. 1970. Behavior and allelic variations in enzyme activity and coat color at the *C* locus of the mouse. *Behav. Genet.* 1: 257–67
242. Thoday, J. M. 1972. Genetics and educability. *J. Biol. Educ.* 6:323–30
243. Thoday, J. M., Gibson, J. B. 1970. Environmental and genetical contributions to class difference: a model experiment. *Science* 167:990–92
244. Treiman, D. M., Fulker, D. W., Levine, S. 1970. Interaction of genotype and environment as determinants of corticosteroid response to stress. *Develop. Psychobiol.* 3:131–40
245. Tyler, P. A., McClearn, G. E. 1970. A quantitative genetic analysis of runway learning in mice. *Behav. Genet.* 1:57–69
246. Vale, J. R., Ray, D. 1972. A diallel analysis of male mouse sex behavior. *Behav. Genet.* 2:199–209
247. Vale, J. R., Vale, C. A. 1973. Diallel analyses of water intake, body weight, and percent hemoconcentration in male mice. *Behav. Genet.* 3:187–92
248. Vale, J. R., Ray, D., Vale, C. A. 1972. The interaction of genotype and exogenous neonatal androgen: agonistic behavior in female mice. *Behav. Biol.* 7:321–34
249. Vale, J. R., Ray, D., Vale, C. A. 1973. Interaction of genotype and exogenous neonatal estrogen: aggression in female mice. *Physiol. Behav.* 10:181–84
250. Vale, J. R., Ray, D., Vale, C. A. 1973. The interaction of genotype and exogenous neonatal androgen and estrogen: sex behavior in female mice. *Develop. Psychobiol.* 6:319–28
251. Vale, J. R., Vale, C. A., Harley, J. P. 1971. Interaction of genotype and population number with regard to aggressive behavior, social grooming and adrenal and gonadal weight in male mice. *Commun. Behav. Biol.* 6:209–21
252. Vandenberg, S. G. 1970. A comparison of heritability estimates of U.S. negro and white high school students. *Acta Genet. Med. Gemellol.* 19:280–84
253. Vandenberg, S. G. 1971. What do we know today about the inheritance of intelligence and how do we know it? See Ref. 29, 182–220
254. Vandenberg, S. G. 1972. Assortative mating, or who marries whom? *Behav. Genet.* 2:127–57
255. Vandenberg, S. G. 1974. Twin studies. See Ref. 134
257. Wahlsten, D. 1972. Genetic experiments with animal learning: a critical review. *Behav. Biol.* 7:143–82
258. Wahlsten, D. 1972. Phenotypic and genetic relations between initial response to electric shock and rate of avoidance in mice. *Behav. Genet.* 2:211–40
259. Ibid 1973. Contributions of the genes albinism (*c*) and retinal degeneration (*rd*) to a strain-by-training procedure

interaction in avoidance learning. 3: 303–16

260. Waller, J. H. 1971. Achievement and social mobility: relationships among IQ score, education, and occupation in two generations. *Soc. Biol.* 18:252–59
261. Ibid. Differential reproduction: its relation to IQ test score, education, and occupation, 122–36
262. Weizmann, F. 1971. Correlational statistics and the nature-nurture problem. *Science* 171:589
263. Wender, P. H., Rosenthal, D., Kety, S. S., Schulsinger, F., Welner, J. 1973. Social class and psychopathology in adoptees: a natural experimental method for separating the roles of genetic and experiential factors. *Arch. Gen. Psychiat.* 28:318–25
264. Whitney, G. 1970. Aggression and open field behavior in male mice. *Psychon. Sci.* 18:167–68
265. Whitney, G. 1972. Relationship between alcohol preference and other behaviors in laboratory mice. See Ref. 80, 151–61
266. Whitney, G. 1973. Vocalization of mice influenced by a single gene in a heterogeneous population. *Behav. Genet.* 3: 57–64
267. Whitney, G., McClearn, G. E., DeFries, J. C. 1970. Heritability of alcohol preference in laboratory mice and rats. *J. Hered.* 61:165–69
268. Wilcock, J. 1971. Gene action and behavior: a clarification. *Psychol. Bull.* 75:106–8
269. Wilcock, J. 1972. Comparative psychology lives on under an assumed name—psychogenetics! *Am. Psychol.* 27:531–38
270. Wilcock, J. 1972. Water-escape in weanling rats: a link between behaviour and biological fitness. *Anim. Behav.* 20:543–47
271. Wilcock, J., Fulker, D. W. 1973. Avoidance learning in rats: genetic evidence for two distinct behavioral processes in the shuttle-box. *J. Comp. Physiol. Psychol.* 82:247–53
272. Willerman, L. 1972. Premature closure. *Contemp. Psychol.* 17:585–86
273. Willerman, L., Stafford, R. E. 1972. Maternal effects on intellectual functioning. *Behav. Genet.* 2:321–25
274. Willerman, L., Naylor, A. F., Myrianthopoulos, N. C. 1970. Intellectual development of children from interracial matings. *Science* 170:1329–31
275. Wilson R. S. 1972. Twins: early mental development. *Science* 175:914–17
276. Wilson, R. S., Harpring, E. B. 1972. Mental and motor development in infant twins. *Develop. Psychol.* 7:277–87
277. Wilson, R. S., Brown, A. M., Matheny, A. P. Jr. 1971. Emergence and persistence of behavioral differences in twins. *Child Develop.* 42:1381–98
278. Winokur, G. 1970. Genetic findings and methodological considerations in manic-depressive disease. *Brit. J. Psychiat.* 117:267–74
279. Woolf, C. M. 1972. Genetic analysis of geotactic and phototactic behavior in selected strains of *Drosophila pseudoobscura*. *Behav. Genet.* 2:93–106
280. Wyatt, R. J. et al 1973. Reduced monoamine oxidase activity in platelets: a possible genetic marker for vulnerability to schizophrenia. *Science* 173:916–18
281. Yanai, J., McClearn, G. E. 1972. Assortative mating in mice. I. Female mating preference. *Behav. Genet.* 2:173–83
282. Ibid 1973. Assortative mating in mice. II. Strain differences in female mating preference, male preference and the question of possible sexual selection. 3: 65–74
283. Ibid. Assortative mating in mice. III. Genetic determination of female mating preference. 3:75–84

SOCIAL AND CULTURAL INFLUENCES ON PSYCHOPATHOLOGY[1]

Bruce P. Dohrenwend[2]
Department of Psychiatry, Columbia University, New York City

Barbara Snell Dohrenwend
Department of Psychology, The City College of the City University of New York

Social and cultural influences have been studied in relation to four distinct though related aspects of psychopathology: its diagnosis; its occurrence and distribution; public attitudes; and treatment. A chapter with the title above, new for the *Annual Review of Psychology,* might well contain sections on all of these topics (cf. 18, 22, 51, 59, 74, 132, 171). Such inclusiveness, however, would require far more space than is available. Our first problem, therefore, is to find a sensible basis on which to narrow the focus.

The key questions about the role of social and cultural factors in the occurrence and distribution of psychopathology, and in relation to attitudes and to treatment, reflect underlying unsolved problems of definition and etiology. Of these three areas, it is the occurrence and distribution of psychopathology that we know most about and which holds, in our opinion, the most important clues to understanding the role of social and cultural factors in etiology. It is here as well that problems of how to define, measure, and diagnose various types of psychopathology present themselves in the most comprehensive form. Given the need to be selective, these considerations

[1]See NAPS document No. 02130 for 31 pages of supplementary material. Order from ASIS/NAPS c/o Microfiche Publications, 305 E. 46th Street, New York, NY 10017. Remit in advance for each NAPS accession number $1.50 for microfiche or $5.00 for photocopies up to 30 pages, 15¢ for each additional page. Make checks payable to Microfiche Publications.

[2]The preparation of this review was supported by Research Grant MH-10328 and by Research Scientist Award K5-MH-14,663 from the National Institute of Mental Health, U.S. Public Health Service.

seem decisive to us. The focus of this review, therefore, will be research on the occurrence and distribution of psychopathology in general populations.

We can further rationalize our choice by noting that interested readers of the *Annual Review of Psychology* are likely to be familiar from previous volumes with much of the relevant literature on relations between social and cultural factors and treatment. They will have heard, for example, of the important research by Hollingshead & Redlich in the 1950s on social class and types of treatment (77) and the various replications, extensions, and related studies of other researchers over the years since. Moreover, they have available two unusual chapters that are extraordinary in the ways they contrast with and complement each other: one by Howard & Orlinsky in 1972, portraying and analyzing the social and cultural contexts of psychotherapy in the United States (78); the other by Cowen in 1973 on Social and Community Interventions (25). This material could be usefully supplemented, however, by more extended consideration of controversies surrounding what has come to be known as the labeling or societal reaction approaches (e.g. 64, 150) and by studies of mental hospitals as social systems (e.g. 19, 58, 141, 160, 173).

Looking for discussion of research on public attitudes towards psychopathology in previous volumes is like searching for a needle in a haystack. Such attitudes, as we are now only too aware from what has become known as "the Eagleton affair," can affect the destinies of candidates for high political office as well as the course of more usual careers. They are important determinants of who is dealt with by what agencies for what problems (cf. 78). It is fortunate for our rationalization, therefore, that recent reviews by Rabkin are now available to make up for our omission of research on public attitudes from the present chapter (139, 140).

INTRODUCTION TO RESEARCH ON THE OCCURRENCE AND DISTRIBUTION OF PSYCHOPATHOLOGY

A Brief Review of the Annual Review of Psychology

Volumes of this *Annual Review* series contain only brief and scattered references to research on the occurrence and distribution of psychopathology in general populations. Up to 1958 these consisted for the most part of citations of the early publications of Hollingshead & Redlich and their colleagues on rates of treated psychiatric disorder in New Haven (77).

The first and only subsection of a review with the title "epidemiology" was in the 1958 issue when Garner, after raising some methodological questions, commented thus about the Midtown Manhattan study: ". . . the very magnitude of the . . . effort ensures its influence as a stimulus to further methodological advance in this area" (53, p. 412).

A year later Blake & Mouton suggested in their chapter on personality that research on "the prevalence of mental illness and milder failures of adjustment" contributes to an "awareness of widespread tensions, frictions and strains of modern living" (13, p. 226). The reason for this suggestion became abundantly clear with the publication in 1962 and 1963 of monographs reporting the main findings from the Midtown Manhattan study (159) and from an investigation that is in some ways its rural counterpart, the Stirling County study (100). These monographs detailed conclusions, anticipated in the more preliminary reports in journals, that rates of psychopathology in the communities studied, including untreated as well as treated cases, were extraordinarily high: almost a quarter of the adult population in Midtown and over half the adult population in Stirling County. In his 1965 chapter on Psychotherapeutic Processes, Matarazzo expressed skepticism about the magnitude of these rates (113). Nevertheless, the Midtown study and Stirling County study monographs were listed by Zubin in his chapter on Classification of the Behavior Disorders as among the "outstanding books" appearing in the 1960–1965 period covered by his review (179), and there is recurrent reference to them, usually in terms of the great unmet need for psychiatric treatment that they portray, the most recent in Cowen's chapter in Volume 24 (25).

We found no references to other epidemiological studies of the "true" prevalence of psychiatric disorders in our review of the *Annual Review of Psychology* through 1973. As the reader will see, however, there are indeed other studies. Moreover, their main importance for our problem, like the importance of the Midtown and Stirling research, is less in any individual study than in the cumulatively consistent relationships that they report between social and cultural factors and psychopathology.

The Inadequacy of Studies Based on Treated Rates

In contrast to the Midtown and Stirling County studies, the majority of investigations of relations between social and cultural factors and psychopathology have defined psychopathology in terms of admission to psychiatric treatment. Although operationally the clearest definition of a "case," this is also the one with the most ambiguous implications. Since treatment rates vary with the availability of facilities and with public attitudes toward their use (e.g., 43,48, 80, 84, 125), either of these conditions may account for correlations between social and cultural factors and rates of psychopathology measured by number of cases in treatment. Thus, when the issue is the possible significance of social and cultural factors in the etiology of psychopathology, correlations involving only treated cases may be seriously misleading. Our own analysis of the evidence bearing on this problem has led us to dismiss from consideration for the most part studies dealing solely with treated rates (33).

The Studies of "True" Prevalence

In 1855, Edward Jarvis, a physician in the state of Massachusetts, submitted a report on what was probably the most complete and influential attempt to investigate the true prevalence of psychopathology conducted in the 19th century (80). This study was done almost half a century before the beginning of the "Kraepelinian era" in psychiatry (119, pp. 419–89), and Jarvis' main nosological distinction was between "insanity" and "idiocy." His procedure was to conduct an incredibly thorough survey of general practitioners, supplemented by reports of other key informants such as clergymen where sufficient information from general practitioners was not available. These informant reports were checked against the records of mental hospitals and other official agencies and the resulting data analyzed according to such demographic variables as sex, place of birth, and economic status.

Jarvis believed that only by analyzing statistics resulting from such research "can we come to the true causes of insanity, and the real influences that remove it" (80, p. 43). Some of the issues he raised on the basis of his findings are vivid forerunners of the major issues of explanation that we face today.

Since the turn of the century at least 58 different investigators or teams of investigators in different parts of the world have attempted to count not only the treated cases but also the untreated cases of psychopathology in the communities that they studied. Excluded from consideration are studies in which the investigators have reported scores measuring symptomatology but have not indicated what is to be considered a case (e.g. 28, 68, 88, 95, 128, 129, 133).

Typically, the whole population in a specified geographical area is included in each of these investigations. Where studies have relied on sample estimates, the *n*s have usually been large: for example, the Midtown study of a probability sample of 1660 adults in a section of New York City (159) and the Stirling County Study of 1010 adults sampled on a probability basis from a rural maritime county in Canada (100).

In most of the studies the rates that we have extracted represent prevalence (the number of cases existing regardless of time of onset) during a period of a few months to a few years. In four exceptions the investigators presented lifetime prevalence rates, and the Stirling County researchers refer to their estimates of "total reportable prevalence" as something more than current prevalence and something less than lifetime prevalence (100, p. 118). In addition, one study (71) has provided 10-year incidence rates (the rates of new cases arising in a 10-year period). By and large, these differences in type of rate employed appear to make less difference in the results than a number of other factors that will be discussed below.

In the sections that follow, we will update the coverage of this literature that we published in our 1969 monograph (33) by adding to the 44 studies covered there the 26 studies that we have discovered since (1, 7–9, 27, 52, 69, 76, 81, 85, 90, 91, 102, 110–112, 117, 118, 136, 151, 153, 164, 166, 167, 176, 178). We will also extend our analyses of what these epidemiological studies and related research have to tell us about relationships between social and cultural factors and psychopathology.

In this review we shall mean by "psychopathology" the types of problematic behaviors described in diagnostic manuals such as the DSM-II (4) as operationalized by the various epidemiological investigators. Moreover, wherever the data permit, we shall restrict the focus to nosological types with no known organic basis—the types of behaviors for which the etiological significance of social and cultural factors is at issue. This restriction limits us very little, since the etiology of most of the psychiatric disorders is still largely unknown. Even for schizophrenia, there is controversy about the magnitude of the demonstrated etiological role of genetic factors (cf. 103) and no comparably persuasive demonstrations of any role for physiological (cf. 162), biochemical (cf. 122), or social and cultural factors (cf. 147, p. 426).

The legacy that the epidemiological studies of "true" prevalence have left us comes in two parts. One is a Pandora's box of problems with regard to case definition and measurement. The second part of the legacy stands out sharply against this background of methodological problems. It is a set of relationships, highly consistent from study to study, between various social and cultural factors and certain types of psychopathology.

Space limitations require that we present summary tables only in the following analyses of these two parts of the legacy. The detailed bibliography and tables of rates on which these summaries are based can be obtained by interested readers according to the procedures described in footnote 1.

THE METHODOLOGICAL PROBLEMS

In the large majority of investigations, cases were defined by applying clinical judgment to symptom data collected mainly on the basis of personal interviews with subjects. Two general approaches to securing these judgmental evaluations have been used. First, in most of the European and Asian research, a single psychiatrist or a small team headed by a psychiatrist personally interviewed community residents and recorded diagnostic judgments on the basis of these interviews. As a rule, the interview procedures were not made explicit in this type of approach (e.g. 7, 71, 85, 101).

In the second type, by contrast, standard and explicit data collection procedures were used. Although the interviews were sometimes done by psychiatrists and clinical psychologists and sometimes by lay interviewers, in all instances case identification depended on psychiatrists' evaluations of protocols compiled from the interview responses and, sometimes, from ancillary data from key informants, official records, and interviewers' observations. The Midtown study and the Stirling County study referred to above pioneered this approach, and some recent studies have adopted their procedures (54, 142, 153). This approach is relatively economical when, as in the Midtown and Stirling County studies, lay interviewers rather than clinicians are used to collect the data to be evaluated. More important, the written protocols that form the basis of the evaluation can be edited to remove direct clues to social and cultural background factors such as social class that could bias the clinical judgments (cf. 137).

On the other hand, the procedure has a distinct disadvantage since it makes a difference whether the clinicians see and talk to the subject directly; the evidence is that clinicians tend to be overimpressed by pathology when working from written records alone (16, 36, 63, 152). The question of what information is required to make an informed clinical judgment and the question of what information is likely to bias such judgment are two horns of a dilemma that has received considerably less attention in the epidemiological studies and in the field of clinical assessment in general than it deserves.

Even more economical than having clinicians rate protocols constructed from data collected by lay interviewers is dispensing with clinical judgments altogether and using objectively scored measures of psychopathology. A growing number of investigators have been doing just that (e.g. 27, 117, 134). Unfortunately, however, their decisions to use objective rather than judgmental measures have been based on considerations of practicality and cost rather than on tests of the relative accuracy of these mechanical vs nonmechanical modes of combining data (115, 149).

The objective measure used most often is a 22-item screening instrument developed by the Midtown study researchers on a purely actuarial basis to provide an approximation of their Mental Health Rating of psychiatric impairment (94). A similar although less widely used measure consisting of 20 Health Opinion Survey questions has been developed by the Stirling County study researchers as well (106). Both have as their core a portion of the items from the Psychosomatic Scale of the Neuropsychiatric Screening Adjunct, developed as an aid to Selective Service screening during World War II (161).

As would be expected from the source of many of them in the NSA, almost half of the questions in these instruments are physiological in content while the others appear on their face to touch on aspects of anxiety and depression. They are more relevant to aspects of neurosis than to psychosis or personality disorder. Such structured questions with fixed alternative response categories are easy to administer and have been subject, unlike the judgmental measures, to a considerable amount of methodological investigation. As a result, they have their proponents (e.g. 152, 156, 164) and their critics (e.g. 26, 28, 30, 32, 108, 135, 136).

Their proponents are impressed that these instruments have been shown to be reliable, to relate strongly to a host of demographic variables, and to discriminate between nonpatients and psychiatric patients, especially when a large portion of the latter were diagnosed as neurotic. Their critics worry about their lack of face validity as a representative sample of the range and variety of symptoms described in diagnostic manuals, their tendency to overrepresent distress in some groups, the fact that the more physiological items among them are confounded with physical illness, and their susceptibility to response styles—in short, an all too familiar catalog of assets and liabilities for personality measures constructed on actuarial bases.

The application of these various judgmental and objective measures have led to dramatically different estimates of the "true" prevalence of psychopathology in different communities. In some communities, rates of 1 percent or less have been reported and in others rates of 50 percent and more. What could account for variability of this magnitude?

Table 1 shows the medians and ranges in total rates reported for the communities studied, grouped according to geopolitical area and according to whether the study site was rural or urban. The range in rates within areas is in most cases so much greater than the differences in the medians between areas that these contrasts in setting do not appear to account for the variation from study to study.

As we have shown in previous analyses—and there is no reason to change our earlier conclusions on the basis of the studies now added—the main sources of the variability between studies have to do far less with substantive factors than with methodological factors such as thoroughness of data collection procedures and contrasting conceptions of what constitutes a case (33). Let us illustrate the manner and scope of the impact of these factors on the rates reported.

Table 1 Medians and ranges of percentages of psychopathology according to geopolitical area and rural versus urban study site

Site		North America	South America	Europe	Middle East	Africa	Asia	Australia
Rural	Median	17.3	–	11.9	9.9	–	1.0	–
	Range	1.7–69.0	–	1.1–28.6	4.5–14.9	40.0	0.4–54.0	5.4–6.8
	Number of studies	12	0	15	3	1	14	2
Urban	Median	21.0	18.4	15.5	–	–	1.8	25.9
	Range	1.8–32.0	17.5–29.8	1.0–33.0	47.4	11.8–45.0	0.8–3.0	25.4–29.4
	Number of studies	12	4	5	1	2	3	3

Contrasting Conceptions of What Constitutes a "Case"

As readers of *Annual Review* chapters on Abnormal Behavior and Classification of the Behavior Disorders over the years must be aware, there has been "a clamor against established categories of behavior disorder" (172, p. 290); "The present status of the classification of behavior disorders is, to say the least, chaotic" (179, pp. 375–76); and the field of behavior disorders is in "a period of ferment, controversy, and innovation" (137, p. 447). It should come as no surprise, therefore, that the single largest source of variability in the rates reported in these epidemiological studies is a function of contrasting conceptions of what constitutes a "case."

The great expansion of psychiatric nomenclatures following World War II affords a vivid opportunity to show the impact of contrasting conceptions of psychopathology on the results of the epidemiological studies. As Raines noted of the clinical experience of psychiatrists in the military in his foreword to the 1952 Diagnostic and Statistical Manual of the American Psychiatric Association:

> Only about 10% of the total cases seen fell into any of the categories ordinarily seen in public mental hospitals. Military psychiatrists, induction station psychiatrists, and Veterans Administration psychiatrists found themselves operating within the limits of a nomenclature specifically not designed for 90% of the cases handled (3, p. vi).

The 1952 DSM was a direct outgrowth of these experiences and its 1968 revision (DSM-II) (4) confirms the expansion and includes modifications which bring the American Psychiatric Association's official nomenclature more nearly into line with that of a somewhat modified World Health Organization nomenclature (157).

We would expect on the basis of these changes in nomenclature to find the rates reported in epidemiological studies published before 1950 to be much lower than the rates reported in studies published in 1950 or later.

As Table 2 shows, the median rates for the more recent studies are far higher than those for the earlier ones. Moreover, the factor of directness of contact is dwarfed in importance by contrast with the time the study was done.

It is tempting to see the results in Table 2 as reflecting not so much changes in the researchers' conceptions as representing a true increase in the amount of disorder as a function of the stress of modern life. However, this explanation flies in the face of what we know about the direction of expansion of nomenclatures over time. Most persuasive of all, it is inconsistent with internal evidence from epidemiological studies in which investigators who applied more and less inclusive standards to the same population obtained dramatic contrasts in rates. Essen-Möller, for example, reported a rate of 13.6 percent for "diagnoses constituting the main subject of most psychiatric populations studies" (44, p. 95) but an average of 54.7 percent (calculation by B. S. Dohrenwend) for whom pathology was not definitely absent. A similar contrast is offered by the figures 23.4 percent in the impaired group and 81.5 percent judged less than "well" in the Midtown study (159, p. 138). The Leightons and their colleagues reported that over 50 percent of the sample studied would be cases as defined by the 1952 Diagnostic Manual (100, p. 121), but for only 3 percent would psychiatric attention be judged " 'mandatory' according to current notions of medical care" (100, p. 143.)

Furthermore, the judgmental measures developed have not always been easy to export. For example, the Leightons and their colleagues concluded concerning their own studies in Canada and Nigeria that "the differences and similarities between the Yoruba and Stirling figures are to an unknown degree under the influence of differences in the procedures employed in the two studies" (99, p. 124). And when D. C. Leighton rated a subsample of the data collected by another team of researchers who had attempted to use the Stirling County rating procedures, the proportion she rated as cases was considerably lower than theirs (153).

Results with objective measures show similar trends. As Langner demonstrated, the proportion among respondents psychiatrically evaluated as "impaired" in the Midtown sample who were identified as cases by the 22 item scale varied markedly with the cutting point employed on the screening measure (94). Paralleling his results are reports of case rates of 27.5 percent in a New Hampshire sample using a cutting point of four or more symptoms (134); 10.8 percent in a sample from three Plains State communities with a cutting point of 7 or more (117); and 3.4 percent in Kalamazoo County, Michigan when a cutting point of 10 or more symptoms was used (109).

Problem of Validity

Given the great variability in rates resulting from these differences in concepts and methods, the question arises as to whether the procedures used in some of the studies

Table 2 Medians and ranges of percentages of psychopathology reported according to directness of contact with subjects and date of publication

Directness of contact with subjects		Date of publication: Before 1950	Date of publication: 1950 or after
Indirect contacts: records and/or informants	Median	2.3	3.0
	Range	1.1–9.0	1.2–14.8
	Number of rates	5	6
Partial direct contact: records and/or informants, and interviews with some subjects	Median	1.3	9.9
	Range	0.8–6.4	1.4–28.6
	Number of rates	5	9
Direct contact: Interviews with all subjects	Median	3.6	18.2
	Range	2.7–12.4	0.4–69.0
	Number of rates	6	40
Interviews with physical examinations of all or most subjects	Median	–	18.0
	Range	–	10.9–64.0
	Number of rates	0	7

are better than the procedures used in others. If so, we would be able to concentrate on the superior studies in our investigation of relations between social and cultural factors and psychopathology. This question is one of evidence—evidence for reliability and validity.

Clearly the methods are unreliable for comparisons of rates across studies, as the results in Tables 1 and 2 show. Within studies, however, the evidence suggests that the assessment procedures—objective or judgmental—are of satisfactory reliability for research purposes. The Stirling County and Midtown researchers, for example, reported quite high agreement among the psychiatrist-raters for the main ratings used (100, 159). Moreover, more recent research supports the proposition that when there is a common data base, reliability of clinical judgment is not as difficult to achieve as had sometimes been supposed from work where nonstandard data bases have been employed (cf. 24). A far more serious problem is the validity of the assessment procedures.

In most of the studies based on psychiatric judgments as to whether subjects were cases, the validity of the results was assumed to be implicit in the diagnostic process, a shaky assumption in light of documented lack of success with psychiatric screening in World War II (55). The tacit request by the researchers that the validity of their findings be accepted on the basis of faith in the clinical training and experience of the clinicians participating in these studies is characteristic, by and large, even of the relatively more sophisticated investigations such as the Midtown study and the Stirling County study. In general, with the possible exception of an incompletely reported Polish investigation (57, 138) and a study conducted by Hogarty, Katz & Lowery (76) that was carefully designed on an actuarial basis for a specific practical purpose, there is little evidence for content validity, criterion-oriented validity, or construct validity in any of these studies. We presented a detailed analysis of the problem in 1969 (33), and although considerable methodological research is now underway, it has been too preliminary thus far to lead to major innovations in the epidemiological studies that we have discovered since that review. For example, a computer program now being developed to make the Stirling County study assessment procedures completely explicit has not been used so far as we know in any of the studies that have modeled themselves on the Stirling County approach (124).

Psychologists familiar with methodological advances in the field of personality research in general could well be appalled at the lack of sophistication of these epidemiological studies. After reading chapters in past volumes of the *Annual Review of Psychology* on personality, abnormal behavior, and related matters in preparation for this review, however, we are inclined to temper our criticism. These reveal a "dismal overall picture" in personality research (89, p. 307); that there is a proliferation of un-or semi-validated measures (13, p. 207); that "most measures used to tap presumably stable personality characteristics have been attacked as not measuring what they purport to measure" (21, p. 201); that the "criterion problem" with regard to what constitutes improvement in psychotherapy remains unsolved (174, p. 367); that "after all these years, and after literally hundreds of studies on anxiety, there is still no general agreement as to what the commonly used scales are measuring" (2, p. 233); that personality measurement is in a "state of chaos" (49, p. 50). Against this background, it is more sensible to regret the lack of sophistication about methodological problems in the epidemiological research than to indict the researchers for having failed to solve them.

We are in a situation then where different concepts and methods of assessment in the epidemiological studies have led to vastly different assessments of rates of psychopathology. Moreover, there is no way to choose, on the basis of the evidence, a subset of these studies in which more valid procedures have been employed.

Note, however, that the diagnostic difficulties are not so different from those faced by genetically oriented researchers who have so successfully employed twin and adoption strategies in the study of schizophrenia. As Lindzey and co-workers pointed out, reported concordance rates for monozygotic twins vary from 6 percent to 69 percent as a function of methodological factors (103). These problems have not, however, prevented the research from demonstrating impressively consistent relationships between degree of genetic similarity and concordance for schizophrenia. What is the reason for this?

Meehl in 1959 published an intriguing defense of formal psychiatric diagnosis. He wrote:

> The fundamental argument for the utility of formal diagnosis can be put either causally or statistically, but it amounts to the same kind of thing one would say in defending formal diagnosis in organic medicine. One holds that there is a sufficient amount of etiological and prognostic homogeneity among patients belonging to a given diagnostic group, so that assignment of a patient to this group has probability implications which it is clinically unsound to ignore (116, p. 103).

Although the epidemiological investigators differ in their concepts [e.g. "symptom patterns" of a particular nosological type in the Stirling County study (100) rather than diagnoses as in the majority of studies], methods, and beliefs about etiology and prognosis, most present their findings in terms at least of broad nosological distinctions. Moreover, there appears to be considerable agreement among them on these vividly contrasting sets of symptom complexes despite differences in where they draw the boundaries among the different types and between all of the types of psychopathology and "normality." Our reason for believing that such basic agreement exists is that we found in previous analyses that there were consistent *relationships* from study to study between various types of psychopathology and various social and cultural factors (33). Such consistencies we take as evidence of the meaningfulness, "the truth," of these broad nosological distinctions as manifested in the epidemiological investigations.

These grounds seem sufficient to warrant extending our analyses on the basis of the expanded number of investigations that we now have available to see what more we can learn. In doing so we shall give each investigation equal weight in our search for firm relationships, excluding studies only when they do not present data on relevant types of psychopathology or on relevant types of social and cultural factors for some of the questions that we will ask of them.

RELATIONS BETWEEN SOCIAL AND CULTURAL FACTORS AND PSYCHOPATHOLOGY

Most researchers concerned with etiology would agree today with Hamburg and his colleagues that "By now, it is clear that serious disorders of behavior may arise from many influences—biological, psychological, and social" (72, p. 86). They would disagree, however, in their hunches about the relative importance of these influences (cf. 73, 147).

The position that attributes greatest importance to social and cultural factors has been summarized by Slotkin as follows:

> Man inherits a limited repertory of responses. Most of his responses are learned, and the majority of these are learned from others, i.e., culturally acquired. Consequently, it is to be expected that the individual's responses, abnormal as well as normal, are greatly influenced by his cultural milieu. And cultures vary tremendously (155, p. 274).

Two corollaries of this point of view, as stated by the same author, are that "cultural disorganization will lead to personality disorganization" (155, p. 271) and that "sheer complexity of civilization contributes to personality disorganization" (155, p. 271). At the extreme, as Burgess pointed out, this orientation has led to the argument that:

> Among primitive societies . . . psychoneuroses and psychoses as we know them are absent or occur very seldom. These societies are static. They are in adjustment to life conditions. They provide satisfying roles for their members (17, p. 13).

This picture contrasts with one drawn of our own society:

> There is a growing realization among thoughtful persons that our culture is sick, mentally disordered, and in need of treatment. . . . Our so-called social problems . . . are to be viewed as arising from the frantic efforts of individuals, lacking any sure direction and sanctions or guiding conception of life, to find some way of protecting themselves or of merely existing on any terms they can manage in a society being remade by technology. Having no strong loyalties and no consistent values or realizable ideals to cherish, the individual's conduct is naturally conflicting, confused, neurotic and antisocial . . . (50, pp. 335, 339–40).

This is Lawrence K. Frank writing in 1936. It is a vivid example of similar statements made before and since—by editorial writers, clergymen, politicians, university students, and the man in the street, as well as by behavioral scientists. The broad social causation position that it illustrates provides a rationale for the contemporary efforts of community psychologists to secure primary prevention of psychopathology through strategies of social and community interventions (25).

It seems to us that these statements of the social causation orientation assume, *at a minimum,* that they are not contradicted by the answers to certain questions of fact. They assume that types of psychopathology are different in different cultures and that, at the extreme, cultures exist that immunize their citizens against the development of psychopathology. Similarly, such statements assume that the stresses and strains of modern mass society produce more psychopathology today than in the past and, by extension, that rates of psychopathology are higher in urban than in rural settings. They assume that in our "sick society" some parts are inflamed and hurting or, in terms of the process involved, that social disorganization within society is producing higher rates of psychopathology in some groups than in others.

The "facts" most often cited with reference to such assumptions have come mainly from studies of psychiatric patients and anecdotal accounts (cf. 11, 132, 168, 169, 175). Let us, therefore, examine these assumptions in light of the best evidence that we have available—the results of epidemiological studies that have attempted to investigate the occurrence and distribution of psychopathology independently of treatment status in general populations.

Are There Cultures That Immunize Their Members Against the Development of Psychopathology?

In 1955 M. J. Field, an English psychiatrist and anthropologist, began a remarkable study in rural Ghana (47). It included a subproject on chronic schizophrenia in 12 Ashanti country towns and villages that is of direct relevance to our question. Using key informant techniques and direct observation, she diagnosed 41 chronic schizophrenics out of a total population of 4283 residents of these villages, a rate of 9.6 per 1000. We have reviewed elsewhere 31 studies from which we could extract "true" prevalence rates for schizophrenia (34). Although these rates do not distinguish between chronic and acute types, and should thus be diagnostically more inclusive than Field's, only one study reported a rate of schizophrenia as high as hers (15). Two more reported higher rates, but these were for the occurrence of symptom patterns of a schizophrenic type rather than for diagnosed cases of schizophrenia (99, 159).

Further evidence is provided by five studies that gave estimates of the overall rates of psychopathology in contemporary preindustrial cultures. These studies yielded rates ranging from 0.8 percent in two relatively isolated aboriginal groups in Taiwan (143) to the highest rate reported in any study to date, 69 percent for an American Indian group in the northwestern United States (153). In between are rates of 1.7 percent reported for the Hutterites, a culturally distinct religious sect which will be discussed further (43), and 5.4 percent and 6.8 percent reported by two studies of aboriginal groups in Australia (90, 91). Only the American Indian study is based on procedures for case identification similar to those used in an industrialized culture (153). Since Shore and his colleagues who conducted the study modeled their procedures on that of the Leightons, their rate of 69 percent can be considered in relation to somewhat over 50 percent reported by the Leightons for a rural maritime county in Canada (100). Clearly this comparison does not support the "noble savage" hypothesis, nor does the Leightons' own study of the Yoruba villages in Nigeria, where they found rates of about 40 percent (99).

It can be argued, of course, that we are not hearing about cultures of the kind that Burgess discussed as being "static" and "in adjustment to life conditions," because they no longer exist. Rather, the reports are of psychopathology shown by natives of cultures under the disruptive impact of contact with industrialized societies (cf. 132). In a sense the argument is academic since there is no way that we can construct a time machine to send teams of psychiatrists back into precontact periods of history (cf. 11). However, there are ethnic enclaves that have been remarkably successful in preserving their traditions in the face of contact with modern mass society. Fortunately, a study of one of them provides valuable data on our question.

On the basis of their review of the literature, Eaton & Weil pointed out that speculations about the absence of psychopathology in some primitive societies were based on limited contact, resulting in observations of uncertain validity (43, p. 22). To provide more systematic data, they set out to study the Hutterites, a group with a strong reputation for excellent mental health based on just such anecdotal accounts.

The Hutterites are an ethnic enclave of about 8500 persons who had lived for over 75 years in the United States and Canada at the time of the research. They comprised a religiously oriented and self-sufficient communal society with a secure agrarian economy. The authors convincingly estimate that less than 5 percent of the males had left their communities never to return, and that the rate among females was much lower. There was a record of only one divorce and four separations in the history of the group. And no Hutterite had ever been allowed to become a public charge as long as he remained a member of his community. This extraordinarily stable society had been highly effective in providing cradle to grave support for its members. Did it also protect them from developing psychopathology?

Eaton & Weil's expectation when the study was initiated was "that few cases of mental disorder would be found" (43, p. 229). If they had restricted their study to treated rates, they would have confirmed their hypothesis since there were no Hutterites in mental hospitals or under treatment by psychiatrists in other settings at the time their fieldwork was done.

On the basis of direct interviews with subjects or key informant reports from members of the Hutterite population, however, Eaton & Weil arrived at a rate of psychosis that ranked the Hutterites as third highest of ten populations for whom they computed age-sex adjusted rates—higher, for example, than the urban and far from affluent Eastern Health District of Baltimore. The researchers were aware, however, that population comparisons are difficult to make across these studies, and they suspected that if the other studies had used comparable procedures, the Hutterite rate would have ranked relatively much lower. Be this as it may, given our question as stated and the initial expectations with which Eaton & Weil began their research, it is difficult not to accept their conclusion that the "findings do not confirm the hypothesis that a simple and relatively uncomplicated way of life provides virtual immunity from mental disorders" (43, p. 209). It would seem that the burden of proof is on those who would locate a symptom-free Utopia in the real world.

Nevertheless, it should be noted that persistent and severe antisocial behavior was indeed close to being absent among Hutterites. Only four Hutterites were diagnosed as having personality disorders and only two of these involved antisocial behavior that posed persistent problems to the community. Even here the problems were relatively mild, taking the form of property thefts in the one case and misuse of colony funds in the others. Beyond this there were only minor law violations by Hutterites, usually on a one-time-only basis. These results are especially remarkable in that the key informant techniques of data collection that Eaton & Weil used should be especially effective in securing adequate coverage of this kind of psychopathology.

Moreover, although the rate of functional psychosis that Eaton & Weil found was appreciable, the subtypes—if not a function of some form of idiosyncratic diagnostic procedure—showed an unusual distribution. By contrast with the high ratio of schizophrenia to manic-depressive psychosis usually reported, the cases of manic-depressive psychosis far outnumbered cases of schizophrenia among the Hutterites. The Hutterite rate for the latter, in fact, was the lowest we found in the 31 studies we reviewed that reported "true" prevalence rates for schizophrenia (34)—which brings us to our next question of fact.

Are Types of Psychopathology Different in Different Cultures?

This question has at least four parts: Do the types of psychopathology that we find in Western societies exist in non-Western cultures, or are Western classifications simply inapplicable? If the Western classifications of types of psychopathology do apply, are the distributions of these types the same in all cultures, or are there culturally predominant types? Are there new types of psychopathology to be found in non-Western cultures? If not new types, are there different symptom manifestations of types of psychopathology that are otherwise familiar to us?

THE APPLICABILITY OF WESTERN NOSOLOGIES In their 1971 *Annual Review* chapter on Classification of Behavior Disorders, Phillips & Draguns concluded that although these things are matters of controversy, "The majority opinion of the field holds that diagnostic categories are universal in representation, though different in distribution" (137, p. 469). We would agree, though the evidence supporting the first part is considerably firmer than the evidence supporting the second part of the opinion.

Wherever psychiatric epidemiologists have attempted to conduct studies in non-Western societies marked by their own distinctively different traditions and a relative absence of modern technology, one of their main goals has been to see whether Western psychiatric classifications are applicable. We know of no instance in the "true" prevalence studies where investigators have attempted to use Western classifications in non-Western societies and felt them to be inapplicable (e.g. 10, 47, 98, 178).

If you doubt the applicability of Western classifications of psychopathology to these vastly different cultures and have had clinical training, we suggest that you look at Field's descriptions of a sample of the more than 2500 cases that she observed at religious shrines in rural Ghana (47). She presents descriptions of the cases in considerable detail and also her own diagnoses, based on Western nosology. See if you agree with her clinical judgments.

ARE THERE DIFFERENCES IN DISTRIBUTION AMONG THE CATEGORIES OF PSYCHOPATHOLOGY? The question of whether the relatively familiar types of psychopathology are differently distributed in non-Western societies is more difficult to answer. This is an area rich in anecdotal evidence that tends to evaporate when more extensive studies are conducted. A good example was the belief that depressive symptomatology is extremely rare in rural African communities (11). In the Yoruba study, depression was found to be the most frequent symptom among African women (99), as it was among the women who brought their problems to rural shrines in Ghana (47). The earlier reported absence of depression may stem from the focus on persons in treatment or persons defined by local norms as deviant. Such definitions of disorder can be very misleading about the types of psychopathology found in general populations, as Katz' comparisons of hospital patients and community samples from contrasting ethnic groups in Hawaii suggested (86).

Although there is far less cultural contrast between the United States and England than between, say, the residents of Stirling County and the residents of Yoruba villages, a much higher proportion of schizophrenia compared to manic-depressive psychosis was found among hospitalized patients in the United States than in the United Kingdom. When diagnostic criteria between the two countries were standardized, however, this difference largely disappeared (24). It is possible that the unusually high ratio of manic-depressive psychosis to schizophrenia found by Eaton & Weil among the Hutterites is also similarly a diagnostic artifact. The fact is that comparisons of rates for types of psychopathology across different investigators using different methodologies is hazardous. The boundaries of the different types of psychopathology are simply not drawn with sufficient consistency from study to study.

Nevertheless, we believe it is likely that types of psychopathology are indeed differently distributed in contrasting cultural settings. The main reason is a set of highly consistent findings of differences in types of psychopathology between groups governed by different social norms within communities. These findings will be discussed in detail in a later section.

ARE THERE DIFFERENT SYMPTOM MANIFESTATIONS OF TYPES OF PSYCHOPATHOLOGY THAT ARE OTHERWISE FAMILIAR TO US? It is by now so well recognized that symptoms can take on coloration from the culture that we shall simply join the chorus by agreeing with this conclusion (cf. 10, 20, 47, 87, 98, 137, 178). Cows and witches, for example, occupy a more important place in the content of symptomatology in rural Ghana (47) than in the content of symptomatology shown by residents of Midtown Manhattan (159). Research subjects from lower class backgrounds are more likely to express psychological distress in somatic terms than research subjects from higher class backgrounds (e.g. 26, 77). So are Puerto Ricans by contrast with Blacks, Jews, and Irish (33). And screening instruments composed of symptoms such as those in the 22-item measure from the Midtown study are more representative of female than of male modes of expressing distress (14, 45, 136).

Such cultural differences in modes of expressing distress are interesting in their own right. They also pose serious measurement difficulties when the research problem is to compare groups that differ in social and cultural background—a methodological problem that has received very little systematic attention. Our own efforts to deal with this problem of valid cross-group comparison yielded a strategy so complex that it is reminiscent of a Rube Goldberg (39). Perhaps as more attention is focused on this issue a simpler solution will develop.

DOES SOME OF THE EXOTIC SYMPTOMATOLOGY OBSERVED IN NON-WESTERN CULTURES INDICATE THE PRESENCE OF TYPES OF PSYCHOPATHOLOGY THAT ARE NOT INCLUDED IN WESTERN NOMENCLATURES? With this question, we are back again in the realm of controversy (e.g. 137). Yap, for example, argued that such exotic syndromes as *amok* and *latah* can be placed in the context of modern clinical psychiatry (177). Murphy, by contrast, treated them as distinct disorders (127). Which is the more useful view, we think, depends in part on the particular research purpose, for there is no way to resolve the issue without increased knowledge of etiology.

Amok and *latah* are vivid enough to have left traces that can be analyzed in their own right—as Murphy's historical detective work shows. In such analyses of trends over time, he has every reason to consider them separate types of psychopathology. By contrast, as Yap emphasized, common classification systems are needed for communication and comparison. It is thus the bias of the epidemiologist under the usual circumstances of his trade to want to employ standard categories for comparative purposes. The broader issue, as Yap well states it, is "how to integrate new knowledge into old, or, conversely, how to allow the application of accumulated knowledge to fresh clinical problems" (177, p. 34).

Is There More Psychopathology Today Than in the Past?

Some types of symptomatology leave traces over time in that they are damaging enough or exotic enough so that they will be recorded or recalled, as in the case of *amok* and *latah* (127). Or they are associated with a physical condition that will invariably bring afflicted persons into treatment or will show up on autopsy, as in the case with some types of ulcer (165). There is considerable evidence that rates of such phenomena vary considerably over time (127, 165). What of change over time in rates of the broad types of psychopathology described in Western classifications?

In what must surely be a classic study, Goldhamer & Marshall capitalized on an unusually fine set of historical records in Massachusetts to investigate hospital first admissions between 1840 and 1940 (61). From statistical evidence it is clear that hospital admissions for psychiatric disorders up until recent innovations in services have indeed tended to increase markedly over time (e.g. 107), undoubtedly influenced by increases in facilities, improved diagnoses, changes in public attitudes, and changes in the age composition of the population. If, therefore, Goldhamer & Marshall had reported just one more study finding an increase in treated rates, we would be entirely justified in dismissing their findings as being irrelevant to our question. What makes their actual results important, however, is that in circumstances biased against such an outcome, they found *no increase* in rates of the functional psychoses of the early and middle years.

Goldhamer & Marshall speculated that perhaps by 1840 the processes of industrialization were far enough along in Massachusetts so that the 100-year period did not extend back far enough in time to permit changes to be detected. As Grob has pointed out, psychiatrists in the middle of the 19th century tended at the time to see insanity as part of the price being paid for increasing urbanization (66). Moreover, the Goldhamer & Marshall findings tell us nothing about whether rates for the neuroses and for the personality disorders have increased over time.

Once again we lack the time machine that would send psychiatric epidemiologists back into history to conduct the required research. At the very least, however, Goldhamer & Marshall's findings should give pause to facile speculation about increases in rates of the functional psychoses with the stresses and strains of modern mass society as we know it today—as opposed to what appears to be the all too recent yesterday of our great grandfathers!

Are Rates of Psychopathology Higher in Urban Than in Rural Areas?

As we implied earlier, there is a widely held belief that the stresses and strains of modern technological societies are concentrated in their urban centers. A corollary of this belief is that high rates of psychopathology—along with slums, crime, and riots—are similarly concentrated in such centers. The empirical basis for such opinion, however, has been slim. While it is true that investigators have typically found much higher rates of first admissions to mental institutions from urban than from rural areas (cf. 146), this information tells us little about the true rural-urban distribution even of hospitalizable psychopathology. On the contrary, it has long been known that rural and urban rates of treated cases differ in part as a function of the lesser availability of treatment facilities and the greater resistance to their use in rural areas (80, 125).

Given the contrasts in their concepts and methods, comparisons of the rates obtained by different investigators is frustrating and uninformative so far as substantive questions are concerned. However, eight investigators have reported data from both rural and urban segments of the populations they studied, with two reporting data for two segments, each divided into rural and urban portions. Thus we can look at 10 pairs of rural and urban rates from studies within which uniform procedures were used.

As Table 3 shows, in one comparison the total rate for all psychopathology combined is higher in the rural setting; there is one tie; and in the remaining eight comparisons, the urban rate is higher than the rural rate. We must point out, however, that although quite consistent, the differences are not large; the median difference for total rates is only 1.1 percent and the range is from an excess of 0.9 percent in the rural area to an excess of 13.9 percent in the urban area.

The remaining results in Table 3 provide some indication as to why most of the differences in total rates are small. While some types of psychopathology were found to be more prevalent in the urban setting, others were found more frequently in the rural setting. That is, total rates for all psychoses combined tended to be higher in the rural than in the urban area in these comparisons, and this appears to be so as well for the manic-depressive subtype though not for schizophrenia which may be

Table 3 Comparison of rural and urban rates of psychopathology reported for studies that included both rural and urban areas

Type of psychopathology	Number of studies reporting higher rate in:	
	Rural area	Urban area
All[a]	1	8
Psychosis	5	2
Schizophrenia	2	3
Manic-depressive psychosis	3	1
Neurosis	1	5
Personality disorder	1	5

[a]In addition, one study reported the same rate for rural and urban areas.

equally frequent in rural and urban settings. By contrast, the rates of neurosis and personality disorder are higher in the urban than in the rural setting in all but one of the six pairs of comparisons for which we could extract data on each of these types of psychopathology.

These results are obtained, of course, on the basis of only ten pairs of rural versus urban comparisons and can hardly be considered representative in any systematic sense of the term. Moreover, the absolute rural-urban difference in rates—especially the overall rate—tend to be small (35). We are inclined, nevertheless, to assign more importance to them than others might (e.g. 158). Our reason is that the studies have publication dates from 1942 to 1972; take place in the United States, Europe, Asia, and Africa; involve cities as different as Tokyo, Reykjavik, and Abeokuta (in Nigeria); and report overall rates of psychopathology ranging from 0.8 percent to 45.0 percent. The consistency in direction of many of the urban-rural differences reported in these studies—despite the diversity of time, place, and method of assessing psychopathology—suggests to us that the results be taken seriously. On the basis of this evidence—and it is the best that we have available—the most reasonable hypothesis appears to be that total rates of psychopathology are somewhat higher in urban than in rural areas, due at least in part to an excess of neurosis and personality disorder in the urban areas. Whether these differences are a function of harsher stress on residents of urban settings, however, is quite another matter.

However harsh and threatening cities may sometimes be, they also provide concentrations of industry and commerce, wealth and power, art and entertainment that make them magnets for rural people. Migrants seeking greater opportunity, challenge, or perhaps anonymity than rural environments provide are drawn to cities in large numbers. The possibility cannot be overlooked, therefore, that they bring with them the types of psychopathology that appear to be more concentrated in urban areas rather than developing them in reaction to the stressful circumstances of the urban environment.

Straightforward evidence to resolve this issue is not available. That is, no one has yet surveyed members of a rural population for evidence of psychopathology, or perhaps a proneness to develop such disorder, at one point in time and then followed this population to determine which members migrated to urban areas and what the migrants' impact was on the rates of psychopathology in the areas to which they migrated. Our analysis of the more indirect evidence bearing on this problem (5, 75, 126, 130) has led us to conclude that the issue is unresolved (35).

Are Rates of Psychopathology Within Societies Higher in Some Groups Than in Others?

Not all of the "true" prevalence studies provide data broken down by the major types of psychopathology in which we are interested; still more present no data on either total rates or on subtypes for all of the social categories that we would like to examine; and for some factors such as age, the subclassifications across studies are far from standard, greatly complicating the analysis (33). Thus the analyses that we shall summarize below are restricted to two sets of factors for which consistent trends could be established on the basis of an appreciable number of studies. The two sets of factors are important: they are sex and social class.

SEX DIFFERENCES In 1850, Jarvis published an analysis of reports from about 250 American and European hospitals that suggested to him that men were more prone to insanity than women (79). Grob, summarizing Jarvis' long-standing interest in sex differences in this investigation and other writings, noted that Jarvis believed that the explanation lay in the dissimilar roles of men and women in society with men "more exposed to sensual temptation and the drive for materialistic rewards; women, having a more sympathetic and sensible personality, were more exposed to emotional factors" (66, p. 49).

In a recent review, Gove & Tudor found much in the writing of contemporary social scientists to suggest quite a different picture for our time from Jarvis' picture of his. Gove & Tudor argued that now ". . . women find their position in society to be more frustrating and less rewarding than do men and that this may be a relatively recent development" (65, p. 816). Accordingly, they "postulate that, because of the difficulties associated with the feminine role in modern Western societies, more women than men become mentally ill" (65, p. 816).

To investigate this question, Gove & Tudor focused on research conducted since World War II, in the belief that this time was a high point of change in women's role with significant portions of married women entering the work force for the first time. They also restricted their coverage to research conducted in industrialized countries of North America and Europe. The most important data that they brought to bear on the issue came from some of the same "true" prevalence studies with which we have been concerned, and from community studies using various symptom measures, such as the 22-item Midtown scale, but not indicating what is to be considered a "case." The results are remarkably consistent with their hypothesis. However, they made a decision about the definition of psychopathology that badly compromised their treatment of the question.

They defined "mental illness" as consisting of neurotic disorders and functional psychoses if the studies provided data in the form of diagnoses, or as "personal discomfort" as indicated by measures of subjective distress and anxiety if the studies provided data in the form of symptom scores only (65, p. 812). In doing so, they combined disparate types of psychopathology and they excluded a major diagnostic category, personality disorder. The unfortunate consequences of these decisions will soon become apparent.

In our previous reviews of the "true" prevalence studies, we found that overall rates of psychopathology did not show consistent differences according to sex, nor did rates of psychosis in general (33) or schizophrenia in particular (34). In sharp contrast, we found in our 1969 review that consistently higher rates of neurosis were reported for women while consistently higher rates of personality disorder were reported for men (33). The studies that we have added since the earlier review change this broad picture very little with respect to rates of psychosis, rates of neurosis, and rates of personality disorder according to sex. However, whereas in our 1969 review we found 12 studies showing higher overall rates for males and 18 for females, the tally now is 16 in which men and 27 in which women show the higher total rates of psychopathology.

Gove & Tudor reported that when they divided the North American and European studies that we included in our 1969 review into pre-World War II and post-World War II groups, overall rates were consistently higher for men in the earlier studies and for women in the later studies. Given the biased definition of "mental illness" that they used in their own analysis of the literature, it would seem that this is the strongest support that they have for their hypothesis, other things equal. Other things, however, are not equal.

Women's roles in North America and Europe should be less traditional and hence, by extension of Gove & Tudor's argument, more stressful in urban than in rural areas, especially in urban areas following World War II. Thus, neurosis and functional psychosis, the two broad types of psychopathology that Gove & Tudor combined with measures of anxiety and distress to indicate "mental illness," should *each* be more likely to show higher rates for females in the later studies than in the earlier and in the urban than in the rural settings—assuming as Gove & Tudor do that environmentally induced stress is the major factor responsible for these types of psychopathology.

Unfortunately, few of the studies published prior to and early in World War II (there is a gap in publications between 1943 and 1950) provide data on psychosis, neurosis, and personality disorder according to sex. As Table 4 shows, no clear trends emerge for these types of psychopathology in these earlier studies. The later studies, however, show higher rates of neurosis for women than for men in *both* rural and urban settings, while for psychosis, the results are just the opposite of what Gove & Tudor's position implies, as women tend to show higher rates in rural settings while men tend to show higher rates in urban settings. The latter finding is more congruent with Jarvis' beliefs about sex roles in the "modern industrial society" of 19th century Massachusetts than Gove & Tudor's ideas about sex roles in the "modern industrial society" of today.

The question remains as to why in Table 4 overall rates of psychopathology should be higher for males in 7 out of the 9 earlier studies while overall rates for females are higher in 18 out of the 19 later studies. This is further documentation

Table 4 Comparison of male and female rates of different types of psychopathology reported in European and North American studies according to rural and urban study sites and date of publication

		Study site					
		Rural		Urban		Mixed	
		Number of studies in which rate is higher for:					
Date of publication	Type of psychopathology	Males	Females	Males	Females	Males	Females
Before 1950	All	4	1	1	1	2	0
	Psychosis	2	1	1	1	0	1
	Neurosis	1	1	0	1	–	–
	Personality disorder	3	0	–	–	–	–
1950 or After	All	1	13	0	5	–	–
	Psychosis	1	6	3	1	–	–
	Neurosis	0	9	0	4	–	–
	Personality disorder	5	2	2	1	–	–

of the reversal over time so perceptively noted and incorrectly interpreted by Gove & Tudor on the basis of our 1969 review of a smaller number of studies.

The key to the answer lies, we believe, in the fact that the overall rates of psychopathology in the later studies show the same relation to sex in Table 4 as does neurosis—consistently higher rates for females in rural as well as in urban settings. As in the case of neurosis, this is hardly what we would expect on the basis of Gove & Tudor's role change argument and the reasonable assumption that women's roles are more traditional in rural settings. However, it is what we would expect in terms of another set of considerations that have to do with methodological differences between the earlier studies and the later studies: first, the use of expanded nomenclatures following World War II; second, the use of symptom items such as the 22-item scale from the Midtown study and a battery of similar items developed by the Stirling County researchers in many of the later studies. As we showed earlier, the expanded nomenclature is largely responsible for the increase in overall rates shown by the studies published in 1950 or later. Moreover, as was also noted, the 22-item scale and similar measures tend to sample neurotic types of symptomatology rather than symptoms of psychosis or personality disorder. These methodological considerations, rather than the role hypotheses of either Jarvis or of Gove & Tudor, seem to provide the most parsimonious explanation of the reversal over time in overall rates according to sex shown in Table 4.

Nevertheless, there is a major substantive issue posed by some of the results in Table 4 and it lies in the contrasting excess of women among neurotics and of men among those diagnosed as having a personality disorder. The contrasts are general for rural and urban areas and tend to hold as well in the studies, excluded from Table 4 above, done outside of North America and Europe. Either social factors that define sex differences are more constant or biological bases of such differences are more potent than social causation theorists have supposed.

Annual Review authors have been pointing out scattered but interesting reports of sex differences and calling for more research for years—and at an accelerating pace in more recent volumes (82, 104, 148, 154). As Bardwick's recent book (6) and Maccoby's review of it (105) suggest, the issue of the relative contribution of biological factors and social factors to these differences is very much alive. We would suggest that the issue comes to an interesting focus in the sex differences in neurosis and personality disorder summarized above.

SOCIAL CLASS On the basis of previous analyses of the "true" prevalence studies, we found that the most consistent result reported was an inverse relationship between overall rates of psychopathology and social class (33). As Table 5 shows, this relationship holds when we add additional findings from among the studies that we have located since our 1969 review. Of the 33 communities for which the relevant data were reported, 28 yielded the highest rate in the lowest class. Moreover, although an earlier, less complete compilation of findings led us to speculate that this inverse relationship between social class and overall rates of psychopathology did not hold in rural areas (35), the expanded coverage of studies, reported in Table 5, no longer suggests as clear a difference in this respect between rural and urban areas.

Table 5 Comparison of rates of different types of psychopathology in lowest and other than lowest social classes within rural and urban study sites

	Study site					
	Rural		Urban		Mixed[a]	
	Number of studies in which rate is highest for:					
Type of psychopathology	Lowest class	Other than lowest class	Lowest class	Other than lowest class	Lowest class	Other than lowest class
All	9	4	17	1	2	0
Psychosis	1	5	3	3	2	1
Neurosis	3	3	4	3	0	2
Personality disorder	4	2	5	1	2	0

[a]Data reported for sites that are not predominantly rural or urban with no separation of rural and urban rates.

We have been able to add few data on the major subtypes of psychopathology and what we have added produced little change in the trends that we reported in our earlier review. Personality disorder shows a consistent inverse relationship with class; neurosis and psychosis do not.

It should be noted, however, that the broad category of psychosis masks some strong differences between two subtypes, manic-depressive psychosis and schizophrenia. Only seven studies reported data on schizophrenia and manic-depressive psychosis according to class (33). Of these seven none reported the highest rate of manic-depressive psychosis in the lowest class while, by contrast, five of the seven reported the highest rate of schizophrenia in the lowest class. In addition, the Midtown study researchers, who did not report data in the form of specific diagnoses, found an inverse relationship between class and symptom patterns judged to be of a schizophrenic type (97). The only exceptions to this inverse relationship are studies done in two Japanese communities, and they may be exceptions in Japan also. That is, Kato, a Japanese epidemiologist, has informed us that they are at variance with unpublished findings from his nationwide study of untreated as well as treated disorder (85).

Furthermore, studies of schizophrenia based only on treated rates have usually shown the same inverse relationship with class (41, 46, 70, 77, 123, 170). Among these studies of treated cases—and there are about a dozen reported or reviewed in the references cited above—only one did not show the highest treated rates of schizophrenia in the lowest social stratum (23).

Altogether then there is considerable evidence of a high concentration of psychopathology in the lower class compared to all other classes. Why should this be so?

In 1939, Faris & Dunham published their classic ecological study of psychiatric disorder in Chicago (46). Their well-known finding was that hospital first admission rates for most psychoses, including schizophrenia, were highest in the central slum sections of the city and decreased regularly as one moved out toward the well-to-do suburban areas. Consider the explanation that Faris & Dunham favored for their results:

> In these most disorganized sections of the city and, for that matter, of our whole civilization, many persons are unable to achieve a satisfactorily conventional organization of their world. The result may be a lack of any organization at all, resulting in a confused, frustrated, and chaotic personality, or it may be a complex but unconventional original organization. In either case there is a serious divergence from the conventional organization which makes communication and understanding impossible and, for that matter, makes any form of cooperation difficult. It is just this type of unintelligible behavior which becomes recognized as mental disorder (46, p. 159).

This view that social location is a cause of psychopathology is reflected in the theoretical explanations supplied in most of the best known epidemiological studies conducted by U.S. investigators. The study, for example, by Hollingshead & Redlich of treated rates of psychopathology according to social class in New Haven was motivated by, and the findings explained in terms of, a view that "psychiatrists work with phenomena that are essentially social in origin" (77, p. 11). The central theoretical hypothesis of the Stirling County study (100) and the Yoruba study (99) was that "social disintegration" is causally related to psychopathology, and the results of the studies were interpreted as being consistent with this hypothesis. Similarly, the Midtown study investigators took as their "most fundamental postulate" the proposition that "sociocultural conditions . . . have measurable consequences reflected in the mental health differences to be observed within a population" (159, pp. 12–13), and they interpreted their main findings in terms of the pathogenic consequences of a "poverty complex" and of processes of "stigmatize-rejection" and "role discontinuity" (159, pp. 366–71), further elaborated in terms of a theory of environmentally induced "stress" and "strain" (97).

There have also been at least two ambitious extensions of these approaches along more social psychological lines, each strongly influenced by the work of Merton (120). One of the approaches was developed in an investigation of drinking and related problem behavior in a town and its surrounding rural area in southwestern Colorado (83); the other focused on explaining symptoms and diagnoses in, respectively, a community sample and a psychiatric patient sample of Blacks in Philadelphia (133). Both theoretical formulations postulate that a major source of stress is created by environmentally induced dysjunctions between goals and the means to achieve them and in related discrepancies between aspirations and achievements.

All of these theoretical positions are examples of social causation orientations. In each, psychopathology is viewed as in large part a consequence of environmentally induced stress on the individual. To varying degrees these approaches are quite compatible with Frank's "sick society" analogy, with the addition that they locate the sources of the social organism's greatest inflammation and pain in its slums and low status groups.

Foreshadowing the findings that we have been discussing, Jarvis reported in 1855 that "the pauper class furnishes, in ratio of its numbers, sixty-four times as many cases of insanity as the independent class" (80, pp. 52–53). His explanation for this finding differed sharply from the environmentalist views described above, however. He wrote:

> Men of unbalanced mind and uncertain judgment do not see the true nature and relation of things, and they manifest this in mismanagement of their common affairs. They do not adapt the means which they possess or use to the ends which they desire to produce. Hence they are unsuccessful in life; their plans of obtaining subsistence for themselves or their families, or of accumulating property, often fail; and they are consequently poor, and often paupers. . . . the cause of . . . their mental derangement lies behind, and is anterior to, their outward poverty (80, pp. 55–56).

In this interpretation Jarvis provides an early example of what has come to be known as the social selection explanation of relationships between social position and psychopathology (40). This type of explanation was encountered previously with regard to the rural-urban differences, in the suggestion that rural migrants to cities may bring psychopathology with them rather than developing it in response to the stress of urban living. It stems from a theoretical orientation more characteristic of epidemiological researchers in Europe today than in the United States (131, 163).

By contrast with the social stress theorists, social selection theorists see social position not as a cause but as a consequence of psychopathology. And just as a social stress explanation is consistent with an environmentalist orientation to etiology, so is a social selection explanation consistent with a genetic view.

In his essay introducing present-day readers to Jarvis' 1855 report, Grob makes an interesting comment on Jarvis' interpretation of the relationship he found between poverty and insanity that helps to put this issue in prespective:

> Like others coming from the same background, Jarvis saw the genteel New England society that he loved and valued being eroded. . . . In a very real sense, therefore, some of the points that he attempted to make . . . were a reflection of his own social ideology. . . . What Jarvis did was to take a series of statistics and read them in the light of his own moral assumptions . . . (66, p. 56).

Would Grob be less critical, however, of the social stress interpretations of the results of the more recent epidemiological investigations that have reported findings so similar to Jarvis'? We doubt it.

As early critics of Faris & Dunham have argued, downward social drift of previously ill persons could explain plausibly the concentration of cases in the slums of Chicago (e.g. 121). Nor does a finding in the New Haven study that most lower class cases of psychopathology had originated in that class rather than having drifted down to it resolve the problem. As Gruenberg pointed out, in a society such as our own where upward social mobility is the norm, it is quite possible that the healthy members of the lower class have been selected upward, leaving behind a "residue" of ill (67). Both downward "drift" and this notion of "residues" are major varieties of what was designated above in broader terms as the social selection hypothesis.

Some findings from the Midtown Study illustrate the difficulties involved in choosing between social stress and social selection explanations of the relation between rate of psychopathology and social position. In an advance over previous epidemiological studies, the Midtown researchers investigated parental class position, a factor clearly antecedent to the current psychiatric condition of their adult respondents. Finding a significant inverse relation between their respondents' symptomatology and the socioeconomic status of their respondents' parents, the investigators suggested that environmental deprivation in childhood is a causal factor in psychopathology. However, they also found that the relation between parental socioeconomic status and impairing symptoms was weaker than the relation of respondents' own socioeconomic status to impairing symptoms. Moreover, respondents rated impaired were most likely to be found among those who were downwardly mobile relative to their parents, and least likely to be found among those who were upwardly mobile. Accordingly, the Midtown researchers concluded that perhaps both social stress, in the form of childhood deprivation, and social selection, in the form of intergeneration mobility, contribute to the strong inverse relation between psychopathology and the respondent's own socioeconomic status (159, pp. 212–13, 228–29). However, as implied by Michael, one of the Midtown researchers, genetic predisposition could, with equal plausibility, be substituted for childhood deprivation in this interpretation (159, pp. 329–30).

Like Jarvis' research, the more recent epidemiological investigations have been cross-sectional, each conducted at one time and in one place and without experimental controls. Like his research, they were not designed to test competing social stress versus social selection hypotheses. Thus it appears that it is the *Zeitgeist* that changed from his time to theirs far more than the empirical basis for choosing between opposing social stress and social selection explanations of relations between social location and psychopathology.

TOWARD A RESOLUTION OF THE SOCIAL STRESS–SOCIAL SELECTION ISSUE

A number of recent studies with data on social mobility have shown that social selection processes play a part in relations between social class and psychopathology, especially schizophrenia and antisocial personality (e.g. 12, 42, 60, 144, 170). How large a part they play relative to social stress, however, has remained at issue (33) and has, in fact, become a matter of sharp controversy in efforts to explain the inverse relationship between social class and schizophrenia (92, 93, 114).

The social stress–social selection issue is a key one. Its resolution would move research on relations between social and cultural factors and psychopathology off the dead center to which the cumulative results of the "true" prevalence studies have brought us—a center marked out by vivid, consistent, and highly challenging relationships that lend themselves all too promiscuously to equally vivid but opposing theoretical explanations. Let us, therefore, summarize our own approach to this venerable issue by way of an illustration of where we think this field will be moving in the future.

A Quasi-Experimental Strategy for Testing of the Social Stress–Social Selection Issue

More impressive research has been done on the etiology of schizophrenia thus far than on any of the other types of psychopathology with no known organic basis. The strongest of this research has been made possible by the identification of natural experiments. The prime examples are the control of heredity provided by the phenomenon of monozygotic twins (e.g. 62) and the strategies centering on adoption (e.g. 147). In such strategies, however, the powerful contrasts so far have been on genetic rather than on the social environmental side of the nature-nurture issue. Are there other natural contrasts that would make it possible to develop quasi-experimental strategies for investigating the etiological implications of the relation between social class and psychopathology?

We have argued that at least one such set of conditions does exist and that it provides, potentially, a key to a crucial test of the social stress–social selection issue for types of psychopathology such as schizophrenia and antisocial personality that are inversely related to social class (28, 33). The set of conditions is provided by the processes whereby ethnic groups are assimilated in relatively open-class societies. Let us try to summarize the main ideas involved in this quasi-experimental strategy.

SOME SOCIAL HISTORY Jarvis reported in 1855 not only that paupers had disproportionately high rates of insanity but that disproportionately high numbers of the poor and insane were new Irish immigrants. While he thought that both environmental factors and heredity were responsible, he believed that the latter was more important, speculating that:

> The Irish laborers have less sensibility and fewer wants to be gratified than the Americans, and yet they more commonly fail to supply them. They have also a greater irritability; they are more readily disturbed when they find themselves at variance with the circumstances about them, and less easily reconciled to difficulties they cannot overcome.
>
> Unquestionably much of their insanity is due to their intemperance, to which the Irish seem to be peculiarly prone . . . (80, p. 62).

The reason for his findings, he implied, was selective migration to the United States by those Irish whose inherited weaknesses had predisposed them to both poverty and insanity (80, pp. 62–63). Consider Jarvis' views on this matter in the context of the history of ethnic groups in New York City.

The urban history of New York has been marked by successive waves of new immigrant groups: the Irish and Germans in the 1840s, the Jews and Italians starting in the 1880s, the Blacks after World War I, and the Puerto Ricans after World War II (56). With the possible exception of non-Jewish Germans, the initial conditions of these new groups in the city, like the Irish of Jarvis' time in Massachusetts, were poverty, slums, and working-class jobs. The Jews, the Irish, and, to a lesser extent, the Italians have moved up *over succeeding generations* into relatively affluent and largely middle class circumstances in New York. In this process of assimilation, these three ethnic groups have achieved a substantial share in the wealth and power of the city, as have, of course, the Irish in Massachusetts.

It has often been thought that one of the tragedies of the human condition is that man does not live long enough to become wise. This is certainly true on this particular count for Jarvis. If he were alive today, he would see that the Irish as a group have indeed assimilated to middle class circumstances, sharing in the wealth and power of the state, and he would be forced to abandon his hypothesis about the constitutional inferiority of this immigrant group. In the light of the history of ethnic assimilation, it seems an equally poor explanation for the low status of Blacks and Puerto Ricans, the newest groups of immigrants to New York City, who are now concentrated geographically in its slums and occupationally in its low-paying unskilled and semiskilled jobs.

THE ALTERNATIVE PREDICTIONS Members of new immigrant groups in our urban centers have faced great social pressures in the form, for example, of prejudice and discrimination. This was true for the Irish immigrants of Jarvis' time (e.g. 66); it is true for Black and Puerto Rican New Yorkers in ours (e.g. 56). It is hardly surprising, therefore, that from a *social stress orientation,* we would predict that Blacks and Puerto Ricans would have higher rates of psychopathology *than their class counterparts* among more advantaged ethnic groups such as WASPS, Jews, and Irish in New York City.

Far less apparent, however, is that from a *social selection orientation,* we would predict just the opposite. For if social pressure is greater on disadvantaged ethnic groups such as Blacks and Puerto Ricans, we would expect more of their healthier members to be kept in lower class positions, thereby diluting the lower class psychopathology. By contrast, with less pressure to block them, the tendency of healthy members of more advantaged ethnic groups to rise or be able to maintain the higher class status to which the groups had been assimilated would leave behind a relatively undiluted residue of disabled persons. Thus social selection processes should function to give a higher rate of psychopathology among WASPs, Jews, and Irish than among Blacks and Puerto Ricans, *social class held constant.*

State of the Evidence

If the theoretical analysis briefly summarized above is correct, we may have something quite rare—a major substantive issue that could turn on what deceptively appear to be simple questions of fact: the question of whether, for example, rates of psychopathology are higher or lower among Blacks and Puerto Ricans in New York City relative to the rates for their class counterparts in more advantaged ethnic groups. We could substitute other sets of advantaged and disadvantaged ethnic groups in other urban centers for Blacks and Puerto Ricans in New York City in the question; for example, Indians and Pakistanis versus other Londoners or southern migrants versus northern residents of Milan. Such replications would provide a cumulatively powerful test.

Some limited but nevertheless informative comparisons may soon become available from Robins' extension of her remarkable program of life history research on antisocial personality (144) to a follow-up study of lower class Black schoolboys (145), Langner's following after 5 years of a children's sample that included Black and Puerto Rican teenagers (96), and from further analysis of Dunham's data on schizophrenia in a Detroit community that contains lower class Blacks and Whites (41). By and large, however, the facts to answer this question are not available from previous research. The "true" prevalence studies do not provide adequate data on different types of psychopathology for contrasting ethnic groups with social class controlled (33). Nor are measures currently available for which there is persuasive evidence of validity, particularly when comparisons are to be made across ethnic groups.

Thus the two parts of the legacy from the "true" prevalence studies have become inseparable: It is impossible to resolve the substantive issues that they pose without coming to terms as well with what we described as the Pandora's box of methodological problems involved in the conceptualization and measurement of psychopathology in general populations. Since measures used in the epidemiological studies have not been adequately tested for validity, the problem has become one of how to test existing measures and/or develop and test new measures. Our views on how this problem can best be tackled, as well as some of the results of our ongoing efforts to solve it, have been presented elsewhere (29–32, 36–39).

We believe that there are four key sets of problems to be solved in conceptualizing and measuring psychopathology in contrasting class and ethnic groups from the general population:

1. Cultural differences in modes of expressing distress.
2. Relations between physical illness and some types of psychiatric symptomatology —especially those thought of as psychophysiological.
3. Relations between symptoms of disturbance of cognition, affect and volition on the one hand and ability and disability in role functioning on the other.
4. The extent to which symptomatology is situationally specific and the extent to which it is relatively independent of changes in external circumstances.

Barring breakthroughs in biochemical research, we believe that how such matters are dealt with will determine in large part the adequacy of measures of psychopathology in general populations.

CONCLUSIONS

A body of epidemological data on the "true" prevalence of psychopathology and its distribution in community populations around the world has accumulated since the early 20th century. These data suggest that some currently popular speculations about relations between social and cultural factors and psychopathology do not represent the best hypotheses to guide future research. The results of these studies give pause, for example, to speculations about an increase in psychopathology as a function of the stresses and strains of modern society, and about an excess of psychopathology among women as a function of their changing role in modern society.

While these studies taken cumulatively have, we believe, generated less parochial hypotheses than any single study or any set of studies done in one area or period, they do not settle the basic issues about the role of social and cultural factors in psychopathology. Nor do we think that future research will settle these issues until it moves from cross-sectional surveys to quasi-experimental studies that exploit contrasts provided by ongoing social processes in order to test specific alternative hypotheses.

This field has reached the stage where a fascinating body of descriptive data has posed a set of major substantive issues. It is moving toward the stage in which increasing sophistication will be brought to bear on the methodological problems that stand in the way of resolution of these issues. We would suggest that it is precisely at this point in its development that a field becomes an exciting one in which to work.

Literature Cited

1. Abramson, J. H. 1966. Emotional disorder, status inconsistency and migration. *Milbank Mem. Fund Quart.* 44:23–48
2. Adelson, J. 1969. Personality. *Ann. Rev. Psychol.* 20:217–52
3. Am. Psychiat. Assoc. Comm. Nomencl. Statist. 1952. *Diagnostic and Statistical Manual: Mental Disorders.* Washington, D.C.: Am. Psychiat. Assoc. 132 pp.
4. Am. Psychiat. Assoc. Comm. Nomencl. Statist. 1968. *DSM-II: Diagnostic and Statistical Manual of Mental Disorders.* Washington, D.C.: Am. Psychiat. Assoc. 134 pp.
5. Astrup, C., Ødegaard, Ø. 1960. Internal migration and disease in Norway. *Psychiat. Quart.* 34 suppl.: 116–30
6. Bardwick, J. M. 1971. *Psychology of Women.* New York: Harper & Row. 242 pp.
7. Bash, K. W. 1967. Untersuchungen über die Epidemiologie neuropsychiatrischer Erkrankungen unter der Landbevölkerung der Provinz Fars, Iran. *Aktuel. Fragen Psychiat. Neurol.* 5: 162–78
8. Bash, K. W., Bash-Liechti, J. 1969. Studies on the epidemiology of neuropsychiatric disorders among the rural population of the province of Khuzestan, Iran. *Soc. Psychiat.* 4:137–43
9. Bautista, C. M. 1970. Epidemiologia neuropsiquica en adolescentes y adultos jóvenes. *Rev. Neuropsychiat.* 33:286–300
10. Beiser, M., Ravel, J.-L., Collomb, H., Egelhoff, C. 1972. Assessing psychiatric disorder among the Serer of Senegal. *J. Nerv. Ment. Dis.* 154: 141–51
11. Benedict, P. K., Jacks, I. 1954. Mental illness in primitive societies. *Psychiatry* 17:377–89
12. Birtchnell, J. 1971. Social class, parental social class, and social mobility in psychiatric patients and general population controls. *Psychol. Med.* 1:209–21
13. Blake, R. R., Mouton, J. S. 1959. Personality. *Ann. Rev. Psychol.* 10:203–32
14. Blumenthal, M. D. 1967. Sex as a source of heterogeneity in a mental health survey. *J. Psychiat. Res.* 5:75–87
15. Böök, J. A. 1953. A genetic and neuropsychiatric investigation of a north Swedish population, with special regard to schizophrenia and mental deficiency. *Acta Genet. Statist. Med.* 4:1–100
16. Buehler, J. H. 1966. Two experiments in psychiatric inter-rater reliability. *J. Health Hum. Behav.* 7:192–202
17. Burgess, E. W. 1955. Mental health in modern society. In *Mental Health and Mental Disorder,* ed. A. M. Rose, 3–17. New York: Norton. 626 pp.
18. Caplan, G., Arieti, S., Eds. *American Handbook of Psychiatry,* Vol. 3. Rev. ed. In press
19. Caudill, W. 1958. *The Psychiatric Hospital as a Small Society.* Cambridge: Harvard Univ. Press. 406 pp.
20. Chance, N. A. 1962. Conceptual and methodological problems in cross-cultural health research. *Am. J. Public Health* 52:410–17

21. Christie, R., Lindauer, F. 1963. Personality structure. *Ann. Rev. Psychol.* 14: 201–30
22. Clausen, J. A. 1959. The sociology of mental illness. In *Sociology Today,* ed. R. K. Merton, L. Broom, L. S. Cottrell Jr., 485–508. New York: Basic Books. 623 pp.
23. Clausen, J. A., Kohn, M. L. 1959. Relation of schizophrenia to the social structure of a small city. In *Epidemiology of Mental Disorder,* ed. B. Pasamanick, 69–94. Washington, D.C.: Am. Assoc. Advan. Sci. 295 pp.
24. Cooper, J. E. et al 1972. *Psychiatric Diagnosis in New York and London.* New York: Oxford Univ. Press. 152 pp.
25. Cowen, E. L. 1973. Social and community interventions. *Ann. Rev. Psychol.* 24:423–72
26. Crandell, D. L., Dohrenwend, B. P. 1967. Some relations among psychiatric symptoms, organic illness, and social class. *Am. J. Psychiat.* 123:1527–38
27. Denis, G., Tousignant, M., Laforest, L. Prevalence de cas d'interet psychiatrique dans une region du Quebec. *J. Assoc. Méd. Can.* Submitted for publication
28. Dohrenwend, B. P. 1966. Social status and psychological disorder: an issue of substance and an issue of method. *Am. Sociol. Rev.* 31:14–34
29. Dohrenwend, B. P. 1970. Psychiatric disorder in general populations: Problem of the untreated "case." *Am. J. Public Health* 60:1052–64
30. Dohrenwend, B. P. Key problems in the conceptualization and measurement of psychiatric disorders in general populations. In *Measuring Psychosocial Stress: Brief Mental Health Scales for Community Studies,* ed. R. Prince, H. B. M. Murphy. Baltimore: Nat. Educ. Press. In press
31. Dohrenwend, B. P., Chin-Shong, E., Egri, G., Mendelsohn, F. R., Stokes, J. 1970. Measures of psychiatric disorder in contrasting class and ethnic groups: a preliminary report of on-going research. See Ref. 74, 159–202
32. Dohrenwend, B. P., Crandell, D. L. 1970. Psychiatric symptoms in community, clinic, and mental hospital groups. *Am. J. Psychiat.* 126: 1611–21
33. Dohrenwend, B. P., Dohrenwend, B. S. 1969. *Social Status and Psychological Disorder.* New York: Wiley. 207 pp.
34. Dohrenwend, B. P., Dohrenwend, B. S. Epidemiological and related research on the problem of schizophrenia: findings and implications. In *Schizophrenia: Implications of Research Findings for Treatment and Teaching,* ed. R. Littlestone, M. Katz, M. Roath, M. Tuma. New York: Basic Books. In press
35. Dohrenwend, B. P., Dohrenwend, B. S. Psychiatric disorders in urban settings. See Ref. 18
36. Dohrenwend, B. P., Egri, G., Mendelsohn, F. 1971. Psychiatric disorder in general populations: a study of the problem of clinical judgment. *Am. J. Psychiat.* 127:1304–12
37. Dohrenwend, B. S. 1973. Life events as stressors: a methodological inquiry. *J. Health Soc. Behav.* 14:167–75
38. Dohrenwend, B. S. Social status and stressful life events. *J. Pers. Soc. Behav.* In press
39. Dohrenwend, B. S., Dohrenwend, B. P. 1973. An approach to the problem of valid comparison of psychiatric disorders in contrasting class and ethnic groups from the general population. See Ref. 73, 13–31
40. Dunham, H. W. 1961. Social structures and mental disorders: competing hypotheses of explanation. In *Causes of Mental Disorders: A Review of Epidemiological Knowledge, 1959,* 227–65. New York: Milbank Mem. Fund. 383 pp.
41. Dunham, H. W. 1965. *Community and Schizophrenia: an Epidemiological Analysis.* Detroit: Wayne State Univ. Press. 312 pp.
42. Dunham, H. W., Phillips, P., Srinivasan, B. 1966. A research note on diagnosed mental illness and social class. *Am. Sociol. Rev.* 31:223–27
43. Eaton, J. W., Weil, R. J. 1955. *Culture and Mental Disorders.* Glencoe, Ill.: Free Press. 254 pp.
44. Essen-Möller, E. 1956. Individual traits and morbidity in a Swedish rural population. *Acta Psychiat. Neurol. Scand. Suppl.* 100
45. Fabrega, H., Rubel, A. J., Wallace, C. A. 1967. Some social and cultural features of working class Mexican psychiatric outpatients. *Arch. Gen. Psychiat.* 16:704–12
46. Faris, R. E. L., Dunham, H. W. 1939. *Mental Disorders in Urban Areas: an Ecological Study of Schizophrenia and Other Psychoses.* Chicago Univ. Press. 270 pp.
47. Field, M. J. 1960. *Search for Security.* Evanston: Northwestern Univ. Press. 478 pp.

48. Fink, R., Shapiro, S., Goldensohn, S. S., Daily, E. F. 1969. The "filter-down" process to psychotherapy in a group practice medical care program. *Am. J. Public Health* 59:245–57
49. Fiske, D. W., Pearson, P. H. 1970. Theory and techniques of personality measurement. *Ann. Rev. Psychol.* 21:49–86
50. Frank, L. K. 1936. Society as the patient. *Am. J. Sociol.* 42:335–44
51. Freeman, H. E., Giovannoni, J. M. 1969. Social psychology of mental health. In *Handbook of Social Psychology,* ed. G. Lindzey, E. Aronson, 5:660–719. Reading, Mass.: Addison-Wesley. 786 pp. 2nd ed.
52. Gaitz, C. M., Scott, J. 1972. Age and the measurement of mental health. *J. Health Soc. Behav.* 13:55–67
53. Garner, A. M. 1958. Abnormalities of behavior. *Ann. Rev. Psychol.* 9:391–418
54. Gillis, L. S., Lewis, J. B., Slabbert, M. 1968. Psychiatric disorder amongst the coloured people of the Cape Peninsula: An epidemiological study. *Brit. J. Psychiat.* 114:1575–87
55. Ginzberg, E., Anderson, J. K., Ginsburg, S. W., Herma, J. L. 1959. *The Lost Divisions.* New York: Columbia Univ. Press. 225 pp.
56. Glazer, N., Moynihan, D. P. 1963. *Beyond the Melting Pot.* Cambridge: MIT Press. 360 pp.
57. Gnat, T., Henisz, J., Sarapata, A. 1964. *A Psychiatric-Socio-Statistical Study of Two Polish Towns.* Presented at 1st Int. Congr. Soc. Psychiat., London
58. Goffman, E. 1961. *Asylums.* New York: Doubleday-Anchor. 386 pp.
59. Golann, S. E., Eisdorfer, C., Eds. 1972. *Handbook of Community Mental Health.* New York: Appleton-Century-Crofts. 982 pp.
60. Goldberg, E. M., Morrison, S. L. 1963. Schizophrenia and social class. *Brit. J. Psychiat.* 109:785–802
61. Goldhamer, H., Marshall, A. W. 1953. *Psychoses and Civilization.* Glencoe, Ill.: Free Press. 126 pp.
62. Gottesman, I. I., Shields, J. 1972. *Schizophrenia and Genetics: A Twin Study Vantage Point.* New York: Academic. 452 pp.
63. Gottheil, E., Kramer, M., Hurvich, M. S. 1966. Intake procedures and psychiatric decisions. *Compr. Psychiat.* 7: 207–15
64. Gove, W. 1970. Societal reaction as an explanation of mental illness: an evaluation. *Am. Sociol. Rev.* 35:873–84
65. Gove, W. R., Tudor, J. F. 1973. Adult sex roles and mental illness. *Am. J. Sociol.* 78:812–35
66. Grob, G. N. 1971. Introduction. In *Insanity and Idiocy in Massachusetts: Report of the Commission on Lunacy, 1855,* 1–71. See Ref. 80
67. Gruenberg, E. M. 1961. Comments on "Social structures and mental disorders: competing hypotheses of explanation" by H. W. Dunham. See Ref. 40, 265–70
68. Gurin, G., Veroff, J., Feld, S. 1960. *Americans View Their Mental Health.* New York: Basic Books. 444 pp.
69. Haese, P. N., Meile, R. L. 1967. The relative effectiveness of two models for scoring the Midtown Psychological Index. *Community Ment. Health J.* 3: 335–42
70. Häfner, H., Reimann, H. 1970. Spatial distribution of mental disorders in Mannheim, 1965. See Ref. 74, 341–54
71. Hagnell, O. 1966. *A Prospective Study of the Incidence of Mental Disorder.* Stockholm: Svenska Bokförlaget Norstedts-Bonniers. 175 pp.
72. Hamburg, D. A. et al 1970. *Psychiatry as a Behavioral Science.* Englewood Cliffs, N.J.: Prentice-Hall. 114 pp.
73. Hammer, M., Salzinger, K., Sutton, S., Eds. 1973. *Psychopathology.* New York: Wiley. 588 pp.
74. Hare, E. H., Wing, J. K., Eds. 1970. *Psychiatric Epidemiology: An International Symposium.* New York: Oxford Univ. Press. 379 pp.
75. Helgason, T. 1964. Epidemiology of mental disorders in Iceland. *Acta Psychiat. Scand. Suppl.* 173
76. Hogarty, G. E., Katz, M. M., Lowery, H. A. 1967. Identifying candidates from a normal population for a community mental health program. In *Psychiatric Epidemiology and Mental Health Planning,* ed. R. R. Monroe, G. D. Klee, E. B. Brody, 220–34. Washington, D.C.: Am. Psychiat. Assoc. 374 pp.
77. Hollingshead, A. B., Redlich, F. C. 1958. *Social Class and Mental Illness.* New York: Wiley. 442 pp.
78. Howard, K. I., Orlinsky, D. E. 1972. Psychotherapeutic processes. *Ann. Rev. Psychol.* 23:615–68
79. Jarvis, E. 1850. On the comparative liability of males and females to insanity, and their comparative curability and mortality when insane. *Am. J. Insanity* 7:142–71
80. Jarvis, E., Ed. 1971. *Insanity and Idiocy in Massachusetts: Report of the Com-*

mission on Lunacy, 1855. Cambridge: Harvard Univ. Press. 213 pp.
81. Jayasundera, M. G. 1969. Mental health surveys in Ceylon. In *Mental Health Research in Asia and the Pacific,* ed. W. Caudill, T. Lin, 54–65. Honolulu: East-West Center Press. 487 pp.
82. Jensen, A. R. 1958. Personality. *Ann. Rev. Psychol.* 9:295–322
83. Jessor, R., Graves, T. D., Hanson, R. C., Jessor, S. L. 1968. *Society, Personality, and Deviant Behavior: A Study of a Tri-Ethnic Community.* New York: Holt, Rinehart & Winston. 500 pp.
84. Kaplan, B., Reed, R. B., Richardson, W. 1956. A comparison of the incidence of hospitalized and non-hospitalized cases of psychosis in two communities. *Am. Sociol. Rev.* 21:472–79
85. Kato, M. 1969. Psychiatric epidemiological surveys in Japan: the problem of case finding. See Ref. 81, 92–104
86. Katz, M. M. 1970. The classification of depression: normal, clinical and ethnocultural variations. In *Depression in the 70's,* ed. R. R. Fieve, 31–40. Excerpta Med. 120 pp.
87. Katz, M. M., Gudeman, H., Sanborn, K. 1969. Characterizing differences in psychopathology among ethnic groups: a preliminary report on Hawaii-Japanese and Mainland-American schizophrenics. See Ref. 81, 148–63
88. Kellert, S., Williams, L. K., Whyte, W. F., Alberti, G. 1967. Culture change and stress in rural Peru. *Milbank Mem. Fund Quart.* 45:391–415
89. Kelly, E. L. 1954. Theory and techniques of assessment. *Ann. Rev. Psychol.* 5:281–310
90. Kidson, M. A. 1967. Psychiatric disorders in the Walbiri of Central Australia. *Aust. New Zeal. J. Psychiat.* 1:14–22
91. Kidson, M. A., Jones, I. H. 1968. Psychiatric disorders among aborigines of the Australian western desert. *Arch. Gen. Psychiat.* 19:413–17
92. Kohn, M. L. 1972. Class, family, and schizophrenia: a reformulation. *Soc. Forces:* 50:295–304
93. Ibid. Rejoinder to David Mechanic, 310–13
94. Langner, T. S. 1962. A twenty-two item screening score of psychiatric symptoms indicating impairment. *J. Health Soc. Behav.* 3:269–76
95. Langner, T. S. 1965. Psychophysiological symptoms and women's status in Mexico. In *Approaches in Cross-Cultural Psychiatry,* ed. J. M. Murphy, A. H. Leighton, 360–92. Ithaca: Cornell Univ. Press. 406 pp.
96. Langner, T. S., Herson, J. H., Greene, E. L., Jameson, J. D., Goff, J. A. 1970. Children of the city: affluence, poverty and mental health. In *Psychological Factors in Poverty,* ed. V. L. Allen, 185–209. Chicago: Markham. 392 pp.
97. Langner, T. S., Michael, S. T. 1963. *Life Stress and Mental Health.* New York: Free Press of Glencoe. 517 pp.
98. Leighton, A. H. 1969. Cultural relativity and the identification of psychiatric disorders. See Ref. 81, 448–62
99. Leighton, A. H. et al 1963. *Psychiatric Disorder Among the Yoruba.* Ithaca: Cornell Univ. Press. 413 pp.
100. Leighton, D. C., Harding, J. S., Macklin, D. B., Macmillan, A. M., Leighton, A. H. 1963. *The Character of Danger.* New York: Basic Books. 545 pp.
101. Lin, T. 1953. A study of the incidence of mental disorder in Chinese and other cultures. *Psychiatry* 16:313–36
102. Lin, T., Rin, H., Yeh, E., Hsu, C., Chu, H. 1969. Mental disorders in Taiwan, fifteen years later: a preliminary report. See Ref. 81, 66–91
103. Lindzey, G., Loehlin, J., Manosevitz, M., Thiessen, D. 1971. Behavioral genetics. *Ann. Rev. Psychol.* 22:39–94
104. Maccoby, E. E. 1964. Developmental psychology. *Ann. Rev. Psychol.* 15: 203–50
105. Maccoby, E. E. 1972. The meaning of being female. *Contemp. Psychol.* 17: 369–72
106. Macmillan, A. M. 1957. The Health Opinion Survey: technique for estimating prevalence of psychoneurotic and related types of disorder in communities. *Psychol. Rep.* 3:325–39
107. Malzberg, B. 1940. *Social and Biological Aspects of Mental Disease.* Utica, NY: State Hosp. Press. 360 pp.
108. Manis, J. G., Brawer, M. J., Hunt, C. L., Kercher, L. C. 1963. Validating a mental health scale. *Am. Sociol. Rev.* 28:108–16
109. Manis, J. G., Brawer, M. J., Hunt, C. L., Kercher, L. C. 1964. Estimating the prevalence of mental illness. *Am. Sociol. Rev.* 29:84–89
110. Maoz, B., Levy, S., Brand, N., Halevi, H. S. 1966. An epidemiological survey of mental disorders in a community of newcomers in Israel. *J. Coll. Gen. Pract.* 11:267–84
111. Marconi, J., Munoz, M. 1968. Vision general de la investigacion epidemiologica en salud mental en Chile. In *Relato Offic. V Congr. Latino amer. Psiquiat.* 17–21
112. Mariategui, J., Alva y Ovidio de Leon, V. 1969. *Epidemiologia Psiquiatrica de un Distrito Urbano de Lima.* Lima,

Peru: Revista de Neuro-Psiquiatría. 115 pp.
113. Matarazzo, J. D. 1965. Psychotherapeutic processes. *Ann. Rev. Psychol.* 16:181–224
114. Mechanic, D. 1972. Social class and schizophrenia: some requirements for a plausible theory of social influence. *Soc. Forces* 50:305–9
115. Meehl, P. E. 1954. *Clinical vs. Statistical Prediction.* Minneapolis: Univ. Minnesota Press. 149 pp.
116. Meehl, P. E. 1959. Some ruminations on the validation of clinical procedures. *Can. J. Psychol.* 13:102–28
117. Meile, R. L., 1972. The 22-item index of psychophysiological disorder: Psychological or organic symptoms? *Soc. Sci. Med.* 6:125–35
118. Meile, R. L., Haese, P. N. 1969. Social status, status incongruence and symptoms of stress. *J. Health Soc. Behav.* 10:237–44
119. Menninger, K., Mayman, M., Pruyser, P. 1963. *The Vital Balance.* New York: Viking 531 pp.
120. Merton, R. K., Ed. 1957. Social structures and anomie. In *Social Theory and Social Structure,* 131–60. Glencoe, Ill.: Free Press. 645 pp.
121. Meyerson, A. 1940. Review of "Mental Disorder in Urban Areas: an Ecological Study of Schizophrenia and Other Psychoses." *Am. J. Psychiat.* 96:995–97
122. Mirskey, A. F. 1969. Neuropsychological bases of schizophrenia. *Ann. Rev. Psychol.* 20:321–48
123. Mishler, E. G., Scotch, N. A. 1965. Sociocultural factors in the epidemiology of schizophrenia: a review. *Int. J. Psychiat.* 10:101–18
124. Moses, L. E., Goldfarb, A., Glock, C. Y., Stark, R. W., Eaton, M. L. 1971. A validity study using the Leighton instrument. *Am. J. Public Health* 61: 1785–93
125. Mott, F. D., Roemer, M. I., 1948. *Rural Health and Medical Care.* New York: McGraw Hill. 608 pp.
126. Murphy, H. B. M. 1965. Migration and the major mental disorders. In *Mobility and Mental Health,* ed. M. B. Kantor, 5–29. Springfield, Ill.: Thomas. 247 pp.
127. Murphy, H. B. M. 1973. History and the evolution of syndromes: the striking case of latah and amok. See Ref. 73, 33–55
128. Myers, J. K., Lindenthal, J. J., Pepper, M. P., 1971. Life events and psychiatric impairment. *J. Nerv. Ment. Dis.* 152: 149–57
129. Myers, J. K., Lindenthal, J. J., Pepper, M. P., Ostrander, D. K., 1972. Life events and mental status: a longitudinal study. *J. Health Soc. Behav.* 13:398–406
130. Ødegaard, Ø. 1945. Distribution of mental diseases in Norway: A contribution to the ecology of mental disorder. *Acta Psychiat. Neurol.* 20:247–84
131. Ødegaard, Ø. 1956. The incidence of psychoses in various occupations. *Int. J. Soc. Psychiat.* 2:11–22
132. Opler, M. K. 1967. *Culture and Social Psychiatry.* New York: Atherton. 434 pp.
133. Parker, S., Kleiner, R. J. 1966. *Mental Illness in the Urban Negro Community.* New York: Free Press. 408 pp.
134. Phillips, D. L., 1966. The "true prevalence" of mental illness in a New England state. *Community Ment. Health J.* 2:35–40
135. Phillips, D. L., Clancy, K. J. 1972. Some effects of "social desirability" in survey studies. *Am. J. Sociol.* 77: 921–40
136. Phillips, D. L., Segal, B. E. 1969. Sexual status and psychiatric symptoms. *Am. Sociol. Rev.* 34:58–72
137. Phillips, L., Draguns, J. G. 1971. Classification of the behavior disorders. *Ann. Rev. Psychol.* 22:447–82
138. Piotrowski, A., Henisz, J., Gnat, T. 1968. Individual interview and clinical examination to determine prevalence of mental disorders. *Proc. 4th World Congr. Psychiat., Madrid, 1966. Excerpta Med. Int. Congr. Ser. No. 150:* 2477–78
139. Rabkin, J. G. 1972. Opinions about mental illness: a review of the literature. *Psychol. Bull.* 77:153–71
140. Rabkin, J. G. Public attitudes toward mental illness: a review of the literature. *Schizophrenia Bull.* In press
141. Rapoport, R. N. 1960. *Community as Doctor.* Springfield, Ill.: Thomas. 325 pp.
142. Rin, H., Chu, H., Lin, T. 1966. Psychophysiological reactions of a rural and suburban population in Taiwan. *Acta Psychiat. Scand.* 42:410–72
143. Rin, H., Lin, T. 1962. Mental illness among Formosan aborigines as compared with the Chinese in Taiwan. *J. Ment. Sci.* 108:134–46
144. Robins, L. N. 1966. *Deviant Children Grown Up.* Baltimore: Williams & Wilkins. 351 pp.
145. Robins, L. N., Murphy, G. E., Woodruff, R. A., King, L. J. 1971. Adult psychiatric status of Black schoolboys. *Arch. Gen. Psychiat.* 24:338–45
146. Rose, A. M., Stub, H. R. 1955. Summary of studies on the incidence of men-

tal disorders. In *Mental Health and Mental Disorder: A Sociological Approach,* ed. A. M. Rose, 87–116. New York: Norton. 626 pp.

147. Rosenthal, D., Kety, S. S., Eds. 1968. *Transmission of Schizophrenia.* London: Pergamon. 433 pp.
148. Sarason, I. G., Smith, R. E. 1971. Personality. *Ann. Rev. Psychol.* 22:393–446
149. Sawyer, J. 1966. Measurement and prediction, clinical and statistical. *Psychol. Bull.* 66:178–200
150. Scheff, T. J. 1966. *Being Mentally Ill.* Chicago: Aldine 210 pp.
151. Schwab, J. J., McGinnis, N. H., Warheit, G. J. 1973. Social psychiatric impairment: racial comparisons. *Am. J. Psychiat.* 130:183–87
152. Shader, R. I., Ebert, M. H., Harmatz, J. S. 1971. Langner's psychiatric impairment scale: a short screening device. *Am. J. Psychiat.* 128:596–601
153. Shore, J. H., Kinzie, J. D., Hampson, J. L., Pattison, E. M. 1973. Psychiatric epidemiology of an Indian village. *Psychiatry* 36:70–81
154. Singer, J. L., Singer, D. G. 1972. Personality. *Ann. Rev. Psychol.* 23:375–412
155. Slotkin, J. S. 1955. Culture and psychopathology. *J. Abnorm. Soc. Psychol.* 51:269–75
156. Spiro, H. R., Siassi, I., Crocetti, G. M. 1972. What gets surveyed in a psychiatric survey? *J. Nerv. Ment. Dis.* 154:105–14
157. Spitzer, R. L., Wilson, P. T. 1968. A guide to the American Psychiatric Association's new diagnostic nomenclature. *Am. J. Psychiat.* 124:1619–29
158. Srole, L. 1973. Reply to "Mental health and the city" by B. S. Dohrenwend. *Am. Sci.* 61:8
159. Srole, L., Langner, T. S., Michael, S. T., Opler, M. K., Rennie, T. A. C. 1962. *Mental Health in the Metropolis.* New York: McGraw-Hill. 428 pp.
160. Stanton, A. H., Schwartz, M. S. 1954. *The Mental Hospital.* New York: Basic Books. 492 pp.
161. Star, S. A. 1950. The screening of psychoneurotics in the army: technical development of tests. In *Measurement and Prediction,* ed. S. A. Stouffer et al, 4:486–547. Princeton Univ. Press. 756 pp.
162. Stern, J. A., McDonald, D. G. 1965. Physiological correlates of mental disease. *Ann. Rev. Psychol.* 16:225–64
163. Strömgren, E. 1950. Statistical and population studies within psychiatry: methods and principal results. In *Actualités Scientifiques et Industrielles. Congr. Int. Psychiat., VI, Psychiat. Soc.,* 155–88. Paris: Herman & Cie
164. Summers, G. F., Seiler, L. H., Hough, R. L. 1971. Psychiatric symptoms: Cross-validation with a rural sample. *Rural Soc.* 36:367–78
165. Susser, M. 1967. Causes of peptic ulcer. *J. Chronic Dis.* 20:435–56
166. Tarnopolsky, A., Olmo, G. D., Valdemarín, D. 1970. Prevalencia de enfermedad mentales en el Partido de Lanús. Informe preliminar. In *Estudios Sobre Epidemiologia Psiquiatria en America Latina,* ed. J. Mariategui, G. A. Castro, 17–27. Buenos Aires: ACTA
167. Tauss, W. 1967. A note on the prevalence of mental disturbance. *Aust. J. Psychol.* 19:121–23
168. Triandis, H. C., Malpass, R. S., Davidson, A. R. 1972. Cross-cultural psychology. *Bien. Rev. Anthropol. 1971:* 1–84
169. Triandis, H. C., Malpass, R. S., Davidson, A. R. 1973. Psychology and culture. *Ann. Rev. Psychol.* 24:355–78
170. Turner, R. J., Wagonfeld, M. O. 1967. Occupational mobility and schizophrenia: an assessment of the social causation and social selection hypotheses. *Am. Sociol. Rev.* 32:104–13
171. Wechsler, H., Solomon, L., Kramer, B. M., Eds. 1970. *Social Psychology and Mental Health.* New York: Holt, Rinehart & Winston. 842 pp.
172. White, R. W. 1953. Abnormalities of behavior. *Ann. Rev. Psychol.* 4:273–94
173. Wing, J. K., Brown, G. W. 1970. *Institutionalism and Schizophrenia.* Cambridge Univ. Press. 260 pp.
174. Wirt, R. D., Wirt, A. L. 1963. Psychotherapeutic processes. *Ann. Rev. Psychol.* 14:365–90
175. Wittkower, E. C., Termansen, P. E. 1969. Cultural psychiatric research in Asia. See Ref. 81, 433–47
176. Yancey, W. L., Rigsby, L., McCarthy, J. D. 1972. Social position and self-evaluation: the relative importance of race. *Am. J. Sociol.* 78:338–59
177. Yap, P. M. 1969. The culture-bound reactive syndromes. See Ref. 81, 33–53
178. Yoo, P. S. 1961. Mental disorders in Korean rural communities. In *Proc. 3rd World Congr. Psychiat.,* 2:1305–9. Montreal: McGill Univ. Press
179. Zubin, J. 1967. Classification of the behavior disorders. *Ann. Rev. Psychol.* 18:373–406

STATISTICS AND DATA ANALYSIS

❖224

William M. Meredith[1]
Carl H. Frederiksen
Donald H. McLaughlin[2]
Department of Psychology, University of California, Berkeley

INTRODUCTION

In attempting to organize the mass of material we felt deserved coverage, we found it necessary to impose a classificatory structure on it. The structure we imposed is in terms of the nature of the dependent variables and the number of populations of measurements (e.g. treatments) being explored. There is a considerable degree of arbitrariness in our classification scheme, and the classes turn out not to be fully mutually exclusive. We feel, however, the reader will find the system useful and convenient. We have attempted to write this chapter at a level which will be accessible to the sophisticated researcher in psychology and to the relatively advanced graduate student. Some papers cited, however, require a considerable degree of mathematical sophistication on the part of the reader for full understanding. We wish to encourage readers to realize that it is not necessary to be able to follow mathematical proofs in detail in order to apply the results.

Our classification scheme's first order concerns whether single or multiple dependent variables are under study; that is, the traditional dichotomy between multivariate and univariate analyses. The second order of classification considers whether a single or multiple populations (treatments, experimental conditions, etc) are involved. With single populations, the questions considered are ordinarily the testing of some hypothesis or fitting of some structural model; multiple populations ordinarily involve testing hypotheses about population differences.

So far we have a fourfold order of classification. The remaining order of classification is in terms of the nature of the measurements involved and has three levels: (*a*) continuous interval scale data; (*b*) ordinal data, and (*c*) categorical data. These

[1]Preparation of this review was supported in part by research grant NSF-GB-30779 from the National Science Foundation.

[2]Now at American Institutes of Research, Palo Alto, California.

levels appear to be somewhat idealized, for in practice they almost reduce to the following categories:

(*a*) Continuous interval scale—ordinary parametric analyses with normality assumptions.

(*b*) Ordinal data—nonparametric analyses.

(*c*) Categorical data—dichotomous data or chi-square analyses. Some cells of the resulting twelvefold system were found to contain so little of interest that they are not mentioned at all.

SINGLE DEPENDENT VARIABLE, SINGLE POPULATION

Continuous Interval Data

This section could contain discussion of classical and Bayesian estimation problems, classical (fixed predictor) regression and curve fitting problems, and discussion of some goodness-of-fit tests, all involving a continuous random variable. In reviewing the literature, we have found it convenient to ignore estimation problems, as we find the recent literature on estimation to be too specialized for a general psychological audience. The same statement applies to goodness-of-fit tests in this context. Nonparametric or distribution-free goodness-of-fit tests are discussed elsewhere.

Regression analysis will be dealt with fairly extensively in both the fixed and random predictor forms. Regression on predictors which are random variates should be dealt with in another section, but for economy and ease of treatment, we shall not make the distinction here.

We might remark that in this context, continuous generally can be interpreted to mean normal random variates.

This section is broken down into a number of subtopics. At the outset we wish to bring attention to the book by Draper & Smith (132) that the user of regression analysis will find helpful. In addition, the book by Goldberger (182), written for an audience of economists, provides fresh and novel insights into many aspects of regression analysis ordinarily ignored by psychologists.

REGRESSION MODELS The question of whether to use multiple regression weights or some simpler alternative has been discussed in three papers. Wang & Stanley (485) provide a lengthy review of theoretical and empirical work on differential weighting problems generally. Claudy (89) explored different weighting procedures empirically, and Schmidt (430) by Monte Carlo techniques. Both conclude that for small samples relative to the number of predictor variables, equal raw score weights should be preferred.

A series of thoughtful papers by Werts & Linn (491, 493) and Linn, Werts & Tucker (321) merit considerable study by psychologists who utilize multiple regression techniques. These papers are directed at the problem of inferring the magnitude of an effect in studies involving school and student characteristics and in choice of a change or growth variable as the dependent variable in regression analysis. In one paper they demonstrate that hypotheses of school effects can either be rejected or confirmed, depending on the method of analysis with a given set of data. These findings, of course, have considerable generality beyond the school effects model they take as a paradigm.

Conger (97) presents a unified treatment of the suppressor variable problem and introduces the notion of reciprocal suppression. Papers by Rutemiller & Bowers (425), Jacquez, Mather & Crawford (247), and Lancaster (310) take up the problem of heteroscedastic regression from different points of view. The first deals with a situation in which the error about regression is linear in the fixed predictors. A maximum likelihood technique is developed and compared with ordinary least squares in two sets of data. The maximum likelihood methods clearly perform better. In the second paper, no specification is imposed on the variance about regression, but it is assumed that several replicates of each value of a single predictor are available. Weighted least squares, maximum likelihood, and ordinary least squares are compared by Monte Carlo methods. It is recommended that weighted least squares be used whenever the number of replicates per cell exceeds the number of cells. Lancaster (310) deals with yet another approach in which the error about regression is a power function in a single predictor variable. He develops grouping estimators based on the mean values of dependent and independent variables in upper and lower sections of the range of the independent variable.

STATISTICAL ISSUES Several other papers deal with statistical problems in regression analysis. Gardner (168) explores the bias in variance about regression estimates when a regression equation from one sample is applied to another. He treats a variety of situations. King (287), in an excellent paper, deals with the question of what estimate of a regression coefficient is best in a new sample. He shows that a modification of the traditional weight is best over a large part of the sample space when sample size is small. Sclove (434) deals with a modified James-Stein estimator for regression weights. Aitkin (9) develops simultaneous fixed-width confidence intervals for a pair of regression lines. Davies (121) discusses the use of absolute deviations rather than squares.

STEPWISE REGRESSION The technique of stepwise multiple regression analysis continues to elicit a substantial degree of attention (133, 309, 333, 339, 418). Generally, stepwise multiple regression is becoming known as a method within the framework of data analysis, rather than strict statistical methodology (93). An excellent paper by Anscombe (16) describes the potential of an interactive computer-based stepwise system in which the investigator chooses the variable to be entered or deleted at each step. Several papers (159, 226, 309, 359) deal with the problem of examining all possible regressions for determination of the best possible subset of a given size. Beale, Kendall & Mann (36) provide a useful discussion, with examples, of this approach. Williams & Lindem (496, 497) describe an interesting procedure for what could be called setwise stepwise multiple regression in which subsets of variables play the role ordinarily taken by individual variates.

Draper, Guttman & Kanemasu (130) show that the significance level for entry of a variable in stepwise analysis should be approximately $p\alpha$, where p is the number of predictor variables instead of α. Their results were obtained assuming mutual independence of the predictors but may provide a useful rule of thumb for the commonly encountered situation.

MISSING DATA Several papers attack the problem of missing data in regression analysis. Afifi & Elashoff (2–5) consider the two-variable case with missing data on both X and Y variates. They discuss several methods of estimation and provide detailed tables and analyses of their behaviors under different conditions. Dagenais (115–118) considers problems that arise when predictor variable data only are missing. Guertin (197), using data from a large scale study, concludes that there is little gained by adopting any procedure other than that of simply ignoring missing computing intercorrelations from available data and then entering this correlation matrix into a multiple regression program. Kelejian (281) studies a similar problem.

NONLINEAR REGRESSION Nonlinear regression problems have attracted attention recently. In this connection we include the use of moderator variables and piecewise regression. Moderator variables have been studied extensively by Zedeck (503–505) and Conger (96). Piecewise linear (and nonlinear) regression has been studied by Bogartz (62, 63), Wainer (482), and others (311, 343). Classical nonlinear regression problems and procedures have been studied extensively (28, 449). An excellent pair of papers by Sclove (435) and Hoel (229) merit careful reading by any investigator interested in nonlinear regression. Thornby (466) has developed an extremely useful distribution-free test of linear regression against a general class of concave alternatives. A related problem is that of estimating linear regression coefficients subject to restraints (i.e. positivity); Mantel (332), McGuire et al (344), and Lovell & Prescott (327) have explored this problem and proposed solutions.

SINGLE DEPENDENT VARIABLE, MULTIPLE POPULATIONS

Continuous Interval Data

The problems we consider here deal with the reasonableness of assumptions and meaningfulness and appropriateness of statistical results. These problems have been the topics of numerous recent papers, but they appear primarily in statistics journals, or are written in a mathematical jargon that makes them next to impossible to comprehend, let alone apply. However, there are a number of results that are readable, if you have a Berlitz-like phrase book for mathematics and realize that you don't have to read the proofs or even the theorems in many of the articles.

What are the problems? Problem A: The *cost* of collecting the data will constrain the completeness of any study. The more one gets involved in a study, the larger the number of factors in the design will become; and there has been some progress in the recent past in constructing designs that make the most out of a given amount of data. For example, careful consideration of the alternatives to the null hypothesis that are of most interest, and use of assumptions of zero higher level implications before experimentation, can reduce the size and number of samples. Problem B: The choice of the best *testing procedure* can make a great deal of difference in the usefulness of data relative to theoretical questions. There have been a larger number of recent studies of the relative power and the robustness of competing test procedures and a much smaller number of creative proposals for new and better test procedures. Problem C: *Badly behaved data,* which violate some of the assumptions of the simplest testing procedures, seem to occur with a very high frequency, and a number of ways of legally fudging such data have been developed; for example, transforming the data to obtain normally distributed errors. In order to apply these procedures, all that is needed is a method of evaluating statistical significance for these new procedures. The work reviewed below is partitioned among these three problems, although some fudging is necessary due to the overlap among the problems, and some subjective interpretation is used, such as the assumption that unequal sample sizes constitute badly behaved data.

PROBLEM A The problem is to decide the pattern of sampling to jointly minimize the cost of the experiment (by minimizing the total sample size) and maximize the precision of the conclusions reached, subject to the constraints of the assumptions made. For example, if one can assume that the interactions between some factors in an experiment are zero, one need only run a small subset of the groups that would otherwise be needed, or if one can tolerate less precision (larger variances of estimates of parameters or larger probabilities of wrong conclusions from tests), fewer replications within each experimental group are necessary. Cohen (94), Bowman (66, 67), Hodges & Lehmann (228), and Tiku (470) provide tables for the relations among sample size and the probabilities of Type I and Type II errors for standard t-tests and analyses of variance (ANOVA).

There are three directions in which progress has been made recently in improving upon the standard designs. First, there is continuing work on randomized blocks designs (in which some or all of the factors are varied within experimental units, such as subjects). Second, there has been a great deal of work on incomplete blocks and fractional factorial designs (in which only a few of the combinations of the independent factors are run). Third, one can consider a sequential design in which a decision is made at various points during the experiment of whether to continue sampling or to stop and state the conclusions. For an introduction to designs of the first two types, there is an excellent book by Kirk (288) and reviews of recent advances by Addelman (1) and Herzberg & Cox (223). Sequential designs are thoroughly covered in De Grott's book (125).

In order to read many of the articles on experimental design, especially those dealing with unequal sample sizes (unbalanced designs, in general), one must become familiar with the notation of the design matrix and the concept of the generalized inverse of a matrix, because most authors have switched to this notation because it is much more compact than the usual summation notation. Briefly, in these terms, the data ($\mathbf{Y}$) are an $N \times 1$ vector and are assumed to be linearly related to an $\mathbf{M} \times 1$ vector of parameters (Θ) by the equation $\mathbf{Y} = \mathbf{X}\Theta + \mathbf{E}$, where $\mathbf{X}$ is an $N \times \mathbf{M}$ matrix of ones and zeros indicating the contributions of the parameters to the data and $\mathbf{E}$ is a vector of random errors that are subject to the usual assumptions. Now $\mathbf{X}^{-1}\mathbf{Y}$ would yield a vector of estimates of the parameters, but unless $\mathbf{M} = N$

and **X** has full rank, $\mathbf{X}^{-1}$ is not defined. Therefore, the generalized inverse of **X** $(\mathbf{X}'\mathbf{X})^{-1}\mathbf{X}'$, has been developed and used extensively. See, for example, Searle (436) for this concept.

Problem A, solution 1 Randomized blocks designs improve the precision of the estimation of parameters at the cost of requiring that one assume that the correlational structure of the observations within units is simple. ANOVA for single subject designs is set forth in articles by Shine (445, 446), and the rationale for such randomized and block designs, in general, is discussed by Youden (502) and Box & Guttman (68). Pearce (377, 378) investigates the relative efficiency of blocks designs, and Calinski (81) describes some desirable patterns in block designs. Koch (291) and Rees (410) present analyses of classes of randomized blocks designs called "split plot" designs, and Naruboodiri (368) describes some "changeover" designs.

One problem with repeated measures within a unit is to minimize undesirable sources of variance. Atkinson (23) gives a correction for the effects of measures on adjacent measures, and Phillips (381) gives tables for order of observations which minimize the linear trend effect across repeated measurements.

Problem A, solution 2 Incomplete and fractional designs purposely confound different sources of variance in order to reduce the size of the experiment. In order to use these designs, the experimenter assumes that certain higher order interactions are zero to eliminate the confounding. This allows one to investigate a large number of factors in an experiment that is not prohibitively large. For example, if one is willing to assume that all third-order and higher interactions are zero but wants to estimate all main effects and second-order interactions (called a Resolution V plan), he can investigate 10 two-level factors with 56 experimental runs, instead of 1024 runs. Addelman (1) reviews most of the recent work on fractional factorial designs. An alternative method of choosing a factorial design, the $|\mathbf{X}'\mathbf{X}|$ criterion, is described by Box (70); and a method for expressing experimental contrasts in factorial designs as linear combinations of a set of basis contrasts is developed by Das & Jain (120).

Latin squares are the best known type of confounded designs and are covered by Kirk (288). Pearce (375) points out several variations on Latin squares that may be of interest if you wish, for example, to test several treatments against a control.

There have been several papers (Pearce 376, Clatworthy 88, Afonja 6, Basson 34, Cunningham & Henderson 110, Robinson 417, and John, Wolock & David 252) on incomplete block designs; that is, designs in which each block receives only a subset of the treatments. These papers are concerned with procedures for generating the combinations of treatments and blocks, with procedures for estimating parameters in such designs, and with the relative efficiencies of the designs.

Finally, two recent papers have investigated the consequences of using nested designs in which different numbers of levels of the nested factors appear within each level of the higher stage factors, unbalanced nested designs. Leone et al (313) present examples of the method for analyzing these designs; and Goldsmith & Gaylor (184) generate and evaluate the relative efficiency of 61 different three-stage unbalanced designs.

Problem A, solution 3 Sequential sampling procedures are characterized by the performance of an intermediate statistical test on a subset of the potential data to be collected to determine whether it is worthwhile to collect more data. Therefore, they include the cost of collecting the data as a relevant term in the intermediate statistical test, which must be balanced against the cost of making an error in the conclusions of the study. In most cases, the form of the intermediate statistical tests is analogous to standard tests, although the interpretation is different. A thorough understanding of these procedures depends on an understanding of stochastic processes in general, as presented, for example, in De Groot's book on optimal statistical decisions (125). However, several recent articles have spelled out specific procedures that can be applied without a great deal of sophistication in stochastic processes.

For a fairly straightforward problem, the estimation of a population mean, two recent studies propose two-stage procedures. Arnold & Al-Bayyati (18) considered the problem of estimating the mean when a prior estimate is available. If the sample mean of a first sample is sufficiently far from the prior estimate of the population mean, a second sample is collected and the pooled mean used as the estimate. This procedure is shown to compare favorably with the usual procedure in efficiency. In a different case, where two populations are known to have a common mean but differing variances, Alam (10) developed a procedure which consists of initially balanced sampling from the two populations, and after determining which has the smaller variance, continued sampling from the population with the smaller variance. In particular, he solves the problem of determining how large the initial samples should be when the total of all the samples is fixed.

For the Behrens-Fisher problem, deciding whether two population means differ when the variances are different, Robbins et al (415) developed a sequential procedure which holds the standard deviations of the sample means from the two populations approximately equal. A nonparametric procedure for testing equality of location of two samples, a sequential signed rank test, was developed by Miller (355).

For the comparison of more than two populations, Ghosh (175) has developed a sequential procedure for various ANOVA designs; and Bechhofer et al (39) have developed sequential procedures for choosing the best (highest mean) of several populations with unknown variance.

Finally, before leaving Problem A, we mention two contributions to the sampling problem by Sedransk. In one study (439) he describes a sampling scheme for multifactor designs when the error variance is known, based on criteria of prescribed precision of estimates; and in another paper (440) he investigates the problems involved in using systematic sampling as opposed to random sampling.

PROBLEM B Most of the studies reviewed in the section on k-group univariate data analysis were concerned in one way or another with the choice of estimation and hypothesis testing procedures, developing new procedures, extending procedures, and evaluating the relative efficiencies of alternative procedures. The type of procedure you will use depends on whether you are interested in measures of location, or measures of dispersion, or the shape of a distribution.

The recent work in this area falls roughly into 11 categories, most of which are related to ANOVA, and we shall consider these categories sequentially.

Preliminary tests A preliminary test procedure is a statistical test whose outcome determines which of alternative tests of a main hypothesis will be used. Kale & Bancroft (279), Han & Bancroft (210), and Arnold (17) have investigated procedures for estimating the mean of a population which use the sample mean along with the mean of a sample from a second population if the two sample means are not too far apart according to a preliminary test. Mehta & Gurland (351) and Davis & Arnold (123) present analogous procedures for the estimation of a population variance, using information from a sample from a second population.

Testing equality of variances Gartside (169) compared empirically seven different methods of testing for homogeneity of variance in k groups and made recommendations based on relative power that were based partly on what kind of departure from homoscedasticity one expects. Generally, Bartlett's statistic compared favorably with the others. Sugiura & Nagao (461) developed mathematical results for Bartlett's test and compared it with Lehmann's asymptotically UMP invariant test. Burr & Foster (79) presented yet another test for equality of variances; and Han (209) has developed a multiple correlation test for use in two-factor designs. Bechhofer (38) has developed a method of ranking the variances of a set of populations to be used, for example, to determine which population has the smallest variance for further sampling.

Testing normality The second of the two main assumptions of the ANOVA model is that the errors are not only distributed with equal variances but are normally distributed. Shapiro, Wilk & Chen (443) compared 9 tests for normality empirically for 45 alternative distributions and recommended use of a statistic developed previously by Shapiro and Wilk. Wilk & Shapiro (495) extended the use of this statistic to the joint assessment of normality of several independent samples. D'Agostino & Cureton (119) presented a test for normality that is powerful against skewness.

Robustness Robustness of a procedure refers to the invariance of the outcome of the procedure with respect to variations in the true error distribution from that assumed in developing the procedure. In ANOVA, the variations are from homoscedasticity, normality, or independence of the errors. If you question these assumptions for your particular data, it is recommended that you use either nonparametric procedures or a function to transform your data prior to analysis. ANOVA has a reputation for being robust, although Bradley (71) has attacked this reputation in a large empirical study which found that when assumptions were violated, the significance levels became dependent on such factors as sample size and correlation of estimates of the mean and variance. For departures from normality, Arvesen (19) applied Tukey's jackknife method to provide a more robust ANOVA; and for departures from homogeneity of variances and covariances in repeated measures designs, Collier et al (95) presented an adjusted F-test which improved upon the standard procedure.

A particular deviation from normality has received continued attention recently: the case of (very) discrete measures. Hsu & Feldt (237) investigated the effect on the one-way F-test of using from two- to five-point scales for criterion scores and found only small differences in the test outcome from continuous scales. In 2-way designs, Gabrielsson & Seeger (163) found similar results with dichotomous data. In case you are still worried about the problem, McNeil (347) has furnished results of exploring consistent statistics in this case, using inverses of the assumed "discretizing" or grouping function.

ANOVA procedures There have been several recent papers on methods for performing the analysis. Most of them are on the difficult problem of estimation of variance components in experiments with unequal n's and will be mentioned under Problem C. A Fortran program for ANOVA is given in (80) and a PL/I program is described in (164). Cunningham (109) describes an algorithm for unusually large designs in ANOVA and analysis of covariance (ANOCOVA). Jones (257) gives a procedure for use with stratified subsamples. Pinneau & Ender (385) have shown the relationship of univariate ANOVA to principal component analysis of the correlations between treatment levels and observations, and Mandel (330) has given a method of analyzing interactions in ANOVA designs in terms of principal components. Hogg (230) describes a more powerful ANOVA procedure for use when the alternatives to the null hypothesis are restricted. To aid in the planning of the analysis of designed experiments, Anderson (14) suggests the conceptual use of a "restriction" source of variance which has no degrees of freedom or associated sum of squares but serves to clarify the analysis of experiments in which randomization is restricted, as in randomized blocks designs. When the analysis problem is simply to choose a subset of the treatments which contains the treatment with the smallest population mean, a procedure described by Desu & Sobel (127) can be used.

Measures of the magnitude of experimental effects are the topics of papers by Fleiss (149) and by Friedman (155, 156). Estimation of the components of variance in the random effects model, even when sample sizes are equal, is subject to a defect that is the topic of papers by Wang (486) and Federer (143): that the estimates may be negative, although the population values are by definition non-negative. Federer gave an improvement over the procedure of merely substituting zero for a negative estimate, and Wang compared the relative efficiencies of five different estimation procedures.

ANOCOVA A Fortran program for analysis of covariance is described by Walsh (484). An article by Reisch & Webster (411) points out that ANOCOVA has uneven power with respect to different alternative hypotheses and suggests a procedure to reduce that unevenness. Problems in applying and interpreting the results of ANOCOVA when the covariates are uncontrolled and may possibly be related to experimental groups are discussed by Werts (493, 494), Mallios (329), and Sprott (455). The use of ANOCOVA for the analysis of paired comparison data is set forth by Bechtel (40).

Residual error Winer (499) discussed several aspects of the concept of error in statistical models, and Cox & Snell (105, 106) and Andrews (15) investigated the general definition of residuals and proposed statistical tests based on residuals. Johnson & Graybill (255) present a method for estimating error variance in a two-way design with interaction, based on the pattern of 2 X 2 contrasts; and Gnanadesikan & Wilk (181) present a maximum likelihood estimation procedure for the error variance in complex designs. Hill (225) broadens the one-way ANOVA procedure to allow for negatively correlated residuals.

Multiple comparisons When more than two groups are present in an experiment, the investigator is usually interested not only in whether there is a significant main effect but also in which groups differ significantly from each other. The problem of evaluating this latter significance is nontrivial because of the multitude of tests being simultaneously performed on the same data, and there have been many suggested procedures. Games (166) and Aitkin (7) have recently surveyed alternative procedures. Rodger (419, 420) has proposed an alternative version of Scheffe's procedure. Smith (450) has recently shown that Tukey's "honest significant difference" procedure is robust with respect to the requirement of equal group sample sizes. Bechhofer (37) described a multiple comparison procedure for group variances, related to his earlier paper (38).

Problems of inference Comparisons of alternative methods of combining the significance levels of independent test statistics have been conducted by van Zwet & Oosterhoff (479) and by Littell & Folks (322). Although there is no uniformly best procedure, Fisher's method compares favorably with its competitors. Concerning the question of experimenter bias, Rosenthal (421) criticized a review by Barber & Silver (26) which indicated that experimenter bias is not a frequent or strong effect. Levin & Marascuilo (315) discuss the problem of Type IV errors, that is, making the wrong conclusion after performing an admissible data analysis.

Likelihood and Bayes procedures Comparison of the likelihood functions for data under competing hypothetical models is a common method of developing a statistical test, and the large sample approximation to the logarithm of the likelihood ratio is well known. Sprott & Kalbfleisch (456) point out that with computers, however, one can frequently avoid using the large sample approximation and that for some examples the approximation is not a good one.

An introduction to Bayesian procedures is given in De Groot's book (125). A few authors recently applied Bayesian procedures, the alteration of a priori hypotheses as a result of the ration of likelihood functions, to ANOVA designs. Box & Tiao (69) apply Bayesian estimation to the one-way random effects model; Farrell (142) considers two-way designs; Tiao & Box (468) consider nested designs; and Tiao &

Draper (469) apply Bayesian analysis to balanced incomplete blocks designs. Other recent papers on Bayesian procedures are by Ericson (141) on estimation of a population mean; by Hudimoto (240) on an empirical Bayes approach to multiple, repeated, decision problems; by Pitz (386) comparing Bayesian and standard procedures for a perception experiment; and by Maritz (337) on an empirical Bayesian approach to the compound decision problem.

Other estimation and testing procedures Seven papers reviewed do not fit into any of the categories above but are worth mention. Blumenthal (56) has compared five procedures for estimating the larger of two population means. Gardner (167) developed a procedure for detecting whether changes occur in the mean of a sequence of n observations. Salsburg (426) demonstrated the use of the jackknife procedure for testing proportions near zero or one. For testing whether a set of binomial, multinomial, or Poisson distributions have homogeneous parameters, Potthoff & Whittinghill (390, 391) have described testing procedures. Slakter (447) empirically investigated an estimate of the power of the chi-square goodness-of-fit test. Finally, Juola (272) has developed a criterion for deciding whether a population is symmetrically distributed; a continuous random variable X is symmetric if and only if $\mathrm{pr}(X \leq t^2/X = 1/2)$ for all $t \geq 0$.

PROBLEM C In this section we consider procedures for handling data which do not fit into more standard models because of the violation of basic assumptions. There are two solutions to the problem: to transform the data to a form that does satisfy the assumptions, or to develop a method for handling the data in their unpleasant form. We first consider papers dealing with the first solution and then papers dealing with the analyses of data which are heteroscedastic or have unequal sample sizes.

Transforming to normality Kowalski & Tarter (295) demonstrated that transforming to normally distributed scores improved the test for correlation and discussed general methods for performing the transformation. Riffenburgh (413) considered the problems involved in transforming a bounded random variable to a normal, and therefore unbounded, variable. Draper & Cox (129) consider a power transformation to achieve normality. A Fortran program for the direct transformation to normality by transforming to ranks and then from the ranks to normal quantiles, is described by Astin et al (22).

Transforming to minimize sources of variance Bogartz & Wackwitz (64), Draper & Hunter (131), and Fraser (153) have developed transformation procedures for fitting simpler forms of the linear model; and in related work, Levine (316, 317) has explored transformations that render curves parallel or of the same shape. Schlesselman, in a thesis under Tukey (429), has considered transformations for two-way ANOVA which simultaneously reduce interaction and heterogeneity of variance.

Filling in missing data Preece (392) has recently discussed iterative procedures for filling in missing values in such a way that the estimate of error variance is minimized in factorial designs. Walsh (483) describes a Fortran procedure for filling in missing data in performing ANOVA.

Heteroscedasticity The problem of testing whether the means of two populations differ when the variances differ is known as the Behrens-Fisher problem. Use of the student's *t* statistic in this case leads to erroneous error levels. However, Bhattacharjee (50) and Mehta & Srinivasan (352) have considered approximations to the *t* distribution which improve the test, as has Patil (374) for the three group case. Scheffé (428) compares six different solutions to the problem, and Eaton (136) develops a multivariate version of a solution suggested by Scheffé.

The problem of heteroscedasticity in regression and covariance analysis has been the target of procedures developed by Ashford & Brown (20), Bain (25), and McLaughlin (346).

Unequal sample sizes The estimation of variance components in ANOVA when the sample sizes are unequal has been attacked recently in at least three different ways. Searle (438) discusses many of the problems involved. Hartley & Rao (217) and Cunningham & Henderson (111) have developed maximum likelihood procedures for the mixed model, which has been extended to nested designs; for example, by Searle (437) and Rudan & Searle (424). Afonja (6) gives minimal sufficient statistics for variance components in randomized blocks and balanced incomplete blocks designs. A least-squares estimation procedure is described by Harvey (218). Rao (406), Rao & Subrahmaniam (409), and Rao (407) have described a different criterion for estimation, the MINQUE or minimum normed quadratic unbiased estimator, for linear models. The MINQUE procedure appears to be the easiest and most efficient of those methods so far developed.

Milliken & Graybill (356, 357) have extended the general linear model and applied it, for example, to testing for interaction in cases of missing data. Koch (290) and Low (328) have developed a procedure for estimation of the population mean in random effects models by minimizing a function that is sensitive to shifts in location.

In some cases, the sample size can be treated as a random variable which may be related to the effect of the treatment. Bartholomew (32) has treated the problem of hypothesis testing when the sample size is random in general, and Harville (219, 220) has considered the problem for one-way and two-way designs in ANOVA.

Ordinal Data

Nonparametric statistics, or rank order statistics, are estimation and testing procedures that are characterized by a transformation of the data to ranks or to signums, indicators of the sign of a difference. The pattern of the transformed data is then either compared to chance distributions or is transformed for testing to scores of some known distribution, such as the normal distribution. How can one choose between a standard procedure and a nonparametric procedure in a given situation? The primary criterion is whether the data one has, or the theory that predicts data to be observed, deviates from the assumptions of the standard procedure. ANOVA assumes normally distributed error, and deviations from normality can, for example, lead to incorrect Type I error levels. It is well known, on the other hand, that use of a nonparametric method when the standard procedure is appropriate, loses some power or efficiency. The recurring conclusion from recent studies is, however, that for many nonparametric methods, this loss is very small, and, in some cases, nonexistent. A secondary criterion is ease of computation, which especially favors the sign test as a method of quick, offhand, data analysis. The studies we consider here fall into three categories: estimation of location and dispersion, two-sample tests, and k-sample tests, for k greater than two.

ESTIMATION OF LOCATION AND DISPERSION If a choice is to be made of which of a family of distributions $F_i(x)$ best fits a set of data, and the distribution functions are related by the equation $F_i(x) = F_j(x - \theta)$, then θ is a location parameter, to be estimated. If the equation is $F_i(x) = F_j(x/\theta)$, then θ is a dispersion parameter. Hollander (232) has considered nonparametric estimates of each type and the relations between them, such as correlation. In general, estimates of location will have small correlations, if any, with estimates of dispersion. Tamura (463) has investigated the properties of a two-stage estimation procedure using the median, analogous to those mentioned above in the section on preliminary tests. Yanagawa (501) has developed an estimator of location in the form of a mean of medians and shown evidence of its robustness.

Estimates for scale or dispersion parameters have been developed by Kakeshita & Yanagawa (278) and by Prescott (394, 395). Mood's squared ranks test statistic has been refined by Mielke (353), who gave a correction for ties.

TWO-SAMPLE TEST PROCEDURES A fine but selective review of recent advances in this area is given by Savage (427), including nonparametric Bayesian procedures. A survey of sign tests is given by Bradley (72), and McNeil (349) has developed two-stage testing procedures, the first stage consisting of a kind of sign test which is easier to perform than more exact tests. Concerning the Mann-Whitney statistic, Buckle (77) have given a better large sample approximation than the normal approximation, based on the sum of uniform variables; and Hollander (231) has given two competitors which compare favorably in efficiency, unless the alternative hypothesis is a pure shift in location. Cureton (112) provided an appropriate correction for ties in the normal approximation to the Wilcoxon signed rank statistic. A comparison between the sign test, the signed rank test, and Fisher's randomization test was carried out by Kempthorne & Doerflor (283), who prefer the randomization test. Edgington (137, 138) has proposed an alternative to exact randomization tests, which suffer mainly from requirements of excessive computation: one can randomly sample among the randomization patterns. McNeil (348) investigated the loss of efficiency in several of these procedures when the data are grouped into class intervals, found it to be relatively small, but recommends that one break ties by randomization rather than averaging ranks.

The asymptotic efficiency of the two-sample Kolmogorov-Smirnov test was investigated by Klotz (289) who found it insensitive to differences of scale; and Steck (458) has derived distributions for this test, characterizing it as a rank test. Bell et al (41, 42, 44) have developed test statistics based on normal order statistics, either using tables of the expected values of these statistics or drawing a random sample from a distribution known to be normal, and have compared this procedure with other nonparametric tests. Birnbaum (51) considered the problem of evaluating the robust efficiency of two-sample rank tests. A variation of the median test has been developed by Gastwirth (170); and Gibbons & Gastwirth (176) have developed rank tests based on only the extreme ranks of the two samples.

MORE-THAN-TWO-SAMPLE TEST PROCEDURES Gilbert (177) has recently conducted an empirical study of the relative power of three alternative rank tests for an ANOVA design. Doksum (128) and Spjøtvoll (454) provide rank procedures for estimation and testing in some designs, Crouse (108) analyzes a 2^m factorial design with rank sum statistics, and Koch (292) explores rank procedures for complex split plot experiments.

Jonckheere's k-sample test against ordered alternatives has been investigated by Odeh (371, 372) and May & Konkin (338), who provide tables of significance and power of the test. Odeh (370) and Conover (99) have developed other rank procedures for determining whether k groups have identical location. Rizvi (414) have described ranking procedures for comparing several groups with a control, and Barlow & Gupta (29) have developed procedures for the selection of a subset of treatments containing the "best" treatment.

Quade (402) has developed a rank ANOCOVA, for which Labinowich & Brewer (304) have provided a Fortran program. Puri & Sen (400) have generalized and refined this analysis.

CENSORED DATA Censored data are data which are allowed to take on only a bounded set of values, although the underlying distribution process may be unbounded. The censoring may occur because of some process inherent in the data, or the experiment may trim the sample to avoid erroneous conclusions based on "outliers" that contaminate the data.

Prescott (393) has recently given an estimator of the standard deviation of a normal population based on censored samples. Hettmansperger (224) has investigated the Mann-Whitney statistic for trimmed samples, and Sobel (452) has generalized the Wilcoxon rank sum test to censored samples. Another generalization of the Wilcoxon test was developed by Gehan and refined by Mantel (331) and Gehan & Thomas (173). Breslow (73) has extended Gehan's test to more than two censored samples.

MULTIPLE COMPARISONS Nonparametric multiple comparison procedures have been developed by Tobach et al (472), Slivka (448), Rhyne & Steel (412), and Roberge (416). Slivka's procedure is for comparison of treatments versus a control, and Roberge's includes the description of a Fortran program for the analysis.

MULTIPLE DEPENDENT VARIABLES, SINGLE POPULATION

This section will review work related to the analysis of multivariate data obtained from a single population of subjects. In this section we will consider models for the analysis of continuous, ordinal, and categorical (nominal) data, and, with the exception of models for the analysis of categorical data which deal with interaction and independence in multidimensional contingency tables, this section will not consider group differences. Work on multivariate analysis of group differences is reviewed in the next section. We will consider first the analysis of continuous multivariate data, followed by ordinal and then categorical data. For each type of data, papers will be reviewed under the topical headings: structural models, regression, estimation, hypothesis testing, and distribution theory.

Continuous Interval Data

LINEAR STRUCTURAL MODELS: COVARIANCE STRUCTURES Suppose that we have obtained a set of p measurements $X_1, \ldots, X_p$ on a random sample of $n + 1$ individuals drawn from a population in which we assume that the jth variate ($j = 1, \ldots, p$) is distributed normally with mean μ_j and variance σ_j^2. In addition, we assume the joint distribution of the p variates is multivariate normal with mean vector $\mu' = (\mu_1, \ldots, \mu_p)$ and covariance matrix $\Sigma = (\sigma_{ij})$ (a prime indicates the transpose of a column vector, $\sigma_{jj} = \sigma_j^2$, and $\sigma_{ij} = \text{cov}(X_i, X_j)$. Let $\mathbf{x}' = (x_1, \ldots, x_p)$ be a vector of observed scores obtained from a single randomly sampled individual. A linear structural model represents this vector of observed scores as given by linear regression on a set of latent (unobservable) random variables plus an additive unique (residual or error) component representing that portion of the observed scores which is not predictable by linear regression from the latent variables. Thus, if $\mathbf{v}$ is a vector of scores of a randomly selected individual on r latent variables, $\mathbf{z}$ is a p-element vector of residual scores uncorrelated with the latent variables, and $\Lambda(p \times r)$ is a matrix of regression weights; the linear structural model is given by the matrix equation $\mathbf{x} = \mu + \Lambda\mathbf{y} + \mathbf{z}$. The estimation problem involves finding a linear structural model which fits the observed scores obtained from a given sample of people and inferring the likelihood that the structural model is valid in the population from which the sample of subjects was drawn.

Since in the linear structural model just described one can replace Λ with $\Lambda\mathbf{T}$ and $\mathbf{y}$ with $\mathbf{T}^{-1}\mathbf{y}$ (where $\mathbf{T}$ is any nonsingular $r \times r$ matrix) and not affect the residual vector $\mathbf{z}$, in order to obtain a unique set of parameter estimates for the structural model it is necessary to impose additional restrictions on the model. Thus, in the model just given, it is minimally necessary to specify a measurement scale for the latent variables (e.g. by specifying unit variance) and to uniquely identify the elements of Λ by requiring that the latent variables be uncorrelated (or have fixed correlations), by setting certain of the elements of each column of Λ equal to specified values (e.g. zero), or by specifying a unique "rotation" for the columns of Λ. In general, the purpose is to make a sufficient number of assumptions so that each parameter which remains to be estimated is uniquely specified by the model (i.e. can have only one value). Such a model is said to be identified. Dunn (134) has stated sufficiency conditions for uniqueness of a restricted factor matrix Λ in the above model, and Werts, Jöreskog & Linn (489) have discussed the identification problem for certain ordered-variate models.

Any linear structural model which does not constrain the mean vector can be expressed in terms of the covariance matrix of the observed variables. Thus, if (using what has become standard notation) Φ represents an $r \times r$ symmetric matrix of covariances of the r latent variables $\mathbf{y}$ of the above structural model, and Ψ represents a $p \times p$ diagonal matrix containing the variances of the residual variates $\mathbf{z}$ on its main diagonal, the model can be expressed in terms of the covariance matrix as follows:

$$\Sigma = \Lambda\Phi\Lambda' + \Psi^2 \qquad 1.$$

The covariance structure form of a linear structural model is especially convenient since all parameters of the model are represented in the model equation. Thus, linear structural models are often expressed as models for the structure of a covariance (or correlation) matrix.

Jöreskog (260) has presented a general model for covariance structures which includes Model 1 as a special case. Jöreskog's model assumes that the population variance-covariance matrix has the form

$$\Sigma = \mathbf{B}\,(\Lambda\Phi\Lambda' + \Psi^2)\,\mathbf{B}' + \Theta^2 \qquad 2.$$

where $\mathbf{B} = (\beta_{ik})$ is a $p \times q$ matrix of regression weights, $\Lambda = (\lambda_{km})$ is a $q \times r$ matrix of regression weights, Φ is as defined previously, and the diagonal matrices $\Psi^2 = (\psi^2{}_k)$ $(q \times q)$ and $\Theta^2 = (\Theta_i{}^2)$ $(p \times p)$ contain unique variances. Note that by setting $\mathbf{B} = \mathbf{I}$, a $p \times p$ identity matrix, and $\Theta^2 = (0)$, a matrix of zeros, the model is equivalent to No. 1 with $q = p$. As in Model 1, the mean vector is assumed to be unconstrained so that all relevant information from the sample is contained in the sample variance-covariance (or correlation) matrix. In the review of work on linear structural models which follows, three principal classes of structural models will be identified which, in most cases, can be represented as special cases of Jöreskog's general Model 2 but which differ in the particular assumptions that are made concerning which elements of the parameter matrices are free (unconstrained), constrained (to be equivalent to other elements), or fixed (to specified values). The three classes of structural models are as follows: (*a*) reduced rank models which specify $r < p$ in Model 1, $\Phi = \mathbf{I}$ (an $r \times r$ identity matrix), and fix the columns of Λ by requiring either that $\Lambda'\Psi^{-2}\Lambda$ be diagonal or that $\Lambda'\Lambda$ be diagonal; (*b*) classificatory models which may or may not reduce rank and in which a large number of elements of Λ (in Model 1) or Λ and $\mathbf{B}$ (in Model 2) are fixed and set equal to zero; and (*c*) ordered variate models in which parameters in Model 2 are fixed in such a way as to impose a stochastic order (or partial order) on the observed variables such that one variate is derivable from another by linear regression in an ordered sequence. Reduced rank models include test theory models ($r = 1$), and the familiar unrestricted factor analysis (UFA) model ($1 < r < p$). Classificatory models include cluster analysis methods and restricted factor analysis (RFA) models in which a factor structure is specified by setting factor loadings (in Λ) equal to zero. Variance and covariance components models in which (e.g. in Model 1) Λ is a completely fixed design matrix containing zeros and ones have also been considered in which the observed variables are viewed as classified according to an experimental design with random effects. Ordered variate models include simplex models [for longitudinal growth or learning data, (cf. 260, 262) and path models (cf. 55, 492)] which can be fitted using general Model 2; and also include continuous state stochastic process models (e.g. certain time series models) and path models which require a structural model which is still more general than Model 2. Mixtures of these three classes of linear structural models have also been considered.

Reduced rank models Here we consider special cases of Model 1 in which $r < p$, but in which no elements of Λ are restricted to be zero. This model is the traditional unrestricted factor analysis (UFA) model which is appropriate in situations in which one either is concerned solely with dimensionality (i.e. the number of factors) or wants to examine the configuration of test vectors in common factor space by attempting to transform the estimated factor matrix Λ according to some criterion for factor rotation, either analytic (cf. 203, 273, 275–277 for recent work concerned with analytic rotation), subjective (graphical rotation to simple structure), or combining analytic with judgmental criteria (389). For purposes of identification and estimation under the UFA model, it is usually required that the factors be uncorrelated (i.e. that $\Phi = \mathbf{I}$) and that either $\Lambda'\Psi^{-2}\Lambda$ be diagonal (the canonical factor characterization) (403) or $\Lambda'\Lambda$ be diagonal (the principal factor characterization). In the former case, the columns of $\Psi^{-1}\Lambda$ are the r characteristic vectors of $\Psi^{-1}\mathbf{S}\Psi^{-1}$ (which has rank r and in which $\mathbf{S}$ is the sample covariance matrix); in the latter case, the columns of Λ are the r principal components of $\mathbf{S} - \Psi^2$. For purposes of obtaining maximum likelihood (ML) estimates, the former assumption is convenient. Bentler (46) has provided a rationale for the canonical factor model in terms of psychometric sampling by defining a coefficient of internal consistency for an observed score composite and then showing that if weights are found which maximize this coefficient, the composites thus defined correspond to factors defined by the canonical factor model.

Jöreskog (259) has provided us with an efficient computational procedure for obtaining ML estimates for the parameters of the UFA model. Using the fact that under the canonical factor characterization for fixed r the conditional likelihood function for given Ψ^2 can be written explicitly in terms of the p-r smallest characteristic roots of $\Psi^{-1}\mathbf{S}\Psi^{-1}$, Jöreskog directly determines those values of Ψ^2 which make the conditional likelihood function a maximum using the Fletcher-Powell algorithm. The algorithm converges rapidly and the maximum likelihood solution can be determined very accurately. Jöreskog found that improper solutions (negative elements of Ψ^2) occur rather frequently and proposed a general procedure for dealing with such cases. Jöreskog's procedure also provides asymptotic standard error of estimate and confidence intervals for all estimated parameters. Browne (75) has published an extensive study comparing a number of approximate factor analytic techniques with the ML solution for artificial data. Browne obtained ML estimates using the "maximum determinant" procedure suggested by Bargmann (27) and Howe (236). His approximate techniques included principal components with diagonal elements of the sample correlation matrix replaced by squared multiple correlations, the iterated principle factor method, and the centroid method.

Browne concluded that ML estimates are superior and should not be rejected for reasons of computation time. Browne also found that the ML procedure for determining the number of factors—successive significance tests with different values of r—was satisfactory. However, Tucker & Lewis (477) have observed that for a large sample of individuals, the likelihood ratio statistic as a criterion for determining the number of factors could indicate that an otherwise acceptable model does not reproduce the sample covariance matrix. They proposed a reliability coefficient which represents a ratio of the amount of variance associated with a model to total variance as an index of quality of representation of the sample covariances.

Jöreskog & Goldberger (268) have proposed that generalized least squares (GLS) be considered as an alternative statistical estimation procedure which provides estimates that are scale free, asymptotically efficient, and (if $\sqrt{n}\,(\mathbf{S}-\Sigma)$ is asymptotically multinormal) have the same asymptotic properties as ML estimates (viz. limiting multinormal distribution of parameter estimates, the same asymptotic variance covariance matrix, and the same asymptotic chi-square test). They proposed that the following three criteria be minimized: unweighted least-squares (ULS), $\frac{1}{2}\mathrm{tr}[(\mathbf{S}-\Sigma)^2]$; weighted (generalized) least squares (GLS), $\frac{1}{2}\mathrm{tr}[(\mathbf{S}^{-1}\Sigma-\mathbf{I})^2]$; and maximum likelihood (ML), $\mathrm{tr}(\Sigma^{-1}\mathbf{S}) - \ln|\Sigma^{-1}\mathbf{S}| - p$. Jöreskog & van Thillo (270) have programmed rapid algorithms using all three criteria. Each of these iterative procedures requires that initial estimates of the elements of Ψ^2 be provided. Kaiser (274) has suggested that when a correlation matrix is analyzed, Ψ^2 initially should be set equal to an identity matrix since the number of positive characteristic roots on the first iteration would then correspond to Guttman's (199) weaker lower bound for the number of common factors.

The special case of the UFA model in which $r = 1$ is of particular interest as a general model within which various test theory models can be expressed. In particular, four structural models have been described by Jöreskog (265, 266) for the covariance matrix of a set of congeneric tests (i. e. tests which are assumed to measure the same thing). The weakest model (i.e. the model which makes the fewest assumptions), the congeneric true score model, assumes only that $r = 1$ in Model 1 and that the single latent "true score" has unit variance. This model implies that all tests are derived by linear regression from a single latent "true score" and does not require homogeneous regression or error variance. The strongest model considered is the parallel test model of classical true score theory (325) which requires that the elements of the column vector Λ be constrained to be equal and that the elements of Ψ^2 also be constrained to be equal (equal error or residual variances). Two intermediate models can also be considered: a model for tau-equivalent tests (325) in which the equal residual variance assumption is dropped from the classical model; and a model due to Kristof (298) for tests which differ only in length. The parameter estimation program ACOVS (269) for the general Model 2 can be used to obtain ML estimates of the parameters of each model and goodness-of-fit test performed. The problem of instrument calibration by estimating pairwise linear structural relationships among a set of p measures which is encountered in biometric work (30, 31) represents a special case of the congeneric test theory model, and thus parameter estimates could be obtained using ACOVS.

Schönemann (432) and Schönemann & Wang (433) have given renewed attention to the problem of indeterminacy of factor scores previously discussed by Guttman (200). The indeterminacy issue (not to be confused with identifiability problems associated with factor rotation) involves the fact that there exists more than one vector **y** of factor scores for each person which satisfies Model 1 for a given set of parameter values. Schöneman discussed relations between the characteristic values obtained in ML estimation and the indeterminacy problem, and he derived bounds for the minimum average correlation between equivalent sets of scores on correlated factors which depend on the characteristic roots of the factor correlation matrix Φ. He argued against the practice of "estimating" factor scores and suggested that factor analysis be employed solely as a procedure for investigating the structure of covariance matrices. Tucker (476), on the other hand, has examined "external characteristics" of four methods of estimating (or defining) factor scores, i.e. relations of these methods to measures not included in the factor analysis. The four methods examined were: least squares, Bartlett's (33) method, regression estimates, and Anderson & Rubin's (13) proposed method for uncorrelated factors. Tucker concluded that none of the estimates has correlations with external measures equal to the "theoretic" values implied by the model, and he offered specific recommendations for choosing factor score estimates for use in regression studies and in studies of group differences.

McDonald (342) has been interested in developing a generalization of the UFA model to two or more groups of variables. The idea is, following Tucker (475), to determine factors common to two groups of variables as well as factors specific to a single group of variables. McDonald generalized the UFA model by relaxing the requirement that the matrix Ψ^2 in Model 1 be diagonal. Instead, if the variables in the score vector **x** are arranged in groups and the covariance matrix Σ is partitioned according to these groups, Ψ^2 is block diagonal, a block corresponding to each group of variables. McDonald also suggests that the covariance matrices contained in the diagonal of Ψ^2 also be factored, resulting in battery-specific factors as well as in interbattery factors. Three alternative models are considered, the most realistic of which is probably a "group canonical factor" model which generalizes the canonical factor model. An alternative treatment of groups of variables has been presented by Jöreskog (265, 267) for multitrait-multimethod data (82) and by Jöreskog (263) and Werts, Jöreskog & Linn (490) for multitest-multioccasion data using the restricted factor (RFA) model. Jöreskog presents a number of alternative models, each of which represents a special case of Model 2.

In spite of the advances made in statistical estimation, approximate procedures for estimating the parameters of the UFA model continue to be used. These methods will probably remain important in exploratory work and in obtaining start values for input to iterative estimation programs in fitting restricted factor models. Among approximate procedures, that of calculating principal components of a sample correlation matrix, retaining characteristic vectors associated with characteristic roots greater than one, followed by normal varimax rotation still appears to be the most popular single method of factor analysis. Kaiser (273, 276) has concluded that this method needs revision and has presented a revised procedure which modifies this procedure in a number of ways. The new procedure results in correlated factors.

A number of investigators have conducted Monte Carlo studies to explore possible capitalization on chance in unrestricted factor analysis and analytic factor rotation. Tobias & Carlson (473) applied Bartlett's test of sphericity to a random correlation matrix and suggested that this test be applied before any further structural analysis of a correlation matrix is undertaken. Cliff (91) reported a Monte Carlo study of the sampling characteristics of the characteristic vectors of a correlation matrix with its diagonal elements replaced with the squared multiple correlations of each variable with all the remaining variables. Humphreys & Ilgen (242) studied three approximate methods with real data, making independent parallel analyses of random normal deviates, and compared the characteristic roots of the real and random correlation matrices to attempt to determine the number of statistically reliable factors. Resulting characteristic roots were also compared to the likelihood ratio chi-squares obtained in fitting a UFA model with number of factors equal to the ordinal number of the characteristic root. In another study, Humphreys et al (243) were concerned with possible capitalization on chance in factor rotation —either to a target matrix or using an analytic criterion. Correlation matrices generated from distributions of random normal deviates were analyzed using the iterated principal factor method. The authors concluded that seemingly meaningful rotated factors can be obtained from random data using either type of rotation. It may be that the only satisfactory solution to this problem is to approach the problem of analysis of covariance structures as a problem of comparative model fitting using restricted factor analysis (RFA) classificatory models.

Classificatory models Problems of classification are of two sorts. One problem involves classifying a set of p statistical variates into a set of distinct or mutually overlapping classes based on the intercovariances of the variates. Examples of statistical models corresponding to this problem are the linear structural Models 1 and 2 with the restriction that some of the elements of Λ and $\mathbf{B}$ are constrained to be zero. If the elements of Λ (say) in Model 1 are all zeros and ones, the model corresponds to a classification of variables in which a variable is either a member of a class or not a member [variance and covariance component models (57, 60, 260, 266, 267)]. If values of Λ not specified to be zero are free to vary (are estimated), then the model corresponds to a classification which allows for degrees of membership of a variate in a category (RFA models). A second problem involves classifying a sample of $n + 1$ objects (individuals) into object-classes based on a set of p measurements obtained on the objects. The statistical model associated with the problem of object classification has been described as a problem of unmixing a mixture of multivariate distributions by Wolfe (500), who has developed a computer program based on ML theory for unmixing mixtures of multivariate normal or multivariate Bernoulli distributions. In general, the problem of classifying variates involves the pairwise statistical dependence of the variates; the problem of object classification involves interobject distances and the statistical dependence of the variates (65). Fleiss & Zubin (150) have pointed out that these two distinct problems often have been confused and argue persuasively against the practice of correlating individuals as a basis for classifying them. In this section, we will consider the problem of classifying variates. Certain heuristic clustering procedures which were developed for object classification but which are applicable to the problem of clustering variates, will also be reviewed here.[3]

Two types of classificatory models have been considered: single order, in which the variables are classified at only one level, and hierarchical, in which the clusters of variates at one level are themselves clustered at the next level. A complete hierarchical clustering (214, 256) consists of a series of levels, ranging from one in which each variable is represented as a separate cluster to one in which all p objects are grouped together as a single cluster. Single level classificatory models can be represented as special cases of Model 1 by fixing appropriate elements of Λ equal to zero. Two-level (second order) models can be fit using Model 2. Hierarchical models requiring more than two levels require still more elaborate structural models and thus have been implemented only as heuristic clustering procedures.

A number of special cases of Model 2 in which elements in Λ or $\mathbf{B}$ are fixed equal to zero are of general interest (cf. 260, 266, 267 for a summary of models which may be represented as special cases of Model 2). Consider first models for the analysis of sets of congeneric tests (265). A model for a single set of congeneric tests already has been described. This model may be generalized to several sets of congeneric tests by setting up a column of Λ for each true score containing zeros for each test not in the set measuring that true score. In the case in which all tests in each set are parallel, this model leads to a model of compound symmetry (480) which requires symmetry within each set of variables (equal variances and covariances) and with respect to variables in all sets. Under either model, the intercorrelations of the true scores can be estimated. A procedure for testing the hypothesis that the correlation coefficient corrected for attenuation between two tests (i.e. the correlation between their true scores) is equal to unity is obtained by specializing the model for sets of congeneric tests to the case of two sets each consisting of two tests. In this case, there is a single correlation ϕ in Φ (under Model 1) to be estimated. A likelihood ratio test is obtained by taking the ratio of the likelihood when ϕ_{12} is restricted to unity, to the likelihood when ϕ_{12} is estimated. The test can also be made under the more restrictive assumptions of parallel tests. See (324), (152), and (299) for other recent work on this problem. If Model 2 is used, and $\Gamma = \Lambda\Phi\Lambda' + \Psi^2$ contains the intercorrelations of the true scores obtained from fitting the model for sets of congeneric tests, then the factor structure of the true scores can be studied by

[3]In addition to Wolfe's (500) paper and the heuristic clustering procedures reviewed in this section, a number of other approaches have been made to the problem of object classification. For example, Friedman & Rubin (157) attempted to obtain that partition of a set of objects into j groups which maximizes the sum of squared Mahalanobis' distances between the groups (i.e. the multivariate F statistic for that grouping). Borucki, Card & Lyle (65), attempting to provide a means of distinguishing between predictive clusters and clusters which may have arisen due to chance fluctuations in the data, presented a method which first clusters the observations and computes spatial boundaries for the clusters and then classifies the clusters into groups that represent statistical dependence between two or more variates, groups that represent the coincidence of peaks in the marginal distributions, and those that represent statistical fluctuation in the data.

specifying a structure for Γ. Such a model represents a special case of a second order restricted factor analysis model in which the first level factors specified by the matrix **B** are nonoverlapping. Jöreskog (265) has also described a model for the use of sets of congeneric tests in multitrait-multimethod studies in which a number of different traits (true scores) are measured each with a number of different methods or measuring instruments (multiple indicators).

Other applications of Model 2 which have been studied include restricted factor analysis (RFA) models, both first order (Model 1) and second order (Model 2); components of variance models (57, 60, 260, 266, 267); models for multitest-multioccasion correlation matrices (263); models for studying change (490); and classificatory models with dimensions of quantitative variation (124). An RFA model is a factor analysis model in which the factors are specified a priori by the locations of the zeros in the factor matrix. Such a model is appropriate for confirmatory studies in which hypothetical structure is to be verified against a sample covariance matrix. In exploratory studies in which the investigator cannot specify a structural hypothesis, an heuristic procedure may be used to initially locate the zeros. In both confirmatory and exploratory studies, alternative models may be fit to a covariance matrix until one is found which best reproduces the sample covariances. In most instances, more than one hypothetical structure will be considered, and often there will be a natural order in which alternative hypotheses are considered. For example, often one proceeds from models containing fewer parameters to more elaborate models containing more parameters to be estimated. Jöreskog (263) has suggested such a sequence of models for studying the structure of multitest-multioccasion correlation matrices such as might be obtained in longitudinal growth studies or studies of learning (including a model which contains stochastically ordered variates). Werts, Jöreskog & Linn (490) presented a specialization of certain of these models to studies of growth in which multiple indicators of initial and final status on a growth variable are obtained, and multiple measures are also obtained of one (or more) traits which are regarded as determinants of growth. Substantive inferences about growth may be based on estimates of the parameters of their model, and various commonly used formulas for reliability of differences, correlation of true initial status with true gain, and correlations of true scores over time can be derived by imposing appropriate restrictions on their model.

Degerman (124) has described an interesting problem in which quantitative dimensions are superimposed on a discrete class structure and observed measures reflect mixtures of class and quantitative variation. Degerman described heuristic procedures for first clustering the measures into discrete classes and then determining within-cluster dimensions of quantitative variation. Gebhardt (172) has treated a similar problem in which it is supposed that some of the factors underlying a covariance matrix are known, while others are to be investigated using the UFA model. Both of these problems involve mixed reduced-rank and classificatory models.

Heuristic procedures generally do not specify a classificatory structure a priori but rather seek to classify a set of variates through a series of operations on a similarity matrix containing pairwise similarity measures. If variates are to be classified, the similarity matrix is usually a correlation matrix; if objects are to be classified, the matrix contains interobject distances. Heuristic clustering schemes may be single level (the number of clusters unspecified or specified) or hierarchical. Hierarchical procedures may be agglomerative or divisive (148). A clustering may be invariant over monotone transformations of the similarities, or may treat similarities as measured on an interval or ratio scale. Fisher & van Ness (148) have defined nine properties which they feel should be satisfied by any reasonable clustering procedure, and they have investigated the admissibility of a number of kinds of clustering procedures with regard to these properties. Any clustering procedure involves a similarity function defined for single objects or variables and for clusters and a criterion for merging (or dividing) clusters. Johnson (256) has described two procedures for hierarchical clustering which differ with respect to how the similarity function is defined for clusters. Thus, if x and y are two objects or variables which are clustered at level j but not at level j - 1, and z is any third object not in a cluster with x and y, the distance $d[x,y]$, z of the cluster $[x,y]$ to z may be taken either as the minimum of $d(x,y)$ or $d(y,z)$, or the maximum. The rule for merging clusters at level j is: search the matrix of similarities at level j - 1, find the minimal nonzero similarity, and merge the pair of objects (variables, clusters) with this similarity. A frequently used third way of defining the similarity function (cf. 286, 326, 474) is to define similarity for clusters in terms of cluster centroids. Hierarchical clustering procedures have been described in a number of papers (214, 215, 238, 239, 256, 286, 350, 442). A single level clustering can always be obtained from a hierarchical procedure by stopping when the required number of clusters has been obtained. Several authors (114, 326, 474) have described single level clustering algorithms and a number of papers compare several clustering algorithms (239, 386, 350). While most are maximum, minimum, or centroid procedures, some procedures seek to find a clustering which minimizes an objective function of the data. For example, King (286) described a procedure which minimizes Wilks' statistic to test the hypothesis of independence between two groups. McQuitty's methods include his "iterative intercolumnar correlational analysis" (350). Shafto (442) has explicated this method by showing that it achieves a solution by transforming the test vectors toward a bipolar, one-factor structure. He offers two alternative methods for extracting a single bipolar factor ("linear contrast") directly from the similarity matrix.

Ordered variate models Suppose we have a set of p variables and that p - 1 of the variables are each derivable from others in the set by linear regression. In particular, consider the first order case in which each of the p - 1 variables is derivable by linear regression from only one other variable in the set. If the p variables form an ordered sequence such that variable j is derivable from variable j - 1 in the sequence (j = 2, . . ., p), then the p variables are completely ordered by the linear structural model. A set of p variables may also be partially ordered by a system of linear structural equations which specifies a network of linear dependency relations for the variables. In most instances, the order or partial order is given a priori and the statistical problem is to determine whether the sample covariance matrix reflects the hypothetical order or partial order.

The most common situation involving a complete order is a continuous state discrete parameter stochastic process (in time) or time series, with p measurements made sequentially and with a constant interval of time between observations. The simplest situation involving observations ordered in time is a pretest-posttest design involving only two observations (cf. 490). In an important paper, Cronbach & Furby (107) have reviewed previously proposed procedures for measuring change in pretest-posttest situations, offered an alternative procedure for estimating true residual gain scores, and then have proceeded to recommend procedures for various research problems involving change which do not require estimation of change scores for individuals. Gottman, McFall & Barnett (190) have argued that a better research strategy than the pretest-posttest design is a time series design in which successive observations are obtained throughout a programmed intervention and in which the characteristics of a change process can be assessed. Time series research designs permit one to study both the characteristics of a stochastic process in time and to detect changes in time-dependent stochastic process. Such changes may be experimentally induced or they may be spontaneous. Two aspects of a stochastic process are of interest in both cases: trends (which may be present in the means; in the variances; and in the means, variances, and covariances) and stochastic dependency (i.e. autoregression) which may be present in the structure of the $p \times p$ matrix of serial correlations. With respect to detection of change, Gottman, McFall & Barnett (190) considered change in trend using both curve fitting and moving-average approaches, and Jones, Crowell & Kapuniai (258) have described a model for detecting change from stationarity in multivariate stationary stochastic processes. Murray, Wiley & Wolfe (367) and Jöreskog (263) have presented discussions of the use of linear structural models in longitudinal developmental research.

A number of papers have appeared on the subject of first order autoregressive or simplex models (262, 364, 365, 431). Jöreskog (262) defined six types of (mean-nonstationary) first order autoregressive models, including a covariance-stationary model (Wiener simplex) and a covariance-nonstationary model (Markov simplex). The first order autoregressive series is

$$x_j = \mu_j + \beta_j(x_{j-1} - \mu_{j-1}) + \zeta_j, \qquad j = 2, \ldots, p,$$

where the residuals ζ_j are uncorrelated and β_j is a regression coefficient. In the Wiener simplex, β_j is a constant (which may be set equal to one) while in the Markov simplex β_j is time dependent. Since error of measurement may be present in the p variables, the autoregression holding for the true scores, Jöreskog (196) also identified models incorporating an additional error component which he refers to as quasi-Wiener and quasi-Markov simplex models. Jöreskog has represented each of these models as a special case of Model 2. Thus, ML estimates of all free and constrained parameters can be obtained using ACOVS and likelihood ratio chi-squares obtained. It is well known that simplex models are likely to be appropriate for longitudinal growth or learning data. Mukherjee (364) has derived the ML solution for the quasi-Wiener simplex and Schöneman (431) has developed a least-squares procedure for both the quasi-Wiener and quasi-Markov simplex models.

Groen (196) has discussed the connection between discrete state Markov processes considered in mathematical learning theory and the Markov simplex.

Several investigators have worked with more general autoregressive models. Subba Rao (460) has presented weighted least-squares estimation procedures for nonstationary time series models of order k. Note that autoregressive models of order $k \geq 2$ require a more general structural model than Model 2. Gottman, McFall & Barnett (190) have argued that a first-order autoregression is likely to be sufficient for most applications in psychology. Jones, Crowell & Kapuniai (258) considered multivariate time series models and presented a model for detecting change in a multivariate time series in which repeated observations are made on r variables (an r-dimensional multivariate stochastic process). Their procedure involves fitting a covariance-stationary k-order autoregressive model to the serial covariance matrix based on observations made before an intervention, obtaining the residuals from predicting observations after the intervention, and then testing the residual variances for an increase produced by the intervention. Such a technique would appear to be valuable in many psychological applications. Likelihood ratio tests of the effect of an intervention can be made for first-order univariate stationary processes using Jöreskog's program if a quasi-Wiener simplex is appropriate and can be fit to the serial correlation matrix obtained prior to an intervention, by testing the fit of the stationary (quasi-Wiener) model to the serial correlation matrix which includes correlations based on observations obtained both before and after the intervention.

Other papers concerned with problems involving time series which may be of interest include papers on inverse autocorrelations and their application in fitting moving average models (90), linear regression with time-dependent residuals (12, 171, 467), multiple regression with regression weights which are the realization of a stationary stochastic process (78), serial correlation (212, 358, 396), tests for trend in dispersion in times series (404), and tests for nonstationarity in time series (397).

Path models involving networks of linear structural relationships have been employed in economics and sociology to attempt to assess causal relationships among sets of linearly related random variables (55) and in biology for instrument calibration (30, 31) and for certain problems in genetics (318). Goldberger (183) has written a very interesting paper on similarities of linear structural models used in economics and psychology, and Werts & Linn (492) have discussed psychological applications of path models. Many path models can be represented as specifications of the general Model 2, and examples of such models have been presented by Jöreskog (260, 266, 267). However, since many problems exist for which a more general model is required, Jöreskog (261) has presented a still more general model which is similar to that used in economics (55, 183, 280). Jöreskog's model is different from that used in economics in that it represents a system of linear structural relations on the true scores and thus allows for errors of measurement as well as errors in equations. Jöreskog & van Thillo (271) have written an ML estimation program for this general model. Their computer program is still more general in that it allows for multiple indicators for the true scores. It should be noted that a simplex model is a special case of a path model in which the variables form an ordered sequence. Jöreskog

(267) has presented numerous examples to illustrate how path diagrams may be used to represent any linear structural model in which variables are classified or ordered. Since the determination of identifiability of parameters may often be an algebraicly complex problem, Werts, Jöreskog & Linn (489) have demonstrated how a visual inspection of the path diagram for a model can be used to simplify the identification problem.

The model of Jöreskog & van Thillo is an example of a structural model which is both classificatory and ordered. Mixed classificatory-ordered variate structural models have also been suggested for multitest-multioccasion correlation matrices (263), for dynamic structural analyses which emphasize changes in factor structure (423), for analysis of lagged multiple time series (367), and for the study of alternative sources of observed stochastic growth in several correlated measurements (154). The problem investigated in this latter paper involves seeking to determine by comparative model fitting whether observed growth in one measure is due to growth in other variables with which the measure is correlated.

CANONICAL CORRELATION There have been a number of suggestions for generalizing canonical correlation analysis to three or more sets of variables (84, 234, 235, 340, 345). The problem is to identify canonical variates which isolate and summarize linear relationships among several sets of variables and to measure the degree of relationship. It is also reasonable to require of any procedure that it reduce to Hotelling's classical procedure when the number of sets of variables is two. Kettenring (285) has presented a comprehensive treatment of the canonical analysis of several sets of variables, and in addition to formulating earlier procedures in terms of random variables, he has provided a treatment which is general and within which he has introduced two new procedures. Suppose we are given m sets of variables ${}_1\mathbf{x}, \ldots, {}_m\mathbf{x}$ with p_j variables in each set. At each of several stages s, we want to derive from the variables a set of m standardized canonical variates

$$\mathbf{z}^{(s)\prime} = ({}_1z^{(s)}, \ldots, {}_mz^{(s)})$$

which are linear composites of ${}_1\mathbf{x}, \ldots, {}_m\mathbf{x}$, respectively, and such that $\mathbf{z}^{(s)}$ maximizes or minimizes a particular function of its correlation matrix $\Phi^{(s)}$. At each stage after the first, new sets of canonical variates must satisfy additional restrictions. For example, successive variates may be required to be uncorrelated within sets. At the first stage, the five criteria identified by Kettenring are: 1. SUMCOR: maximize the sum of elements of $\Phi^{(1)}, (\mathbf{1}'\Phi^{(1)}\mathbf{1})$; 2. MAXVAR: maximize the largest eigenvalue of $\Phi^{(1)}$, $\lambda^{(1)}{}_1$; 3. SSQCOR: maximize the sum of squares of the elements of $\Phi^{(1)}$ (the sum of squares of its eigenvalues $\lambda_1{}^{(1)2} + \ldots + \lambda_m{}^{(1)2}$); 4. MINVAR: minimize the smallest eigenvalue of $\Phi^{(1)}$, $\lambda_m{}^{(1)}$; and 5. GENVAR: minimize the generalized variance of $\mathbf{z}^{(1)}$,

$$|\Phi^{(1)}| = \prod_{i=1}^{m} \lambda_i^{(1)}.$$

Criteria 1 and 2 are due to Horst (234), 3 and 4 are introduced by Kettenring. Criteria 1, 3, and 5 require iterative computations. All procedures generate canonical variates which make $\Phi^{(1)}$ as far as possible from an identity matrix. Each of these procedures reduces to the classical procedure for $m = 2$. In his paper, Kettenring first presents a development for each of these criteria. He then treats the problem of choosing restrictions for higher stage canonical variates and presents computational procedures for each of the five criteria. The paper includes a comparison of results obtained in applying the five procedures to real data.

Following Rozeboom (422) and Stewart & Love (459), Miller & Farr (354) have suggested a measure of interbattery association for two sets of variables which can be obtained in the absence of a canonical correlation analysis. The measure of association between sets of orthogonalized measures is the proportion of total variance in a battery explained through each of its components (any orthogonal linear composites such as principal components or canonical variates) by the other battery. The association measure developed is directional and asymmetric and is independent of methods employed to orthogonalize the sets of variables.

LINEAR COMPOSITES A great many problems in multivariate analysis involve seeking a weighted linear combination of a set of variates such that the linear composite has some optimal property or properties. McDonald (340) has presented a unified treatment of weighting problems which define best weights according to the following common property: choose a normalized vector of weights associated with one or more extreme values of a quadratic or bilinear form whose matrix consists of covariances or correlations. McDonald has shown in his paper that eight different weighting procedures can be treated as special cases of a single, reasonable general weighting procedure corresponding to this property. The eight weighting problems considered are multiple regression, canonical correlation analysis, principal components of a correlation matrix, principal components of scale analysis, maximizing the correlation between two multicategory items, maximizing composite reliability, and canonical factor analysis.

Another linear weighting problem involves finding least-squares linear composites of predictors for estimating several criteria which satisfy the restriction that the composites have an arbitrary specified correlation matrix. The optimal weights without any restriction on the correlations of the composites are the multiple regression weights for predicting each criterion variable. Green (191) has presented a solution to this problem which is more general than previous treatments of the problem and whose derivation depends on a general result concerning best-fitting orthonormal transformations. The procedure is applicable to the problem of obtaining regression estimates of factor scores whose correlations are the same as the factor correlation estimates obtained in fitting the factor model.

ESTIMATION: PARAMETERS OF CONTINOUS MULTIVARIATE DISTRIBUTIONS We consider first bivariate distributions. Several papers have appeared concerning effects of selection and restriction of range on the product moment correlation coefficient for a bivariate normal distribution. Pearson's formula for correcting for univariate selection is based on the assumption of normality of variates before and after selection. Brewer & Hills (74) examined empirically the influence of skew upon estimated correlation using Pearson's adjustment for univariate selection. They generated symmetric bivariate distributions and then introduced different levels of correlation and skewness in the predictor marginal distribution. The corrected correlation was computed for each cumulative tenth of cases from each direction of the predictor variable and in this manner effects of size of correlation, degree of skew, and degree of restriction were studied. Brewer & Hills concluded that "even with essentially symmetric distributions, a large proportion of the data is necessary to obtain reasonably precise estimates of low correlations. With increasing skew, estimates become increasingly erroneous, the direction of the error depending upon which tail of the distribution is the basis of the estimates." Effects of truncating a bivariate normal distribution on sample variances have been studied by Rao (405). Bryant & Gokhale (76) presented a formula for correcting a correlation for restriction in range for the special case in which the variances of the two variables in the unrestricted sample are known. Their formula is appropriate in situations in which the selection is on some unknown variable and assumes that the distribution after selection is bivariate normal. Several other papers on correction for restriction of range have appeared (151, 314, 488).

Fhanér (144) applied an information measure in an empirical study of information loss when Pearson r is applied to non-normal data. Elston & Stewart (140) proposed a new test statistic for detecting association between two continuous random variables. Connor & Mosimann (98) have considered concepts of independence for non-negative continuous random variables which sum to one. For data which consist of proportion scores for individual subjects, their treatment may be appropriate. A concept of neutrality is developed and related to a concept of independence for proportions.

A frequently encountered problem in multivariate analysis is that of obtaining sample estimates of the parameters of a multivariate normal population when the sample data are incomplete. One approach to the missing data problem is to estimate values for the missing data points and then compute sample statistics based on both observed and estimated values. Timm (471) has published an empirical comparison using simulated data of four such methods of estimating correlation and covariance matrices when observations are missing at random from the data matrices. The effects of sample size, number of variables, percent of missing data, and average intercorrelation of variables were examined for the four methods. Methods investigated were: (*a*) a method involving decomposing a score matrix into its known and unknown parts and using principal components of the known part to estimate the unknown part; (*b*) substituting the sample mean of each unknown variable (based on known data) for unknown values; (*c*) multiple regression estimates; and (*d*) using only the complete data. While no uniformly best technique was found, methods *a* and *c* were found to be superior independently of sample size and number of variates when 1%, 10% and 20% of the data were missing. Games (165) has described an efficient computer algorithm for method *d*.

A second approach to the missing data problem involves attempting to obtain ML esimates of parameters under normality assumptions, based on the available observations. Individual missing data points are not estimated. One problem with these procedures is that they can yield estimates of Σ which are not positive definite (i.e. for which all characteristic roots are not greater than zero). Hartley & Hocking

(216) have attempted to provide a taxonomy for incomplete data problems and to develop a unified method of analysis based on ML estimation. An earlier paper (Hocking & Smith 227) presented a method for estimating the parameters in a multinormal distribution in which missing observations are not restricted to follow specific systematic patterns. Morrison (361) has presented a procedure for a single incomplete and q complete variates.

HYPOTHESIS TESTING We will consider first hypotheses on correlation coefficients. When two correlation coefficients are calculated from a single sample, they are not statistically independent and the usual methods for testing equality do not apply. Dunn & Clark (135) have investigated power curves for several large sample tests based on Fisher's z-transformation and have also investigated possible alternative simple methods suitable for small samples using Monte Carlo methods to determine level of significance and power. Choi (86) has presented a sequential test for correlation coefficients. The sequential test permits a substantial reduction in average sample size compared to that required in a fixed sample test. Jennrich (248) has described an asymptotic chi-square test for the equality of two correlation matrices.

In testing for a treatment effect, an experimenter may have to use the same subjects for control and experimental groups. Independence no longer holds, and tests of bivariate symmetry may be appropriate. Bell & Doksum (43) have shown that bivariate symmetry is not equivalent to univariate symmetry, and they discussed alternative tests for this hypothesis. Repeated measures analysis of variance models require that the covariance matrix of the repeated observations have compound symmetry (480). In the case in which constant correlation can be assessed, it may be desired to test the hypothesis of homogeneity of variance for the correlated variables. Han (207) has proposed four test procedures for this hypothesis and compared the four tests. A number of papers have dealt with problems involved in testing the assumption of multivariate normality and proposed tests of this hypothesis (8, 323, 335, 481).

DISTRIBUTION THEORY This section will identify papers of two sorts: those that consider the distribution of statistics which arise in testing correlations or various multivariate hypotheses, and papers on generating multivariate data. Kristof (297) has discussed properties of a statistic arising in testing correlation and applied the statistic to the psychometric problem of testing point hypotheses on coefficient α based on dividing a test into two parts. Papers on the distribution of various multivariate test statistics include: multiple correlation (198); likelihood ratio criteria for tests of independence of sets of variates (101), compound symmetry (103), bipolarity of a covariance matrix (102), and sphericity in a p-variate normal distribution (100, 254); largest characteristic roots of covariance and other symmetric matrices (221, 462); traces of Wishart matrices (249); and the ratio of two generalized variances (24). Capra & Elster (83) discussed a procedure for generating N multinormal observations on p-variates where the p-variates have specified means, variances, and covariances; and Smith & Hocking (451) have described a subroutine for generating a covariance matrix from a Wishart distribution.

Ordinal Data

STRUCTURAL MODELS Structural models for ordinal data have been developed both in the context of factor analysis (cf. 201, 202, 319, 320) and multidimensional scaling [cf. the reviews of Zinnes (506) and Cliff (92), the recent book edited by Shepard, Romney & Nerlove (444), and the bibliography prepared by Harris (213)]. Ordinal ("nonmetric") structural models for matrices of ordinal similarities may be rank reducing (spatial) or classificatory. Rank reducing models seek to generate a configuration of points in a Euclidean space of smallest (or specified) dimensionality which is capable of reproducing the rank-order of the similarities of the objects so represented. Classificatory models seek to generate an object classification from which ordinal similarities can be reproduced. As yet only heuristic estimation procedures have been produced for structural analysis of ordinal data (Kruskal & Carroll 300). Work on classificatory models for ordinal similarities has already been reviewed. Research on rank reducing models is regularly reviewed in the *Annual Review* chapter on scaling and will not be covered here (92, 139, 506).

CONTINGENCY TABLES WITH ORDERED CATEGORIES Frequently it is necessary to measure association between variables that are rank orderings in which many ties occur among the rankings. Such data are often presented in a cross-tabulation. It may be of interest to extend commonly used measures of association to multiway cross classifications and to develop measures analogous to partial and multiple correlation coefficients for such tables. Davis (122) has defined a partial coefficient γ_{ABC} in a manner analogous to Goodman & Kruskal's interpretation of their coefficient γ. They define γ_{ABC} as "how much more probable it is to get like than unlike orders in measures A and B when pairs of individuals differing on A and on B and tied on C but unselected on any other measure are chosen at random from the population" (p. 190). They show that this coefficient is a weighted sum of the values of γ in the various strata defined by the categories of C. Somers (453), seeking to provide a measure of partial association in three-way tables which takes account of the ordered nature of the control variable, has presented a coefficient based on Kendall's partial coefficient but modified to distinguish the independent from the dependent variable.

Two very general models for the analysis of contingency tables with ordered categories have been presented by Williams & Grizzle (498). Their methods apply a recently developed linear models approach to the analysis of interaction in contingency tables, and the analysis can be performed using the weighted regression methods of Grizzle, Starmer & Koch (194). The models permit investigation of experimental design variables with category effects and utilize information contained in the ordered responses. These methods will be described in the next section on discrete (categorical) data. Finally, Weisberg (487) has developed an approach to the problem of comparing two multinomial distributions with k categories in which the categories are ordered.

Categorical Data

ADDITIVE COMPONENT STRUCTURAL MODELS A major development during the period reviewed is a general model for the analysis of categorical data arranged in multidimensional contingency tables. The approach taken in this work is to transform observed proportions contained in the cells of a multidimensional contingency table by means of a specified response function which may be linear, log-linear, or logistic, and to represent the transformed data by means of an additive component structural model analogous to that used in analysis of variance. Thus a design matrix can be specified to estimate any effects which are of interest and the effects then may be polled for hypothesis testing. Hypotheses that can be considered may involve the analysis of main effects or interaction effects in tables based on multiple independent samples, they may involve tests of conditional independence in multivariate tables based on a single sample, or they may involved both independence and interaction effects. Since the statistical treatment of these hypotheses is identical, work on the application of the linear models approach to the study of group differences in contingency tables will be included in this section.

The analysis of categorical data by linear models has been approached using minimum chi-square (weighted least squares), maximum likelihood, minimum discrimination information, and minimum Pearson chi-square estimation. We will outline first the general model for the analysis of a multidimensional contingency table as presented by Grizzle, Starmer & Koch (194) for an s x r table using weighted least squares, and then discuss other approaches to estimation. Suppose we have an s x r contingency table with observed proportions p_{ij} which estimate the probabilities π_{ij}. Let the rows represent different populations and the columns represent different categories of response. Let

$$\pi'_i = (\pi_{i1}, \ldots, \pi_{ir}),$$

the ith row of the expected contingency table, and

$$\mathbf{p}'_i = (p_{i1}, \ldots, p_{ir}),$$

the corresponding sample estimate. Let

$$\pi' = (\pi'_1, \ldots, \pi'_r)$$

contain the entire table "strung out" into an rs element vector. Then var $(\mathbf{p}_i) = \mathrm{V}(\pi_i)_{(r \times r)}$, a function of π_{ij} (for all cells), and the corresponding sample estimate $\mathrm{V}(\mathbf{p}_i)$ can be computed. Let $\mathrm{V}(\mathbf{p})$ be a block diagonal matrix having $\mathrm{V}(\mathbf{p}_i)$ on the main diagonal. Then arbitrary response functions of the elements of π, $f_m(\pi)$ may be defined ($m = 1, \ldots, u$) such that each function has partial derivatives up to second order with respect to the elements of π, and the functions are jointly independent. Let $f_m(\mathbf{p})$ be the mth function evaluated at

$\pi = \mathbf{p}$, and let $\mathbf{F}' = (f_1(\mathbf{p}), \ldots, f_u(\mathbf{p}))$

which estimates $\mathrm{F}(\pi)'$. The covariance matrix of $\mathbf{F}$ is $\mathbf{S} = \mathbf{HV(p)H}'$ of rank u where

$$\underset{u \times rs}{\mathbf{H}} = \left(\frac{\partial f_m(\Pi)}{\partial \Pi_{ij}} \,\middle|\, \Pi_{ij} = \mathrm{P}_{ij} \right)$$

(284, p. 232). When $f_m(\mathbf{p})$ is a linear function of the elements of $\mathbf{p}$, $\mathbf{S}$ is the exact covariance matrix of $\mathbf{F}$; otherwise it is the asymptotic covariance matrix.

Now assume the linear structural model $F(\pi) = X\beta$ where $X(u \times v)$ is a known design matrix of rank $v \leq u$ and β is a vector of v unknown parameters. A weighted least-squares estimate **b** of β is obtained by finding that vector **b** which minimizes

$$(\mathbf{F} - \mathbf{Xb})' \mathbf{S}^{-1}(\mathbf{F} - \mathbf{Xb}).$$

From here on the treatment is conventional weighted least-squares regression, and hypotheses may be tested in the same manner as in the linear models approach to analysis of variance if the model fits. All test statistics have asymptotic chi-square distributions with appropriate degrees of freedom. Particular models may be specified by choosing the response functions **F** and specifying a design matrix **X**. Chi-squares are additive and may be pooled to test specific hypotheses.

The maximum likelihood (ML) approach begins with an assumed sampling distribution for the sample observations. Three sampling schemes lead to identical unique ML estimates for complete or incomplete tables [if the zero cells are sampling zeros rather than structural, i.e. a priori zeros, (146)]; independent Poisson variates for each cell, a single multinomial sampling scheme, and a set of independent multinomial sampling schemes. All three sampling models lead to the log likelihood-ratio statistic $L = 2\Sigma\, n_{ij} \ln (n_{ij}/m_{ij}) = 2n\Sigma\, p_{ij} \ln (p_{ij}/\pi_{ij})$ where n_{ij} is a cell frequency, m_{ij} is an ML estimate of n_{ij}, $n = \Sigma\, n_{ij}$, and the summations are over all the cells in the table. L has an asymptotic chi-square distribution with degrees of freedom obtained in the usual way. If it is desired to transform the proportions and assume a linear structural model for the transformed proportions, the likelihood function can be written as a function of the parameters of the linear model. The most frequent assumption is the log-linear model: $\ln m_{ij} = u + u_{1(i)} + u_{2(j)} + u_{12(ij)}$ for each cell in the table. ML estimates of the parameters of this model are thus obtained, and the ML chi-squares for different hypotheses are additive. Fienberg (145) has described an iterative procedure for obtaining ML estimates for this model. The minimum discrimination information approach of Ku & Kullback (301) leads to estimates that are identical to the ML estimates. Statistical properties of the different estimates have been thoroughly discussed by Grizzle, Starmer & Koch (194), Fienberg (146), Bishop (53), and Goodman (188).

It remains to identify particular response functions $f(\pi)$ which have been used and to indicate specific hypotheses which can be tested using each function. Four classes of response function can be defined which cover all the applications we have found in our review. The classes of response functions are as follows: 1. linear functions: $F(\pi) = \mathbf{A}\pi$, where **A** is a $u \times rs$ matrix of arbitrary specified constants (cf. 194, 195, 293). 2. Logarithmic-linear functions: $F(\pi) = \mathbf{K} \ln \mathbf{A}\pi$, where **A** is as given under 1, **K** is a $t \times u$ matrix of arbitrary constants, and $F(\pi)$ is a $t \times 1$ column vector (53, 54, 146, 186–189, 194, 195, 293). Note that the logistic response function logit $p_{ij} = \ln(p_{ij}/(1 - p_{ij}))$ is a special case of 2 (47, 48, 53, 194, 498). 3. Exponential-logarithmic linear functions: $F(\pi) = \exp[\mathbf{K} \ln \mathbf{A}\pi]$ (293). 4. Inverse normal ogive (normit) response function: $F(\pi) = \Phi^{-1}(\pi)$, where $\Phi^{-1}(\pi_{ij})$ is the unit normal deviate corresponding to the cumulative normal probability π_{ij}. This latter function is used principally in bioassay and in item analysis. It is well known that the logit and normit functions yield values that are practically equivalent except for extremely small or large probabilities.

The references cited after the definitions of each response function above contain numerous examples of analyses applying linear models to transformed proportions. Several classes of hypotheses may be identified. First consider categorical data collected on a single population tabulated in a multiway contingency table to study the associations among the attributes associated with the ways of classification. Hypotheses that can be considered in this case using response function 1 are homogeneity of marginal distributions (194) and symmetry and marginal (conditional) homogeneity (244). Hypotheses using response function 2 are independence (195), quasi-independence both in tables containing structural zero frequencies (146, 186) and in tables with incomplete response patterns (195, 293), and partial or conditional independence (195). When categorical data are collected on several populations (groups of individuals, treatment groups), the linear model analysis is very similar to analysis of variance for continuous data. Hypotheses involving several populations can be studied using any of the above response functions. Hypotheses include main effects, interactions (53, 194, 293), and hypotheses involving ordered response classes (498). The advances represented by this work make it possible now to perform the same kind of detailed analyses on qualitative data that have long been possible for quantitative data.

LINEAR STRUCTURAL MODELS Consider a set of binary classifications on p discrete random variables (or items). It may be of interest not only to investigate hypotheses regarding the independence of the variates arranged in a p-way contingency table but also to study the dependence structure of the variates in a manner analagous to that employed in the study of structural relations of p continuous random variables. The approach taken to this problem is similar to that developed for the analysis of multidimensional contingency tables using additive component models. The items are assumed to represent dichotomous (or polychotomous) random variables that are derived from underlying continuous random variables by a process such as that for item i, $p_i = \text{Prob}\,(y_i \geq h_i)$ for some cutting point h_i. A linear structural model can then be assumed for the p element vector $\mathbf{y}$. If $\mathbf{y}$ is assumed to be p-variate multinormal, the cases of general Model 2 can be considered. Response functions that have been considered for the proportions p_i are the linear (312, 341), the logistic (47, 52), and the normal ogive function (21, 58, 59, 61, 87). The most frequently assumed structural model that has been considered is the one-factor (rank one) model. Bock & Wood (61) have recently reviewed this work for the 1971 *Annual Review of Psychology* in their chapter on test theory. An interesting application of the one-factor model in bioassay is provided by Ashford & Sowden's (21) paper on multivariate probit analysis. If the general Model 2 (or still more general models) is to be applied to the problem of analyzing dichotomous variables, one can adopt the normal ogive response function and assume $\mathbf{y}$ is p-variate multinormal with covariance matrix satisfying Model 2. Christofferson (87) has recently attempted to develop an estimation procedure for the RFA model. Since ML estimation of parameters will lead to large amounts of computation and therefore severely limit the number of items that can be analyzed, Christofferson suggested estimation procedures based on the marginal distributions for single and pairs of items. Two procedures are developed: a generalized least-squares procedure and a simple two step least-squares procedure. The former estimators are asymptotically efficient among estimators that use the same amount of information and the function minimized is asymptotically chi-square. Unfortunately, the method requires an extremely large amount of computer storage. The estimation problem associated with fitting linear structural models to dichotomous (or polychotomous) variables is in much need of further development.

TETRACHORIC CORRELATION Bock & Lieberman (60) found that they were able to get heuristic estimates of the parameters of the one-factor normal ogive model by fitting a one-factor model to the matrix of inter-item tetrachoric correlations using Jöreskog's program, provided the tetrachoric correlation coefficients were computed to a high degree of accuracy. They obtained accurate estimates (to nearly four figures) by interpolating in a table of the bivariate normal distribution. In the interest of finding a fast and accurate method, Froemel (158) compared several existing approaches using tabled probabilities for the bivariate normal distribution to generate data. A computer routine by Saunders was identified as most accurate for the widest range of data. Other papers on tetrachoric correlation are (113, 185, 204, 205).

DISCRETE STRUCTURAL MODELS Murray (366) has recently presented a general model for fitting discrete structural models to an m-way contingency table in which each classification corresponds to response categories for one of m items. Let

$$p_{a_1, a_2, \ldots, a_m}$$

be the observed proportion for the $a_1, a_2, \ldots, a_{m\text{th}}$ cell ($a_i = 1, \ldots, N_i$ response categories for the ith item), and let

$$\pi_{\alpha_1, \ldots, \alpha m}$$

denote a latent (theoretical) probability parameter for the $\alpha_1, \ldots, \alpha_{m\text{th}}$ cell. The latent probabilities are assumed to be specified functions of some smaller set of basic latent parameters Θ. Let

$$Q^i_{a_i\, \alpha_i}$$

denote a misclassification probability for the ith item; i.e. the probability that a member of the $\alpha_{i\text{th}}$ latent state (category) is observed in category a_i. Let **p** be a vector containing the observed proportions, π a vector containing the corresponding latent probabilities,

$$Q^i = (q^i_{a_i \alpha_i})$$

be an (N_i x N_i) matrix of misclassification probabilities for the ith item, and $Q = Q^1 \otimes Q^2 \otimes \ldots \otimes Q^m$ be an N X N matrix for all latent and observed cells (where $\otimes$ denotes a Kronecker product). Murray has shown that under the assumption that misclassifications are independent from item to item for subjects in the same latent state, $\mathbf{p} = \mathbf{Q}\boldsymbol{\pi}$. The procedure is to constrain the latent probabilities π by means of an assumed structural model and obtain ML estimates of parameters by maximizing the likelihood function subject to the constraints imposed by the model. Models considered by Murray are pure Guttman scales, discrete state Markov processes, and causal models. Applications of the models to developmental data are presented.

REGRESSION WITH CATEGORICAL DEPENDENT VARIABLES Neter & Maynes (369) have discussed the appropriateness of the correlation coefficient with dichotomous dependent variables in an interesting paper which focuses on problems relating to curvilinearity and the nature of the prediction being made. They concluded that the correlation ratio is likely to be a better measure than the coefficient of determination because it is free of restrictions on the functional form of the relationship. Alternative measures are also considered. Morrison (362) has considered the problem of evaluating prediction models that generate probabilities for binary outcomes. Morrison suggests that a correlation between the binary outcomes and the prediction probabilities can yield meaningful results. Finally, Stanley (457) has discussed a similarity between biserial r and Glass's (178) biserial r for ranks.

MULTIPLE DEPENDENT VARIABLES, MULTIPLE POPULATIONS

Continuous Interval Data

The developments to be described in this section almost all assume multivariate normality and consist of extensions of multivariate analysis of variance techniques and discriminant analysis. This seems to be an appropriate place to mention that a number of new and useful books on multivariate analysis have appeared in recent years. We single out Cooley & Lohnes (104), Dempster (126), Morrison (360), and Tatsuoka (465) as especially worthy.

Several review articles have appeared recently that the student or novice user of multivariate technique should find illuminating. The articles by Pruzek (398), Bay (35), Finn (147), and Porebski (388) illustrate various multivariate methodologies for studying group differences within the context of multivariate analysis of variance and discriminant analysis. A significant review of recent work at a more technical level is provided by Rao. (408) Joe & Anderson (251) have developed a series of potentially useful measures of association between treatments and effects in multivariate ANOVA correspondence to the various test statistics (e.g. likelihood-ratio, Hotelling's trace) commonly used in these setups. Another review paper worth careful perusal is Kempthorne's (282), in which he raises questions about the utility and purposes of multivariate analysis generally. See also the papers by Healy (222) and Hummel (241).

SIMULTANEOUS TEST PROCEDURES Perhaps the most exciting and potentially useful recent work in multivariate ANOVA is the work on simultaneous test procedure.

Roughly speaking, simultaneous test procedures provide post hoc comparisons given that a significant overall result has been observed. In the multivariate case, this may involve studying particular variables and subsets of variables or linear composites of variables as well as comparing pairs of treatment groups and other contrasts on treatment groups. Thus these procedures permit some resolution of overall significant results down to single variables and contrasts. The test procedures are based on the eigenvalues of the product of the hypothesis and within-groups dispersion matrices. Gabriel (160–162) discusses test procedures based on all the usual multivariate significance tests (e.g. largest root, etc). His papers are quite readable, though technical, and merit extensive scrutiny by psychologists. Gabriel recommends the largest root procedures in general but points out that if the experimenter is merely interested in comparing all pairs of groups on all single variables, a battery of ordinary *t*-tests cannot be improved upon. Note, however, that significance levels are not calculated in the ordinary way as for one pair of groups and one variable. Other useful papers on simultaneous inference are those of Krishnaiah (296) and Jensen (250).

DATA ANALYSIS Another set of exciting developments in multivariate methodology involve what are becoming known as data-analytic methods. Cooley & Lohnes have adopted an explicitly data-analytic outlook in their revision (104) of their well-known book. Briefly put, data analysts, as opposed to statisticians, adopt a somewhat cavalier attitude toward classical estimations and significance testing and are primarily concerned with heuristics and algorithms for data reduction, exposure of structure, and exploration of nonlinearities and nonsingularities. Graphical procedures play a large role in univariate data analysis and have been adapted successfully to several multivariate situations (179). Gnanadesikan & Wilk have provided an excellent overview of the area (180).

DISCRIMINANT ANALYSIS Discriminant analysis continues to attract attention in all its varieties. Two excellent and readable papers by Porebski (387, 388) summarized current knowledge and illustrated the application of discriminant analysis technology. Urbakh (478) showed that the loss of discriminating power due to deletion of a single variate is

$$\Delta^2 - \beta^2{}_k/\mathrm{P}^{kk}$$

where Δ^2 is the Mahalanobis distance, β_k is the standardized discriminant coefficient, and P^{kk} is the diagonal element out of the inverse of the correlation matrix. This formula, of course, is directly analogous to the formula for the reduction in squared multiple correlation. Han (206, 208) discussed discriminant analysis with unequal covariance matrices, and Lachenbruch (305–308) in a series of papers explored misclassification probabilities as related to sample size and other factors. Geisser (174) introduced some Bayesian notions into discriminant analysis.

MANOVA In the rest of this section, we briefly review some other recent developments related to MANOVA and discriminant analysis. The robustness of multivariate techniques with respect to heteroscedasticity and lack of normality has been studied by Mardia (336) and Ito (245). Both authors reported that multivariate test procedures are robust to non-normality when testing hypotheses about mean vectors but not necessarily so when testing hypotheses about variance-covariance matrices. Heteroscedasticity can be a severe problem, and Ito (245) developed some alternative test statistics for use when marked heteroscedasticity is present. Korin (294), however, reported substantial robustness. Holloway (233) examined the robustness of Hotelling's T^2 statistic.

Two papers (193) discussed the analysis of growth curves by multivariate techniques. Grizzle's (192) paper on this topic also illustrates the use of planned comparisons in MANOVA. Two papers dealt with the problem of missing data in discriminant analysis. Jackson (246) and Chan & Dunn (85) found substitution of the mean for missing values to be a satisfactory procedure compared with other alternatives.

One-sided multivariate significance tests have been investigated by Kudo (302), Kudo & Fujisawa (303), and Perlman (379, 380). Generally speaking, these tests can be applied to one-sample cases with hypotheses that the mean vector is zero against an alternative that all the components have "slipped to the right." It appears that further work will be necessary before fully usable procedures are available, although clearly a significant start has been made.

A number of papers have dealt with the distribution of test statistics used in MANOVA and other types of multivariate analysis. These papers generally are quite technical and beyond the reach of a psychological audience. Several, however, contain useful results or tables and are cited here (211, 249, 253, 363, 382–384).

In closing this section, we want to draw special attention to the recent work of Jöreskog (264) on simultaneous factor analysis in several populations. This promises to be an extraordinarily useful statistical technique with numerous psychological applications. Briefly, his method consists of determining maximum likelihood estimators of factor pattern matrices, factor intercorrelation matrices, and uniquenesses under models of increasing degrees of stringency and evaluating the likelihood ratio test statistic for each model.

Ordinal Data

In this section we are going to deal solely with a new class of nonparametric multivariate procedures for testing the hypothesis of equality of location parameters for two or more goups. These procedures have been discussed by Puri & Sen (399, 401), Anderson (11), Bhapkar (49), and Bell & Smith (45). Work is under way to extend multivariate nonparametric methods to general linear (MANOVA) models and include estimation problems as well (401, 441).

Consider a p-dimensional random vector with continuous distribution function $F_k(X)$, where the subscript $k(=1, \ldots, K)$ indexes various treatments or experimental groups. We suppose a location shift as a consequence of experimental treatments, i.e.

$F_k(X) = F(X + \Theta_k)$

where Θ_k is a vector of constants. Otherwise the multivariate distributions are identical. We desire to test the null hypotheses

$H_o: \Theta_k = \mathbf{O}$

for all k versus

$H_a : \Theta_k \neq \mathbf{O}$.

Suppose n_k observations have been made on the random vector **x** under treatment condition k. We now rank all

$\Sigma_1^k n_k (=N)$

observations on each of the p-variables separately and form the ranks into an $N \times p$ matrix **R** in which the first n_1 rows correspond to the sample of observations obtained under treatment conditions one, etc. The ranks can be transformed further. For example: let

(i) $P_{ij} = \begin{cases} 1 \text{ if } r_{ij} \leq (N+1)½ \\ 0 \text{ otherwise} \end{cases}$

(ii) $P_{ij} = r_{ij}/(N + 1)$

(iii) $P_{ij} = \Phi^{-1}(r_{ij})/(N + 1)$

These lead to a median test, a rank-sum test, and normal scores test, respectively, if Φ^{-1} denotes the inverse normal transformation. The test statistic involves calculating the mean vector of the **P** matrix for each subsample and the grand mean vector. Denote by $\mathbf{T}_k$ the mean vector of **P** corresponding to the kth sample or treatment, by **P** the grand mean. Further, calculate a variance-covariance matrix **V** from the matrix **P.** The proposed test statistic is

$L = \Sigma_1^k n_k[\mathbf{T}_k - \mathbf{P}]' \mathbf{V}^{-1}[\mathbf{T}_k - \mathbf{P}]$.

This statistic is not fully distribution-free since it depends on the rank correlations of the observations, but a distribution-free test can be determined by considering the permutation rank order distribution of the statistic. Puri & Sen (399, 401) have shown that for large samples, the permutation distribution of L is asymptotically chi-square with $p(K - 1)$ degrees of freedom. For small samples, the permutation distribution of L would have to be determined for each separate case.

Modifications of the foregoing procedures have been discussed by Patel & Bradley (373). Tamura (464) has developed methods for comparing each treatment with a control. Mantel (334) and Anderson (11) have described approaches alternative to the permutation rank order procedures that appear very interesting. Most of this literature is highly technical. A less technical review paper with applications is sorely needed for the applied worker.

Literature Cited

1. Addelman, S. 1972. Recent developments in the design of factorial experiments. *J. Am. Statist. Assoc.* 67:103–11
2. Afifi, A. A., Elashoff, R. M. 1967. Missing observations in multivariate statistics II. Point estimation in a simple linear regression. *J. Am. Statist. Assoc.* 62:10–29
3. Afifi, A. A., Elashoff, R. M. 1968. Analysis of a group of balanced block experiments having error variance and some treatments in common. *Biometrics* 64: 389–400
4. Afifi, A. A., Elashoff, R. M. 1969. Missing observations in multivariate statistics III. Large sample analysis of simple linear regression. *J. Am. Statist. Assoc.* 62:337–58
5. Ibid. Missing observations in multivariate statistics IV. A note on simple linear regression, 359–65
6. Afonja, B. 1972. Minimal sufficient statistics for variance components for a general class of designs. *Biometrika* 59: 295–302
7. Aitkin, M. A. 1970. Multiple comparisons in psychological experiments. *Brit. J. Math. Statist. Psychol.* 23:193–98
8. Aitkin, M. A. 1972. A class of tests for multivariate normality based on linear functions of order statistics. *ETS Res. Bull. 72–16*
9. Aitkin, M. A. 1972. Fixed-width confidence intervals in linear regression with applications to the Johnson-Neyman technique. *ETS Res. Bull. 72–18*
10. Alam, K. 1967. A two-sample estimate of a common mean. *Ann. Inst. Statist. Math.* 19:261–70
11. Anderson, T. W. 1966. Some nonparametric procedures based on statistically equivalent blocks. In *Multivariate Analysis,* ed. P. R. Krishnaiah, 1–35. New York: Academic
12. Anderson, T. W. 1970. Efficient estimation of regression coefficients in time series. *Proc. 6th Berkeley Symp. Math. Statist. Probab.,* 1:471–82. Berkeley: Univ. California Press
13. Anderson, T. W., Rubin, H. 1956. Statistical inference in factor analysis. *Proc. 3rd Berkeley Symp. Math. Statist. Probab.* 5:111–50
14. Anderson, V. L. 1970. Restriction errors for linear models (an aid to develop models for designed experiments). *Biometrics* 26:255–68
15. Andrews, D. F. 1971. Significance tests based on residuals. *Biometrika* 58: 139–48
16. Anscombe, F. J. 1967. Topics in the investigation of linear relations fitted by the method of least squares. *J. Roy. Statist. Soc. B.* 29:1–52
17. Arnold, B. C. 1970. Hypothesis testing incorporating a preliminary test of significance. *J. Am. Statist. Assoc.* 65: 1590–96
18. Arnold, J. C., Al-Bayyati, H. A. 1970. On double-stage estimation of the mean using prior knowledge. *Biometrics* 26: 787–800
19. Arvesen, J. N. 1970. Robust procedures for variance component problems using the jackknife. *Biometrics* 26:677–86
20. Ashford, J. R., Brown, S. 1969. Generalised covariance analysis with unequal error variances. *Biometrics* 25:715–24
21. Ashford, J. R., Sowden, R. R. 1970. Multivariate probit analysis. *Biometrics* 26:535–46
22. Astin, A. W., Richardson, G. T., Salmon, M. 1967. A computer program for normalizing distributions of variables. *Educ. Psychol. Meas.* 27:153–57
23. Atkinson, A. C. 1969. The use of residuals as a concomitant variable. *Biometrika* 56:33–41
24. Bagai, O. P. 1967. The distribution of the ratio of two generalized variances. *J. Indian Statist. Assoc.* 5:30
25. Bain, L. B. 1967. Reducing a random sample to a smaller set, with applications. *J. Am. Statist. Assoc.* 62:510–19
26. Barber, T. X., Silver, M. J. 1968. Fact, fiction, and the experimenter bias effect. *Psychol. Bull.* 70:1–29
27. Bargmann, R. E. 1957. A study of independence and dependence in multivariate normal analysis. Chapel Hill: Univ. North Carolina Inst. Statist. Mimeo Ser. 186
28. Barham, R. H., Drane, W. 1972. An algorithm for least squares estimation of nonlinear parameters when some of the parameters are linear. *Technometrics* 14:757–66
29. Barlow, R. E., Gupta, S. S. 1969. Selection procedures for restricted families of probability distributions. *Ann. Math. Statist.* 40:905–17
30. Barnett, V. D. 1969. Simultaneous pairwise linear structural relationships. *Biometrics* 25:129–42
31. Barnett, V. D. 1970. Fitting straight lines—the linear functional relationship with replicated observations. *J. Roy. Statist. Soc. C* (*Appl. Statist.*) 19: 135–44

32. Bartholomew, D. J. 1967. Hypothesis testing when the sample size is treated as a random variable. *J. Roy. Statist. Soc. B* 29:53–82
33. Bartlett, M. S. 1937. The statistical conception of mental factors. *Brit. J. Psychol.* 28:97–104
34. Basson, R. P. 1970. A comparison of variances of some estimators in the balanced incomplete block (BIB) variance components model. *Biometrics* 26: 657–69
35. Bay, K. S. 1971. Applications of multivariate analysis of variance to educational and psychological research: Hypothesis testing by MANOVA programs. *Multivar. Behav. Res.* 6:325–62
36. Beale, E. M. L., Kendall, M. G., Mann, D. W. 1967. The discarding of variables in multivariate analysis. *Biometrika* 54:357–66
37. Bechhofer, R. E. 1968. Multiple comparisons with a control for multiple-classified variances of normal populations. *Technometrics* 10:715–18
38. Ibid. Single-stage procedures for ranking multiple-classified variances of normal populations, 693–714
39. Bechhofer, R. E. 1970. An undesirable feature of a sequential multiple-decision procedure for selecting the best one of several normal populations with a common unknown variance. *Biometrics* 26:347–49
40. Bechtel, G. G. 1971. A covariance analysis of multiple paired comparisons. *Psychometrika* 36:35–55
41. Bell, C. B., Doksum, K. A. 1964. *Some new distribution-free statistics.* San Diego State Coll. and Univ. California, Berkeley, NSFG–25220, 203–14
42. Bell, C. B., Doksum, K. A. 1966. "Optimal" one-sample distribution-free tests and their two-sample extensions. *Ann. Math. Statist.* 37:120–32
43. Ibid 1969. Bivariate symmetry tests: parametric and nonparametric. 40: 259–69
44. Bell, C. B., Moser, J. M., Thompson, R. 1966. Goodness criteria for two-sample distribution-free tests. *Ann. Math. Statist.* 37:133–42
45. Bell, C. B., Smith, P. J. 1969. Some nonparametric tests for the multivariate goodness-of-fit, multisample, independence, and symmetry problems. *Multivar. Anal.* 2:3–23
46. Bentler, P. M. 1968. Alpha-maximized factor analysis (alphamax): its relation to alpha and canonical factor analysis. *Psychometrika* 33:335–45
47. Berkson, J. 1968. Application of minimum logit X^2 estimate to a problem of Grizzle with a notation on the problem of "no interaction." *Biometrics* 24: 75–95
48. Ibid 1972. Minimum discrimination information, the "no interaction" problem, and the logistic function. 28:443–68
49. Bhapkar, V. P. 1966. Some nonparametric tests for the multivariate several sample location problem. See Ref. 11
50. Bhattacharjee, G. P. 1968. Non-normality and heterogeneity in two-sample T-test. *Ann. Inst. Statist. Math.* 20: 239–54
51. Birnbaum, A. 1967. Efficiency robust two-sample rank tests. *Am. Statist. Assoc. J.* 1241–51
52. Birnbaum, A. 1968. Some latent trait models and their use in inferring an examinee's ability. See Ref. 325, 397–472
53. Bishop, Y. M. M. 1969. Full contingency tables, logits, and split contingency tables. *Biometrics* 25:383–99
54. Bishop, Y. M. M., Fienberg, S. E. 1969. Incomplete two-dimensional contingency tables. *Biometrics* 25:119–28
55. Blalock, H. M., Ed. 1971. *Causal Models in the Social Sciences.* Chicago: Aldine-Atherton
56. Blumenthal, S. 1968. Estimation of the larger of two normal means. *J. Am. Statist. Assoc.* 63:861–76
57. Bock, R. D. 1960. Components of variance analysis as a structural and discriminal analysis for psychological tests. *Brit. J. Statist. Psychol.* 13: 151–63
58. Bock, R. D. 1972. Estimating item parameters and latent ability when responses are scored in two or more nominal categories. *Psychometrika* 37:29–51
59. Bock, R. D., Bargmann, R. E. 1966. Analysis of covariance structures. *Psychometrika* 31:507–34
60. Bock, R. D., Lieberman, M. 1970. Fitting a response model for dichotomously scored items. *Psychometrika* 35:179–97
61. Bock, R. D., Wood, R. 1971. Test theory. *Ann. Rev. Psychol.* 22:161–92
62. Bogartz, R. S. 1968. A least-squares method for fitting intercepting line segments to a set of data points. *Psychol. Bull.* 70:749–55
63. Ibid 1971. Least squares methods for locating function shifts and disturbance regions. 75:294–96
64. Bogartz, R. S., Wackwitz, J. H. 1971. Polynomial response scaling and func-

tional measurement. *J. Math. Psychol.* 8:418–43

65. Borucki, W. J., Card, D. H., Lyle, G. C. 1973. *A practical method for identifying clusters that represent statistical dependencies in multivariate data.* Ames Res. Center, N.A.S.A., Moffett Field, Calif. (mimeo)
66. Bowman, K. O. 1970. Sample size requirements: one-way analysis of variance. *Biometrika* 57:421–30
67. Ibid. Sample size requirements: randomized block designs, 573–77
68. Box, G. E. P., Guttman, I. 1966. Some aspects of randomization. *J. Roy. Statist. Soc. B* 28:543–58
69. Box, G. E. P., Tiao, G. C. 1968. Bayesian estimation of means for the random effect model. *Am. Statist. Assoc.* 63: 174–81
70. Box, M. J. 1971. Factorial designs, the $|X'X|$ criterion and some related matters. *Technometrics* 13:731–42
71. Bradley, J. V. 1964. Studies in research methodology VI. The central limit effect for a variety of populations and the robustness of Z, t, and F. *Tech. Rep. AMRL-TR-64-123, Wright-Patterson AFB, Ohio.* 290 pp.
72. Bradley, J. V. 1969. A survey of sign tests based on the binomial distribution. *J. Qual. Technol.* 1:89–101
73. Breslow, N. 1970. A generalized Kruskal-Wallis test for comparing K samples subject to unequal patterns of censorship. *Biometrika* 57:579–94
74. Brewer, J. K., Hills, J. R. 1969. Univariate selection: the effects of size of correlations, degree of skew, and degree of restriction. *Psychometrika* 34:347–61
75. Browne, M. W. 1968. A comparison of factor analytic techniques. *Psychometrika* 33:267–334
76. Bryant, N. D., Gokhale, S. 1972. Correcting correlations for restrictions in range due to selection on an unmeasured variable. *Educ. Psychol. Meas.* 32:305–10
77. Buckle, N., Kraft, C., van Eeden, C. 1969. An approximation to the Wilcoxon-Mann-Whitney distribution. *J. Am. Statist. Assoc.* 64:591–99
78. Burnett, T. D., Guthrie, D. 1970. Estimation of stationary stochastic regression parameters. *J. Am. Statist. Assoc.* 65:1547–53
79. Burr, I. W., Foster, L. A. 1972. *A test for equality of variances.* Purdue Univ. and Valparaiso Univ. Dep. Statist., Div. Math. Sci., Mimeo. Ser. 282. 26 pp.
80. Butler, D. H., Kamlet, A. S., Monty, R. A. 1969. A multipurpose analysis of variance Fortran IV computer program. Aberdeen Res. Develop. Center, AMCMS Code 5011.11.84100, Aberdeen proving ground, Md. *Psychon. Monogr. Suppl.* 2:301–20
81. Calinski, T. 1971. On some desirable patterns in block designs. *Biometrics* 27:275–90
82. Campbell, D. T., Fiske, D. W. 1959. Convergent and discriminant validation by the multitrait-multimethod matrix. *Psychol. Bull.* 56:81–105
83. Capra, J. R., Elster, R. S. 1971. A note on generating multivariate data with desired means, variances, and covariances. *Educ. Psychol. Meas.* 31:749–52
84. Carroll, J. D. 1968. Generalization of canonical correlation to three or more sets of variables. *Proc. 76th Ann. Conv. APA,* 227–28
85. Chan, L. S., Dunn, O. J. 1972. The treatment of missing values in discriminant analysis—1. The sampling experiment. *J. Am. Statist. Assoc.* 67:473–77
86. Choi, S. C. 1971. Sequential test for correlation coefficients. *J. Am. Statist. Assoc.* 66:575–76
87. Christofferson, A. 1973. *Factor analysis of dichotomized variables.* Res. Rep. 73–4, Univ. Uppsala Dep. Statist., Uppsala, Sweden
88. Clatworthy, W. H. 1967. Some new families of partially balanced designs of the Latin square type and related designs. *Technometrics* 9:229–44
89. Claudy, J. G. 1972. A comparison of five variable weighting procedures. *Educ. Psychol. Meas.* 32:311–22
90. Cleveland, W. S. 1972. The inverse autocorrelations of a time series and their applications. *Technometrics* 14:277–93
91. Cliff, N. 1970. The relation between sample and population characteristic vectors. *Psychometrika* 35:163–78
92. Cliff, N. 1973. Scaling. *Ann. Rev. Psychol.* 24:473–506
93. Cohen, J. 1968. Multiple regression as a general data-analytic system. *Psychol. Bull.* 70:426–43
94. Cohen, J. 1970. Approximate power and sample size determination for common one-sample and two-sample hypothesis tests. *Educ. Psychol. Meas.* 30:811–31
95. Collier, R. O. Jr. 1967. Estimates of test size for several test procedures based on conventional variance ratios in the repeated measures design. *Psychometrika* 32:339–53
96. Conger, A. J. 1969. An analysis of Ghiselli's moderator variable. *Psychol. Rep.* 25:519–27

97. Conger, A. J. 1971. *A revised definition for suppressor variables: A guide to their identification and interpretation.* L. L. Thurstone Psychometric Lab. Rep. 96, Univ. North Carolina. 18 pp.
98. Connor, R. J., Mosimann, J. E. 1969. Concepts of independence for proportions with a generalization of the Dirichlet distribution. *J. Am. Statist. Assoc.* 64:194–206
99. Conover, W. J. 1968. Two K-sample slippage tests. *J. Am. Statist. Assoc.* 63:614–26
100. Consul, P. C. 1967. On the exact distributions of likelihood ratio criteria for testing independence of sets of variates under the null hypothesis. *Ann. Math. Statist.* 38:1160–69
101. Ibid. On the exact distributions of the criterion W for testing sphericity in *p* -variate normal distribution, 1170–74
102. Consul, P. C. 1968. On the distribution of Votaw's likelihood ratio criterion L for testing the bipolarity of a covariance matrix. *Math. Nachr.* 36:1–13
103. Consul, P. C. 1969. On the exact distributions of Votaw's criteria for testing compound symmetry of a covariance matrix. *Ann. Math. Statist.* 40:836
104. Cooley, W. W., Lohnes, P. R. 1971. *Multivariate Data Analysis.* New York: Wiley
105. Cox, D. R., Snell, E. J. 1968. a general definition of residuals. *J. Roy. Statist. Soc. B* 30:248–75
106. Cox, D. R., Snell, E. J. 1971. On test statistics calculated from residuals. *Biometrika* 58:589–94
107. Cronbach, L. J., Furby, L. 1970. How we should measure "change"—or should we? *Psychol. Bull.* 74:68–80
108. Crouse, C. F. 1968. A distribution-free method of analyzing a 2^m factorial experiment. *S. Afr. Statist. J.* 2:101–8
109. Cunningham, E. P. 1970. A program for large-scale non-orthogonal analysis of variance and covariance. *J. Roy. Statist. Soc. C* 19:160–72
110. Cunningham, E. P., Henderson, C. R. 1966. Analytical techniques for incomplete block experiments. *Biometrics* 22:829–42
111. Ibid 1968. An interative procedure for estimating fixed effects and variance components in mixed model situations. 24:13–25
112. Cureton, E. E. 1967. The normal approximation to the signed-rank sampling distribution when zero differences are present. *J. Am. Statist. Assoc.* 62: 1068–69
113. Cureton, E. E. 1968. Tetrachoric correlation by the Camp approximation. *Educ. Psychol. Meas.* 28:239–44
114. Cureton, E. E., Cureton, L. W., Durfee, R. C. 1970. A method of cluster analysis. *Multivar. Behav. Res.* 5:101–16
115. Dagenais, M. G. 1971. Further suggestions concerning the utilization of incomplete observations in regression analysis. *J. Am Statist. Assoc.* 66:93–98
116. Dagenais, M. G. 1972. Asymptotic behavior and small sample performance: Experiments on regression parameter estimation with incomplete observations. To appear in *European Economic Review,* cah. 7213. 25 pp.
117. Dagenais, M. G. 1972. Small sample estimation of regression parameters in the three-variable linear model, with incomplete observations. Sponsored by the Canada Council of Arts and the Ministère de l'Education du Québec. 17 pp. (mimeo)
118. Dagenais, M. G. Using incomplete observations in multiple regression analysis: A generalized least square approach. Submitted to *J. Econometrics*
119. D'Agostino, R. B., Cureton, E. E. 1972. Test of normality against skewed alternatives. *Psychol. Bull.* 78:262–65
120. Das, M. N., Jain, R. C. 1970. On component analysis of factorial and fractional factorial experiments. *Biometrics* 26:823–33
121. Davies, M. 1967. Linear approximation using the criterion of least total deviations. *J. Roy. Statist. Soc. B* 29:101–9
122. Davis, J. A. 1967. A partial coefficient for Goodman and Kruskal's Gamma. *J. Am. Statist. Assoc.* 62:189–93
123. Davis, R. L., Arnold, J. C. 1970. An efficient preliminary test estimator for the variance of a normal population when the mean is unknown. *Biometrika* 57:674–77
124. Degerman, R. 1970. Multidimensional analysis of complex structure: mixtures of class and quantitative variation. *Psychometrika* 35:475–91
125. DeGroot, M. H. 1970. *Optimal Statistical Decisions.* New York: McGraw-Hill
126. Dempster, A. P. 1969. *Elements of Continuous Multivariate Analysis.* Reading, Mass.: Addison-Wesley
127. Desu, M. M., Sobel, M. 1968. A fixed subset-size approach to the selection problem. *Biometrika* 55:401–10
128. Doksum, K. 1967. Robust procedures for some linear models with one observation per cell. *Ann. Math. Statist.* 38: 878–83

129. Draper, N. R., Cox, D. R. 1969. On distributions and their transformation to normality. *J. Roy. Statist. Soc.* 31: 472–76
130. Draper, N. R., Guttman, I., Kanemasu, H. 1971. The distribution of certain regression statistics. *Biometrika* 58:1–4
131. Draper, N. R., Hunter, W. G. 1969. Transformations: Some examples revisited. *Technometrics* 11:23–40
132. Draper, N. R., Smith, H. 1966. *Applied Regression Analysis.* New York: Wiley
133. Draper, N. R., Smith, H. 1969. Methods for selecting variables from a given set of variables for regression analysis. *ISI Bull.* 43:7–15
134. Dunn, J. E. 1973. A note on a sufficiency condition for uniqueness of a restricted factor matrix. *Psychometrika* 38:141–43
135. Dunn, O. J., Clark, V. 1969. Correlation coefficients measured on the same individuals. *J. Am. Statist. Assoc.* 64: 366–77
136. Eaton, M. L. 1969. Some remarks on Scheffé's solution to the Behrens-Fisher problem. *J. Am. Statist. Assoc.* 64: 1318–22
137. Edgington, E. S. 1969. Approximate randomization tests. *J. Psychol.* 72: 143–49
138. Ibid 1971. Randomization tests with statistical control over concomitant variables. 79:13–19
139. Ekman, G., Sjöberg, L. 1965. Scaling. *Ann. Rev. Psychol.* 16:451–74
140. Elston, R. C., Stewart, J. 1970. A new test of association for continuous variables. *Biometrics* 26:305–14
141. Ericson, W. A. 1970. On the posterior mean and variance of a population mean. *J. Am. Statist. Assoc.* 65:649–52
142. Farrell, R. H. 1969. On the Bayes character of a standard model II analysis of variance test. *Ann. Math. Statist.* 40: 1094–97
143. Federer, W. T. 1968. Non-negative estimators for components of variance. *Appl. Statist.* 2:171–74
144. Fhaner, S. 1967. Information loss when ρ is applied in non-normal cases. *Scand. J. Psychol.* 8:127–31
145. Fienberg, S. E. 1970. An iterative procedure for estimation in contingency tables. *Ann. Math. Statist.* 41:907–17
146. Fienberg, S. E. 1972. The analysis of incomplete multiway contingency tables. *Biometrics* 28:177–202
147. Finn, J. D. 1969. *Multivariate analysis of repeated measures data.* Multivar. Behav. Res., State Univ. New York at Buffalo, abstr., 391–413
148. Fisher, L., van Ness, J. W. 1971. Admissible clustering procedures. *Biometrika* 58:91–104
149. Fleiss, J. L. 1969. Estimating the magnitude of experimental effects. *Psychol. Bull.* 72:273–76
150. Fleiss, J. L., Zubin, J. 1969. On the methods and theory of clustering. *Multivar. Behav. Res.* 4:235–50
151. Forsyth, R. A. 1971. An empirical note on correlation coefficients corrected for restriction in range. *Educ. Psychol. Meas.* 31:115–23
152. Forsyth, R. A., Feldt, L. S. 1969. An investigation of empirical sampling distributions of correlation coefficients corrected for attenuation. *Educ. Psychol. Meas.* 29:61–71
153. Fraser, D. A. S. 1967. Data transformations and the linear model. *Ann. Math. Statist.* 38:1456–65
154. Frederiksen, C. H. 1972. *The goodness-of-fit of alternative Markov simplex models for language comprehension data.* Presented at Psychometric Soc. Meet., Princeton, N. J.
155. Friedman, H. 1968. Magnitude of experimental effect and a table for its rapid estimation. *Psychol. Bull.* 70: 245–51
156. Friedman, H. 1969. A simplified table for the estimation of magnitude of experimental effect. *Psychon. Sci.* 14:193–95
157. Friedman, H. P., Rubin, J. 1967. On some invariant criteria for grouping data. *J. Am. Statist. Assoc.* 62:1157–77
158. Froemel, E. C. 1971. A comparison of computer routines for the calculation of the tetrachoric correlation coefficient. *Psychometrika* 36:165–74
159. Furnival, G. M. 1971. All possible regressions with less computation. *Technometrics* 13:403–8
160. Gabriel, K. R. 1968. Simultaneous test procedures for one-way ANOVA and MANOVA based on rank scores. *Sankhyā* 30:303–12
161. Gabriel, K. R. 1968. Simultaneous test procedures in multivariate analysis of variance. *Biometrics* 55:489–504
162. Gabriel, K. R. 1969. A comparison of some methods of simultaneous inference in MANOVA. *Multivar. Anal.* 2: 67–86
163. Gabrielsson, A., Seeger, P. 1971. Tests of significance in two-way designs (mixed model) with dichotomous data. *Brit. J. Math. Statist. Psychol.* 24: 111–16
164. Galosy, R. A., Adams, W. A. 1971. A multipurpose four-dimensional analysis

of variance program. *Behav. Res. Methods Instrum.* 3:205–10
165. Games, P. A. 1967. A missing observations correlation program. *Educ. Psychol. Meas.* 27:715–18
166. Games, P. A. 1971. Multiple comparisons of means. *Am. Educ. Res. J.* 8: 531–65
167. Gardner, L. A. Jr. 1969. On detecting changes in the mean of normal variates. *Ann. Math. Statist.* 40:116–26
168. Gardner, M. J. 1972. On using an estimated regression line in a second sample. *Biometrika* 59:263–74
169. Gartside, P. S. 1972. A study of methods for comparing several variances. *J. Am. Statist. Assoc.* 67:342–46
170. Gastwirth, J. L. 1968. The first-median test: A two-sided version of the control median test. *J. Am. Statist. Assoc.* 63: 692–706
171. Geary, R. C. 1966. The average critical value method for adjudging relative efficiency of statistical tests in time series regression analysis. *Biometrika* 53: 109–19
172. Gebhardt, F. 1971. Maximum likelihood solution to factor analysis when some factors are completely specified. *Psychometrika* 36:155–63
173. Gehan, E. A., Thomas, D. G. 1969. The performance of some two-sample tests in small samples with and without censoring. *Biometrika* 56:127–32
174. Geisser, S. 1967. Estimation associated with linear discriminants. *Ann. Math. Statist.* 38:807–17
175. Ghosh, B. K. 1967. Analysis of variance under random and mixed models. *Am. Statist. Assoc. J.* 62:1401–17
176. Gibbons, J. D., Gastwirth, J. L. 1970. Properties of the percentile modified rank tests. *Ann. Inst. Statist. Math.* Suppl. 6:95–114
177. Gilbert, R. O. 1972. A Monte Carlo study of analysis of variance and competing rank tests for Scheffé's mixed model. *J. Am. Statist. Assoc.* 67:71–75
178. Glass, G. V. 1966. Note on rank biserial correlation. *Educ. Psychol. Meas.* 26: 623–31
179. Gnanadesikan, R., Lee, E. T. 1970. Graphical techniques for internal comparisons amongst equal degree of freedom groupings in multiresponse experiments. *Biometrika* 57:229–37
180. Gnanadesikan, R., Wilk, M. B. 1969. Data analytic methods in multivariate statistical analysis. *Multivar. Anal.* 2: 593–638
181. Gnanadesikan, R., Wilk, M. B. 1970. Use of maximum likelihood for estimating error variance from a collection of analysis of variance mean squares. *Ann. Math. Statist.* 41:292–304
182. Goldberger, A. S. 1968. *Topics in Regression Analysis.* New York: Macmillan
183. Goldberger, A. S. 1971. Econometrics and psychometrics: a survey of communalities. *Psychometrika* 36:83–107
184. Goldsmith, C. H., Gaylor, D. W. 1970. Three-stage nested designs for estimating variance components. *Technometrics* 12:487–98
185. Goldstein, S. G., Linden, J. D., Baker, T. T. 1967. Programs for the determination of the coefficient and standard error of the tetrachoric correlation. *Educ. Psychol. Meas.* 27:723–27
186. Goodman, L. A. 1968. The analysis of cross-classified data: independence, quasi-independence, and interaction in contingency tables with or without missing entries. *J. Am. Statist. Assoc.* 63:1091–1131
187. Ibid 1970. The multivariate analysis of qualitative data interactions among multiple classifications. 65:226–56
188. Goodman, L. A. 1971. The analysis of multidimensional contingency tables: stepwise procedures and direct estimation methods for building models for multiple classifications. *Technometrics* 13:33–61
189. Goodman, L. A. 1971. Partitioning of chi-square, analysis of marginal contingency tables, and estimation of expected frequencies in multidimensional contingency tables. *J. Am. Statist. Assoc.* 66: 339–44
190. Gottman, J. M., McFall, R. M., Barnett, J. T. 1969. Design and analysis of research using time series. *Psychol. Bull.* 72:229–306
191. Green, B. F. 1969. Best linear composites with a specified structure. *Psychometrika* 34:301–18
192. Grizzle, J. E. 1969. An example of the analysis of a series of response curves and an application of multivariate multiple comparisons. *Essays Probab. Statist.* 15:311–26
193. Grizzle, J. E., Allen, D. M. 1968. *Analysis of growth and dose response curves.* Inst. Statist. Mimeo Ser. 576. 37 pp. Supported by NIH, Inst. Gen. Med. Sci., Grant No. GM-12868-04
194. Grizzle, J. E., Starner, C. F., Koch, G. G. 1969. Analysis of categorical data by linear models. *Biometrics* 25:489–504

195. Grizzle, J. E., Williams, O. D. 1972. Log linear models and tests of independence for contingency tables. *Biometrics* 28:137–56
196. Groen, G. J. 1971. Stochastic processes and the Guttman simplex. *Psychometrika* 36:289–302
197. Guertin, W. H. 1968. Comparison of three methods of handling missing observations. *Psychol. Rep.* 22:896
198. Gurland, J. 1968. A relatively simple form of the distribution of the multiple correlation coefficient. *J. Roy. Statist. Soc. B.* 30:276–83
199. Guttman, L., 1954. Some necessary conditions for common factor analysis. *Psychometrika* 19:149–61
200. Guttman, L. 1955. The determinancy of factor score matrices with implications for five other basic problems of common-factor theory. *Brit. J. Statist. Psychol.* 8:65–81
201. Guttman, L. 1967. The development of nonmetric space analysis: A letter to John Ross. *Multivar. Behav. Res.* 2: 71–82
202. Guttman, L. 1968. A general nonmetric technique for finding the smallest coordinate space for a configuration of points. *Psychometrika* 33:469–506
203. Hakstian, A. R. 1971. A comparative evaluation of several prominent methods of oblique factor transformation. *Psychometrika* 37:175–93
204. Hamdan, M. A. 1970. The equivalence of tetrachoric and maximum likelihood estimates of ρ in 2 X 2 tables. *Biometrika* 57:212–14
205. Hamdan, M. A. 1971. On the polychoric series method for estimation of ρ in contingency tables. *Psychometrika* 36:253–59
206. Han, C.-P. 1968. Testing the homogeneity of a set of correlated variances. *Biometrika* 55:317–26
207. Ibid. A note on discrimination in the case of unequal covariance matrices, 586–87
208. Han, C.-P. 1969. Distribution of discriminant function when covariance matrices are proportional. *Ann. Math. Statist.* 40:979–85
209. Han, C.-P. 1969. Testing the homogeniety of variances in a two-way classification. *Biometrics* 25:153–58
210. Han, C.-P., Bancroft, T. A. 1968. On pooling means when variance is unknown. *J. Am. Statist. Assoc.* 63: 1333–42
211. Hanumara, R. C., Thompson, W. A. Jr. 1968. Percentage points of the extreme roots of a Wishart matrix. *Biometrika* 55:505–12
212. Haq, M. S. 1970. Structural analysis for the first order autoregressive stochastic models. *Ann. Math. Statist.* 41:970–78
213. Harris, G. G. 1972. Multidimensional scaling (1910–1971). *Biblio. No. 205.* Bell Telephone Lab., Libraries and Information Systems, Murray Hill, NJ
214. Hartigan, J. A. 1967. Representation of similarity matrices by trees. *J. Am. Statist. Assoc.* 62:1140–58
215. Ibid 1972. Direct clustering of a data matrix. 67:123–29
216. Hartley, H. O., Hocking, R. R. 1971. The analysis of incomplete data. *Biometrics* 783–823
217. Hartley, H. O., Rao, J. N. K. 1967. Maximum-likelihood estimation for the mixed analysis of variance model. *Biometrika* 54:93–108
218. Harvey, W. R. 1970. Estimation of variance and covariance components in the mixed model. *Biometrics* 26:485–504
219. Harville, D. A. 1967. Statistical dependence between random effects and the numbers of observations on the effects for the unbalanced one-way random classification. *J. Am. Statist. Assoc.* 62: 1375–86
220. Ibid 1968. Statistical dependence between subclass means and the numbers of observations in the subclasses for the two-way completely random classification. 63:1484–94
221. Hayakawa, T. 1969. On the distribution of the latent roots of a positive definite random symmetric matrix. I. *Ann. Inst. Statist. Math.* 21:1
222. Healy, M. J. R. 1969. Rao's paradox concerning multivariate tests of significance. *Biometrics* 25:2
223. Herzberg, A. M., Cox, D. R. 1969. Recent work on the design of experiments: A bibliography and a review. *J. Roy. Statist. Soc. A* 132:29–67
224. Hettmansperger, T. P. 1968. On the trimmed Mann-Whitney statistic. *Ann. Math. Statist.* 39:1610–14
225. Hill, B. N. 1967. Correlated errors in the random model. *J. Am. Statist. Assoc.* 62:1387–1400
226. Hocking, R. R., Leslie, R. N. 1967. Selection of the best subset in regression analysis. *Technometrics* 9:531–40
227. Hocking, R. R., Smith, W. B. 1968. Estimation of parameters in the multivariate normal distribution with missing observations. *J. Am. Statist. Assoc.* 63: 159–73

228. Hodges, J. L. Jr., Lehmann, E. L. 1968. A compact table for power of the *T*-test. *Ann. Math. Statist.* 39:1629–37
229. Hoel, P. G. 1968. On testing for the degree of a polynomial. *Technometrics* 10:757–67
230. Hogg, R. V. 1965. On models and hypotheses with restricted alternatives. *J. Am. Statist. Assoc.* 60:1153–62
231. Hollander, M. 1967. Asymptotic efficiency of two nonparametric competitors of Wilcoxon's two-sample test. *J. Am. Statist. Assoc.* 62:939–49
232. Ibid 1968. Certain uncorrelated nonparametric test statistics. 63:707–14
233. Holloway, L. N. 1967. The robustness of Hotelling's T^2. *J. Am. Statist. Assoc.* 62:124–36
234. Horst, P. 1961. Relations among m sets of measures. *Psychometrika* 26:129–49
235. Horst, P. 1965. *Factor Analysis of Data Matrices.* New York: Holt, Rinehart & Winston
236. Howe, W. G. 1955. *Some contributions to factor analysis.* Oak Ridge Nat. Lab. Rep. No. ORNL-1919
237. Hsu, T.-C., Feldt, L. S. 1969. The effect of limitations on the number of criterion score values on the significance level of the F-test. *Am. Educ. Res. J.* 6:515–27
238. Hubert, L. 1973. Monotone invariant clustering procedures. *Psychometrika* 38:47–62
239. Ibid. MIN and MAX hierarchical clustering using asymmetric similarity measures, 63–72
240. Hudimoto, H. 1971. Empirical Bayes approach to multiple decision. *J. Jap. Statist. Soc.* 2:27–32
241. Hummel, T. J. 1971. Empirical comparison of univariate and multivariate analysis of variance procedures. *Psychol. Bull.* 76:49–57
242. Humphreys, L. G., Ilgen, D. R. 1969. Note on a criterion for the number of common factors. *Educ. Psychol. Meas.* 29:571–78
243. Humphreys, L. G., Ilgen, D. R., McGrath, D., Montanelli, R. 1969. Capitalization on chance in rotation of factors. *Educ. Psychol. Meas.* 29: 259–71
244. Ireland, C. T., Ku, H. H. Kullback, S. 1969. Symmetry and marginal homogeneity of an r x r contingency table. *J. Am. Statist. Assoc.* 64:1323–41
245. Ito, K. 1969. On the effect of heteroscedasticity and non-normality upon some multivariate test procedures. See Ref. 296, 87–110
246. Jackson, E. C. 1968. Missing values in linear multiple discriminant analysis. *Biometrics* 24:835–44
247. Jacquez, J. A., Mather, F. J., Crawford, C. R. 1968. Linear regression with non-constant, unknown error variances: Sampling experiments with least squares, weighted least squares and maximum likelihood estimators. *Biometrics* 24:607–26
248. Jennrich, R. I. 1970. An asymptotic X^2 test for the equality of two correlation matrices. *J. Am. Statist. Assoc.* 65: 904–12
249. Jensen, D. R. 1970. The joint distribution of traces of Wishart matrices and some applications. *Ann. Math. Statist.* 41:133–45
250. Jensen, D. R. 1972. Some simultaneous multivariate procedures using Hotelling's T^2 statistics. *Biometrics* 28:39–53
251. Joe, G. W., Anderson, H. E. Jr. 1969. Mean differences and association. *Multivar. Behav. Res.,* 379–89 (abstr.)
252. John, J. A., Wolock, F. W., David, H. A. 1972. *Cyclic designs.* Nat. Bur. Stand. Appl. Math. Ser. 62. 76 pp. (U.S. Dep. Commerce)
253. John, S. 1971. Some optimal multivariate tests. *Biometrika* 58:123–27
254. Ibid 1972. The distribution of a statistic used for testing sphericity of normal distributions. 59:169–73
255. Johnson, D. E., Graybill, F. A. 1972. Estimation of ^{2} in a two-way classification model with interaction. *J. Am. Statist. Assoc.* 67:388–94
256. Johnson, S. C. 1967. Hierarchical clustering schemes. *Psychometrika* 32: 241–54
257. Jones, H. L. 1968. The analysis of variance of data from stratified subsamples. *J. Am. Statist. Assoc.* 63:64–86
258. Jones, R. H., Crowell, D. H., Kapuniai, L. E. 1970. Change detection model for serially correlated mutlivariate data. *Biometrics* 26:269–80
259. Jöreskog, K. G. 1967. Some contributions to maximum likelihood factor analysis. *Psychometrika* 32:443–82
260. Jöreskog, K. G. 1970. A general method for analysis of covariance structures. *Biometrika* 57:239–51
261. Jöreskog, K. G. 1970. A general method for estimating a linear structural equation system. *ETS Res. Bull. 70–54*
262. Jöreskog, K. G. 1970. Estimation and testing of simplex models. *Brit. J. Math. Statist. Psychol.* 23:121–45
263. Jöreskog, K. G. 1970. Factoring the multitest-multioccasion correlation ma-

trix. In *Current Problems and Techniques in Multivariate Psychology,* ed. C. E. Lunneborg, 68–100. Seattle: Univ. Washington Press

264. Jöreskog, K. G. 1971. Statistical analysis of sets of congeneric tests. *Psychometrika* 36:109–33
265. Ibid. Simultaneous factor analysis in several populations, 409–26
266. Jöreskog, K. G. 1973. Analysis of covariance structures. In *Multivariate Analysis III,* ed. P. R. Krishnaiah. New York: Academic
267. Jöreskog, K. G. 1973. Analyzing psychological data by structural analysis of covariance matrices. *Res. Rep. 73–2.* Univ. Uppsala Dep. Statist., Uppsala, Sweden
268. Jöreskog, K. G., Goldberger, A. S. 1972. Factor analysis by generalized least squares. *Psychometrika* 37:243–60
269. Jöreskog, K. G., Gruvaeus, G. T., van Thillo, M. 1970. ACOVS: A general computer program for analysis of covariance structures. *ETS Res. Bull. 70–15*
270. Jöreskog, K. G., van Thillo, M. 1971. New rapid algorithms for factor analysis by unweighted least squares, generalized least squares and maximum likelihood. *ETS Memo. 71–5*
271. Jöreskog, K. G., van Thillo, M. 1972. LISREL—A general computer program for estimating linear structural relationships. *ETS Res. Bull. 72–56*
272. Juola, R. C. 1970. Population symmetry and the regions. *Biometrika* 57:668–69
273. Kaiser, H. F. 1970. A second-generation little Jiffy. *Psychometrika* 35: 401–16
274. Kaiser, H. F. 1973. *A computational starting point for Rao's canonical factor analysis.* Univ. California, Berkeley (mimeo)
275. Kaiser, H. F. 1973. *A note on the Equamax criterion.* Univ. California, Berkeley (mimeo)
276. Kaiser, H. F. 1973. *Little Jiffy, Mark IV.* Univ. California, Berkeley (mimeo)
277 Kaiser, H. F. 1973. *Three comments on oblimax.* Univ. California, Berkeley (mimeo)
278. Kakeshita, S., Yanagawa, T. 1967. Estimates for scale based on u-statistics. *Kyushu Univ. Ser. A. (Math.)* 21:139–52. Reprinted from Memoirs of Faculty of Science, Jukuoka, Japan
279. Kale, B. K., Bancroft, T. A. 1967. Inference for some completely specified models involving normal approximations to discrete data. *Biometrics* 23:335–48
280. Kaufman, G. M. 1969. Conditional prediction and unbiasedness in structural equations. *Econometrika* 37:44–49
281. Kelejian, H. H. 1969. Missing observations in multivariate regression: efficiency of a first-order method. *J. Am. Statist. Assoc.* 64:1609–16
282. Kempthorne, O. 1966. Multivariate responses in comparative experiments. See Ref. 11
283. Kempthorne, O., Doerfler, T. E. 1969. The behavior of some significance tests under experimental randomization. *Biometrika* 56:231–48
284. Kendall, M. G., Stuart, A. 1969. *The Advanced Theory of Statistics,* Vol. 1. London:Griffin
285. Kettenring, J. R. 1971. Canonical analysis of several sets of variables. *Biometrika* 58:433–51
286. King, B. 1967. Step-wise clustering procedures. *J. Am. Statis. Assoc.* 62:86–101
287. King, N. 1972. An alternative for the linear regression equation when the predictor variable is uncontrolled and the sample size is small. *J. Am. Statist. Assoc.* 67:217–19
288. Kirk, R. E. 1968. *Experimental Design: Procedures for the Behavioral Sciences.* Belmont, Calif.:Brooks/Cole
289. Klotz, J. 1967. Asymptotic efficiency of the two-sample Kolmogorov-Smirnov test. *J. Am. Statist. Assoc.* 62:932–38
290. Koch, G. G. 1967. A procedure to estimate the population mean in random effects models. *Technometrics* 9:577–85
291. Koch, G. G. 1969. Some aspects of the statistical analysis of "split plot" experiments in completely randomized layouts. *J. Am. Statist. Assoc.* 64:485–505
292. Koch, G. G. 1970. The use of non-parametric methods in the statistical analysis of a complex split plot experiment. *Biometrics* 26:105–28
293. Koch, G. G., Imrey, P. B., Reinfurt, D. W. 1972. Linear model analysis of categorical data with incomplete response vectors. *Biometrics* 28:663–92
294. Korin, B. P. 1972. Some comments on the homoscedasticity criterion M and the multivariate analysis of variance tests T^2, W, and R. *Biometrika* 59: 215–16
295. Kowlaski, C. J., Tarter, M. E. 1969. Coordinate transformations to normality and the power of normal tests for independence. *Biometrika* 56:139–48
296. Krishnaiah, P. R. 1969. Simultaneous test procedure under general MANOVA models. In *Multivariate*

Analysis, Vol. 2, ed. P. R. Krishnaiah. New York:Academic

297. Kristof, W. 1971. On a statistic arising in testing correlation. *ETS Res. Bull. 71–21*
298. Kristof, W. 1971. On the theory of a set of tests which differ only in length. *Psychometrika* 36:207–25
299. Ibid 1973. Testing a linear relation between true scores of two measures. 38: 101–11
300. Kruskal, J. B., Carroll, J. D. 1969. Geometrical models and badness-of-fit functions. See Ref. 296, 639–72
301. Ku, H. H., Kullback, S. 1968. Interaction in multidimensional contingency tables; an information theoretic approach. *J. Res. Nat. Bur. Stand.-Math. Sci.* 72B:159–99
302. Kudo, A. 1963. A multivariate analog of the one-sided test. *Biometrika* 50:403–18
303. Kudo, A., Fujisawa, H. 1966. Some multivariate tests with restricted alternative hypotheses. See Ref. 11
304. Labinowich, E. P., Brewer, J. K. 1971. Computer programs for rank analysis of covariance. *Educ. Psychol. Meas.* 31: 295–96
305. Lachenbruch, P. A. 1966. Discriminant analysis when the initial samples are misclassified. *Technometrics* 8:657–62
306. Lachenbruch, P. A. 1967. An almost unbiased method of obtaining confidence intervals for the probability of misclassification in discriminant analysis. *Biometrics* 23:639–45
307. Ibid 1968. On expected probabilities of misclassification in discriminant analysis, necessary sample size, and a relation with the multiple correlation coefficient. 24:823–34
308. Lachenbruch, P. A., Mickey, M. R. 1968. Estimation of error rates in discriminant analysis. *Technometrics* 10: 1–11
309. LaMotte, L. R., Hocking, R. R. 1970. Computational efficiency in the selection of regression variables. *Technometrics* 12:83–93
310. Lancaster, T. 1968. Grouping estimators on heteroscedastic data. *J. Am. Statist. Assoc.* 63:182–91
311. Lawton, W. H., Sylvestre, E. A., Maggio, M. S. 1972. Self-modeling nonlinear regression. *Technometrics* 14: 513–32
312. Lazarsfeld, P. F., Henry, N. 1968. *Latent Structure Analysis.* New York: Houghton-Mifflin
313. Leone, F. C. et al 1968. Sampling distributions of variance components. II. Empirical studies of unbalanced nested designs. *Technometrics* 10:719–37
314. Levin, J. 1972. The occurrence of an increase in correlation by restriction of range. *Psychometrika* 37:93–97
315. Levin, J. R., Marascuilo, L. A. 1972. Type IV errors and interactions. *Psychol. Bull.* 78:368–74
316. Levine, M. V. 1970. Transformations that render curves parallel. *J. Math. Psychol.* 7:410–43
317. Ibid 1972. Transforming curves into curves with the same shape. 9:1–16
318. Li, C. C. 1968. Fisher, Wright, and path coefficients. *Biometrics* 24:471–83
319. Lingoes, J. C. 1966. Recent computational advances in nonmetric methodology for the behavioral sciences. *Proc. Int. Symp. Math. Comput. Methods in Soc. Sci. Rome,* 1–38
320. Lingoes, J. C. 1971. Some boundary conditions for a monotone analysis of symmetric matrices. *Psychometrika* 36:195–203
321. Linn, R. L., Werts, C. E., Tucker, L. R. 1971. The interpretation of regression coefficients in a school effects model. *Educ. Psychol. Meas.* 31:85–93
322. Littell, R. C., Folks, J. L. 1971. Asymptotic optimality of Fisher's method of combining independent tests. *J. Am. Statist. Assoc.* 66:802–6
323. Lockhart, R. S. 1967. The assumption of multivariate normality. *Brit. J. Math. Statist. Psychol.* 20:63–69
324. Lord, F. M. 1973. Testing if two measuring procedures measure the same dimension. *Psychol. Bull.* 79:71–72
325. Lord, F. M., Novick, M. R. 1968. *Statistical Theories of Mental Test Scores.* Reading, Mass: Addison-Wesley
326. Lorr, M., Radhakrishnan, B. K. 1967. A comparison of two methods of cluster analysis. *Educ. Psychol. Meas.* 27: 47–53
327. Lovell, M. C., Prescott, E. 1970. Multiple regression with inequality constraints: Pretesting bias, hypothesis testing and efficiency. *J. Am. Statist. Assoc.* 65:913–25
328. Low, L. 1970. An application of majorization to comparison of variances. *Technometrics* 12:141–45
329. Mallios, W. S. 1967. A structural regression approach to covariance analysis when the covariance is uncontrolled. *J. Am. Statist. Assoc.* 62:1037–49
330. Mandel, J., 1969. The partitioning of interaction in analysis of variance. *J. Res.* 73B:309–28

331. Mantel, N. 1967. Ranking procedures for arbitrarily restricted observation. *Biometrics* 23:65–78
332. Mantel, N. 1969. Restricted least squares regression and convex quadratic programming. *Technometrics* 11: 763–73
333. Ibid 1970. Why stepdown procedures in variable selection? 12:621–25
334. Mantel, N., Valand, R. S. 1970. A technique of nonparametric multivariate analysis. *Biometrics* 26:547–58
335. Mardia, K. V. 1970. Measures of multivariate skewness and kurtosis with applications. *Biometrika* 57:519–30
336. Ibid 1971. The effect of nonnormality on some multivariate tests and robustness to nonnormality in the linear model. 58:105–21
337. Maritz, J. S. 1968. On the smooth empirical Bayes approach to testing of hypotheses and the compound decision problem. *Biometrika* 55:83–100
338. May, R. B., Konkin, P. R. 1970. A nonparametric test of an ordered hypothesis for k independent samples. *Educ. Psychol. Meas.* 30:251–58
339. McCornack, R. L. 1970. A comparison of three predictor selection techniques in multiple regression. *Psychometrika* 35:257–71
340. McDonald, R. P. 1968. A unified treatment of the weighting problem. *Psychometrika* 33:351–81
341. McDonald, R. P. 1969. The common factor analysis of multicategory data. *Brit. J. Math. Statist. Psychol.* 22: 165–75
342. McDonald, R. P. 1970. Three common factor models for groups of variables. *Psychometrika* 35:111–28
343. McGee, V. E., Carleton, W. T. 1970. Piecewise regression. *J. Am. Statist. Assoc.* 65:1109–26
344. McGuire, T. W. et al 1968. Estimation and inference for linear models in which subsets of the dependent variable are constrained. Reprint No. 400, 1201–13, Grad. Sch. Ind. Admin., Carnegie-Mellon Univ., Pittsburgh
345. McKeon, J. J. 1966. Canonical analysis: some relations between canonical correlation, factor analysis, discriminant analysis, and sealing theory. *Psychometric Monogr.* 13
346. McLaughlin, D. H. A likelihood ratio test for homogeneity of regression without homogeneity of variance. *Educ. Psychol. Meas.* In press
347. McNeil, D. R. 1966. Consistent statistics for estimating and testing hypotheses from grouped samples. *Biometrika* 53:545–57
348. McNeil, D. R. 1967. Efficiency loss due to grouping in distribution-free tests. *J. Am. Statist. Assoc.* 62:954–65
349. McNeil, D. R. 1968. Quick powerful tests with grouped data. *Biometrika* 55:264–67
350. McQuitty, L. 1971. A comparative study of some selected methods of pattern analysis. *Educ. Psychol. Meas.* 31: 607–26
351. Mehta, J. S., Gurland, J. 1969. On utilizing information from a second sample in estimating variance. *Biometrika* 56:527–32
352. Mehta, J. S., Srinivasan, R. 1970. On the Behrens-Fisher problem. *Biometrika* 57:649–55
353. Mielke, P. W. Jr. 1967. Note on some squared rank tests with existing ties. *Technometrics* 9:312–14
354. Miller, J. K., Farr, S. D. 1971. Bimultivariate redundancy: a comprehensive measure of interbattery relationship. *Multivar. Behav. Res.* 6:313–24
355. Miller, R. G. Jr. 1969. *A sequential signed-rank test.* Dep. Statist. Tech. Rep. 14, Stanford Univ. 28 pp.
356. Milliken, G. A., Graybill, F. A. 1970. Extensions of the general linear hypothesis model. *J. Am. Statist. Assoc.* 65: 797–807
357. Milliken, G. A., Graybill, F. A. 1971. Tests for interaction in the two-way model with missing data. *Biometrics* 27:1079–83
358. Moran, P. A. P. 1970. A note on serial correlation coefficients. *Biometrika* 57: 670–72
359. Morgan, J. A., Tatar, J. F. 1972. Calculation of the residual sum of squares for all possible regressions. *Technometrics* 14:317–25
360. Morrison, D. F. 1967. *Multivariate Statistical Methods.* New York:McGraw-Hill
361. Morrison, D. F. 1971. Expectations and variances of maximum likelihood estimates of the multivariate normal distribution parameters with missing data. *J. Am. Statist. Assoc.* 66:602–4
362. Morrison, D. G. 1972. Upper bounds for correlations between binary outcomes and probabilistic predictions. *J. Am. Statist. Assoc.* 67:68–70
363. Muirhead, R. J. 1970. Asymptotic distributions of some multivariate tests. *Ann. Mater. Statist.* 41:1002
364. Mukherjee, B. N. 1966. Derivation of likelihood-ratio tests for Guttman

quasi-simplex covariance structures. *Psychometrika* 31:97–123
365. Mukherjee, B. N. 1969. Invariance of the Guttman quasi-simplex linear model under selection. *Brit. J. Math. Statist. Psychol.* 22:1–28
366. Murray, J. R. 1971. *Statistical models for qualitative data with classification errors.* Unpublished PhD dissertation. Univ. Chicago
367. Murray, J. R., Wiley, D. E., Wolfe, R. G. 1971. New statistical techniques for evaluating longitudinal models. *Hum. Develop.* 14:142–48
368. Naruboodiri, N. K. 1972. Experimental designs in which each subject is used repeatedly. *Psychol. Bull.* 77:54–64
369. Neter, J., Maynes, E. S. 1970. On the appropriateness of the correlation coefficient with a 0, 1 dependent variable. *J. Am. Statist. Assoc.* 65:501–9
370. Odeh, R. E. 1967. The distribution of the maximum sum of ranks. *Technometrics* 9:271–78
371. Ibid 1971. On Jonckheere's K-sample test against ordered alternatives. 13: 912–18
372. Odeh, R. E. 1972. On the power of Jonckheere's K-sample test against ordered alternatives. *Biometrika* 59: 467–71
373. Patel, K. M., Bradley, R. A. 1967. *Approximate small-sample distributions for multivariate two-sample nonparametric tests.* FSU Statist. Rep. M128, Florida State Univ., Tallahassee. 18 pp.
374. Patil, V. 1969. Approximation to the generalized Behrens-Fisher distribution involving three variates. *Biometrika* 56:687–88
375. Pearce, S. C. 1968. Alternatives to a latin square. *Biometrics* 24:657–62
376. Pearce, S. C. 1968. The mean efficiency of equi-replicate designs. *Biometrika* 55:251–53
377. Pearce, S. C. 1970. The efficiency of block designs in general. *Biometrika* 57: 339–46
378. Ibid 1971. Precision in block experiments. 58:161–67
379. Perlman, M. D. 1969. One-sided testing problems in multivariate analysis. *Ann. Math. Statist.* 40:549–67
380. Perlman, M. D. 1971. Multivariate one-sided testing problems involving Fisher's discriminant function. *Sankhyā, Ser. A* 33:19–34
381. Phillips, J. P. N. 1968. Methods of constructing one-way and factorial designs balanced for trend. *Appl. Statist.* 17: 162–70
382. Pillai, K. C. S. 1967. Upper percentage points of the largest root of a matrix in multivariate analysis. *Biometrika* 54: 189–94
383. Pillai, K. C. S., Gupta, A. K. 1969. On the exact distribution of Wilks's criterion. *Biometrika* 56:109–18
384. Pillai, K. C. S., Jayachandran, K. 1968. Power comparisons of test of equality of two covariance matrices based on four criteria. *Biometrika* 55:335–42
385. Pinneau, S. R., Ender, P. B. 1971. Analysis of component variance. *Percept. Mot. Skills* 33:327–35
386. Pitz, G. F. 1968. An example of Bayesian hypothesis testing: The perception of rotary motion in depth. *Psychol. Bull.* 70:252–55
387. Porebski, O. R. 1966. Discriminatory and canonical analysis of technical college data. *Brit. J. Math. Statist. Psychol.* 19:215–36
388. Ibid. On the interrelated nature of the multivariate statistics used in discriminatory analysis, 197–214
389. Porebski, O. R. 1968. A semi-orthogonal dependent factor solution. *Psychometrika* 3:451–68
390. Potthoff, R. F., Whittinghill, M. 1966. Testing for homogeneity I. The binomial and multinomial distributions. *Biometrika* 53:167–82
391. Ibid. Testing for homogeneity II. The Poisson distribution, 183–90
392. Preece, D. A. 1971. Iterative procedures for missing values in experiments. *Technometrics* 13:743–53
393. Prescott, P. 1970. Estimation of the standard deviation of a normal population from doubly censored samples using normal scores. *Biometrika* 57:409–19
394. Ibid 1971. Distribution of the normal scores estimator of the standard deviation of a normal population. 58:631–36
395. Ibid. Use of a simple range-type estimator of σ in tests of hypotheses, 33–40
396. Press, S. J. 1969. On serial correlation. *Ann. Math. Statist.* 49:188
397. Priestly, M. B., Rao, T. S. 1969. A test for non-stationarity of time series. *J. Roy. Statist. Soc. B (Methodological)* 31:140–49
398. Pruzek, R. M. 1971. Methods and problems in the analyses of multivariate data. *Rev. Educ. Res.* 41:163–90
399. Puri, M. L., Sen, P. K. 1966. On a class of multivariate multisample rank-order tests. *Sankhyā, Ser. A* 28:353–76

400. Puri, M. L., Sen, P. K. 1969. Analysis of covariance based on general rank scores. *Ann Math. Statist.* 40:610–18
401. Puri, M. L., Sen, P. K. 1971. *Nonparametric Methods in Multivariate Analysis.* New York:Wiley
402. Quade, D. 1967. Rank analysis of covariance. *J. Am. Statist. Assoc.* 62: 1187–1200
403. Rao, C. R. 1955. Estimation and tests of significance in factor analysis. *Psychometrika* 20:93–111
404. Rao, C. R. 1968. A note on the asymptotic relative efficiencies of Cox & Stuart's tests for testing trend in dispersion of a p-dependent time series. *Biometrika* 55:381–85
405. Rao, C. R. 1969. Correlation between the sample variances in a singly truncated bivariate normal distribution. *Biometrika* 55:433
406. Rao, C. R. 1970. Estimation of heteroscedastic variances in linear models. *J. Am. Statist. Assoc.* 65:161–72
407. Ibid 1972. Estimation of variance and covariance components in linear models. 67:112–15
408. Rao, C. R. 1972. Recent trends of research work in multivariate analysis. *Biometrics* 28:3–22
409. Rao, J. N. K., Subrahmaniam, K. 1971. Combining independent estimators and estimation in linear regression with unequal variances. *Biometrics* 27:971–90
410. Rees, D. H. 1969. The analysis of variance of some non-orthogonal designs with split plots. *Biometrika* 56:43–54
411. Reisch, J. S., Webster, J. T. 1969. The power of a test in covariance analysis. *Biometrics* 25:701–14
412. Rhyne, A. L., Steel, R. G. D. 1967. A multiple comparisons sign test: All pairs of treatments. *Biometrics* 23: 539–49
413. Riffenburgh, R. H. 1969. Half-rectified truncated distributions: Sampling theory and hypothesis testing. *Technometrics* 11:47–59
414. Rizvi, M. H., Sobel, M., Woodworth, G. G. 1968. *Nonparametric ranking procedures for comparison with a control.* Dep. Statist. Tech. Rep. 133, Stanford Univ., California. 38 pp.
415. Robbins, H., Simons, G., Starr, N. 1967. A sequential analogue of the Behrens-Fisher problem. *Ann. Math. Statist.* 38:1384–91
416. Roberge, J. J. 1971. A computer program for nonparametric post hoc multiple comparisons. *Educ. Psychol. Meas.* 31:755–60
417. Robinson, J. 1967. Incomplete split plot designs. *Biometrics* 23:793–802
418. Rock, D. A. et al 1970. A comparison of predictor selection techniques using Monte Carlo methods. *Educ. Psychol. Meas.* 30:873–84
419. Rodger, R. S. 1967. Type I errors and their decision basis. *Brit. J. Math. Statist. Psychol.* 20:51–62
420. Ibid. Type II errors and their decision basis, 187–204
421. Rosenthal, R. 1968. Experimenter expectancy and the reassuring nature of the null hypothesis decision procedure. *Psychol. Bull. Monogr. Suppl.* 70: 30–47
422. Rozeboom, W. W. 1965. Linear correlations between sets of variables. *Psychometrika* 30:57–71
423. Rozeboom, W. W. 1972. *Dynamic analysis of multivariate process data.* Univ. Alberta Center Advan. Study Theoret. Psychol. (mimeo)
424. Rudan, J. W., Searle, S. R. 1971. Large sample variances of maximum likelihood estimators of variance components in the 3-way nested classification, random model, with unbalanced data. *Biometrics* 27:1087–91
425. Rutemiller, H. C., Bowers, D. A. 1968. Estimation in a heteroscedastic regression model. *J. Am. Statist. Assoc.* 63: 552–57
426. Salsburg, D. 1971. Testing dose responses on proportions near zero or one with the jackknife. *Biometrics* 27: 1035–41
427. Savage, I. R. 1969. Nonparametric statistics: A personal review. *Sankhyā, Ser. A* 31:107–44
428. Scheffé, H. 1970. Practical solutions of the Behrens-Fisher problem. *J. Am. Statist. Assoc.* 65:1501–8
429. Schlesselman, J. J. 1971. Data transformation in two-way analysis of variance. *ETS Res. Bull. 71–33.* 228 pp.
430. Schmidt, F. L. 1971. The relative efficiency of regression and simple unit predictor weights in applied differential psychology. *Educ. Psychol. Meas.* 31: 699–714
431. Schönemann, P. H. 1970. Fitting a simplex symmetrically. *Psychometrika* 35: 1–21
432. Ibid 1971. The minimum average correlation between equivalent sets of uncorrelated factors. 36:21–30
433. Schönemann, P. H., Wang, M. 1972. Some new results on factor indeterminancy. *Psychometrika* 37:61–91
434. Sclove, S. L. 1968. Improved estimators for coefficients in linear regression. *J. Am. Statist. Assoc.* 63:596–606

435. Sclove, S. L. 1972. (Y vs. X) or (log Y vs. X)? *Technometrics* 14:391–403
436. Searle, S. R. 1966. *Matrix Algebra for the Biological Sciences.* New York: Wiley
437. Searle, S. R. 1970. Large sample variances of maximum likelihood estimators of variance components using unbalanced data. *Biometrics* 26:505–24
438. Ibid 1971. Topics in variance components estimation. 27:1–76
439. Sedransk, J. 1967. Designing some multi-factor analytical studies. *J. Am. Statist. Assoc.* 62:1121–39
440. Sedransk, J. 1969. Some elementary properties of systematic sampling. Reprinted from *Skand. Aktuarietidskrift,* 39–47
441. Sen, P. K., Puri, M. L. 1969. On robust nonparametric estimation in some multivariate linear models. See Ref. 296, 33–54
442. Shafto, M. 1972. Cluster analysis by linear contrasts. *ETS Res. Bull.* 72–35
443. Shapiro, S. S., Wilk, M. B., Chen, H. J. 1968. A comparative study of various tests for normality. *J. Am. Statist. Assoc.* 63:1343–73
444. Shepard, R., Romney, A. K., Nerlove, S. B., Eds. 1972. *Multidimensional Scaling.* Vol. I: *Theory;* Vol. 2: *Applications.* New York: Seminar Press
445. Shine, L. C. II. A multi-way analysis of variance for single-subject designs. *Educ. Psychol. Meas.* To be published
446. Shine, L. C. II, Bower, S. M. 1971. A one-way analysis of variance for single-subject designs. *Educ. Psychol. Meas.* 31:105–13
447. Slakter, M. J. 1968. Accuracy of an approximation to the power of the chi-square goodness-of-fit test with small but equal expected frequencies. *J. Am. Statist. Assoc.* 63:912–18
448. Slivka, J. 1970. A one-sided nonparametric multiple comparison control percentile test: treatments versus control. *Biometrika* 57:431–38
449. Smith, F. B. Jr., Shanno, D. F. 1971. An improved Marquardt procedure for nonlinear regressions. *Technometrics* 13:63–74
450. Smith, R. A. 1971. The effect of unequal group size on Tukey's HSB procedure. *Psychometrika* 36:31–34
451. Smith, W. B., Hocking, R. R. 1972. Wishart variate generator. *Appl. Statist.* 21:341–52
452. Sobel, M. 1966. *On a generalization of Wilcoxon's rank sum test for censored data.* Tech. Rep. 69, Univ. Minnesota (revised)
453. Somers, R. H. 1970. A partitioning of ordinal information in a three-way cross-classification. *Multivar. Behav. Res.* 5:217–39
454. Spjotvøll, E. 1968. A note on robust estimation in analysis of variance. *Ann. Math. Statist.* 39:1486–92
455. Sprott, D. A. Use of the analysis of covariance. Manuscript, Univ. Waterloo. 12 pp.
456. Sprott, D. A., Kalbfleisch, J. D. 1969. Examples of likelihoods and comparison with point estimates and large sample approximations. *J. Am. Statis. Assoc.* 64:468–84
457. Stanley, J. C. 1968. An important similarity between biserial *r* and the Brogden-Cureton-Glass biserial *r* for ranks. *Educ. Psychol. Meas.* 28:249–53
458. Steck, G. P. 1969. The Smirnov two-sample tests as rank tests. *Ann. Math. Statist.* 40:1449–66
459. Stewart, D., Love, W. 1968. A general canonical correlation index. *Psychol. Bull.* 70:160–63
460. Subba Rao, T. 1970. The fitting of non-stationary time-series models with time-dependent parameters. *J. Roy. Statist. Soc. B* 32:312–22
461. Sugiura, N., Nagao, H. 1969. On Bartlett's test and Lehmann's test for homogeneity of variances. *Ann. Math. Statist.* 40:2018–32
462. Sugiyama, T. 1967. On the distribution of the largest latent root of the covariance matrix. *Ann. Math. Statist.* 38: 1198
463. Tamura, R. 1967. Small sample properties of a "sometimes pool estimate" in the nonparametric case. Reprinted from *Bull. Math. Sci.* 12:75–83
464. Tamura, R. 1969. Some multivariate comparison procedures based on ranks. *Ann. Math. Statist.* 40:1486–91
465. Tatsuoka, M. M. 1971. *Multivariate Analysis.* New York: Wiley
466. Thornby, J. I. 1972. A robust test for linear regression. *Biometrics* 28:533–43
467. Tiao, G. C., Ali, M. M. 1971. Analysis of correlated random effects: linear model with two random components. *Biometrika* 58:37–51
468. Tiao, G. C., Box, G. E. P. 1967. Bayesian analysis of a three-component hierarchical design model. *Biometrika* 54:109–25
469. Tiao, G. C., Draper, N. R. 1968. Bayesian analysis of linear models with two random components with special reference to the balanced incomplete block design. *Biometrika* 55:101–17

470. Tiku, M. L. 1967. Tables of the power of the F-test. *J. Am. Statist. Assoc.* 62: 525–39
471. Timm, N. H. 1970. The estimation of variance-covariance and correlation matrices from incomplete data. *Psychometrika* 35:417–37
472. Tobach, E. et al 1967. A table for making rank sum multiple paired comparisons. *Technometrics* 9:561–67
473. Tobias, S., Carlson, J. E. 1969. Bartlett's test of sphericity and chance findings in factor analysis. *Multivar. Behav. Res.* 4:375–78
474. Tryon, R. C., Bailey, D. E. 1970. *Cluster Analysis.* New York: McGraw-Hill
475. Tucker, L. R. 1958. An inter-battery method of factor analysis. *Psychometrika* 23:111–36
476. Ibid 1971. Relations of factor score estimates to their use. 36:427–36
477. Tucker, L. R., Lewis, C. 1973. A reliability coefficient for maximum likelihood factor analysis. *Psychometrika* 38:1–10
478. Urbakh, V. Y. 1971. Linear discriminant analysis: Loss of discriminating power when a variate is omitted. *Biometrics* 27:531–34
479. van Zwet, W. R., Oosterhoff, J. 1967. On the combination of independent test statistics. *Ann. Math. Statist.* 38: 659–80
480. Votaw, D. F. Jr. 1948. Testing compound symmetry in a normal multivariate distribution. *Ann. Math. Statist.* 19:447–73
481. Wagle, B. 1968. Multivariate beta distribution and a test for multivariate normality. *J. Roy. Statist. Soc. B* 30:511
482. Wainer, J. 1971. Piecewise regression: A simplified procedure. *Brit. J. Math. Statist. Psychol.* 24:83–92
483. Walsh, J. F. 1971. Use of a general analysis of variance program in missing data situations. *Behav. Res. Methods Instrum.* 3:202
484. Ibid. Using a general analysis of variance algorithm for covariance designs, 203
485. Wang, M. D., Stanley, J. C. 1970. Differential weighting: A review of methods and empirical studies. 663–705. Baltimore: Johns Hopkins Univ.
486. Wang, Y. Y. 1967. A comparison of several variance component estimators. *Biometrika* 54:301–5
487. Weisberg, H. I. 1972. Bayesian comparison of two ordered multinomial populations. *Biometrics* 28:859–67
488. Wells, D. G. 1970. Correcting the correlation coefficient for explicit restriction on both variables. *Educ. Psychol. Meas.* 30:925–34
489. Werts, C. E., Jöreskog, K. G., Linn, R. L. 1971. Identification and estimation in path analysis with unmeasured variables. *ETS Res. Bull. 71–39*
490. Werts, C. E., Jöreskog, K. G., Linn, R. L. 1973. A multitrait-multimethod model for studying growth. *Educ. Psychol. Meas.* 33. In press
491. Werts, C. E., Linn, R. L. 1968. Analyzing school effects: How to use the same data to support different hypotheses. Growth Study Paper 27. *ETS Res. Bull. 68–60.* 18 pp.
492. Werts, C. E., Linn, R. L. 1970. Path analysis: psychological examples. *Psychol. Bull.* 67:193–212
493. Werts, C. E., Linn, R. L. 1971. Analyzing school effects: ANCOVA with a fallible covariance. *Educ. Psychol. Meas.* 31:95–104
494. Ibid. Considerations when making inferences within the analysis of covariance model, 407–16
495. Wilk, M. B., Shapiro, S. S. 1968. The joint assessment of normality of several independent samples. *Technometrics* 10:825–39
496. Williams, J. D., Lindem, A. C. Jr. 1971. *Setwise linear regression.* Spec. Rep. 30, UND Computer Center, Grand Rapids. 23 pp.
497. Williams, J. D., Lindem, A. C. Jr. 1971. Setwise regression analysis—A stepwise procedure for sets of variables. *Educ. Psychol. Meas.* 31:747–48
498. Williams, O. D., Grizzle, J. E. 1972. Analysis of contingency tables having ordered response categories. *J. Am. Statist. Assoc.* 67:55–63
499. Winer, B. J. 1968. The error. *Psychometrika* 33:391–403
500. Wolfe, J. H. 1970. Pattern clustering by multivariate mixture analysis. *Multivar. Behav. Res.* 5:329–50
501. Yanagawa, T. 1968. A small sample robust competitor of Hodges-Lehmann estimate. Reprinted from *Bull. Math. Statist.* 13. 14 pp.
502. Youden, W. J. 1972. Randomization and experimentation. *Technometrics* 14:13–22
503. Zedeck, S. 1971. Identification of moderator variables by discriminant analysis in a multipredictable group validation model. *J. Appl. Psychol.* 55: 364–71
504. Zedeck, S. 1971. Problems with the use of "moderator" variables. *Psychol. Bull.* 76:295–310
505. Zedeck, S. et al 1971. Comparison of "joint moderators" in three prediction techniques. *J. Appl. Psychol.* 55:234–40
506. Zinnes, J. L. 1969. Scaling. *Ann Rev. Psychol.* 20:447–78

REPRINTS

The conspicuous number aligned in the margin with the title of each article in this volume is a key for use in ordering reprints.

Available reprints are priced at the uniform rate of \$1 each postpaid. Payment must accompany orders less than \$10. A discount of 20% will be given on orders of 20 or more. For orders of 200 or more, any Annual Reviews article will be specially printed.

The sale of reprints of articles published in the Reviews has been expanded in the belief that reprints as individual copies, as sets covering stated topics, and in quantity for classroom use will have a special appeal to students and teachers.

AUTHOR INDEX

H

Q

R

SUBJECT INDEX

C

U

CUMULATIVE INDEXES

CONTRIBUTING AUTHORS VOLUMES 22-25

CHAPTER TITLES VOLUMES 22-25